The Mammoth Book of Eye-Witness History

Also available

The Mammoth Book of Classic Science Fiction
The Mammoth Book of Golden Age Science Fiction
The Mammoth Book of Vintage Science Fiction
The Mammoth Book of New Age Science Fiction
The Mammoth Book of Fantastic Science Fiction
The Mammoth Book of Modern Science Fiction
The Mammoth Book of Private Eye Stories
The Mammoth Book of Great Detective Stories
The Mammoth Book of Spy Thrillers
The Mammoth Book of True Murder
The Mammoth Book of True Crime
The Mammoth Book of True Crime 2
The Mammoth Book of Short Horror Novels
The Mammoth Book of True War Stories
The Mammoth Book of Modern War Stories
The Mammoth Book of the Western
The Mammoth Book of Ghost Stories
The Mammoth Book of Ghost Stories 2
The Mammoth Book of the Supernatural
The Mammoth Book of Astounding Puzzles
The Mammoth Book of Terror
The Mammoth Book of Vampires
The Mammoth Book of Killer Women
The Mammoth Book of Zombies
The Mammoth Book of Historical Whodunnits
The Mammoth Book of Werewolves
The Mammoth Book of Golden Age Detective Stories
The Mammoth Book of Contemporary SF Masters
The Mammoth Book of Erotica
The Mammoth Book of Frankenstein
The Mammoth Book of Battles
The Mammoth Book of Astounding Word Games
The Mammoth Book of Mindbending Puzzles
The Mammoth Book of Historical Detectives
The Mammoth Book of Victorian & Edwardian Ghost Stories
The Mammoth Book of Dreams
The Mammoth Book of Symbols
The Mammoth Book of Brainstorming Puzzles
The Mammoth Book of Great Lives
The Mammoth Book of International Erotica
The Mammoth Book of Pulp Fiction
The Mammoth Book of The West
The Mammoth Book of Love & Sensuality
The Mammoth Book of Chess
The Mammoth Book of Fortune Telling
The Mammoth Puzzle Carnival
The Mammoth Book of Dracula
The Mammoth Book of Gay Short Stories
The Mammoth Book of Fairy Tales
The Mammoth Book of New Sherlock Holmes Adventures
The Mammoth Book of Gay Erotica
The Mammoth Book of the Third Reich at War
The Mammoth Book of Best New Horror

The Mammoth Book of
Eye-Witness History

Edited by
JON E. LEWIS

Carroll & Graf Publishers, Inc.
NEW YORK

For Freda, Tristram and Penny Lewis-Stempel

Carroll & Graf Publishers, Inc.
19 West 21st Street
Suite 601
New York
NY 10010–6805

First published in the UK by Robinson Publishing 1998

Cover pictures: *The Defeat of the French and the English in Combat* from The Bayeux Tapestry, Bridgeman Art Library, with special authorisation of the City of Bayeux; *The Death of Nelson*, by Daniel Maclise, Bridgeman Art Library; Moon Landing, Getty Images.

First Carroll & Graf edition 1998

ISBN 0–7867–0534–5

Printed and bound in the United Kingdom

10 9 8 7 6 5 4 3 2 1

CONTENTS

INTRODUCTION

In the beginning was the word. The ancient Sumerians invented writing, and thus begat history. For it is only with writing that we have direct records – whether as diaries, temple accounts, letters, or memoirs – of what people did and thought. Before the coming of the written word lies the shadowy lost land of 'pre-history', where what passed and why have to be guessed with the help of the archaeologist's trowel.

It was probably around 3500 BC, at Uruk, that writing first emerged. Five and a half millennia of human history have passed since then. And what history: the rise of empires (and their inevitable fall), the Black Death pandemic, the discovery of America, the triumph of manned flight, such implausibly beautiful works of art as Michelangelo's Sistine Chapel ceiling, the crucifixion of Christ, the French Revolution, the slave trade, the creation of the steam machine, the assassination of John F. Kennedy, and always, of course, wars, wars galore. Of all these major historical events, and more, the following pages offer an armchair view. They are written by 'those who were there': eye-witnesses to the deed. (There are a handful of exceptions to the rule of direct eye-witness: but only where the importance of the incident justifies it, and where the report is obviously based on eye-witness accounts of others. An example is Nicolaus of Damascus' story of Julius Caesar's assassination.)

Eye-witness history is far more vivid than the sifted, sorted words of recorded history. If the strength of the latter is its studied analysis, the pure joy of eye-witness history lies in the vicarious thrill of experiencing the event. Sometimes it can even allow intimate eavesdropping over time, such as Napoleon's love letter to Josephine. Many of the eye-witnesses themselves are the movers and shakers of history (Oliver Cromwell, Friedrich Engels, St John, Nebuchadnezzar, Benito Mussolini); others are people caught up by chance in the great affairs of their time. Not until the nineteenth century do professional recorders of events – journalists – crowd the page.

And yet this book is about much more than the great, world-changing events. History is revealed in the minutiae too, from Cato's instructions in 70 BC on 'How to keep a Slave' to Franciscus' account of London's streets in 1497, words which catch the flavour of an age or a glimpse of its mind-set. And these social snippets reveal, I think, an often forgotten truth of history – which is how much remains the same. The Sumerian schoolboy reciting his day in 2000 BC and Minucius Felix's children skipping stones beside the Tiber in AD 300 are startlingly familiar. So too, but more darkly, is Arnaud de Verniolles' account of paedophilia in AD 1300. History does not 'progress' in linear fashion: it zigzags, it leaps, and some aspects of humanity hardly change at all. An ancient Sumerian might be bewildered by the technology in the last scene in this book, the arrival by air of the coffin of a dead princess in 1997, but the stunned grief of the crowd would be almost reassuringly recognizable.

As ever, my thanks are due to all at Robinson Publishing, especially Nick Robinson and Krystyna Green. Thanks, too, to Julian Alexander of Lucas Alexander Whitley, the staff of the British Library and, naturally, Penny Stempel.

CHRONOLOGY

KEY DATES	HISTORY, POLITICS, WAR	RELIGION, SCIENCE, CULTURE	SOCIAL LIFE
9000 BC			Farming begins in Near East.
c. 3500 BC	Sumerian city-states founded.	Invention of writing, Sumer.	
c. 3000	Canaanites settle Syria. Minoans establish civilisation in Crete.	Bronze produced in Sumer.	
2780	Old Kingdom founded in Egypt.	Building of the Step Pyramid at Saqqara.	
2300			Wheeled carts in use in Europe.
2000	Aryans from Caucasian steppes conquer Indus Valley.	*Epic of Gilgamesh* written down.	Oil lamps in Middle East.
1792	Babylonian empire of Hammurabi (until 1750).		Code of Hammurabi provides first legal system.
1700		Use of iron by Hittites, Turkey. Minoan palaces built.	

KEY DATES	HISTORY, POLITICS, WAR	RELIGION, SCIENCE, CULTURE	SOCIAL LIFE
1600	Shang Dynasty founded in China.		
1560	New Kingdom founded in Egypt.		
1500		Building of Stonehenge, England.	
1360		Monotheistic worship of Aton, Egypt.	
1347		Tutankhamun reintroduces Egyptian polytheism.	
1194–1184	Trojan War		
1116	Tiglath-pileser, founder of Assyrian empire, born (d. 1077).		
1000	Accession of David to throne of Judah and Israel. Beginnings of Kush civilization in E. Africa.		
800		*Iliad* and *Odyssey* written by Homer. First recorded music, Sumer.	Iron utensils in use.
776			First recorded Olympic Games.
753	Rome founded.		
701	Sennacherib of Assyria besieges Jerusalem.		Iron weapons in Central Europe.
600		Nebuchadnezzar II builds 'Hanging Gardens' of Babylon.	
551		Confucius born.	
546	Persian empire founded by Cyrus.		

KEY DATES	HISTORY, POLITICS, WAR	RELIGION, SCIENCE, CULTURE	SOCIAL LIFE
534		Buddha begins teaching.	
500	Olmecs establish civilization in Mexico. Hinduism consolidated in N. India by Aryans.	Theseum erected, Athens.	
449	Greeks defeat Persians at Salamis.		Celts settle Britain. Population of Greece reaches 3 million (inc 1 million slaves).
432	Peloponnesian War (until 404); Sparta defeats Athens.	Zenith of Greek culture, led by the democratic Athens of Pericles.	
430			Plague in Athens.
399		Socrates executed, Athens.	
336	Reign of Alexander the Great (until 323).		First Roman coins.
323		Euclid's *Elements*.	
264	First Punic War between Rome and Carthage (until 241).		
215			Great Wall of China.
206			Han dynasty in China institutes civil service examinations.
202	Scipio Africanus defeats Hannibal at Zuma, ending Second Punic War (begun 219).		
149–146	Third Punic War ends with destruction of Carthage. Greece annexed by Rome.		

KEY DATES	HISTORY, POLITICS, WAR	RELIGION, SCIENCE, CULTURE	SOCIAL LIFE
71	Slave revolts of Spartacus ended by Pompey.		
58	Julius Caesar conquers Gaul.		
48	Caesar defeats Pompey to become dictator of Rome.		
44	Julius Caesar assassinated.		
43	Roman colonization of Britain.		
30	Egypt annexed by Rome.		
4 BC	Jesus Christ now thought to have been born.		
0			
AD 30		Christ executed in Judaea.	
64	Fire of Rome.	First persecution of Christians.	
70	Temple of Jerusalem destroyed by Romans.		
74			Silk Road opened between China and Rome.
79	Eruption of Vesuvius; Pompeii buried.		
c. 100	Roman Empire (under Tragan) reaches greatest extent.		
220	Han dynasty collapses in China.		
380		Christianity becomes state religion of Rome.	

KEY DATES	HISTORY, POLITICS, WAR	RELIGION, SCIENCE, CULTURE	SOCIAL LIFE
c. 400	Mexican civilization in golden age.		
410	Visigoths sack Rome.		
419	Saxons, Angles, Jutes colonize Britain.		
431		St Patrick begins mission to Ireland.	
452			Venice founded.
476	End of Western Roman Empire.		
529		Benedict of Nuria draws up rules for monastic life.	
553	Narses annexes Rome for Byzantine.		
570		Muhammad born.	
600	Sasanid (Persian) Empire at height.	Books printed in China by Buddist monks.	
601		St Augustine becomes first Archbishop of Canterbury.	
604		Shotoko Taishi Code requires veneration of Buddha in Japan.	
637	Jerusalem captured by Muhammadans.		
650	Bosnia occupied by Croats and Serbs.		
664	Synod of Whitby; England adopts Roman Catholicism. Kingdom of Ghana founded, Africa.		Easter eggs used by Christians.

KEY DATES	HISTORY, POLITICS, WAR	RELIGION, SCIENCE, CULTURE	SOCIAL LIFE
732	Franks halt Arab invasion of Europe at Tours		Beginning of feudalism in Europe. Beds become fashionable in parts of W. Europe.
771	Charlemagne becomes sole ruler of Frankish kingdom.		
787	First Viking raid on Britain.		
814		Doge's palace, Venice, begun.	
845			Paper money in China causes inflation.
878	Alfred defeats Danes ar Eddington.		
885	Vikings besiege Paris.		
c. 900	Viking raids destroy golden age of Irish Celtic civilization.		
982	Eric the Red establishes Viking colonies in Greenland.		Cane sugar arrives in W. Europe.
1066	Normans invade Britain.		Chinese under Sung dynasty establish iron and steel manufactories in esp. Kaifeng. Use of gunpowder widespread in China.
1085	Alfonso VI takes Toledo from Arabs.		
c. 1090			Water-powered clock invented, China.
1093	Malcolm of Scotland killed invading England.		

KEY DATES	HISTORY, POLITICS, WAR	RELIGION, SCIENCE, CULTURE	SOCIAL LIFE
1096	First Christian Crusade to Holy Land.		
1128	Khmers of Cambodia expand into Vietnam.		
1135	Stephen of Boulogne becomes King of England; civil war follows with supporters of Matilda, daughter of Henry I.		
1163		Notre Dame built, Paris.	
1167		Oxford University founded.	
1170	Thomas à Becket, Archbishop of Canterbury murdered.	Chrétien de Troyes' courtly love romance, *Lancelot.*	Glass windows in English houses.
1187	Mohammed of Ghor conquers Punjab. Saladin takes Jerusalem.		
1189	Massacre of Jews at coronation of King Richard I, England.		
1194		Gothic Cathedral at Chartres.	
1215	King John seals Magna Carta.		'St George's Day' becomes national holiday, England. Crusaders bring leprosy to Europe.
1237	Mongols conquer Russia.		
1248		Alhambra palace, Spain.	
1271	Marco Polo travels to China.		Glass mirror invented.

KEY DATES	HISTORY, POLITICS, WAR	RELIGION, SCIENCE, CULTURE	SOCIAL LIFE
1272	Kublai Khan conquers Sung of China.		
1290	Osman founds Ottoman Turkish Empire.		
1306	Philip IV expels Jews from France.		
1314	Scots under Robert Bruce defeat English at Bannockburn.		
1321		Dante writes *Divine Comedy*.	
1328	Ivan I makes Moscow capital.		
1337	Beginning of Hundred Years War between England and France.		
1346	Battle of Crécy; French defeated by English longbow.		
1347			Black Death pandemic in Europe; fifth of population dies.
1364		Aztecs build Tenochtitlan.	
1365	Charles V crowned King of Burgundy.		
1368	Ming dynasty expels Mongols, China.		
1381	Peasants Revolt, England.		
1399	Tamerlane's Mongols sack Delhi.		

KEY DATES	HISTORY, POLITICS, WAR	RELIGION, SCIENCE, CULTURE	SOCIAL LIFE
c. 1400	All Europe Christian. In N. Italy Renaissance begins. Tea-drinking introduced in Japan.		
1414	Medici become bankers to papacy.		
1415	Henry V defeats French at Agincourt.		
1429	Jean of Arc raises siege of Orleans.		
1453	Fall of Constantinople to Turks; end of East Roman (Byzantine) Empire.		
1456		Paolo Uccello paints *Battle of San Romano* – introduction of scientific perspective.	
1467			Scots prohibit golf and 'fute-ball'.
1474		William Caxton prints first book in English.	
1479	Castile and Aragon united under Ferdinand and Isabella.		
1484		Botticelli paints *Birth of Venus*.	
1487		Aztecs dedicate temple of sun god, Tenochtitlan, with sacrifice of 24,000 captives.	

KEY DATES	HISTORY, POLITICS, WAR	RELIGION, SCIENCE, CULTURE	SOCIAL LIFE
1492	Columbus lands on Watling Island, Bahamas. Spanish conquer Granada, last Moorish state in Spain.		
1497	Cabot lands in Canada.		
1500			First recorded Caesarean operation, Switzerland
1505	Ivan the Great of Russia dies, having ended Mongol 'Golden Horde' influence in Muscovy (Moscow).		
1508		Michelangelo begins painting ceiling of Sistine Chapel, Rome (until 1512).	
1512		Copernicus' *Commentariolus* declares that Earth moves around Sun.	
1514	Peasant's Revolt, Hungary.		
1517	Magellan embarks on first circumnavigation of globe (one ship successful, returning 1522).	Martin Luther posts 95 Theses on door of Wittenberg Church: Protestantism founded.	
1519	Hernando Cortés enters Mexico	Leonardo da Vinci dies.	Hops introduced into England.
1527	Sack of Rome by imperial troops of Charles V.		

KEY DATES	HISTORY, POLITICS, WAR	RELIGION, SCIENCE, CULTURE	SOCIAL LIFE
1529	Turks reach gates of Vienna.		
1531	Henry VIII becomes Supreme Head of Church in England: Reformation begins in England.		
1534	John of Leiden founds commutarian state of Anabaptists in Westphalia.	Jesuit Order begun by Ignatius Loyola.	
1542	Portuguese become first Westerners to reach Japan.		
1543	Spanish Inquisition burns first Protestants.		First records of cricket.
1558	Elizabeth I accedes to throne of England.		
1562	John Hawkins begins slave trade between Africa and West Indies.		
1565	Spanish colonize Florida.		Tobacco introduced into England.
1569			First public lottery in England.
1571	Christian alliance breaks Turkish sea-power at Lepanto.		
1582	English establish colony in Newfoundland.		Forks appear at French court.
1586	Spanish Armada leaves for England; defeated in Channel, scattered by storms.		
1587	Mary, Queen of Scots executed.		

KEY DATES	HISTORY, POLITICS, WAR	RELIGION, SCIENCE, CULTURE	SOCIAL LIFE
1598		Invention of first knitting machine.	
1590		Shakespeare's *Henry VI*, parts 2 and 3 completed.	Water closets installed at Queen's Palace, Richmond.
1596	English sack Cadiz.		
1603	Elizabeth I dies; succeeded by James VI of Scotland as James I of England and Ireland.		
1605	Catholic Gunpowder Plot to blow up Parliament and James I.		
1611		Authorized Version of Bible ('King James Bible').	
1618	Beginning of religious Thirty Years War in Central Europe.		
1620	Pilgrim Fathers reach New England.		
1627	Dutch Republic pre-eminent mercantile nation of world.	Rembrandt paints *The Money-Changer.*	
1637		Descartes, *Discourse on Method.*	
1642	English Civil War (until 1649); ends in execution of Charles I and establishment of republic under Cromwell.		

KEY DATES	HISTORY, POLITICS, WAR	RELIGION, SCIENCE, CULTURE	SOCIAL LIFE
1643	Louis XIV succeeds to throne of France. Reigns until 1715, the last of the great Renaissance despots.		
1660	Restoration of monarchy in England.		
1661			Famine in India.
1665		Newton discovers gravity.	Great Plague in London.
1666			Great Fire of London.
1682	French court moves to Versailles.		
1683	Turks besiege Vienna.		
1694	Bank of England founded.		
1701	Captain Kidd, pirate, executed.		
1707	Aurangzib, last great Mughal emperor of India dies; anarchy ensues.		
1739	Persians sack Delhi.		
1755			Lisbon earthquake kills 30,000.
1756	British soldiers murdered by Nawab in the 'Black Hole of Calcutta'.		
1770	James Cook discovers Botany Bay, Australia.		
1775	American Revolution (until 1783).	James Watt perfects steam engine.	

KEY DATES	HISTORY, POLITICS, WAR	RELIGION, SCIENCE, CULTURE	SOCIAL LIFE
1776	Thomas Jefferson drafts Declaration of Independence, America.	Adam Smith, *An Inquiry into the Nature and Causes of the Wealth of Nations.*	
1779			First outbreaks of 'machine-wrecking' in England.
1783	Britain recognizes independence of USA. Slave trade to New World at peak.	Montgolfier brothers make first balloon flight, France.	
1786		Mozart, writes opera *Marriage of Figaro*	Internal gas lighting in England.
1789–1791	French Revolution.	First steam-powered cotton-mill, Manchester.	
1793	Napoleonic Wars between France and England (until 1815).		France introduces compulsory schooling from age 6.
1794	Paris Commune abolished.		
1798	French capture Rome, Naples and Egypt.		
1799	George Washington dies.		
1800	US capital established at Washington DC.	Alessandro Volta constructs first electrical battery.	Population of New York reaches 65,000.
1803	'Louisiana' (most of the American West) bought by US from France.		
1805	Nelson defeats combined French and Spanish fleet at Trafalgar. Napoleon victorious over Austro-Russian army at Austerlitz.		

KEY DATES	HISTORY, POLITICS, WAR	RELIGION, SCIENCE, CULTURE	SOCIAL LIFE
1812	Napoleon enters Moscow but forced to retreat (only 10,000 troops of initial 500,000 survive campaign). US declares war on Britain.		'Luddism' at peak. Waltz popular.
1813	Mexico declares independence from Spain. Bolivar becomes dictator of Venezuela.	Jane Austen writes *Pride and Prejudice.*	
1814	Peace between US and Britain.	George Stephenson constructs first locomotive.	
1815	Wellington defeats Napoleon at Waterloo.		
1818		First steanship crossing of Atalntic.	
1819	Army attacks reform marchers at 'Peterloo', Manchester.		
1829	Greece freed from Turkish rule; Ottoman Empire in decline.		
1831			Cholera pandemic sweeps much of Europe. Horse-drawn buses, already established in Europe, appear in New York.
1836	Dutch Boers make 'Great Trek' to found Orange Free State and others. Battle of the Alamo; in aftermath Texas wins independence from Mexico.		Chartism, the first working-class political organization in Britain, seeks universal suffrage.
1838	Coronation of Queen Victoria.		

KEY DATES	HISTORY, POLITICS, WAR	RELIGION, SCIENCE, CULTURE	SOCIAL LIFE
1839			Baseball invented by Abner Doubleday.
1845		Engels, *The Condition of the Working Class in England.*	Irish potato famine.
1847	First California gold rush.		
1848	Worker uprisings throughout Europe.	Marx and Engels, *The Communist Manifesto.*	
1856	Dr Livingstone becomes first white to see Victoria Falls, Africa.		
1857–1858	Indian Mutiny.		
1859	Construction of Suez Canal begins.	Darwin, *Origin of Species.*	
1860	Garibaldi liberates Sicily from Bourbons.		
1861	Serfs emancipated, Russia. American Civil War begins as proslavery Southern states fight to secede from Union.		
1864	Massacre of Cheyenne at Sand Creek. In American Civil War, Sherman marches through Georgia and defeats Confederates at Atlanta.		
1865	Confederates surrender at Appomattox. President Lincoln assassinated.		Ku Klux Klan established.
1867		Zola, *Thérèse Raquin.*	
1870	Franco-Prussian War (until 1871).		
1871	Paris Commune is suppressed after 2 months. Italy unified.		FA Cup founded.

KEY DATES	HISTORY, POLITICS, WAR	RELIGION, SCIENCE, CULTURE	SOCIAL LIFE
1876	Custer and 7th Cavalry defeated by Sioux at Little Big Horn.	Alexander Graham Bell invents telephone.	
1879	Zulus massacre British at Isandhlwana.		
1881	Billy the Kid, outlaw, assassinated.		Height of cattle-ranching on Great Plains.
1882	Britain occupies Egypt.		
1885		Van Gogh paints *The Potato Eaters*.	
1890	Massacre at Wounded Knee ends Indian Wars in US. First General Election in Japan.		Global influenza endemic.
1892	Keir Hardie becomes first Labour MP, Britain.		
1893		Karl Benz builds his first motor car. Advent of art nouveau.	
1896	Italy defeated by Abyssinians (Ethiopians) at Adowa; almost uniquely, Abyssinia survives the 'scramble for Africa' which has seen the rest of the continent colonized by European powers.	Puccini's opera *La Bohème*	
1898	Spanish–American War; Spains cedes Cuba and Philippines.	Marie and Pierre Curie discover radium.	Métro opens in Paris.
1899	Boer War between Britain and Boers (until 1901).	Rutherford discovers alpha and beta rays.	
1900	Nationalist Boxer Rebellion in China.	Freud, *The Interpretation of Dreams*.	

KEY DATES	HISTORY, POLITICS, WAR	RELIGION, SCIENCE, CULTURE	SOCIAL LIFE
1901	Death of Queen Victoria.	Marconi sends radio signal across Atlantic.	
1903		First powered air flight, Kitty Hawk, USA.	Henry Ford founds Ford Motor Co.
1904	Russo–Japanese War (until 1905).		
1905	'Bloody Sunday', St Petersburg: peaceful democratic protest attacked by Czarist troops. Sinn Fein founded, Ireland.	Einstein proposes Special Theory of Relativity.	
1906		Upton Sinclair, *The Jungle.*	San Francisco earthquake.
1909	Commander Peary reaches North Pole.	Blériot flies the Channel. Bakelite invented.	
1910	Coal miners riot in Tonypandy, Wales. Mexican Revolution (until 1912). Japan annexes Korea.	Post-Impressionist Exhibition, London.	Labour Exchanges open, Britain.
1911	Amundsen reaches South Pole. China becomes a republic under Sun Yat-sen.		
1913	Suffragette demonstrations in London. War in the Balkans.	Première of Stravinsky's *Rite of Spring.*	
1914	Assassination of Archduke Franz Ferdinand, Sarajevo. World War begins. Germany invades Low Countries and France.	Gershwin, *Rhapsody in Blue*	

KEY DATES	HISTORY, POLITICS, WAR	RELIGION, SCIENCE, CULTURE	SOCIAL LIFE
1915	WWI: Gallipoli campaign; *Lusitania* torpedoed; Zeppelins raid London.	Einstein expounds General Theory of Relativity. D.W.Griffiths movie, *Birth of a Nation.*	
1916	WWI: Battles of Verdun and Somme on Western Front; tanks introduced by British; Battle of Jutland in North Sea. Sinn Fein launches Easter Rising in Dublin.	Jazz gains popularity in USA. Daddaism invented by Tristan Tzatra.	Daylight Saving in Britain.
1917	WWI: opening of battle of Passchendaele; tank battle at Cambrai: US declares war on Germany. Russian Revolution: Bolsheviks under Lenin seize power; civil war with 'Whites' continues until 1920.		
1918	WWI: Germany tries last gamble on Western Front; Armistice on 11 November – WWI ends, with Allies victorious. Tsar Nicholas and family shot. Worker uprisings in Berlin. Suffrage for women over 30 inroduced in Britain.		
1919	Treaty of Versailles: Germany disarmed, stripped of colonies and forced to pay reparations. Spartacist Revolution in Berlin; counter-revolutionaries murder Karl Liebknecht and Rosa Luxemburg. Mussolini founds Fascist movement, Italy.		

KEY DATES	HISTORY, POLITICS, WAR	RELIGION, SCIENCE, CULTURE	SOCIAL LIFE
1920	League of Nations formed. 19th Amendment in US gives women vote. Unemployment insurance in Britain.		Prohibition in USA.
1921		Schoenberg, 'Piano Suite Op 25'.	
1922	Fascists take power, Italy. Irish Free State proclaimed.	James Joyce, *Ulysses.*	
1923	Turkey becomes a republic. Hyperinflation in Germany.		
1926	General Strike, Britain.		
1927			Babe Ruth hits 60 home runs for NY Yankees.
1928		D.H. Lawrence, *Lady Chatterley's Lover.*	
1929	Wall Street Crash.		'Talkies' end silent movie era.
1930	In India Gandhi leads 200-mile civil disobedience march.		
1931	Hunger March in Washington. All German banks close.	Jehovah's Witnesses founded.	First woman senator, USA.
1933	Hitler appointed Chancellor of Germany; uses pretext of the Reichstag fire to introduce Nazi dictatorship.		

KEY DATES	HISTORY, POLITICS, WAR	RELIGION, SCIENCE, CULTURE	SOCIAL LIFE
1934	Civil Works Emergency Relief in USA.		
1935	Show trials in USSR Italy invades Abyssinia.		First TV broadcast by BBC; Metro opens in Moscow.
1936	Spanish Civil War (until 1939). Trotsky exiled from USSR. Chang Kai-shek declares war on Japan.		Black athelete Jesse Owens wins four gold medals in Berlin Olympics.
1937		Whittle builds first jet engine.	Airship *Hindenburg* crashes, NY.
1938	Austria annexed by Germany.	Laslo Biro invents ballpoint pen.	
1939	World War II begins: Britain and France declare war on Germany. Germany invades Poland. USSR occupies eastern Poland.		Nylon stockings become fashionable.
1940	WWII: Germany occupies Norway, Denmark, Low Countries and France. Churchill becomes British PM. Luftwaffe launches 'Blitz' on London. Trotsky assassinated by Stalinist agent.		
1941	WWII: German offensive in North Africa led by Rommel, attacks Tobruk; Germans invade Russia, reach outskirts of Moscow; Japan bombs Pearl Harbor; USA enters war.	Orson Welles' film, *Citizen Kane.*	Clothes rationing in Britain.

KEY DATES	HISTORY, POLITICS, WAR	RELIGION, SCIENCE, CULTURE	SOCIAL LIFE
1942	WWII: Japanese capture Singapore, lose battles of Coral Sea and Midway; in North Africa, Rommel loses battle of El Alamein. Nazis begin mass extermination of Jews in gas chambers.	Albert Camus, *The Outsider.*	
1943	WWII: German Sixth Army surrenders at Stalingrad; Germans lose campaign in North Africa; Allies invade Italy; Italy surrenders; Japanese forced from Guadalcanal.		
1944	WWII: Allied 'D-Day' landings in Normandy; France liberated; Allied troops cross German border; Warsaw uprising; US troops land in Philippines; Russians occupy Hungary; V–2 rockets land on England.	Aaron Copland, *Appalachian Spring.*	
1945	WWII: Russian offensive in east reaches Berlin; Hitler commits suicide; Germany surrenders on May 7; US drops atomic bombs on Hiroshima and Nagasaki; Japan surrenders – end of WWII. Landslide Labour government in Britain.	George Orwell, *Animal Farm.*	

KEY DATES	HISTORY, POLITICS, WAR	RELIGION, SCIENCE, CULTURE	SOCIAL LIFE
1947	India granted independence from Britain.		
1948	Israel declares independence.		Bread rationing ends in Britain.
1949	Communist People's Republic proclaimed, China; Britain recognizes independence of Eire; Democratic Republic established in East Germany.		
1950	Korean War (until 1953).		
1951	McCarthyite anti-Communist witch hunts in full spate, USA.		Colour TV introduced in USA.
1953	Stalin dies.	Hillary and Tenzing Norgay climb Everest; Arthur Miller, *The Crucible*.	
1956	Anti-Stalinist revolution, Hungary; Egypt nationalizes Suez canal – Britain stages abortive invasion; Castro sails to Cuba with small rebel force.		The birth of rock 'n' roll.
1957	Desegregation protests at Little Rock, Arkansas.	Jack Kerouac, *On the Road*. USSR launches Sputnik I.	
1959	Castro's rebels oust Batista from power, Cuba.		First motorway opens in Britain.

KEY DATES	HISTORY, POLITICS, WAR	RELIGION, SCIENCE, CULTURE	SOCIAL LIFE
1960	Massacre of black demonstrators against apartheid, Sharpeville; John F. Kennedy elected President of US.		
1961	Building of the Berlin Wall; CIA sponsors abortive Bay of Pigs invasion, Cuba.		
1962	Cuban Missile Crisis.	Bob Dylan records 'Blowin' in the Wind'.	
1963	Great Train Robbery, England; Freedom March on Washington; President John F. Kennedy assassinated, Dallas.		
1964	USA becomes embroiled in conflict in Vietnam; *de facto* start of Vietnam War (until 1975).	The Beatles film, *Hard Day's Night.*	Cassius Clay wins world heavyweight boxing title.
1965	Winston Churchill dies (aged 91).		
1966			England win World cup. 'Summer of love' – Hippie youth movement at peak.
1967	Six Day War between Israel and Arab states.		
1968	Student riots in Paris spark virtual revolution in France.		
1969	British troops sent to Northern Ireland.	Neil Armstrong and Buzz Aldrin land on Moon.	Woodstock rock festival.

KEY DATES	HISTORY, POLITICS, WAR	RELIGION, SCIENCE, CULTURE	SOCIAL LIFE
1972	British troops massacre 13 civil rights protesters, N. Ireland; national miners' strike, Britain.		
1973	Elected Marxist government overthrown by military, Chile.		Worldwide petroleum crisis caused by Arab embargo.
1974	US President Richard Nixon resigns over Watergate scandal; floods kill 2500 in Bangladesh.		Muhammad Ali beats George Foreman in Zaïre to regain world heavyweight title.
1975	North Vietnamese Communists occupy South Vietnam; US evacuates troops – end of Vietnam War.		
1976		Sex Pistols record, 'Anarchy in the UK' – the birth of punk rock.	Bjorn Borg wins men's singles tennis title, Wimbledon.
1979	Islamic fundamentalists overthrow Shah of Iran; Conservative government, led by Margaret Thatcher, elected, Britain.		
1980	SAS troops relieve siege at Iranian Embassy, London; Lech Walesa leads *Solidarnosc* protests in Poland.		
1981	Falklands/Malvinas War.		
1984	Miners' Stike, Britain (until 1985).		

KEY DATES	HISTORY, POLITICS, WAR	RELIGION, SCIENCE, CULTURE	SOCIAL LIFE
1986	Army lead overthrow of President Marcos, Philippines.		
1987			AIDS endemic in Africa.
1989	Pro-democracy students shot, Tianenmen Square, China; Fall of the Berlin Wall; Stalinist regimes of Romania, Bulgaria, East Germany overthrown. Yugoslavia fragments into civil war.		
1991	Persian Gulf War.		
1992	Los Angeles riot.		
1994	End of apartheid in South Africa.		
1997	Diana, Princess of Wales, and lover, Dodi Fayed, die in car crash, Paris; Labour government elected in Britain.		

Part One

The Ancient World

3500 BC–AD 500

INTRODUCTION

There have been many calculations of the age of the world. In the seventeenth century Archbishop James Armagh announced, with the certainty of faith, that the world was created in 4004 BC. Modern astronomy suggests that the archbishop missed his mark by around 5000 million years. Relative to this, the human race has existed for a mere blink in time, emerging around 4 million BC. What we know as 'civilization' has been around for even less.

The first of the great river civilizations of the ancient world, Sumeria, arose in about 3500 BC, when the people of the fertile lands between the Tigris and the Euphrates developed (through an irrigation system supervised by warrior-kings) an agriculture that could support largescale population levels. Whereas their primitive hunter-gather ancestors needed hundreds of acres to support a family unit, the Sumerian farmer needed less than twenty-five. More food meant more mouths could be fed. And, gradually, the owners of these mouths came to live a sedentary life based around the temple and the storehouse. By 3000 BC the Sumerians had built thirteen cities, some of them boasting populations of over 50,000.

Thus did civilization – from the Latin *civitas*, 'living in a city' – begin. For the first time human beings lived in an environment shaped entirely by their own hands, with the material resources to be spared the constant hunt and labour for food. City life demanded new, complex forms of organization. City life, by thronging together a mass of people, made cultural and technological innovation more likely. So it was that the Sumerians devised the first calendar and the first system of numbers; they made the first wheeled vehicles; Sumerian smiths, their endeavours supported by the agricultural surplus, added tin to copper and produced the first bronze. (The 'Bronze Age' would last until 1200 BC, when the Mycenae were wiped out by the iron swords of the Dorians.) Perhaps the crowning achievement of the Sumerians was their creation of the first hieroglyphic script, probably at the temple at Uruk (the Bible's Erech), where it was used to record grain transactions. With the invention of writing, works of literature soon followed. The Sumerian tale, *The Epic of Gilgamesh*, is the oldest in the world, written down some time after 2000 BC.

By this time Sumerian civilization was in decline. But civilization itself had already filtered through to Egypt (in around 3100 BC), India (2500 BC) and would shortly reach China. Like Sumer, these other major early civilizations were irrigation or 'hydraulic' societies, built around agriculture and the management of unpredictable water supplies. They had other similarities with Sumer, too. All were bound together by polytheistic religions. (There were partial exceptions in China, where the idea of the universe being controlled by the forces of nature predominated and in the unsuccessful attempt by the fourteenth-century BC Egyptian pharoah Akhenaton to establish a monotheistic religion around the sun-god Aton.) All were authoritarian monarchies. And all rested on slavery.

Initially, slavery was relatively unimportant to the ancient world. The labour which built the ziggurats (temple-towers) of Sumer, even the earliest pyramid tombs of the Egyptians, was the enforced labour of the people themselves. In the Near and Middle East, however, this state of affairs did not last beyond 2000 BC. One of the discoveries of war – which was endemic across the ancient world, for imperial conquest or for the defence of wealth from barbarian raiders – was that the conquered could be enslaved. Put another way, human beings as well as animals could be domesticated. Soon there was a thriving traffic in slaves, even between nations. As a commodity, slaves had a particular asset; they could be multiplied by captive breeding.

The 'classical' societies of the ancient world which arose in the southern Mediterranean were likewise slave states. Indeed, if anything, slavery was more important to Greece and Rome than to the river civilizations, or the host of minor states which emulated them. With the rise of the Greek city-states from 800 BC came advancements in culture (the plays of Sophocles, the rational philosophical method of Socrates), and science (Leucippus and Democritus' fifth-century BC proposal that all matter was composed of atoms, the theorem of Pythagoras) which still inform Western civilization. These advancements included the first experiments in political democracy (a Greek word, from *demos* 'the people', and *krateo* 'to rule'), at Chios and Athens. A democracy, however, which excluded the Asiatic and Black Sea peoples, whose forced labour, in houses, textile shops, mines and plantations made the city-states rich. The numbers of the enslaved were almost incalculable; Athens alone had 390,000 men, women and children in slavery.

At the beginning of their armed march to dominance over the ancient world, the Romans had no substantial slave labour. The building of an empire which stretched from Britain to Egypt soon changed this. If Rome needed a slave-state model to follow, she may have found it in the conquered nations of Carthage and Greece. In any case the logic of empire building left little alternative: what else was to be done with captive peoples? Slaves by the million – Pompey's campaigns in Asia in the first century BC alone enslaved 2 million – were sent back to Rome, many to work in plantations in Sicily and the south of Italy.

The glory that was the Roman Empire lasted four centuries. *Pax Romana* brought order, just laws, fine roads and aqueducts to most of Europe, much of Asia Minor and North Africa. Enervated by a continuing fiscal crisis, deterioration in the prestige of the emperor, bloated with discontented slaves and a parasitic aristocracy (the latter two went hand in hand), the Empire was unable to resist the waves of barbarian nomads who fell on its frontiers in the fourth century. Rome itself was captured by the Visigoths in AD 410, and in 476 the last nominal emperor, the boy Romulus Augustulus, was pensioned off by the barbarian general Odacer. With this ignominy, the Roman Empire in the West was effectively ended (the Empire in the East, based at Constantinople on the Bosphorus, continued) and Europe would enter the Dark Ages.

A SCHOOLBOY'S DAY, SUMER, *c.* 2000 BC

Anon.

The Sumerians of Mesopotamia (now Iraq), built the first cities, the first state. They invented writing and the formal education of children.

Arriving at school in the morning I recited my tablet, ate my lunch, prepared my new tablet, wrote it, finished it, then they assigned me my oral work . . . When school was dismissed, I went home, entered the house, and found my father sitting there. I told my father of my written work, then recited my tablet to him, and my father was delighted.

THE PALACE OF BABYLON IS REBUILT IN SPLENDOUR, BABYLONIA, *c.* 600 BC

Nebuchadnezzar

With the fall and decline of Sumerian civilization, other empires arose in Mesopotamia, pre-eminent among them Babylon. In 689 BC Babylon was attacked by Sennacherib of Assyria – 'The city and its houses, from its foundation to its top, I destroyed, I devastated, I burnt with fire . . . Through the midst of that city I dug canals. I flooded with water, and its very foundations thereof I destroyed' – but was later rebuilt by Nebuchadnezzar in a splendour unseen in the known world.

I laid the foundation of the new palace firmly, and built it mountain high with bitumen and baked bricks. Huge cedars I caused to be laid for its roof, door leaves of cedar mounted with copper, thresholds and hinges made of bronze I fitted to its gates. Silver, gold, precious stones, ornaments of exaltedness I stored within it, and immense abundance of royal treasures I accumulated in it.

HUNTING CROCODILES, EGYPT, *c.* 450 BC

Herodotus

The crocodile is a four-footed land and marsh creature which eats nothing for the four winter months. It lays its eggs on the bank, where it leaves them, spends most of the day on dry-land and the whole of the night in the river, for the water is warmer than the clear open sky and the dew. We know of no animal which starts so small and grows so large. The eggs it lays are not much bigger than those of a goose, and the young crocodile is proportionate in size to the egg, but it grows to a length of twenty-seven feet or more. It has pig-like eyes, and large tusk-like teeth to match its body. It is the only animal to have no tongue. It does not move its lower jaw, but is again the only animal to bring its upper jaw down on to the lower. It has strong claws and a scaly skin, unpierceable over its back. It is blind in the water, but very sharp-sighted out of it. As it spends so much time in the water, its mouth is quite full of leeches. All birds and animals avoid it, except the sandpiper which makes itself useful and so has a covenant with it. When the crocodile climbs out of the water and lies with its mouth wide open (which it normally does facing the west), then the bird hops into its mouth and eats up the leeches. The crocodile is pleased with this assistance and does the bird no harm.

Some of the Egyptians hold the crocodile as sacred, but others do not, and hunt it as an enemy. Those that live in the neighbourhood of Thebes and the lake of Moeris consider it to be extremely sacred. Each community rears one crocodile which is trained to come to hand; they put glass and gold ornaments on its ears and bracelets on its front feet, giving it special food and divine offerings, and treating it extremely well as long as it lives. On its death it is embalmed and placed in sacred coffins. But the inhabitants of the city of Elephantine do not think of them as sacred, and even eat them . . .

There are all sorts of methods of hunting them. I will just describe the one that seems to me to be the cleverest. They bait a hook with a pig's chine and float it in the middle of the river. Then they hold a live pig on the bank and beat it. The crocodile hears the pig's squeals and makes for the sound. Coming across the chine, it gobbles it down; whereupon the hunters drag it ashore. When it has been brought to land, they first of all smear its eyes with mud. You can easily despatch a crocodile if you do that first, but only with considerable difficulty if you do not.

THE PLAGUE IN ATHENS, 430 BC

Thucydides

Shortly after the commencement of the Peloponnesian War between Athens and Sparta, plague (probably typhus) broke out in Athens.

The plague was said to have started in Egypt above the cataracts. From there it spread into Egypt proper, to Libya and most of the Persian Empire. Its onset in Athens was very sudden. It first attacked men in the Piraeus, which made the inhabitants spread the rumour that the Peloponnesians had thrown poison into the water-cisterns (there were no wells there at the time). It then spread to the city itself, and the death rate increased considerably. I expect that everyone, doctor and layman alike, will give his personal views about its likely origin and the reasons which he thinks explain why it became virulent enough to cause such a catastrophe. I will merely describe its symptoms, adding such points as will help anyone to a knowledge of the disease in the event of any future occurrence. I can do this as an actual victim of the plague, and as a witness of other people's suffering.

It is generally agreed that this year was completely free from other complaints; and even if anyone caught some other disease, it always ended up in this. It struck the healthy without warning, starting with high fever in the head, and a reddening and inflammation of the eyes. Internally, the throat and tongue became immediately inflamed, and the breath was laboured and foul. Sneezing and sore throats followed, and soon the trouble descended to the chest, causing a severe cough. On entering the stomach it produced acute indigestion and every type of purging of bile that is known to medical science. Pain was acute, for most were affected by a hollow retching accompanied by violent spasms which lasted for different times in different cases. The outside of the body was not excessively hot to the touch nor pallid, but rather reddish and blotchy, breaking out into small pustules and sores. But internally the fever was so intense that men could not stand even the lightest clothes of muslin being thrown on them. They much preferred to lie quite naked, and would with pleasure have thrown themselves into cold water. Indeed, many of those unattended were afflicted with an unquenchable thirst and did actually hurl themselves into wells. But it made no difference whether they drank little or much; sufferers were all quite unable to lie still or get any sleep. There was no wasting of the body while the disease was at its height, but it seemed to resist the complaint in an astonishing fashion. Most, then, died from the internal fever on the seventh or ninth day with their bodily strength unimpaired. Those who survived past that found the disease entering their intestines, where severe ulcerations and acute diarrhoea meant that weakness was the most likely cause of death for those who still survived.

The disease started in the head and spread downwards through the whole body. If anyone survived the first attacks he still was marked by the loss of his extremities, for it attacked the genitals and the tips of the hands and feet. Many lost these, or even their eyes, and lived. An immediate and total amnesia affected those who recovered. They even forgot who they were, and failed to recognize close relations. The nature of the disease really beggars description and was far too severe for the human frame to stand. Its difference from the normal types of sickness was most marked. The birds and animals which scavenge around corpses never went near the many dead bodies lying about unburied, or if they did so and touched the body, they died. As evidence may be cited the obvious absence of such birds, not one of which was seen near a corpse or anywhere else, while dogs provided a clear proof of the consequences because of their domesticity.

This, then, to omit individual peculiarities, was the general nature of the plague. As said above, none of the normal diseases occurred while the plague lasted, or if they did they ended up in this. Men died whether receiving every attention or left uncared for. There was virtually no remedy which could be applied to do any good, for what assisted one sufferer harmed another. No physique seemed strong enough to withstand the attack which removed even those who received every attention. The very worst thing about the calamity was the despair which anyone felt if he thought that he was sickening. Thrown into utter dejection, he let himself go and stopped trying to resist the disease. Some caught it from nursing others and they died like sheep. This, indeed, caused the highest death toll. For if men shrank from visiting others, they died by themselves, and many households were wiped out through lack of attention. If they did pay visits the result was just the same, and this particularly affected those who made any pretensions to virtue. When the very relations of the dead were quite overcome by the disaster and had even stopped bewailing their loss, good men went to their help out of a sense of shame, and were unsparing of their own lives. Survivors showed the most pity for the sick and dying because of their personal knowledge of the pain. They also felt very confident, for the disease never attacked the same man twice, at least not fatally. They also received the congratulations of others, and in their immediate joy even entertained the vain hope that they would never be killed by any other disease in the future.

The evacuation from the countryside into the town greatly increased the trouble, especially for the evacuees who had no houses to go to, and lived in stifling hovels at the hottest time of the year. Death came upon them without warning. Corpses lay where they died on top of each other, and the dying lurched around the streets and wells in their crying need for water. The sacred places, also, where they squatted, were filled with the corpses of those who died there. For as the disease gained strength men had no idea what would become of them, and the natural reaction was to belittle all sacred and holy things. Their previous observances about burial were disregarded, and they buried the dead as best they might. Many were buried in unhallowed ground, as most of their relatives had already been destroyed. Some men took corpses to a pyre which was meant for another, threw them on and set light to it, while some even hurled their load onto a pyre that was already burning and ran off. In addition to its other effects, the plague caused a great increase in lawlessness.

THE GREEKS MARCH TO THE SEA, KURDISTAN-ARMENIA, 401 BC

Xenophon

Recruited by Cyrus in his abortive attempt to seize the Persian throne, 10,000 Greek mercenaries under Xenophon fought an epic retreat through the mountains of Kurdistan and Armenia to the Black Sea.

Having got their kit and baggage together, they at once began their march through deep snow with several guides . . . with the north wind blowing in their teeth, drying up everything and benumbing the men. Here one of the seers suggested to them to do sacrifice to Boreas, and sacrifice was done. The effect was obvious to all in the diminished fierceness of the blast. But there was six feet of snow, so that many of the baggage animals and slaves were lost, and about thirty of the men themselves.

They spent the whole night in kindling fires; for there was fortunately no dearth of wood at the halting-place; only those who came late into camp had no wood. Accordingly those who had arrived a good while and had kindled fires were not for allowing these late-comers near their fires, unless they would in return give a share of their corn or of any other victuals they might have. Here then a general exchange of goods was set up. Where the fire was kindled the snow melted, and great trenches formed themselves down to the bare earth, and here it was possible to measure the depth of the snow.

Leaving these quarters, they marched the whole of the next day over snow, and many of the men were afflicted with 'boulimia' (or hunger-faintness). Xenophon, who was guarding the rear, came upon some men who had dropt down, and he did not know what ailed them; but someone who was experienced in such matters suggested to him that they had evidently got boulimia; and if they got something to eat, they would revive. Then he went the round of the baggage train, and laying an embargo on any eatables he could see, doled out with his own hands, or sent off other able-bodied agents to distribute to the sufferers, who as soon as they had taken a mouthful got on their legs again and continued the march.

On and on they marched, and about dusk Cheirisophus reached a village, and surprised some women and girls who had come from the village to fetch water at the fountain outside the stockade. These asked them who they were. The interpreters answered for them in Persian: 'They were on their way from the king to the satrap'; in reply to which the women gave them to understand that the satrap was not at home, but was away a parasang farther on. As it was late they entered with the water-carriers within the stockade to visit the headman of the village. Accordingly Cheirisophus and as many of the troops as were able got into cantonments there, while the rest of the soldiers – those namely who were unable to complete the march – had to spend the night out, without food and without fire; under the circumstances some of the men perished.

On the heels of the army hung perpetually bands of the enemy, snatching away disabled baggage animals and fighting with each other over the carcases. And in its track not seldom were left to their fate disabled soldiers, struck down with snow-blindness or with toes mortified by frost-bite. As to the eyes, it was some alleviation against the snow to march with something black before them; for their feet, the only remedy was to keep in motion without stopping for an instant, and to loose the sandal at night. If they went to sleep with the sandals on, the thong worked into the feet, and the sandals were frozen fast to them. This was partly due to the fact that, since their old sandals had failed, they wore untanned brogues made of newly flayed ox-hides. It was owing to some such dire necessity that a party of men fell out and were left behind, and seeing a black-looking patch of ground where the snow had evidently disappeared, they conjectured it must have been melted; and this was actually so, owing to a spring of some sort which was to be seen steaming up in a dell close by. To this they had turned aside and sat down, and were loth to go a step further. But Xenophon, with his rearguard, perceived them, and begged and implored them by all manner of means not to be left behind, telling them that the enemy were after them in large packs pursuing; and he ended by growing angry. They merely bade him put a knife to their throats; not one step farther would they stir. Then it seemed best to frighten the pursuing enemy if possible, and prevent their falling upon the invalids. It was already dusk, and the pursuers were advancing with much noise and hubbub, wrangling and disputing over their spoils. Then all of a sudden the rearguard, in the plenitude of health and strength, sprang up out of their lair and ran upon the enemy, whilst those weary wights bawled out as loud as their sick throats could sound, and clashed their spears against their shields; and the enemy in terror hurled themselves through the snow into the dell, and not one of them ever uttered a sound again.

After this they marched into the country of the Taochians – and provisions failed; for the Taochians lived in strong places, into which they had carried up all their stores. Now when the army arrived before one of these strong places – a mere fortress, without city or houses, into which a motley crowd of men and women and numerous flocks and herds were gathered – Cheirisophus attacked at once. When the first regiment fell back tired, a second advanced, and again a third, for it was impossible to surround the place in full force, as it was encircled by a river. Presently Xenophon came up with the rearguard, consisting of both light and heavy infantry, whereupon Cheirisophus hailed him with the words: 'In the nick of time you have come; we must take this place, for the troops have no provisions, unless we take it.' Thereupon they consulted together, and to Xenophon's inquiry, 'What it was which hindered their simply walking in?' Cheirisophus replied, 'There is just this one narrow approach which you see; but when we attempt to pass by it they roll down volleys of stones from yonder overhanging crag,' pointing up, 'and this is the state in which you find yourself, if you chance to be caught;' and he pointed to some poor fellows with their legs or ribs crushed to bits. 'But when they have expended their ammunition,' said Xenophon, 'there is nothing else, is there, to hinder our passing? Certainly, except yonder handful of fellows, there is no one in front of us that we can see; and of them, only two or three apparently are armed, and the distance to be traversed under fire is, as your eyes will tell you, about one hundred and fifty feet as near as can be, and of this space the first hundred is thickly covered with great pines at intervals; under cover of these, what harm can come to our men from a pelt of stones, flying or rolling? So then, there is only fifty feet left to cross, during a lull of stones.' 'Ay,' said Cheirisophus, 'but with our first attempt to approach the bush a galling fire of stones commences.' 'The very thing we want,' said the other, 'for they will use up their ammunition all the quicker; but let us select a point from which we shall have only a brief space to run across, if we can, and from which it will be easier to get back, if we wish.'

Thereupon Cheirisophus and Xenophon set out with Callimachus the Parrhasian, the captain in command of the officers of the rearguard that day; the rest of the captains remained out of danger. That done, the next step was for a party of about seventy men to get away under the trees, not in a body, but one by one, every one using his best precaution; and Agasias the Stymphalian, and Aristonymus the Methydrian, who were also officers of the rearguard, were posted as supports outside the trees; for it was not possible for more than a single company to stand safely within the trees. Here Callimachus hit upon a pretty contrivance – he ran forward from the tree under which he was posted two or three paces, and as soon as the stones came whizzing, he retired easily, but at each excursion more than ten wagon-loads of rocks were expended. Agasias, seeing how Callimachus was amusing himself, and the whole army looking on as spectators, was seized with the fear that he might miss his chance of being first to run the gauntlet of the enemy's fire and get into the place. So, without a word of summons to his next neighbour, Aristonymus, or to Eurylochus of Lusia, both comrades of his, or to any one else, off he set on his own account, and passed the whole detachment. But Callimachus, seeing him tearing past, caught hold of his shield by the rim, and in the meantime Aristonymus the Methydrian ran past both, and after him Eurylochus of Lusia; for they were one and all aspirants to valour, and in that high pursuit, each was the eager rival of the rest. So in this strife of honour, the four of them took the fortress, and when they had once rushed in, not a stone more was hurled from overhead.

And here a terrible spectacle displayed itself: the women first cast their infants down the cliff, and then they cast themselves after their fallen little ones, and the men likewise. In such a scene, Aeneas the Stymphalian, an officer, caught sight of a man with a fine dress about to throw himself over, and seized hold of him to stop him; but the other caught him to his arms, and both were gone in an instant headlong down the crags, and were killed. Out of this place the merest handful of human beings were taken prisoners, but cattle and asses in abundance and flocks of sheep.

From this place they marched through the Chalybes seven stages, fifty parasangs. These were the bravest men whom they encountered on the whole march, coming cheerily to close quarters with them. They wore linen corselets reaching to the groin, and instead of the ordinary 'wings' or basques, a thickly plaited fringe of cords. They were also provided with greaves and helmets, and at the girdle a short sabre, about as long as the Laconian dagger, with which they cut the throats of those they mastered and after severing the head from the trunk they would march along carrying it, singing and dancing, when they drew within their enemy's field of view. They carried also a spear fifteen cubits long, lanced at one end. This folk stayed in regular townships, and whenever the Hellenes passed by they invariably hung close on their heels fighting. They had dwelling-places in their fortresses, and into them they had carried up their supplies, so that the Hellenes could get nothing from this district, but supported themselves on the flocks and herds they had taken from the Taochians . . .

On the fifth day they reached the mountain, the name of which was Theches. No sooner had the men in front ascended it and caught sight of the sea than a great cry arose, and Xenophon, with the rearguard, catching the sound of it, conjectured that another set of enemies must surely be attacking in front; for they were followed by the inhabitants of the country, which was all aflame; indeed the rearguard had killed some and captured others alive by laying an ambuscade; they had taken also about twenty wicker shields, covered with the raw hides of shaggy oxen.

But as the shout became louder and nearer, and those who from time to time came up, began racing at the top of their speed towards the shouters, and the shouting continually recommenced with yet greater volume as the numbers increased, Xenophon settled in his mind that something extraordinary must have happened, so he mounted his horse, and taking with him Lycius and the cavalry, he galloped to the rescue. Presently they could hear the soldiers shouting and passing on the joyful word, *The sea! the sea!*

Thereupon they began running, rearguard and all, and the baggage animals and horses came galloping up. But when they had reached the summit, then indeed they fell to embracing one another – generals and officers and all – and the tears trickled down their cheeks. And on a sudden, someone, whoever it was, having passed down the order, the soldiers began bringing stones and erecting a great cairn, whereon they dedicated a host of untanned skins, and staves, and captured wicker shields, and with his own hand the guide hacked the shields to pieces, inviting the rest to follow his example. After this the Hellenes dismissed the guide with a present raised from the common store, to wit, a horse, a silver bowl, a Persian dress, and ten darics; but what he most begged to have were their rings, and of these he got several from the soldiers. So, after pointing out to them a village where they would find quarters, and the road by which they would proceed towards the land of the Macrones, as evening fell, he turned his back upon them in the night and was gone.

THE EXECUTION OF THE PHILOSOPHER SOCRATES, ATHENS, 399 BC

Plato

Along with Aristotle, Socrates was the pivotal figure in ancient philosophy, shifting its focus from the world of nature to that of man, especially man's ethics and politics. The enterprise always carried the faint tinge of sedition and at the age of seventy he was found guilty by an Athenian state court of 'corrupting the minds of the young'. Rejecting the option of merely paying a fine, he was sentenced to death by drinking hemlock (*Conium maculatum*).

Crito made a sign to the servant, who was standing by; and he went out, and after some time returned with the jailer carrying the cup of poison. Socrates said: My good friend, you are an expert in these matters; what must I do? The man answered: You have only to walk about until your legs are heavy, and then to lie down, and the poison will act. At the same time he handed the cup to Socrates, who very cheerfully and without the least tremor or change of colour or feature, glancing upwards and looking the man full in the face, Echecrates, as his manner was, took the cup and said: What about making a libation out of this cup? May I, or not? The man answered: We only prepare, Socrates, just so much as we think enough. I understand, he said: but I may and must ask the gods to prosper my journey from this to the other world – even so –

and so be it according to my prayer. Then raising the cup to his lips, quite readily and cheerfully he drank of the poison. Till then most of us had been able to control our sorrow; but now when we saw him drinking, and saw too that he had finished the draught, we could do it no longer, and in spite of myself my own tears were flowing fast; so that I covered my face and wept, not for him, but at the thought of my own calamity in having to part from such a friend. Nor was I the first; for Crito, when he found himself unable to restrain his tears, had got up, and I followed; and at that moment Apollodorus, who had been in tears all the time, broke out in a loud and passionate cry which made cowards of us all. Socrates alone retained his calmness: What are you doing, you strange people? he said. I sent away the women mainly in order that they might not strike this false note, for I have been told that a man should die in peace. Be quiet then, and have patience. When we heard his words we were ashamed, and checked our tears; and he walked about until, as he said, his legs began to fail, and then he lay on his back, according to the directions, and the man who gave him the poison now and then looked at his feet and legs; and after a while he pressed his foot hard, and asked him if he could feel; and he said, No; and then his leg, and so upwards and upwards, and showed us that he was cold and stiff. Then he felt them again, and said: When the poison reaches the heart, that will be the end. He was beginning to grow cold about the groin, when he uncovered his face, for he had covered himself up, and said: Crito, I owe a cock to Asclepius; will you remember to pay the debt? The debt shall be paid, said Crito; is there anything else? There was no answer to this question; but in a minute or two a movement was heard, and the attendants uncovered him; his eyes were set, and Crito closed his eyes and mouth.

Such was the end, Echecrates, of our friend; of whom I may truly say, that of all the men of his time whom I have known, he was the wisest and justest and best.

THE DEATH OF ALEXANDER THE GREAT, BABYLON, 323 BC

Arrian

Alexander was the son of Philip II of Macedon. In 334 BC Alexander crossed into Asia on an eleven-year campaign that would take him as far east as India. He died at the age of thirty-three. Arrian was one of several biographers of Alexander in antiquity; as he makes clear, his account is based on the official diaries of Alexander's march.

A few days later he (Alexander) had performed the divine sacrifices, those prescribed for good fortune and others suggested by the priests, and was drinking far into the night with some friends. He is said to have distributed sacrificial victims and wine to the army by detachments and companies. Some state that he wanted to leave the drinking-party and go to bed, but then Medius met him, the most trusty of his Companions, and asked him to a party, for he promised that it would be a good one.

Day 1

The Royal Diaries tell us that he drank and caroused with Medius. Later he rose, had a bath and slept. He then returned to have dinner with Medius and again drank far into the night. Leaving the drinking, he bathed, after which he had a little to eat and went to sleep there. The fever was already on him.

Day 2

Each day he was carried on his couch to perform the customary sacrifices, and after their completion he lay down in the men's apartments until dusk. During this time he gave instructions to his officers about the coming expedition and sea-voyage, for the land forces to be ready to move on the fourth day, and for those sailing with him to be prepared to cast off a day later. He was carried thence on his couch to the river, where he boarded a boat and sailed across to the garden where he rested again after bathing.

Day 3

The next day, he again bathed and performed the prescribed sacrifices. He then entered his room, lay down and talked to Medius. After ordering the officers to meet him in the morning, he had a little food. Carried back to his room, he lay now in continual fever the whole night.

Day 4

In the morning he bathed and sacrificed. Nearchus and the other officers were instructed to get things ready for sailing two days later.

Day 5

The following day, he again bathed and sacrificed, and after performing them, he remained in constant fever. But in spite of that he summoned the officers and ordered them to have everything quite ready for the journey. After a bath in the evening, he was now very ill.

Day 6

The next day, he was carried to the house by the diving place, where he sacrificed, and in spite of being very poorly, summoned the senior officers to give them renewed instructions about the voyage.

Day 7

The next day he was carried with difficulty to perform the sacrifices, and continued to give orders just the same to his officers about the voyage.

Day 8

The next day, though very weak, he managed to sacrifice. He asked the generals to stay in the hall, with the brigadiers and colonels in front of the doors. Now extremely sick, he was carried back from the garden to the Royal Apartments. As the officers entered, he clearly recognized them, but he said not a word to them.

Day 9 and 10

He had a high fever that night, all the next day and for another day as well.

This information comes from the Royal Diaries, where we also learn that the soldiers wanted to see him, some hoping to see him before he died and others because there was a rumour that he was already dead, and they guessed that his death was being kept back by his personal guard, or so I think. Many pressed into the room in their grief and longing to see Alexander. They say that he remained speechless as the army filed past him. Yet he welcomed each one of them by a nod with his head or a movement of his eyes. The Royal Diaries say that Peithon, Attalus, Demophon, Peucestas, Cleomenes, Menidas and Seleucus spent the night in the temple of Serapis and asked the god whether it would be better and more profitable for Alexander to be carried into the temple to pray the god for his recovery. A reply came from the god that he should not be brought into the temple, but that it would be better for him to remain where he was. The Companions brought this news, and, shortly after, Alexander died; for this was what was better.

HOW TO KEEP A SLAVE, ROME, *c.* 170 BC

Cato

Rations for the slaves

For the actual labourers four pecks of wheat in the winter months, and four and a half in summer. The overseer, housekeeper, foreman and head-shepherd should receive three pecks. The chain-gang should receive four pounds of bread a day in winter, five from the time when they begin to dig the vines until the figs start to ripen, and then back to four again.

Wine for the slaves

For three months after the harvest, they should drink rough wine. In the fourth month, half a pint a day, or about two gallons a month. For the fifth, sixth, seventh and eighth months, the ration should be a pint a day, or four gallons a month. For the remaining four months, give them one and a half pints a day, or six gallons a month. For the feasts of the Saturnalia and Compitalia (December) there should be an extra ration per man of two and a half gallons. The total wine issue per man for a year should be about forty-two gallons. An additional amount can be given as a bonus to the chain-gang, depending on how well they work. A reasonable quantity for them to have to drink per annum is about sixty gallons.

Relish for the slaves

Keep all the windfall olives you can. Then keep the ripe olives from which only a small yield could be gained. Issue them sparingly to make them last as long as possible. When the olives are finished, give them fish-pickle and vinegar. Give each man a pint of oil a month. A peck of salt should be enough for a man for a year.

Clothes for the slaves

A tunic three and a half feet long and a blanket-cloak every other year. When you issue a tunic or cloak, take in the old one to make rough clothes. You ought to give them a good pair of clogs every other year.

JULIUS CAESAR INVADES BRITAIN, 55 BC

Julius Caesar

Caesar's invasion was intended to prevent the Britons from aiding their subjugated kinsmen in Gaul. He writes in the third person.

. . . and so it was about 10 a.m. when Caesar arrived off Britain with the leading ships. Armed men could be seen stationed on all the heights, and the nature of the place was such, with the shore edged by sheer cliffs, that missiles could be hurled onto the beach from the top. Caesar considered this a totally unsuitable place for disembarkation, and waited at anchor till 3 p.m. for the rest of his invasion fleet to assemble. He then summoned a meeting of his brigade and battalion commanders, revealed the news he had from Volusenus, and outlined his orders. He wanted them to be ready to act immediately, on the slightest sign from him. For military practice demanded this, especially in a naval attack, which was liable to rapid, unexpected changes of circumstance. Dismissing his officers, he waited for a favourable combination of wind and tide, and then gave the signal to weigh anchor. Sailing on for about seven miles, he halted his line opposite an open, level beach.

The barbarians had discovered Caesar's plan by sending forward cavalry units and charioteers (a very common method of fighting with them). Their main force which had followed later was now in a position to prevent our men from disembarking. This caused considerable difficulty. The ships could only be drawn up in deep water because of their draught. The soldiers were faced with unknown ground and had their hands impeded, while they were burdened with a very heavy load of arms. And yet they had to leap down from the ships, keep their footing in the waves and fight the enemy. The latter, on the other hand, could either resist from dry land or by moving just a little forward into the shallows. So, completely unencumbered and with full knowledge of the ground, they boldly hurled their missiles, badly disturbing the horses which were totally unused to the conditions. Our men were shaken by these circumstances through lack of experience of this style of warfare, and failed to show the same dash and enthusiasm as they did in land battles.

As Caesar noticed this, he gave orders to the warships to row off slightly to the enemy's open flank away from the cargo ships. These ships were less well known to the barbarians and much more manoeuvrable. They were to halt, attack and move the enemy back by the use of slings, arrows and other missiles. All this helped our men considerably. The barbarians were affected by the strange shape of the ships, by the motion of the oars and the unusual type of catapult. Halting their advance, they slowly began to retire.

Our troops, however, were still hesitating, largely because of the depth of the sea, when the standard-bearer of the Tenth legion, with a prayer to the gods for a happy outcome for his legion, shouted, 'Jump down, men, unless you want the enemy to get your standard. You will not find me failing in my duty to my country or my leader.' This he yelled at the top of his voice, and then springing off the boat began to bear the eagle forward against the enemy. Our troops, with mutual words of encouragement not to commit a terrible wrong, all jumped down into the sea. Their fellows in the next boats saw what they were doing, followed suit and came to grips with the enemy . . .

Fighting was tough on both sides. My men could not keep in line, get a firm foothold or keep to their own standards. Each man joined the nearest unit irrespective of his ship and chaos reigned. The enemy knew the lie of the shoals and when they saw from the beach isolated groups disembarking they made a mounted charge and attacked them in their difficulties. These they outnumbered and surrounded, while their comrades raked the main party with an enfilade. Caesar assessed the situation and had both the boats of the warships and the sloops packed with soldiers to help wherever he saw need. Our men reached the land and were there reinforced by all those behind.

Then came the assault which routed the enemy, but we could not follow up satisfactorily as the cavalry had failed to hold its course and make the island. The enemy lost the day. As soon as they could stop bolting they sent a peace delegation to Caesar. Commius, the Atrebatian, came along with it. It was he whom Caesar had sent to Britain to bring that general's instructions; but they had seized him as soon as he stepped ashore and clapped him in irons. The outcome of our victory was his release. In sueing for peace they attributed this outrage to the lower classes and asked him to let it pass as an act of their folly. Caesar protested at their unprovoked aggression after they had taken it upon themselves to send a delegation over to the continent to make peace with him. Yet he forgave their folly and demanded hostages. Some they delivered on the spot but promised to send for the others from up-country in a few days. Meanwhile they demobilized the tribesmen, and the chiefs came in from all quarters to surrender themselves and their countries to Caesar. Thus peace was made within four days of the landing in Britain.

A CHARIOT FIGHT, BRITAIN, 55 BC

Julius Caesar

Meanwhile the Seventh legion was out on a routine foraging mission without any thought of action as there were still people on the farms and traffic in and out of the camp. Suddenly the guards at the gate reported to Caesar an exceptional quantity of dust where the legion had gone. Caesar rightly sensed a new native stratagem. He told the two duty cohorts to follow him and the other two to relieve them, and the rest to arm and follow at once. After a short march he saw his troops pressed by the enemy almost to breaking point with the legion undeployed and subject to cross-fire. For the corn had been reaped in every district except one and the enemy had guessed they would go there and had prepared an ambush by night in the woods. Our men were scattered, busy reaping with arms piled, when the attack began. They killed some, put the others into confusion and surrounded them with both cavalry and chariots.

A chariot fight is like this: first they scour the field shooting and this often breaks the line just with the fear of the horses and the din of wheels. When they have infiltrated among the cavalry units they jump down and fight as infantry. Meanwhile the drivers withdraw a bit to wait where they can quickly escape to base if compelled by weight of numbers. Thus they show the dash of cavalry and the steadiness of infantry in action. Daily drill teaches them the habit of checking their steeds even in full career down a steep slope, of lightning turns and of running along the pole, standing on the yoke and getting back quickly into the chariot.

Caesar brought help in the nick of time to our men for they were dismayed by such novel tactics.

Caesar withdrew from Britain in 55 BC, only to reinvade in the following year. However, troubles in Gaul forced another retreat; it was not until AD 43, under the Emperor Claudius, that the Romans successfully colonized England. Scotland remained unconquered.

A DICTATOR COMES TO DINNER, ROME, 45 BC

Marcus Tullius Cicero

The Roman lawyer Cicero had long been an opponent of Julius Caesar – hence the tone of amused cynicism here.

Oh, what a formidable guest to have had! and yet *je ne m'en plains pas*, because he was in a very agreeable mood. But after his arrival at Philippus's house on the evening of the second day of the Saturnalia the whole establishment was so crowded with soldiers that even the room where Caesar himself was to dine could hardly be kept clear from them; it is a fact that there were two thousand men! Of course I was nervous about what might be the case with me next day, and so Cassius Barba came to my assistance; he set some men on guard. The camp was pitched out of doors; my villa was made secure. On the third day of the Saturnalia he stayed at Philippus's till near one, and admitted nobody (accounts with Balbus, I suppose); then took a walk on the beach. After two to the bath: then he heard about Mamurra; he made no objection. After the toilet he sat down to dinner. He was under the 'emetic cure', and consequently he ate and drank *sans peur*; and with much satisfaction. And certainly everything was very good, and well served; nay more, I may say that

> 'Though the cook was good,
> 'Twas Attic salt that flavoured best the food.'

There were three dining-rooms besides, where there was a very hospitable reception for the gentlemen of his *suite*; while the inferior class of freedmen and slaves had abundance at any rate; for as to the better class, they had a more refined table. In short, I think I acquitted myself like a man. The guest however was not the sort of person to whom you would say 'I shall be most delighted if you will come here again on your way back'; once is enough. Nothing was said *au grand sérieux*; much on 'literary' chat. In short, he was greatly pleased, and seemed to enjoy himself. He told me that he should be one day at Puteoli, and the next near Baiae. Here you have the story of his visit – or, I may call it, his *billeting* – which, as I told you, was a thing one would shrink from, but did not give much trouble. I am for Tusculum next after a short stay here.

When he was passing Dolabella's house, but nowhere else, the whole guard was paraded in arms on either side of him as he rode; I have it from Nicias.

Cicero was executed in 43 BC for opposing the military triumvirate of Marcus Antonius (Mark Anthony), Octavian and Lepidus. His head and hands were severed from his body and put on public display.

THE ASSASSINATION OF JULIUS CAESAR, ROME, 15 March 44 BC

Nicolaus of Damascus

The conspirators never met openly, but they assembled a few at a time in each other's homes. There were many discussions and proposals, as might be expected, while they investigated how and where to execute their design. Some suggested that they should make the attempt as he was going along the Sacred Way, which was one of his favourite walks. Another idea was for it to be done at the elections during which he had to cross a bridge to appoint the magistrates in the Campus Martius; they should draw lots for some to push him from the bridge and for others to run up and kill him. A third plan was to wait for a coming gladiatorial show. The advantage of that would be that, because of the show, no suspicion would be aroused if arms were seen prepared for the attempt. But the majority opinion favoured killing him while he sat in the Senate, where he would be by himself since non-Senators would not be admitted, and where the many conspirators could hide their daggers beneath their togas. This plan won the day. Chance, too, played a part, for it made him settle on a definite day for the Senate to meet to discuss his intended measures.

When the day came, they assembled, with everything ready, in Pompey's Stoa, their normal meeting-place. The impression might be gained from his evil genius that all this was quite by accident and subject to chance, but in fact it led him into his enemy's place, in which he was to lie dead in front of Pompey's statue, and be murdered near the image of a man now dead whom, when alive, he had defeated. But if any attention is paid to such things, his destiny had the stronger force. For his friends were alarmed at certain rumours and tried to stop him going to the Senate-house, as did his doctors, for he was suffering from one of his occasional dizzy spells. His wife, Calpurnia, especially, who was frightened by some visions in her dreams, clung to him and said that she would not let him go out that day. But Brutus, one of the conspirators who was then thought of as a firm friend, came up and said, 'What is this, Caesar? Are you a man to pay attention to a woman's dreams and the idle gossip of stupid men, and to insult the Senate by not going out, although it has honoured you and has been specially summoned by you? But listen to me, cast aside the forebodings of all these people, and come. The Senate has been in session waiting for you since early this morning.' This swayed Caesar and he left.

While this was happening, the conspirators were making their preparations and arranging their seats, some next to him, some facing him and some behind. Before he entered the chamber, the priests brought up the victims for him to make what was to be his last sacrifice. The omens were clearly unfavourable. After this unsuccessful sacrifice, the priests made repeated other ones, to see if anything more propitious might appear than what had already been revealed to them. In the end they said that they could not clearly see the divine intent, for there was some transparent, malignant spirit hidden in the victims. Caesar was annoyed and abandoned divination till sunset, though the priests continued all the more with their efforts. Those of the murderers present were delighted at all this, though Caesar's friends asked him to put off the meeting of the Senate for that day because of what the priests had said, and he agreed to do this. But some attendants came up, calling him and saying that the Senate was full. He glanced at his friends, but Brutus approached him again and said, 'Come, good sir, pay no attention to the babblings of these men, and do not postpone what Caesar and his mighty power has seen fit to arrange. Make your own courage your favourable omen.' He convinced Caesar with these words, took him by the right hand, and led him to the Senate which was quite near. Caesar followed in silence.

The Senate rose in respect for his position when they saw him entering. Those who were to have part in the plot stood near him. Right next to him went Tillius Cimber, whose brother had been exiled by Caesar. Under pretext of a humble request on behalf of this brother, Cimber approached and grasped the mantle of his toga, seeming to want to make a more positive move with his hands upon Caesar. Caesar wanted to get up and use his hands, but was prevented by Cimber and became exceedingly annoyed. That was the moment for the men to set to work. All quickly unsheathed their daggers and rushed at him. First Servilius Casca struck him with the point of the blade on the left shoulder a little above the collar-bone. He had been aiming for that, but in the excitement he missed. Caesar rose to defend himself, and in the uproar Casca shouted out in Greek to his brother. The latter heard him and drove his sword into the ribs. After a moment, Cassius made a slash at his face, and Decimus Brutus pierced him in the side. While Cassius Longinus was trying to give him another blow, he missed and struck Marcus Brutus on the hand. Minucius also hit out at Caesar and hit Rubrius in the thigh. They were just like men doing battle against him. Under the mass of wounds, he fell at the foot of Pompey's statue. Everyone wanted to seem to have had some part in the murder, and there was not one of them who failed to strike his body as it lay there, until, wounded thirty-five times, he breathed his last.

JESUS CHRIST IS CRUCIFIED, JERUSALEM, *c.* AD 30

St John

One of the Twelve Apostles, St John – by tradition, at least – composed the Gospel which bears his name before dying at an advanced age near Ephesus.

Then Pilate therefore took Jesus, and scourged *him*.
2 And the soldiers platted a crown of thorns, and put *it* on his
head, and they put on him a purple robe,
3 And said, Hail, King of the Jews! and they smote him with
their hands.
4 Pilate therefore went forth again, and saith unto them, Behold, I
bring him forth to you, that ye may know that I find no fault in him.
5 Then came Jesus forth, wearing the crown of thorns, and the
purple robe. And *Pilate* saith unto them, Behold the man!
6 When the chief priests therefore and officers saw him, they
cried out, saying, Crucify *him*, crucify *him*. Pilate saith unto them,
Take ye him, and crucify *him*: for I find no fault in him.
7 The Jews answered him, We have a law, and by our law he
ought to die, because he made himself the Son of God.
8 ¶ When Pilate therefore heard that saying, he was the more
afraid;

9 And went again into the judgment hall, and saith unto Jesus, Whence art thou? But Jesus gave him no answer.

10 Then saith Pilate unto him, Speakest thou not unto me? Knowest thou not that I have power to crucify thee, and have power to release thee?

11 Jesus answered, Thou couldest have no power *at all* against me, except it were given thee from above: therefore he that delivered me unto thee hath the greater sin.

12 And from thenceforth Pilate sought to release him: but the Jews cried out, saying, If thou let this man go, thou art not Cæsar's friend: whosoever maketh himself a king speaketh against Caesar.

13 ¶ When Pilate therefore heard that saying, he brought Jesus forth, and sat down in the judgment seat in a place that is called the Pavement, but in the Hebrew, Gabbatha.

14 And it was the preparation of the passover, and about the sixth hour: and he saith unto the Jews, Behold your King!

15 But they cried out, Away with *him*, away with *him*, crucify him, Pilate saith unto them, Shall I crucify your King? The chief priests answered, We have no king but Caesar.

16 Then delivered he him therefore unto them to be crucified. And they took Jesus, and led *him* away.

17 And he bearing his cross went forth into a place called *the place* of a skull, which is called in the Hebrew Golgotha:

18 Where they crucified him, and two other with him, on either side one, and Jesus in the midst.

19 ¶ And Pilate wrote a title, and put *it* on the cross. And the writing was, JESUS OF NAZARETH THE KING OF THE JEWS.

20 This title then read many of the Jews: for the place where Jesus was crucified was nigh to the city: and it was written in Hebrew, *and* Greek, *and* Latin.

21 Then said the chief priests of the Jews to Pilate, Write not, The King of the Jews; but that he said, I am King of the Jews.

22 Pilate answered, What I have written I have written.

23 ¶ Then the soldiers, when they had crucified Jesus, took his garments, and made four parts, to every soldier a part; and also *his* coat: now the coat was without seam, woven from the top throughout.

24 They said therefore among themselves, Let us not rend it, but cast lots for it, whose it shall be: that the scripture might be fulfilled, which saith, They parted my raiment among them, and

for my vesture they did cast lots. These things therefore the soldiers did.

25 ¶ Now there stood by the cross of Jesus his mother, and his mother's sister, Mary the *wife* of Cleophas, and Mary Magdalene.

26 When Jesus therefore saw his mother, and the disciple standing by, whom he loved, he saith unto his mother, Woman, behold thy son!

27 Then saith he to the disciple. Behold thy mother! And from that hour that disciple took her unto his own *home*.

28 ¶ After this, Jesus knowing that all things were now accomplished, that the scripture might be fulfilled, saith, I thirst.

29 Now there was set a vessel full of vinegar: and they filled a sponge with vinegar, and put *it* upon hyssop, and put *it* to his mouth.

30 When Jesus therefore had received the vinegar, he said, It is finished: and he bowed his head, and gave up the ghost.

GLADIATORIAL GAMES, ROME, *c.* AD 50

Seneca

There is nothing so ruinous to good character as to idle away one's time at some spectacle. Vices have a way of creeping in because of the feeling of pleasure that it brings. Why do you think that I say that I personally return from shows greedier, more ambitious and more given to luxury, and, I might add, with thoughts of greater cruelty and less humanity, simply because I have been among humans?

The other day, I chanced to drop in at the midday games, expecting sport and wit and some relaxation to rest men's eyes from the sight of human blood. Just the opposite was the case. Any fighting before that was as nothing; all trifles were now put aside – it was plain butchery. The men had nothing with which to protect themselves, for their whole bodies were open to the thrust, and every thrust told. The common people prefer this to matches on level terms or request performances. Of course they do. The blade is not parried by helmet or shield, and what use is skill or defence? All these merely postpone death. In the morning men are thrown to bears or lions, at midday to those who were previously watching them. The crowd cries for the killers to be paired with those who will kill them, and reserves the victor for yet another death. This is the only release the gladiators have. The whole business needs fire and steel to urge men on to fight.

'But he was a robber.' What of it; did he kill anyone? 'Yes, he did.' Well, just because he committed murder, did he deserve to suffer this? And you, poor man, what have you done to deserve to have to watch it? 'Kill him, lash him, brand him! Why is he so frightened of running against cold steel? Why does he die so feebly? Why is he so reluctant to die or to be driven to his death by the lash? They must both inflict wounds on each other's bare chests. Ah, now there's an interval. Let's have some men strangled to fill in the time.'

THE FIRE OF ROME, AD 64

Tacitus

Nero now tried to make it appear that Rome was his favourite abode. He gave feasts in public places as if the whole city were his own home. But the most prodigal and notorious banquet was given by Tigellinus. To avoid repetitious accounts of extravagance, I shall describe it, as a model of its kind. The entertainment took place on a raft constructed on Marcus Agrippa's lake. It was towed about by other vessels, with gold and ivory fittings. Their rowers were degenerates, assorted according to age and vice. Tigellinus had also collected birds and animals from remote countries, and even the products of the ocean. On the quays were brothels stocked with high-ranking ladies. Opposite them could be seen naked prostitutes, indecently posturing and gesturing.

At nightfall the woods and houses nearby echoed with singing and blazed with lights. Nero was already corrupted by every lust, natural and unnatural. But he now refuted any surmises that no further degradation was possible for him. For a few days later he went through a formal wedding ceremony with one of the perverted gang called Pythagoras. The emperor, in the presence of witnesses, put on the bridal veil. Dowry, marriage bed, wedding torches, all were there. Indeed everything was public which even in a natural union is veiled by night.

Disaster followed. Whether it was accidental or caused by a criminal act on the part of the emperor is uncertain – both versions have supporters. Now started the most terrible and destructive fire which Rome had ever experienced. It began in the Circus, where it adjoins the Palatine and Caelian hills. Breaking out in shops selling inflammable goods, and fanned by the wind, the conflagration instantly grew and swept the whole length of the Circus. There were no walled mansions or temples, or any other obstructions, which could arrest it. First, the fire swept violently over the level spaces. Then it climbed the hills – but returned to ravage the lower ground again. It outstripped every counter-measure. The ancient city's narrow winding streets and irregular blocks encouraged its progress.

Terrified, shrieking women, helpless old and young, people intent on their own safety, people unselfishly supporting invalids or waiting for them, fugitives and lingerers alike – all heightened the confusion. When people looked back, menacing flames sprang up before them or outflanked them. When they escaped to a neighbouring quarter, the fire followed – even districts believed remote proved to be involved. Finally, with no idea where or what to flee, they crowded on to the country roads, or lay in the fields. Some who had lost everything – even their food for the day – could have escaped, but preferred to die. So did others, who had failed to rescue their loved ones. Nobody dared fight the flames. Attempts to do so were prevented by menacing gangs. Torches, too, were openly thrown in, by men crying that they acted under orders. Perhaps they had received orders. Or they may just have wanted to plunder unhampered.

Nero was at Antium. He returned to the city only when the fire was approaching the mansion he had built to link the Gardens of Maecenas to the Palatine. The flames could not be prevented from overwhelming the whole of the Palatine, including his palace. Nevertheless, for the relief of the homeless, fugitive masses he threw open the Field of Mars, including Agrippa's public buildings, and even his own Gardens. Nero also constructed emergency accommodation for the destitute multitude. Food was brought from Ostia and neighbouring towns, and the price of corn was cut to less than 1/4 sesterce a pound. Yet these measures, for all their popular character, earned no gratitude. For a rumour had spread that, while the city was burning, Nero had gone on his private stage and, comparing modern calamities with ancient, had sung of the destruction of Troy.

By the sixth day enormous demolitions had confronted the raging flames with bare ground and open sky, and the fire was finally stamped out at the foot of the Esquiline Hill. But before panic had subsided, or hope revived, flames broke out again in the more open regions of the city. Here there were fewer casualties; but the destruction of temples and pleasure arcades was even worse.

This new conflagration caused additional ill-feeling because it started on Tigellinus' estate in the Aemilian district. For people believed that Nero was ambitious to found a new city to be called after himself.

Of Rome's fourteen districts only four remained intact . . .

THE DESTRUCTION OF THE TEMPLE AT JERUSALEM, 8 September AD 70

Josephus

The end play in Rome's suppression of the Jewish Revolt of AD 66. Josephus was a Jewish general who defected to the Roman army under Titus.

At this moment one of the soldiers, not waiting for orders and without any dread of such an act but driven on by some frenzy, snatched a brand from the blazing fire and, lifted up by a comrade, hurled the torch through the golden door which gave access to the buildings of the Temple Precinct from the north side. As the flames surged up, a great cry to match their feelings arose from the Jews, and they rushed to the defence, reckless of their lives and prodigal of their strength once they saw that the purpose of their previous watch was gone.

A message was quickly brought to Titus, who was in his tent during a lull in the battle. He leapt up just as he was, and rushed to the Temple to control the blaze, followed by all the officers, with the common soldiers accompanying them in a flutter. The shouts and noise were on a scale to be expected from such a force in such a disorderly move. Titus by verbal orders and gestures signalled to those fighting to put out the fire, but they did not hear his voice as their ears were filled with the greater volume of noise, and they paid no attention to his hand-signals, distracted as they were by the passion of battle. As the legionaries rushed in, neither warning nor threat checked their frenzy, but fury was their general. Many, as they pushed about the entrances, were trampled on by each other or fell on the still hot, smouldering ruins of the porches, and suffered the same fate as the vanquished. As they approached the Temple, they pretended not to hear Titus's instructions, but encouraged those in front to throw in the brands. The rebels were by now incapable of resisting, and death and flight were everywhere. For the most part it was the weak, defenceless citizens who were butchered where caught, and the pile of corpses grew around the altar, as the blood ran deep down the Temple steps and bodies of the slain slipped down from above.

As the fire gained strength, Titus found that he could not restrain the surge of his enthusiastic soldiers. Going into the Temple with his officers, he gazed at the Holy of Holies and its contents, much finer than the normal report of them which is circulated, and not a whit below their reputation and glory among the Jews themselves. The flames had not yet got inside, but were consuming the surrounding buildings. Titus quite rightly thought that the Temple could still be saved, and, leaping forward, he tried to get the soldiers to douse the fire, ordering Liberalius, the centurion of his bodyguard of lancers, to strike with his club anyone who disobeyed, and force him to help. But their obedience to Titus and their fear of the officers who were trying to control them was mastered by their passion, their hatred of the Jews and the wilder lust for battle. Most were driven on by the hope of loot, for they thought that the inside of the building must be full of money if the outside, which they could see, was made of gold. One of those who had got in forestalled the attempts of Titus who had rushed in to check them, and hurled a brand against the hinges of the door. Suddenly flames appeared from within, which forced back Titus and his officers, leaving those outside to kindle the blaze unhindered. In this way, though much against Titus's will, the Temple was burnt . . .

THE ERUPTION OF VESUVIUS, BAY OF NAPLES, ITALY, 4 August AD 79

Pliny the Younger

My uncle was stationed at Misenum, in active command of the fleet. On 24 August, in the early afternoon, my mother drew his attention to a cloud of unusual size and appearance. He had been out in the sun, had taken a cold bath, and lunched while lying down, and was then working at his books. He called for his shoes and climbed up to a place which would give him the best view of the phenomenon. It was not clear at that distance from which mountain the cloud was rising (it was afterwards known to be Vesuvius); its general appearance can best be expressed as being like an umbrella pine, for it rose to a great height on a sort of trunk and then split off into branches, I imagine because it was thrust upwards by the first blast and then left unsupported as the pressure subsided, or else it was borne down by its own weight so that it spread out and gradually dispersed. Sometimes it looked white, sometimes blotched and dirty, according to the amount of soil and ashes it carried with it. My uncle's scholarly acumen saw at once that it was important enough for a closer inspection, and he ordered a boat to be made ready, telling me I could come with him if I wished. I replied that I preferred to go on with my studies, and as it happened he had himself given me some writing to do.

As he was leaving the house he was handed a message from Rectina, wife of Tascius whose house was at the foot of the mountain, so that escape was impossible except by boat. She was terrified by the danger threatening her and implored him to rescue her from her fate. He changed his plans, and what he had begun in a spirit of inquiry he completed as a hero. He gave orders for the warships to be launched and went on board himself with the intention of bringing help to many more people besides Rectina, for this lovely stretch of coast was thickly populated. He hurried to the place which everyone else was hastily leaving, steering his course straight for the danger zone. He was entirely fearless, describing each new movement and phase of the portent to be noted down exactly as he observed them. Ashes were already falling, hotter and thicker as the ships drew near, followed by bits of pumice and blackened stones, charred and cracked by the flames: then suddenly they were in shallow water, and the shore was blocked by the debris from the mountain. For a moment my uncle wondered whether to turn back, but when the helmsman advised this he refused, telling him that Fortune stood by the courageous and they must make for Pomponianus at Stabiae. He was cut off there by the breadth of the bay (for the shore gradually curves round a basin filled by the sea) so that he was not as yet in danger, though it was clear that this would come nearer as it spread. Pomponianus had therefore already put his belongings on board ship, intending to escape if the contrary wind fell. This wind was of course full in my uncle's favour, and he was able to bring his ship in. He embraced his terrified friend, cheered and encouraged him, and thinking he could calm his fears by showing his own composure, gave orders that he was to be carried to the bathroom. After his bath he lay down and dined; he was quite cheerful, or at any rate he pretended he was, which was no less courageous.

Meanwhile on Mount Vesuvius broad sheets of fire and leaping flames blazed at several points, their bright glare emphasized by the darkness of night. My uncle tried to allay the fears of his companions by repeatedly declaring that these were nothing but bonfires left by the peasants in their terror, or else empty houses on fire in the districts they had abandoned. Then he went to rest and certainly slept, for as he was a stout man his breathing was rather loud and heavy and could be heard by people coming and going outside his door. By this time the courtyard giving access to his room was full of ashes mixed with pumice-stones, so that its level had risen, and if he had stayed in the room any longer he would never have got out. He was wakened, came out and joined Pomponianus and the rest of the household who had sat up all night. They debated whether to stay indoors or take their chance in the open, for the buildings were now shaking with violent shocks, and seemed to be swaying to and fro as if they were torn from their foundations. Outside on the other hand, there was the danger of falling pumice-stones, even though these were light and porous; however, after comparing the risks they chose the latter. In my uncle's case one reason outweighed the other, but for the others it was a choice of fears. As a protection against falling objects they put pillows on their heads tied down with cloths.

Elsewhere there was daylight by this time, but they were still in darkness, blacker and denser than any ordinary night, which they relieved by lighting torches and various kinds of lamp. My uncle decided to go down to the shore and investigate on the spot the possibility of any escape by sea, but he found the waves still wild and dangerous. A sheet was spread on the ground for him to lie down, and he repeatedly asked for cold water to drink. Then the flames and smell of sulphur which gave warning of the approaching fire drove the others to take flight and roused him to stand up. He stood leaning on two slaves and then suddenly collapsed, I imagine because the dense fumes choked his breathing by blocking his windpipe which was constitutionally weak and narrow and often inflamed. When daylight returned on the 26th – two days after the last day he had seen – his body was found intact and uninjured, still fully clothed and looking more like sleep than death.

Meanwhile my mother and I were at Misenum . . . After my uncle's departure I spent the rest of the day with my books, as this was my reason for staying behind. Then I took a bath, dined, and then dozed fitfully for a while. For several days past there had been earth tremors which were not particularly alarming because they are frequent in Campania: but that night the shocks were so violent that everything felt as if it were not only shaken but overturned. My mother hurried into my room and found me already getting up to wake her if she were still asleep. We sat down in the forecourt of the house, between the buildings and the sea close by. I don't know whether I should call this courage or folly on my part (I was only seventeen at the time) but I called for a volume of Livy and went on reading as if I had nothing else to do. I even went on with the extracts I had been making. Up came a friend of my uncle's who had just come from Spain to join him. When he saw us sitting there and me actually reading, he scolded us both – me for my foolhardiness and my mother for allowing it. Nevertheless, I remained absorbed in my book.

By now it was dawn, but the light was still dim and faint. The buildings round us were already tottering, and the open space we were in was too small for us not to be in real and imminent danger if the house collapsed. This finally decided us to leave the town. We were followed by a panic-stricken mob of people wanting to act on someone else's decision in preference to their own (a point in which fear looks like prudence), who hurried us on our way by pressing hard behind in a dense crowd. Once beyond the buildings we stopped, and there we had some extraordinary experiences which thoroughly alarmed us. The carriages we had ordered to be brought out began to run in different directions though the ground was quite level, and would not remain stationary even when wedged with stones. We also saw the sea sucked away and apparently forced back by the earthquake: at any rate it receded from the shore so that quantities of sea creatures were left stranded on dry sand. On the landward side a fearful black cloud was rent by forked and quivering bursts of flame, and parted to reveal great tongues of fire, like flashes of lighting magnified in size.

At this point my uncle's friend from Spain spoke up still more urgently: 'If your brother, if your uncle is still alive, he will want you both to be saved; if he is dead, he would want you to survive him – why put off your escape?' We replied that we would not think of considering our own safety as long as we were uncertain of his. Without waiting any longer, our friend rushed off and hurried out of danger as fast as he could.

Soon afterwards the cloud sank down to earth and covered the sea; it had already blotted out Capri and hidden the promontory of

Misenum from sight. Then my mother implored, entreated and commanded me to escape as best I could – a young man might escape, whereas she was old and slow and could die in peace as long as she had not been the cause of my death too. I refused to save myself without her, and grasping her hand forced her to quicken her pace. She gave in reluctantly, blaming herself for delaying me. Ashes were already falling, not as yet very thickly. I looked round: a dense black cloud was coming up behind us, spreading over the earth like a flood. 'Let us leave the road while we can still see,' I said, 'or we shall be knocked down and trampled underfoot in the dark by the crowd behind.' We had scarcely sat down to rest when darkness fell, not the dark of a moonless or cloudy night, but as if the lamp had been put out in a closed room. You could hear the shrieks of women, the wailing of infants, and the shouting of men; some were calling their parents, others their children or their wives, trying to recognize them by their voices. People bewailed their own fate or that of their relatives, and there were some who prayed for death in their terror of dying. Many besought the aid of the gods, but still more imagined there were no gods left, and that the universe was plunged into eternal darkness for evermore. There were people, too, who added to the real perils by inventing fictitious dangers: some reported that part of Misenum had collapsed or another part was on fire, and though their tales were false they found others to believe them. A gleam of light returned, but we took this to be a warning of the approaching flames rather than daylight. However, the flames remained some distance off; then darkness came on once more and ashes began to fall again, this time in heavy showers. We rose from time to time and shook them off, otherwise we should have been buried and crushed beneath their weight. I could boast that not a groan or cry of fear escaped me in these perils, had I not derived some poor consolation in my mortal lot from the belief that the whole world was dying with me and I with it.

At last the darkness thinned and dispersed into smoke or cloud; then there was genuine daylight, and the sun actually shone out, but yellowish as it is during an eclipse. We were terrified to see everything changed, buried deep in ashes like snowdrifts. We returned to Misenum where we attended to our physical needs as best we could, and then spent an anxious night alternating between hope and fear. Fear predominated, for the earthquakes went on, and several hysterical individuals made their own and other people's calamities seem ludicrous in comparison with their frightful predictions.

THE MARTYRDOM OF POLYCARP, SMYRNA, *c.* AD 155

Anon

For three hundred years after the crucifixion, Christians in the Roman Empire remained a persecuted sect. The martyred included Polycarp, Bishop of Smyrna, whose fate was recorded in an anonymous letter from the Church at Smyrna to the Church at Philomelium. For the Roman authorities, Emperor worship was a constitutional necessity; in refusing a pinch of incense for Caesar, Polycarp became guilty of treason.

Now the glorious Polycarp at the first, when he heard it, so far from being dismayed, was desirous of remaining in town; but the greater part persuaded him to withdraw. So he withdrew to a farm not far distant from the city; and there he stayed with a few companions, doing nothing else night and day but praying for all men and for the churches throughout the world; for this was his constant habit. And while praying he falleth into a trance three days before his apprehension; and he saw his pillow burning with fire. And he turned and said unto those that were with him: 'It must needs be that I shall be burned alive'.

And as those that were in search of him persisted, he departed to another farm; and forthwith they that were in search of him came up; and not finding him, they seized two slave lads, one of whom confessed under torture; for it was impossible for him to lie concealed, seeing that the very persons who betrayed him were people of his own household. And the captain of the police, who chanced to have the very name, being called Herod, was eager to bring him into the stadium, that he himself might fulfil his appointed lot, being made a partaker with Christ, while they – his betrayers – underwent the punishment of Judas himself.

So taking the lad with them, on the Friday about the supper hour, the gendarmes and horsemen went forth with their accustomed arms, hastening *as against a robber*. And coming up in a body late in the evening, they found the man himself in bed in an upper chamber in a certain cottage; and though he might have departed thence to another place, he would not, saying, *The will of God be done*. So when he heard that they were come, he went down and conversed with them, the bystanders marvelling at his age and his constancy, and wondering how there should be so much eagerness for the apprehension of an old man like him. Thereupon forthwith he gave orders that a table should be spread for them to eat and drink at that hour, as much as they desired. And he persuaded them to grant him an hour that he might pray unmolested; and on their consenting, he stood up and prayed, being so full of the grace of God, that for two hours he could not hold his peace, and those that heard were amazed, and many repented that they had come against such a venerable old man.

But when at length he brought his prayer to an end, after remembering all who at any time had come in his way, small and great, high and low, and all the universal Church throughout the world, the hour of departure being come, they seated him on an ass and brought him into the city, it being a high sabbath. And he was met by Herod the captain of police and his father Nicetes, who also removed him to their carriage and tried to prevail upon him, seating themselves by his side and saying, 'Why, what harm is there in saying, Caesar is Lord, and offering incense', with more to this effect, 'and saving thyself?' But he at first gave them no answer. When however they persisted, he said, 'I am not going to do what ye counsel me'. Then they, failing to persuade him, uttered threatening words and made him dismount with speed, so that he bruised his shin, as he got down from the carriage. And without even turning round, he went on his way promptly and with speed, as if nothing had happened to him, being taken to the stadium; there being such a tumult in the stadium that no man's voice could be so much as heard.

But as Polycarp entered into the stadium, a voice came to him from heaven: 'Be strong, Polycarp, and play the man'. And no one saw the speaker, but those of our people who were present heard the voice. And at length, when he was brought up, there was a great tumult, for they heard that Polycarp had been apprehended. When then he was brought before him, the proconsul inquired whether he were the man. And on his confessing that he was, he tried to persuade him to a denial saying, 'Have respect to thine age', and other things in accordance therewith, as it is their wont to say; 'Swear by the genius of Caesar; repent and say, Away with the atheists'. Then Polycarp with solemn countenance looked upon the whole multitude of lawless heathen that were in the stadium, and waved his hand to them; and groaning and looking up to heaven he said, 'Away with the atheists'. But when the magistrate pressed him hard and said, 'Swear the oath, and I will release thee; revile the Christ,' Polycarp said, 'Fourscore and six years have I been His servant, and He hath done me no wrong. How then can I blaspheme my King who saved me?' . . .

Saying these things and more besides, he was inspired with courage and joy, and his countenance was filled with grace, so that not only did it not drop in dismay at the things which were said to him, but on the contrary the proconsul was astounded and sent his own herald to proclaim three times in the midst of the stadium, 'Polycarp hath confessed himself to be a Christian'. When this was proclaimed by the herald, the whole multitude both of Gentiles and of Jews who dwelt in Smyrna cried out with ungovernable wrath and with a loud shout, 'This is the teacher of Asia, the father of the Christians, the puller down of our gods, who teacheth numbers not to sacrifice nor worship'. Saying these things, they shouted aloud and asked the Asiarch Philip to let a lion loose upon Polycarp. But he said that it was not lawful for him, since he had brought the sports to a close. Then they thought fit to shout out with one accord that Polycarp should be burned alive. For it must needs be that the matter of the vision should be fulfilled, which was shown him concerning his pillow, when he saw it on fire while praying, and turning round he said prophetically to the faithful who were with him, 'I must needs be burned alive'.

These things then happened with so great speed, quicker than words could tell, the crowds forthwith collecting from the workshops and baths timber and faggots, and the Jews more especially assisting in this with zeal, as is their wont. But when the pile was made ready, divesting himself of all his upper garments and loosing his girdle, he endeavoured also to take off his shoes, though not in the habit of doing this before, because all the faithful at all times vied eagerly who should soonest touch his flesh. For he had been treated with all honour for his holy life even before his grey hairs came. Forthwith then the instruments that were prepared for the pile were placed about him; and as they were going likewise to nail him to the stake, he said, 'Leave me as I am; for He that hath granted me to endure the fire will grant me also to remain at the pile unmoved, even without the security which ye seek from nails'.

In spite of the efforts of the Romans, Christianity thrived in the Empire. (Ironically enough, the Roman genius for building roads, and the establishment of civil order, positively aided Christian proselytizers.) Eventually, in the fourth century, it was adopted by Constantine, as the Empire's official religion.

EMPEROR SEPTIMIUS SEVERUS IS MADE A GOD, ROME, AD 211

Herodian

It is the Roman custom to give divine status to those of their emperors who die with heirs to succeed them. This ceremony is called deification. Public mourning, with a mixture of festive and religious ritual, is proclaimed throughout the city, and the body of the dead man is buried in the normal way with a costly funeral. Then they make an exact wax replica of the man, which they put on a huge ivory bed, strewn with gold-threaded coverings, raised high up in the entrance to the palace. This image, deathly pale, rests there like a sick man. Either side of the bed is attended for most of the day, the whole Senate sitting on the left, dressed in black, while on the right are all the women who can claim special honours from the position of their husbands or fathers. Not one of these can be seen wearing gold or adorned with necklaces, but they are all dressed in plain white garments, giving the appearance of mourners.

This continues for seven days, during each of which doctors come and approach the bed, take a look at the supposed invalid and announce a daily deterioration in his condition. When at last the news is given that he is dead, the bed or bier is raised on the shoulders of the noblest members of the Equestrian Order and chosen young Senators, carried along the Sacred Way, and placed in the Forum Romanum, where the Roman magistrates usually lay down their office. Tiers of seats rise up on either side, and on one flank a chorus of children from the noblest and most respected families stands facing a body of women selected on merit. Each group sings hymns and songs of thanksgiving in honour of the dead emperor, composed in a solemn and mournful key.

After this the bier is raised and carried outside the city walls to the Campus Martius, where on the widest part of the plain a square structure is erected, looking like a house, made from only the largest timbers jointed together. The whole inside is filled with firewood, and the outside is covered with golden garments, ivory decorations and rich pictures. On top of this rests another structure, similar in design and finish but smaller, with doors and open panels. Third and fourth storeys, decreasing in size, are topped by a fifth, the smallest of all. The shape of the whole might be compared with a lighthouse at the entrance to a harbour which guides ships on safe courses at night by its light. (Such a lighthouse is commonly called a *Pharos*.) When the bier has been taken to the second storey and put inside, aromatic herbs and incense of every kind produced on earth, together with flowers, grasses and juices collected for their smell, are brought and poured in in heaps. Every nation and city, every person without distinction of rank or position competes in bringing these last gifts in honour of their emperor. When the pile of aromatic material is very high and the whole space filled, a mounted display is held around the structure. The whole Equestrian Order rides round, wheeling in well-disciplined circles in the Pyrrhic style. Chariots also circle in the same formations, the charioteers dressed in purple and carrying images with the masks of famous Roman generals and emperors.

The display over, the heir to the throne takes a brand and sets it to the building. All the spectators crowd in and add to the flame. Everything is very easily and readily consumed by the fire because of the mass of firewood and incense inside. From the highest and smallest storey, as from some battlement, an eagle is released and carried up into the sky with the flames. The Romans believe that this bird bears the soul of the emperor from earth to heaven. Thereafter the dead emperor is worshipped with the rest of the gods.

CHILDREN PLAYING, ROME, *c.* AD 300

Minucius Felix

Then our party came to a place where several small boats, having been drawn up on the shore, rested above ground on oaken rollers so as to prevent rot. There we saw a group of small boys, who were eagerly vying with one another in a game of ducks and drakes. This is what the game is all about: you choose a well-rounded shell from the shore – one that has been rubbed smooth by the pounding of the waves – and holding it horizontally in your fingers while stooping as low to the ground as you can get, you send it spinning across the water. Once thrown, it should either skim the surface of the sea, gliding smoothly along, or conversely shave the tops of the waves, only to resurface time and time again. Among the boys, the one whose shell has gone the farthest and skipped the most declares himself the winner.

THE HUNS, *c.* AD 370

Ammianus Marcellinus

Marcellinus was a Roman soldier. The Huns were the most feared of the barbarian nomads who eventually engulfed the Roman Empire in the West.

The Huns have been but lightly touched on in old records. They live beyond the Sea of Azov, by the frozen Ocean, and their barbarity passes all bounds. From their earliest childhood, babies' faces are deeply scored with steel and these puckered scars slow down the growth of hair that comes with adolescence. So they grow up beardless, but without any charm, like eunuchs. All have strong, well-knit limbs and sturdy necks, and are so appallingly misshapen and deformed that you would take them for animals standing on two legs, or for the posts crudely fashioned into images which are used for the balustrades of bridges.

They may be horribly ugly as men, but they are so tough in their way of life that they have no need of fire or of good-tasting food. Their diet consists of the roots of wild plants and half-raw meat from some animal or other. They warm this meat up a little by putting it between their thighs and the backs of their horses. They never live in houses, which they avoid like tombs set apart from common use. You cannot even find among them a hut roofed over with reeds, but they wander and roam through the mountains and woods, and from their cradles have grown accustomed to bearing with frost, hunger and thirst. They never enter strangers' houses, unless forced by dire necessity, for they feel no safety in being under a roof.

They wear clothes made of linen or the skins of wood-mice, and the same dress serves them inside and outside the home. Once a tunic of some dull colour has been put over their necks, it is not taken off or changed until it is in tatters and has shredded into rags from the constant use. They cover their heads with round caps, and their hairy legs in goat-skins. Their shoes are not fashioned on lasts, and this prevents them from walking freely. This means that they are not very adept at infantry battles.

They are almost glued to their horses, which are sturdy but ugly creatures. They sometimes sit on them side-saddle to perform their usual tasks. It is on horseback that all Huns remain day and night, to buy and sell, to eat and drink, and, leaning forward on the narrow necks of their mounts, they collapse into a sleep deep enough to allow all manner of dreams. It is on horseback too that they all consult together when any discussion arises about some important matter.

They are disciplined by no king, but are content with the wild leadership of chiefs under whom they burst through any obstacle. When provoked to battle they enter the fight in wedge formation with horrible discordant yells. They are lightly armed for speed and surprise, and so they suddenly disperse on purpose for the assault. Charging in no definite ranks, they rush around dealing out widespread slaughter. You will never catch them attacking earthworks or hurling their javelins at enemy camps because of their preoccupation with speed. They easily earn the reputation thereby of being the fiercest warriors on earth. Their missiles are hurled from a distance and instead of arrow tips have sharpened bones fastened on most cleverly. Then they gallop over the intervening ground, and, reckless of their own lives, use their swords in hand-to-hand combat. While their opponents are on their guard against sword-thrusts, they lasso them with twisted nooses and by enmeshing their limbs make them totally incapable of riding or walking.

No one ever ploughs or touches a plough among them, for the whole people wanders about without fixed abode, with no homestead, no laws, no habitual diet. They always look like fugitives, as they travel with the wagons in which they live. In these wagons, their wives weave their coarse garments, have intercourse with their husbands, and give birth to their children whom they bring up to puberty. None of them, if asked, can tell you where he comes from, for he was conceived in one place, born in another far away, and brought up in a third yet more distant spot.

They are faithless and inconstant in observing truce, wafted on the faintest breeze of any new hope, and give their all to utter violence and madness. Like senseless animals, they are completely ignorant of the distinction between right and wrong, and in parleys they are ambiguous and deceitful, bound by no reverence for religion or superstition. Gold enflames their desires inordinately. They are so changeable and easily angered that they are often estranged from friends more than once on the same day, although there is no cause for annoyance, and are reconciled again, although no one brings them together.

DINNER WITH ATTILA THE HUN, *c.* AD 450

Priscus

Priscus was an envoy sent from the Eastern Roman Empire to make peace with Attila, King of the Huns.

When we had returned to our tent, Orestes' father came to say that Attila invited both parties of us to dine with him about 3 o'clock that afternoon. We waited for the time of the invitation, and then all of us, the envoys from the Western Romans as well, presented ourselves in the doorway facing Attila. In accordance with the national custom the cupbearers gave us a cup for us to make our libations before we took our seats. When that had been done and we had sipped the wine, we went to the chairs where we would sit to have dinner. All the seats were ranged down either side of the room, up against the walls. In the middle Attila was sitting on a couch with a second couch behind him. Behind that a few steps led up to his bed, which for decorative purposes was covered in ornate drapes made of fine linen, like those which Greeks and Romans prepare for marriage ceremonies. I think that the more distinguished guests were on Attila's right, and the second rank on his left, where we were with Berichos, a man of some renown among the Scythians, who was sitting in front of us. Onegesios was to the right of Attila's couch, and opposite him were two of the king's sons on chairs. The eldest son was sitting on Attila's own couch, right on the very edge, with his eyes fixed on the ground in fear of his father.

When all were sitting properly in order, a cupbearer came to offer Attila an ivy-wood bowl of wine, which he took and drank a toast to the man first in order of precedence. The man thus honoured rose to his feet and it was not right for him to sit down again until Attila had drunk some or all of the wine and had handed the goblet back to the attendant. The guests, taking their own cups, then honoured him in the same way, sipping the wine after making the toast. One attendant went round to each man in strict order after Attila's personal cupbearer had gone out. When the second guest and then all the others in their turn had been honoured, Attila greeted us in like fashion in our order of seating.

After everyone had been toasted, the cupbearers left, and a table was put in front of Attila and other tables for groups of three or four men each. This enabled each guest to help himself to the things put on the table without leaving his proper seat. Attila's servant entered first with plates full of meat, and those waiting on all the others put bread and cooked food on the tables. A lavish meal, served on silver trenchers, was prepared for us and the other barbarians, but Attila just had some meat on a wooden platter, for this was one aspect of his self-discipline. For instance, gold or silver cups were presented to the other diners, but his own goblet was made of wood. His clothes, too, were simple, and no trouble was taken except to have them clean. The sword that hung by his side, the elasps of his barbarian shoes and the bridle of his horse were all free from gold, precious stones or other valuable decorations affected by the other Scythians. When the food in the first plates was finished we all got up, and no one, once on his feet, returned to his seat until he had, in the same order as before, drunk the full cup of wine that he was handed, with a toast for Attila's health. After this honour had been paid him, we sat down again and second plates were put on each table with other food on them. This also finished, everyone rose once more, drank another toast and resumed his seat.

As twilight came on torches were lit, and two barbarians entered before Attila to sing some songs they had composed, telling of his victories and his valour in war. The guests paid close attention to them, and some were delighted with the songs, others excited at being reminded of the wars, but others broke down and wept if their bodies were weakened by age and their warrior spirits forced to remain inactive. After the songs a Scythian entered, a crazy fellow who told a lot of strange and completely false stories, not a word of truth in them, which made everyone laugh. Following him came the moor, Zerkon, totally disorganized in appearance, clothes, voice and words. By mixing up the languages of the Italians with those of the Huns and Goths, he fascinated everyone and made them break out into uncontrollable laughter, all that is except Attila. He remained impassive, without any change of expression, and neither by word or gesture did he seem to share in the merriment except that when his youngest son, Ernas, came in and stood by him, he drew the boy towards him and looked at him with gentle eyes. I was surprised that he paid no attention to his other sons, and only had time for this one. But the barbarian at my side, who understood Italian and what I had said about the boy, warned me not to speak up, and said that the seers had told Attila that his family would be banished but would be restored by this son. After spending most of the night at the party, we left, having no wish to pursue the drinking any further.

Part Two

The Age of Faith

The Medieval World 501–1517

'Deliver us, O Lord, from the fury of the Norsemen!'
A Medieval Prayer

INTRODUCTION

With the swamping of Roman civilization, the West entered the Dark Ages. For four centuries, Europe was in almost constant flux as barbarian tribes uprooted and migrated under pressure of the advancing nomads from the East. England alone endured invasions by Angles, Saxons and Jutes from north Germany and Denmark. Then, in the 780s, the Vikings of Scandinavia bore down on the country in their longships. At first there was stout resistance, but by 1016 England had become part of the empire of the Danish king, Canute. Fifty years later, the Normans (from 'Norsemen'), descendants of the Vikings from France, occupied the country. With war came, always, attendants of famine and pestilence. Population stagnated.

England was not particularly unfortunate – most other western realms endured similar changes of tenure. And yet in the midst of this anarchy, the Christian Church endured, indeed triumphed, for the story of the Middle Ages is the story of the growth of faith. Successive popes, beginning with Pope Gregory the Great (590–604) sent out missions to heathen lands, their efforts consolidated by the vigorous monastic movement inaugurated by Benedict of Nursia. Everywhere they were founded, monasteries acted as centres of worship, and also of scholarship (exemplified by the *Book of Kells*, a 680-page illuminated version of the Gospels), and even welfare centres for the local poor. By the year 700 most of Western Europe had been converted. In 732, a tribe of former heathens, the Franks, saved Christian Europe from an invasion by followers of another dynamic monotheistic religion – Islam, founded by the prophet Muhammad (AD 570–632). The Arab Muslim onrush into Europe was stopped at Tours by a Frankish force under Charles Martel. The Muslims were forced to retreat, although they would continue to hold parts of Spain until the fifteenth century. The militant faiths of Islam and Christianity would clash again, most spectacularly during the 200 years which followed Pope Urban II's call in 1095 for the Crusaders of Christendom to march on the Holy Land.

The Muslims may have lost the battle of Tours, but indirectly they were responsible for establishing the social system that would prevail throughout medieval Europe. At Tours, the Muslim cavalry had impressed Martel with their use of stirrups, which enabled them to fight on horseback with either swords or lances. Martel created a similar cadre of horsemen, giving them land in return for an oath of service. The grant of land was called, in Latin, *feudum*. In essence, 'feudalism' was service in return for land; at first the service was of a military nature, but gradually became agricultural, whereby the toiling serfs worked on their masters' estates in return for three or four acres of land on which to support themselves. (Usually the land was scattered in strips, far apart, and of varying quality.) The ties of feudalism were all-encompassing: a serf could not move, even marry, without his lord's permission.

And yet, the lord himself was a tenant – of the king. The king in turn was a vassal of the emperor. The feudal system was intricate and elaborate, a towering pyramid of rigid class gradations. For centuries, feudalism and Church held the medieval world together (indeed they would maintain Eastern Europe in thrall until the nineteenth century), but it was never a marriage made in heaven.

As the Christian Church grew, so did its power. This power – which encompassed its own courts, taxes, right to offer sanctuary – was viewed with mistrust by the powerful monarchs who headed the emergent nation-states of Western Europe. It was precisely the insistence of Archbishop Thomas à Becket that the Crown had no power over the clergy that caused Henry II of England to call, previously, for his murder in 1170. Moreover, as the centuries rolled on, other aspects of the Church came under criticism. Where it was wealthy, it was frequently corrupt. 'God has given us the papacy,' said the Borgia Pope Alexander VI, 'now let us enjoy it.' Where the Church was poor, it staffed pulpits with clergy scarcely more theologically literate than their flock. There were periodic reform movements of the Church, such as those of John Wycliffe of

England and Jan Hus of Bohemia, but they achieved little, except to fragment the authority of the Church.

By the middle of the fourteenth century it was obvious to many that the twin hierarchies of Church and State were losing their historic grip on society. This was most apparent in Italy with a revival of interest (later to be dubbed the 'Renaissance' by the historian Jules Michelet) in the classical civilizations of antiquity. Against the otherworldly concerns of medieval thinkers and artists, the craftsmen of the Renaissance took pride in worldly affairs and even Man himself. In Michelangelo Buonarroti's painting *Creation of Adam*, the father of man is the focus, dominating even God.

Michelangelo was the archetypal 'Renaissance Man', magnificent as painter, poet and sculptor alike. There were other such cultural prodigies – Leonardo da Vinci, Raphael, Benvenuto Cellini among them. Underpinning their achievements was patronage by a wealthy merchant class. One of the by-products of the Crusades had to been to stimulate trade in such north Italian cities as Genoa, Florence, Milan and Venice. The rich merchant families – led by the Medicis in Florence – largely paid for the Renaissance. The self same merchants were the harbingers of capitalism; it was the money of the towns which sounded the death knell for feudalism.

The humanistic, enquiring spirit of the Renaissance, however, was not confined to artistic endeavour. Above all it caused men to explore the world around them.

Exploration was not merely a matter of the mind's desire. It was predicated on technological developments. Apart from the Atlantic voyages of the Vikings in the tenth century and Marco Polo's overland journey to China, medieval Europeans had made few long-distance explorations. A chief reason was the poor manoeuvrability of the medieval 'cog' ship, with its single square sail and lack of navigational aids. Medieval ships rarely sailed out of sight of land. But by the end of the fifteenth century, the cog had been replaced by the three-master with variable sails and a stern rudder. The magnetic compass had also arrived (probably from China, via the Arabs, who had sent an embassy to China as early as 651). Thus equipped, European sailors could sail far over the Ocean Blue.

One who did so, in 1492, was Christopher Columbus. A Genoese in the employ of the Spanish throne, Columbus was possessed by the revolutionary idea that by sailing westwards across the

Atlantic he would reach Asia – this at a time when almost everyone thought the world was flat. After 69 days afloat Columbus landed in the Bahamas. Inadvertently, he had discovered a New World. The importance of Christopher Columbus's journey is difficult to overestimate. Because of him, other Europeans sailed to America and colonized it; because of him Ferdinand Magellan would lead an expedition that circumnavigated the globe for the first time; because of him Europe would come to dominate the modern world.

If the precise moment when the medieval became the modern world is impossible to pin down, 1517 is as good a year as any. The New World had been discovered and the Renaissance was at its apogee. Capitalism was seeded in the merchant towns of Europe, and in Germany a little-known theologian by the name of Martin Luther would in this year pin a set of proclamations on a church door in Wittenberg. Thus was Protestantism established – the first successful challenge to the power of the Roman Catholic Church which for so long had dominated Western society.

THE SYNOD OF WHITBY, ENGLAND, AD 664

Eddius Stephanus

At which it was decided that Britain should follow the customs of Rome, not the native Celtic church.

On a certain occasion in the days of Colman, bishop of York and metropolitan, while Oswiu and Alhfrith his son were reigning, the abbots and priests and men of all ranks in the order of the Church gathered together in a monastery called Whitby, in the presence of the holy mother and most pious nun Hilda, as well as of the kings and two bishops, namely Colman and Agilbert, to consider the question of the proper date for the keeping of Easter – whether in accordance with the British and Scottish manner and that of the whole of the northern district, Easter should be kept on the Sunday between the fourteenth day of the moon and the twenty-second, or whether the plan of the apostolic see was better, namely to celebrate Easter Sunday between the fifteenth day of the moon and the twenty-first. The opportunity was granted first of all to Bishop Colman, as was proper, to state his case in the presence of all. He boldly spoke in reply as follows: 'Our fathers and their predecessors, plainly inspired by the Holy Spirit as was Columba, ordained the celebration of Easter on the fourteenth day of the moon, if it was a Sunday, following the example of the Apostle and Evangelist John 'who leaned on the breast of the Lord at supper' and was called the friend of the Lord. He celebrated Easter on the fourteenth day of the moon and we, like his disciples Polycarp and others, celebrate it on his authority; we dare not change it, for our fathers' sake, nor do we wish to do so. I have expressed the opinion of our party, do you state yours.'

Agilbert the foreign bishop and Agatho his priest bade St Wilfrid, priest and abbot, with his persuasive eloquence explain in his own tongue the system of the Roman Church and of the apostolic see. With his customary humility he answered in these words: 'This question has already been admirably investigated by the three hundred and eighteen most holy and learned fathers gathered together in Nicaea, a city of Bithynia. They fixed amongst other decisions upon a lunar cycle which recurs every nineteen years. This cycle never shows that Easter is to be kept on the fourteenth day of the moon. This is the fixed rule of the apostolic see and of almost the whole world, and our fathers, after many decrees had been made, uttered these words: ' "he who condemns any one of these let him be accursed." '

Then, after St Wilfrid the priest had finished his speech, King Oswiu smilingly asked them all: 'Tell me which is greater in the kingdom of heaven, Columba or the Apostle Peter?' The whole synod answered with one voice and one consent: 'The Lord settled this when he declared: 'Thou art Peter and upon this rock I will build my Church and the gates of hell shall not prevail against it. And I will give thee the keys of the kingdom of heaven; and whatsoever thou shalt bind on earth shall be bound in heaven; and whatsoever thou shalt loose on earth shall be loosed in heaven." '

The king wisely replied: 'He is the porter and keeps the keys. With him I will have no differences nor will I agree with those who have such, nor in any single particular will I gainsay his decisions so long as I live.'

THE VIKINGS RAID BRITAIN, AD 787–93

The Anglo-Saxon Chronicle

787 [789]. In this year Beorhtric took to wife Eadburh, daughter of king Offa. And in his days came first three ships of Norwegians from Hörthaland [around Hardanger Fjord]: and then the reeve

rode thither and tried to compel them to go to the royal manor, for he did not know what they were: and then they slew him. These were the first ships of the Danes to come to England.

793. In this year terrible portents appeared over Northumbria, and miserably frightened the inhabitants: these were exceptional flashes of lightning, and fiery dragons were seen flying in the air. A great famine soon followed these signs; and a little after that in the same year on 8 January the harrying of the heathen miserably destroyed God's church in Lindisfarne by rapine and slaughter. In this year . . . Northumbria was ravaged by the heathen, and Ecgfrith's monastery at *Donemup* [Jarrow] looted; and there one of their leaders was slain, and some of their ships besides were shattered by storms: and many of them were drowned there, and some came ashore alive and were at once slain at the river mouth.

CREMATION OF A VIKING CHIEFTAIN, THE VOLGA, AD 922

Ibn Fadlan

Fadlan was an Arab traveller; the warrior whose funerary rites he observed was a Rus, a Swedish Viking.

One day I learnt that one of their chieftains had died. He was placed apart in a grave which was covered over for ten days until clothing for him had been cut out and stitched. If the dead man were poor, a small boat was made, in which the corpse was placed and then burnt. But if he were wealthy, his property and goods were divided into three portions: one for his family, another to meet the cost of his clothing, the third to make *nabid* (funeral beer) which was drunk on the day when the dead man's slave was burnt with him . . .

When one of their chiefs died, his family demanded of his men and women slaves: 'Which among you wish to die with him?' Then, one of them would say, 'I will', and whoever said that would be forced to undergo it, it was not possible to withdraw. If she wished to do so, it would not be allowed. Those who volunteered were nearly always female slaves.

So it was that when this man died, the slaves were asked: 'Which among you wishes to die with him?' One of the female slaves replied: 'I will'. From that moment she would be under constant guard by two other servants who took care of her to the extent of washing her feet with their own hands. Preparations were made for the dead man, his clothing made etc., while every day the condemned girl would drink and sing, as though in preparation for a joyous event. When the day arrived for the chief and his slave to be burnt, I went to the river where his boat was moored. It had been hoisted up on to the bank. Then there were placed around it something which looked like a great scaffolding of wood . . .

People began to walk around it speaking in a tongue unknown to me, but the corpse was lying all the time in his grave; they never disturbed it again. They then brought a bier, placed it on the boat, and covered it over with carpets and cushions of *dibag* (brocaded silk) from Byzantium. Then there arrived an old woman whom they called the 'Angel of Death', and she it was who spread the cushions on the bier. She, too, was in charge of the whole ceremony, from the dressing of the cadaver to the execution of the slave.

I noticed that the Angel of Death was a strapping woman, massively built and austere of countenance. When they arrived at the grave the earth was removed from the wooden lid and then the wood itself was taken away. Next the corpse was stripped of the garments in which he had died. I noticed that his body had turned black from the intense cold.

When they had placed the body in the grave, they had also put there beer, fruit and a lute, all things which they now took away. Most surprisingly, the corpse has not changed at all save for the colour of his flesh. They took a pride in their duty of clothing him in drawers, trousers, boots, a tunic and cloak of *dibag* embellished with gold buttons: the corpse was then given a cap of *dibag* and sable; then he was carried to a tent set over the boat *Nabid,* fruits and aromatic herbs were then brought and placed all around his body; they also brought bread, meat and onions which they threw down before him.

That done, they took a dog and, after cutting it in two, they threw the pieces into the ship. Afterwards they brought all his weapons and laid them by his side. Then they took two horses, drove them until they sweated, and then cut them in pieces with swords and threw their flesh into the boat; the same was done with two cows. Next they killed a cock and a hen and threw them in too.

Meanwhile, the slave who had volunteered to be killed went hither and thither, entering each tent in turn, and the master of each household had sexual intercourse with her, saying: 'Tell your master that I do this thing for the love of him.'

When Friday afternoon came, they led the slave girl to something they had made which resembled a door frame. Then she mounted on to the palms of the men's hands high enough to look down over the framework, and when they lowered her again she said something in a strange tongue. They lifted her up again and she behaved exactly as before. They lowered her again, then once more raised her up and she repeated what she had done the first and second times. Then they gave her a hen; she cut off its head and threw it away; they took the hen and threw it into the boat.

I asked my interpreter what she had said. He replied: 'The first time she was lifted up, she said: "Look. I see my father and mother!" The second time: "Behold, I see my dead relatives seated around." The third time, she had said: "Behold! I see my master in Paradise, and Paradise is green and fair, and with him are men and young boys. He is calling me. Let me go to him!" '

Then they led her towards the ship. Next she took off two bracelets she was wearing and gave them to the old woman, the Angel of Death, who was going to kill her. She then took off the two finger-rings she was wearing and gave them to the daughters of the Angel of Death.

Then they raised her on to the ship, but they did not let her enter the tent. After that many men came with wooden shields and she was given a beaker of *nabid*. She sang as she drank it. My interpreter told me then: 'It is thus that she bids farewell to her friends.' Then she was given a second cup. She took it and sang for a long time: but the old woman told her to make haste, to drink up and go into the tent where she would find her master. I looked at her at that moment and she seemed completely bewildered. She wanted to enter the tent but only managed to put her head between it and the ship. The old woman took hold of her head and made her enter the tent, following her in.

Then it was that the men began to beat their shields with wooden sticks, to stifle the cries of the slave girl, so that other girls would not take fright and refuse to die with their masters. Six men then entered the tent and all had sexual intercourse with her. Then they made her lie at the side of her dead master. Two held her hands and two her feet, and the Angel of Death wound a noose round her neck ending in a knot at both ends which she placed in the hands of two men, for them to pull. She then advanced with a broad-bladed dagger which she plunged repeatedly between the ribs of the girl while the men strangled her until she was dead.

Then the closest relative of the dead man came. He seized a piece of wood and started a fire. In this fashion was set alight the wood which had been piled under the ship after the dead slave girl had been placed beside her master. Finally, people came with kindling and firewood; each man carried a firebrand which he threw upon the wood-pile, so that the wood was engulfed in flames, then the ship, the tent and the man, the slave and everything in it.

DEVILS TAKE THE WITCH OF BERKELEY'S SOUL, ENGLAND, 1065

William of Malmesbury

At the same time something similar occurred in England, not by divine miracle, but by infernal craft; which when I shall have related, the credit of the narrative will not be shaken, though the minds of the hearers should be incredulous; for I have heard it from a man of such character, who swore he had seen it, that I should blush to disbelieve.

There resided at Berkeley a woman addicted to witchcraft, as it afterwards appeared, and skilled in ancient augury . . . and of bad character. On a certain day, as she was regaling, a jack daw, which was a very great favourite, chattered a little more loudly than usual. On hearing which the woman's knife fell from her hand, her countenance grew pale, and deeply groaning, 'This day,' said she, 'my plough has completed its last furrow; to-day I shall hear of, and suffer, some dreadful calamity.' While yet speaking, the messenger of her misfortunes arrived; and being asked, 'why he approached with so distressed an air', 'I bring news,' said he, 'from that village,' naming the place, 'of the death of your son, and of the whole family, by a sudden accident.' At this intelligence, the woman, sorely afflicted, immediately took to her bed, and perceiving the disorder rapidly approaching the vitals, she summoned her surviving children, a monk, and a nun, by hasty letters; and, when they arrived, with faltering voice, addressed them thus: 'Formerly, my children, I constantly administered to my wretched circumstances by demoniacal arts: I have been the sink of every vice, the teacher of every allurement: yet, while practising these crimes, I was accustomed to soothe my hapless soul with the hope of your piety. Despairing of myself, I rested my expectations on you; I advanced you as my defenders against evil spirits, my safe guards against my strongest foes. Now, since I have approached the end of my life, and shall have those eager to punish, who lured me to sin, I entreat you by your mother's breasts, if you have any regard, any affection, at least to endeavour to alleviate my torments; and, although you cannot revoke the sentence already passed upon my soul, yet you may perhaps rescue my body, by these means: sew up my corpse in the skin of a stag; lay it on its back in a stone coffin; fasten down the lid with lead and iron; on this lay a stone, bound round with three iron chains of enormous weight; let there be psalms sung for fifty nights, and masses said for an equal number of days, to allay the ferocious attacks of my adversaries. If I lie thus secure for three nights, on the fourth day bury your mother in the ground; although I fear, lest the earth, which has been so often burdened with my crimes, should refuse to receive and cherish me in her bosom.' They did their utmost to comply with her injunctions: but alas! vain were pious tears, vows, or entreaties; so great was the woman's guilt, so great the devil's violence. For on the first two nights, while the choir of priests was singing psalms around the body, the devils, one by one, with the utmost ease bursting open the door of the church, though closed with an immense bolt, broke asunder the two outer chains; the middle one being more laboriously wrought, remained entire. On the third night, about cock-crow, the whole monastery seemed to be overthrown from its very foundation, by the clamour of the approaching enemy. One devil, more terrible in appearance than the rest, and of loftier stature, broke the gates to shivers by the violence of his attack. The priests grew motionless with fear, their hair stood on end, and they became speechless. He proceeded, as it appeared, with haughty step towards the coffin, and calling on the woman by name, commanded her to rise. She replying that she could not on account of the chains: 'You shall be loosed,' said he, 'and to your cost': and directly he broke the chain, which had mocked the ferocity of the others, with as little exertion as though it had been made of flax. He also beat down the cover of the coffin with his foot, and taking her by the hand, before them all, he dragged her out of the church. At the doors appeared a black horse, proudly neighing, with iron hooks projecting over his whole back; on which the wretched creature was placed, and, immediately, with the whole party, vanished from the eyes of the beholders; her pitiable cries, however, for assistance, were heard for nearly the space of four miles.

THE NORMAN INVASION, ENGLAND, September–October 1066

William of Poitiers

With the death of Edward the Confessor, Harold II was chosen as king of England; however, his claim was disputed by Duke William of Normandy, who landed in England on 29 September 1066. William of Poitiers was the Duke's chaplain.

Rejoicing greatly at having secured a safe landing, the Normans seized and fortified first Pevensey and then Hastings, intending that these should serve as a stronghold for themselves and as a refuge for their ships. Marius and Pompey the Great, both of whom earned their victories by courage and ability (since the one brought Jugurtha in chains to Rome while the other forced Mithridates to take poison), were so cautious when they were in enemy territory that they feared to expose themselves to danger even by separating themselves with a legion from their main army: their custom was (like that of most generals) to direct patrols and not to lead them. But William, with twenty-five knights and no more, himself went out to gain information about the neighbourhood and its inhabitants. Because of the roughness of the ground he had to return on foot, a matter doubtless for laughter, but if the episode is not devoid of humour it none the less deserves serious praise. For the duke came back carrying on his shoulder, besides his own hauberk, that of William fitz Osbern, one of his companions. This man was famed for his bodily strength and courage, but it was the duke who relieved him in his necessity of the weight of his armour.

A rich inhabitant of the country who was a Norman by race, Robert, son of Wimarc, a noble lady, sent a messenger to Hastings to the duke who was his relative and his lord. 'King Harold,' he said, 'has just given battle to his brother and to the king of Norway, who is reputed to be the greatest warrior under heaven, and he has killed both of them in one fight, and has destroyed their mighty armies. Heartened by this success he now hastens towards you at the head of innumerable troops all well equipped for war, and against them your own warriors will prove of no more account than a pack of curs. You are accounted a wise man, and at home you have hitherto acted prudently both in peace and war. Now therefore take care for your safety lest your boldness lead you into a peril from which you will not escape. My advice to you is to remain within your entrenchments and not at present to offer battle.' But the duke replied to the messenger thus: 'Although it would have been better for your master not to have mingled insults with his message, nevertheless I thank him for his advice. But say this also to him: I have no desire to protect myself behind any rampart, but I intend to give battle to Harold as soon as possible. With the aid of God I would not hesitate to oppose him with my own brave men even if I had only ten thousand of these instead of the sixty thousand I now command.'

One day when the duke was visiting the guards of his fleet, and was walking about near the ships, he was told that a monk had arrived sent to him by Harold. He at once accosted him and discreetly said: 'I am the steward of William, duke of Normandy, and very intimate with him. It is only through me you will have an opportunity of delivering your message. Say therefore what you have to say to me, and I will deliver a faithful report of your message, for no one is dearer to him than I am. Afterwards through my good offices you may in person say to him whatever you wish.' The monk then delivered his message without further delay, and the duke at once caused him to be well housed and kindly entertained. At the same time he carefully considered with his followers what reply he should make to the message.

The next day, seated in the midst of his magnates, he summoned the monk to his presence and said: 'I am William, by the grace of God, prince of the Normans. Repeat now therefore in the presence of these men what you said to me yesterday.' The envoy then spoke: 'This is what Harold bids you know. You have come into his land with he knows not what temerity. He recalls that King Edward at first appointed you as his heir to the kingdom of England, and he remembers that he was himself sent by the king to Normandy to give you an assurance of the succession. But he knows also that the same king, his lord, acting within his rights, bestowed on him the kingdom of England when dying. Moreover, ever since the time when blessed Augustine came to these shores it has been the unbroken custom of the English to treat death-bed bequests as inviolable. It is therefore with justice that he bids you return with your followers to your own country. Otherwise he will break the friendship and the pacts he made with you in Normandy. And he leaves the choice entirely to you.'

When the duke had heard this message he asked the monk whether he would conduct his messenger safely into Harold's presence, and the monk promised that he would take as much care for his safety as for his own. Then the duke ordered a certain monk of Fécamp to carry this message forthwith to Harold: 'It is not with temerity nor unjustly but after deliberation and in defence of right that I have crossed the sea into this country. My lord and kinsman, King Edward, made me the heir of this kingdom even as Harold himself has testified; and he did so because of the great honours and rich benefits conferred upon him and his brother and followers by me and my magnates. He acted thus because among all his acquaintance he held me to be the best capable of supporting him during his life and of giving just rule to the kingdom after his death. Moreover his choice was not made without the consent of his magnates since Archbishop Stigand, Earl Godwine, Earl Leo-fric and Earl Siward confirmed it, swearing in his hands that after King Edward's death they would serve me as lord, and that during his lifetime they would not seek to have the country in any way occupied so as to hinder my coming. He gave me the son and the nephew of Godwine as hostages. And finally he sent me Harold himself to Normandy that in my presence he might personally take the oath which his father and the others had sworn in my absence. While he was on his way to me Harold fell into a perilous captivity from which he was rescued by my firmness and prudence. He made himself my man by a solemn act of homage, and with his hands in mine he pledged to me the security of the English kingdom. I am ready to submit my case against his for judgment either by the law of Normandy or better still by the law of England, whichever he may choose; and if according to truth and equity either the Normans or the English decide that the kingdom is his by right, let him possess it in peace. But if it be decided that in justice the kingdom should be mine, let him yield it up. Moreover, if he refuses these conditions, I do not think it right that either my men or his should perish in conflict over a quarrel that is none of their making. I am therefore ready to risk my life against his in single combat to decide whether the kingdom of England should by right be his or mine.'

We have been careful to record all this speech in the duke's own words rather than our own, for we wish posterity to regard him with favour. Anyone may easily judge that he showed himself wise and just, pious and brave. On reflection it will be considered that the strength of his argument was such that it could not have been shaken by Tully himself, the glory of Roman eloquence; and it brought to brought the claims of Harold. The duke (it will be seen) was ready to accept the judgment prescribed by the law of nations, since he did not desire that his enemies, the English, should perish because of his quarrel, but rather he wanted to decide the issue by means of a single combat and at the peril of his own life. When Harold advanced to meet the duke's envoy and heard this message he grew pale and for a long while remained as if dumb. And when the monk had asked more than once for a reply he first said: 'We march at once,' and then added, 'We march to battle.' The envoy besought him to reconsider this reply, urging that what the duke desired was a single combat and not the double slaughter of two armies. (For that good and brave man was willing to renounce something that was just and agreeable to him in order to prevent the death of many: he wished for Harold's head, knowing that it was defended by less fortitude than his own, and that it was not protected by justice.) Then Harold, lifting up his face to heaven, exclaimed: 'May the Lord decide this day between William and me, and may he pronounce which of us has the right.' Thus, blinded by his lust for dominion, and in his fear unmindful of the wrongs he had committed, Harold made his conscience his judge and that to his own ruin.

In the meantime trusty knights who had been sent out by the duke on patrol came back in haste to report the approach of the enemy. The king was the more furious because he had heard that the Normans had laid waste the neighbourhood of their camp, and he planned to take them unawares by a surprise or night attack. Further, in order to prevent their escape, he sent out a fleet of seven hundred armed vessels to block their passage home. Immediately the duke summoned to arms all those within the camp, for the greater part of his host had gone out foraging. He himself attended mass with the greatest devotion, and fortified both his body and soul by partaking of the Body and Blood of our Lord. With great humility he hung round his neck the relics on which Harold had sworn the oath he had now broken, and whose protection he had therefore lost. The duke had with him two bishops from Normandy, Odo, bishop of Bayeux, and Geoffrey, bishop of Coutances;

and there were also with him many secular clergy and not a few monks. This company made ready to fight for him with their prayers. Anyone but the duke would have been alarmed at seeing his hauberk turn to the left when he put it on, but he merely laughed and did not allow the unlucky omen to disturb him.

Although no one has reported to us in detail the short harangue with which on this occasion he increased the courage of his troops, we doubt not it was excellent. He reminded the Normans that with him for their leader they had always proved victorious in many perilous battles. He reminded them also of their fatherland, of its noble history, and of its great renown. 'Now is the time,' he said, 'for you to show your strength, and the courage that is yours.' 'You fight,' he added, 'not merely for victory but also for survival. If you bear yourselves valiantly you will obtain victory, honour and riches. If not you will be ruthlessly butchered, or else led ignominiously captive into the hands of pitiless enemies. Further, you will incur abiding disgrace. There is no road for retreat. In front, your advance is blocked by an army and a hostile countryside; behind you, there is the sea where an enemy fleet bars your flight. Men worthy of the name do not allow themselves to be dismayed by the number of their foes. The English have again and again fallen to the sword of an enemy; often, being vanquished, they have submitted to a foreign yoke; nor have they ever been famed as soldiers. The vigorous courage of a few men armed in a just cause and specially protected by heaven must prevail against a host of men unskilled in combat. Only be bold so that nothing shall make you yield, and victory will gladden your hearts.'

He then advanced in good order with the papal banner which had been granted to him borne aloft at the head of his troops. In the van he placed foot-soldiers equipped with arrows and crossbows; in the second rank came the more heavily armed infantry clad in hauberks; and finally came the squadrons of knights in the midst of whom he rode himself, showing invincible courage and in such a position that he could give his orders by hand or by voice. If any ancient writer had described the host of Harold, he would have said that at its passage the rivers became dry and the forests were turned into plains. From all the provinces of the English a vast host had gathered together. Some were moved by their zeal for Harold, but all were inspired by the love of their country which they desired, however unjustly, to defend against foreigners. The land of the Danes who were allied to them had also sent copious reinforcements. But fearing William more than the king of Norway and not daring to fight with him on equal terms, they took up their position on higher ground, on a hill abutting the forest through which they had just come. There, at once dismounting from their horses, they drew themselves up on foot and in very close order. The duke and his men in no way dismayed by the difficulty of the ground came slowly up the hill, and the terrible sound of trumpets on both sides signalled the beginning of the battle. The eager boldness of the Normans gave them the advantage of attack, even as in a trial for theft it is the prosecuting counsel who speaks first. In such wise the Norman foot drawing nearer provoked the English by raining death and wounds upon them with their missiles. But the English resisted valiantly, each man according to his strength, and they hurled back spears and javelins and weapons of all kinds together with axes and stones fastened to pieces of wood. You would have thought to see our men overwhelmed by this death-dealing weight of projectiles. The knights came after the chief, being in the rearmost rank, and all disdaining to fight at long range were eager to use their swords. The shouts both of the Normans and of the barbarians were drowned in the clash of arms and by the cries of the dying, and for a long time the battle raged with the utmost fury. The English, however, had the advantage of the ground and profited by remaining within their position in close order. They gained further superiority from their numbers, from the impregnable front which they preserved, and most of all from the manner in which their weapons found easy passage through the shields and armour of their enemies. Thus they bravely withstood and successfully repulsed those who were engaging them at close quarters, and inflicted losses upon the men who were shooting missiles at them from a distance. Then the foot-soldiers and the Breton knights, panic-stricken by the violence of the assault, broke in flight before the English and also the auxiliary troops on the left wing, and the whole army of the duke was in danger of retreat. This may be said without disparagement to the unconquerable Norman race. The army of the Roman emperor, containing the soldiers of kings accustomed to victory on sea and land, sometimes fled on the report, true or false, that their leader was dead. And in this case the Normans believed that their duke and lord was killed. Their flight was thus not so much shameful as sad, for their leader was their greatest solace.

Seeing a large part of the hostile host pursuing his own troops, the prince thrust himself in front of those in flight, shouting at them and threatening them with his spear. Staying their retreat, he took off his helmet, and standing before them bareheaded he cried: 'Look at me well. I am still alive and by the grace of God I shall yet prove victor. What is this madness which makes you fly, and what way is open for your retreat? You are allowing yourselves to be pursued and killed by men whom you could slaughter like cattle. You are throwing away victory and lasting glory, rushing into ruin and incurring abiding disgrace. And all for naught since by flight none of you can escape destruction.' With these words he restored their courage, and, leaping to the front and wielding his death-dealing sword, he defied the enemy who merited death for their disloyalty to him their prince. Inflamed by his ardour the Normans then surrounded several thousands of their pursuers and rapidly cut them down so that not one escaped. Heartened by this success, they then furiously carried their attack on to the main body of the English host, which even after their losses scarcely seemed diminished in number. The English fought confidently with all their strength, striving in particular to prevent the attackers from penetrating within their ranks, which indeed were so closely massed together that even the dead had not space in which to fall. The swords of the bravest warriors hewed a gap in some places, and there they were followed by the men of Maine, by the French, by the Bretons and the men of Aquitaine, and by the Normans who showed the greatest valour.

A certain Norman, Robert, son of Roger of Beaumont, being nephew and heir to Henry, count of Meulan, through Henry's sister, Adeline, found himself that day in battle for the first time: he was as yet but a young man and he performed feats of valour worthy of perpetual remembrance. At the head of the troop which he commanded on the right wing, he attacked with the utmost bravery and success. It is not, however, our purpose, or within our capacity, to describe as they deserve the exploits of individuals. Even a master of narrative who had actually been present that day would find it very difficult to narrate them all in detail. For our part we shall hasten to the point at which, having ended our praise of William the count, we shall begin to describe the glory of William the king.

Realising that they could not without severe loss overcome an army massed so strongly in close formation, the Normans and their allies feigned flight and simulated a retreat, for they recalled that only a short while ago their flight had given them an advantage. The barbarians thinking victory within their grasp shouted with triumph, and heaping insults upon our men, threatened utterly to destroy them. Several thousand of them, as before, gave rapid pursuit to those whom they thought to be in flight; but the Normans suddenly wheeling their horses surrounded them and cut down their pursuers so that not one was left alive. Twice was this ruse employed with the utmost success, and then they attacked those that remained with redoubled fury. This army was still formidable and very difficult to overwhelm. Indeed this was a battle of a new type: one side vigorously attacking; the other resisting as if rooted to the ground. At last the English began to weary, and as if confessing their crime in their defeat they submitted to their punishment. The Normans threw and struck and pierced. The movements of those who were cut down to death appeared greater than that of the living; and those who were lightly wounded could not escape because of the density of their formation but were crushed in the throng. Thus fortune crowned the triumph of William.

There were present in this battle: Eustace, count of Boulogne; William, son of Richard, count of Evreux; Geoffrey, son of Rotrou, count of Mortagne; William fitz Osbern; Haimo, *vicomte* of Thouars; Walter Giffard; Hughe of Montfort-sur-Risle; Rodulf of Tosny; Hugh of Grantmesnil; William of Warenne; and many other most renowned warriors whose names are worthy to be commemorated in histories among the bravest soldiers of all time. But Duke William excelled them all both in bravery and soldier-craft, so that one might esteem him as at least the equal of the most praised generals of ancient Greece and Rome. He dominated this battle, checking his own men in flight, strengthening their spirit, and sharing their dangers. He bade them come with him, more often than he ordered them to go in front of him. Thus it may be understood how he led them by his valour and gave them courage. At the mere sight of this wonderful and redoubtable knight, many of his enemies lost heart even before they received a scratch. Thrice his horse fell under him; thrice he leapt upon the ground; and thrice he quickly avenged the death of his steed. It was here that one could see his prowess, and mark at once the strength of his arm and the height of his spirit. His sharp sword pierced shields, helmets and armour, and not a few felt the weight of his shield.

His knights seeing him thus fight on foot were filled with wonder, and although many were wounded they took new heart. Some weakened by loss of blood went on resisting, supported by their shields, and others unable themselves to carry on the struggle, urged on their comrades by voice and gesture to follow the duke. 'Surely,' they cried, 'you will not let victory slip from your hands.' William himself came to the rescue of many . . .

Evening was now falling, and the English saw that they could not hold out much longer against the Normans. They knew they had lost a great part of their army, and they knew also that their king with two of his brothers and many of their greatest men had fallen. Those who remained were almost exhausted, and they realised that they could expect no more help. They saw the Normans, whose numbers had not been much diminished, attack them with even greater fury than at the beginning of the battle, as if the day's fighting had actually increased their vigour. Dismayed at the implacable bearing of the duke who spared none who came against him and whose prowess could not rest until victory was won, they began to fly as swiftly as they could, some on horseback, some on foot, some along the roads, but most over the trackless country. Many lay on the ground bathed in blood, others who struggled to their feet found themselves too weak to escape, while a few, although disabled, were given strength to move by fear. Many left their corpses in the depths of the forest, and others were found by their pursuers lying by the roadside. Although ignorant of the countryside the Normans eagerly carried on the pursuit, and striking the rebels in the back brought a happy end to this famous victory. Many fallen to the ground were trampled to death under the hooves of runaway horses.

But some of those who retreated took courage to renew the struggle on more favourable ground. This was a steep valley intersected with ditches. These people, descended from the ancient Saxons (the fiercest of men), are always by nature eager for battle, and they could only be brought down by the greatest valour. Had they not recently defeated with ease the king of Norway at the head of a fine army?

The duke who was following the victorious standards did not turn from his course when he saw these enemy troops rallying. Although he thought that reinforcements had joined his foes he stood firm. Armed only with a broken lance he was more formidable than others who brandished long javelins. With a harsh voice he called to Eustace of Boulogne, who with fifty knights was turning in flight, and was about to give the signal for retreat. This man came up to the duke and said in his ear that he ought to retire since he would court death if he went forward. But at the very moment when he uttered the words Eustace was struck between the shoulders with such force that blood gushed out from his mouth and nose, and half dead he only made his escape with the aid of his followers. The duke, however, who was superior to all fear and dishonour, attacked and beat back his enemies. In this dangerous phase of the battle many Norman nobles were killed since the nature of the ground did not permit them to display their prowess to full advantage.

Having thus regained his superiority, the duke returned to the main battlefield, and he could not gaze without pity on the carnage, although the slain were evil men, and although it is good and glorious in a just war to kill a tyrant. The bloodstained battle-ground was covered with the flower of the youth and nobility of England. The two brothers of the king were found near him, and Harold himself stripped of all badges of honour could not be identified by his face, but only by certain marks on his body. His corpse was brought into the duke's camp, and William gave it for burial to William, surnamed Malet, and not to Harold's mother, who offered for the body of her beloved son its weight in gold. For the duke thought it unseemly to receive money for such merchandise, and equally he considered it wrong that Harold should be buried as his mother wished, since so many men lay unburied because of his avarice. They said in jest that he who had guarded the coast with such insensate zeal should be buried by the seashore . . .

THE ANARCHY OF THE BARONS, ENGLAND, 1137–54

The Anglo-Saxon Chronicle

When King Stephen landed in England he held his council at Oxford, and there he arrested Roger, bishop of Salisbury, and his 'nephews', Alexander, bishop of Lincoln, and the chancellor Roger. He put them all in prison until they surrendered their castles. When the traitors saw that Stephen was a good-humoured, kindly, and easy-going man who inflicted no punishment, then they committed all manner of horrible crimes. They had done him homage and sworn oaths of fealty to him, but not one of their oaths was kept.

They were all forsworn and their oaths broken. For every great man built him castles and held them against the king; and they filled the whole land with these castles. They sorely burdened the unhappy people of the country with forced labour on the castles; and when the castles were built, they filled them with devils and wicked men. By night and by day they seized those whom they believed to have any wealth, whether they were men or women; and in order to get their gold and silver, they put them into prison and tortured them with unspeakable tortures for never were martyrs tortured as they were. They hung them up by the feet and smoked them with foul smoke. They strung them up by the thumbs, or by the head, and hung coats of mail on their feet. They tied knotted cords round their heads and twisted it till it entered the brain. They put them in dungeons wherein were adders and snakes and toads, and so destroyed them. Some they put into a 'crucethus'; that is to say, into a short, narrow, shallow chest into which they put sharp stones; and they crushed the man in it until they had broken every bone in his body. In many of the castles were certain instruments of torture so heavy that two or three men had enough to do to carry one. It was made in this way: a weight was fastened to a beam which was attached to a sharp iron put round the man's throat and neck so that he could move in no direction, and could neither sit, nor lie, nor sleep, but had to bear the whole weight of the iron. Many thousands they starved to death.

I know not how to, nor am I able to tell of, all the atrocities nor all the cruelties which they wrought upon the unhappy people of this country. It lasted throughout the nineteen years that Stephen was king, and always grew worse and worse. At regular intervals they levied a tax, known as 'tenserie' [protection money] upon the villages. When the wretched people had no more to give, they plundered and burned all the villages, so that you could easily go a day's journey without ever finding a village inhabited or a field cultivated. Then was corn dear and flesh and cheese and butter, for there was none in the land. The wretched people perished with hunger; some, who had been great men, were driven to beggary, while others fled from the country.

Never did a country endure greater misery, and never did the heathen act more vilely than they did. Contrary to custom, they spared neither church nor churchyard, but seized everything of value that was in it, and afterwards burned the church and all it contained. They spared not the lands of bishops, nor of abbots, nor of priests, but plundered the monks and the clergy; and every man who could robbed his neighbour. If two or three men came riding towards a village, all the villagers fled for fear of them, believing that they were robbers. The bishops and the clergy were for ever cursing them, but that was nothing to them, for they were all excommunicated and forsworn and lost.

Wherever the ground was tilled the earth bore no corn, for the land was ruined by such doings; and men said openly that Christ and His saints slept. Such things and others more than we know how to relate we suffered nineteen years for our sins.

THE MURDER OF THOMAS À BECKET, CANTERBURY, ENGLAND, 29 December 1170

Edward Grim

Formerly Henry II's chancellor, Thomas à Becket was appointed archbishop of Canterbury in 1162; in this office he became an enthusiastic supporter of ecclesiastical claims against lay powers. Henry's expressed wish to be rid of 'this turbulent priest', led to four knights – Hugh de Merville, Reginald Fitzurse, Richard le Breton and William de Tracy – murdering Becket in Canterbury cathedral.

. . . After the monks had retreated within the precincts of the church, the four knights came following hard on their heels . . . All the onlookers were in tumult and consternation, for by this time those who had been singing vespers had rushed up to the scene of death.

In a spirit of mad fury the knights called out, 'Where is Thomas Becket, traitor to the king and the realm?' When he returned no answer, they cried out the more loudly and insistently, 'Where is the archbishop?' At this quite undaunted . . . he descended from the steps, whither he had been dragged by the monks . . ., and in a perfectly clear voice answered, 'Lo! here am I, no traitor to the king, but a priest. What do you seek from me? . . . I am ready to suffer in His Name who redeemed me by His Blood. Far be it from me to flee from your swords, or to depart from righteousness.' . . . 'Absolve,' they cried, and restore to communion those whom you have excommunicated . . .' He answered, 'There has been no satisfaction made, and I will not absolve them.' 'Then you shall die this instant,' they cried, 'and receive your desert.' 'I, too,' said he, 'am ready to die for my Lord, that in my blood the Church may obtain peace and liberty; but in the name of Almighty God I forbid you to harm any of my men, whether clerk or lay.' . . .

Then they made a rush at him and laid sacrilegious hands upon him, pulling and dragging him roughly and violently, endeavouring to get him outside the walls of the church and there slay him, or bind him and carry him off prisoner . . . But as he could not easily be moved from the pillar, one of them seized hold of him and clung to him more closely. The archbishop shook him off vigorously, . . . saying, 'Touch me not, Reginald; you owe me fealty and obedience; you are acting like a madman; you and your accomplices.' All aflame with a terrible fury at this rebuff, the knight brandished his sword against that, consecrated head. Neither faith, he cried; 'nor obedience do I owe you against my fealty to my lord the king.' Then the unconquered martyr understood that the hour was approaching that should release him from the miseries of this mortal life. Whereupon . . . he commended his cause and that of the Church to God and St Mary and the blessed martyr, St Denys. Scarce had he uttered the words than the wicked knight . . . leapt suddenly upon him and wounded the sacrificial lamb of God in the head, cutting off the top of the crown which the unction of the sacred charism [consecrated oil] had dedicated to God, and by the same stroke he almost cut off the arm of him who tells the story. For he, when all the others, both monks and clerks had fled, steadfastly stood by the saintly archbishop and held his arms around him, till the one he opposed to the blow was almost severed . . .

Next he received a second blow on the head but still he stood firm and immovable. At the third blow he tell on his knees and elbows, . . . saying in a low voice, 'For the Name of Jesus and the protection of the Church I am ready to embrace death.' But the third knight inflicted a terrible wound as he lay prostrate. The fourth knight warded off any who sought to intervene. . . . But the fifth – no knight he but . . . [a] clerk who had entered with the knights – . . . placed his foot on the neck of the holy priest and precious martyr and horrible to relate scattered the brains and blood about the pavement crying out to the others, Let us away, knights this fellow will rise no more.' . . .

Becket was canonized in 1173, and Henry II did public penance at his tomb the following year. The shrine of St Thomas of Canterbury was a popular place of pilgrimage for several centuries.

THE CRUSADES: SALADIN RECAPTURES JERUSALEM, 25 September 1187

Ibn-al-Qalansi

Jerusalem, the holy city of the Jews, Christians and Muslims, was seized by the Crusaders in 1099; in 1187 it was recaptured by Saladin, sultan of Egypt and Syria. The author was Saladin's secretary.

On Friday 20 rajab [25 September] the Sultan moved to the northern side and pitched his tent there, cutting the Frankish lines and opening up the way to death. He mounted the catapults, and by this means milked the udders of slaughter, making the Rock groan under the impact of missiles; his reward was the hosts of evil behind the wall. They could no longer put a head outside the gates without meeting death and the day of disaster, and casting their souls into perdition. The Templars clamoured, the barons leapt to their destruction in Hell, the Hospitallers went to damnation, the 'Brethren' found no escape from death. No band of soldiers cast itself between the stones from the catapults and their objective; in every heart on either side burned the fire of longing, faces were exposed to the blade's kiss, Bahan of Ibelin asked for an amnesty for his people. But the Sultan refused and upheld his claims, saying: 'Neither amnesty nor mercy for you! Our only desire is to inflict perpetual subjection upon you; tomorrow will make us your masters by main force. We shall kill and capture you wholesale, spill men's blood and reduce the poor and women to slavery.' He absolutely refused to grant them an amnesty, and their response was without bravura; they feared the consequences of a sudden decision, and communicated their fear. They said: 'If we must despair of your mercy and fear your power and lose all hope of your magnanimity, and if we are sure that there is no escape or way out, no peace or safety, no grace or generosity, then we shall seek death, and shall fight like men who sell their lives dearly . . . No one will be wounded before he has first wounded ten men himself, no one will shake hands with death before he has been seen to stave off destruction with open hands. We shall burn the houses and pull down the Dome, and leave to you to enjoy the grief of losing it; we shall kill every Muslim prisoner in our hands, and we have thousands, since it is well known that each one of us spurns dishonour and honours his reputation. As for our possessions, we shall destroy them rather than hand them over, and as for our sons, we shall be quick to slay them; you shall not find us slow to do it. What advantage do you gain from this ungenerous spirit of negation, you who would only lose everything by such a gain? What delusions are born of the hope of success, when only peace will repair the evil! How many men, forced to make a journey in the dark, have wandered from the path in the gloom of night before the dawn appeared!'

Then the Sultan called a council meeting and sent for the leaders of his victorious hosts, consulting with them on the question, discussing with them in secret and in the open. He begged them to reveal to him their innermost thoughts and to display their hidden opinions; he wanted to light the spark in them, he asked to know their minds, he beguiled them into pronouncing the best solution and conferred with them on the most profitable peace treaty . . . So after repeated requests and consultations and messages and importunings and intercessions an amount was fixed that satisfied us and would act as weighty caution, for which they were to ransom themselves and their possessions and save their men, women, and children. Under the treaty, at the end of forty days, whoever was unable to pay what he owed or refused to pay it was to become our slave by right and come into our possession. The tax was ten dinar for each man, five for a woman, and two for a boy or girl. Ibn Barzan and the Patriarch and the Grand Masters of the Temple and the Hospital stood guarantee, and Ibn Barzan gave 30,000 dinar for the poor, fulfilling his word faithfully and without default . . . Once the tax had been fixed they surrendered the city on Friday 27 rajab [2 October], surrendering it under duress like ill-gotten gains rather than a legitimate deposit. There were more than 100,000 persons in the city, men, women, and children. The gates were closed upon them all, and representatives appointed to make a census and demand the sum due. An emir or representative was appointed to each gate, to keep count of those coming and going; those who paid, went out, while those who did not settle their debt remained prisoners within . . . There was great negligence and widespread peculation [embezzlement] and anyone who paid a bribe was allowed to get out, for the officials strayed from the path of honesty to accept bribes. Some people were let down from the walls on ropes, some carried out hidden in luggage, some changed their clothes and went dressed as Muslim soldiers . . .

The Franks began selling their possessions and taking their precious things out of safe-keeping to sell them for nothing in the market of abjection. People made bargains with them and bought the goods at very low prices . . . The Grand Patriarch gathered up all that stood above the Sepulchre, the gold-plating and gold and silver artifacts, and collected together the contents of the church of the Resurrection, precious things of both metals and of the two sorts of fabric. Then I said to the Sultan: 'These are great riches, their value is quite clearly 200,000 dinar; free exit is permitted to personal property but not to that of churches and convents; do not allow these rascals to keep this in their grasp.' But he replied: 'If we interpret the treaty to their disadvantage they will accuse us of breaking the faith and of being ignorant of the true essence of the thing. I prefer to make them obey the letter of the treaty, so that they are then unable to accuse the Believers of breaking their word, but will tell others of the benefits we have bestowed upon them.' So they left the heavy objects and carried away the most precious and the lightest, and shook from their hands the dust of their heritage and the sweepings of their dung heap [the Holy Sepulchre].

When Jerusalem was purified of the filth of the hellish Franks and had stripped off her vile garments to put on the robe of honour, the Christians, after paying their tax, refused to leave, and asked to be allowed to stay on in safety, and gave prodigious service and worked for us with all their might, carrying out every task with discipline and cheerfulness. They paid 'the tax for protection permitted to them, humbly.' They stood ready to accept whatever might be inflicted on them, and their affliction grew as they stood waiting for it. Thus they became in effect tribute-payers, reliant upon [Muslim] protection; they were used and employed in menial tasks and in their position they accepted these tasks as if they were gifts.

THE CRUSADES: A FRENCH KNIGHT IN COMBAT, MANSOURAH, SYRIA, AD 1250

Jean de Joinville

In the meantime, I and my knights had decided to go and attack some Turks who were loading their baggage in their camp on our left; so we fell on them. As we were pursuing them through the camp I caught sight of a Saracen on the point of mounting his horse; one of his knights was holding the bridle. At the moment he had both his hands on the saddle to pull himself up, I gave him a thrust with my lance just under the arm-pits and struck him dead. On seeing this, his knight left his lord and the horse, and thrusting his lance at me as I passed, caught me between the shoulders, pinning me down to the neck of my horse in such a way that I could not draw the sword at my belt. I therefore had to draw the sword attached to my horse. When he saw me with my sword drawn he withdrew his lance and left me.

When I and my knights came out of the Saracens' camp we found what we reckoned to be about six thousand Turks, who had left their tents and retreated into the fields. As soon as they saw us they came charging towards us, and killed Hugues de Trichâtel, Lord of Conflans, who was with me bearing a banner. I and my knights spurred on our horses and went to the rescue of Raoul de Wanou, another of my company, whom they had struck to the ground.

As I was coming back, the Turks thrust at me with their lances. Under the weight of their attack my horse was brought to its knees, and I went flying forward over its ears. I got up as soon as ever I could, with my shield at my neck and sword in hand. One of my knights, named Érard de Siverey – may God grant him grace! – came to me and advised our drawing back towards a ruined house where we could wait for the king, who was on his way. As we were going there, some on foot and some on horseback, a great body of Turks came rushing at us, bearing me to the ground and riding over my body, so that my shield went flying from my neck.

As soon as they had passed, Érard de Siverey came back to me and took me with him to the walls of the tumble-down house. Here we were joined by Hugues d'Écot, Frédéric de Loupey, and Renaud de Menoncourt. While we were there the Turks attacked us from all sides. Some of them got into the house and pricked us with their lances from above. My knights asked me to hold on to their horses' bridles, which I did, for fear the beasts should run away. Then they put up a vigorous defence against the Turks, for which, I may say, they were afterwards highly praised by all men of good standing in the army, both those who witnessed their bravery and those who heard of it later.

During this incident, Hugues d'Écot received three wounds in the face from a lance, and so did Raoul de Wanou, while Frédéric de Loupey had a lance-thrust between his shoulders, which made so large a wound that the blood poured from his body as if from the bung-hole of a barrel. A blow from one of the enemy's swords landed in the middle of Érard de Siverey's face, cutting through his nose so that it was left dangling over his lips.

VIOLENT DEATHS, ENGLAND, 1267–87

Calendar of Inquisitions

Death by misadventure, 1267

On Wednesday before Ascension day 51 Henry III William de Stangate came down a road called Burleyesdam [in Sussex] with a cross-bow on his left shoulder and a poisoned arrow, and he met Desiderata, late the wife of Robert le Champeneys, who was his child's godmother, and a particular friend. And she asked him in jest, whether he were one of the men who were going about the country with cross-bows and other weapons, to apprehend robbers and evildoers by the king's order; adding that she could overcome and take two or three like him. And putting out her arm she caught him by the neck and crooking her leg behind his without his noticing it, she upset him and fell on him. And in falling she struck herself in the side with the arrow which he had under his belt, piercing to the heart, and died on the spot. *Verdict.* Death by misadventure.

A wedding brawl, 1268

A certain stranger being new-married was taking his wife and others who were with her to one end of the town of Byrun, when William Selisaule asked for a ball, which it is the custom to give; and they having no ball gave him a pair of gloves for a pledge; afterwards other men of Byrun asked for a ball, and they said they would not give one, because they had already given a pledge for one, and the men of Byrun would not believe them, but still asked for the said ball; and so there arose a dispute, and the wedding party, being slightly drunk, assaulted the men of Byrun with axes and bows and arrows, and wounded very many; and the said William hearing the noise, and thinking it was for the ball for which he had a pledge, ran with a stick to appease the dispute; and when he had come near, one William son of Ralph de Rotil[?]

drew an arrow at him and hit him in the breast, so that he thought he had got his death; as the said William son of Ralph, not yet content, was meaning to shoot at him again, he saw that he could only escape the arrow by hitting him back, so as to hinder his drawing; so he ran up to the said William son of Ralph to hit him on the arm, but by mischance, hit the said Adam [de Auwerne], who unwittingly came between them, so he died. Thus the said William Selisaule killed the said Adam by mischance, and not of malice prepense.

A stabbing, 1287

John de Quercubus of Scottes Acton killed Hugh de Weston, chaplain, in self defence. On Christmas day 16 Edward I after sunset there were some men singing outside a tavern kept by Richard son of William de Skottesacton in that town. And Hugh came by the door immensely drunk, and quarreled with the singers. Now John was standing by, singing, and Hugh hated him a little because he sang well, and desired the love of certain women who were standing by in a field and whom Hugh much affected. So Hugh took a naked sword in his hand and ran at John, striking him once, twice, thrice, on the head, and nearly cutting off two fingers of his left hand. And John went on his knees, and raised his hands asking God's peace and the king's, and then ran into a corner near the street under a stone wall. And Hugh ran after him and tried to kill him, so he drew his knife and wounded Hugh in the chest, killing him instantly.

KUBLAI-KHAN'S SUMMER PALACE, SHANDU, CHINA, *c.* 1275

Marco Polo

The Mongol emperor Kublai-Khan ruled most of the Eurasian continent, including China, at the time of Marco Polo's travels. His description of the Khan's summer palace prompted Coleridge to write two of the most well-known lines: 'In Xanadu [Shandu] did Kubla Khan/A pleasure dome decree.'

Departing from the city last mentioned [Changa-nor], and proceeding three days' journey in a north-easterly direction, you arrive at a city called Shandu, built by the Grand Khan Kublai, now reigning. In this he caused a palace to be erected, of marble and other handsome stones, admirable as well for the elegance of its design as for the skill displayed in its execution. The halls and chambers are all gilt, and very handsome. It presents one front towards the interior of the city, and the other towards the wall; and from each extremity of the building runs another wall to such an extent as to enclose sixteen miles in circuit of the adjoining plain, to which there is no access but through the palace. Within the bounds of this royal park there are rich and beautiful meadows, watered by many rivulets, where a variety of animals of the deer and goat kind are pastured, to serve as food for the hawks and other birds employed in the chase, whose mews are also in the grounds. The number of these birds is upwards of two hundred; and the Grand Khan goes in person, at least once in the week, to inspect them. Frequently, when he rides about this enclosed forest, he has one or more small leopards carried on horseback, behind their keepers; and when he pleases to give direction for their being slipped, they instantly seize a stag, or goat, or fallow deer, which he gives to his hawks, and in this manner he amuses himself. In the centre of these grounds, where there is a beautiful grove of trees, he has built a royal pavilion, supported upon a colonnade of handsome pillars, gilt and varnished. Round each pillar a dragon, likewise gilt, entwines its tail, whilst its head sustains the projection of the roof, and its talons or claws are extended to the right and left along the entablature. The roof is of bamboo cane, likewise gilt, and so well varnished that no wet can injure it. The bamboos used for this purpose are three palms in circumference and ten fathoms in length, and being cut at the joints, are split into two equal parts, so as to form gutters, and with these (laid concave and convex) the pavilion is covered; but to secure the roof against the effect of wind, each of the bamboos is tied at the ends to the frame. The building is supported on every side (like a tent) by more than two hundred very strong silken cords, and otherwise, from the lightness of the materials, it would be liable to oversetting by the force of high winds. The whole is constructed with so much ingenuity of contrivance that all the parts may be taken asunder, removed, and again set up, at his majesty's pleasure. This spot he has selected for his recreation on account of the mild temperature and salubrity of the air, and he accordingly makes it his residence during three months of the year, namely, June, July, and August; and every year, on the twenty-eighth day of the moon, in the last of these months, it is his established custom to depart from thence, and proceed to an appointed place, in order to perform certain sacrifices, in the following manner. It is to be understood that his majesty keeps up a stud of about ten thousand horses and mares, which are white as snow; and of the milk of these mares no person can presume to drink who is not of the family descended from Chingis-khan, with the exception only of one other family, named Boriat, to whom that monarch gave the honourable privilege, in reward of valorous achievements in battle, performed in his own presence. So great, indeed, is the respect shown to these horses that, even when they are at pasture in the royal meadows or forests, no one dares to place himself before them, or otherwise to impede their movements. The astrologers whom he entertains in his service, and who are deeply versed in the diabolical art of magic, having pronounced it to be his duty, annually, on the twenty-eighth day of the moon in August, to scatter in the wind the milk taken from these mares, as a libation to all the spirits and idols whom they adore for the purpose of propitiating them and ensuring their protection of the people, male and female, of the cattle, the fowls, the grain and other fruits of the earth; on this account it is that his majesty adheres to the rule that has been mentioned, and on that particular day proceeds to the spot where, with his own hands, he is to make the offering of milk. On such occasions these astrologers, or magicians as they may be termed, sometimes display their skill in a wonderful manner; for if it should happen that the sky becomes cloudy and threatens rain, they ascend the roof of the palace where the Grand Khan resides at the time, and by the force of their incantations they prevent the rain from falling and stay the tempest; so that whilst, in the surrounding country, storms of rain, wind, and thunder are experienced, the palace itself remains unaffected by the elements.

PAEDOPHILIA, PAMIERS, FRANCE, *c.* 1300

Arnaud de Verniolles

In an effort to destroy the heretical sect of Albigensianism, Bishop Jacques Fournier – the future Pope Benedict XII – organized an Inquisition in his diocese of Pamiers in the Comte de Foix. It turned up deviations other than theological ones.

My father had sent me to learn grammar with Master Pons de Massabucu, a schoolteacher who later became a Dominican friar.

I shared a bedroom with Master Pons and his other pupils, Pierre de l'Isle (of Montaigu), Bernard Balessa (of Pamiers), and Arnaud Auriol, the son of Pierre Auriol, the knight. Arnaud was from La Bastide-Serou; he had already started to shave, and now he is a priest. My brother Bernard de Verniolles was also there, and other pupils whose names I have forgotten.

In the bedroom shared by master and pupils, I slept for a good six weeks in the same bed as Arnaud Aurio . . . On the fourth or fifth night we spent together, when Arnaud thought that I was fast asleep, he began to embrace me and put himself between my thighs . . . and to move about there as if I was a woman. And he went on sinning thus every night. I was still no more than a child, and I did not like it. But I was so ashamed I did not dare tell anyone of this sin.

THE BATTLE OF CRÉCY, FRANCE, 26 September 1346

Sir John Froissart

Fought in pursuit of the claim by King Edward III of England to the throne of France.

You must know that the French troops did not advance in any regular order, and that as soon as their King came in sight of the English his blood began to boil, and he cried out to his marshals, 'Order the Genoese forward and begin the battle in the name of God and St Denis.' There were about 15,000 Genoese crossbow men; but they were quite fatigued, having marched on foot that day six leagues, completely armed and carrying their crossbows, and accordingly they told the Constable they were not in a condition to do any great thing in battle. The Earl of Alençon hearing this, said, 'This is what one gets by employing such scoundrels, who fall off when there is any need for them.' During this time a heavy rain fell, accompanied by thunder and a very terrible eclipse of the sun; and, before this rain, a great flight of crows hovered in the air over all the battalions, making a loud noise; shortly afterwards it cleared up, and the sun shone very bright; but the French had it in their faces, and the English on their backs. When the Genoese were somewhat in order they approached the English and set up a loud shout, in order to frighten them; but the English remained quite quiet and did not seem to attend to it. They then set up a second shout, and advanced a little forward; the English never moved. Still they hooted a third time, advancing with their crossbows presented, and began to shoot. The English archers then advanced one step forward, and shot their arrows with such force and quickness, that it seemed as if it snowed. When the Genoese felt these arrows, which pierced through their armour, some of them cut the strings of their crossbows, others flung them to the ground, and all turned about and retreated quite discomfited.

The French had a large body of men-at-arms on horseback to support the Genoese, and the King, seeing them thus fall back, cried out, 'Kill me those scoundrels, for they stop up our road without any reason.' The English continued shooting, and some of their arrows falling among the horsemen, drove them upon the Genoese, so that they were in such confusion, they could never rally again.

In the English army there were some Cornish and Welsh men on foot, who had armed themselves with large knives, these advancing through the ranks of the men-at-arms and archers, who made way for them, came upon the French when they were in this danger, and falling upon earls, barons, knights, and squires, slew many, at which the King of England was exasperated. The valiant King of Bohemia was slain there; he was called Charles of Luxembourg, for he was the son of the gallant king and emperor, Henry of Luxembourg, and, having heard the order for the battle, he inquired where his son the Lord Charles was; his attendants answered that they did not know, but believed he was fighting. Upon this, he said to them, 'Gentlemen, you are all my people, my friends, and brethren at arms this day; therefore, as I am blind, I request of you to lead me so far into the engagement that I may strike one stroke with my sword.' The knights consented, and in order that they might not lose him in the crowd, fastened all the reins of their horses together, placing the King at their head that he might gratify his wish, and in this manner advanced towards the enemy. The Lord Charles of Bohemia, who already signed his name as King of Germany, and bore the arms, had come in good order to the engagement; but when he perceived that it was likely to turn out against the French he departed. The King, his father, rode in among the enemy, and he and his companions fought most valiantly; however, they advanced so far that they were all slain, and on the morrow they were found on the ground with all their horses tied together.

The Earl of Alençon advanced in regular order upon the English, to fight with them, as did the Earl of Flanders in another part. These two lords with their detachments, coasting, as it were, the archers, came to the Prince's battalion, where they fought valiantly for a length of time. The King of France was eager to march to the place where he saw their banners displayed, but there was a hedge of archers before him: he had that day made a present of a handsome black horse to Sir John of Hainault, who had mounted on it a horse ran off with the knight and forced his way through the English army, and when about to return, stumbled and fell into a ditch and severely wounded him; he did not, however, experience any other inconvenience than from his horse, for the English did not quit their ranks that day to make prisoners: his page alighted and raised him up, but the French knight did not return the way he came, as he would have found it difficult from the crowd. This battle, which was fought on Saturday, between La Broyes and Crécy, was murderous and cruel; and many gallant deeds of arms were performed that were never known: towards evening, many knights and squires of the French had lost their masters, and wandering up and down the plain, attacked the English in small parties; but they were soon destroyed, for the English had determined that day to give no quarter, nor hear of ransom from anyone.

Early in the day some French, Germans, and Savoyards had broken through the archers of the Prince's battalion, and had engaged with the men-at-arms; upon this the second battalion came to his aid, and it was time they did so, for otherwise he would have been hard pressed. The first division, seeing the danger they were in, sent a knight off in great haste to the King of England, who was posted upon an eminence near a windmill. On the knight's arrival he said, 'Sir, the Earl of Warwick, the Lord Stafford, the Lord Reginald Cobham, and the others who are about your son, are vigorously attacked by the French, and they entreat that you will come to their assistance with your battalion, for if numbers should increase against him, they fear he will have too much to do.' The King replied, 'Is my son dead, unhorsed, or so badly wounded that he cannot support himself?' 'Nothing of the sort, thank God,' rejoined the knight, 'but he is in so hot an engagement that he has great need of your help.' The King answered, 'Now, Sir Thomas, return to those that sent you, and tell them from me not to send again for me this day, nor expect that I shall come, let what will happen, as long as my son has life; and say that I command them to let the boy win his spurs, for I am determined, if it please God, that all the glory of this day shall be given to him, and to those into whose care I have entrusted him.' The knights returned to his lords and related the King's answer, which mightily encouraged them, and made them repent they had ever sent such a message.

It is a certain fact, that Sir Godfrey de Harcourt, who was in the prince's battalion, having been told by some of the English that they had seen the banner of his brother engaged in the battle against him, was exceedingly anxious to save him; but he was too late, for he was left dead on the field, and so was the Earl of Aumarle, his nephew. On the other hand, the Earls of Alençon and Flanders were fighting lustily under their banners with their own people; but they could not resist the force of the English, and were there slain, as well as many other knights and squires, who were attending on, or accompanying them.

The Earl of Blois, nephew to the King of France, and the Duke of Lorraine, his brother-in-law, with their troops, made a gallant defence; but they were surrounded by a troop of English and Welsh, and slain in spite of their prowess. The Earl of St Pol, and the Earl of Auxerre, were also killed, as well as many others. Late after vespers, the King of France had not more about him than sixty men, every one included. Sir John of Hainault, who was of the number, had once remounted the King, for his horse had been killed under him by an arrow: and seeing the state he was in, he said, 'Sir, retreat whilst you have an opportunity, and do not expose yourself so simply; if you have lost this battle, another time you will be the conqueror.' After he had said this he took the bridle of the King's horse and led him off by force, for he had before entreated him to retire. The King rode on until he came to the castle of La Broyes, where he found the gates shut, for it was very dark: he ordered the Governor of it to be summoned, who, after some delay, came upon the battlements, and asked who it was that called at such an hour. The King answered, 'Open, open, Governor, it is the fortune of France.' The Governor hearing the King's voice immediately descended, opened the gate, and let down the bridge; the King and his company entered the castle, but he had with him only five barons: Sir John of Hainault, the Lord Charles of Montmorency, the Lord of Beaujeu, the Lord of Aubigny, and the Lord of Montfort. It was not his intention, however, to bury himself in such a place as this, but having taken some refreshments, he set out again with his attendants about midnight, and rode on under the direction of guides, who were well acquainted with the country, until about daybreak he came to Amiens, where he halted. This Saturday the English never quitted their ranks in pursuit of anyone, but remained on the field guarding their position and defending themselves against all who attacked them. The battle ended at the hour of vespers, when the King of England embraced his son and said to him, 'Sweet son, God give you perseverance: you are my son; for most loyally have you acquitted yourself; you are worthy to be a sovereign.' The Prince bowed very low, giving all honour to the King, his father. The English during the night made frequent thanksgivings to the Lord for the happy issue of the day; and with them there was no rioting, for the King had expressly forbidden all riot or noise.

On the following day, which was Sunday, there were a few encounters with the French troops; however, they could not withstand the English, and soon either retreated or were put to the sword. When Edward was assured that there was no appearance of the French collecting another army, he sent to have the number and rank of the dead examined. This business was entrusted to Lord Reginald Cobham and Lord Stafford, assisted by three heralds to examine the arms, and two secretaries to write down the names. They passed the whole day upon the field of battle, and made a very circumstantial account of all they saw: according to their report it appeared that 80 banners, the bodies of 11 princes, 1200 knights, and about 30,000 common men were found dead on the field.

THE BLACK DEATH, BRITAIN, 1348–9

Anon

A form of bubonic plague which may have carried away a third or more of Europe's 25 million population. Around 2 million died in Britain.

The pestilence which had first broken out in the land occupied by the Saracens became so much stronger that, sparing no dominion, it visited with the scourge of sudden death the various parts of all the kingdoms, extending from that land to the northward, including even Scotland, destroying the greater part of the people. For it began in England in Dorsetshire . . . in the year of the Lord 1348, and immediately advancing from place to place it attacked men without warning and for the most part those who were healthy. Very many of those who were attacked in the morning it carried out of human affairs before noon. And no one whom it willed to die did it permit to live longer than three or four days. There was moreover no choice of persons, with the exception, at least, of a few rich people. In the same day twenty, forty or sixty corpses, and indeed many times as many more bodies of those who had died, were delivered to church burial in the same pit at the same time. And about the feast of All Saints, reaching London, it deprived many of their life daily, and increased to so great an extent that from the feast of the Purification till after Easter there were more than two hundred bodies of those who had died buried daily in the cemetery which had been then recently made near Smithfield, besides the bodies which were in other graveyards of the same city. The grace of the Holy Spirit finally intervening, that is to say about the feast of Whitsunday, it ceased at London, proceeding continously northward. In these parts it ceased about the feast of St Michael, in the year of the Lord, 1349.

'NEITHER BEAST NOR BIRD WOULD TOUCH THEM': BRITAIN AFTER THE BLACK DEATH, 1348

Henry Knighton

In the same year there was a great murrain of sheep everywhere in the kingdom, so that in one place in a single pasture more than 5000 sheep died; and they putrefied so that neither bird nor beast would touch them. Everything was low in price because of the fear of death, for very few people took any care of riches or property of any kind. A man could have a horse that had been worth 40*s* for half a mark [6*s* 8*d*], a fat ox for 4*s*, a cow for 12*d*, a heifer for 6*d*, a fat wether for 4*d*, a sheep for 3*d*, a lamb for 2*d*, a large pig for 5*d*; a stone of wool [24 lbs] was worth 9*d*. Sheep and cattle ran at large through the fields and among the crops, and there was none to drive them off or herd them; for lack of care they perished in ditches and hedges in incalculable numbers throughout all districts, and none knew what to do. For there was no memory of death so stern and cruel since the time of Vortigern, King of the

Britons, in whose day, as Bede testifies, the living did not suffice to bury the dead.

In the following autumn a reaper was not to be had for a lower wage than 8*d*, with his meals; a mower for not less than 10*d*, with meals. Wherefore many crops wasted in the fields for lack of harvesters. But in the year of the pestilence, as has been said above, there was so great an abundance of every kind of grain that almost no one cared for it.

The Scots, hearing of the dreadful plague among the English, suspected that it had come about through the vengeance of God, and, according to the common report, they were accustomed to swear 'be the foul deth of Engelond'. Believing that the wrath of God had befallen the English, they assembed in Selkirk forest with the intention of invading the kingdom, when the fierce mortality overtook them, and in a short time about 5000 perished. As the rest, the strong and the feeble, were preparing to return to their own country, they were followed and attacked by the English, who slew countless numbers of them.

Master Thomas of Bradwardine was consecrated by the Pope Archbishop of Canterbury, and when he returned to England he came to London, but within two days was dead . . .

Meanwhile the King sent proclamation into all the counties that reapers and other labourers should not take more then they had been accustomed to take, under the penalty appointed by statute. But the labourers were so lifted up and obstinate that they would not listen to the King's command, but if anyone wished to have them he had to give them what they wanted, and either lose his fruit and crops, or satisfy the lofty and covetous wishes of the workmen. And when it was known to the King that they had not observed his command, and had given greater wages to the labourers, he levied heavy fines upon abbots, priors, knights, greater and lesser, and other great folk and small folk of the realm, of some 100*s*, of some 40*s*, of some 20*s*, from each according to what he could give. And afterwards the King had many labourers arrested, and sent them to prison; many withdrew themselves and went into the forests and woods; and those who were taken were heavily fined. Their ringleaders were made to swear that they would not take daily wages beyond the ancient custom, and then were freed from prison. And in like manner was done with the other craftsmen in the boroughs and villages . . . After the aforesaid pestilence, many buildings, great and small, fell into ruins in every city, borough, and village for lack of inhabitants, likewise many villages and hamlets became desolate, not a house being left in them, all having died who dwelt there; and it was probable that many such villages would never be inhabited.

FLAGELLANTS, LONDON, Michaelmas 1349

Robert of Avesbury

Usually members of the Dominican and Franciscan orders, flagellants underwent public voluntary whipping in atonement for society's sins. Their numbers increased dramatically in the wake of the Black Death (which, in medieval eyes, was seeming, punishment by God.)

About Michaelmas 1349 over six hundred men came to London from Flanders, mostly of Zeeland and Holland origin. Sometimes at St Paul's and sometimes at other points in the city they made two daily public appearances wearing cloths from the thighs to the ankles, but otherwise stripped bare. Each wore a cap marked with a red cross in front and behind. Each had in his right hand a scourge with three tails. Each tail had a knot and through the middle of it there were sometimes sharp nails fixed. They marched naked in a file one behind the other and whipped themselves with these scourges on their naked and bleeding bodies. Four of them would cant in their native tongue and, another four would chant in response like a litany. Thrice they would all cast themselves on the ground in this sort of procession, stretching out their hands like the arms of a cross. The singing would go on and, the one who was in the rear of those thus prostrate acting first, each of them in turn would step over the others and give one stroke with his scourge to the man lying under him. This went on from the first to the last until each of them had observed the ritual to the full tale of those on the ground. Then each put on his customary garments and always wearing their caps and carrying their whips in their hands they retired to their lodgings. It is said that every night they performed the same penance.

FRAUDULENT BEGGARS, LONDON, 1380

City of London Letter-Book

On the 24th day of October, in the 4th year of Richard II, John Warde, of the County of York, and Richard Lynham, of the

County of Somerset, two impostors, were brought to the Hall of the Guildhall of London, before John Hadlee, Mayor, the Aldermen, and the Sheriffs, and questioned for that, whereas they were stout enough to work for their food and raiment, and had their tongues to talk with, they, the same John Warde and Richard Lynham, did there pretend that they were mutes, and had been deprived of their tongues; and went about in divers places of the city aforesaid, carrying in their hands two ell measures, an iron hook and pincers, and a piece of leather, in shape like part of a tongue, edged with silver, and with writing around it, to this effect – THIS IS THE TONGUE OF JOHN WARDE – with which instruments, and by means of divers signs, they gave many persons to understand that they were traders, in token whereof they carried the said ell measures; and that they had been plundered by robbers of their goods; and that their tongues had also been drawn out with the said hook, and then cut off with the pincers; they making a horrible noise, like unto a roaring, and opening their mouths; where it seemed to all who examined the same, that their tongues had been cut off: to the defrauding of other poor and infirm persons, and in manifest deceit of the whole of the people.

Wherefore, they were asked how they would acquit themselves thereof; upon which, they acknowledged that they had done all the things above imputed to them. And as it appeared to the Court that of their evil intent and falsity they had done the things aforesaid, and in deceit of all the people; and to the end that other persons might beware of such and the like evil intent, falsity, and deceit, it was awarded that they should be put upon the pillory on three different days, each time for one hour in the day; namely, on the Wednesday, Friday, and Saturday, before the Feast of St Simon and St Jude; the said instruments being hung about their necks each day . . . which punishment being completed, they were instructed to have them taken back to the Gaol of Newgate, there to remain until orders should be given for their release.

THE PEASANTS' REVOLT REACHES LONDON, 13–15 June 1381

City of London Letter-Book

The Peasants' Revolt was triggered by opposition to the Statute of Labourers, which tried to set maximum wages in the wake of the Black

Death, and end the Poll Tax of 1379. Riots broke out all over England and 60,000 peasants, led by Wat Tyler, marched on the English capital.

Among the most wondrous and hitherto unheard-of prodigies that ever happened in the City of London, that which took place there on the Feast of Corpus Christi, the 13th day of June, in the 4th year of the reign of King Richard the Second, seems deserving to be committed to writing, that it may not be unknown to those to come.

For on that day, while the King was holding his Council in the Tower of London, countless companies of the commoners and persons of the lowest grade from Kent and Essex suddenly approached the said City, the one body coming to the town of Southwark, and the other to the place called 'Mileende', without Algate. By the aid also of perfidious commoners within the City, of their own condition, who rose in countless numbers there, they suddenly entered the City together, and, passing straight through it, went to the mansion of Sir John [of Gaunt], Duke of Lancaster, called 'le Savoye', and completely levelled the same with the ground, and burned it. From thence they turned to the Church of the Hospital of St John of Jerusalem, without Smethefeld, and burnt and levelled nearly all the houses there, the church excepted.

On the next morning, all the men from Kent and Essex met at the said place called 'Mileende', together with some of perfidious persons of the City aforesaid; whose numbers in all were past reckoning. And there the King came to them from the Tower, accompanied by many knights and esquires, and citizens on horseback, the lady his mother following him also in a chariot. Where, at the prayer of the infuriated rout, our Lord the King granted that they might take those who were traitors against him, and slay them, wheresoever they might be found. And from thence the King rode to his Wardrobe, which is situate near to Castle Baynard; while the whole of the infuriated rout took its way towards the Tower of London; entering which by force, they dragged forth from it Sir Simon, Archbishop of Canterbury, Chancellor of our Lord the King, and Brother Robert Hales, Prior of the said Hospital of St John of Jerusalem, the King's Treasurer; and, together with them, Brother William Appeltone, of the Order of Friars Minors, and John Leg, Serjeant-at-arms to the King, and also, one Richard Somenour, of the Parish of Stebenhuthe; all of whom they beheaded in the place called

'Tourhille', without the said Tower; and then carrying their heads through the City upon lances, they set them up on London Bridge, fixing them there on stakes.

Upon the same day there was also no little slaughter within the City, as well of natives as of aliens. Richard Lions, citizen and vintner of the said City, and many others, were beheaded in Chepe. In the Vintry also, there was a very great massacre of Flemings, and in one heap there were lying about forty headless bodies of persons who had been dragged forth from the churches and their houses; and hardly was there a street in the City in which there were not bodies lying of those who had been slain. Some of the houses also in the said City were pulled down, and others in the suburbs destroyed, and some too, burnt.

Such tribulation as this, greater and more horrible than could be believed by those who had not seen it, lasted down to the hour of Vespers on the following day, which was Saturday, the 15th of June; on which day God sent remedy for the same, and His own gracious aid, by the hand of the most renowned man, Sir William Walworthe, the then Mayor; who in Smethefelde, in presence of our Lord the King and those standing by him, lords, knights, esquires, and citizens on horseback, on the one side, and the whole of this infuriated rout on the other, most manfully, by himself, rushed upon the captain of the said multitude, 'Walter Tylere' by name, and, as he was altercating with the King and the nobles, first wounded him in the neck with his sword, and then hurled him from his horse, mortally pierced in the breast; and further, by favour of the divine grace, so defended himself from those who had come with him, both on foot and horseback, that he departed from thence unhurt, and rode on with our Lord the King and his people, towards a field near to the spring that is called 'Whitewellebeche'; in which place, while the whole of the infuriated multitude in warlike manner was making ready against our Lord the King and his people, refusing to treat of peace except on condition that they should first have the head of the said Mayor, the Mayor himself, who had gone into the City at the instance of our Lord the King, in the space of half an hour sent and led forth therefrom so great a force of citizen warriors in aid of our Lord the King, that the whole multitude of madmen was surrounded and hemmed in; and not one of them would have escaped, if our Lord the King had not commended them to be gone.

Therefore our Lord the King returned into the City of London with the greatest of glory and honour, and the whole of this profane multitude in confusion fled forthwith for concealment, in their affright.

For this same deed our Lord the King, beneath his standard, in the field, with his own hands decorated with the order of knighthood the said Mayor, and Sir Nicholas Brembre, and Sir John Phelipot, who had already been Mayors of the said City; as also, Sir Robert Launde.

A COMPLAINT AGAINST PETS IN THE NUNNERY, ENGLAND, 1387

William of Wykeham, Bishop of Winchester

A letter written to the Abbess of Romsey.

Item, because we have convinced ourselves by clear proofs that some of the nuns of your house bring with them to church birds, rabbits, hounds and such like frivolous things, whereunto they give more heed than to the offices of the church, with frequent hindrance to their own psalmody and that of their fellow nuns and to the grievous peril of their souls; therefore we strictly forbid you, all and several, in virtue of the obedience due unto us, that you presume henceforward to bring to church no birds, hounds, rabbits or other frivolous things that promote indiscipline; and any nun who does to the contrary, after three warnings shall fast on bread and water on one Saturday for each offence, notwithstanding one discipline to be received publicly in chapter on the same day . . . Item, whereas through the hunting-dogs and other hounds abiding within your monastic precincts, the alms that should be given to the poor are devoured and the church and cloister and other places set apart for divine and secular services are foully defiled, contrary to all honesty, and whereas, through their inordinate noise, divine service is frequently troubled, therefore we strictly command and enjoin you, Lady Abbess, in virtue of obedience, that you remove these dogs altogether and that you suffer them never henceforth, nor any other such hounds, to abide within the precincts of your nunnery.

PAGEANTS FOR THE WEDDING OF ISABELLA AND CHARLES VII, PARIS, 22 August 1389

Jean Froissart

At the outer gate of Saint-Denis as one enters the city of Paris, near the place known as La Bastide, there was a representation of the starry firmament, and within it were young children dressed as angels, singing most melodiously. There was, moreover, a living tableau of Our Lady holding in her arms a child playing with a windmill made from a large walnut. The upper part of the firmament was richly emblazoned with the arms of France and Bavaria, and a golden sun in its glory – the king's badge in the jousting tournaments to follow. The Queen of France and her ladies were delighted with all these as they passed, as indeed were all the others who went by.

When they had seen it the queen and her ladies went slowly on to the fountain in the rue Saint-Denis, which was covered all round about with a fine blue cloth powdered with golden fleurs-de-lis; the pillars surrounding the fountain bore the arms of several of the principal lords of the kingdom of France, and from its spouts the fountain gave forth streams of excellent claret and spiced wine. Ranged about the fountain were gaily dressed girls with fine caps of gold, singing very tunefully; it was most agreeable to listen to them, and they held in their hands golden cups and goblets, offering drink to all who wanted some. As she passed, the queen halted to enjoy the spectacle and delight in the way it had been arranged; all the ladies and maidens and all the men who passed did likewise.

Further on, in front of the Hospital of the Trinity, a wooden platform had been set up in the street, and on it a castle in front of which was a representation by living actors of the battle with Saladin, the Christians on one side and the Saracens on the other. All the most famous barons, who took part in the battle were shown, each armed in the style of that time. A little above them was a man who represented the King of France, with the twelve peers of France round him, each wearing his own coat-armour. When the Queen of France in her litter had reached the platform King Richard (Cœur-de-Lion) left his companions in the play and approached the King of France to ask his permission to attack the Saracens. When it was granted to him he returned to his companions and they arrayed themselves and went to attack Saladin and the Saracens. Then followed a mock-battle which was very fierce and lasted some time, affording a most interesting spectacle.

Then the procession passed on and came to the inner gate of Saint-Denis, where they had built a castle like the one at the outer gate, with a coloured sky sprinkled with stars, in which sat God in His majesty – Father, Son and Holy Spirit – and in the sky were choir-boys dressed as angels singing most sweetly. At the moment the queen passed in her litter under the arch of the gate, the heavens opened and two angels came down, holding in their hands a golden crown richly studded with precious stones which they laid very gently on the queen's head, and as they did this they sang:

O Lady, girl with fleurs-de-lis,
Queen are you now of fair Paris,
Of France, and all this rich country.
– Now back to Paradise we flee.

When they came in front of the Chapelle Saint-Jacques the lords and ladies saw another platform which had been erected on the right-hand side of the street, sumptuously constructed and hung with lofty curtains as if it were a room, and in the room were men playing sweet music on organs. The whole length of the rue Saint-Denis was covered over with camlet or silk in such profusion one would have thought the stuff was to be had for the asking – as if one lived in Alexandria or Damascus. I, the author of this book, was a witness of all these things, and when I saw such profusion of stuffs I wondered how it could all have been obtained. All the houses on both sides of the great rue Saint-Denis as far as the Chatelet, indeed as far as the Grand Pont, were hung with tall tapestries representing various scenes so that the whole street was a source of pleasure to the eye. And so the concourse of ladies in their litters with their escorting lords reached the gate of the Chatelet at a walking pace, and there they again halted to watch other scenes that had been prepared for them.

In front of this gate a fortress had been constructed in wood and equipped with watch-turrets, strong enough to last for forty years. On each of the turrets was a man fully armed; within the castle was a ceremonial bed, as richly hung as if it were for the King's bed-chamber, and this throne was called the Bed of Justice. On it sat a woman representing Saint Anne. In front of the castle was a large flat space arranged with bushes to look like a warren; among the bushes were large numbers of hares, rabbits and small birds who kept darting out, only to fly back again at once for fear of the vast crowds of people. From the side on which the ladies had approached a white hart came out of the undergrowth and stepped towards the Bed of Justice; then from the bushes on the opposite side came a lion and an eagle, skilfully counterfeited, who went up to the hart before the throne. At this there emerged from the bushes a dozen young maidens, richly clad and wearing golden chaplets, each with a naked sword in her hand, and they placed themselves between the hart and the eagle and lion. With their swords they showed that they would protect the hart and the Bed of Justice, an allegory that appealed greatly to the queen and those about her.

From there they went on towards the Grand Pont, so finely decorated that the work could not have been improved, and covered over with an awning of green and crimson samite in the form of a starry sky. All the streets were decorated as far as the church of Notre-Dame, and when the ladies had crossed the Grand Pont and were nearing the church it was already late, for throughout the length of the journey from Saint-Denis their speed had never been faster than a walking pace.

THE ENGLISH LONGBOW WINS THE BATTLE OF AGINCOURT, FRANCE, 25 October 1415

Jehan de Wavrin

A battle in the Hundred Years War between England and France in which, as at Crécy, the superior technology of the English defeated the greater numbers of the French. Around 10,000 men under Henry V faced the 50,000 French troops of Constable Charles I d'Albret.

Of the mortal battle of Azincourt, in which the King of England discomfited the French.

It is true that the French had arranged their battalions between two small thickets, one lying close to Azincourt, and the other to Tramecourt. The place was narrow, and very advantageous for the English, and, on the contrary, very ruinous for the French, for the said French had been all night on horseback, and it rained, and the pages, grooms, and others, in leading about the horses, had broken up the ground, which was so soft that the horses could with difficulty step out of the soil. And also the said French were so loaded with armour that they could not support themselves or move forward. In the first place they were armed with long coats of steel, reaching to the knees or lower, and very heavy, over the leg harness, and besides plate armour also most of them had hooded helmets; wherefore this weight of armour, with the softness of the wet ground, as has been said, kept them as if immovable, so that they could raise their clubs only with great difficulty, and with all these mischiefs there was this, that most of them were troubled with hunger and want of sleep. There was a marvellous number of banners, and it was ordered that some of them should be furled. Also it was settled among the said French that everyone should shorten his lance, in order that they might be stiffer when it came to fighting at close quarters. They had archers and cross-bowmen enough, but they would not let them shoot, for the plain was so narrow that there was no room except for the men-at-arms.

Now let us return to the English. After the parley between the two armies was finished, as we have said, and the delegates had returned, each to their own people, the King of England, who had appointed a knight called Sir Thomas Erpingham to place his archers in front in two wings, trusted entirely to him, and Sir Thomas, to do his part, exhorted every one to do well in the name of the king, begging them to fight vigorously against the French in order to secure and save their own lives. And thus the knight, who rode with two others only in front of the battalion, seeing that the hour was come, for all things were well arranged, threw up a baton which he held in his hand, saying 'Nestrocq' [? 'Now Strike!'], which was the signal for attack; then dismounted and joined the king, who was also on foot in the midst of his men, with his banner before him. Then the English, seeing this signal, began suddenly to march, uttering a very loud cry, which greatly surprised the French. And when the English saw that the French did not approach them, they marched dashingly towards them in very fine order, and again raised a loud cry as they stopped to take breath.

Then the English archers, who, as I have said, were in the wings, saw that they were near enough, and began to send their arrows on the French with great vigour. The said archers were for the most part in their doublets, without armour, their stockings rolled up to their knees, and having hatchets and battle-axes or great swords hanging at their girdles; some were bare-footed and bare-headed, others had caps of boiled leather, and others of osier, covered with harpoy or leather.

Then the French, seeing the English come towards them in this fashion, placed themselves in order, every one under his banner, their helmets on their heads. The constable, the marshal, the admirals, and the other princes earnestly exhorted their men to fight the English well and bravely; and when it came to the approach the trumpets and clarions resounded everywhere; but the French began to hold down their heads, especially those who had no bucklers, for the impetuosity of the English arrows, which fell so heavily that no one durst uncover or look up. Thus they went forward a little, then made a little retreat, but before they could come to close quarters, many of the French were disabled and wounded by the arrows; and when they came quite up to the English, they were, as has been said, so closely pressed one against another that none of them could lift their arms to strike against their enemies . . .

COLUMBUS REACHES THE AMERICAS, BAHAMAS, 12 October 1492

Christopher Columbus

Seeking a new trade route to the East on behalf of Imperial Spain, the explorer sailed west, reaching the Bahamas two months later. He was not the first European to reach the New World (the Viking Bjarni Herjolfsson had explored the coast of Labrador as early as AD 985), but he did unveil the continent's existence to Europe.

I was on the poop deck at ten o'clock in the evening when I saw a light. It was so indistinct that I could not be sure it was land, but I called Gutiérrez, the Butler of the King's Table and told him to look at what I thought was a light.

He looked and saw it. I also told Rodrigo Sánchez de Segovia, Your Majesties' observer on board, but he saw nothing because he was standing in the wrong place. After I had told them, the light appeared once or twice more, like a wax candle rising and falling. Only a few people thought it was a sign of land, but I was sure we were close to a landfall.

Then the *Pinta*, being faster and in the lead, sighted land and made the signal as I had ordered. The first man to sight land was called Rodrigo de Triana. The land appeared two hours after midnight, about two leagues away. We furled all sail except the *treo*, the mainsail with no bonnets, and we jogged off and on until Friday morning, when we came to an island. We saw naked people, and I went ashore in a boat with armed men, taking Martín Alonso Pinzón and his brother Vicente Yáñez, captain of the *Nina*. I took the royal standard, and the captains each took a banner with the Green Cross, which each of my ships carries as a device, with the letters F and Y, surmounted by a crown, at each end of the cross.

When we stepped ashore we saw fine green trees, streams everywhere and different kinds of fruit. I called to the two captains to jump ashore with the rest, who included Rodrigo de Escobedo, secretary of the fleet, and Rodrigo Sánchez de Segovia, asking them to bear solemn witness that in the presence of them all I was taking possession of this island for their Lord and Lady the King and Queen, and I made the necessary declaration which are set down at greater length in the written testimonies.

Soon many of the islanders gathered round us. I could see that they were people who would be more easily converted to our Holy Faith by love than by coercion, and wishing them to look on us with friendship I gave some of them red bonnets and glass beads which they hung round their necks, and many other things of small value, at which they were so delighted and so eager to please us that we could not believe it. Later they swam out to the boats to bring us parrots and balls of cotton thread and darts, and many other things, exchanging them for such objects as glass beads and hawk bells. They took anything, and gave willingly whatever they had.

However, they appeared to me to be a very poor people in all respects. They go about as naked as the day they were born, even the women, though I saw only one, who was quite young. All the men I saw were quite young, none older than thirty, all well built, finely bodied and handsome in the face. Their hair is coarse, almost like a horse's tail, and short; they wear it short, cut over the brow, except a few strands of hair hanging down uncut at the back.

Some paint themselves with black, some with the colour of the Canary islanders, neither black nor white, others with white, others with red, others with whatever they can find. Some have only their face painted, others their whole body, others just their eyes or nose. They carry no weapons, and are ignorant of them;

when I showed them some swords they took them by the blade and cut themselves. They have no iron; their darts are just sticks without an iron head, though some of them have a fish tooth or something else at the tip.

They are all the same size, of good stature, dignified and well formed. I saw some with scars on their bodies, and made signs to ask about them, and they indicated to me that people from other islands nearby came to capture them and they defended themselves. I thought, and still think, that people from the mainland come here to take them prisoner. They must be good servants, and intelligent, for I can see that they quickly repeat everything said to them. I believe they would readily become Christians; it appeared to me that they have no religion. With God's will, I will take six of them with me for Your Majesties when I leave this place, so that they may learn Spanish.

I saw no animals on the island, only parrots.

A TRAVELLER'S LONDON, 1497

Andreas Franciscus

London is defended by handsome walls on the northern side, where they have recently been rebuilt. Within these stands a very strongly defended castle on the banks of the river, where the King of England and his Queen sometimes have their residence. There are also other great buildings, and especially a beautiful and convenient bridge over the Thames, of many marble arches, which has on it many shops built of stone and mansions and even a church of considerable size. Nowhere have I seen a finer or more richly built bridge.

Throughout the town are to be seen many workshops of craftsmen in all sorts of mechanical arts, to such an extent that there is hardly a street which is not graced by some shop or the like, which can also be observed by everyone at Milan. This makes the town exceedingly well-stocked and prosperous, as well as having the immediate effect of adding to its splendour. The working in wrought silver, tin or white lead is very expert here, and perhaps the finest I have ever seen. There are also very many mansions, which do not, however, seem very large from the outside, but inside they contain a great number of rooms and garrets and are quite considerable. Six-inch oak beams are inserted in the walls the same distance apart as their own breadth, and walls built in this way turn out to be of the same material as the houses I described at Maastricht.

All the streets are so badly paved that they get wet at the slightest quantity of water, and this happens very frequently owing to the large number of cattle carrying water, as well as on account of the rain, of which there is a great deal in this island. Then a vast amount of evil-smelling mud is formed, which does not disappear quickly but lasts a long time, in fact nearly the whole year round. The citizens, therefore, in order to remove this mud and filth from their boots, are accustomed to spread fresh rushes on the floors of all houses, on which they clean the soles of their shoes when they come in . . .

Londoners have such fierce tempers and dispositions that they not only despise the way in which Italians live, but actually pursue them with uncontrolled hatred, and whereas at Bruges foreigners are hospitably received and complimented and treated with consideration by everyone, here the Englishmen use them with the utmost contempt and arrogance, and make them the object of insults. At Bruges we could do as we liked by day as well as by night. But here they look askance at us by day, and at night they sometimes drive us off with kicks and blows of the truncheon . . .

They eat very frequently, at times more than is suitable, and are particularly fond of young swans, rabbits, deer and sea birds. They often eat mutton and beef, which is generally considered to be better here than anywhere else in the world. This is due to the excellence of their pastures. They have all kinds of fish in plenty and great quantities of oysters which come from the seashore. The majority, not to say everyone, drink that beverage I have spoken of before, and prepare it in various ways. For wine is very expensive, as the vine does not grow in the island; nor does the olive, and the products of both are imported from France and Spain . . .

They have several harsh laws and customs, one of which, still in force to-day, we would consider the most severe of all. This lays down that, at death, a man must leave all his property to his wife, completely excluding the children, for whom they show no affection, lavishing all their love on their wives. And consequently, since the wives have the same dislike for their children, they choose in the end a husband from among the servants and ignore the children. This custom, apart from being contrary to nature, may also be objected to as impious and profane.

Franciscus, an Italian, misunderstood the English law on property; if a man died, only a third of his estate went to his wife.

'JOUST OF THE WHORES', ROME, 1499

Johann Buchal

An orgy, arranged by the Borgia Pope Alexander VI, to celebrate his son Cesare's marriage to Princess Charlotte D'Albret.

This marriage has been celebrated with such unexampled orgies as were never before seen. His Holiness gave a supper to the cardinals and grandees of his court, placing at the side of each guest two courtesans, whose only dress consisted of a loose garment of gauze and garlands of flowers; and when the meal was over, those women, more than fifty in number, performed lascivious dances – at first alone, afterwards with the guests. At last, at a signal given by Madam Lucrezia, the garments of the women fell down, and the dance went on to the applause of His Holiness.

They afterwards proceeded to other sports. By order of the Pope, there were symmetrically placed in the ballroom, twelve rows of branched candelabras covered with lighted candles; Madam Lucrezia threw upon the floor some handfuls of chestnuts, after which those courtesans, entirely naked, ran on all fours, contending to gather the most, and the swifter and more successful obtained from his Holiness presents of jewels and silk dresses. At last, as there were prizes for the sports, there were premiums for lust, and the women were carnally attacked at the pleasure of the guests; and this time Madam Lucrezia, who presided with the Pope on a platform, distributed the premiums to the victors.

MICHELANGELO PAINTS THE CEILING OF THE SISTINE CHAPEL, ROME, 1508–14

A. Condivi

Whilst he was painting, Pope Julius would often go to see the work, ascending by a ladder; and Michelagnolo used to hold out his hand to him to assist him in mounting the scaffold. And like the man that he was, naturally eager and impatient of waiting, as soon as the half was done, namely, from the door to the middle of the vault, he ordered Michelagnolo to uncover it; although it was still unfinished, and wanted the last touches. The opinion and the expectation that was held of Michelagnolo drew all Rome to see the work; and thither the pope also went, before the dust that was raised by the removal of the scaffold had settled.

After this had been done, Raffaello, having seen the new and marvellous manner, as one who had an admirable gift of imitation, sought, by means of Bramante to paint the rest. At this, Michelagnolo was much perturbed, and having obtained audience of the pope, grievously complained of the injury that Bramante did him, and in his presence deplored it before the pope, disclosing all the persecutions which he had received at his hands; and then revealed many of his faults, and especially, when he pulled down old Saint Peter's, how he threw to the ground those marvellous columns that were in that church, neither caring nor taking heed to prevent their being shattered in pieces, though he might have gently lowered them and preserved them entire; and he showed how easy a thing it was to pile brick upon brick, but to make a column of that kind a most difficult one; together with many other things, which it is not needful to relate: so that the pope, having heard these complaints, ordered that Michelagnolo should proceed; and showed more favours than he had ever shown him. Michelagnolo finished the whole of the work in twenty months without any assistance soever; not even of someone to grind the colours for him. It is true I have heard him say, that it was not finished as he would have wished; having been prevented by the hurry of the pope, who asked him one day when he would finish the chapel, and Michelagnolo replying to him, 'As soon as I shall be able,' added in wrath: 'You wish that I should cause you to be thrown down from that scaffold.' And Michelagnolo hearing this, said to himself: 'You shall not have me thrown down.' And having gone his way, he caused the scaffold to be removed, and uncovered the work on the feast of All Saints; and it was seen with great satisfaction by the pope, who was in chapel that day, and with admiration by all Rome, who flocked together to see it. There were still wanting the retouches of ultramarine 'a secco' and gold in some places, that it might appear the more rich. Julius, his first enthusiasm having abated, wished Michelagnolo to add these; but he, considering the trouble that he would have had in re-erecting the scaffold, replied that what was wanting was not a matter of importance. 'It is, indeed, necessary to retouch it with gold,' replied the pope; to whom Michelagnolo answered familiarly, as he was wont to do with his holiness: 'I know not wherefore these men should wear gold.' And the pope: 'The work will look poor.' To which he replied, 'They who are painted here were poor, even they.' Thus was the retort made in jest, and thus the paintings remain. Michelagnolo received for his work, including all his expenses, three thousand ducats, out of which he spent in colours, as I have heard him say, about twenty, or twenty-five.

When the work was finished, Michelagnolo, in having for so long a time, whilst he was painting, held his eyes raised towards the vault, was afterwards able to see little when looking down; so that if he had to read a letter, or look at some other small object, it was necessary for him to hold it with his arm raised above his head. Nevertheless he afterwards, little by little, accustomed himself to read.

STRANGE CRUELTIES: THE SPANISH SLAUGHTER THE NATIVES, WEST INDIES, *c.* 1513

Bartolome de las Casas

The Spaniards with their Horses, their Speares and Lances, began to commit murders, and strange cruelties: they entered into Townes, Borowes, and Villages, sparing neither children nor old men, neither women with childe, neither them that lay in, but that they ripped their bellies, and cut them in peeces, as if they had beene opening of Lambes shut up in their fold. They laid wagers with such as with one thrust of a sword would paunch or bowell a man in the middest, or with one blow of a sword would most readily and most deliverly cut off his head, or that would best pierce his entrals at one stroake. They tooke the little soules by the heeles, ramping them from the mothers dugges, and crushed their heads against the clifts. Others they cast into the Rivers laughing and mocking, and when they tumbled into the water, they said, now shift for they selfe such a ones corpes. They put others, together with their mothers, and all that they met, to the edge of the sword. They made certaine Gibbets long and low, in such sort, that the feete of the hanged on, touched in a manner the ground, every one enough for thirteene, in honour and worship of our Saviour and his twelve Apostles (as they used to speake) and setting to fire, burned them all quicke that were fastened. Unto all others, whom they used to take and reserve alive, cutting off their two hands as neere as might be, and so letting them hang, they said; Get you with these Letters, to carry tydings to those which are fled by the Mountaines. They murdered commonly the Lords and Nobility on this fashion: They made certaine grates of pearches laid on pickforkes, and made a little fire underneath, to the intent, that by little and little yelling and despairing in these torments, they might give up the Ghost.

One time I saw foure or five of the principall Lords roasted and broyled upon these gredirons. Also I thinke that there were two or three of these gredirons, garnished with the like furniture, and for that they cryed out pittiously, which thing troubled the Captaine that he could not then sleepe: he commanded to strangle them. The Sergeant, which was worse than the Hangman that burned them (I know his name and friends in Sivil) would not have them strangled, but himselfe putting Bullets in their mouthes, to the end that they should not cry, put to the fire, untill they were softly roasted after his desire. I have seene all the aforesaid things and others infinite. And forasmuch as all the people which could flee, hid themselves in the Mountaines, and mounted on the tops of them, fled from the men so without all manhood, emptie of all pitie, behaving them as savage beasts, the slaughterers and deadly enemies of mankinde: they taught their Hounds, fierce Dogs, to teare them in peeces at the first view, and in the space that one may say a Credo, assailed and devoured an Indian as if it had beene a Swine.

MARTIN LUTHER PROTESTS AGAINST THE SALE OF INDULGENCES, WITTENBERG, GERMANY, 1517

Martin Luther

A priest at the University of Wittenberg, Luther attacked the sales of indulgences in 95 theses, which he nailed to a church door, defying the papacy. This act and two centuries of religious persecution and warfare between 'Protestants' and Roman Catholics followed.

It was in the year 1517, when the profligate monk Tetzel, a worthy servant of the pope and the devil – for I am certain that the pope is the agent of the devil on earth – came among us selling indulgences, maintaining their efficacy, and impudently practising on the credulity of the people. When I beheld this unholy and detestable traffic taking place in open day, and thereby sanctioning the most villainous crimes, I could not, though I was then but a young doctor of divinity, refrain from protesting against it in the strongest manner, not only as directly contrary to the Scriptures, but as opposed to the canons of the church itself. Accordingly, in my place at Wittemberg – in which university, by the favor of God and the kindness of the illustrious elector of Saxony, I was honored with the office of professor of divinity – I resolved to oppose the career of this odious monk, and to put the people on their guard against the revival of this infamous imposition on their credulity. When I put this resolution into practice, instead of being abused and condemned, as I have been, by these worthless tyrants and impostors, the pope and his mercenaries, I expected to be warmly encouraged and commended, for I did little more than make use of the pope's own language, as set forth in the decretals, against the rapacity and extortion of the collectors. I cautioned my hearers against the snares which were laid for them, showing them that this was a scheme altogether opposed to religions, and only intended as a source of emolument by these unprincipled men. It was on the festival of All-Hallows Eve that I first drew their attention to the gross errors touching indulgences; and about the same time I wrote two letters, one to the most reverend prelate Jerome, bishop of Brandenburg, within whose jurisdiction Tetzel and his associates were carrying on their scandalous traffic; the other to the most reverend prelate and prince, Albert, archbishop of Magdeburg, pointing out to them the consequences of this imposition, and praying them to silence Tetzel. My letter to the archbishop was in these terms:

' "To the most reverend father in Christ, my most illustrious lord, prince Albert, archbishop of Magdeburg and Mayence, marquis of Brandenburg, &c. Luther to his lord and pastor in Christ, in all submission and reverence.

JESUS

' "The grace and mercy of God, and whatever can be and is. Pardon me, most reverend father in Christ, illustrious prince, that I have the temerity, I who am the lees of mankind, to raise my eyes to your sublimity, and address a letter to you. Jesus, my Lord and Savior, is witness for me, that, long restrained by the consciousness of my own turpitude and weakness, I have long delayed commencing the work which I now undertake with open and upraised brow, impelled by the fidelity I owe to Jesus Christ; deign then, your grace, to cast a look upon the grain of sand who now approaches you, and to receive my prayer with paternal clemency.

' "Persons are now hawking about papal indulgences, under the name and august title of your lordship, for the construction of St Peter's at Rome. I say nothing about the vaporings of the preachers, which I have not myself heard; but I complain bitterly of the fatal errors in which they are involving the common people, men of weak understanding, whom, foolish as they are, these men persuade that they will be sure of salvation if they only buy their letters of plenary indulgence. They believe that souls will fly out of purgatory, the moment that the money paid for their redemption is thrown into the preacher's bag, and that such virtue belongs to these indulgences, that there is no sin, howsoever great, even the violation, which is impossible, of the Mother of God, which the indulgences will not absolutely and at once efface.

' "Great God! And is it thus that men dare to teach unto death, those who are entrusted to your care, oh reverend father, and make more difficult the account which will be demanded from you in the great day! When I saw these things I could remain silent no longer. No; there is no episcopal power which can insure to man his salvation; even the infused grace of our Lord cannot wholly render him secure, our apostle commands us to wash out our salvation in fear and trembling: *The righteous scarcely shall be saved*, so narrow is the way which leads to life. Those who are saved are called in the Scripture, brands saved from the burning; everywhere the Lord reminds us of the difficulty of salvation. How, then, dare these men seek to render poor souls fatally confident of salvation, on the mere strength of purchased indulgences and futile promises? The chiefest work of bishops should be to take care that the people learn truly the gospel, and be full of Christian charity. Never did Christ preach indulgences, nor command them to be preached: what he preached and commanded to be preached, was the gospel. . . . I would implore you to silence these ill preachers, ere some one shall arise, and utterly confuting them and their preachings, cast discredit upon your sublimity, a thing to be avoided, but which I fear must needs occur, unless you take measures for silencing these men . . . I entreat your grace to read and consider the propositions, wherein I have demonstrated the vanity of these indulgences, which the preachers thereof call all-powerful.'

To this letter I received no answer, and indeed I knew not at the time that the archbishop had bargained with the pope to receive one-half of the money raised from these indulgences, and to remit the other half to Rome. These, then, were my first steps in the matter, until the increased insolence and the lying representations of Tetzel, which seemed to be fully sanctioned by the silence of his superiors, as well as my determination to maintain the truth at all hazards, induced me to adopt more decisive measures than a mere personal remonstrance, in a series of cautions to those with whom I was more particularly connected, to beware of these arch impostors and blasphemers. So finding all my remonstrances disregarded, on the festival of All Saints, in November, 1517, I read, in the great church of Wittemberg, a series of propositions against these infamous indulgences, in which, while I set forth their utter inefficiency and worthlessness, I expressly declared in my protest, that I would submit on all occasions to the word of God and the decisions of the church. At the same time I was not so presumptuous as to imagine that my opinion would be preferred above all others, nor yet so blind as to set the fables and decrees of man above the written word of God. I took occasion to express these opinions rather as subjects of doubt than of positive assertion, but I held it to be my duty to print and circulate them throughout the country, for the benefit of all classes – for the learned, that they might detect inaccuracies – for the ignorant, that they might be put on their guard against the villainies and impositions of Tetzel, until the matter was properly determined.

Part Three

The Age of Revolution
The Making of the Modern World, 1518–1899

'The Age of Reason has at length revolved. Long have we been endeavouring to find ourselves men. We now find ourselves so. We will be treated as such.'

Address of the sailors at the Nore
during the naval mutiny of 1797

INTRODUCTION

The faith of the medieval age did not simply disappear. The lives of Western men and women, from birth to death, would continue to be defined by religious rites and rituals. But religion no longer bound society together; on the contrary, it split it asunder. A hundred years of ferocious religious wars followed Luther's pinning of his theses to the church door at Wittenberg. As Protestantism advanced, so it was met by the Catholic 'Counter-Reformation' (particularly Ignatius Loyola's Society of Jesus – the Jesuits – and the forbidding Inquisition). In the name of God, torture, death and repression became Western commonplaces.

Divided, the Church was less able to withstand the eroding waves of science and humanism that still spilled over from the Renaissance. In 1609, in Padua, Galileo Galilei built the first astronomical telescope, which proved conclusively that Nicholas Copernicus's theory that the earth moved around the sun was correct. A central tenet of Christian religion was ended in an instant. Emboldened, Galileo formulated laws governing the speed of falling bodies and concluded that the whole universe obeyed the same physical laws.

By chain intellectual reaction, Galileo's work was taken up by the French philosopher René Descartes. In perhaps the key moment in modern thought, Descartes decided to reject all received wisdom and authority, and begin at the beginning. The one unassailable truth was that his own mind was thinking, and that he himself existed: *Cogito, ergo sum* ('I think, therefore I am'). Descartes' philosophy of Rationalism, as expounded in *Discours de la Methode* (1637) accepted God – but it was a God proven by reason, and not dependent on faith. Fifty years later, Sir Isaac Newton declared that one force – gravity – held the universe together. His *Principia Mathematica* furnished powerful support for Descartes' contention that the great truths of life and the universe might be discovered by the use of reason alone. Galileo, Descartes and Newton did not 'kill' God (Descartes and Newton were highly religious men), but by the 'Age of Enlightenment' – the late seventeenth century to early eighteenth century – it was clear that a revolution had taken place in the minds of many Western men and woman. Phenomena previously attributable to God were now explained by science. Atheism even became respectable.

It was perhaps only a matter of time before someone would suggest that society, as well as the universe, was subject to an all-embracing natural law. And that this law held that all men were free and equal. The philosopher who did so was the Englishman John Locke in *Two Treatises of Government* (1690) which, for good measure, also rejected the Divine Right of kings to rule. Much of Locke's philosophy was not new and drew directly on the practice of English history. The Divine Right of English kings to rule had come to early grief in the 1640s, when Charles I (courtesy of a powerful merchant class and a strong parliament) lost the English Civil War and was beheaded in 1649. The Puritan military dictatorship of Oliver Cromwell followed. Although this proved too austere for English tastes, and the Stuarts were restored in 1660, the monarchy was henceforth highly restricted. When James II failed to please, he was deposed in the Glorious Revolution of 1688. 'Divine Right' was only conspicuous by its absence.

But if Locke's *Treatises of Government* drew on history, they also made it. His contention that any ruling body which offended against natural law should be removed had a direct influence on the American Revolution of 1775, which threw off British colonial rule. Thomas Jefferson's draft Declaration of Independence, based on his reading of John Locke, declared: 'We hold these truths to be self-evident. That all men are created equal, that they are endowed by their Creator with certain inalienable rights, that among these are Life, Liberty and the Pursuit of Happiness.' (There were also more prosaic reasons for rebellion: Britain had taxed the American colonies – to pay for an army to occupy the American colonies.)

Revolution was infectious. In 1789 it reached France, the exemplar of the absolutist state, where Louis XIV, the 'Sun King' and builder of Versailles had once opined 'L'état c'est moi' (I am the state). After the disastrous harvest of 1788, the mob rose. On 14 July 1789 Parisians stormed the Bastille; their example fired France's peasantry, who refused to pay taxes or feudal dues. Within a year, the French monarchy had been swept away, a Republic declared in its place. Eventually, the French – under Napoleon Bonaparte – moved to export their revolution for 'Liberty, Equality, Opportunity' on the end of bayonets and muskets, but the war of European liberation soon turned into a war of French conquest. However the ideals of the French Revolution lived on; in the Romantic movements in the arts, and in the tide of liberal nationalism which swept the world in the early nineteenth century. They shaped the politics of South America, and produced nationalist heroes such as Garibaldi and statesmen such as Abraham Lincoln. Nationalism was the strongest ideological force since the fervour of the Reformation.

Upheaval in the Age of Revolution was not only political. The most fundamental change was economic: the coming of the Industrial Revolution, which began in Britain as early as 1750. New machines, powered and forged by Britain's blessed supplies of coal and iron, brought the factory system into being. Huge urban conurbations sprang up as the rural poor left the land in search of work, often to be crowded into squalid slum housing. Over the course of the nineteenth century, the Industrial Revolution spread across Europe and much of the globe. It brought advantages to some, but it also sowed the seeds of ultimate conflict. Industrialization led to social problems which the 'laissez-faire' style of capitalism ignored, while the division of the world into spheres of imperial interest by the major economic powers would only be resolved by war.

THE CONQUISTADORS ENTER MEXICO CITY, 8 November 1519

Bernal Diaz

After founding Vera Cruz and defeating the Tlaxcala, the Spanish conquistadores *of Hernando Cortés marched on the capital of Aztec civilization.*

Next morning, we came to a broad causeway and continued our march towards Iztapalapa. And when we saw all those cities and villages built in the water, and other great towns on dry land and that straight and level causeway leading to Mexico, we were astounded. These great towns and *cues* and buildings rising from the water, all made of stone, seemed like an enchanted vision from the tale of Amadis. Indeed, some of our soldiers asked whether it was not all a dream. It is not surprising therefore that I should write in this vein. It was all so wonderful that I do not know how to describe this first glimpse of things never heard of, seen or dreamed of before.

When we arrived near Iztapalapa we beheld the splendour of the other *Caciques* who came out to meet us, the lord of that city whose name was Cuitlahuac, and the lord of Culuacan, both of them close relations of Montezuma. And when we entered the city of Iztapalapa, the sight of the palaces in which they lodged us! They were very spacious and well built, of magnificent stone, cedar wood, and the wood of other sweet-smelling trees, with great rooms and courts, which were a wonderful sight, and all covered with awnings of woven cotton.

When we had taken a good look at all this, we went to the orchard and garden, which was a marvellous place both to see and walk in. I was never tired of noticing the diversity of trees and the various scents given off by each, and the paths choked with roses and other flowers, and the many local fruit-trees and rose-bushes, and the pond of fresh water. Another remarkable thing was that large canoes could come into the garden from the lake, through a channel they had cut, and their crews did not have to disembark. Everything was shining with lime and decorated with different kinds of stonework and paintings which were a marvel to gaze on. Then there were birds of many breeds and varieties which came to the pond. I say again that I stood looking at it, and thought that no land like it would ever be discovered in the whole world, because at that time Peru was neither known nor thought of . . . we left Iztapalapa with a large escort of these great *Caciques*, and followed the causeway, which is eight yards wide and goes so straight to the city of Mexico that I do not think it curves at all. Wide though it was, it was so crowded with people that there was hardly room for them all. Some were going to Mexico and others coming away, besides those who had come out to see us, and we could hardly get through the crowds that were there. For the towers and the *cues* were full, and they came in canoes from all parts of the lake. No wonder, since they had never seen horses or men like us before!

With such wonderful sights to gaze on we did not know what to say, or if this was real that we saw before our eyes. On the land side there were great cities, and on the lake many more. The lake was crowded with canoes. At intervals along the causeway there were many bridges, and before us was the great city of Mexico. As for us, we were scarcely four hundred strong, and we well remembered the words and warnings of the people of Huexotzinco and Tlascala and Tlamanalco, and the many other warnings we had received to beware of entering the city of Mexico, since they would kill us as soon as they had us inside. Let the interested reader consider whether there is not much to ponder in this narrative of mine. What men in all the world have shown such daring? But let us go on.

We marched along our causeway to a point where another small causeway branches off to another city called Coyoacan, and there, beside some tower like buildings, which were their shrines, we were met by many more *Caciques* and dignitaries in very rich cloaks. The different chieftains wore different brilliant liveries, and the causeways were full of them. Montezuma had sent these great *Caciques* in advance to receive us, and as soon as they came before Cortes they told him in their language that we were welcome, and as a sign of peace they touched the ground with their hands and kissed it.

There we halted for some time while Cacamatzin, the lord of Texcoco, and the lords of Iztapalapa, Tacuba, and Coyoacan went ahead to meet the great Montezuma, who approached in a rich litter, accompanied by other great lords and feudal *Caciques* who owned vassals. When we came near to Mexico, at a place where there were some other small towers, the great Montezuma descended from his litter, and these other great *Caciques* supported him beneath a marvellously rich canopy of green feathers, decorated with gold work, silver, pearls, and *chalchihuites*, which hung from a sort of border. It was a marvellous sight. The great Montezuma was magnificently clad, in their fashion, and wore sandals of a kind for which their name is *cotaras*, the soles of which are of gold and the upper parts ornamented with precious stones. And the four lords who supported him were richly clad also in garments that seem to have been kept ready for them on the road so that they could accompany their master. For they had not worn clothes like this when they came out to receive us. There were four other great *Caciques* who carried the canopy above their heads, and many more lords who walked before the great Montezuma, sweeping the ground on which he was to tread, and laying down cloaks so that his feet should not touch the earth. Not one of these chieftains dared to look him in the face. All kept their eyes lowered most reverently except those four lords, his nephews, who were supporting him.

When Cortes saw, heard, and was told that the great Montezuma was approaching, he dismounted from his horse, and when he came near to Montezuma each bowed deeply to the other. Montezuma welcomed our Captain, and Cortes, speaking through Doña Marina, answered by wishing him very good health. Cortes, I think, offered Montezuma his right hand, but Montezuma refused it and extended his own. Then Cortes brought out a necklace which he had been holding. It was made of those elaborately worked and coloured glass beads called *margaritas*, of which I have spoken, and was strung on gold cord and dipped in musk to give it a good odour. This he hung round the great Montezuma's neck, and as he did so attempted to embrace him. But the great princes who stood round Montezuma grasped Cortes' arm to prevent him, for they considered this an indignity.

Then Cortes told Montezuma that it rejoiced his heart to have seen such a great prince, and that he took his coming in person to receive him and the repeated favours he had done him as a high honour. After this Montezuma made him another complimentary speech, and ordered two of his nephews who were supporting him, the lords of Texcoco and Coyoacan, to go with us and show us our quarters. Montezuma returned to the city with the other two kinsmen of his escort, the lords of Cuitlahuac and Tacuba; and all those grand companies of *Caciques* and dignitaries who had come with him returned also in his train. And as they accompanied their lord we observed them marching with their eyes downcast so that they should not see him, and keeping close to the wall as they followed him with great reverence. Thus space was made for us to enter the streets of Mexico without being pressed by the crowd.

Who could now count the multitude of men, women, and boys in the streets, on the roof-tops and in canoes on the waterways, who had come out to see us? It was a wonderful sight and, as I write, it all comes before my eyes as if it had happened only yesterday.

They led us to our quarters, which were in some large houses capable of accommodating us all and had formerly belonged to the great Montezuma's father, who was called Axayacatl. Here Montezuma now kept the great shrines of his gods, and a secret chamber containing gold bars and jewels. This was the treasure he had inherited from his father, which he never touched. Perhaps their reason for lodging us here was that, since they called us *Teules* and considered us as such, they wished to have us near their idols. In any case they took us to this place, where there were many great halls, and a dais hung with the cloth of their country for our Captain, and matting beds with canopies over them for each of us.

On our arrival we entered the large court, where the great Montezuma was awaiting our Captain. Taking him by the hand, the prince led him to his apartment in the hall where he was to lodge, which was very richly furnished in their manner. Montezuma had ready for him a very rich necklace, made of golden crabs, a marvellous piece of work, which he hung round Cortes' neck. His captains were greatly astonished at this sign of honour.

After this ceremony, for which Cortes thanked him through our interpreters, Montezuma said: 'Malinche, you and your brothers are in your own house. Rest awhile.' He then returned to his palace, which was not far off.

We divided our lodgings by companies, and placed our artillery in a convenient spot. Then the order we were to keep was clearly explained to us, and we were warned to be very much on the alert, both the horsemen and the rest of us soldiers. We then ate a sumptuous dinner which they had prepared for us in their native style.

So, with luck on our side, we boldly entered the city of Tenochtitlan or Mexico on 8 November in the year of our Lord 1519.

Cordiality did not last. The excesses of Cortés's deputy, Alvarado, prompted an Aztec uprising, and Cortés was obliged to evacuate Tenochitlan with terrible losses in the 'Night of Sorrows'. He returned, however, with a reassembled army, laid siege to the city and, after defeating a vastly larger Aztec army, razed it to the ground. A new, Spanish Mexico City was built in its place.

THE DEATH OF FERDINAND MAGELLAN, THE PHILIPPINES, 1521

Antonio Pigafetta

After discovering the strait at the southern tip of the Americas which now bears his name, Ferdinand Magellan eventually reached an ocean he named 'pacific'. It was on crossing this sea that he chanced upon an inhabited island, probably Cebu in the Philippines archipelago.

When morning came, forty-nine of us leaped into the water up to our thighs, and walked through water for more than two crossbow flights before we could reach the shore. The boats could not approach nearer because of certain rocks in the water. The other eleven men remained behind to guard the boats. When we reached land, those men had formed in three divisions to the number of more than 1,500 persons. When they saw us, they charged down upon us with exceeding loud cries, two divisions on our flanks and the other on our front. When the captain saw that, he formed us into two divisions, and thus did we begin to fight.

The musketeers and crossbowmen shot from a distance for about a half-hour, but uselessly; for the shots only passed through the shields which were made of thin wood and the arms. The captain [Magellan] cried to them, 'Cease firing! cease firing!' but his order was not at all heeded. When the natives saw that we were shooting our muskets to no purpose, crying out they determined to stand firm, but they redoubled their shouts. When our muskets were discharged, the natives would never stand still, but leaped hither and thither, covering themselves with their shields. They shot so many arrows at us and hurled so many bamboo spears (some of them tipped with iron) at the captain-general, besides pointed stakes hardened with fire, stones, and mud, that we could scarcely defend ourselves. Seeing that, the captain-general sent some men to burn their houses in order to terrify them.

When they saw their houses burning, they were roused to greater fury. Two of our men were killed near the houses, while we burned twenty or thirty houses. So many of them charged down upon us that they shot the captain through the right leg with a poisoned arrow. On that account, he ordered us to retire slowly, but the men took to flight, except six or eight of us who remained with the captain. The natives shot only at our legs, for the latter were bare; and so many were the spears and stones that they hurled at us that we could offer no resistance. The mortars in the boats could not aid us as they were too far away. So we continued to retire for more than a good crossbow flight from the shore, always fighting up to our knees in the water. The natives continued to pursue us, and picking up the same spear four or six times, hurled it at us again and again. Recognizing the captain, so many turned upon him that they knocked his helmet off his head twice, but he always stood firmly like a good knight, together with some others.

Thus did we fight for more than one hour, refusing to retire further. An Indian hurled a bamboo spear into the captain's face, but the latter immediately killed him with his lance, which he left in the Indian's body. Then, trying to lay hand on sword, he could draw it out but halfway, because he had been wounded in the arm with a bamboo spear. When the natives saw that, they all hurled themselves upon him. One of them wounded him on the left leg with a large cutlass, which resembles a scimitar, only being larger. That caused the captain to fall face downward, when immediately they rushed upon him with iron and bamboo spears and with their cutlasses, until they killed our mirror, our light, our comfort, and our true guide. When they wounded him, he turned back many times to see whether we were all in the boats. Thereupon, beholding him dead, we, wounded, retreated as best we could to the boats, which were already pulling off. The Christian king would have aided us, but the captain charged him before we landed, not to leave his balanghai, but to stay to see how we fought. When the king learned that the captain was dead, he wept.

Had it not been for that unfortunate captain, not a single one of us would have been saved in the boats, for while he was fighting the others retired to the boats. I hope through the efforts of your most illustrious Lordship that the fame of so noble a captain will not become effaced in our times. Among the other virtues which he possessed, he was more constant than ever anyone else in the greatest of adversity. He endured hunger better than all the others, and more accurately than any man in the world did he understand sea charts and navigation. And that this was the truth was seen openly, for no other had had so much natural talent nor the boldness to learn how to circumnavigate the world, as he had almost done.

A single ship of Magellan's fleet, the *Victoria*, captained by Juan Sebastian del Cano and navigated by Pigafetta, completed the first navigation of the world, reaching Spain in 1522. There were just eighteen survivors on board out of a crew of 241 who had begun Magellan's expedition.

THE SACK OF ROME: CELLINI BISECTS A SPANIARD, 1527

Benvenuto Cellini

Rome was invaded by troops of Charles V as part of the Spanish emperor's bid to possess Italy. Pope Clement VII was forced into refuge in the Castel Sant'Angelo. Cellini's greater reputation rests on his art as a Renaissance goldsmith and sculptor.

One day the Pope happened to be walking along round the keep when he noticed in the Prati a Spanish officer who had once been in his service and whom he recognized from certain characteristics that he had. As he was staring down at him he started to talk about the man. Meanwhile, knowing nothing about all this, I merely looked down from the top of the Angel and noticed that there was someone directing the digging of trenches. He had a lance in his hand and was dressed in a rose-coloured uniform. I began to wonder how I could get at him, took one of the falconets that was near me – the falconet is bigger and longer than the swivel gun and very like a demi-culverin – cleared it, and then loaded with a hefty charge of fine powder, mixed with coarse. I aimed carefully at the man who was dressed in red, elevating the gun way up in the air, as he was too far away for me to be sure of accuracy with a gun of that kind. Then I fired and hit him exactly in the middle.

With typical Spanish swagger he was wearing his sword across his front. The result was that the shot struck the sword and cut him in two. The Pope who was taken by surprise was astonished and delighted, but he found it impossible to understand how a gun could be fired accurately at such range, or how on earth the man could have been cut in two. So he sent for me and asked me to explain.

I told him how painstaking I had been in aiming the gun, and as for why he was cut in two, I said that neither he nor I could ever understand. And then falling on my knees, I begged him to absolve me of that homicide, and of the others I had committed while serving the Church in the castle. At this the Pope raised his hand, carefully made a great sign of the cross above my head, and said that he gave me his blessing and that he forgave me all the homicides I had ever committed and all those I ever would commit in the service of the Apostolic Church.

INCONTINENT WITH PISS, ENGLAND, *c.* 1535

Lord Edmund Howard

The medicine mentioned in Howard's letter to Lady Lisle was probably derived from dandelion, a common medieval diuretic (hence its colloquial name, 'pissabed'). Howard was the father of the future queen, Catherine Howard.

Madame,

So it is I have this night after midnight taken your medicine, for the which I heartily thank you, for it hath done me much good, and hath caused the stone to break, so that now I void much gravel. But for all that, your said medicine hath done me little honesty, for it made me piss my bed this night, for the which my wife hath sore beaten me, and saying it is children's parts to bepiss their bed. Ye have made me such a pisser that I dare not this day go abroad, wherefore I beseech you to make mine excuse to my Lord and Master Treasurer, for that I shall not be with you this day at dinner. Madame, it is showed me that a wing or a leg of a stork, if I eat thereof, will make me that I shall never piss more in bed, and though my body be simple yet my tongue shall be ever good, and especially when it speaketh of women; and sithence such a medicine will do such a great cure God send me a piece thereof.

all yours,
Edmund Howard

THE REFORMATION IN ENGLAND: A VISITATION TO THE MONASTERIES OF BUCKINGHAMSHIRE, 1537–8

John London, Roger Townsend, Richard Layton, Geoffrey Chamber

The authors were agents of Thomas Cromwell, Henry VIII's Lord Privy Seal, sent to report on the state of the monasteries prior to dissolution.

In my most humble manner I have me commended unto your good lordship, ascertaining the same that I have pulled down the image of Our Lady at Caversham, whereunto was great pilgrimage. The image is plated over with silver, and I have put it in a chest fast locked and nailed up, and by the next barge that cometh from Reading to London it shall be brought to your lordship. I have also pulled down the place she stood in, with all other ceremonies, as lights, shrowds, crosses, and images of wax hanging about the chapel, and have defaced the same thoroughly in eschewing of any further resort thither. This chapel did belong to Notley Abbey, and there always was a canon of that monastery which was called the Warden of Caversham, and he sung in this chapel and had the offerings for his living. He was accustomed to show many pretty relics, among the which were (as he made report) the holy dagger that killed King Henry, and the holy knife that killed St Edward. All these with many other, with the coats of this image, her cap and hair, my servants shall bring unto your lordship this week, with the surrender of the friars under their convent seal, and their seal also. I have sent the canon home again to Notley, and have made fast the doors of the chapel, which is thoroughly well covered with lead, and if it be your lordship's pleasure I shall see it made sure to the King's grace's use. And if it be not so ordered, the chapel standeth so wildly that the lead will be stolen by night, as I was served at the Friars. For as soon as I had taken the Friars' surrender, the multitude of the poverty of the town resorted thither, and all things that might be had they stole away, insomuch that they had conveyed the very clappers of the bells. And saving that Mr Fachell, which made me great cheer at his house, and the Mayor did assist me, they would have made no little spoil . . .

Please it your good lordship to be advertised that . . . the Abbot of Langdon passeth all other that ever I knew in profound bawdry; the drunkennest knave living. All his canons be even as he is, not one spark of virtue amongst them; arrant bawdy knaves every man. The Abbot caused his chaplain to take an whore, and instigate him to it, brought her up into his own chapter, took one of his feather-beds off his own bed, and made his chaplain's bed in the inner chamber, within him, and there caused him to go to bed with his whore that the Abbot had provided for him. To rehearse you the whole story, it were long and too abominable to hear. The house is in utter decay and will shortly fall down. You must needs depose him and suddenly sequestrate the fruits, and take an inventory of the goods. You can do no less of justice . . .

My singular good lord, my duty remembered unto your lordship, this shall be to advertise the same that upon the defacing of the late monastery of Boxley, and plucking down the images of the same, I found in the image of the Rood called the Rood of Grace, the which heretofore hath been had in great veneration of the people, certain engines and old wire, with old rotten sticks in the back of the same, that did cause the eyes of the same to move and stare in the head thereof, like unto a living thing; and also the nether lip in like wise to move as though it should speak, which, so famed, was not a little strange to me and other that was present at the plucking down of the same, whereupon the abbot, hearing this bruit, did thither resort, whom to my little wit and cunning, with other of the old monks, I did examine of their knowledge of the premises; who do declare themselves to be ignorant of the same.

THE MURDER OF RIZZIO, EDINBURGH, 9 March 1566

Lord Ruthven

David Rizzio was an Italian chorister who rose to become the favourite and private secretary of Mary, Queen of Scots. His influence discontented the nobility, who conspired to be rid of him. The conspirators included Mary's husband, Lord Darnley.

The said Earl Morton, Lords Ruthven and Lindsay, with their accomplices, entering the Palace . . . and through the chamber to the cabinet, where they found her Majesty at supper, at a little table, the Lady Argyll at the one end, and David at the other end, his cap on his head, the King speaking with her Majesty, with his hand about her waist.

The said Lord Ruthven at his entering in, said unto the Queen's Majesty, 'let it please your Majesty that yonder man David come forth of your privy chamber, where he hath been overlong'. The Queen answered, 'what offence hath he done?' Ruthven answered, that he made a greater and more heinous offence to her Majesty's honour, the King her husband, the Nobility and the Commonwealth. 'If it please your Majesty, he hath offended your honour, which I dare not be so bold to speak of. As to the King your husband's honour, he hath hindered him of the Crown-Matrimonial, which your Grace promised him, besides many other things which are not necessary to be expressed; and hath caused your Majesty to banish a great part of the Nobility, and to forfeit them, that he might be made a Lord . . .

Then the said Lord Ruthven said to the King, 'Sir, take the Queen your wife and sovereign to you', who stood all amazed, and wist not what to do. Then her Majesty rose upon her feet, and stood before David, he holding her Majesty by the plates of her gown, leaning back over the window, his dagger drawn in his hand, and Arthur Erskine, and the Abbot of Holyroodhouse, and the Lord Keith, master of the household, with the French pothecary; and one of the chamber began to lay hands on the Lord Ruthven, none of the King's party being there present. Then the said Lord Ruthven pulled out his dagger, and defended himself until more came in, and said to them, 'Lay no hands on me, for I will not be handled.' At the coming in of others into the cabinet, the said Lord Ruthven put up his dagger; and with the rushing in of men, the board fell into the wall, meat and candles being thereon, and the Lady of Argyll took one of the candles in her hand. At the same instant the Lord Ruthven took the Queen in his arms and put her into the King's arms, beseeching her Majesty not to be afraid, for there was no man there that would do her body any more harm than they would do their own hearts; and assured her Majesty that all that was done was the King's own deed. And the remnant of the gentlemen being in the cabinet took David out of the window, and after they had him out of the Queen's chamber, the said Lord Ruthven followed, and bade take him away down to the King's chamber the privy way; and the said Lord returned to the cabinet, thinking that the said David had been taken down to the King's chamber; the press of the people hurled him forth to the outer-chamber, where there was a great number standing who were vehemently moved against him, so that they could not abide any longer, but slew him at the Queen's foredoor in the other chamber . . . and David was thrown down the stairs from the Palace where he was slain, and brought to the Porter's lodge, who taking off his clothes said, 'this was his destiny; for upon this chest was his first bed when he came to this place, and now he lieth a very niggard and misknown knave'. The King's dagger was found sticking in his side. The Queen enquired at the King where his dagger was? who answered that he wist not well. 'Well,' said the Queen, 'it will be known hereafter.'

A PRISONER OF THE INQUISITION, MEXICO CITY, 1574–5

Miles Phillips

The author, along with 140 other English sailors, had been abandoned on the coast of Spanish Mexico by Sir John Hawkins' disastrous third slave-trading expedition (1567).

Now after that six years were fully expired since our first coming into the Indies, in which time, we had been imprisoned and served in the said country, as is before truly declared: in the year of our Lord 1574, the Inquisition began to be established in the Indies; very much against the minds of many of the Spaniards themselves. For never until this time, since their first conquering and planting in the Indies, were they subject to that bloody and cruel Inquisition.

The Chief Inquisitor was named Don Pedro Moya de Contreres, and Juan de Bouilla, his companion; and Juan Sanchis, the Fiscal; and Pedro de la Rios, the Secretary.

They being come and settled, and placed in a very fair house near unto the White Friars (considering with themselves that they must make an entrance and beginning of that their most detestable Inquisition here in Mexico, to the terror of the whole country) thought it best to call us that were Englishmen first in question. We were sent for, and sought out in all places of the country, and Proclamation made, upon pain of losing of goods and excommunication, that no man should hide or keep secret any Englishman or any part of his goods.

By means whereof, we were all soon apprehended in all places, and all our goods seized and taken for the Inquisitors' use. And so, from all parts of the country, we were conveyed and sent as prisoners to the city of Mexico; and there committed to prison, in sundry dark dungeons, where we could not see but by candle light; and were never past two together in one place: so that we saw not one another, neither could one of us tell what was become of another.

Thus we remained close imprisoned for the space of a year and a half, and others for some less time: for they came to prison ever as they were apprehended.

During which time of our imprisonment, at the first beginning, we were often called before the Inquisitors alone; and there severely examined of our faith; and commanded to say the *Pater noster*, the *Ave Maria*, and the *Creed* in Latin: which, God knoweth! a great number of us could not say otherwise than in the English tongue. And having the said Robert Sweeting, who was our friend at Tescuco always present with them for an interpreter, he made report for us, that in our own country speech, we could say them perfectly, although not word for word as they were in the Latin.

Then did they proceed to demand of us, upon our oaths, 'What we did believe of the Sacrament?' and 'Whether there did remain any bread or wine, after the words of consecration, Yea or No?' and 'Whether we did not believe that the Host of bread which the priest did hold up over his head, and the wine that was in the chalice, was the very true and perfect body and blood of our Saviour Christ, Yea or No?'

To which, if we answered not 'Yea!' then there was no way but death.

Then they would demand of us, 'What did we remember of ourselves, what opinions we had held or been taught to hold contrary to the same, whiles we were in England?'

So we, for the safety of our lives, were constrained to say that, 'We never did believe, nor had been taught otherwise than as before we had said.'

Then would they charge us that 'We did not tell them the truth. That they knew to the contrary, and therefore we should call ourselves to remembrance, and make them a better answer at the next time, or else we should be racked, and made to confess the truth whether we would or not!'

And so coming again before them, the next time, we were still demanded of 'our belief whiles we were in England, and how we had been taught'; and also what we thought, or did know of such of our own company as they did name unto us. So that we could never be free from such demands.

And, at other times, they would promise us that if we would tell them truth, then should we have favour and be set at liberty; although we very well knew their fair speeches were but means to intrap us, to the hazard and loss of our lives.

Howbeit, God so mercifully wrought for us, by a secret means that we had, that we kept us still to our first answer; and would still say that 'we had told the truth unto them; and knew no more by ourselves, nor any other of our fellows than as we had declared; and that for our sins and offences in England, against God, and

Our Lady, and any of His blessed Saints; we were right heartily sorry for the same, and did cry God, mercy!' And besought the Inquisitors, 'For God's sake, considering that we came unto those countries by force of weather, and against our wills; and that we had never, in all our lives, either spoken or done anything contrary to their laws; that therefore they would have mercy upon us!' Yet all this would not serve.

About the space of three months before [i.e., in January 1575] they proceeded to their severe judgment, we were all racked; and some enforced to utter against themselves, which afterwards cost them their lives.

And having thus got, from our own mouths, sufficient for them to proceed in judgment against us; they caused a large scaffold to be made in the midst of the Market Place in Mexico, right over against the Head Church: and fourteen or fifteen days before the day of their judgment, with the sound of trumpet and the noise of their *attabalies* (which are a kind of drums) they did assemble the people in all parts of the city; before whom it was then solemnly proclaimed that 'whosoever would, upon such a day, repair to the Market Place, they should hear the sentence of the Holy Inquisition against the English heretics, Lutherans; and also see the same put in execution'.

Which being done, and the time approaching of this cruel judgment; the night before, they came to the prison where we were, with certain Officers of that Holy Hellish House, bringing with them certain fools' coats, which they had prepared for us, being called in their language, *San Benitos*, which coats were made of yellow cotton, and red crosses upon them both before and behind.

They were so busied in putting on their coats about us, and in bringing us out into a large yard, and placing and pointing us in what order we should go to the scaffold or place of judgment upon the morrow, that they did not once suffer us to sleep all that night long.

The next morning being come, there was given to every one of us, for our breakfast, a cup of wine and a slice of bread fried in honey; and so about eight of the clock in the morning, we set forth of the prison: every man alone, in his yellow coat, and a rope about his neck, and a great green wax candle in his hand unlighted; having a Spaniard appointed, to go upon either side of every one of us.

So marching in this order and manner towards the Scaffold in the Market Place, which was a bow shot distant or thereabouts, we found a great assembly of people all the way, and such a throng that certain of the Inquisitors' Office, on horseback, were constrained to make way.

So coming to the Scaffold, we went up by a pair of stairs, and found seats ready made, and prepared for us to sit down on, every man in the order as he should be called to receive his judgment.

We being thus set down as we were appointed: presently the Inquisitors came up another pair of stairs; and the Viceroy and all the Chief Justices with them.

When they were set down under the Cloth of Estate, and placed according to their degrees and calling; then came up also a great number of Friars, White, Black, and Grey. They, being about the number of 300 persons, were set in the places appointed for them there.

There was there a solemn *Oyez!* made; and silence commanded.

And then presently began their severe and cruel judgment.

The first man that was called, was one Roger, the Chief Armourer of the *Jesus*: and he had judgment to have 300 stripes on horseback; and, after, was condemned to the galleys, as a slave, for ten years.

After him, were called John Gray, John Browne, John Rider, John Moon, James Collier, and one Thomas Browne. These were adjudged to have 200 stripes on horseback; and, after, to be committed to the galleys for the space of eight years.

Then was called John Keies, and was adjudged to have 100 stripes on horseback; and condemned to serve in the galleys for the space of six years.

Then were severally called, to the number of fifty-three; one after another: and every man had his several judgment. Some to have 200 stripes on horseback, and some 100; and condemned for slaves in the galleys, some for six years, some for eight, and some for ten.

And then was I, Miles Phillips, called; and was adjudged to serve in a Monastery for five years without any stripes; and to wear a fool's coat, or *San Benito*, during all that time.

Then were called John Story, Richard Williams, David Alexander, Robert Cooke, Paul Horsewell, and Thomas Hull. These six were condemned to serve in Monasteries without stripes; some for three years, and some for four, and to wear the *San Benito* during all the said time.

Which being done, and it now drawing towards night, George Rivelie, Peter Momfrie, and Cornelius the Irishman were called:

and had their judgment to be burnt to ashes. And so were presently sent away to the place of execution in the Market Place, but a little from the Scaffold: where they were quickly burned and consumed.

And as for us that had received our judgment, being 68 in number; we were carried back that night to prison again.

And the next day, in the morning, being Good Friday, the year of our Lord 1575, we were all brought into a court of the Inquisitors' Palace; where we found a horse in a readiness for every one of our men which were condemned to have stripes, and to be committed to the galleys, which were in number 61.

So they being enforced to mount up on horseback, naked from the middle upwards, were carried to be shewed as a spectacle for all the people to behold throughout the chief and principal streets of the city; and had the number of stripes appointed to every one of them, most cruelly laid upon their naked bodies with long whips, by sundry men appointed to be the executioners thereof. And before our men there went a couple of Criers, which cried as they went, 'Behold these English dogs! Lutherans! enemies to God!' And all the way as they went, there were some of the Inquisitors themselves, and of the Familiars of that rakehell Order, that cried to the executioners, 'Strike! Lay on those English heretics! Lutherans! God's enemies!'

So this horrible spectacle being shewed round about the city; and they returned to the Inquisitor's House, with their backs all gore blood, and swollen with great bumps: they were then taken from their horses; and carried again to prison, where they remained until they were sent into Spain to the galleys, there to receive the rest of their martyrdom.

I, and the six others with me, which had judgment, and were condemned amongst the rest, to serve an apprenticeship in the Monasteries, were taken presently, and sent to certain Religious Houses appointed for the purpose.

THE DISCOVERY OF VIRGINIA, AMERICA, July 1576

Captain John Smith

The second of July they fell with the coast of Florida in shoal water, where they felt a most delicate sweet smell, though they saw no land, which ere long they espied, thinking it the continent: an hundred and twenty miles they sailed not finding any harbour. The first that appeared with much difficulty they entered, and anchored; and after thanks to God they went to view the next land adjoining, to take possession of it for the Queen's most excellent Majesty: which done, they found their first landing place very sandy and low, but so full of grapes that the very surge of the sea sometimes overflowed them: of which they found such plenty in all places, both on the sand, the green soil and hills, as in the plains as well on every little shrub, as also climbing towards the tops of high cedars, that they did think in the world were not the like abundance.

We passed by the sea-side towards the tops of the next hills being not high: from whence we might see the sea on both sides, and found it an isle of twenty miles in length and six in breadth, the valleys replenished with goodly tall cedars. Discharging our muskets, such a flock of cranes, the most white, arose by us, with such a cry as if an army of men had shouted all together. This isle hath many goodly woods and deer, conies, and fowl in incredible abundance, and using the author's own phrase, the woods are not such as you find in Bohemia, Muscovy, or Hercynia, barren and fruitless, but the highest and reddest cedars of the world, bettering those of the Azores, Indies, or Libanus; pines, cypress, sassafras, the lentisk that beareth mastic, and many other of excellent smell and quality. Till the third day we saw not any of the people, then in a little boat three of them appeared. One of them went on shore, to whom we rowed, and he attended us without any sign of fear; after he had spoke much though we understood not a word, of his own accord he came boldly aboard us. We gave him a shirt, a hat, wine and meat, which he liked well; and after he had well viewed the barks and us, he went away in his own boat; and within a quarter of a mile of us in half an hour, had laden his boat with fish, with which he came again to the point of land, and there divided it in two parts, pointing one part to the ship, the other to the pinnace, and so departed.

The next day came divers boats, and in one of them the king's brother, with forty or fifty men, proper people, and in their behaviour very civil; his name was Granganameo, the king is called Wingina, the country Wingandacoa. Leaving his boats a little from our ships, he came with his train to the point, where spreading a mat he sat down. Though we came to him well armed, he made signs to us to sit down without any show of fear, stroking his head and breast, and also ours, to express his love. After he had made a long speech unto us, we presented him with divers toys, which he kindly accepted. He was greatly regarded by his people, for none of them did sit nor speak a word, but four, on whom we bestowed presents also, but he took all from them, making signs all things did belong to him.

The king himself, in a conflict with a king, his next neighbour and mortal enemy, was shot in two places through the body and the thigh, yet recovered: whereby he lay at his chief town six days' journey from thence.

A day or two after showing them what we had, Granganameo taking most liking to a pewter dish, made a hole in it, hung it about his neck for a breastplate: for which he gave us twenty deer skins, worth twenty crowns: and for a copper kettle, fifty skins, worth fifty crowns. Much other truck we had, and after two days he came aboard, and did eat and drink with us very merrily. Not long after he brought his wife and children; they were of mean stature, but well favoured and very bashful. She had a long coat of leather, and about her forehead a band of white coral, and so had her husband; in her ears were bracelets of pearl, hanging down to her middle, of the bigness of great peas. The rest of the women had pendants of copper, and the noblemen five or six in an ear; his apparel as his wives', only the women wear their hair long on both sides, and the men but on one; they are of colour yellow, but their hair is black, yet we saw children that had very fair chestnut coloured hair.

After that these women had been here with us, there came down from all parts great store of people, with leather, coral, and divers kind of dyes, but when Granganameo was present, none durst trade but himself and them that wore red copper on their heads, as he did. Whenever he came, he would signify by so many fires he came with so many boats, that we might know his strength. Their boats are but one great tree, which is but burnt in the form of a trough with gins and fire, till it be as they would have it. For an armour he would have engaged us a bag of pearl, but we refused, as not regarding it, that we might the better learn where it grew. He was very just of his promise, for oft we trusted him, and he would come within his day to keep his word. He sent us commonly every day a brace of bucks, conies, hares and fish, sometimes melons, walnuts, cucumbers, peas and divers roots. This author saith, their corn groweth three times in five months; in May they sow, in July reap; in June they sow, in August reap; in July sow, in

August reap. We put some of our peas in the ground, which in ten days were fourteen inches high.

The soil is most plentiful, sweet, wholesome, and fruitful of all other; there are about fourteen several sorts of sweet smelling timber trees; the most parts of the underwood, bays and such like, such oaks as we, but far greater and better . . .

This discovery was so welcome into England that it pleased her Majesty to call this country of Wingandacoa, Virginia.

THE VIRTUES OF TOBACCO, VIRGINIA, AMERICA, 1585

Thomas Heriot

The writer was a member of Sir Richard Grenville's unsuccessful attempt to establish an English colony at Roanoke.

There is an herbe which is sowed apart by itselfe, and is called by the inhabitants Uppowoc; in the West Indies it hath divers names, according to the severall places and countreys where it groweth and is used; the Spanyards generally call it Tabacco. The leaves thereof being dried and brought into pouder, they use to take the fume or smoake thereof, by sucking it thorow pipes made of clay, into their stomacke and head; from whence it purgeth superfluous fleame and other grosse humours, and openeth all the pores and passages of the body: by which meanes the use thereof not onely preserveth the body from obstructions, but also (if any be, so that they have not bene of too long continuance) in short time breaketh them; whereby their bodies are notably preserved in health, and know not many grievous diseases, wherewithall we in England are often times afflicted.

This Uppowoc is of so precious estimation amongst them, that they thinke their gods are marvellously delighted therewith: whereupon sometime they make hallowed fires, and cast some of the pouder therin for a sacrifice: being in a storme upon the waters, to pacifie their gods, they cast some up into the aire and into the water: so a weare for fish being newly set up, they cast some therein and into the aire: after an escape from danger, they cast some into the aire likewise: but all done with strange gestures, stamping, sometime dancing, clapping of hands, holding up of hands, and staring up into the heavens, uttering therewithall, and chattering strange words and noises.

We ourselves, during the time we were there, used to sucke it after their manner, as also since our return, and have found many rare and woonderfull experiments of the vertues thereof: of which the relation would require a volume by it selfe: the use of it by so many of late, men and women of great calling, as els, and some learned Physicians also, is of sufficient witnesse.

THE EXECUTION OF MARY, QUEEN OF SCOTS, FOTHERINGAY, ENGLAND, 8 February 1586

R. Wynkfielde

After fleeing Scotland, Mary Stuart threw herself on the mercy of her English cousin, Elizabeth I. But Mary's presence was a source of constant unease to the English government, since the country's Catholic minority looked to her as a potential restorer of the old faith. On the evidence of letters seemingly approving Elizabeth's murder, Mary was sentenced to death.

. . . Her prayers being ended, the executioners, kneeling, desired her Grace to forgive them her death: who answered, 'I forgive you with all my heart, for now, I hope, you shall make an end of all my troubles.' Then they, with her two women, helping her up, began to disrobe her of her apparel: then she, laying her crucifix upon the stool, one of the executioners took from her neck the *Agnus Dei*, which she, laying hands off it, gave to one of her women, and told the executioner he should be answered money for it. Then she suffered them, with her two women, to disrobe her of her chain of pomander beads and all other her apparel most willingly, and with joy rather than sorrow, helped to make unready herself, putting on a pair of sleeves with her own hands which they had pulled off, and that with some haste, as if she had longed to be gone.

All this time they were pulling off her apparel, she never changed her countenance, but with smiling cheer she uttered these words, 'that she never had such grooms to make her unready, and that she never put off her clothes before such a company' . . .

This done, one of the women having a Corpus Christi cloth lapped up three-corner-ways, kissing it, put it over the Q. of Sc. face, and pinned it fast to the caule of her head. Then the two women departed from her, and she kneeling down upon the cushion most resolutely, and without any token or fear of death, she spake aloud this Psalm in Latin, *In Te Domine confido, non confundar in eternam*, etc. Then, groping for the block, she laid down her head, putting her chin over the block with both her hands, which, holding there still, had been cut off had they not been espied. Then lying upon the block most quietly, and stretching out her arms cried, *In manus tuas, Domine*, etc. three or four times. Then she, lying very still upon the block, one of the executioners holding her slightly with one of his hands, she endured two strokes of the other executioner with an axe, she making very small noise or none at all, and not stirring any part of her from the place where she lay: and so the executioner cut off her head, saving one little gristle, which being cut asunder, he lift up her head to the view of all the assembly and bade *God save the Queen*. Then, her dress of lawn falling from off her head, it appeared as grey as one of threescore and ten years old, polled very short, her face in a moment being so much altered from the form she had when she was alive, as few could remember her by her dead face. Her lips stirred up and down a quarter of an hour after her head was cut off . . .

Then one of the executioners, pulling off her garters, espied her little dog which was crept under her clothes, which could not be gotten forth but by force, yet afterward would not depart from the dead corpse, but came and lay between her head and her shoulders, which being imbrued with her blood was carried away and washed . . .

THE ARMADA: A COMMANDER REPORTS, 31 July 1588

Sir John Hawkins

The Spanish invasion fleet was sighted off the coast of England on Friday 19 July. Hawkins, one of the English fleet's commanders, was the first Englishman to traffic in slaves.

My bounden duty humbly remembered unto your good Lordship: – I have not busied myself to write often to your Lordship in this great cause, for that my Lord Admiral doth continually advertise the manner of all things that doth pass. So do others that understand the state of all things as well as myself. We met with this fleet somewhat to the westward of Plymouth upon Sunday in the morning, being the 21st of July, where we had small fight with them in the afternoon. By the coming aboard one of the other of the Spaniards, a great ship, a Biscayan, spent her foremast and bowsprit; which was left by the fleet in the sea, and so taken up by Sir Francis Drake the next morning. The same Sunday there was, by a fire chancing by a barrel of powder, a great Biscayan spoiled and abandoned, which my Lord took up and sent away.

The Tuesday following, athwart of Portland, we had a sharp fight with them, wherein we spent a great part of our powder and shot; so as it was not thought good to deal with them any more till that was relieved.

The Thursday following, by the occasion of the scattering of one of the great ships from the fleet, which we hoped to have cut off, there grew a hot fray, wherein some store of powder was spent; and after that, little done till we came near to Calais, where the fleet of Spain anchored, and our fleet by them; and because they should not be in peace there, to refresh their water or to have conference with those of the Duke of Parma's party, my Lord Admiral, with firing of ships, determined to remove them; as he did, and put them to the seas; in which broil the chief galleass spoiled her rudder, and so rode ashore near the town of Calais, where she was possessed of our men, but so aground as she could not be brought away.

That morning, being Monday, the 29th of July, we followed the Spaniards, and all that day had with them a long and great fight, wherein there was great valour showed generally of our company. In this battle there was spent very much of our powder and shot; and so the wind began to blow westerly, a fresh gale, and the Spaniards put themselves somewhat to the northward, where we follow and keep company with them. In this fight there was some hurt done among the Spaniards. A great ship of the galleons of Portugal, her rudder spoiled, and so the fleet left her in the sea. I doubt not but all these things are written more at large to you Lordship than I can do; but this is the substance and material of matter that hath passed.

Our ships, God be thanked, have received little hurt, and are of great force to accompany them, and of such advantage that with some continuance at the seas, and sufficiently provided of shot and powder, we shall be able, with God's favour, to weary them out of the sea and confound them . . .

The Armada was driven into the North Sea, where the English were forced to abandon the chase due to a lack of gunpowder. Less than half the Spanish fleet returned home.

THE TORTURING OF A JESUIT PRIEST, THE TOWER OF LONDON, ENGLAND, April 1597

Father John Gerard

On the third day the warder came to my room straight from his dinner. Looking sorry for himself, he said the Lords Commissioners had arrived with the Queen's Attorney-General and that I had to go down to them at once.

'I am ready,' I said, 'but just let me say an *Our Father* and *Hail Mary* downstairs.'

He let me go, and then we went off together to the Lieutenant's lodgings inside the walls of the Tower. Five men were there waiting for me, none of whom, except Wade, had examined me before. He was there to direct the charges against me . . .

'You say,' said the Attorney-General, 'you have no wish to obstruct the Government. Tell us, then, where Father Garnet is. He is an enemy of the state, and you are bound to report on all such men.'

'He isn't an enemy of the state,' I said . . . 'But I don't know where he lives, and if I did, I would not tell you.'

'Then we'll see to it that you tell us before we leave this place.'

'Please God you won't,' I answered.

Then they produced a warrant for putting me to torturé. They had it ready by them and handed it to me to read. (In this prison a special warrant is required for torture.)

I saw the warrant was properly made out and signed, and then I answered: 'With God's help I shall never do anything which is unjust or act against my conscience or the Catholic faith. You have me in your power. You can do with me what God allows you to do – more you cannot do.'

Then they began to implore me not to force them to take steps they were loath to take. They said they would have to put me to torture every day, as long as my life lasted, until I gave them the information they wanted.

'I trust in God's goodness,' I answered, 'that He will prevent me from ever committing a sin such as this – the sin of accusing innocent people. We are all in God's hands and therefore I have no fear of anything you can do to me.'

This was the sense of my answers, as far as I can recall them now.

We went to the torture-room in a kind of solemn procession the attendants walking ahead with lighted candles.

The chamber was underground and dark, particularly near the entrance. It was a vast place and every device and instrument of human torture was there. They pointed out some of them to me and said I would try them all. Then they asked me again whether I would confess.

'I cannot,' I said.

I fell on my knees for a moment's prayer. Then they took me to a big upright pillar, one of the wooden posts which held the roof of this huge underground chamber. Driven into the top of it were iron staples for supporting heavy weights. Then they put my wrists into iron gauntlets and ordered me to climb two or three wicker steps. My arms were then lifted up and an iron bar was passed through the rings of one gauntlet, then through the staple and rings of the second gauntlet. This done, they fastened the bar with a pin to prevent it slipping, and then, removing the wicker steps one by one from under my feet, they left me hanging by my hands and arms fastened above my head. The tips of my toes, however, still touched the ground, and they had to dig away the earth from under them. They had hung me up from the highest staple in the pillar and could not raise me any higher, without driving in another staple.

Hanging like this I began to pray. The gentlemen standing around asked me whether I was willing to confess now.

'I cannot and I will not,' I answered.

But I could hardly utter the words, such a gripping pain came over me. It was worst in my chest and belly, my hands and arms. All the blood in my body seemed to rush up into my arms and hands and I thought that blood was oozing from the ends of my fingers and the pores of my skin. But it was only a sensation caused by my flesh swelling above the irons holding them. The pain was so intense that I thought I could not possibly endure it, and added to it, I had an interior temptation. Yet I did not feel any inclination or wish to give them the information they wanted. The Lord saw my weakness with the eyes of His mercy, and did not permit me to be tempted beyond my strength. With the temptation He sent me relief. Seeing my agony and the struggle going on in my mind, He gave me this most merciful thought: the utmost and worst they can do is to kill you, and you have often wanted to give your life for your Lord God. The Lord God sees all you are enduring – He can do all things. You are in God's keeping. With these thoughts, God in His infinite goodness and mercy gave me the grace of resignation, and with a desire to die and a hope (I admit) that I would, I offered Him myself to do with me as He wished. From that moment the conflict in my soul ceased, and even the physical pain seemed much more bearable than before, though it must, in fact, I am sure, have been greater with the growing strain and weariness of my body . . .

Sometime after one o'clock, I think, I fell into a faint. How long I was unconscious I don't know, but I think it was long, for the men held my body up or put the wicker steps under my feet until I came to. Then they heard me pray and immediately let me down again. And they did this every time I fainted – eight or nine times that day – before it struck five . . .

A little later they took me down. My legs and feet were not damaged, but it was a great effort to stand upright . . .

AN AUDIENCE WITH QUEEN ELIZABETH I, LONDON, 8 December 1597

André Hurault

Hurault was an Ambassador Extraordinary from Henry IV of France to the court of Queen Elizabeth. In 1597 Elizabeth was sixty years old, and in the fortieth year of her reign.

She kept the front of her dress open, and one could see the whole of her bosom, and passing low, and often she would open the front of this robe with her hands as if she was too hot. The collar of the robe was very high, and the lining of the inner part all adorned with rubies and pearls, very many, but quite small. She had also a chain of rubies and pearls about her neck. On her head she wore a garland of the same material and beneath it a great reddish-coloured wig, with a great number of spangles of gold and silver, and hanging down over her forehead some pearls, but of no great worth. On either side of her ears hung two great curls of hair, almost down to her shoulders and within the collar of her robe, spangled as the top of her head. Her bosom is somewhat wrinkled, as well as one can see for the collar that she wears round her neck, but lower down her flesh is exceeding white and delicate, so far as one could see.

As for her face, it is and appears to be very aged. It is long and thin, and her teeth are very yellow and unequal, compared with what they were formerly, so they say, and on the left side less than on the right. Many of them are missing, so that one cannot understand her easily when she speaks quickly. Her figure is fair and tall and graceful in whatever she does; so far as may be she keeps her dignity, yet humbly and graciously withal.

All the time she spoke she would often rise from her chair and appear to be very impatient with what I was saying. She would complain that the fire was hurting her eyes, though there was a great screen before it and she six or seven feet away; yet did she give orders to have it extinguished, making them bring water to pour on it. She told me she was well pleased to stand up, and that she used to speak thus with ambassadors who came to seek her, and used sometimes to tire them, of which they would on occasion complain. I begged her not to overtire herself in any way, and I rose when she did; and then she sat down again, and so did I.

'MY COCK IS LIKE A DRAWBRIDGE': THE INFANTILE ERECTIONS OF LOUIS XII, PARIS, *c. 1602–5*

Heroard

Heroard was a physician at the French court. His account of Louis XIII's infancy is summarized here by Philip Aries.

Louis XIII was not yet one year old: 'He laughed uproariously when his nanny waggled his cock with her fingers.' An amusing trick which the child soon copied. Calling a page, 'he shouted "Hey, there!" and pulled up his robe, showing him his cock.'

He was one year old: 'In high spirits,' notes Heroard, 'he made everybody kiss his cock.' This amused them all. Similarly everyone considered his behaviour towards two visitors, a certain de Bonières and his daughter, highly amusing: 'He laughed at him, lifted up his robe and showed him his cock, but even more so to his daughter, for then, holding it and giving his little laugh, he shook the whole of his body up and down.' They thought this so funny that the child took care to repeat a gesture which had been such a success; in the presence of a 'little lady', 'he lifted up his coat, and showed her his cock with such fervour that he was quite beside himself. He lay on his back to show it to her.'

When he was just over a year old he was engaged to the Infanta of Spain; his attendants explained to him what this meant, and he understood them fairly well. 'They asked him: "Where is the Infanta's darling?" He put his hand on his cock.'

During his first three years nobody showed any reluctance or saw any harm in jokingly touching the child's sexual parts. 'The Marquise [de Verneuil] often put her hand under his coat; he got his nanny to lay him on her bed where she played with him, putting her hand under his coat.' Mme de Verneuil wanted to play with him and took hold of his nipples; he pushed her away, saying: 'Let go, let go, go away.' He would not allow the Marquise to touch his nipples, because his nanny had told him: 'Monsieur, never let anybody touch your nipples, or your cock, or they will cut it off." He remembered this.' Again: 'When he got up, he would not take his shirt and said: "Not my shirt, I want to give you all some milk from my cock." We held out our hands, and he pretended to give us all some milk, saying: "Pss, pss," and only then agreeing to take his shirt.'

It was a common joke, repeated time and again, to say to him: 'Monsieur, you haven't got a cock.' Then 'he replied: "Hey, here it is!" – laughing and lifting it up with one finger.' These jokes were not limited to the servants, or to brainless youths, or to women of easy virtue such as the King's mistress. The Queen, his mother, made the same sort of joke: 'The Queen, touching his cock, said: "Son, I am holding your spout." ' Even more astonishing is this passage: 'He was undressed and Madame too [his sister], and they were placed naked in bed with the King, where they kissed and twittered and gave great amusement to the King. The King asked him: "Son, where is the Infanta's bundle?" He showed it to him, saying: "There is no bone in it, Papa." Then, as it was slightly distended, he added: "There is now, there is sometimes." '

The Court was amused, in fact, to see his first erections: 'Waking up at eight o'clock, he called Mlle Bethouzay and said to her: "Zezai, my cock is like a drawbridge; see how it goes up and down." And he raised it and lowered it.'

By the age of four, 'he was taken to the Queen's apartments, where Mme de Guise showed him the Queen's bed and said to him: "Monsieur, this is where you were made." He replied: "With Mamma?" ' 'He asked his nanny's husband: "What is that?" "That," came the reply, "is one of my silk stockings." "And those?" [after the manner of parlour-game questions] "Those are my breeches." "What are they made of?" "Velvet." "And that?" "That is a cod-piece." "What is inside?" "I don't know, Monsieur." "Why, a cock. Who is it for?" "I don't know, Monsieur." "Why, for Madame Doundoun [his nanny]." '

THE ENGLISH LOVE OF HUNTING, 1602

Philip Julius, Duke of Pomerania-Wolgast

The English hold the chase in high esteem; there is scarcely any royal residence, or even a nobleman's house, which has not at least one deer park – sometimes two, or even three, may be found.

Good level ground is left between them for following the deer and wounding them in the chase, there being no other large game.

If a man finds strange dogs in his deer park, he hangs them, however valuable they may be, as an insult to the huntsman.

This is also done with game killed by a strange huntsman, it being believed that the arrows, still frequently used, are poisoned.

The hunting parties are, however, generally arranged in honour of the ladies. As soon as a stag or other animal is killed, the lady is expected to give it the first cut with the hunting-knife on the shoulder, the rest of the work being left to the huntsman.

Coursing hares is practised very often in England, and affords great sport, and as there is coppice and thickets in plenty, they are rarely baited by dogs, but only followed by them until they get fatigued or fall down. We were told that, after having followed a hare for pleasure's sake a whole day, the hunter would often leave the animal to his dogs, taking a rabbit instead.

The reason is that the game is thought less of than the amusement. This is the case even with the peasants, who also are permitted to hunt; they keep fine big dogs, at little expense, for with a little money they can procure the heads, entrails and feet of lambs and calves, which in England are always thrown away, with the exception of the tongue . . .

THE DEATH OF QUEEN ELIZABETH I, RICHMOND PALACE, SURREY, ENGLAND, 24 March 1603

Sir Robert Carey

When I came to court, I found the Queen ill disposed, and she kept her inner lodging; yet she, hearing of my arrival, sent for me. I found her in one of her withdrawing chambers sitting low upon her cushions. She called me to her; I kissed her hand, and told her, it was my chiefest happiness to see her in safety and in health, which I wished might long continue. She took me by the hand, and wrung it hard; and said 'No, Robin, I am not well!' and then discoursed with me of her indisposition, and that her heart had been sad and heavy for ten or twelve days; and, in her discourse, she fetched not so few as forty or fifty great sighs. I was grieved, at the first, to see her in this plight: for, in all my lifetime before, I never knew her fetch a sigh, but when the Queen of Scots was beheaded; then, upon my knowledge, she shed many tears and sighs, manifesting her innocence that she never gave consent to the death of that Queen. I used the best words I could to persuade her from this melancholy humour; but I found by her it was too deep rooted in her heart, and hardly to be removed. This was upon a Saturday night: and she gave command that the great closet should be prepared for her to go to chapel the next morning.

The next day, all things being in a readiness, we long expected her coming. After eleven o'clock, one of the grooms came out, and bade make ready for the private closet; she would not go to the great. There we stayed long for her coming: but at last she had cushions laid for her in the privy chamber, hard by the closet door; and there she heard service. From that day forwards she grew worse and worse. She remained upon her cushions four days and nights, at the least. All about her could not persuade her, either to take any sustenance or go to bed. I, hearing that neither the physicians, nor none about her, could persuade her to take any course for her safety, feared her death would soon after ensue. I could not but think in what a wretched estate I should be left, most of my livelihood depending on her life. And hereupon I bethought myself with what grace and favour I was ever received by the King of Scots, whensoever I was sent to him. I did assure myself it was neither unjust nor unhonest for me to do for myself, if God at that time should call her to his mercy. Hereupon I wrote to the King of Scots, knowing him to be the right heir to the crown of England, and certified him in what state her Majesty was. I desired him not to stir from Edinburgh: if of that sickness she should die, I would be the first man that should bring him news of it.

The Queen grew worse and worse, because she would be so: none about her being able to persuade her to go to bed. My Lord Admiral was sent for, who, by reason of my sister's death that was his wife, had absented himself some fortnight from court. What by fair means, what by force, he gat her to bed. There was no hope of her recovery, because she refused all remedies. On Wednesday, the 23rd of March, she grew speechless. That afternoon, by signs, she called for her Council: and by putting her hand to her head, when the King of Scots was named to succeed her, they all knew he was the man she desired should reign after her. About six at night, she made signs for the Archbishop, and her chaplains to come to her; at which time, I went in with them, and sat upon my knees full of tears to see that heavy sight. Her Majesty lay upon her back, with one hand in the bed and the other without. The bishop kneeled down by her, and examined her first of her faith; and she so punctually answered all his several questions by lifting up her eyes and holding up her hand, as it was a comfort to all beholders. Then the good man told her plainly, what she was and what she was to come to, and though she had been long a great Queen here upon earth, yet shortly she was to yield an accompt of her stewardship to the King of Kings. After this he began to pray, and all that were by did answer him. After he had continued long in prayer, till the old man's knees were weary, he blessed her, and meant to rise and leave her. The Queen made a sign with her hand. My sister Scroop, knowing her meaning, told the bishop, the Queen desired he would pray still. He did so for a long half-hour after, and then thought to leave her. The second time she made sign to have him continue in prayer. He did so for half an hour more, with earnest cries to God for her soul's health, which he uttered with that fervency of spirit as the Queen, to all our sight, much rejoiced thereat, and gave testimony to us all of her Christian and comfortable end. By this time, it grew late, and every one departed, all but her women that attended her. This that I heard with my ears and did see with my eyes, I thought it my duty to set down, and to affirm it for a truth upon the faith of a Christian; because I know there have been many false lies reported of the end and death of that good lady.

I went to my lodging, and left word with one in the cofferer's chamber to call me, if that night it was thought she would die; and gave the porter an angel to let me in at any time, when I called. Between one and two of the clock on Thursday morning, he that I left in the cofferer's chamber, brought me word the Queen was dead. I rose and made all haste to the gate, to get in. There I was answered, I could not enter: the Lords of the Council having been with him and commanded him that none should go in or out, but by warrant from them. At the very instant, one of the Council, the Comptroller, asked whether I was at the gate. I said 'Yes.' He said, if I pleased, he would let me in. I desired to know how the Queen was. He answered, 'Pretty well.' I bade him good night. He replied and said, 'Sir, if you will come in, I will give you my word and credit you shall go out again at your own pleasure.' Upon his word, I entered the gate, and came up to the cofferer's chamber: where I found all the ladies weeping bitterly. He led me from thence to the privy chamber, where all the Council was assembled. There I was caught hold of; and assured I should not go for Scotland till their pleasures were further known. I told them I came of purpose to that end. From thence, they all went to the secretary's chamber: and, as they went, they gave a special command to the porters, that none should go out at the gates but such servants as they should send to prepare their coaches and horses for London.

There was I left, in the midst of the court, to think my own thoughts till they had done counsel. I went to my brother's chamber, who was in bed, having been overwatched many nights before. I got him up with all speed; and when the Council's men were going out of the gate, my brother thrust to the gate. The porter, knowing him to be a great officer, let him out. I pressed after him, and was stayed by the porter. My brother said angrily to the porter, 'Let him out, I will answer for him!' Whereupon I was suffered to pass; which I was not a little glad of. I got to horse, and rode to the Knight Marshal's lodging by Charing Cross; and there stayed till the Lords came to Whitehall Garden. I stayed there till it was nine o'clock in the morning; and hearing that all the Lords were in the old orchard at Whitehall, I sent the Marshal to tell them that I had stayed all that while to know their pleasures; and that I would attend them, if they would command me any service. They were very glad when they heard I was not gone: and desired the Marshal to send for me; and I should, with all speed, be dispatched for Scotland. The Marshal believed them; and sent Sir Arthur Savage for me. I made haste to them. One of the Council, my Lord of Banbury that now is, whispered the Marshal in the ear, and told him, if I came they would stay me and send some other in my stead. The Marshal got from them and met me coming to them, between the two gates. He bade me be gone, for he had learned, for certain, that if I came to them, they would betray me.

I returned, and took horse between nine and ten o'clock; and that night rode to Doncaster. The Friday night I came to my own house at Witherington, and presently took order with my deputies to see the Borders kept in quiet; which they had much to do: and gave order, the next morning, the King of Scotland should be proclaimed King of England, and at Morpeth and Alnwick. Very early, on Saturday, I took horse for Edinburgh, and came to Norham about twelve at noon, so that I might well have been with the King at supper time. But I got a great fall by the way; and my horse, with one of his heels, gave me a great blow on the head, that made me shed much blood. It made me so weak, that I was forced to ride a soft pace after: so that the King was newly gone to bed by the time I knocked at the gate. I was quickly let in; and carried up to the King's Chamber. I kneeled by him, and saluted him by his title of 'England, Scotland, France and Ireland.' He gave me his hand to kiss, and bade me welcome. After he had long discoursed of the manner of the Queen's sickness, and of her death, he asked what letters I had from the Council. I told him, none: and acquainted him how narrowly I escaped from them. And yet I brought him a blue ring from a fair lady, that I hoped would give him assurance of the truth that I had reported. He took it, and looked upon it, and said, 'It is enough. I know by this you are a true messenger.' Then he committed me to the charge of my Lord Hume, and gave straight command that I should want nothing. He sent for his chirurgeons to attend me; and when I kissed his hand, at my departure, he said to me these gracious words: 'I know you have lost a near kinswoman and a loving mistress: but take here my hand, I will be as good a master to you, and will requite you this service with honour and reward.' So I left him that night, and went with my Lord Hume to my lodging: where I had all things fitting for so weary a man as I was. After my head was dressed, I took leave of my Lord and many others that attended me, and went to my rest.

The next morning, by ten o'clock, my Lord Hume was sent to me from the King, to know how I had rested: and withal said, that his Majesty commanded him to know of me, what it was that I desired most that he should do for me; bade me ask, and it should be granted. I desired my Lord to say to his Majesty from me, that I had no reason to importune him for any suit; for that I had not, as yet, done him any service: but my humble request to his Majesty was to admit me a gentleman of his bedchamber; and hereafter, I knew, if his Majesty saw me worthy, I should not want to taste his bounty. My Lord returned this answer, that he sent me word back, 'With all his heart, I should have my request.' And the next time I came to court, which was some four days after at night, I was called into his bedchamber: and there, by my Lord of Richmond, in his presence, I was sworn one of the gentlemen of his bedchamber; and presently I helped to take off his clothes, and stayed till he was in bed. After this, there came, daily, gentlemen and noblemen from our court; and the King set down a fixed day for his departure towards London.

THE GUNPOWDER PLOT, ENGLAND, 5 November 1605

Guy Fawkes

The Gunpowder Plot was a conspiracy to advance the Catholic cause in England by blowing up the King and the Houses of Parliament. The foiling of the plot is still celebrated in England, with a annual burning of an effigy of the conspirator Guy Fawkes.

I confesse, that a practise in generall was first broken unto me, against his Maiestie for reliefe of the Catholic cause, and not invented or propounded by my selfe. And this was first propounded unto mee about Easter Last was twelve moneth beyond the seas, in the Lowe Countreys of the *Archdukes* obeissance, by *Thomas Winter*, who came thereupon with mee into England, and there we imparted our purpose to three other Gentlemen more, namely, *Robert Catesby*, *Thomas Percy* and *Iohn Wright*, who all five consulting together of the means how to execute the same, and taking a vow among our selves for secrecie, *Catesby* propounded to have it performed by Gunpowder, and by making a Myne under the upper House of Parliament: which place wee made a choice of the rather because Religion having been unjustly suppressed there, it was fittest that Iustice and punishment should be executed there.

This being resolved amongst us, *Thomas Percy* hired an House at Westminster for that purpose, neere adioyning to the Parliament House, and there we begun to make our Myne about the II of December 1604.

The five that first entred into the worke were *Thomas Percy*, *Thomas Catesby*, *Thomas Winter*, *Iohn Wright* and myselfe: and soone after wee tooke another unto us, *Christopher Wright* having Sworne him also, and taken the Sacrament for secrecie.

When we came to the very foundation of the Wall of the House, which was about three yards thicke, and found it a matter of great difficultie, wee tooke unto us another Gentleman *Robert Winter*, in like maner with oath and sacrament as afore said.

It was about Christmas when we brought our myne unto the Wall, and about Candlemas we had wrought the wall halfe through: and whilst they were in working, I stood as Sentinell to descrie any man that came neere, whereof I gave them warning, and so they ceased until I gave notice againe to proceede.

All we seven lay in the House, and had Shot and Powder, being resolved to die in that place before we should yield or be taken. As they were working upon the wall they heard a rushing in the Cellar of remooving of Coales, whereupon we feared we had been discovered: and they sent me to go to the Cellar, who finding that the Coales were a-selling and that the Cellar was to bee let, viewing the commoditie thereof for our purpose, *Percy* went and hired the same for yeerely rent.

We had before this provided and brought into the House twentie Barrels of Powder, which we remooved into the Cellar, and covered the same with Billets and Faggots, which were provided for that purpose.

About Easter, the Parliament being prorogued till October next, we dispersed ourselves and I retired into the Low countreys by advice and direction of the rest, as well to aquaint *Owen* with the particulars of the Plot, as also lest by my longer stay I might have growen suspicious, and so have come in question.

In the meantime *Percy* having the key of the Cellar, laide in more Powder and wood into it. I returned about the beginning of September next, and then receiving the key againe of Percy, we brought in more Powder and Billets to cover the same againe, and so I went for a time into the Countrey till the 30 of October.

It was a further resolve amongst us that the same day that this act should have been performed, some other of our Confederates should have surprised the person of Lady Elizabeth the King's eldest daughter, who was kept in Warwickshire at Lo. *Harrington's* house, and presently have her proclaimed as Queen, having a proiect of a Proclamation ready for that purpose, wherein we made no mention of altering of Religion, nor would have avowed the deede to be ours, untill we should have had power enough to make our partie good and then we would have avowed both.

Concerning Duke Charles, the King's second sonne, wee had sundry consultations how to seise on his Person. But because we found no means how to to compasse it (the Duke being kept neere London, where we had not Forces y-nough) we resolved to serve our turn with the Lady Elizabeth.

THE NAMES OF OTHER PRINCIPALL persons, that were made privy afterwards to this horrible conspiracie

SHIPWRECKED BY A HURRICANE, NEW ENGLAND, AMERICA, 16 August 1635

Anthony Thacher

But now with the leaf I must alter my matter and subject and turn my drowned pen with my shaking hand to write other news and to rouse up my heavy heart and sadded spirits to indite the story of such sad news as never before this happened in New England and been lamented both in the public on the pulpit and concourse of the people and in private in the closet and in the same places hath God's name been magnified for his great mercy and wonderful deliverance of me out of the bottom of the angry sea.

The story is thus. First there was a league of perennial friendship solemnly made between my cousin Avary and myself made in Mr Graves his ship never to forsake each other to the death but to be partaker each of other's misery or welfare as also of habitation in one place. Now it pleased God immediately on our arrival unto New England there was an offer made unto us, and my cousin Avary was invited to Marblehed by the men of that place to be their pastor, there being as yet no church there planted but there a town appointed by the whole country to be planted there, intended for the good of the whole country to set up the trade of fishing. Now because that many there (the most being fishers) were something loose and remiss in their carriage and behavior, my cousin was unwilling to go thither, and so refusing it we went to Newberry to Mr Parker and others of his acquaintance, intending there to sit down and plant, but being solicited so often both by the men of the place and by the magistrates, and counselled to it by Mr Cotten and most of the ministers in the patent, alleging what a benefit we might do both to the people there and also unto the country and commonweal to settle there a plantation, at length we embraced it and there consented to go. The men of Marblehed forthwith sent a pinnace for us and our goods, and we were at Ipswich on Tuesday the twelfth of August, 1635, embarked ourselves and all and every one of our families with all our goods and substance for Marblehed, we being in all twenty-three souls, to wit eleven in my cousin's family and seven in mine and one Master William Elliott and four mariners. Whence the next morning having recommended ourselves unto the Lord with cheerful and contented hearts we hoisted sail for Marblehed.

But the Lord suddenly turned our cheerfulness into mourning and sad lamentation. Thus on Friday the fourteenth of August 1635 in the evening about ten of the clock our sails being old and torn, we, having a fine fresh gale of wind, were split. Our sailors, because it was something dark would not put on new sails presently but determined to cast their sheet anchor and so to ride at anchor until the next morning and then to put [them] on. But before daylight it pleased God to send so mighty a storm as the like was never felt in New England since the English came there nor in the memory of any of the Indeans. It was [so] furious that our anchor came home, whereupon our mariners let slip more cable, yea, even to the utmost end thereof, and so made it fast only about the bit, whence it slipped away end for end. Then our sailors knew not what to do but were driven as pleased the storm and waves. My cousin and we, perceiving our danger, solemnly recommended ourselves to God, the Lord both of earth and seas, expecting with every wave to be swallowed up and drenched in the deeps. And as my cousin, his wife and children and maid servant, my wife and my tender babes sat comforting and cheering on the other in the Lord against ghastly death, which every moment stares us in the face and sat triumphingly on each other's forehead, we were by the violence of the waves and fury of the winds by the Lord's permission lifted up upon a rock between two high rocks yet all was but one rock but ragged, with the stroke whereof the water came into the pinnace. So as we were presently up to the middle in water as wet, the waters came furiously and violently over us and against us but by reason of the rock's proportion could not lift us off but beat her all to pieces. Now look with me upon our distresses and consider of my misery, who beheld the ship broken, the water in her and violently overwhelming us, my goods and provision swimming in the seas, my friends almost drowned and mine own poor children so untimely (if I may so term it without offence) before mine eyes half drowned and ready to be swallowed up and dashed to pieces against the rocks by the merciless waves and myself ready to accompany them.

But I must go on to an end of this woeful relation. In the same room with us sat he that went master of the pinnace, not knowing what to do. Our foremast was cut down, our mainmast broken in three pieces, the forepart of our pinnace beaten away, our goods swimming about the seas, my children bewailing me as not pitying themselves, and myself bemoaning them, poor souls whom I had occasioned to such an end in their tender years whenas they could scarce be sensible of death. And so likewise my cousin, his wife and his children and both of us bewailing each other in Our Lord and only Savior Jesus Christ, in whom only we had comfort and cheerfulness, insomuch that from the greatest to the least of us there was not one screech or outcry made, but all as silent sheep were contentedly resolved to die together lovingly as since our acquaintance we had lived together friendly.

Now as I was sitting in the cabinroom door, lo, one of the sailors by a wave being washed out of the pinnace was gotten in again, and coming into the cabinroom over my back, cried out, 'oh, we are all cast away. Lord, have mercy on us. I have been washed overboard into the sea and am gotten in again.' His speeches made me look forth, and looking toward the sea and seeing how we were, I turned myself toward my cousin and the rest and these words, 'Oh, cousin, it hath pleased God here to cast us between two rocks, and the shore not far off from us, for I saw the top of trees when I looked forth.' Whereupon the said master of the pinnace, looking up at the s[c]uttle hole of the half deck went out of it, but I never saw him afterward. Then he that had been in the sea went out again by me and leaped overboard toward the rock, whom afterward also I could never see.

Now none were left in the bark that I knew or saw, but my cousin and his wife and children, myself and mine and his maidservant. I put [on] my great coat, a waistcoat of cotton but had neither sleeves nor skirts, a thin pair of breeches, a pair of boots without stockings. My coat I put off me and laid it under my poor babe's feet to raise it out of the water (a poor supporter), but my cousin thought I would have fled from him and said unto me, 'Oh, cousin, leave us not. Let us die together,' and reached forth his hand unto me. Then I, letting go my son Peter's hand, took him by the hand and said to him, 'I purpose it not whither shall I go. I am willing and ready here to die with you. And my poor children, God be merciful to us,' adding these words, 'The Lord is able to help and to deliver us.' He replied, saying, 'True, cousin, but what His pleasure is, we know not; I fear we have been too unthankful for former mercies. But He hath promised to deliver us from sin and condemnation, through the all-sufficient satisfaction of Jesus Christ. This, therefore, we may challenge of him.' To which I, replying, said, 'That is all the deliverance I now desire and expect,' which words I had no sooner spoken but by a mighty wave I was with a piece of the bark washed out upon part of the rock, where the wave left me almost drowned. But recovering my feet, [I] saw above me on the rock my daughter Mary, to whom I was no sooner gotten but my cousin Avary and his eldest son came to us, being all four of us washed out with one and the same wave. We went all into a small hole on the top of the rock, whence we called to those in the pinnace to come unto us. Supposing we had been in more safety than they were in, my wife, seeing us there, was crept into the scuttle of the half deck to come unto us, but presently another wave dashing the pinnace all to pieces carried away my wife in the scuttle as she was with the greater part of the half deck [carried] to the shore, where she was safely cast, but her legs were something bruised, and much timber of the vessel being there also cast, she was some time before she could get away, washed with the waves. All the rest that were in the bark were drowned in the merciless seas.

We four by that wave were clean swept away from off the rock also into the sea, the Lord in one instant of time disposing of the souls of us to his good pleasure and will. His wonderful mercy to me was thus. Standing on the rock as before you heard with my eldest daughter, my cousin, and his eldest son, [I was] looking upon and talking unto them in the bark whenas we were by that cruel wave washed off the rock as before you heard. God in his mercy caused me to fall by the stroke of the wave flat on my face, for my face was toward the sea insomuch that I was sliding down the rock into the sea. The Lord directed my toes into a joint in the rock's side as also the tops of some of my fingers with my right hand by means whereof, the waves leaving me, I remained so, having only my head above the water. On my left hand I espied a board or plank of the pinnace, and as I was reaching out my left hand to lay hold on it, by another wave coming on the top of the rock I was washed away from the rock and by the violence of the waves was driven hither and thither in the sea a great while and had many dashes against the rocks. At length past hope of life and wearied both in body and spirit I even gave out to nature, and being ready to receive in the waters of death I lifted up both my heart and hands to the God of heaven (for, note, I had my senses remaining and perfect with me all the time I was under and in the water), who at that instant lifted my head clean above the top of waters that so I might breathe without hindrance by the waters. I stood bolt upright as if I stood upon my feet but I felt no bottom nor had any footing for to stand upon but the waters. While I was thus above the waters I saw a piece of the mast as I supposed about three foot long which I labored to catch into my arms, but suddenly I was overwhelmed with water and driven to and fro again and at last I felt the ground with my right foot. Immediately I was violently thrown grovelling on my face. When presently I recovered my feet [I] was in the water up to my breast and through God's great mercy had my face to the shore and not to the sea. I made haste to get out but was thrown down on my hands with the waves and so with safety crept forth to the dry shore, where, blessing God, I turned about to look for my children and friends but saw neither them nor any part of the pinnace where I left them as I supposed, but I saw my wife about a butt-length from me, getting herself forth from amongst the timber of the broken bark, but before I could get unto her she was gotten to the shore. When we were come each to other we went up into the land and sat us down under a cedar tree, which the winds had thrown down, where we sat about an hour, even dead with cold, for I was glad to put off my breeches, they being rent all to pieces in the rocks.

But now the storm was broken up and the wind was calm, but the sea remained rough and fearful to us. My legs was much bruised and so was my heart, and other hurt had I none, neither had I taken in much water. But my heart would not suffer me to sit still any longer, but I would go to see if any more was gotten to the land in safety, especially hoping to have met with some of mine own poor children, but I could find none, neither dead nor yet living. You condole with me my further miseries, who now began to consider of my losses. Now [I] called to my remembrance the time and manner how and when I last saw and left my children and friends. One was severed from me sitting on the rock at my feet, the other three in the pinnace, my little babe (ah, poor Peter) sitting in his sister Edith's arms, who to the utmost of her power sheltered him out of the waters, my poor William standing close unto her, all three of them looking ruefully on me on the rock, their very countenance calling unto me to help them, whom I could not go unto, neither could they come unto me, neither could the merciless waves afford me space or time to use any means at all, either to help them or myself.

Oh I yet see their cheeks, poor, silent lambs, pleading pity and help at my hands. Then on the other side to consider the loss of my dear friends with the spoil and loss of all our goods and provisions, myself cast upon an unknown land in a wilderness, I know not where, and how to get there we did not know. Then it came into my mind how I had occasioned the death of my children, who had occasioned them out of their native land, who might have left them there, yea and might have sent some of them back again and cost me nothing. These and many such thoughts do press down my heavy heart very much, but I leave this till I see your face, before which time I fear I shall never attain comfort. Now having no friend to whom I can freely impart myself, Mr Cotten is now my chiefest friend to whom I have free welcome and access, as also Mr Mavericke, Mr Warde, Mr Ward, Mr Hocker, Mr Weles, Mr Warhad, and Mr Parker also, Mr Noyes, who use me friendly. This is God's goodness to me, as also to set the eyes of all the country on me, especially of the magistrates who much favor and comfort me.

But I let this pass and will proceed on in the relation of God's goodness unto me. While I was in that desolate island on which I was cast, I and my wife were almost naked, both of us, and wet and cold even unto death. When going down to the shore as before I said I found cast on the shore a snapsack in which I had a steel and a flint and a powder horn. Going further I found a drowned goat. Then I found a hat and my son Will's coat, both which I put on. My wife found one of her own petticoats which she put on. I found also two cheeses and some butter driven ashore. Thus the Lord sent us some clothes to put on and food to sustain our new lives which he had given lately unto us, and means also to make fire, for in my horn I had some gunpowder, which to my own and other men's admiration was dry. So, taking a piece of my wife's neckcloth, which I dried in the sun, I struck fire and so dried and warmed our wet bodies, and then skinned the goat, and having found a small brass pot we boiled some of it. Our drink was brackish water.

Bread we had none. There we remained until the Monday following, where about three o'clock in the afternoon in a boat that came that way, we went off that desolate island, which I named after my own name, 'Thacher's Woe,' and the rock I named 'Avary his Fall,' to the end their fall and loss and mine own might be had in perpetual remembrance. In the island lieth buried the body of my cousin's eldest daughter, whom I found dead on the shore. On the Tuesday following in the afternoon we arrived at Marblehed, where I am now remaining in health and good respect though very poor, and thus you have heard such relation as never before happened in New England, and as much bewailed as it was strange. What I shall do or what course I shall take I know not. The Lord in his mercy direct me that I may so lead the new life which he hath given me as may be most to his own glory.

Praise God and pray to God for me.

A PORTRAIT OF OLIVER CROMWELL, LONDON, November 1640

Sir Philip Warwick

Born in 1599, the son of a country squire, Cromwell rose to become commander of the New Model Army in the English Civil War. After the eventual defeat of the Royalist side, Cromwell was declared the Lord Protector of England.

I have no mind to give an ill character of Cromwell, for in his conversation towards me he was ever friendly, though at the latter end of the day, finding me ever incorrigible and having some inducements to suspect me a tamperer, he was sufficiently rigid. The first time that ever I took notice of him was in the very beginning of the Parliament held in November 1640, when I vainly thought myself a courtly young gentleman (for we courtiers valued ourselves much upon our good clothes). I came one morning into the House well clad, and perceived a gentleman speaking (whom I knew not) very ordinarily apparelled, for it was a plain-cloth suit, which seemed to have been made by an ill country tailor: his linen was plain and not very clean, and I remember a speck or two of blood upon his little band, which was not much larger than his collar. His hat was without a hat-band. His stature was of good size, his sword stuck close to his side, his countenance swollen and reddish, his voice sharp and untunable, and his eloquence full of fervour, for the subject matter would not bear much of reason, it being in behalf of a servant of Mr Prynne's, who had dispersed libels against the Queen for her dancing and such like innocent and courtly sports: and he aggravated the imprisonment of this man by the Council-Table unto that height that one would have believed the very government itself had been in great danger by it.

THE ENGLISH CIVIL WAR: THE BATTLE OF MARSTON MOOR, YORKSHIRE, 1 July 1644

Oliver Cromwell

It was Cromwell's surprise cavalry charge late in the day which won Marston Moor for the 'Roundheads'. With the Royalist Northern Army routed, the tide of Civil War turned ineluctably in Parliament's favour. Cromwell's letter below is addressed to his brother-in-law, Colonel Valentine Walton.

It's our duty to sympathize in all mercies; and to praise the Lord together in chastisements or trials, that so we may sorrow together.

Truly England and the Church of God hath had a great favour from the Lord, in this great victory given unto us, such as the like never was since this war began. It had all the evidences of an absolute victory obtained by the Lord's blessing upon the Godly Party principally. We never charged but we routed the enemy. The Left Wing, which I commanded, being our own horse, saving a few Scots in our rear, beat all the Prince's horse. God made them as stubble to our swords. We charged their regiments of foot with our horse, and routed all we charged. The particulars I cannot relate now; but I believe, of twenty thousand the Prince hath not four thousand left. Give glory, all the glory, to God.

Sir, God hath taken away your eldest son by a cannon-shot. It brake his leg. We were necessitated to have it cut off, whereof he died.

Sir, you know my own trials this way: but the Lord supported me with this, That the Lord took him into the happiness we all pant for and live for. There is your precious child full of glory, never to know sin or sorrow any more. He was a gallant young man, exceedingly gracious. God give you His comfort. Before his death he was so full of comfort that to Frank Russel and myself he could not express it, 'It was so great above his pain.' This he said to us. Indeed it was admirable. A little after, he said, One thing lay upon his spirit. I asked him, What that was? He told me it was, That God had not suffered him to be any more the executioner of His enemies. At his fall, his horse being killed with the bullet, and as I am informed three horses more, I am told he bid them, Open to the right and left, that he might see the rogues run. Truly he was exceedingly beloved in the Army, of all that knew him. But few knew him; for he was a precious young man, fit for God. You have cause to bless the Lord. He is a glorious Saint in Heaven; wherein you ought exceedingly to rejoice. Let this drink up your sorrow; seeing these are not feigned words to comfort you, but the thing is so real and undoubted a truth. You may do all things by the strength of Christ. Seek that, and you shall easily bear your trial. Let this public mercy to the Church of God make you to forget your private sorrow. The Lord be your strength: so prays

Your truly faithful and loving brother,

OLIVER CROMWELL

THE ENGLISH CIVIL WAR: FRIENDS DIVIDED, SOUTHAMPTON, July 1644

Edmund Ludlow

Ludlow was a leader of the Parliamentarian Forces during the Civil War.

Two days after my coming to Southampton Col. Norton received advice, that the enemy was preparing to send some forces, in order to beat off those of ours that blocked up Basing House. He being then before Winchester, and resolving to march with his troop to reinforce the besiegers, desired me with my troop to supply his place at Winchester till his return. Being unwilling to refuse any public service, tho my men were very much harassed, I marched thither; and that those in the castle might see they were not at liberty to ravage the country, I drew out my troop and faced them; upon which they sent out what horse they had to skirmish with us; amongst whom observing one Mr William Neale, who was of my acquaintance, and formerly my schoolfellow, I called to him telling him, that I was sorry to see him there; but since it was so, I offered to exchange a shot with him, and riding up to that purpose, he retreated towards his party, where making a stand, he called to me to come on, which I did; but he retreated again till he came within the shelter of their foot, and one with him dismounting, fired a musquet at me loaded with a brace of bullets, of which one went into the belly of my horse, the other struck upon my breast-plate, within half an inch of the bottom of it: my horse carried me off, but died that night.

THE ENGLISH CIVIL WAR: THE EXECUTION OF CHARLES I, 30 January 1649

Philip Henry

At the later end of the year 1648 I had leave [from Oxford University] to goe to London to see my Father, & during my stay there at that time at Whitehal it was that I saw the Beheading of King Charles the first; He went by our door on Foot each day that hee was carry'd by water to Westminster, for he took Barge at Gardenstayres where we liv'd & once he spake to my Father & sayd Art thou alive yet! On the day of his execution, which was Tuesday, Jan. 30, I stood amongst the crowd in the street before Whitehal gate, where the scaffold was erected, and saw what was done, but was not so near as to hear any thing. The Blow I saw given, & can truly say with a sad heart; at the instant whereof, I remember well, there was such a Grone by the Thousands then present, as I never heard before & desire I may never hear again. There was according to Order one Troop immediately marching from-wards charing-cross to Westm[r] & another from-wards Westm[r] to charing-cross purposely to masker the people, & to disperse & scatter them, so that I had much adoe amongst the rest to escape home without hurt.

THE ENGLISH CIVIL WAR: THE STORMING OF DROGHEDA, IRELAND, 10–11 September 1649

Oliver Cromwell

Fearing that Ireland might become the launching place for a Royalist invasion of England, Cromwell determined on its conquest.

It hath pleased God to bless our endeavours at Tredah [Drogheda]. After battery, we stormed it. The enemy were about 3000 strong in the Town. They made a stout resistance; and near 1000 of our men being entered, the Enemy forced them out again. But God giving a new courage to our men, they attempted again, and entered; beating the enemy from their defences.

The Enemy had made three retrenchments, both to the right and left of where we entered; all which they were forced to quit. Being thus entered, we refused them quarter; having, the day before, summoned the Town. I believe we put to the sword the whole number of the defendants. I do not think Thirty of the whole number escaped with their lives. Those that did, are in safe custody for the Barbadoes. Since that time, the Enemy quitted to us Trim and Dundalk. In Trim they were in such haste that they left their guns behind them.

This hath been a marvellous great mercy. The Enemy, being not without some considerable loss; Colonel Castle being there shot in the head, whereof he presently died; and divers officers and soldiers doing their duty killed and wounded. There was a Tenalia to flanker the south Wall of the Town, between Duleek Gate and the corner Tower before mentioned; – which our men entered, wherein they found some forty or fifty of the Enemy, which they put to the sword. And this 'Tenalia' they held: but it being without the Wall, and the sally-port through the Wall into that Tenalia being choked up with some of the Enemy which were killed in it, it proved of no use for an entrance into the Town that way.

Although our men that stormed the breaches were forced to recoil, as is before expressed; yet, being encouraged to recover their loss, they made a second attempt; wherein God was pleased so to animate them that they got ground of the enemy, and by the goodness of God, forced him to quit his entrenchments. And after a very hot dispute, the Enemy having both horse and foot, and we only foot, within the Wall – they gave ground, and our men became masters both of their retrenchments and of the Church; which, indeed, although they made our entrance the more difficult, yet they proved of excellent use to us; so that the Enemy could not now annoy us with their horse, but thereby we had the advantage to make good the ground, that so we might let in our own horse; which accordingly was done, though with much difficulty.

Divers of the Enemy retreated into the Mill-Mount: a place very strong and difficult of access; being exceedingly high, having a good graft, and strong palisadoed. The Governor, Sir Arthur Ashton, and divers considerable Officers being there, our men getting up to them, were ordered by me to put them all to the sword. And indeed, being in the heat of action, I forbade them to spare any that were in arms in the Town: and, I think, that night they put to the sword about 2000 men; – divers of the officers and soldiers being fled over the Bridge into the other part of the Town, where about 100 of them possessed St Peter's Church-steeple, some the west Gate, and others a strong Round Tower next the Gate called St Sunday's. These being summoned to yield to mercy, refused. Whereupon I ordered the steeple of St Peter's Church to be fired, when one of them was heard to say in the midst of the flames: 'God damn me, God confound me; I burn, I burn.'

The next day, the other two Towers were summoned; in one of which was about six or seven score; but they refused to yield themselves: and we knowing that hunger must compel them, set only good guards to secure them from running away until their stomachs were come down. From one of the said Towers, notwithstanding their condition, they killed and wounded some of our men. When they submitted, their officers were knocked on the head; and every tenth man of the soldiers killed; and the rest shipped for the Barbadoes. The soldiers in the other Tower were all spared, as to their lives only; and shipped likewise for the Barbadoes.

I am persuaded that this is a righteous judgement of God upon these barbarous wretches, who have imbrued their hands in so much innocent blood; and that it will tend to prevent the effusion of blood for the future. Which are the satisfactory grounds to such actions, which otherwise cannot but work remorse and regret. The officers and soldiers of this Garrison were the flower of their army. And their great expectation was, that our attempting this place would put fair to ruin us . . . And now give me leave to say how it comes to pass that this work is wrought. It was set upon some of our hearts, That a great thing should be done, not by power or might, but by the Spirit of God. And is it not so, clearly? That which caused your men to storm so courageously, it was the Spirit of God, who gave your men courage, and took it away again; and gave the Enemy courage, and took it away again; and gave your men courage again, and therewith this happy success. And therefore it is good that God alone have all the glory . . .

Your most obedient servant,

OLIVER CROMWELL.

UNCONSUMMATED CHILD MARRIAGE, ENGLAND, 1651

Court Records

John Bridge v Elizabeth Bridge

. . . the said John wold Eate no meate at supper . . . and whan hit was bed tyme, the said John did wepe to go home with his father, he beynge at that tyme at her brothers house. Yet nevertheles, bie his fathers intreating, and bie the perswasion of the priest, the said John did comme to bed to this Respondent far in the night; and there lay still, till in the morning, in suche sort as this deponent might take unkindnes with hym; for he lay with his backe toward her all night; and neither then, nor anie tyme els, had carnall dole with her, nor never after came in her companie, more than he had never knowne her.

. . . the said John was, at the tyme of the said marriage, above the age of xii yeres, and vnder xiii.

HIGHWAY ROBBERY, KENT, ENGLAND, 11 June 1652

John Evelyn

The weather being hot, and having sent my man on before, I rode negligently under favour of the shade, till within three miles of Bromley, at a place called Procession Oak, two cut-throats started out, and striking with long staves at the horse and taking hold of the reins threw me down, took my sword, and haled me into a deep thicket some quarter of a mile from the highway, where they did might securely rob me, as they soon did. What they got of money was not considerable, but they took two rings, the one an emerald with diamonds, the other an onyx, and a pair of buckles set with rubies and diamonds, which were of value, and after all bound my hands behind me, and my feet, having before pulled off my boots; they then set me up against an oak, with the most bloody threats to cut my throat if I offered to cry out or make any noise, for they should be within hearing, I not being the person they looked for. I told them, if they had not basely surprised me they should not have had so easy a prize, and that it would teach me never to ride near a hedge, since had I been midway they durst not have adventured on me; at which they cocked their pistols, and told me they had long guns too, and were 14 companions. I begged for my onyx, and told them it being engraven with my arms would betray them, but nothing prevailed. My horse's bridle they slipt, and searched the saddle, which they pulled off, but let the horse graze, and then turning again bridled him and tied him to a tree, yet so as he might graze, and thus left me bound. My horse was perhaps not taken because he was marked and cropped on both ears, and well known on that road. Left in this manner grievously was I tormented with flies, ants, and the sun, nor was my anxiety little how I should get loose in that solitary place, where I could neither hear or see any creature but my poor horse, and a few sheep straggling in the copse. Afternear two hours attempting I got my hands to turn palm to palm, having been tied back to back, and then it was long before I could slip the cord over my wrists to my thumb, which at last I did, and then soon unbound my feet, and saddling my horse and roaming awhile about I at last perceived dust to rise, and soon after heard the rattling of a cart, towards which I made, and by the help of two countrymen I got back into the highway. I rode to Col. Blount's, a great judiciary of the times, who sent out hue and cry immediately. The next morning, sore as my wrists and arms were, I went to London and got 500 tickets printed and dispersed by an officer of Goldsmiths Hall, and within two days had tidings of all I had lost except my sword which had a silver hilt and some trifles. The rogues had pawned one of my rings for a trifle to a goldsmith's servant before the tickets had come to the shop, by which means they escaped; the other ring was bought by a victualler, who brought it to a goldsmith, but he having seen the ticket seized the man. I afterwards discharged him on protestation of innocence. Thus did God deliver me from these vilains, and not only so, but restored what they took, as twice before he had graciously done, both at sea and land; I mean when I was robbed by pirates, and was in danger of a considerable loss at Amsterdam; for which, and many, many signal preservations, I am extremely obliged to give thanks to God my Saviour.

THE PRODIGIOUS BOYHOOD OF SIR ISAAC NEWTON, *c.* 1660

Dr Stukeley

Every one that knew Sir Isaac, or have heard of him, recount the pregnancy of his parts when a boy, his strange inventions, and extraordinary inclination for mechanics. That instead of playing among the other boys, when from school, he always busied himself in making knick-knacks and models of wood in many kinds. For which purpose he had got little saws, hatchets, hammers, and all sorts of tools, which he would use with great dexterity. In particular they speak of his making a wooden clock. About this time, a new windmill was set up near Grantham, in the way to Gunnerby, which is now demolished, this country chiefly using water mills. Our lad's imitating spirit was soon excited and by frequently prying into the fabric of it, as they were making it, he became master enough to make a very perfect model thereof, and it was said to be as clean and curious a piece of workmanship, as the original. This sometimes he would set upon the house-top, where he lodged, and clothing it with sail-cloth, the wind would readily turn it; but what was most extraordinary in its composition was, that he put a mouse into it, which he called the miller, and that the mouse made the mill turn round when he pleased; and he would joke too upon the miller eating the corn that was put in. Some say that he tied a string to the mouse's tail, which was put into a wheel, like that of turn-spit dogs, so that pulling the string, made the mouse go forward by way of resistance, and this turned the mill. Others suppose there was some corn placed above the wheel, this the mouse endeavouring to get to, made it turn.

THE GREAT FIRE OF LONDON, 2 September 1666

Samuel Pepys

After the Great Plague of 1665, fire visited the English capital. The son of a tailor, Samuel Pepys was an official with the Admiralty. He was also an assiduous diarist, recording entries daily from 1660 until 1669, when his eyesight failed him. Written in shorthand code, the diary was not deciphered until 1825.

Diary: 1666, September 2 (Lord's day). Some of our maids sitting up late last night to get things ready against our feast to-day, Jane called us up about three in the morning, to tell us of a great fire they saw in the City. So I rose, and slipped on my night-gown, and went to her window; and thought it to be on the backside of Mark Lane at the farthest; but being unused to such fires as followed, I thought it far enough off; and so went to bed again, and to sleep. About seven rose again to dress myself, and there looked out at the window, and saw the fire not so much as it was, and farther off. So to my closet to set things to rights, after yesterday's cleaning. By and by Jane comes and tells me that she hears that above 300 houses have been burned down to-night by the fire we saw, and that it is now burning down all Fish Street, by London Bridge. So I made myself ready presently, and walked to the Tower; and there got up upon one of the high places, Sir J. Robinson's little son going up with me; and there I did see the houses at that end of the bridge all on fire, and an infinite great fire on this and the other side the end of the bridge; which, among other people, did trouble me for poor little Michell and our Sarah on the bridge. So down, with my heart full of trouble, to the Lieutenant of the Tower, who tells me that it began this morning in the King's baker's house in Pudding Lane, and that it hath burned down St Magnus's Church and most part of Fish Street already. So I down to the waterside, and there got a boat, and through bridge, and there saw a lamentable fire. Poor Michell's house, as far as the Old Swan, already burned that way, and the fire running farther, that in a very little time it got as far as the Steelyard, while I was there. Everybody endeavouring to remove their goods, and flinging into the river, or bringing them into lighters that lay off; poor people staying in their houses as long as till the very fire touched them, and then running into boats, or clambering from one pair of stairs, by the waterside, to another. And, among other things, the poor pigeons, I perceive, were loath to leave their houses, but hovered about the windows and balconies, till they burned their wings, and fell down. Having stayed, and in an hour's time seen the fire rage every way; and nobody, to my sight, endeavouring to quench it, but to remove their goods, and leave all to the fire; and having seen it get as far as the Steelyard, and the wind mighty high and driving it into the City; and everything, after so long a drought, proving combustible, even the very stones of churches, and, among other things, the poor steeple by which pretty Mrs — lives, and whereof my old schoolfellow Elborough is parson, taken fire in the very top, and there burned till it fell down; I to Whitehall, with a gentleman with me, who desired to go off from the Tower, to see the fire, in my boat; and there up to the King's closet in the Chapel, where people came about me, and I did give them an account dismayed them all, and word was carried in to the King. So I was called for, and did tell the King and Duke of York what I saw; and that unless his Majesty did command houses to be pulled down nothing could stop the fire. They seemed much troubled, and the King commanded me to go to my Lord Mayor from him, and command him to spare no houses, but to pull down before the fire every way. The Duke of York bid me tell him that if he would have any more soldiers he shall; and so did my Lord Arlington afterwards, as a great secret. Here meeting with Captain Cocke, I in his coach, which he lent me, and Creed with me to Paul's; and there walked along Watling Street as well as I could, every creature coming away loaden with goods to save, and here and there sick people carried away in beds. Extraordinary good goods carried in carts and on backs. At last met my Lord Mayor in Canning Street, like a man spent, with a handkercher about his neck. To the King's message he cried, like a fainting woman, 'Lord! what can I do? I am spent: people will not obey me. I have been pulling down houses; but the fire overtakes us faster than we can do it.' That he needed no more soldiers; and that, for himself, he must go and refresh himself, having been up all night. So he left me, and I him, and walked home, seeing people all almost distracted, and no manner of means used to quench the fire. The houses, too, so very thick thereabouts, and full of matter for burning, as pitch and tar, in Thames Street; and warehouses of oil, and wines, and brandy, and other things. Here I saw Mr Isaac Houblon, the handsome man, prettily dressed and dirty, at his door at Dowgate, receiving some of his brother's things, whose houses were on fire; and, as he says, have been removed twice already; and he doubts, as it soon proved, that they must be in a little time removed from his house also, which was a sad consideration. And to see the churches all filling with goods by people who themselves should have been quietly there at this time. By this time it was about twelve o'clock; and so home, and there find my guests, who were Mr Wood and his wife Barbary Sheldon, and also Mr Moone; she mighty fine, and her husband, for aught I see, a likely man. But Mr Moone's design and mine, which was to look over my closet, and please him with the sight thereof, which he hath long desired, was wholly disappointed; for we were in great trouble and disturbance at this fire, not knowing what to think of it. However, we had an extraordinary good dinner, and as merry as at this time we could be. While at dinner, Mrs Batelier came to enquire after Mr Woolfe and Stanes, who, it seems, are related to them, whose houses in Fish Street are all burned, and they in a sad condition. She would not stay in the fright. Soon as dined, I and Moone away, and walked through the City, the streets full of nothing but people and horses and carts loaden with goods, ready to run over one another, and removing goods from one burned house to another. They now removing out of Canning Street, which received goods in the morning, into Lombard Street, and farther; and, among others, I now saw my little goldsmith, Stokes receiving some friend's goods, whose house itself was burned the day after. We parted at Paul's; he home, and I to Paul's Wharf, where I had appointed a boat to attend me, and took in Mr Carcasse and his brother, whom I met in the street, and carried them below and above bridge to and again to see the fire, which was now got farther, both below and above, and no likelihood of stopping it. Met with the King and Duke of York in their barge, and with them to Queenhithe, and there called Sir Richard Browne to them. Their order was only to pull down houses apace, and so below bridge at the waterside; but little was or could be done, the fire coming upon them so fast. Good hopes there was of stopping it at the Three Cranes above and at Buttulph's Wharf below bridge, if care be used; but the wind carries it into the City, so as we know not by the waterside what it do there. River full of lighters and boats taking in goods, and good goods swimming in the water; and only I observed that hardly one lighter or boat in three that had the goods of a house in, but there was a pair of virginals in it. Having seen as much as I could now, I away to Whitehall by appointment, and there walked to St James's Park; and there met my wife, and Creed, and Wood and his wife, and walked to my boat; and there upon the water again, and to the fire up and down, it still increasing, and the wind great. So near the fire as we could for smoke; and all over the Thames, with one's face in the wind, you were almost burned with a shower of fire-drops. This is very true; so as houses were burned by these drops and flakes of fire, three or four, nay, five or six houses, one from another. When we could endure no more upon the water, we to a little alehouse on the Bankside, over against the Three Cranes, and there stayed till it was dark almost, and saw the fire grow; and, as it grew darker, appeared more and more, and in corners and upon steeples, and between churches and houses, as far as we could see up the hill of the City, in a most horrid, malicious, bloody flame, not like the fine flame of an ordinary fire. Barbary and her husband away before us. We stayed till, it being darkish, we saw the fire as only one entire arch of fire from this to the other side the bridge, and in a bow up the hill for an arch of above a mile long: it made me weep to see it. The churches, houses, and all on fire, and flaming at once; and a horrid noise the flames made, and the cracking of houses at their ruin.

THE GREAT FROST, LONDON, 1684

John Evelyn

[Sunday] Jan. 1st, 1684. The weather continuing intolerably severe, streetes of booths were set upon the Thames; the air was so very cold and thick, as of many years there had not ben the like. The small pox was very mortal . . .

9th. I went crosse the Thames on the ice, now become so thick as to beare not onely streetes of boothes, in which they roasted meate, and had divers shops of wares, quite across as in a towne, but coaches, carts and horses, passed over. So I went from Westminster Stayres to Lambeth, and din'd with the Archbishop . . .

16th. The Thames was fill'd with people and tents, selling all sorts of wares as in the Citty.

24th. The frost continuing more and more severe, the Thames before London was still planted with boothes in formal streetes, all sortes of trades and shops furnish'd and full of commodities, even to a printing presse, where the people and ladyes tooke a fancy to have their names printed, and the day and yeare set down when printed on the Thames: this humour tooke so universally, that 'twas estimated the printer gain'd £5 a day, for printing a line onely, at sixpence a name, besides what he got by ballads, &c. Coaches plied from Westminster to the Temple, and from several other staires to and fro, as in the streetes, sleds, sliding with skeetes, a bull-baiting, horse and coach races, puppet plays and interludes, cookes, tipling, and other lewd places, so that it seem'd to be a bacchanalian triumph or carnival on the water, whilst it was a severe judgement on the land, the trees not onely splitting as if lightning-struck, but men and cattle perishing in divers places, and the very seas so lock'd up with ice, that no vessels could stir out or come in. The fowles, fish, and birds, and all our exotiq plants and greenes universally perishing. Many parkes of deer were destroied, and all sorts of fuell so deare that there were great contributions to preserve the poore alive. Nor was this severe weather much less intense in most parts of Europe, even as far as Spaine and the most southern tracts. London, by reason of the excessive coldnesse of the aire hindering the ascent of the smoke, was so filled with the fuliginous steame of the sea-coale, that hardly could one see crosse the streets, and this filling the lungs with its grosse particles, exceedingly obstructed the breast, so as one could hardly breath. Here was no water to be had from the pipes and engines, nor could the brewers and divers other tradesmen worke, and every moment was full of disastrous accidents.

Feb. 4th. I went to Says Court to see how the frost had dealt with my garden, where I found many of the greenes and rare plantes utterly destroied. The oranges and mirtalls very sick, the rosemary and laurells dead to all appearance, but ye cypress likely to indure it.

5th. It began to thaw, but froze againe. My coach crossed from Lambeth to the Horseferry at Millbank, Westminster. The booths were almost all taken downe, but there was first a map or landskip cut in copper representing all the manner of the camp, and the several actions, sports, and pastimes thereon, in memory of so signal a frost . . .

8th. The weather was set in to an absolute thaw and raine, but ye Thames still frozen.

TRIAL FOR WITCHCRAFT, ESSEX, ENGLAND, 1699

John Bufton

Although England escaped the worst excesses of the great witch-hunt, which began in the Western world in the fifteenth century, there were isolated trials for witchcraft as late as the 1690s (as there were in America, notably at Salem).

Diary: 1699, July 13. The widow Comon was put into the river to see if she would sink, because she was suspected to be a witch – and she did not sink, but swim. And she was tried again July 19, and then she swam again, and did not sink.

24. The widow Comon, was tried a third time by putting her into the river, and she swum and did not sink.

Dec. 27. The widow Comon, that was counted a witch, was buried.

SMALL-POX INGRAFTING, ADRIANOPLE, TURKEY, 1 April 1717

Lady Mary Wortley Montagu

The writer was the wife of the English ambassador to Turkey.

Those dreadful stories you have heard of the *plague* have very little foundation in truth. I own I have much ado to reconcile myself to the sound of a word which has always given me such terrible ideas, though I am convinced there is little more in it than in a fever. As a proof of this, let me tell you that we passed through two or three towns most violently infected. In the very next house where we lay (in one of those places) two persons died of it. Luckily for me I was so well deceived that I knew nothing of the matter; and I was made believe, that our second cook had only a great cold. However, we left our doctor to take care of him, and yesterday they both arrived here in good health; and I am now let into the secret that he has had the *plague*. There are many that escape it; neither is the air ever infected. I am persuaded that it would be as easy a matter to root it out here as out of Italy and France; but it does so little mischief, they are not very solicitous about it, and are content to suffer this distemper instead of our variety, which they are utterly unacquainted with.

A propos of distempers, I am going to tell you a thing that will make you wish yourself here. The small-pox, so fatal, and so general amongst us, is here entirely harmless by the invention of *ingrafting*, which is the term they give it. There is a set of old women who make it their business to perform the operation every autumn, in the month of September, when the great heat is abated. People send to one another to know if any of their family has a mind to have the small-pox: they make parties for this purpose, and when they are met (commonly fifteen or sixteen together), the old woman comes with a nut-shell full of the matter of the best sort of small-pox, and asks what vein you please to have opened. She immediately rips open that you offer to her with a large needle (which gives you no more pain than a common scratch), and puts into the vein as much matter as can lie upon the head of her needle, and after that binds up the little wound with a hollow bit of shell; and in this manner opens four or five veins. The Grecians have commonly the superstition of opening one in the middle of the forehead, one in each arm, and one on the breast, to mark the sign of the cross; but this has a very ill effect, all these wounds leaving little scars, and is not done by those that are not superstitious, who choose to have them in the legs, or that part of the arm that is concealed. The children or young patients play together all the rest of the day, and are in perfect health to the eighth. Then the fever begins to seize them, and they keep their beds two days, very seldom three. They have very rarely above twenty or thirty in their faces, which never mark; and in eight days' time they are as well as before their illness. Where they are wounded, there remain running sores during the distemper, which I don't doubt is a great relief to it. Every year thousands undergo this operation; and the French ambassador says pleasantly, that they take the small-pox here by way of diversion, as they take the waters in other countries. There is no example of any one that has died in it; and you may believe I am well satisfied of the safety of this experiment, since I intend to try it on my dear little son.

I am patriot enough to take pains to bring this useful invention into fashion in England; and I should not fail to write to some of our doctors very particularly about it, if I knew any one of them that I thought had virtue enough to destroy such a considerable branch of their revenue for the good of mankind. But that distemper is too beneficial to them, not to expose to all their resentment the hardy wight that should undertake to put an end to it. Perhaps, if I live to return, I may, however, have courage to war with them. Upon this occasion admire the heroism in the heart of your friend, etc., etc.

A PUBLIC EXECUTION, LONDON, c. 1750

Samuel Richardson

Richardson was the author of *Clarissa*. The letter below is addressed to his brother.

I have this day been satisfying a curiosity, I believe natural to most people, by seeing an execution at Tyburn: The sight has had an extraordinary effect upon me, which is more owing to the unexpected oddness of the scene, than the affecting concern which is unavoidable in a thinking person, at a spectacle so awful, and so interesting, to all who consider themselves of the same species with the unhappy sufferers.

That I might the better view the prisoners, and escape the pressure of the mob, which is prodigious, nay, almost incredible, if we consider the frequency of these executions in London, which is once a month; I mounted my horse, and accompanied the melancholy cavalcade from Newgate to the fatal tree. The criminals were five in number. I was much disappointed at the unconcern and carelessness that appeared in the faces of three of the unhappy wretches: The countenances of the other two were spread with that horror and despair which is not to be wonder'd at in men whose period of life is so near, with the terrible aggravation of its being hastened by their own voluntary indiscretion and misdeeds. The exhortation spoken by the bell-man, from the wall of St Sepulchre's churchyard, is well intended; but the noise of the officers, and the mob, was so great, and the silly curiosity of people climbing into the cart to take leave of the criminals, made such a confused noise, that I could not hear the words of the exhortation when spoken; tho' they are as follow:

'All good people pray heartily to God for these poor sinners, who now are going to their deaths; for whom this great bell doth toll.

'You that are condemned to die, repent with lamentable tears. Ask mercy of the Lord for the salvation of your own souls, thro' the merits, death, and passion, of Jesus Christ, who now sits at the right-hand of God, to make intercession for as many of you as penitently return unto him.

'*Lord have mercy upon you! Christ have mercy upon you!*' – Which last words the bell-man repeats three times.

All the way up Holborn the croud was so great, as, at every twenty or thirty yards, to obstruct the passage; and wine, notwithstanding a late good order against that practice, was brought the malefactors, who drank greedily of it, which I thought did not suit well with their deplorable circumstances: After this, the three thoughtless young men, who at *first* seemed not enough concerned, grew most shamefully daring and wanton; behaving themselves in a manner that would have been ridiculous in men in any circumstance whatever: They swore, laugh'd, and talked obscenely; and wish'd their wicked companions good luck, with as much assurance as if their employment had been the most lawful.

At the place of execution, the scene grew still more shocking; and the clergyman who attended was more the subject of ridicule, than of their serious attention. The psalm was sung amidst the curses and quarrelling of hundreds of the most abandon'd and profligate of mankind: Upon whom (so stupid are they to any sense of decency) all the preparation of the unhappy wretches seems to serve only for the subject of a barbarous kind of mirth, altogether inconsistent with humanity. And as soon as the poor creatures were half-dead, I was much surprised, before such a number of peace-officers, to see the populace fall to haling and pulling the carcases with so much earnestness, as to occasion several warm rencounters, and broken heads. These, I was told, were the friends of the persons executed, or such as, for the sake of tumult, chose to appear so, and some persons sent by private surgeons to obtain bodies for dissection. The contests between these were fierce and bloody, and frightful to look at: so that I made the best of my way out of the croud, and, with some difficulty, rode back among a large number of people, who had been upon the same errand with myself. The face of every one spoke a kind of mirth, as if the spectacle they had beheld had afforded pleasure instead of pain, which I am wholly unable to account for.

In other nations, common criminal executions are said to be little attended by any beside the necessary officers, and the mournful friends, but here, all was hurry and confusion, racket and noise, praying and oaths, swearing and singing psalms; I am unwilling to impute this difference in our own from the practice of other nations, to the cruelty of our natures; to which, foreigners, however, to our dishonour, ascribe it. In most instances, let them say what they will, we are humane beyond what other nations can boast; but in this, the behaviour of my countrymen is past my accounting for; every street and lane I passed through, bearing rather the face of a holiday, than of that sorrow which I expected to see, for the untimely deaths of five members of the community.

One of their bodies was carried to the lodging of his wife, who not being in the way to receive it, they immediately hawked it about to every surgeon they could think of, and when none would buy it, they rubb'd tar all over it, and left it in a field hardly cover'd with earth.

This is the best description I can give you of a scene that was no way entertaining to me, and which I shall not again take so much pains to see.

CAPTURED BY SLAVE TRADERS, EASTERN NIGERIA, *c.* 1756

Olaudah Equiano

My father . . . had a numerous family, of which seven lived to grow up, including myself and sister, who was the only daughter. As I was the youngest of the sons, I became, of course, the greatest favorite with my mother, and was always with her; and she used to take particular pains to form my mind. I was trained up from my earliest years in the art of war: my daily exercise was shooting and throwing javelins, and my mother adorned me with emblems, after the manner of our greatest warriors. In this way I grew up till I had turned the age of eleven, when an end was put to my happiness in the following manner: Generally, when the grown people in the neighborhood were gone far in the fields to labor, the children assembled together in some of the neighboring premises to play; and commonly some of us used to get up a tree to look out for any assailant, or kidnapper, that might come upon us – for they sometimes took those opportunities of our parents' absence, to attack and carry off as many as they could seize.

One day as I was watching at the top of a tree in our yard, I saw one of those people come into the yard of our next neighbor but one, to kidnap, there being many stout young people in it. Immediately on this I gave the alarm of the rogue, and he was surrounded by the stoutest of them, who entangled him with cords, so that he could not escape, till some of the grown people came and secured him. But, alas! ere long it was my fate to be thus attacked, and to be carried off, when none of the grown people were nigh. One day, when all our people were gone out to their works as usual, and only I and my dear sister were left to mind the house, two men and a woman got over our walls, and in a moment seized us both, and, without giving us time to cry out, or make resistance, they stopped our mouths, and ran off with us into the nearest wood. Here they tied our hands, and continued to carry us as far as they could, till night came on, when we reached a small house, where the robbers halted for refreshment, and spent the night. We were then unbound, but were unable to take any food; and, being quite overpowered by fatigue and grief, our only relief was some sleep, which allayed our misfortune for a short time.

The next morning we left the house, and continued travelling all the day. For a long time we had kept [to] the woods, but at last we came into a road which I believed I knew. I had now some hopes of being delivered; for we had advanced but a little way before I discovered some people at a distance, on which I began to cry out for their assistance; but my cries had no other effect than to make them tie me faster and stop my mouth, and then they put me into a large sack. They also stopped my sister's mouth, and tied her hands; and in this manner we proceeded till we were out of sight of these people. When we went to rest the following night, they offered us some victuals, but we refused it; and the only comfort we had was in being in one another's arms all that night, and bathing each other with our tears. But alas! we were soon deprived of even the small comfort of weeping together. The next day proved a day of greater sorrow than I had yet experienced; for my sister and I were then separated, while we lay clasped in each other's arms. It was in vain that we besought them not to part us; she was torn from me, and immediately carried away, while I was left in a state of distraction not to be described. I cried and grieved continually; and for several days did not eat anything but what they forced into my mouth . . .

I was soon put down under the decks, and there I received such a salutation in my nostrils as I had never experienced in my life: so that with the loathsomeness of the stench and crying together, I became so sick and low that I was not able to eat, nor had I the least desire to taste anything. I now wished for the last friend, death, to relieve me; but soon, to my grief, two of the white men offered me eatables, and on my refusing to eat, one of them held me fast by the hands and laid me across I think the windlass, and tied my feet while the other flogged me severely. I had never experienced anything of this kind before, and although, not being used to the water, I naturally feared that element the first time I saw it, yet nevertheless could I have got over the nettings I would have jumped over the side, but I could not; and besides, the crew used to watch us very closely who were not chained down to the decks, lest we should leap into the water: and I have seen some of these poor African prisoners most severely cut for attempting to do so, and hourly whipped for not eating. This indeed was often the case with myself. In a little time after, amongst the poor chained men I found some of my own nation, which in a small degree gave ease to my mind. I inquired of these what was to be done with us; they gave me to understand we were to be carried to these white people's country to work for them.

THE BLACK HOLE OF CALCUTTA, 21 June 1756

J.Z. Holwell

Having captured Calcutta's Fort William, the nawab of Bengal confined 146 British prisoners to the military gaol there – the 300-square-foot 'Black Hole'.

We had been but few minutes confined before every one fell into a perspiration so profuse, you can form no idea of it. This brought on a raging thirst, which increased in proportion as the body was drained of its moisture.

Various expedients were thought of to give more room and air. To obtain the former, it was moved to put off their cloaths; this was approved as a happy motion, and in a few minutes I believe every man was stripped (myself, Mr Court, and the two young gentlemen by me excepted). For a little time they flattered themselves with having gained a mighty advantage; every hat was put in motion to produce a circulation of air, and Mr Baillie proposed that every man should sit down on his hams. This expedient was several times put in practice, and at each time many of the poor creatures, whose natural strength was less than that of others, or who had been more exhausted and could not immediately recover their legs, as others did when the word was given to rise, fell to rise no more; for they were instantly trod to death or suffocated. When the whole body sat down, they were so closely wedged together, that they were obliged to use many efforts before they could put themselves in motion to get up again.

Before nine o'clock every man's thirst grew intolerable, and respiration difficult. Efforts were made again to force the door, but in vain. Many insults were used to the guard to provoke them to fire in upon us. For my own part, I hitherto felt little pain or uneasiness, but what resulted from my anxiety for the sufferings of those within. By keeping my face between two of the bars, I obtained air enough to give my lungs easy play, though my perspiration was excessive, and thirst commencing. At this period, so strong a urinous volatile effluvia came from the prison, that I was not able to turn my head that way, for more than a few seconds at a time.

Now every body, excepting those situated in and near the windows, began to grow outrageous, and many delirious: *Water, water*, became the general cry. And the old Jemmautdaar before mentioned, taking pity on us, ordered the people to bring some skins of water. This was what I dreaded. I foresaw it would prove the ruin of the small chance left us, and essayed many times to speak to him privately to forbid its being brought; but the clamour was so loud, it became impossible. The water appeared. Words cannot paint to you the universal agitation and raving the sight of it threw us into. I flattered myself that some, by preserving an equal temper of mind, might out-live the night; but now the reflection, which gave me the greatest pain, was, that I saw no possibility of one escaping to tell the dismal tale.

Until the water came, I had myself not suffered much from thirst, which instantly grew excessive. We had no means of conveying it into the prison, but by hats forced through the bars; and thus myself and Messieurs Coles and Scott (notwithstanding the pains they suffered from their wounds) supplied them as fast as possible. But those who have experienced intense thirst, or are acquainted with the cause and nature of this appetite, will be sufficiently sensible it could receive no more than a momentary alleviation; the cause still subsisted. Though we brought full hats within the bars, there ensued such violent struggles, and frequent contests to get at it, that before it reached the lips of any one, there would be scarcely a small tea cup full left in them. These supplies, like sprinkling water on fire, only served to feed and raise the flame.

Oh! my dear Sir, how shall I give you a conception of what I felt at the cries and ravings of those in the remoter parts of the prison, who could not entertain a probable hope of obtaining a drop, yet could not divest themselves of expectation, however unavailing! and calling on me by the tender considerations of friendship and affection, and who knew they were really dear to me! Think, if possible, what my heart must have suffered at seeing and hearing their distress, without having it in my power to relieve them: for the confusion now became general and horrid. Several quitted the other window (the only chance they had for life) to force their way to the water, and the throng and press upon the window was beyond bearing; many forcing their passage from the further part of the room, pressed down those in their way, who had less strength, and trampled them to death.

From about nine to near eleven, I sustained this cruel scene and painful situation, still supplying them with water, though my legs were almost broke with the weight against them. By this time I myself was near pressed to death, and my two companions, with Mr William Parker (who had forced himself into the window) were really so . . .

For a great while they preserved a respect and regard to me, more than indeed I could well expect, our circumstances considered; but now all distinction was lost. My friend Baillie, Messrs Jenks, Revely, Law, Buchanan, Simpson, and several others, for whom I had a real esteem and affection, had for some time been dead at my feet: and were now trampled upon by every corporal or common soldier, who, by the help of more robust constitutions, had forced their way to the window, and held fast by the bars over me, till at last I became so pressed and wedged up, I was deprived of all motion.

Determined now to give every thing up, I called to them, and begged, as the last instance of their regard, they would remove the pressure upon me, and permit me to retire out of the window, to die in quiet. They gave way; and with much difficulty I forced a passage into the centre of the prison, where the throng was less by the many dead, (then I believe amounting to one-third) and the numbers who flocked to the windows; for by this time they had water also at the other window.

In the black hole there is a platform corresponding with that in the barrack: I travelled over the dead, and repaired to the further end of it, just opposite to the other window. Here my poor friend Mr Edward Eyre came staggering over the dead to me, and with his usual coolness and good-nature, asked me how I did? but fell and expired before I had time to make him a reply. I laid myself down on some of the dead behind me, on the platform; and, recommending myself to heaven, had the comfort of thinking my sufferings could have no long duration.

My thirst grew now insupportable, and the difficulty of breathing much increased; and I had not remained in this situation, I believe, ten minutes, when I was seized with a pain in my breast, and palpitation of heart, both to the most exquisite degree. These roused and obliged me to get up again; but still the pain, palpitation, thirst, and difficulty of breathing increased. I retained my senses notwithstanding; and had the grief to see death not so near me as I hoped; but could no longer bear the pains I suffered without attempting a relief, which I knew fresh air would and could only give me. I instantly determined to push for the window opposite to me; and by an effort of double the strength I had ever before possessed, gained the third rank at it, with one hand seized a bar, and by that means gained the second, though I think there were at least six or seven ranks between me and the window.

In a few moments the pain, palpitation, and difficulty of breathing ceased; but my thirst continued intolerable. I called aloud for *Water for God's sake*. I had been concluded dead; but as soon as they found me amongst them, they still had the respect and tenderness for me, to cry out, *Give him water, give him water!* nor would one of them at the window attempt to touch it until I had drank. But from the water I had no relief; my thirst was rather increased by it; so I determined to drink no more, but patiently wait the event; and kept my mouth moist from time to time by sucking the perspiration out of my shirt sleeves, and catching the drops as they fell, like heavy rain, from my head and face; you can hardly imagine how unhappy I was if any of them escaped my mouth.

I came into the prison without coat or waistcoat; the season was too hot to bear the former, and the latter tempted the avarice of one of the guards, who robbed me of it, when we were under the Veranda. Whilst I was at this second window, I was observed by one of my miserable companions on the right of me, in the expedient of allaying my thirst by sucking my shirt-sleeve. He took the hint, and robbed me from time to time of a considerable part of my store; though after I detected him, I had even the address to begin on that sleeve first, when I thought my reservoirs were sufficiently replenished; and our mouths and noses often met in the contest. This plunderer I found afterwards was a worthy young gentleman in the service, Mr Lushington, one of the few who escaped from death, and since paid me the compliment of assuring me, he believed he owed his life to the many comfortable draughts he had from my sleeves. Before I hit upon this happy expedient, I had in an ungovernable fit of thirst, attempted drinking my urine; but it was so intensely bitter, there was no enduring a second taste, whereas no Bristol water could be more soft or pleasant than what arose from perspiration . . .

Many to the right and left sunk with the violent pressure, and were soon suffocated; for now a steam arose from the living and the dead, which affected us in all its circumstances, as if we were forcibly held by our heads over a bowl of strong volatile spirit of hartshorn, until suffocated; nor could the effluvia of the one be distinguished from the other; and frequently, when I was forced by the load upon my head and shoulders, to hold my face down, I was obliged, near as I was to the window, instantly to raise it again, to escape suffocation . . .

When the day broke, and the gentlemen found that no intreaties could prevail to get the door opened, it occurred to one of them (I think to Mr Secretary Cooke) to make a search for me, in hopes I might have influence enough to gain a release from this scene of misery. Accordingly Messrs Lushington and Walcot undertook the search, and by my shirt discovered me under the dead upon the platform. They took me from thence, and imagining I had some signs of life, brought me towards the window I had first possession of.

But as life was equally dear to every man (and the stench arising from the dead bodies was grown so intolerable) no one would give up his station in or near the window: so they were obliged to carry me back again. But soon after Captain Mills, (now captain of the company's yacht) who was in possession of a seat in the window, had the humanity to offer to resign it. I was again brought by the same gentlemen and placed in the window.

At this juncture the suba [viceroy of Bengal], who had received an account of the havock death had made amongst us, sent one of his Jemmautdaars to enquire if the chief survived. They shewed me to him; told I had appearance of life remaining; and believed I might recover if the door was opened very soon. This answer being returned to the suba, an order came immediately for our release, it being then near six in the morning.

As the door opened inwards, and as the dead were piled up against it, and covered all the rest of the floor, it was impossible to open it by any efforts from without; it was therefore necessary that the dead should be removed by the few that were within, who were become so feeble, that the task, though it was the condition of life, was not performed without the utmost difficulty, and it was twenty minutes after the order came before the door could be opened.

About a quarter after six in the morning, the poor remains of 146 souls, being no more than three and twenty, came out of the black hole alive, but in a condition which made it very doubtful whether they would see the morning of the next day; among the living was Mrs Carey, but poor Leech was among the dead. The bodies were dragged out of the hole by the soldiers, and thrown promiscuously into the ditch of an unfinished ravelin, which was afterwards filled with earth.

A PERFECT STEAM ENGINE, SCOTLAND, *c.* 1765

John Robinson

At the breaking-up of the College (I think in 1765), I went to the country. About a fortnight after this, I came to town, and went to have a chat with Mr Watt, and to communicate to him some observations I had made on Desaguiliers' and Belidor's account of the steam-engine. I came into Mr Watt's parlour without ceremony, and found him sitting before the fire, having lying on his knee a little tin cistern, which he was looking at. I entered into conversation on what we had been speaking of at last meeting, – something about steam. All the while, Mr Watt kept looking at the fire, and laid down the cistern at the foot of his chair. At last he looked at me, and said briskly, 'You need not *fash* yourself any more about that, man; I have now got an engine that shall not waste a particle of steam. It shall be all boiling hot; – aye, and hot water injected if I please.' So saying, Mr Watt looked with complacency at the little thing at his feet, and, seeing that I observed him, he shoved it away under a table with his foot. I put a question to him about the nature of his contrivance. He answered me rather drily. I did not press him to a further explanation at that time, knowing that I had offended him a few days before by blabbing a pretty contrivance which he had hit on for turning the cocks of the engine. I had mentioned this in presence of an engine-builder who was going to erect one for a friend of mine; and this having come to Mr Watt's ears, he found fault with it.

I was very anxious, however, to learn what Mr Watt had contrived, but was obliged to go to the country in the evening. A gentleman who was going to the same house said he would give me a place in his carriage, and desired me to wait for him on the walk by the river-side. I went thither, and found Mr Alexander Brown; a very intimate acquaintance of Mr Watt's, walking with another gentleman, (Mr Craig, architect). Mr Brown immediately accosted me with, 'Well, have you seen Jamie Watt?' – 'Yes.'– 'He'll be in high spirits now with his engine, isn't he?' 'Yes,' said I, 'very fine spirits.' 'Gad,' says Mr Brown, 'the condenser's the thing: keep it but cold enough, and you may have perfect vacuum, whatever be the heat of the cylinder.' The instant he said this, the whole flashed on my mind at once. I did all I could to encourage the conversation, but was much embarrassed. I durst not appear ignorant of the apparatus, lest Mr Brown should find he had communicated more than he ought to have done. I could only learn that there was a vessel called a condenser which communicated with the cylinder, and that this condenser was immersed in cold water, and had a pump to clear it of the water which was formed in it. I also learned that the great difficulty was to make the piston tight; and that leather and felt had been tried, and were found quite unable to stand the heat. I saw that the whole would be perfectly dry, and that Mr Watt had used steam instead of air to press up his piston, which I thought, by Mr Brown's description was inverted. We parted, and I went home, a very silent companion to the gentleman who had given me a seat. Next day, impatient to see the effects of the separate condensation, I sent to Paisley and got some tin things made there, in completion of the notion I had formed. I tried it as an air-pump, by making my steam-vessel communicate with a tea-kettle, a condenser, and a glass receiver. In less than two minutes I rarefied the air in a pretty large receiver more than twenty times. I could go no farther in this process, because my pump for taking out the air from my condenser was too large, and not tight enough; but I saw that when applied to the mere process of taking out the air generated from the water, the vacuum might be made almost complete. I saw, too, (in consequence of a conversation the preceding day with Mr Watt about the eduction-pipe in Beighton's engine), that a long suck-pipe; or syphon, would take off all the water. In short, I had no doubt that Mr Watt had really made a perfect steam-engine.

THE AMERICAN WAR OF INDEPENDENCE: IN ACTION AGAINST THE BRITISH AT BUNKER HILL, 16–17 June 1775

Israel R. Potter

By the break of day Monday morning I swung my knapsack, shouldered my musket, and with the company commenced my march with a quick step for Charleston, where we arrived about sunset and remained encamped in the vicinity until about noon on the 16th June, when, having been previously joined by the remainder of the regiment from Rhode Island, to which our company was attached, we received orders to proceed and join a detachment of about 1000 American troops, which had that morning taken possession of Bunker Hill and which we had orders immediately to fortify, in the best manner that circumstances would admit of. We laboured all night without cessation and with very little refreshment, and by the dawn of day succeeded in throwing up a redoubt of eight or nine rods square. As soon as our works were discovered by the British in the morning, they commenced a heavy fire upon us, which was supported by a fort on Copp's hill; we however (under the command of the intrepid Putnam) continued to labour like beavers until our breast-work was completed.

About noon, a number of the enemy's boats and barges, filled with troops, landed at Charlestown, and commenced a deliberate march to attack us – we were now harangued by Gen. Putnam, who reminded us, that exhausted as we were, by our incessant labour through the preceding night, the most important part of our duty was yet to be performed, and that much would be expected from so great a number of excellent marksmen – he charged us to be cool, and to reserve our fire until the enemy approached so near as to enable us to see the white of their eyes – when within about ten rods of our works we gave them the contents of our muskets, and which were aimed with so good effect, as soon to cause them to turn their backs and to retreat with a much quicker step than with what they approached us. We were now again harangued by 'old General Put,' as he was termed, and requested by him to aim at the officers, should the enemy renew the attack – which they did in a few moments, with a reinforcement – their approach was with a slow step, which gave us an excellent opportunity to obey the commands of our General in bringing down their officers. I feel but little disposed to boast of my own performances on this occasion and will only say, that after devoting so many months in hunting the wild animals of the wilderness, while an inhabitant of New Hampshire, the reader will not suppose me a bad or inexperienced marksman, and that such were the fare shots which the epauletted red coats presented in the two attacks, that every shot which they received from me, I am confident on another occasion would have produced me a deer skin.

So warm was the reception that the enemy met with in their

second attack, that they again found it necessary to retreat, but soon after receiving a fresh reinforcement, a third assault was made, in which, in consequence of our ammunition failing, they too well succeeded – a close and bloody engagement now ensued – to fight our way through a very considerable body of the enemy, with clubbed muskets (for there were not one in twenty of us provided with bayonets) were now the only means left us to escape the conflict, which was a sharp and severe one, is still fresh in my memory, and cannot be forgotten by me while the scars of the wounds which I then received, remain to remind me of it! Fortunately for me, at this critical moment, I was armed with a cutlass, which although without an edge, and much rust-eaten, I found of infinite more service to me than my musket – in one instance I am certain it was the means of saving my life – a blow with a cutlass was aimed at my head by a British officer, which I parried and received only a slight cut with the point on my right arm near the elbow, which I was then unconscious of, but this slight wound cost my antagonist at the moment a much more serious one, which effectually *dis-armed* him, for with one well-directed stroke I deprived him of the power of very soon again measuring swords with a 'yankee rebel!' We finally however should have been mostly cut off, and compelled to yield to a superior and better equipped force, had not a body of three or four hundred Connecticut men formed a temporary breast work, with rails &c. and by which means held the enemy at bay until our main body had time to ascend the heights, and retreat across the neck; – in this retreat I was less fortunate than many of my comrades – I received two musket ball wounds, one in my hip and the other near the ankle of my left leg. I succeeded however without any assistance in reaching Prospect Hill, where the main body of the Americans had made a stand and commenced fortifying – from thence I was soon after conveyed to the Hospital in Cambridge, where my wounds were dressed and the bullet extracted from my hip by one of the Surgeons; the house was nearly filled with the poor fellows who like myself had received wounds in the late engagement, and presented a melancholy spectacle.

Bunker Hill fight proved a sore thing for the British, and will I doubt not be long remembered by them; while in London I heard it frequently spoken of by many who had taken an active part therein, some of whom were pensioners, and bore indelible proofs of American bravery – by them the Yankees, by whom they were opposed, were not infrequently represented as a set of infuriated beings, whom nothing could daunt or intimidate: and who, after their ammunition failed, disputed the ground, inch by inch, for a full hour with clubbed muskets, rusty swords, pitchforks and billets of wood, against the British bayonets:

THE FIRST AERIAL VOYAGE IN ENGLAND, LONDON, 15 September 1784

Vincent Lunardi

A little before two o'clock on Wednesday, Mr Biggin and myself were prepared for our expedition. His attention was allotted to the philosophical experiments and observations, mine to the conduct of the Machine, and the use of the vertical cars, in depressing the Balloon at pleasure.

The impatience of the multitude made it unadvisable to proceed in filling the Balloon so as to give it the force it was intended to have: the process being therefore stopped, I retired for a few minutes to recollect and refresh myself previous to my departure, when a servant brought me a sudden account that by the falling of one of the masts which had been erected for the purpose of suspending the Balloon while filling, it had received a material injury which might possibly retard, if not prevent my voyage. I hastened instantaneously from the Armory House, where I then was, and though I was happy to find that the accident was prevented by giving the falling fixture an opposite direction, yet I was so extremely shocked at the danger that menaced me, and the word I had received, that I did not possess myself or recover the effect of my apprehension during the remainder of my stay on the earth. The consequence was, that in the convulsion of my ideas, I forgot to supply myself with those instruments of observation which had been appointed for the voyage. On balancing the rising force of the Balloon, it was supposed incapable of taking up Mr Biggin with me, (whether he felt the most regret in relinquishing his design, or I in being deprived of his company it may be difficult to determine) but we were before a Tribunal, where an immediate decision was necessary, for hesitation and delay would have been construed into guilt, and the displeasure impending over us would have been fatal, if in one moment he had not the heroism to leave the gallery, and I the resolution to go alone. I now determined on my immediate ascension, being assured by the dread of any accident which might consign me and my Balloon to the fury of the populace, whose impatience had wrought them up to a degree of ferment. An affecting, because unpremeditated testimony of approbation and interest in my fate, was here given. The Prince of Wales, and the whole surrounding assembly, almost at one instant, took off hats, hailed my resolution, and expressed the kindest and most cordial wishes for my safety and success. At five minutes after two, the last gun was fired, the cords divided, and the Balloon rose, the company returning my signals of adieu with the most unfeigned acclamations and applauses. The effect was, that of a miracle, on the multitudes which surrounded the place; and they passed from incredulity and menace, into the most extravagant expressions of approbation and joy.

At the height of twenty yards,the Balloon was a little depressed by the wind, which had a fine effect; it held me over the ground for a few seconds, and seemed to pause majestically before its departure.

On discharging a part of the ballast, it ascended to the height of two hundred yards. As a multitude lay before me of a hundred and fifty thousand people, who had not seen my ascent from the ground, I had recourse to every stratagem to let them know I was in the gallery, and they literally rent the air with their acclamations and applause, in these stratagems I devoted my flag, and worked my oars, one of which was immediately broken, and fell from me, a pidgeon too escaped, which, with a dog, and cat, were the only companions of my excursions.

When the thermometer had fallen from 68°. to 61°. I perceived a great difference in the temperature of the air. I became very cold and found it necessary to take a few glasses of wine. I likewise ate the leg of a chicken, but my bread and other provisions had been rendered useless, by being mixed with the sand, which I carried as ballast.

When the thermometer was at fifty, the effect of the atmosphere and the combination of circumstances around, produced a calm delight, which is inexpressible, and which no situation on earth could give. The stillness, extent, and magnificence of the scene, rendered it highly awful. My horizon seemed a perfect circle; the terminating line several hundred miles in circumference. This I conjectured from the view of London; the extreme points of which, formed an angle of only a few degrees. It was so reduced on the great scale before me, that I can find no simile to convey an idea of it. I could distinguish Saint Paul's and other churches, from the houses. I saw the streets as lines, all animated with beings, whom I knew to be men and women, but which I should otherwise have had a difficulty in describing. It was an enormous bee-hive, but the industry of it was suspended. All the moving mass seemed to have no object but myself, and the transition from the suspicion, and perhaps contempt of the preceding hour, to the affectionate transport, admiration and glory of the present moment, was not without its effect on my mind. I recollected the puns on my name, and was glad to find myself calm. I had soared from the apprehensions and anxieties of the Artillery Ground, and felt as if I had left behind me all the cares and passions that molest mankind.

THE INDUSTRIAL REVOLUTION: THE MOB DESTROY THE MACHINES, ENGLAND, October 1779

Thomas Bentley

The introduction of technology, widely believed to cause unemployment, was often met by 'wrecking', a movement which reached its British apogee in the Luddism of the early nineteenth century.

I wrote to my dear friend last from Bolton, and I mention'd the mob which had assembled in that neighbourhood; but they had not done much mischief; they only destroyed a small engine or two near Chowbent. We met them on Saturday morning, but I apprehend what we saw were not the main body; for on the same day, in the afternoon, a capital engine or mill, in the manner of Arcrites, and in which he is a partner, near Chorley, was attacked; but from its peculiar situation they could approach to it by one passage only; and this circumstance enabled the owner, with the assistance of a few neighbours, to repulse the enemy and preserve the mill for that time. Two of the mob were shot dead upon the spot, one drowned, and several wounded. The mob had no fire-arms, and did not expect so warm a reception. They were greatly exasperated, and vowed revenge; accordingly they spent all Sunday and Monday morning in collecting fire-arms and ammunition and melting their pewter dishes into bullets. They were now join'd by the Duke of Bridgewater's colliers and others, to the number, we are told, of eight thousand, and march'd by beat of drum and with colours flying to the mill, where they met with a repulse on Saturday. They found Sir Richard Clayton guarding the place with fifty Invalids armed, but this handful were by no means a match for enraged thousands; they (the Invalids) therefore contented themselves with looking on, while the mob completely destroyed a set of mills valued at 10,000*l*.

This was Monday's employment. On Tuesday morning we heard their drum at about two miles distance from Bolton, a little, before we left the place, and their professed design was to take Bolton, Manchester, and Stockport on their way to Crumford, and to destroy all the engines not only on these places, but throughout all England. How far they will be able to put their threats into execution time alone can discover.

THE FRENCH REVOLUTION: THE ARREST OF LOUIS XVI and MARIE ANTOINETTE, VERSAILLES 5 October 1789

Thomas Blaikie

As the fermentation continued and the Assembly pretended they were not free at Versailles and the people emagining the falt of the government so they formed the resolution to go to Versailles and force the King and family with the Assembly to comme to Paris. As this was the project of the Jacobin club who Stuck at nothing all those revolutionary went of for Versailles to bring in the King and endeed such a rable was hardly ever seen; as they approached Versailles the gardes desired to defend the King but he ordered them to make no resistance although several of them was massacred and M. L'Heretier who was with the Paris gardes got into the appartements and saved the Queen who was in the greatest danger as the people hated the Queen as some people ensinuated that it was her that was the cause of the Scarcity of Bread &c Which was all done by other intrigues. However she was conducted into the King's appartement and the whole brought to Paris but the Scene was most chocking to See the poissards mounted up on the Cannon some with one of the gards coats or hatts and the poor gardes obliged to be conducted along with them in this manner and the heads of their comerades that was killed at Versailles brought along with them. The King and Queen and Dauphin was likewise conducted in this humiliating condition; the Maire of Paris was at the Barriere des Bonnes hommes below

Passy to receive them and as a form to present the Keys of the town to the King which might be looked upon rather as a Mockery than otherwise. The people was all roaring out 'Voila le Boulanger et la Boulangere et le Pitit Mitron' saying that now they should have Bread as they now had got the Baker and his wife and Boy. The Queen sat at the bottom of the Coach with the Dauphin on her Knees in this condition while some of the Blackguards in the rable was firing there guns over her head. As I stood by the coach one Man fired and loaded his gun four times and fired it over the Queens head. I told him to desiste but he said he would continue but when I told him I should try by force to stop him and not have people hurt by his imprudence some cryed it was right and so he Sluged of very quietelly and after the corte went on and they lodged the King and his familly in the thuilleries. So that every thing now began to change and the Jacobin club to triump and the royale familly keept as prisoners.

THE FRENCH REVOLUTION: THE CONDEMNED ARE SENT TO THE GUILLOTINE, PARIS, 1793

J. G. Millingen

Never can I forget the mournful appearance of these funereal processions to the place of execution. The march was opened by a detachment of mounted *gendarmes* – the carts followed; they were the same carts as those that are used in Paris for carrying wood; four boards were placed across them for seats, and on each board sat two, and sometimes three victims; their hands were tied behind their backs, and the constant jolting of the cart made them nod their heads up and down, to the great amusement of the spectators. On the front of the cart stood Samson, the executioner, or one of his sons or assistants; *gendarmes* on foot marched by the side; then followed a hackney-coach, in which was the *Rapporteur* and his clerk, whose duty it was to witness the execution, and then return to Fouquier-Tinville, the *Accusateur Publique*, to report the execution of what they called the law.

The process of execution was also a sad and heart-rending spectacle. In the middle of the Place de la Révolution was erected a guillotine, in front of a colossal statue of Liberty, represented seated on a rock, a Phrygian cap on her head, a spear in her hand, the other reposing on a shield. On one side of the scaffold were drawn out a sufficient number of carts, with large baskets painted red, to receive the heads and bodies of the victims. Those bearing the condemned moved on slowly to the foot of the guillotine; the culprits were led out in turn, and, if necessary, supported by two of the executioner's valets, as they were formerly called, but now denominated *élèves de l'Executeur des hautes oeuvres de la justice;* but their assistance was rarely required. Most of these unfortunates ascended the scaffold with a determined step – many of them looked up firmly on the menacing instrument of death, beholding for the last time the rays of the glorious sun, beaming on the polished axe; and I have seen some young men actually dance a few steps before they went up to be strapped to the perpendicular plane, which was then tilted to a horizontal plane in a moment, and ran on the grooves until the neck was secured and closed in by a moving board, when the head passed through what was called, in derision, *la lunette républicaine;* the weighty knife was then dropped with a heavy fall; and, with incredible dexterity and rapidity, two executioners tossed the body into the basket, while another threw the head after it.

THE BATTLE OF TRAFALGAR: THE DEATH OF LORD NELSON, 1 October 1805

Dr William Beatty

Trafalgar, off the port of Cadiz in Spain, was the decisive naval battle of the Napoleonic Wars. But Britain's victory over the combined French and Spanish fleet came at the cost of the life of the Lord Nelson.

It was from this Ship (the *Redoutable*) that Lord Nelson received his mortal wound. About fifteen minutes past one o'clock, which was in the heat of the engagement, he was walking the middle of the quarterdeck with Captain Hardy, and in the act of turning near the hatchway with his face towards the stern of the *Victory*, when the fatal ball was fired from the Enemy's mizen-top; which, from the situation of the two ships (lying on board of each other), was brought just abaft, and rather below, the *Victory's* main-yard, and of course not more than fifteen yards distant from that part of the deck where his Lordship stood. The ball struck the epaulette on his left shoulder, and penetrated his chest. He fell with his face on the deck. Captain Hardy, who was on his right (the side furthest from the Enemy) and advanced some steps before his Lordship, on turning round, saw the Sergeant-Major (Secker) of Marines with two Seamen raising him from the deck; where he had fallen on the same spot on which, a little before, his Secretary had breathed his last, with whose blood his Lordship's clothes were much soiled. Captain Hardy expressed a hope that he was not severely wounded; to which the gallant Chief replied: 'They have done for me at last, Hardy.' 'I hope not,' answered Captain Hardy. 'Yes,' replied his Lordship, 'my backbone is shot through.'

Captain Hardy ordered the Seamen to carry the Admiral to the cockpit; and now two incidents occurred strikingly characteristic of this great man, and strongly marking that energy and reflection which in his heroic mind rose superior even to the immediate consideration of his present awful condition. While the men were carrying him down the ladder from the middle deck, his Lordship observed that the tillar ropes were not yet replaced; and desired one of the Midshipmen stationed there to go up on the quarterdeck and remind Captain Hardy of that circumstance, and request that new ones should be immediately rove. Having delivered this order, he took his handkerchief from his pocket and covered his face with it, that he might be conveyed to the cockpit at this crisis unnoticed by the crew . . .

The *Victory*'s crew cheered whenever they observed an Enemy's Ship surrender. On one of these occasions, Lord Nelson anxiously inquired what was the cause of it; when Lieutenant Pasco, who lay wounded at some distance from his Lordship, raised himself up, and told him that another Ship had struck: which appeared to give him much satisfaction. He now felt an ardent thirst; and frequently called for drink, and to be fanned with paper, making use of these words: 'Fan, fan,' and 'Drink, drink.' This he continued to repeat, when he wished for drink or the refreshment of cool air, till a very few minutes before he expired . . .

His Lordship now requested the Surgeon, who had been previously absent a short time attending Mr Rivers to return to the wounded, and give his assistance to such of them as he could be useful to; 'for,' said he, 'you can do nothing for me.' The Surgeon assured him that the Assistant Surgeons were doing everything that could be effected for those unfortunate men; but on his Lordship's several times repeating his injunctions to that purpose, he left him, surrounded by Doctor Scott, Mr Burke and two of his Lordship's domestics. After the Surgeon had been absent a few minutes attending Lieutenants Peake and Reeves of the

Marines, who were wounded, he was called by Doctor Scott to his Lordship, who said: 'Ah, Mr Beatty! I have sent for you to say, what I forgot to tell you before, that all power of motion and feeling below my breast are gone; and *you*,' continued he, 'very well *know* I can live but a short time.' The emphatic manner in which he pronounced these last words left no doubt in the Surgeon's mind, that he adverted to the case of a man who had some months before received a mortal injury of the spine on board the *Victory*, and had laboured under similar privations of sense and muscular motion. The case had made a great impression on Lord Nelson: he was accordingly explained to him; and he now appeared to apply the situation and fate of this man to himself. The Surgeon answered, 'My Lord, you told me so before': but he now examined the extremities, to ascertain the fact; when his Lordship said, 'Ah, Beatty! I am too certain of it: Scott and Burke have tried it already. *You know* I am gone.' The Surgeon replied: 'My Lord, unhappily for our Country, nothing can be done for you', and having made this declaration he was so much affected, that he turned round and withdrew a few steps to conceal his emotions. His Lordship said: 'I know it. I feel something rising in my breast,' putting his hand on his left side, 'which tells me I am gone.' Drink was recommended liberally, and Doctor Scott and Mr Burke fanned him with paper. He often exclaimed, 'God be praised, I have done my duty': and upon the Surgeon's inquiring whether his pain was still very great, he declared, it continued so very severe, that he wished he was dead. 'Yet,' said he in a lower voice, 'one would like to live a little longer, too': and after a pause of a few minutes, he added in the same tone, 'What would become of poor Lady Hamilton [Nelson's mistress], if she knew my situation!' . . .

Captain Hardy now came to the cockpit to see his Lordship a second time, which was after an interval of about fifty minutes from the conclusion of his first visit. Before he quitted the deck, he sent Lieutenant Hills to acquaint Admiral Collingwood with the lamentable circumstance of Lord Nelson's being wounded. Lord Nelson and Captain Hardy shook hands again: and while the Captain retained his Lordship's hand, he congratulated him, even in the arms of death, on his brilliant victory; 'which,' said he, 'was complete'; though he did not know how many of the Enemy were captured, as it was impossible to perceive every Ship distinctly. He was certain however of fourteen or fifteen having surrendered. His Lordship answered, 'That is well, but I bargained for twenty': and then emphatically exclaimed, '*Anchor*, Hardy, *anchor*!' To this the Captain replied: 'I suppose, my Lord, Admiral Collingwood will now take upon himself the direction of affairs.' 'Not while I live, I hope, Hardy!' cried the dying Chief; and at that moment endeavoured ineffectually to raise himself from the bed. 'No,' added he; 'do *you* anchor, Hardy.' Captain Hardy then said: 'Shall *we* make the signal, Sir?' 'Yes,' answered his Lordship, 'for if I live, I'll anchor.' The energetic manner in which he uttered these his last orders to Captain Hardy, accompanied with his efforts to raise himself, evinced his determination never to resign the Command while he retained the exercise of his transcendent faculties, and that he expected Captain Hardy still to carry into effect the suggestions of his exalted mind; a sense of his duty overcoming the pains of death. He then told Captain Hardy, he felt that in a few minutes he should be no more; adding in a low tone, 'Don't throw me overboard, Hardy.' The Captain answered: 'Oh! no, certainly not', 'Then,' replied his Lordship, 'You know what to do: and', continued he, 'take care of my dear Lady Hamilton, Hardy: take care of poor Lady Hamilton. Kiss me, Hardy.' The Captain now knelt down, and kissed his cheek; when his Lordship said, 'Now I am satisfied. Thank God, I have done my duty.' Captain Hardy stood for a minute or two in silent contemplation: he knelt down again, and kissed his Lordship's forehead. His Lordship said: 'Who is that?' The Captain answered: 'It is Hardy'; to which his Lordship replied, 'God bless you, Hardy!' . . . His thirst now increased; and he called for 'drink, drink,' 'fan, fan,' and 'rub, rub,' addressing himself in the last case to Doctor Scott, who had been rubbing his Lordship's breast with his hand, from which he found some relief. These words he spoke in a very rapid manner, which rendered his articulation difficult: but he every now and then, with evident increase of pain, made a greater effort with his vocal powers, and pronounced distinctly these last words: 'Thank God, I have done my duty'; and this great sentiment he continued to repeat as long as he was able to give it utterance.

THE RETREAT OF NAPOLEON'S GRAND ARMÉE FROM RUSSIA, November 1812

Lieutenant H.A. Vossler

After defeating the Russians at Borodino, Napoleon entered Moscow unopposed on 15 September 1812. The early arrival of the Russian winter made his subsequent withdrawal calamitous. The author was a German serving with the Grand Armée.

In Smolensk I met several officers of my old regiment, which had been dissolved after the Grand Army's retreat from Moscow, and with them I joined forces. We had found a common billet in an empty house, heating the place with furniture and woodwork from neighbouring, unoccupied houses. But for food we had to pay almost its weight in gold. Apart from hunger, our main preoccupation was our next move. No shelter could be found for our horses. Some of them perished from the cold while others were stolen at night, which in turn led to reprisals by our troopers. I myself had already lost two of the four horses I had. At Viazma I had found a serviceable, ownerless carriage to which I had harnessed my horses. But I had been forced to abandon it when we were still three days away from Smolensk, the horses lacking the strength to haul it farther and the general chaos of the retreating army making further progress with it impossible in any case. For four days we held out in Smolensk, stiff with cold, determined not to leave the city before the Emperor did so. We believed that our best chance of keeping on the move was to be among the troops he selected for his escort. If this reduced, for the moment, our chance of getting enough to eat we were quite prepared to put up with it and go on eating horse flesh.

The city of Smolensk by now was little more than a heap of rubble for no night passed without several houses going up in flames. Not a single local inhabitant was left; all had turned their backs on their homes and fled . . .

We had been told that in Smolensk we would find provisions in plenty and, what we needed just as urgently, a corps of 40,000 fresh troops. We were to be cruelly disappointed. There was not so much as a single seasoned regiment, the city being inhabited entirely by the flotsam of the Grand Army.

Our hopes of joining the Emperor's escort came to nothing, but because of the cold we delayed our departure from Smolensk as long as possible. At last, on 13th November, the day after the departure of the Imperial Guard, we, too, resumed our retreat. The first day's march passed without mishap. On the second we were less fortunate. Great swarms of Cossacks kept pace with the vast and motley column on both sides of the road, using every opportunity the terrain afforded to harry us with cannon fire and to wear us down with sporadic attacks. In Krasnoye we caught up with the imperial headquarters which, on the night from the 15th to the 16th, came under fierce but not very successful attack, while we bivouacked half an hour away at Sarokino, anxiously awaiting the outcome of the battle. On the 16th and 17th we passed through Liady and Dubrovno, crossing the Dnieper and reaching Orzha on the 18th. After a day of rest we took the road to Minsk, constantly harassed by Cossacks, and reaching Bobr on the 22nd, where we were allowed another day of rest. Three more days of marching led us through Borisov, where we left the Minsk road and turned due east towards Vilna, and the banks of the Berezina. In a hamlet half an hour's ride from the river we established our billets. Here the remnants of the army drifted past us along the road, each man at his own pace and pleasure. Some abandoned the road for byways in the hope of finding something to eat. A few were lucky, but most paid for their foolhardiness with their lives or at least their liberty.

Near Krasnoye we had overtaken what remained of the army's disciplined core. In Orzha and again in Bobr we rejoined the rabble. As we approached the Berezina the disorganized throng began to crowd together. The regiments that remained intact were involved in constant skirmishes. Hour by hour the rearguard was trying to fend off the Russians pressing close behind. The number of battle-worthy units diminished day by day. We had hoped that our retreat could be halted at Minsk, but before ever we reached the city it had been seized by Admiral Chichagov, cutting off our line of withdrawal and forcing us to veer towards Vilna. On this town our remaining hopes were now centred.

I myself, from Smolensk onward, had been beset by every conceivable danger, hardship and privation. Constantly exposed on the march to enemy shot and shell, once barely escaping capture, in Orzha on the point of being roasted alive in a burning house and the previous day almost drowning in the Dnieper. I left Smolensk reasonably well mounted, all things considered, but by the 16th, in Liady, I had lost my useful little Cossack pony from weakness. My companions, more fortunate with their mounts, parted company with me and I continued on my way alone. At Orzha I had the good fortune to find a pair of top boots, laced, but on the very next day my last horse, a pony carrying my equipment, my top coat and my provisions, was captured together with my temporary servant. It had been several days since this horse was last able to carry me. Now I had lost my best protection against the cold – my coat. Though a Württemberg officer, who did not know me but thought I had an honest face, gave me a loan, first of two ducats, and later of six from his regimental war chest, gold was a poor substitute for food, and of no use whatever against the cold.

On the 24th I was entrusted with the odd and, under the prevailing conditions, preposterous mission of assembling all the stray chasseurs wandering along the road and re-forming them into a fighting unit. Being on foot I had some success by day in gathering and keeping together a few of them, but as soon as night fell and we had to look for sleeping quarters they discovered that I had not so much as a bite of food or anything else to offer them. So away they melted again. Though I realized that I would receive a reprimand if I should happen to meet my commanding officer next day without my retinue, I neither could nor would make even an attempt to force these famished men to stay with me by putting them under formal orders.

The night of the 24th to the 25th I found a barn filled with hay into which I dug myself deep to escape the cold. The next night I spent in a wood, out in the open in the snow, without so much as a fire, and had I not pulled myself together every now and again to walk up and down and keep my circulation going I would undoubtedly have frozen to death. Next day, however, fortune smiled on me, for I met a Frenchman encumbered with two sheepskin coats, one of which he sold me for three ducats. This happy accident revived my spirits and I continued on my way more purposefully. The day after I was even luckier, for as I approached a small village I came upon a Württemberg officer who gladdened me with the splendid news that my servant with my baggage and two horses had just arrived there and was enquiring after me. I hastened on and found that the officer had spoken no less than the truth. I doubt if I ever had a more welcome surprise or felt greater relief and contentment in all my life. Now at last I had some decent clothes to wear and was well mounted once more. From now on I could face the cold in comparative comfort. Though hungry, I set out warmer and in better spirits than for a long time, and at nightfall reached a village where I found, in one house, a sergeant and fifteen chasseurs of my regiment – well mounted, well armed, who had come this far by side roads and had just re-joined the main highway. They had pork meat and honey in plenty, and looked upon me as an honoured guest. I needed no urging and without further ado seized the proffered meat and finally ate my fill – something I had not done for at least four weeks. But this reckless meal of pork, washed down with cold water, was followed by a bout of diarrhoea that plagued me for more than a year before I was completely cured.

Undoubtedly I would have done better to keep to starvation rations. Even as I ate I was uneasily aware that I should have to pay for my excess, but I never imagined that the consequences would be quite so disastrous. Yet such was my famished state that I doubt whether even the foreknowledge of such an outcome – indeed the certainty of imminent death itself – would have held me back from eating till I could eat no more.

When I left Smolensk I had provisions for no more than one day, that is to say, a small bag of flour. By the next day I was already reduced to eating horse flesh and though, from time to time, I did come upon something more palatable it was usually no more than scraps offered me out of kindness by people who had little enough to spare. Never was it enough to still the pangs of hunger. Even of the revolting horse flesh there was never enough to go round. In these circumstances nothing was more natural than the greed with which I fell upon the pork.

The weather had been very changeable during our march from Smolensk to the Berezina. When we left the city the cold was still bitter, but by evening milder weather had set in and by next morning it was thawing. The thaw, accompanied by fierce gales, lasted several days. But as soon as the wind dropped and the sky cleared the cold returned, though not as severe as at Smolensk. Twenty-four hours later the temperature rose again and from then onward until we reached the Berezina remained tolerable.

Roads and footpaths were generally very slippery and made walking or marching something of a penance. The many ravines exhausted the horses' strength as much as the treacherous surface which after the thaw turned to solid ice. On the whole, however, the terrain was less difficult than on the road from Dogorobuzh to Smolensk. In the small towns along our way some of the inhabitants had remained. Most of them were Jews who did a roaring trade with the sale of inferior provisions in exchange for the loot the troops found too burdensome to carry. The Christians, less adept at trade but more venturesome, mostly roamed the countryside, taking revenge on their wretched enemies by robbing and murdering the stragglers among them.

In our hamlet half an hour's ride from the Berezina my chasseurs and I awaited our turn to cross the river, which we expected to come next morning. On the Emperor's orders two bridges had been thrown across the river near the village of Zembin, about fifteen miles above Borisov, a position which had first to be wrested from Admiral Chichagov in bitter fighting with heavy losses on both sides. One bridge was intended for wagons and heavy equipment, the other for cavalry and infantry. By the 27th November both were ready, but fate decreed that only a few were to have the chance of availing themselves of this safe and easy passage. On that day the bulk of the army, hard pressed by the pursuing Russians, was already massing on the banks of the river. But it was not until one o'clock in the morning of the 28th that the crossing began, with men and vehicles now crowding in upon the bridges. That for the wagons soon collapsed under the strain, and though it was repeatedly mended had become quite impassable by midday. No engineers could be found to undertake further repairs, everyone was intent only on saving his own skin. An immense flood of men, horses and wagons now surged towards the other bridge. In the frightful crush men and horses were squeezed and trampled underfoot in their hundreds. The bridge was so narrow that it could only take two or three men abreast. Those lucky enough to reach it pressed on eagerly, but still not fast enough for those behind. At the approaches to the bridge, officers and orderlies tried to maintain some sort of discipline, but they were powerless in the face of the ever increasing pressure. On the bridge itself those who did not move fast enough were pushed over the side. Many waded into the water and tried to get on to the bridge that way, only to find themselves thrust back with sword and bayonet, most of them losing their lives in the attempt. Around one o'clock the cry went up 'the Cossacks are coming'. Those on the periphery knew they would be their first victims. Any speeding up of the movement towards the bridge seemed utterly impossible, but the cry electrified the rabble and spurred everybody to a final effort. Groups of cavalrymen closed ranks and ruthlessly rode down every thing in their path. At the approaches to the bridge all semblance of order had ceased. Officers and orderlies had either fled before the raging mob or, if they stood their ground, had been cut to pieces. By now there were many trying to swim the river, but few succeeded. Most perished in the icy water. The fight for a passage reached its ultimate horror when the Russian guns began to find the range of the milling mass, spreading death and destruction. From now on it was a fight of each man against his neighbour. The stronger trampled their weaker comrades to the ground and struggled on until they, in turn, found their match in others stronger still. This ghastly scene ended only with the approach of darkness, when a detachment of French engineers on the far bank dismantled their end of the bridge, leaving what remained behind – men, horses, guns and wagons of every description – at the Russians' mercy.

This day, and the cruel spectacle of it all, is something I shall never forget as long as I live. Not indeed, that I had an easy time of it myself. With my chasseurs I had set out towards the bridge at three o'clock in the morning. Even at that early hour we found ourselves preceded by an immense mass of humanity. An even greater one pressed on us from behind. Soon I had lost sight of my chasseurs in the crowd. Only my servant and Regimental Quartermaster Veikelmann were still with me. The crush became so intolerable that I would gladly have turned back had it been possible. Towards noon there came a great push from behind and from one side. Many men and horses were thrown to the ground, I among them. I was pinned under my horse, began to be trampled underfoot and resigned myself to the end when the quartermaster, with an immense effort, dragged me clear. Together we succeeded in getting my horse to its feet as well. I remounted and we continued to press on. But it was not long before I got separated from my servant and the quartermaster and finally lost sight of them. Then the warning of the Cossacks' approach arose and spread panic. Despairing of ever reaching the bridge I turned towards the river bank in the hope of getting on to it from there, even if it meant abandoning my horse. But presently I was thrown to the ground once more by a sudden sharp thrust of the mob, caused by the impetus of a group of well-mounted officers, and was severely trampled and bruised. Once more I was about to resign myself to my fate, seeing how remote, in these conditions, was the chance of a helping hand, when I saw looming above me a fellow-German, a Saxon cuirassier. I called out to him, he seized me by the arm, pulled me up and heaved my horse to its feet also. I found it hard to express my relief and gratitude. My plan of making for the river bank and reaching the bridge from there appealed to him. With his huge, powerful horse he pressed ruthlessly on, riding down whatever could not get out of his way in time, and I followed in his wake. By an almost superhuman effort we reached the bank. Here there were no mounted men and only a few on foot, we being among the first to try this desperate expedient. We found ourselves right beside the bridge. Quickly I dismounted and pulled myself up on to it, but was just as quickly pushed off again. The second attempt succeeded. A few sharp blows from the flat of the cuirassier's sword brought my horse leaping up on to the bridge beside me, and leading it at a smart trot I reached the far bank. There I waited for my servant, the quartermaster and the admirable cuirassier. The two former, to my great delight, soon joined me, but there was no sign of the cuirassier. Finally, when the Russian gunfire began to straddle the bridge and all who had got safely across were gone, I too, departed with a heavy heart. I never saw the cuirassier again.

A large part of the army, and all its equipment except for a few guns, were lost at the Berezina. Though most of what remained consisted of sick, wounded, worn-out soldiers without weapons, a few weeks' rest and care could have restored most of them and turned them once more into a formidable army. All who reached the western bank were glad to turn their backs on this ill-fated river and made haste to Vilna. But on the very night following the crossing the skies cleared and a frost set in which grew daily more severe until it reached a degree unheard-of even in these parts. Our road led through Zembin, Radescowiczi, Molodeczno, Smorgonye and Osmyany. All these places had been furnished with garrisons and stores of every kind, but with the news of the disaster that had overtaken us and of the approach of the Russian Army of the South, the former had been pulled back and the latter removed or destroyed. Nowhere did we find provisions, and the few inhabitants who had returned to their homes were as badly off as we.

After our crossing of the Berezina the Russians pursued us less hotly, for they, too, suffered badly from the awful cold. The remnants of our army withdrew as quickly as cold, hunger and exhaustion allowed towards Vilna, harassed less by the enemy than by indescribable misery and hardship. Those who travelled singly hastened ahead of the main army to seize what little food there was. Many fugitives had reached Vilna as early as 6th December, and in the two days that followed the influx was such that it had needed only a river ahead and the Russians behind to reproduce at the gates of the city the scenes of the Berezina crossing. Indeed, on the 9th they *were* re-enacted when the Russian spearhead reached the gates simultaneously with our rear-guard and entered Vilna with them, pillaging and murdering as they went. A goodly number of those who had been lucky enough to reach the western bank of the Berezina perished from the cold before ever they reached Vilna. Even the strongest constitutions succumbed where there was no protection from the climate. Every day I thanked my Maker that in the very nick of time he had provided me with what was, under the circumstances, the most precious possible gift: a fur coat. With Quartermaster Veikelmann and my servant I travelled as far each day as our horses would carry us. Despite our overcoats and furs we suffered pitifully from the cold, and eager though we were to press on we never passed a wayside fire or a burning house without warming ourselves at the flames. In this way we succeeded in keeping up both our spirits and our circulation. Thanks also to the good progress we made we managed to find almost everywhere enough provisions to feed the three of us. My diarrhoea, however, grew ever more violent and greatly sapped my strength. Soon I was incapable of mounting my horse unaided. I therefore resolved to stay in Vilna if ever I got there.

In Radescowiczi we met a Württemberg lieutenant with a detachment of lancers. He was waiting for the rest of his regiment. Two days later he got caught up in a rearguard and the following night froze to death with most of his men while on picket duty. Two newly arrived Neapolitan cavalry regiments, fresh and unscarred by battle, fared little better. We met them two days' march from Vilna, but three days later they were utterly demoralized by the cold and more than half of them had perished. A detachment of some 2,000 Russian foot soldiers captured by the French in the battle for the Berezina crossings and driven with the army towards Vilna suffered a similar fate. Only a handful reached their destination. Most of them froze to death in bivouacs at night and many of the remainder, unable to keep up because of exhaustion or frost-bite, were shot by their guards and left lying by the roadside. On 7th December Quartermaster Veikelmann and I reached Vilna. My servant had died from exhaustion in the little village where we had spent the previous night. The previous day, December 6th, Napoleon had left the remnants of his army at

Smorgonye to return to Paris alone. He put the unfortunate Marshal Murat in charge who led the remains of the Grand Army to final destruction before abandoning them to flee to his kingdom of Naples.

WATERLOO, BELGIUM, 18 June 1815

Ensign Edmund Wheatley, the King's German Legion

The armies of Napoleon and the Duke of Wellington that met at Waterloo, a village in Belgium, were of similar size, at around 70,000 men apiece.

About ten o'clock, the order came to clean out the muskets and fresh load them. Half an allowance of rum was then issued, and we descended into the plain, and took our position in solid Squares. When this was arranged as per order, we were ordered to remain in our position but, if we like, to lay down, which the battalion did [as well as] the officers in the rere.

I took this opportunity of surveying our situation. It was singular to perceive the shoals of Cavalry and artillery suddenly in our rere all arranged in excellent order as if by a magic wand. The whole of the horse Guards stood behind us. For my part I thought they were at Knightsbridge barracks or prancing on St James's Street.

A Ball whizzed in the air. Up we started simultaneously. I looked at my watch. It was just eleven o'clock, Sunday . . . morning. In five minutes a stunning noise took place and a shocking havock commenced.

One could almost feel the undulation of the air from the multitude of cannon shot. The first man who fell was five files on my left. With the utmost distortion of feature he lay on his side and shrivelling up every muscle of the body he twirled his elbow round and round in acute agony, then dropped lifeless, dying as it's called a death of glory, heaving his last breath on the field of fame. *Dieu m'engarde!*

A black consolidated body was soon seen approaching and we distinguished by sudden flashes of light from the sun's rays, the iron-cased cavalry of the enemy. Shouts of 'Stand firm!' 'Stand fast!' were heard from the little squares around and very quickly these gigantic fellows were upon us.

No words can convey the sensation we felt on seeing these heavy-armed bodies advancing at full gallop against us, flourishing their sabres in the air, striking their armour with the handles, the sun gleaming on the steel. The long horse hair, dishevelled by the wind, bore an appearance confounding the senses to an astonishing disorder. But we dashed them back as coolly as the sturdy rock repels the ocean's foam. The sharp-toothed bayonet bit many an adventurous fool, and on all sides we presented our bristly points like the peevish porcupines assailed by clamorous dogs.

The horse Guards then came up and drove them back; and although the sight is shocking 'tis beautiful to see the skirmish of Cavalry.

The French made repeated attacks of this kind. But we stood firm as the ground we stood on, and two long hours were employed in these successive attacks.

About two o'clock the cavalry ceased annoying and the warfare took a new turn. In order to destroy our squares, the enemy filled the air with shells, howitzers and bombs, so that every five or six minutes, the whole Battalion lay on its face then sprang up again when [the danger] was over.

The Prince of Orange gallop'd by, screaming out like a new born infant, 'Form into line! Form into line!' And we obeyed.

About this time the battle grew faint and a mutual cannonade with musketry amused us for one and a half hours, during which time I walked up and down chatting and joking with the young officers who had not [until] then smelt powder.

An ammunition cart blew up near us, smashing men and horses. I took a calm survey of the field around and felt shocked at the sight of broken armour, lifeless bodies, murdered horses, shattered wheels, caps, helmets, swords, muskets, pistols, still and silent. Here and there a frightened horse would rush across the plain trampling on the dying and the dead. Three or four poor wounded animals standing on three legs, the other dangling before [them]. We killed several of these unfortunate beasts and it would have been an equal Charity to have perform'd the same operation on the wriggling, feverish, mortally lacerated soldiers as they rolled on the ground.

About four o'clock the battle was renewed with uncommon ardour. We still stood in line. The carnage was frightful. The balls which missed us mowed down the Dutch behind us, and swept away many of the closely embattled Cavalry behind them.

I saw a cannon ball take away a Colonel of the Nassau Regiment so cleanly that the horse never moved from under him. While [I was] buisy in keeping the men firm in their ranks, closing up the vacuities as the balls swept off the men, inspecting the fallen to detect deception [or] subterfuge, a regiment of Cuirassiers darted like a thunderbolt among us. At the instant a squadron of horse Guards dashed up to our rescue. In the confusion of the moment I made [for] the Colors to defend them. And we succeeded with infinite difficulty in rallying the men again.

I parried with great good fortune a back stroke from a horseman as he flew by me and Captain Sander had a deep slice from the same fellow on the head the instant after.

The battalion once more formed into a solid square, in which we remained the [whole] afternoon.

I felt the ardor of the fight increase very much within me, from the uncommon fury of the engagement.

Just then I fired a slain soldier's musket until my shoulder was nearly jellied and my mouth was begrimed with gunpowder to such a degree that I champed the gritty composition unknowingly.

Nothing could equal the splendor and terror of the scene. Charge after charge succeeded in constant succession. The clashing of swords, the clattering of musketry, the hissing of balls, and shouts and clamours produced a sound, jarring and confounding the senses, as if hell and the Devil were in evil contention.

About this time I saw the Duke of Wellington running from a charge of Cavalry towards the Horse-Guards, waving his hat to beckon them to the encounter.

All our artillery in front fell into the French power, the bombardiers skulking under the carriages. But five minutes put them again into our hands and the men creeping out applied the match and sent confusion and dismay into the retreating enemy.

Several times were these charges renewed and as often defeated. Charge met charge and all was pellmell. The rays of the sun glittered on the clashing swords as the two opposing bodies closed in fearful combat and our balls clattered on the shining breastplates like a hail shower.

As I stood in the square I looked down, I recollect, to take a pinch of snuff and thought of the old ballad, which I had seen somewhere, of the aged Nurse who describes the glorious battles of Marlborough to the child. After each relation of valor and victory, the infant [says]

> 'Ten thousand slain you say and more?
> What did they kill each other for?'

'Indeed I cannot tell,' said she,
'But 'twas a famous victory.'

The field was now thickened with heaps of bodies and shattered instruments. Carcases of men and beasts lay promiscuously entwined. Aide-de-Camps scoured across with inconceivable velocity. All was hurry and indefatigable exertion. The small squares on our right kept up incessant firings and the fight was as obstinate as at the commencement.

The Duke of Wellington passed us twice, slowly and coolly.

No advantage as yet was discernible on either side. The French Cavalry were less annoying. Their brave, repeated assaults had cost them very dear.

About six o'clock a passe-parole ran down the line – not to be disheartened, as the Prussians were coming up to our left, which news we received with loud cheers. And on looking [to] the left I perceived at some distance a dark swarm moving out of a thick wood. In twenty minutes a fresh cannonading began as if in rere of the French and the battle raged with increased vehemence.

A French Regiment of Infantry before us opposite the Farm house called the holy hedge (La Haye Sainte) advanced considerably just then and poured a destructive fire into our Battalion.

Colonel Ompteda ordered us instantly into line to charge, with a strong injunction to 'walk' forward, until he gave the word. When within sixty yards he cried 'Charge', we ran forward huzzaing. The trumpet sounded and no one but a soldier can describe the thrill one instantly feels in such an awful moment. At the bugle sound the French stood until we just reached them. I ran by Colonel Ompteda who cried out, 'That's right, Wheatley!'

I found myself in contact with a French officer but ere we could decide, he fell by an unknown hand. I then ran at a drummer, but he leaped over a ditch through a hedge in which he stuck fast. I heard a cry of, 'The Cavalry! The Cavalry!' But so eager was I that I did not mind it at the moment, and when on the eve of dragging the Frenchman back (his iron-bound hat having saved him from a Cut) I recollect no more. On recovering my senses, I look'd up and found myself, bareheaded, in a clay ditch with a violent head-ache. Close by me lay Colonel Ompteda on his back, his head stretched back with his mouth open, and a hole in his throat. A Frenchman's arm across my leg.

So confused was I that I did not remember I was on the field of

Battle at the moment. Lifting up a little, I look'd over the edge of the ditch and saw the backs of a French Regiment and all the day's employment instantly suggested itself to my mind. Suddenly I distinguished some voices and heard one say '*En voici! En voici!*'

I lay down as dead, retaining my breath, and fancied I was shot in the back of my head. Presently a fellow cries, '*Voici un autre b.*' And a tug at my epaulette bespoke his commission. A thought struck me – he would turn me round to rifle my pockets. So starting up, I leaped up the ditch; but a swimming seized me and I was half on the ground when the fellow thrust his hand in my collar, grinning, '*Ou va's tu, chien?*' I begged of him to let me pick up my cap and he dragged me into the house.

The inside of La Haye Sainte I found completely destroyed, nothing but the rafters and props remaining. The floor, covered with mortar bricks and straw, was strewed with bodies of the German Infantry and French Tirailleurs. A Major in Green lay by the door. The carnage had been very great in this place.

I was taken over these bodies out of a door on the right, through a garden to the back of the house where I found several Officers and men standing. [They] instantly crowded round me. One of my wings was on and the other half off. My oil skin haversac [was] across my shoulder, and my cap fastened to my waist, by running my sash through the internal lining.

A multitude of questions was put to me by the men and Officers while I fastened on my Cap: '*Vous êtes Chef de Battalion, Monsieur?*' . . .

Wheatley was unlucky to be captured so late in the day, for within the hour Wellington would begin the advance which would drive the French from the field.

PETERLOO, MANCHESTER, 16 April 1819

Samuel Bamford

A peaceful demonstration for universal suffrage was, on the orders of local magistrates, attacked by troops of the Cheshire Volunteers, the Manchester Yeomanry and 15th Hussars. Eleven protesters were killed.

In about half an hour after our arrival the sounds of music and reiterated shouts proclaimed the near approach of Mr Hunt and his party; and in a minute or two they were seen coming from

Deansgate, preceded by a band of music and several flags. On the driving seat of a barouche sat a neatly dressed female, supporting a small flag, on which were some emblematical drawings and an inscription. Within the carriage were Mr Hunt, who stood up, Mr Johnson, of Smedley Cottage; Mr Moorhouse, of Stockport; Mr Carlile, of London; Mr John Knight, of Manchester; and Mr Saxton, a sub-editor of the *Manchester Observer*. Their approach was hailed by one universal shout from probably eighty thousand persons. They threaded their way slowly past us and through the crowd, which Hunt eyed, I thought, with almost as much of astonishment as satisfaction. This spectacle could not be otherwise in his view than solemnly impressive. Such a mass of human beings he had not beheld till then. His responsibility must weigh on his mind. Their power for good or evil was irresistible, and who should direct that power? Himself alone who had called it forth. The task was great, and not without its peril. The meeting was a tremendous one. He mounted the hustings; the music ceased; Mr Johnson proposed that Mr Hunt should take the chair; it was seconded, and carried with acclamation; and Mr Hunt, stepping towards the front of the stage, took off his white hat, and addressed the people.

Whilst he was doing so, I proposed to an acquaintance that, as the speeches and resolutions were not likely to contain anything new to us, and as we could see them in the papers, we should retire awhile and get some refreshment, of which I stood much in need, being not in very robust health. He assented, and we had got to nearly the outside of the crowd, when a noise and strange murmur arose towards the church. Some persons said it was the Blackburn people coming, and I stood on tip-toe and looked in the direction whence the noise proceeded, and saw a party of cavalry in blue and white uniform come trotting, sword in hand, round the corner of the garden-wall, and to the front of a row of new houses, where they reined up in a line.

'The soldiers are here,' I said; 'we must go back and see what this means.' 'Oh,' some one made reply, 'they are only come to be ready if there should be any disturbance in the meeting.' 'Well, let us go back,' I said, and we forced our way towards the colours.

On the cavalry drawing up they were received with a shout of good-will, as I understood it. They shouted again, waving their sabres over their heads; and then, slackening rein, and striking spur into their steeds, they dashed forward and began cutting the people.

'Stand fast,' I said, 'they are riding upon us; stand fast.' And there was a general cry in our quarter of 'Stand fast.' The cavalry were in confusion: they evidently could not, with all the weight of man and horse, penetrate that compact mass of human beings; and their sabres were plied to hew a way through naked held-up hands and defenceless heads; and then chopped limbs and wound-gaping skulls were seen; and groans and cries were mingled with the din of that horrid confusion. 'Ah! Ah!' 'for shame! for shame!' was shouted. Then, 'Break! break! they are killing them in front, and they cannot get away'; and there was a general cry of 'break! break!' For a moment the crowd held back as in a pause; then was a rush, heavy and resistless as a headlong sea, and a sound like low thunder, with screams, prayers, and imprecations from the crowd moiled and sabre-doomed who could not escape.

By this time Hunt and his companions had disappeared from the hustings, and some of the yeomanry, perhaps less sanguinarily disposed than others, were busied in cutting down the flag-staves and demolishing the flags at the hustings.

On the breaking of the crowd the yeomanry wheeled, and, dashing whenever there was an opening, they followed, pressing and wounding. Many females appeared as the crowd opened; and striplings or mere youths also were found. Their cries were piteous and heart-rending, and would, one might have supposed, have disarmed any human resentment: but here their appeals were in vain. Women, white-vested maids, and tender youths, were indiscriminately sabred or trampled; and we have reason for believing that few were the instances in which that forbearance was vouchsafed which they so earnestly implored.

In ten minutes from the commencement of the havoc the field was an open and almost deserted space. The sun looked down through a sultry and motionless air. The curtains and blinds of the windows within view were all closed. A gentleman or two might occasionally be seen looking out from one of the new houses before mentioned, near the door of which a group of persons (special constables) were collected, and apparently in conversation; others were assisting the wounded or carrying off the dead. The hustings remained, with a few broken and hewed flag-staves erect, and a torn and gashed banner or two dropping; whilst over the whole field were strewed caps, bonnets, hats, shawls, and shoes, and other parts of male and female dress, trampled, torn, and bloody. The yeomanry had dismounted – some were easing their horses' girths, others adjusting their accoutrements, and some were wiping their sabres. Several mounds of human beings still remained where they had fallen, crushed down and smothered. Some of these still groaning, others with staring eyes, were gasping for breath, and others would never breathe more. All was silent save those low sounds, and the occasional snorting and pawing of steeds. Persons might sometimes be noticed peeping from attics and over the tall ridgings of houses, but they quickly withdrew, as if fearful of being observed, or unable to sustain the full gaze of a scene so hideous and abhorrent.

THE INDUSTRIAL REVOLUTION: THE BLACK COUNTRY, ENGLAND, 1830

James Nasmyth

On leaving Coalbrookdale I trudged my way towards Wolverhampton. I rested at Shiffnal for the night. Next day I was in the middle of the Black Country. I had no letters of introduction to employers in Wolverhampton; so that, without stopping there, I proceeded at once to Dudley. The Black Country is anything but picturesque. The earth seems to have been turned inside out. Its entrails are strewn about; nearly the entire surface of the ground is covered with cinder-heaps and mounds of scoriae. The coal, which has been drawn from below ground, is blazing on the surface. The district is crowded with iron furnaces, puddling furnaces and coal-pit engine furnaces. By day and by night the country is glowing with fire, and the smoke of the ironworks hovers over it. There is a rumbling and clanking of iron forges and rolling mills. Workmen covered with smut, and with fierce white eyes, are seen moving about amongst the glowing iron and dull thud of forge-hammers.

Amidst these flaming, smoky, clanging works, I beheld the remains of what had once been happy farmhouses, now ruined and deserted. The ground underneath them had sunk by the working out of the coal, and they were falling to pieces. They had in former times been surrounded by clumps of trees but only the skeletons of them remained, dilapidated, black, and lifeless. The grass had been parched and killed by the vapours of sulphureous acid thrown out by the chimneys; and every herbaceous object was of a ghastly gray – the emblem of vegetable death in its saddest aspect. Vulcan had driven out Ceres. In some places I heard a sort of chirruping sound, as of some forlorn bird haunting the ruins of the old farmsteads. But no! the chirrup was a vile delusion. It proceeded from the shrill creaking of the coal-winding chains, which were placed in small tunnels beneath the hedgeless road.

I went into some of the forges to see the workmen at their labours. There was no need of introduction; the works were open to all, for they were unsurrounded by walls. I saw the white-hot iron run out from the furnace; I saw it spun, as it were, into bars and iron ribbands, with an ease and rapidity which seemed marvellous. There were also the ponderous hammers and clanking rolling-mills. I wandered from one to another without restraint. I lingered among the blast furnaces, seeing the flood of molten iron run out from time to time, and remained there until it was late. When it became dark the scene was still more impressive. The workmen within seemed to be running about amidst the flames as in a pandemonium; while around and outside the horizon was a glowing belt of fire, making even the stars look pale and feeble. At last I came away with reluctance, and made my way towards Dudley. I reached the town at a late hour. I was exhausted in mind and body, yet the day had been most interesting and exciting. A sound sleep refreshed me, and I was up in the morning early, to recommence my journey of inquiry.

I made my way to the impressive ruins of Dudley Castle, the remnant of a very ancient stronghold, originally built by Dud, the Saxon. The castle is situated on a finely wooded hill; it is so extensive that it more resembles the ruins of a town than of a single building. You enter through a treble gateway, and see the remnants of the moat, the court, and the keep. Here are the central hall, the guard-rooms and the chapel. It must have been a magnificent structure. In the Midlands it was known as the 'Castle of the Woods'. Now it is abandoned by its owners, and surrounded by the Black Country. It is undermined by collieries, and even penetrated by a canal. The castle walls sometimes tremble when a blast occurs in the bowels of the mountain beneath. The town of Dudley lies quite close to the castle, and was doubtless protected by it in ancient times.

The architectural remains are of various degrees of antiquity, and are well worthy of study, as embodying the successive periods which they represent. Their melancholy grandeur is rendered all the more impressive by the coal and iron works with which they are surrounded – the olden type of buildings confronting the modern. The venerable trees struggle for existence under the destroying influence of sulphureous acid; while the grass is withered and the vegetation everywhere blighted. I sat down on an elevated part of the ruins, and looking down upon the extensive district, with its roaring and blazing furnaces, the smoke of which blackened the country as far as eye could reach; and as I watched the decaying trees I thought of the price we had to pay for our vaunted supremacy in the manufacture of iron. We may fill our purses, but we pay a heavy price for it in the loss of picturesqueness and beauty.

FIRST EXCURSION ON THE LIVERPOOL–MANCHESTER RAILWAY, 25 August 1830

Fanny Kemble

A party of sixteen persons was ushered into a large court-yard, where, under cover, stood several carriages of a peculiar construction, one of which was prepared for our reception. It was a long-bodied vehicle with seats placed across it, back to back; the one we were in had six of these benches, and was a sort of uncovered *char à banc*. The wheels were placed upon two iron bands, which formed the road, and to which they are fitted, being so constructed as to slide along without any danger of hitching or becoming displaced, on the same principle as a thing sliding on a concave groove. The carriage was set in motion by a mere push, and, having received this impetus, rolled with us down an inclined plane into a tunnel, which forms the entrance to the railroad. This tunnel is four hundred yards long (I believe), and will be lighted by gas. At the end of it we emerged from darkness, and, the ground becoming level, we stopped. There is another tunnel parallel with this, only much wider and longer, for it extends from the place which we had now reached, and where the steam-carriages start, and which is quite out of Liverpool, the whole way under the town, to the docks. This tunnel is for waggons and other heavy carriages; and as the engines which are to draw the trains along the railroad do not enter these tunnels, there is a large building at this entrance which is to be inhabited by steam-engines of a stationary turn of mind, and different constitution from the travelling ones, which are to propel the trains through the tunnels to the terminus in the town, without going out of their houses themselves. The length of the tunnel parallel to the one we passed through is (I believe) two thousand two hundred yards. I wonder if you are understanding one word I am saying all this while! We were introduced to the little engine which was to drag us along the rails. She (for they make these curious little fire-horses all mares) consisted of a boiler, a stove, a small platform, a bench, and behind the bench a barrel containing enough water to prevent her being thirsty for fifteen miles, – the whole machine not bigger than a common fire-engine. She goes upon two wheels, which are her feet, and are moved by bright steel legs called pistons; these are propelled by steam, and in proportion as more steam is applied to the upper extremities (the hip-joints, I suppose) of these pistons, the faster they move the wheels; and when it is desirable to diminish the speed, the steam, which unless suffered to escape would burst the boiler, evaporates through a safety-valve into the air. The reins, bit, and bridle of this wonderful beast is a small steel handle, which applies or withdraws the steam from its legs or pistons, so that a child might manage it. The coals, which are its oats, were under the bench, and there was a small glass tube affixed to the boiler, with water in it, which indicates by its fulness or emptiness when the creature wants water, which is immediately conveyed to it from its reservoirs. There is a chimney to the stove, but as they burn coke there is none of that dreadful black smoke which accompanies the progress of a steam-vessel. This snorting little animal, which I felt rather inclined to pat, was then harnessed to our carriage, and Mr Stephenson having taken me on the bench of the engine with him, we started at about ten miles an hour. The steam-horse being ill adapted for going up and down hill, the road was kept at a certain level, and appeared sometimes to sink below the surface of the earth, and sometimes to rise above it. Almost at starting it was cut through the solid rock, which formed a wall on either side of it, about sixty feet high. You can't imagine how strange it seemed to be journeying on thus, without any visible cause of progress other than the magical machine, with its flying white breath and rhythmical, unvarying pace, between these rocky walls, which are already clothed with moss and ferns and grasses; and when I reflected that these great masses of stone had been cut asunder to allow our passage thus far below the surface of the earth, I felt as if no fairy tale was ever half so wonderful as what I saw. Bridges were thrown from side to side across the top of these cliffs, and the people looking down upon us from them seemed like pigmies standing in the sky. I must be more concise, or I shall want room. We were to go only fifteen miles, that distance being sufficient to show the speed of the engine, and to take us on to the most beautiful and wonderful object on the road. After proceeding through this rocky defile, we presently found ourselves raised upon embankments ten or twelve feet high; we then came to a moss, or swamp of considerable extent, on which no human foot could tread without sinking, and yet it bore the road which bore us. This had been the great stumbling-block in the minds of the committee of the House of Commons; but Mr Stephenson has succeeded in overcoming it. A foundation of hurdles, or as he called it, basket-work, was thrown over the morass, and the interstices were filled with moss and other elastic matter. Upon this the clay and soil were laid down, and the road *does* float, for we passed over it at the rate of five and twenty miles an hour, and saw the stagnant swamp water trembling on the surface of the soil on either side of us. I hope you understand me. The embankment had gradually been rising higher and higher, and in one place, where the soil was not settled enough to form banks, Stephenson had constructed artificial ones of wood-work, over which the mounds of earth were heaped, for he calculated that though the wood-work would rot, before it did so the banks of earth which covered it would have been sufficiently consolidated to support the road.

We had now come fifteen miles, and stopped where the road traversed a wide and deep valley. Stephenson made me alight and led me down to the bottom of this ravine, over which, in order to keep his road level, he has thrown a magnificent viaduct of nine arches, the middle one of which is seventy feet high, through which we saw the whole of this beautiful little valley. It was lovely and wonderful beyond all words. He here told me many curious things respecting this ravine: how he believed the Mersey had once rolled through it; how the soil had proved so unfavourable for the foundation of his bridge that it was built upon piles, which had been driven into the earth to an enormous depth; how, while, digging for a foundation, he had come to a tree bedded in the earth fourteen feet below the surface of the ground; how tides are caused, and how another flood might be caused; all of which I have remembered and noted down at much greater length than I can enter upon it here. He explained to me the whole construction of the steam-engine, and said he could soon make a famous engineer of me, which, considering the wonderful things he *has* achieved, I dare not say is impossible. His way of explaining himself is peculiar, but very striking, and I understood, without difficulty, all that he said to me. We then rejoined the rest of the party, and the engine having received its supply of water, the carriage was placed behind it, for it cannot turn, and was set off at its utmost speed, thirty-five miles an hour, swifter than a bird flies (for they tried the experiment with a snipe). You cannot conceive what that sensation of cutting the air was; the motion is as smooth as possible, too. I could either have read or written; and as it was, I stood up, and with my bonnet off 'drank the air before me.' The wind, which was strong, or perhaps the force of our thrusting against it, absolutely weighed my eyelids down. When I closed my eyes this sensation of flying was quite delightful, and strange beyond description; yet, strange as it was, I had a perfect sense of security, and not the slightest fear. At one time, to exhibit the power of the engine, having met another steam-carriage which was unsupplied with water, Mr Stephenson caused it to be fastened in front of ours; moreover, a waggon laden with timber was also chained to us, and thus propelling the idle steam-engine, and dragging the loaded waggon which was beside it, and our own carriage full of people behind, this brave little she-dragon of ours flew on. Farther on she met three carts, which being fastened in front of her, she pushed on before her without the slightest delay or difficulty; when I add that this pretty little creature can run with equal facility either backwards or forwards, I believe I have given you an account of all her capacities.

THE INDUSTRIAL REVOLUTION: CHILD LABOUR IN ENGLAND, 1833

Ellen Hootton

Evidence given before the Parliamentary Commission inquiry into child labour in mines and manufactories.

How old are you? – I shall be ten on the 4th August.

How old were you when you began to work in Eccles' factory [at Wigan]? – I wasn't quite eight. Worked there above a year.

Were you beaten and scolded at Eccles'? – Yes. Who by? – William Swanton. What for? – For having my ends down. How often were you beaten by him? – Twice a week. What with? – His hands. Did he hurt you much? – No; but it made my head sore with his hands.

Did Mr Swanton ever tie a weight to you? – Yes, to my back. What was it tied with, a string? – Yes, it was tied with one string round my neck, one round my shoulders, and one round my middle. How heavy was it? – I don't know. It was a great piece of iron, and two more beside. How big were they? – One was as big as this book (pointing to the Lords' Report of 1818). Was it as thick? – No; it was thicker. (Pointing to an unbound octavo book of 419 pages.) As thick as that.

What time of the day was it? – It was after breakfast. How long was it kept on you? – About half an hour. What did you do? – I walked up and down the room. What did you walk up and down the room for? – He made me. Was it that other children might see you with it? – Yes.

Did you ever see such weights tied to other children? – Yes; there was one other that had them tied to his legs. Was there more than one? – Yes, there was two beside him. How long did they wear it? – About an hour. Did they walk up and down the room too? – Yes.

Now mind and don't tell a lie; what had you done? – I did nothing but run away because he beat me. Had you stolen any thing? – No. Did you tell your mother of it? – Yes. She said nothing.

Is your father dead? – I have no father.

ENTERING THE FORBIDDEN CITY, MECCA, 1835

Sir Richard Burton

Burton was one of the more colourful explorers of the African continent. He visited Mecca disguised as an Afghan Muslim.

So, after staying at Medinah for about six weeks, I set out with the Damascus Caravan down the Darb el Sharki, under the care of a very venerable Bedawin, who nicknamed me 'Abu Shuwarib', – meaning 'Father of Moustachios', mine being very large. I found myself standing opposite the Egyptian gate of El Medinah, surrounded by my friends – those friends of a day, who cross the phantasmagoria of one's life. There were affectionate embraces and parting mementoes. The camels were mounted; I and the boy Mohammed in the litter or *shugduf*, and Shaykh Nur in his cot. The train of camels with the Caravan wended its way slowly in a direction from north to north-east, gradually changing to eastward. After an hour's travel, the Caravan halted to turn and take farewell of the Holy City.

We dismounted to gaze at the venerable minarets and the green dome which covers the tomb of the Prophet. The heat was dreadful, the climate dangerous, and the beasts died in numbers. Fresh carcases strewed our way, and were covered by foul vultures. The Caravan was most picturesque. We travelled principally at night, but the camels had to perform the work of goats, and step from block to block of basalt like mountaineers, which being unnatural to them, they kept up a continual piteous moan. The simoom and pillars of sand continually threw them over.

Water is the great trouble of a Caravan journey, and the only remedy is to be patient and not to talk. The first two hours gives you the mastery, but if you drink you cannot stop. Forty-seven miles before we reached Mecca, at El Zaribah, we had to perform the ceremony of El Ihram, meaning 'to assume the pilgrim garb'. A barber shaved us, trimmed our moustaches; we bathed and perfumed, and then we put on two new cotton cloths, each six feet long by three and a half broad. It is white, with narrow red strips and fringe, and worn something as you wear it in the baths. Our heads and feet, right shoulder and arm, are exposed.

We had another fight before we got to Mecca, and a splendid camel in front of me was shot through the heart. Our Sherif Zayd was an Arab Chieftain of the purest blood, and very brave. He took two or three hundred men, and charged our attackers. However, they shot many of our dromedaries and camels, and boxes and baggage strewed the place; and when we were gone the Bedawi would come back, loot the baggage, and eat the camels. On Saturday, the 10th of September, at one in the morning, there was great excitement in the Caravan, and loud cries of 'Mecca! Mecca! Oh, the Sanctuary, the Sanctuary!' All burst into loud praises and many wept. We reached it next morning, after ten days and nights from El Medinah. I became the guest of the boy Mohammed, in the house of his mother.

First I did the circumambulation of the Haram. Early next morning I was admitted to the house of our Lord; and we went to the holy well Zemzem, the holy water of Mecca, and then the Ka'abah, in which is inserted the famous black stone, where they say a prayer for the Unity of Allah. Then I performed the seven circuits round the Ka'abah, called the *Tawaf*. I then managed to have a way pushed for me through the immense crowd to kiss it. While kissing it, and rubbing hands and forehead upon it, I narrowly observed it, and came away persuaded that it is an aerolite. It is curious that almost all agree upon one point, namely, that the stone is volcanic. Ali Bey calls it mineralogically a 'block of volcanic basalt, whose circumference is sprinkled with little crystals, pointed and strawlike, with rhombs of tile-red felspath upon a dark ground like velvet or charcoal, except one of its protuberances, which is reddish'. It is also described as 'a lava containing several small extraneous particles of a whitish and of a yellowish substance'.

All this time the pilgrims had scorched feet and burning heads, as they were always uncovered. I was much impressed with the strength and steadfastness of the Mohammedan religion. It was so touching to see them; one of them was clinging to the curtains, and sobbing as though his heart would break. At night I and Shaykh Nur and the boy Mohammed issued forth with the lantern and praying-carpet.

The moon, now approaching the full, tipped the brow of Abu Kubaya, and lit up the spectacle with a more solemn light. In the midst stood the huge bier-like erection – 'Black as the wings which some spirit of ill o'er a sepulchre flings!' – except where the moonbeams streaked it like jets of silver falling upon the darkest marble. It formed the point of rest for the eyes; the little pagoda-like buildings and domes around it, with all their gilding and framework, faded to the sight. One object, unique in appearance, stood in view – the temple of the one Allah, the God of Abraham, of Ishmael, and of their posterity. Sublime it was, and expressing by all the eloquence of fancy and grandeur of the one idea which vitalized El Islam, and the strength and steadfastness of its votaries.

One thing I remarked, and think worthy of notice, is that ever since Noah's dove, every religion seems to consider the pigeon a sacred bird. For example, every Mosque swarms with pigeons; St Mark's at Venice, and the same exists in most Italian market-places; the Hindoo pandits and the old Assyrian Empire also have them; whilst Catholics make it the emblem of the Holy Ghost.

The day before I went to Arafat, I spent the night in the Mosque, where I saw many strange sights. One was a negro possessed by the devil. There, too, he prayed by the grave of

Ishmael. After this we set out for Arafat, where is the tomb of Adam. (I have seen two since – one at Jerusalem, and one in the mountains behind Damascus!)

It was a very weary journey and, with the sun raining fire on our heads and feet, we suffered tortures. The camels threw themselves on the ground, and I myself saw five men fall out and die. On the Mount there were numerous consecrated shrines to see, and we had to listen to an immensely long sermon. On the great festival day we stoned the Devil, each man with seven stones washed in seven waters, and we said, while throwing each stone, 'In the name of Allah – and Allah is Almighty – I do this in hatred of the Devil, and to his shame.' There is then an immense slaughter of victims (five or six thousand), which slaughter, with the intense heat, swarms of flies, and the whole space reeking with blood, produces the most noisome vapours, and is probably the birthplace of that cholera and smallpox which generally devastate the World after the Haj.

Now we were allowed to doff the pilgrim's garb. We all went to barbers' booths, where we were shaved, had our beards trimmed and our nails cut, saying prayers the while; and, though we had no clothes, we might put our clothes over our heads and wear our slippers, which were a little protection from the heat. We might then twirl our moustachios, stroke our beards, and return to Mecca. At the last moment I was sent for. I thought, 'Now something is going to happen to me. Now I am suspected.'

A crowd stood gathered round the Ka'abah, and I had no wish to stand bareheaded and barefooted in the midday September sun. At the cry of 'Open a path for the Haji (pilgrim) who would enter the House!' the gazers made way. Two stout Meccans, who stood below the door, raised me in their arms, whilst a third drew me from above into the building. At the entrance I was accosted by several officials, dark-looking Meccans, of whom the blackest and plainest was a youth of the Benu Shaybah family, the true blood of the El Hejaz. He held in his hand the huge silver-gilt padlock of the Ka'abah, and presently, taking his seat upon a kind of wooden press in the left corner of the hall, he officially inquired my name, nation, and other particulars. The replies were satisfactory, and the boy Mohammed was authoritatively ordered to conduct me round the building, and to recite the prayers. I will not deny that, looking at the windowless walls, the officials at the door, and a crowd of excited fanatics below – 'And the place death, considering who I was,' my feelings were of the trapped-rat description, acknowledged by the immortal nephew of his uncle Perez. A blunder, a hasty action, a misjudged word, a prayer or bow, not strictly the right shibboleth, and my bones would have whitened the desert sand. This did not, however, prevent my carefully observing the scene during our long prayer, and making a rough plan with a pencil upon my white *ihram*.

I returned home after this *quite* exhausted, performed an elaborate toilet, washing with henna and warm water, to mitigate the pain the sun had caused on my shoulders, and breast, head and feet, and put on my gayest clothes in honour of the festival. When the moon rose, there was a second stoning, or lapidation, to be performed, and then we strolled round the coffee-houses. There was also a little pilgrimage to undertake, which is in honour of Hagar seeking water for her son Ishmael.

I now began to long to leave Mecca. I had done everything, seen everything. The heat was simply unendurable, and the little room where I could enjoy privacy for about six hours a day, and jot my notes down, was a perfect little oven.

I slowly wended my way with a Caravan to Jeddah, with donkeys and Mohammed. I must say that the sight of the sea and the British flag was a pleasant tonic. I went to the British Consulate, but the Dragomans were not very civil to the unfortunate 'Afghan'.

So I was left kicking my heels at the Great Man's gate for a long time, and heard somebody say, 'Let the dirty nigger wait.' Long inured to patience, however, I did wait, and when the Consul consented to see me, I presented him with a bit of paper, as if it were a money order. On it was written, 'Don't recognize me. I am Dick Burton, but I am not safe yet. Give me some money (naming the sum), which will be returned from London, and don't take any notice of me.' He, however, frequently afterwards, when it was dark, sent for me and, once safe in his private room, showed me abundance of hospitality. Necessity compelled me living with Saykh Nur in a room (to myself), swept, sprinkled with water, and spread with mats.

When I went out in gay attire, I was generally mistaken for the Pasha of El Medinah. After about ten days' suspense, an English ship was sent by the Bombay Steam Navigation Company to convey pilgrims from El Hejaz to India, so one day the 'Afghan' disappeared – was supposed to have departed with other dirty pilgrims, but in reality had got on board the *Dwarka*, an English ship, with a first-class passage; he had emerged from his cabin, after washing all his colouring off, in the garb of an English gentleman; experienced the greatest kindness from the Commander and Officers which he much needed, being worn out with fatigue and the fatal fiery heat, and felt the great relief to his mind and body from being able to take his first complete rest in safety on board an English ship; but was so changed that the Turkish pilgrims, who crowded the deck, never recognized their late companion pilgrim.

A SLAVE-MART, NATCHEZ, AMERICA, *c.* 1834

Joseph Ingraham

'Will you ride with me into the country?' said a young planter. 'I am about purchasing a few negroes and a peep into a slave-mart may not be uninteresting to you.' I readily embraced the opportunity and in a few minutes our horses were at the door.

A mile from Natchez we came to a cluster of rough wooden buildings, in the angle of two roads, in front of which several saddle-horses, either tied or held by servants, indicated a place of popular resort.

'This is the slave market,' said my companion, pointing to a building in the rear; and alighting, we left our horses in charge of a neatly dressed yellow boy belonging to the establishment. Entering through a wide gate into a narrow court-yard, partially enclosed by low buildings, a scene of a novel character was at once presented. A line of negroes, commencing at the entrance with the tallest, who was not more than five feet eight or nine inches in height – for negroes are a low rather than a tall race of men – down to a little fellow about ten years of age, extended in a semicircle around the right side of the yard. There were in all about forty. Each was dressed in the usual uniform of slaves, when in market, consisting of a fashionably shaped, black fur hat, roundabout and trowsers of coarse corduroy velvet, precisely such as are worn by Irish labourers, when they first 'come over the water'; good vests, strong shoes, and white cotton shirts, completed their equipment. This dress they lay aside after they are sold, or wear out as soon as may be; for the negro dislikes to retain the indication of his having recently been in the market. With their hats in their hands, which hung down by their sides, they stood perfectly still, and in close order, while some gentlemen were passing from one to another examining for the purpose of buying. With the exception of displaying their teeth when addressed, and rolling their great white eyes about the court – they were so many statues of the most glossy ebony.

As we entered the mart, one of the slave merchants – for a 'lot' of slaves is usually accompanied, if not owned, by two or three individuals – approached us, saying 'Good morning, gentlemen! Would you like to examine my lot of boys? I have as fine a lot as ever came into market.' – We approached them, one of us as a curious spectator, the other as a purchaser; and as my friend passed along the line, with a scrutinizing eye – giving that singular look, peculiar to the buyer of slaves as he glances from head to foot over each individual – the passive subjects of his observations betrayed no other signs of curiosity than that evinced by an occasional glance. The entrance of a stranger into a mart is by no means an unimportant event to the slave, for every stranger may soon become his master and command his future destinies.

*

'For what service in particular did you want to buy?' inquired the trader of my friend, 'A coachman.' 'There is one I think may suit you, sir,' said he; 'George, step out here.' Forthwith a light-coloured negro, with a fine figure and good face, bating an enormous pair of lips, advanced a step from the line, and looked with some degree of intelligence, though with an air of indifference, upon his intended purchaser.

'How old are you, George?' he inquired. 'I don't recollect, sir 'zactly – b'lieve I'm somewere 'bout twenty-dree.' 'Where were you raised?' 'On master R – 's farm in Wirginny.' 'Then you are a Virginia negro.' 'Yes, master, me full blood Wirginny.' 'Did you drive your master's carriage?' 'Yes, master, I drove ole missus' carage, more dan four year.' 'Have you a wife?' 'Yes, master, I lef' young wife in Richmond, but I got new wife here in de lot. I wishy you buy her, master, if you gwine to buy me.'

Then came a series of the usual questions from the intended purchaser. 'Let me see your teeth – your tongue – open your hands – roll up your sleeves – have you a good appetite? are you good tempered? 'Me get mad sometime,' replied George to the last query, 'but neber wid my horses.' 'What do you ask for this boy, sir?' inquired the planter, after putting a few more questions to the unusually loquacious slave. 'I have held him at one thousand dollars, but I will take nine hundred and seventy-five cash.' The bargain was in a few minutes concluded, and my companion took the negro at nine hundred and fifty, giving negotiable paper – the customary way of paying for slaves – at four months. It is, however, generally understood, that if servants prove unqualified for the particular service for which they are bought, the sale is dissolved. So there is general perfect safety in purchasing servants untried, and merely on the warrant of the seller.

George, in the meanwhile, stood by, with his hat in his hand, apparently unconcerned in the negotiations going on, and when the trader said to him, 'George, the gentleman has bought you; get ready to go with him,' he appeared gratified at the tidings, and smiled upon his companions apparently quite pleased, and then bounded off to the buildings for his little bundle. In a few minutes he returned and took leave of several of his companions, who, having been drawn up into line only to be shown to purchasers, were now once more at liberty, and moving about the court, all the visitors having left except my friend and myself. 'You mighty lucky, George,' said one, congratulating him, 'to get sol so quick,' 'Oh, you neber min', Charly,' replied the delighted George; 'your turn come soon too.'

A FEAST WITH A MANDAN CHIEF, NORTH AMERICA, *c.* 1838

George Catlin

Within twenty years of Catlin's meal, the Mandan would be wiped out by smallpox contracted from Caucasian pioneers.

The simple feast which was spread before us consisted of three dishes only, two of which were served in wooden bowls, and the third in an earthen vessel of their own manufacture, somewhat in shape of a bread-tray in our own country. This last contained a quantity of *pem-i-can* and *marrow-fat*; and one of the former held a fine brace of buffalo ribs, delightfully roasted; and the other was filled with a kind of paste or pudding, made of the flour of the '*pomme blanche*', as the French call it, a delicious turnip of the prairie, finely flavoured with the buffalo berries, which are collected in great quantities in this country, and used with divers dishes in cooking, as we in civilized countries use dried currants, which they very much resemble.

A handsome pipe and a tobacco-pouch made of the otter skin, filled with k'nick-k'neck (Indian tobacco), laid by the side of the feast; and when we were seated, mine host took up his pipe, and deliberately filled it; and instead of lighting it by the fire, which he could easily have done, he drew from his pouch his flint and steel, and raised a spark with which he kindled it. He drew a few strong whiffs through it, and presented the stem of it to my mouth, through which I drew a whiff or two while he held the stem in his hands. This done, he laid down the pipe, and drawing his knife from his belt, cut off a very small piece of the meat from the ribs, and pronouncing the word 'Ho-pe-ne-chee wa-pa-shee' (meaning a *medicine* sacrifice), threw it into the fire.

He then (by signals) requested me to eat, and I commenced, after drawing out from my belt my knife (which it is supposed that every man in this country carries about him, for at an Indian feast a knife is never offered to a guest). Reader, be not astonished that I sat and ate my dinner *alone*, for such is the custom of this strange land. In all tribes in these western regions it is an invariable rule that a chief never eats with his guests invited to a feast; but while they eat, he sits by, at their service, and ready to wait upon them; deliberately charging and lighting the pipe which is to be passed around after the feast is over. Such was the case in the present instance, and while I was eating, Mah-to-toh-pa sat cross-legged before me, cleaning his pipe and preparing it for a cheerful smoke when I had finished my meal. For this ceremony I observed he was making unusual preparation, and I observed as I ate, that after he had taken enough of the k'nick-k'neck or bark of the red willow, from his pouch, he rolled out of it also a piece of the '*castor*', which it is customary amongst these folks to carry in their tobacco-sack to give it a flavour; and, shaving off a small quantity of it, mixed it with the bark, with which he charged his pipe. This done, he drew also from his sack a small parcel containing a fine powder, which was made of dried buffalo dung, a little of which he spread over the top, (according also to custom), which was like tinder, having no other effect than that of lighting the pipe with ease and satisfaction. My appetite satiated, I straightened up, and with a whiff the pipe was lit, and we enjoyed together for a quarter of an hour the most delightful exchange of good feelings, amid clouds of smoke and pantomimic signs and gesticulations.

The dish of 'pemican and marrow-fat', of which I spoke, was thus: – The first, an article of food used throughout this country, as familiarly as we use bread in the civilized world. It is made of buffalo meat dried very hard, and afterwards pounded in a large wooden mortar until it is made nearly as fine as sawdust, then packed in this dry state in bladders or sacks of skin, and is easily carried to any part of the world in good order. 'Marrow-fat' is collected by the Indians from the buffalo bones which they break to pieces, yielding a prodigious quantity of marrow, which is boiled out and put into buffalo bladders which have been distended; and after it cools, becomes quite hard like tallow, and has the appearance, and very nearly the flavour, of the richest yellow butter. At a feast, chunks of this marrow-fat are cut off and placed in a tray or bowl, with the pemican, and eaten together.

*

In this dish laid a spoon made of the buffalo's horn, which was black as jet, and beautifully polished; in one of the others there was another of still more ingenious and beautiful workmanship, made of the horn of the mountain-sheep, or 'Gros corn', as the French trappers call them; it was large enough to hold of itself two or three pints, and was almost entirely transparent.

I spoke also of the earthen dishes or bowls in which these viands were served out; they are a familiar part of the culinary furniture of every Mandan lodge, and are manufactured by the women of this tribe in great quantities, and modelled into a thousand forms and tastes. They are made by the hands of the women, from a tough black clay, and baked in kilns which are made for the purpose, and are nearly equal in hardness to our own manufacture of pottery; though they have not yet got the art of glazing, which would be to them a most valuable secret. They make them so strong and serviceable, however, that they hang them over the fire as we do our iron pots, and boil their meat in them with perfect success. I have seen some few specimens of such manufacture, which have been dug up in Indian mounds and tombs in the southern and middle states, placed in our Eastern Museums and looked upon as a great wonder, when here this novelty is at once done away with, and the whole mystery; where women can be seen handling and using them by hundreds, and they can be seen every day in the summer also, moulding them into many fanciful forms, and passing them through the kiln where they are hardened.

Whilst sitting at this feast the wigwam was as silent as death, although we were not alone in it. This chief, like most others, had a plurality of wives, and all of them (some six or seven) were seated around the sides of the lodge, upon robes or mats placed upon the ground, and not allowed to speak, though they were in readiness to obey his orders or commands, which were uniformly given by signs-manual, and executed in the neatest and most silent manner.

When I arose to return, the pipe through which we had smoked was presented to me; and the robe on which I had sat, he gracefully raised by the corners and tendered it to me, explaining by signs that the paintings which were on it were the representations of the battles of his life, where he had fought and killed with his own hand fourteen of his enemies; that he had been two weeks engaged in painting it for me, and that he had invited me here on this occasion to present it to me.

THE MARRIAGE OF VICTORIA AND ALBERT, LONDON, 19 February 1840

Queen Victoria

Monday, 10th February. – Got up at a 1/4 to 9 – well, and having slept well; and breakfasted at 1/2 p. 9. Mamma came before and brought me a Nosegay of orange flowers. My dearest kindest Lehzen gave me a dear little ring. Wrote my journal, and to Lord M. Had my hair dressed and the wreath of orange flowers put on. Saw Albert for the *last* time *alone*, as my *Bridegroom*. Dressed.

Saw Uncle, and Ernest whom dearest Albert brought up. At 1/2 p. 12 I set off, dearest Albert having gone before. I wore a white satin gown with a very deep flounce of Honiton lace, imitation of old. I wore my Turkish diamond necklace and earrings, and Albert's beautiful sapphire brooch. Mamma and the Duchess of Sutherland went in the carriage with me. I never saw such crowds of people as there were in the Park, and they cheered most enthusiastically. When I arrived at St James's, I went into the dressing-room where my 12 young Train-bearers were, dressed all in white with white roses, which had a beautiful effect. Here I waited a little till dearest Albert's Procession had moved into the Chapel. I then went with my Train-bearers and ladies into the Throne-room, where the Procession formed; Lord Melbourne in his fine new dress-coat, bearing the Sword of State, and Lord

Uxbridge and Lord Belfast on either side of him walked immediately before me. Queen Anne's room was full of people, ranged on seats one higher than the other, as also in the Guard room, and by the Staircase, – all very friendly; the Procession looked beautiful going downstairs. Part of the Color Court was also covered in and full of people who were very civil. The Flourish of Trumpets ceased as I entered the Chapel, and the organ began to play, which had a beautiful effect. At the Altar, to my right, stood Albert; Mamma was on my left as also the Dukes of Sussex and Cambridge, and Aunt Augusta; and on Albert's right was the Queen Dowager, then Uncle Ernest, Ernest, the Duchess of Cambridge and little Mary, George, Augusta, and Princess Sophia Matilda. Lord Melbourne stood close to me with the Sword of State. The Ceremony was very imposing, and fine and simple, and I think OUGHT to make an everlasting impression on every one who promises at the Altar to *keep* what he or she promises. Dearest Albert repeated everything very distinctly. I felt so happy when the ring was put on, and by Albert. As soon as the Service was over, the Procession returned as it came, with the exception that my beloved Albert led me out. The applause was very great, in the Color Court as we came through; Lord Melbourne, good man, was very much affected during the Ceremony and at the applause. We all returned to the Throne-room, where the Signing of the Register took place; it was first signed by the Archbishop, then by Albert and me, and all the Royal Family, and by: the Lord Chancellor, the Lord President, the Lord Privy Seal, the Duke of Norfolk (as Earl Marshal), the Archbishop of York, and Lord Melbourne. We then went into the Closet, and the Royal Family waited with me there till the ladies had got into their carriages. I gave all the Train-bearers as a brooch a small *eagle* of turquoise. I then returned to Buckingham Palace alone with Albert; they cheered us really most warmly and heartily; the crowd was immense; and the Hall at Buckingham Palace was full of people; they cheered us again and again. The great Drawing-room and Throne-room were full of people of rank, and numbers of children were there. Lord Melbourne and Lord Clarendon, who had arrived, stood at the door of the Throne-room when we came in. I went and sat on the sofa in my dressing-room with Albert; and we talked together there from 10 m. to 2 till 20 m. p. 2. Then we went downstairs where all the Company was assembled and went into the dining-room – dearest Albert leading me in, and my Train being borne by 3

Pages, Cowell, little Wemyss, and dear little Byng. I sat between dearest Albert and the Duke of Sussex. My health and dearest Albert's were drunk. The Duke was very kind and civil. Albert and I drank a glass of wine with Lord Melbourne, who seemed much affected by the whole. I talked to all after the breakfast, and to Lord Melbourne, whose fine coat I praised. Little Mary behaved so well both at the Marriage and the breakfast. I went upstairs and undressed and put on a white silk gown trimmed with swansdown, and a bonnet with orange flowers. Albert went downstairs and undressed. At 20 m. to 4 Lord Melbourne came to me and stayed with me till 10 m. to 4. I shook hands with him and he kissed my hand. Talked of how well everything went off. 'Nothing could have gone off better,' he said, and of the people being in such good humor and having also received him well; of my receiving the Addresses from the House of Lords and Commons; of his coming down to Windsor in time for dinner. I begged him not to go to the party; he was a little tired; I would let him know when we arrived; I pressed his hand once more, and he said, 'God bless you, Ma'am,' most kindly, and with such a kind look. Dearest Albert came up and fetched me down stairs, where we took leave of Mamma and drove off at near 4; I and Albert alone.

THE INDUSTRIAL REVOLUTION: THE SLUMS OF MANCHESTER, ENGLAND, 1844

Friedrich Engels

I now proceed to describe Manchester's worker districts. First of all, there is the Old Town, which lies between the northern boundary of the commercial district and the Irk. Here the streets, even the better ones, are narrow and winding, as Todd Street, Long Millgate, Withy Grove, and Shude Hill, the houses dirty, old, and tumble-down, and the construction of the side streets utterly horrible. Going from the Old Church to Long Millgate, the stroller has at once a row of old-fashioned houses at the right, of which not one has kept its original level; these are remnants of the old pre-manufacturing Manchester, whose former inhabitants have removed with their descendants into better-built districts, and have left the houses, which were not good enough for them, to a working-class population strongly mixed with Irish blood. Here one is in an almost undisguised working-men's quarter, for even the shops and beerhouses hardly take the trouble to exhibit a trifling degree of cleanliness. But all this is nothing in comparison with the courts and lanes which lie behind, to which access can be gained only through covered passages, in which no two human beings can pass at the same time. Of the irregular cramming together of dwellings in ways which defy all rational plan, of the tangle in which they are crowded literally one upon the other, it is impossible to convey an idea. And it is not the buildings surviving from the old times of Manchester which are to blame for this; the confusion has only recently reached its height when every scrap of space left by the old way of building has been filled up and patched over until not a foot of land is left to be further occupied.

To confirm my statement I have drawn here a small section of the plan of Manchester – not the worst spot and not one-tenth of the whole Old Town.

This drawing will suffice to characterise the irrational manner in which the entire district was built, particularly the part near the Irk.

The south bank of the Irk is here very steep and between fifteen and thirty feet high. On this declivitous hillside there are planted three rows of houses, of which the lowest rise directly out of the river, while the front walls of the highest stand on the crest of the hill in Long Millgate. Among them are mills on the river, in short, the method of construction is as crowded and disorderly here as in the lower part of Long Millgate. Right and left a multitude of covered passages lead from the main street into numerous courts, and he who turns in thither gets into a filth and disgusting grime, the equal of which is not be found – especially in the courts which lead down to the Irk, and which contain unqualifiedly the most horrible dwellings which I have yet beheld. In one of these courts there stands directly at the entrance, at the end of the covered passage, a privy without a door, so dirty that the inhabitants can pass into and out of the court only by passing through foul pools of stagnant urine and excrement. This is the first court on the Irk above Ducie Bridge – in case any one should care to look into it. Below it on the river there are several tanneries which fill the whole neighborhood with the stench of animal putrefaction. Below Ducie Bridge the only entrance to most of the houses is by means of narrow, dirty stairs and over heaps of refuse and filth. The first court below Ducie Bridge, known as Allen's Court, was in such a state at the time of the cholera that the sanitary police ordered it evacuated, swept and disinfected with chloride of lime. Dr Kay gives a terrible description of the state of this court at that time. Since then, it seems to have been partially torn away and rebuilt; at least looking down from Ducie Bridge, the passer-by sees several ruined walls and heaps of *débris* with some newer houses. The view from this bridge, mercifully concealed from mortals of small stature by a parapet as high as a man, is characteristic for the whole district. At the bottom flows, or rather stagnates, the Irk, a narrow, coal-black, foul-smelling stream, full of *débris* and refuse, which it deposits on the shallower right bank. In dry weather, a long string of the most disgusting blackish-green slime pools are left standing on this bank, from the depths of which bubbles of miasmatic gas constantly arise and give forth a stench unendurable even on the bridge forty of fifty feet above the surface of the stream. But besides this, the stream itself is checked every few paces by high weirs, behind which slime and refuse accumulate and rot in thick masses. Above the bridge are tanneries, bonemills, and gasworks, from which all drains and refuse find their way into the Irk, which receives further the contents of all the neighbouring sewers and privies. It may be easily imagined, therefore, what sort of residue the stream deposits. Below the bridge you look upon the piles of *débris*, the refuse, filth, and offal from the courts on the steep left bank; here each house is packed close behind its neighbour and a piece of each is visible, all black, smoky, crumbling, ancient, with broken panes and window-frames. The background is furnished by old barrack-like factory buildings. On the lower right bank stands a long row of houses and mills; the second house being a ruin without a roof, piled with *débris*; the third stands so low that the lowest floor is uninhabitable, and therefore without windows or doors. Here the background embraces the pauper burial-ground, the station of the Liverpool and Leeds railway, and, in the rear of this, the Workhouse, the 'Poor-Law Bastille' of Manchester, which, like a citadel, looks threateningly down from behind its high walls and parapets on the hilltop, upon the working-people's quarter below.

Above Ducie Bridge, the left bank grows more flat and the right bank steeper, but the condition of the dwellings on both banks grows worse rather than better. He who turns to the left here from the main street, Long Millgate, is lost; he wanders from one court to another, turns countless corners, passes nothing but narrow, filthy nooks and alleys, until after a few minutes he has lost all clue, and knows not whither to turn. Everywhere half or wholly ruined buildings, some of them actually uninhabited, which means a great deal here; rarely a wooden or stone floor to be seen in the houses, almost uniformly broken, ill-fitting windows and doors, and a state of filth! Everywhere heaps of *débris*, refuse, and offal; standing pools for gutters, and a stench which alone would make it impossible for a human being in any degree civilised to live in such a district. The newly-built extension of the Leeds railway, which crosses the Irk here, has swept away some of these courts and lanes, laying others completely open to view. Immediately under the railway bridge there stands a court, the filth and horrors of which surpass all the others by far, just because it was hitherto so shut off, so secluded that the way to it could not be found without a good deal of trouble. I should never have discovered it myself, without the breaks made by the railway, though I thought I knew this whole region thoroughly. Passing along a rough bank, among stakes and washing-lines, one penetrates into this chaos of small one-storied, one-roomed huts, in most of which there is no artificial floor; kitchen, living and sleeping-room all in one. In such a hole. Scarcely five feet long by six broad, I found two beds – and such bedsteads and beds! – which, with a staircasé and chimney-place, exactly filled the room. In several others I found absolutely nothing, while the door stood open, and the inhabitants leaned against it. Everywhere before the doors refuse and offal; that any sort of pavement lay underneath could not be seen but only felt, here and there, with the feet. This whole collection of cattle-sheds for human beings was surrounded on two sides by houses and a factory, and on the third by the river, and besides the narrow stair up the bank, a narrow doorway alone led out into another almost equally ill-built, ill-kept labyrinth of dwellings.

Enough! The whole side of the Irk is built in this way, a planless, knotted chaos of houses, more or less on the verge of uninhabitableness, whose unclean interiors fully correspond with their filthy external surroundings. And how could the people be clean with no proper opportunity for satisfying the most natural and ordinary wants? Privies are so rare here that they are either filled up every day, or are too remote for most of the inhabitants to use. How can people wash when they have only the dirty Irk water at hand, while pumps and water pipes can be found in decent parts of the city alone? In truth, it cannot be charged to the account of these helots of modern society if their dwellings are not more clean than the pig sties which are here and there to be seen among them. The landlords are not ashamed to let dwellings like the six or seven cellars on the quay directly below Scotland Bridge, the floors of which stand at least two feet below the low-water level of the Irk that flows not six feet away from them; or like the upper floor of the corner-house on the opposite shore directly above the bridge, where the ground-floor, utterly uninhabitable, stands deprived of all fittings for doors and windows, a case by no means rare in this region, when this open ground-floor is used as a privy by the whole neighbourhood for want of other facilities!

If we leave the Irk and penetrate once more on the opposite side from Long Millgate into the midst of the working-men's dwellings, we shall come into a somewhat newer quarter, which stretches from St Michael's Church to Withy Grove and Shude Hill. Here there is somewhat better order. In place of the chaos of buildings, we find at least long straight lanes and alleys or courts, built according to a plan and usually square. But if, in the former case, every house was built according to caprice, here each lane and court is so built, without reference to the situation of the adjoining ones. The lanes run now in this direction, now in that, while every two minutes the wanderer gets into a blind alley, or on turning a corner, finds himself back where he started from; certainly no one who has not lived a considerable time in this labyrinth can find his way through it.

If I may use the word at all in speaking of this district, the ventilation of these streets and courts is, in consequence of this confusion, quite as imperfect as in the Irk region; and if this quarter may, nevertheless, be said to have some advantage over that of the Irk, the houses being newer and the streets occasionally having gutters, nearly every house has, on the other hand, a cellar dwelling, which is rarely found in the Irk district, by reason of the greater age and more careless construction of the houses. As for the rest, the filth, *débris*, and offal heaps, and the pools in the streets are common to both quarters, and in the district now under discussion, another feature most injurious to the cleanliness of the inhabitants, is the multitude of pigs walking about in all the alleys, rooting into the offal heaps, or kept imprisoned in small pens. Here, as in most of the working-men's quarters of Manchester, the pork-raisers rent the courts and build pig-pens in them. In almost every court one or even several such pens may be found, into which the inhabitants of the court throw all refuse and offal, whence the swine grow fat; and the atmosphere, confined on all four sides, is utterly corrupted by putrefying animal and vegetable substances. Through this quarter, a broad and measurably decent street has been cut, Millers Street, and the background has been pretty successfully concealed. But if any one should be led by curiosity to pass through one of the numerous passages which lead into the courts, he will find this piggery repeated at every twenty paces.

THE IRISH POTATO FAMINE, 1846–8

Elizabeth Smith

Some four million Irish people lived almost entirely on potatoes in the mid nineteenth century. In 1845 and 1846 the annual crop was hit by blight. Around one million people died, and 1,600,000 more emigrated to the United States. The author was the wife of an Irish landowner.

5 November 1846. Hal has just brought in two damaged potatoes the first we have seen of our own for on our hill few have been found as yet.

6 November. Another blustering day after a stormy night, however as there is no rain it will dry the potatoes finely.

11 November. Mr Darker much afraid of this second potato field. The first had hardly a bad potato so that he was unprepared for this.

13 November. *Half* the potatoes in this new field are tainted, some very badly.

16 November. This had been a regular rainy day, the river all over the meadows. The papers still occupied with the potato disease though Lady Odela Villiers and her well managed elopement has been a God-send to them the last few days . . .

30 November. Mr Robinson came down yesterday to collect the rents, the Tennants paid well, were in good spirits, made no complaints, not even of their potatoes, were well dressed, so that altogether it was a most comfortable gale day [rent day]. The potato failure has been much exaggerated, the disease is by no means so far spread as was supposed and the crop so over abundant that the partial failure will be less felt, particularly as the corn harvest was excellent. But people were much frightened and this caused a run on the Savings Bank which might have encreased the evil, that too is luckily over so that the prospects for the winter are brightening. John Robinson said nothing could more fully prove the encreasing prosperity of the country than the multitudes whom this panick proved to have been saving, the very poorest looking people drawing out their fortys, fiftys, hundreds. The crowds were so immense and so excited that horse and foot police were necessary to guard their lives.

12 January 1847. . . . we make daily a large pot of soup which is served gratis to 22 people at present. It is ready at one o'clock and I thought it quite a pretty sight yesterday in the kitchen all the workmen coming in for their portion, a quart with a slice of beef; half of them get this one day for dinner with a bit of their own bread; the other half get milk and the cheap rice we have provided for them. Next day they reverse the order. The Colonel is giving them firing too; so they are really comfortable; there are twelve of them and ten pensioners, old and feeble men and women, or those with large families of children; some of them no longer living on our ground yet having been once connected with us we can't desert them. So far well; but beyond our small circle what a waste of misery; how are we to relieve it? Such a dense population squatted here and there upon neglected properties, dying with want, wretched every year but ruined this. At the Relief Committee yesterday it was resolved to institute soup kitchens at proper stations for general relief, to be supported by subscription, each subscription to have a certain number of tickets. I think the gentlemen are doing this, the ladies must combine for a clothing fund. The rags are hardly coverings for decency; beds and bedding there are none, among the mob, I mean; such miseries crush hope, yet hope I will . . .

16 January. We then went on to Jem Doyle's. Most wretched it was, though very clean, he must go to the poor-house, he and his family. He has an ulcer on his leg, which will prevent his working for weeks and they will starve during this month, that there is no relief going. Widow Mulligan is also starving. So are the widow Quin and fifty more. They must be forced into the poor-house for they cannot otherwise be supported. They are the meanest feeling people ever were, they will accept of charity from anyone, live on it in idleness, but they won't go to the poor-house.

10 October. Sunday. Little in the papers but failures. Cattle dealers in Dublin have gone and caused immense distress, in fact paralysed the markets; not an offer for a beast of any sort at any of the late fairs. Banks, merchants, brokers, agents, all are bankrupt in all places. John Robinson has lost seven thousand pounds by bad debts, trusting people who have failed to pay; he must pay the millers who sent him the flour he so imprudently parted with out of his former profits, his capital, and learn wisdom by this shake.

17 October. Sunday again – the 17th – I hardly know how the week has gone – not a creature has entered the house but the Doctor. We have been as quiet as possible, indeed the country generally is very dull; people are oppressed by this frightful amount of bankruptcies, almost everyone either themselves or their friends affected by some of these numerous failures. Then the winter prospects look very gloomy. The destitution is expected to be wider spread than last year for the very poor will be nearly as ill off while the classes above which then relieved them are all this year in serious difficulties. No money anywhere; the little hoards of cash and goods all spent and nothing to replace either. The ministry says the land must support the people on it. Half the country having been left untilled for want of means to crop it while a million of money was squandered in destroying the roads, much of it finding its way into pockets full enough before. The Queen has ordered the begging box to go round all the English churches for us!

31 January 1848. 6 inches of snow lying evenly over the country. Except that it stops the outwork, we ought to be glad to see it to keep the ground warm, purify the air, and drive fever away. Spite of the worthlessness of our fine peasantry one can't help grieving for their sufferings. We in this district never would give out any out door relief while there were vacancies in the poor-house at any rate; at Ballymore they gave it and it was abused beyond idea. The Government Commissioners have put a stop to it, taken another house in Naas and refused all aid except under what the people consider imprisonment. A report got about that only the able bodied would be forced into the poor-house, that the aged, sickly, etc. would be relieved in their own homes; crowds therefore presented themselves to the Doctor to beg certificates of decrepitude, hale and hearty men and women assuring him they were suffering under every ill that flesh is heir to. This description of consciences last year when only the able bodied were accepted for certain relief works were equally anxious to make themselves out in the rudest health whatever infirmities they had. They are all again beginning to beg, of course, because some are so foolish as to give.

We are little teased, we never refuse a bit of bread, we never give anything else, and they leave us in quiet, for it is money they want, pennies for tobacco and snuff and tea and whiskey.

CANNIBALISM AT THE DONNER CAMPS, CALIFORNIA, 17 April 1847

Captain Fellun

Trapped by snow in the high sierras, a party of California-bound emigrants led by George Donner resorted to eating human flesh. The author led one of the relief expeditions which eventually struggled through to the Donner camps.

April, 17th. Reached the Cabins between 12 and 1 o'clock. Expected to find some of the sufferers alive, Mrs Donner and Kiesburg in particular. Entered the cabins and a horrible scene presented itself, – human bodies terribly mutilated, legs, arms, and sculls scattered in every direction. One body, supposed to be that of Mrs Eddy, lay near the entrance, the limbs severed off and a frightful gash in the scull. The flesh from the bones was nearly consumed and a painful stillness pervaded the place. The supposition was that all were dead, when a sudden shout revived our hopes, and we flew in the direction of the sound, three Indians [who] were hitherto concealed, started from the ground and fled at our approach, leaving behind their bows and arrows. We delayed two hours in searching the cabins, during which we were obliged to witness sights from which we would have fain turned away, and which are too dreadful to put on record. We next started for 'Donner's camp' 8 miles distant over the mountains. After traveling about half way, we came upon a track in the snow, which excited our suspicion, and we determined to pursue it. It brought us to the camp of Jacob Donner, where it had evidently left that morning. There we found property of every discription, books, calicoes, tea, coffee, shoes, purcussion caps, household and kitchen furniture scattered in every direction, and mostly in the water. At the mouth of the tent stood a large iron kettle, filled with human flesh cut up, it was the body of Geo. Donner, the head had been split open, and the brains extracted therefrom, and to the appearance, he had not been long dead, not over three or four days at the most. Near by the kettle stood a chair, and thereupon three legs of a bullock that had been shot down in the early part of the winter, and snowed under before it could be dressed. The meat was found sound and good, and with the exception of a small piece out of the shoulder, wholly untouched. We gathered up some property and camped for the night.

THE GREAT EXHIBITION AT CRYSTAL PALACE, LONDON, 7 June 1851

Charlotte Brontë

Yesterday I went for the second time to the Crystal Palace. We remained in it about three hours, and I must say I was more struck with it on this occasion than at my first visit. It is a wonderful place – vast, strange, new, and impossible to describe. Its grandeur does not consist in *one* thing, but in the unique assemblage of *all* things. Whatever human industry has created you find there, from the great compartments filled with railway engines and boilers, with mill machinery in full work, with splendid carriages of all kinds, with harness of every description, to the glass-covered and velvet spread stands loaded with the most gorgeous work of the goldsmith and silversmith, and the carefully guarded caskets full of real diamonds and pearls worth hundreds of thousands of pounds. It may be called a bazaar or a fair, but it is such a bazaar or fair as Eastern genii might have created. It seems as if only magic could have gathered this mass of wealth from all the ends of the earth – as if none but supernatural hands could have arranged it thus, with such a blaze and contrast of colours and marvellous power of effect. The multitude filling the great aisles seems ruled and subdued by some invisible influence. Amongst the thirty thousand souls that peopled it the day I was there not one loud noise was to be heard, not one irregular movement seen; the living tide rolls on quietly, with a deep hum like the sea heard from the distance.

THE BATTLE OF BALACLAVA: THE CHARGE OF THE LIGHT BRIGADE, CRIMEA, 25 October 1854

William Howard Russell

Russell was the war correspondent for the London *Times*.

If the exhibition of the most brilliant valour, of the excess of courage, and of a daring which would have reflected lustre on the best days of chivalry can afford full consolation for the disaster of today, we can have no reason to regret the melancholy loss which we sustained in a contest with a savage and barbarian enemy.

I shall proceed to describe, to the best of my power, what occurred under my own eyes, and to state the facts which I have heard from men whose veracity is unimpeachable, reserving to myself the exercise of the right of private judgement in making public and in suppressing the details of what occurred on this memorable day . . .

It will be remembered that in a letter sent by last mail from this place it was mentioned that eleven battalions of Russian infantry had crossed the Tchernaya, and that they threatened the rear of our position and our communication with Balaclava. Their bands could be heard playing at night by travellers along the Balaclava road to the camp, but they 'showed' but little during the day and kept up among the gorges and mountain passes through which the roads to Inkermann, Simpheropol, and the south-east of the Crimea wind towards the interior. It will be recollected also that the position we occupied in reference to Balaclava was supposed by most people to be very strong – even impregnable. Our lines were formed by natural mountain slopes in the rear, along which the French had made very formidable intrenchments. Below those intrenchments, and very nearly in a right line across the valley beneath, are four conical hillocks, one rising above the other as they recede from our lines . . . On the top of each of these hills the Turks had thrown up earthen redoubts, defended by 250 men each, and armed with two or three guns – some heavy ship guns – lent by us to them, with one artilleryman in each redoubt to look after them. These hills cross the valley of Balaclava at the distance of about two and a half miles from the town. Supposing the spectator then to take his stand on one of the heights forming the rear of our camp before Sebastopol, he would see the town of Balaclava, with its scanty shipping, its narrow strip of water, and its old forts on his right hand; immediately below he would behold the valley and plain of coarse meadowland, occupied by our cavalry tents, and stretching from the base of the ridge on which he stood to the foot of the formidable heights on the other side; he would see the French trenches lined with Zouaves a few feet beneath, and distant from him, on the slope of the hill; a Turkish redoubt lower down, then another in the valley, then in a line with it some angular earthworks, then, in succession, the other two redoubts up Canrobert's Hill.

At the distance of two or two and a half miles across the valley there is an abrupt rocky mountain range of most irregular and picturesque formation, covered with scanty brushwood here and there, or rising into barren pinnacles and plateaux of rock. In outline and appearance, this position of the landscape is wonderfully like the Trossachs. A patch of blue sea is caught in between the overhanging cliffs of Balaclava as they close in the entrance to the harbour on the right. The camp of the Marines pitched on the hillsides more than one thousand feet above the level of the sea is opposite to you as your back is turned to Sebastopol and your right side towards Balaclava. On the road leading up the valley, close to the entrance of the town and beneath these hills, is the encampment of the 93rd Highlanders.

The cavalry lines are nearer to you below, and are some way in advance of the Highlanders, and nearer to the town than the Turkish redoubts. The valley is crossed here and there by small waves of land. On your left the hills and rocky mountain ranges gradually close in toward the course of the Tchernaya, till at three or four miles' distance from Balaclava the valley is swallowed up in a mountain gorge and deep ravines, above which rise tier after tier of desolate whitish rock garnished now and then by bits of scanty herbage, and spreading away towards the east and south, where they attain the alpine dimensions of Tschatir Dagh. It is very easy for an enemy at the Belbek, or in command of the road of Mackenzie's Farm, Inkermann, Simpheropol, or Bakhchisarai, to debouch through these gorges at any time upon this plain from the neck of the valley, or to march from Sebastopol by the Tchernaya and to advance along it towards Balaclava, till checked by the Turkish redoubts on the southern side or by the fire from the French works on the northern side, i.e., the side which in relation to the valley of Balaclava forms the rear of our position.

At half past seven o'clock this morning an orderly came galloping in to the headquarters camp from Balaclava, with the news that at dawn a strong corps of Russian horse supported by guns and battalions of infantry had marched into the valley, and had already nearly dispossessed the Turks of the redoubt No. 1 (that on Canrobert's Hill, which is farthest from our lines) and that they were opening fire on the redoubts Nos. 2, 3 and 4, which would speedily be in their hands unless the Turks offered a stouter resistance than they had done already.

Orders were dispatched to Sir George Cathcart and to HRH the Duke of Cambridge to put their respective divisions, the 4th and 1st, in motion for the scene of action, and intelligence of the advance of the Russians was also furnished to General Canrobert. Immediately on receipt of the news the General commanded General Bosquet to get the Third Division under arms, and sent a strong body of artillery and some 200 Chasseurs d'Afrique to assist us in holding the valley. Sir Colin Campbell, who was in command of Balaclava, had drawn up the 93rd Highlanders a little in front of the road to the town at the first news of the advance of the enemy. The marines on the heights got under arms; the seamen's batteries and marines' batteries on the heights close to the town were manned, and the French artillerymen and the Zouaves prepared for action along their lines. Lord Lucan's little camp was the scene of great excitement. The men had not had time to water their horses; they had not broken their fast from the evening of the day before, and had barely saddled at the first blast of the trumpet, when they were drawn up on the slope behind the redoubts in front of the camp to operate on the enemy's squadrons. It was soon evident that no reliance was to be placed on the Turkish infantrymen or artillerymen. All the stories we had heard about their bravery behind stone walls and earthworks proved how differently the same or similar people fight under different circumstances. When the Russians advanced the Turks fired a few rounds at them, got frightened at the distance of their supports in the rear, looked round, received a few shots and shell, and then 'bolted', and fled with an agility quite at variance with the commonplace notions of oriental deportment on the battlefield. But Turks on the Danube are very different beings from Turks in the Crimea, as it appears that the Russians of Sebastopol are not at all like the Russians of Silistria.

Soon after eight Lord Raglan and his staff turned out and cantered towards the rear of our position. The booming of artillery, the spattering roll of musketry, were heard rising from the valley, drowning the roar of the siege guns in front before Sebastopol. As I rode in the direction of the firing over the thistles and large stones which cover the undulating plain which stretches away towards Balaclava, on a level with the summit of the ridges above it, I observed a French light infantry regiment (the 27th, I think) advancing with admirable care and celerity from our right towards the ridge near the telegraph house, which was already lined with companies of French infantry, while mounted officers scampered along its broken outline in every direction.

General Bosquet, a stout soldierlike-looking man, who reminds one of the old *genre* of French generals as depicted at Versailles, followed, with his staff and small escort of Hussars, at a gallop. Faint white clouds rose here and there above the hill from the cannonade below. Never did the painter's eye rest upon a more beautiful scene than I beheld from the ridge. The fleecy vapours still hung around the mountain tops and mingled with the ascending volumes of smoke; the patch of sea sparkled freshly in the rays of the morning sun, but its light was eclipsed by the flashes which gleamed from the masses of armed men below.

Looking to the left towards the gorge we beheld six compact masses of Russian infantry which had just debouched from the mountain passes near the Tchernaya, and were slowly advancing with solemn stateliness up the valley. Immediately in their front was a regular line of artillery, of at least twenty pieces strong. Two batteries of light guns were already a mile in advance of them, and were playing with energy on the redoubts, from which feeble puffs of smoke came at long intervals. Behind the guns, in front of the infantry, were enormous bodies of cavalry. They were in six compact squares, three on each flank, moving down *en échelon* towards us, and the valley was lit up with the blaze of their sabres and lance points and gay accoutrements. In their front, and extending along the intervals between each battery of guns, were clouds of mounted skirmishers, wheeling and whirling in the front of their march like autumn leaves tossed by the wind. The Zouaves close to us were lying like tigers at the spring, with ready rifles in hand, hidden chin deep by the earthworks which run along the line of these ridges on our rear, but the quick-eyed Russians were manoeuvring on the other side of the valley, and did not expose their columns to attack. Below the Zouaves we could see the Turkish gunners in the redoubts, all in confusion as the shells burst over them. Just as I came up the Russians had carried No. 1 redoubt, the farthest and most elevated of all, and their horsemen were chasing the Turks across the interval which lay between it and redoubt No. 2. At that moment the cavalry, under Lord Lucan, were formed in glittering masses – the Light Brigade, under Lord Cardigan, in advance of the Heavy Brigade, under Brigadier-General Scarlett, in reserve. They were drawn up just in front of their encampment, and were concealed from the view of the enemy by a slight 'wave' in the plain. Considerably to the rear of their right, the 93rd Highlanders were drawn up in line, in front of the approach to Balaclava. Above and behind them on the heights, the marines were visible through the glass, drawn up under arms, and the gunners could be seen ready in the earthworks, in which were placed the heavy ships' guns. The 93rd had originally been advanced somewhat more into the plain, but the instant the Russians got possession of the first redoubt they opened fire on them from our own guns, which inflicted some injury, and Sir Colin Campbell 'retired' his men to a better position. Meantime the enemy advanced his cavalry rapidly. To our inexpressible disgust we saw the Turks in redoubt No. 2 fly at their approach. They ran in scattered groups across towards redoubt No. 3, and towards Balaclava, but the horse-hoof of the Cossacks was too quick for them, and sword and lance were busily plied among the retreating band. The yells of the pursuers and pursued were plainly audible. As the Lancers and Light Cavalry of the Russians advanced they gathered up their skirmishers with great speed and in excellent order – the shifting trails of men, which played all over the valley like moonlight on water, contracted, gathered up, and the little *peloton* in a few moments became a solid column. Then up came their guns, in rushed their gunners to the abandoned redoubt, and the guns of No. 2 redoubt soon played with deadly effect upon the dispirited defenders of No. 3 redoubt. Two or three shots in return from the earthworks, and all is silent. The Turks swarm over the earthworks and run in confusion towards the town, firing their muskets at the enemy as they run. Again the solid column of cavalry opens like a fan, and resolves itself into the 'long spray' of skirmishers. It laps the flying Turks, steel flashes in the air, and down go the poor Muslim quivering on the plain, split through fez and musket-guard to the chin and breast-belt. There is no support for them. It is evident the Russians have been too quick for us. The Turks have been too quick also, for they have not held their redoubts long enough to enable us to bring them help. In vain the naval guns on the heights fire on the Russian cavalry; the distance is too great for shot or shell to reach. In vain the Turkish gunners in the earthen batteries which are placed along the French intrenchments strive to protect their flying countrymen; their shots fly wide and short of the swarming masses. The Turks betake themselves towards the Highlanders, where they check their flight and form into companies on the flanks of the Highlanders.

As the Russian cavalry on the left of their line crown the hill, across the valley they perceive the Highlanders drawn up at the distance of some half-mile, calmly awaiting their approach. They halt, and squadron after squadron flies up from the rear, till they have a body of some 1500 men along the ridge – Lancers and Dragoons and Hussars. Then they move *en échelon* in two bodies, with another in reserve. The cavalry who have been pursuing the Turks on the right are coming up the ridge beneath us, which conceals our cavalry from view. The heavy brigade in advance is drawn up in two columns. The first column consists of the Scots Greys and of their old companions in glory, the Enniskillens; the second of the 4th Royal Irish, of the 5th Dragoon Guards, and of the 1st Royal Dragoons. The Light Cavalry Brigade is on their left in two lines also. The silence is oppressive; between the cannon bursts, one can hear the champing of bits and the clink of sabres in the valley below. The Russians on their left drew breath for a moment, and then in one grand line dashed at the Highlanders. The ground flies beneath their horses' feet – gathering speed at every stride they dash on towards that thin red streak topped with a line of steel. The Turks fire a volley at 800 yards, and run. As the Russians come within 600 yards, down goes that line of steel in front, and out rings a rolling volley of Minié musketry. The distance is too great. The Russians are not checked, but still sweep onwards with the whole force of horse and man, through the smoke, here and there knocked over by the shot of our batteries above. With breathless suspense everyone awaits the bursting of the wave upon the line of Gaelic rock; but ere they came within 150 yards, another deadly volley flashes from the levelled rifles, and carries death and terror into the Russians. They wheel about, open files right and left, and fly back faster than they came.

'Bravo Highlanders! well done!' shout the excited spectators; but events thicken. The Highlanders and their splendid front are soon forgotten. Men scarcely have a moment to think of this fact that the 93rd never altered their formation to receive that tide of horsemen.

'No,' said Sir Colin Campbell, 'I did not think it worth while to form them even four deep!'

The ordinary British line, two deep, was quite sufficient to repel the attack of these Muscovite chevaliers. Our eyes were, however, turned in a moment on our own cavalry. We saw Brigadier-General Scarlett ride along in front of his massive squadrons.

The Russians – evidently *corps d'élite* – their light-blue jackets embroidered with silver lace, were advancing on their left at an easy gallop, towards the brow of the hill. A forest of lances glistened in their rear, and several squadrons of grey-coated dragoons moved up quickly to support them as they reached the summit. The instant they came in sight the trumpets of our cavalry gave out the warning blast which told us all that in another moment we would see the shock of battle beneath our very eyes. Lord Raglan, all his staff and escort, and groups of officers, the Zouaves, the French generals and officers, and bodies of French infantry on the height, were spectators of the scene as though they were looking on the stage from the boxes of a theatre. Nearly everyone dismounted and sat down, and not a word was said.

The Russians advanced down the hill at a slow canter, which they changed to a trot and at last nearly halted. The first line was at least double the length of ours – it was three times as deep. Behind them was a similar line, equally strong and compact. They evidently despised their insignificant-looking enemy, but their time was come.

The trumpets rang out through the valley, and the Greys and Enniskillens went right at the centre of the Russian cavalry. The space between them was only a few hundred yards; it was scarce enough to let the horses 'gather way', nor had the men quite space sufficient for the full play of their sword arms. The Russian line brings forward each wing as our cavalry advance and threaten to annihilate them as they pass on. Turning a little to their left, so as to meet the Russians' right, the Greys rush on with a cheer that thrills to every heart – the wild shout of the Enniskillens rises through the air at the same moment. As lightning flashes through a cloud the Greys and Enniskillens pierced through the dark masses of the Russians. The shock was but for a moment. There was a clash of steel and a light play of sword blades in the air, and then the Greys and the redcoats disappear in the midst of the shaken and quivering columns. In another moment we see them merging and dashing on with diminished numbers, and in broken order, against the second line, which is advancing against them to retrieve the fortune of the charge.

It was a terrible moment. 'God help them! They are lost!' was the exclamation of more than one man, and the thought of many. With unabated fire the noble hearts dashed at their enemy – it was a fight of heroes. The first line of Russians which had been smashed utterly by our charge, and had fled off at one flank and towards the centre, were coming back to swallow up our handful of men. By sheer steel and sheer courage Enniskillen and Scot were winning their desperate way right through the enemy's squadrons, and already grey horses and redcoats had appeared right at the rear of the second mass, when, with irresistible force, like one bolt from a bow, the 1st Royals, the 4th Dragoon Guards, and the 5th Dragoon Guards rushed at the remnants of the first line of the enemy, went through it as though it were made of pasteboard, and dashing on the second body of Russians, as they were still disordered by the terrible assault of the Greys and their companions, put them to utter rout. This Russian horse in less than five minutes after it met our dragoons was flying with all its speed before a force certainly not half its strength.

A cheer burst from every lip – in the enthusiasm officers and men took off their caps and shouted with delight, and thus keeping up the scenic character of their position, they clapped their hands again and again . . .

And now occurred the melancholy catastrophe which fills us all with sorrow. It appears that the Quartermaster General, Brigadier Airey, thinking that the Light Cavalry had not gone far enough in front when the enemy's horse had fled, gave an order in writing to Captain Nolan, 15th Hussars, to take to Lord Lucan, directing His Lordship 'to advance' his cavalry nearer to the enemy. A braver soldier than Captain Nolan the army did not possess. He was known to all his arm of the service for his entire devotion to his profession, and his name must be familiar to all who take interest in our cavalry for his excellent work published a year ago on our drill and system of remount and breaking horses. I had the pleasure of his acquaintance, and I know he entertained the most exalted opinions respecting the capabilities of the English horse soldier. Properly led, the British Hussar and Dragoon could in his mind break square, take batteries, ride over columns of infantry, and pierce any other cavalry in the world, as if they were made of straw. He thought they had not had the opportunity of doing all that was in their power, and that they had missed even such chances as they had offered to them – that, in fact, they were in some measure disgraced. A matchless rider and a first-rate swordsman, he held in contempt, I am afraid, even grape and canister. He rode off with his orders to Lord Lucan. He is now dead and gone.

God forbid I should cast a shade on the brightness of his honour, but I am bound to state what I am told occurred when he reached His Lordship. I should premise that, as the Russian cavalry retired, their infantry fell back towards the head of the valley, leaving men in three of the redoubts they had taken and abandoning the fourth. They had also placed some guns on the heights over their position, on the left of the gorge. Their cavalry joined the reserves, and drew up in six solid divisions, in an oblique line, across the entrance to the gorge. Six battalions of infantry were placed behind them, and about thirty guns were drawn up along their line, while masses of infantry were also collected on the hills behind the redoubts on our right. Our cavalry had moved up to the ridge across the valley, on our left, as the ground was broken in front, and had halted in the order I have already mentioned.

When Lord Lucan received the order from Captain Nolan and had read it, he asked, we are told, 'Where are we to advance to?'

Captain Nolan pointed with his finger to the line of the Russians, and said, 'There are the enemy, and there are the guns, sir, before them. It is your duty to take them,' or words to that effect, according to the statements made since his death.

Lord Lucan with reluctance gave the order to Lord Cardigan to advance upon the guns, conceiving that his orders compelled him to do so. The noble Earl, though he did not shrink, also saw the fearful odds against him. Don Quixote in his tilt against the windmill was not near so rash and reckless as the gallant fellows who prepared without a thought to rush on almost certain death.

It is a maxim of war that 'cavalry never act without support', that 'infantry should be close at hand when cavalry carry guns, as the effect is only instantaneous', and that it is necessary to have on the flank of a line of cavalry some squadrons in column, the attack on the flank being most dangerous. The only support our Light Cavalry had was the reserve of Heavy Cavalry at a great distance behind them – the infantry and guns being far in the rear. There were no squadrons in column at all, and there was a plain to charge over before the enemy's guns were reached of a mile and a half in length.

At ten past eleven our Light Cavalry Brigade rushed to the front. They numbered as follows, as well as I could ascertain:

	MEN
4th Light Dragoons	118
8th Irish Hussars	104
11th Prince Albert's Hussars	110
13th Light Dragoons	130
17th Lancers	145
Total	607 sabres

The whole brigade scarcely made one effective regiment, according to the numbers of continental armies; and yet it was more than we could spare. As they passed towards the front, the Russians opened on them from the guns in the redoubts on the right, with volleys of musketry and rifles.

They swept proudly past, glittering in the morning sun in all the pride and splendour of war. We could hardly believe the evidence of our senses! Surely that handful of men were not going to charge an army in position? Alas! it was but too true – their desperate valour knew no bounds, and far indeed was it removed from its so-called better part – discretion. They advanced in two lines, quickening their pace as they closed towards the enemy. A more fearful spectacle was never witnessed than by those who, without the power to aid, beheld their heroic countrymen rushing to the arms of death. At the distance of 1200 yards the whole line of the enemy belched forth, from thirty iron mouths, a flood of smoke and flame, through which hissed the deadly balls. Their flight was marked by instant gaps in our ranks, by dead men and horses, by steeds flying wounded or riderless across the plain. The first line was broken – it was joined by the second, they never halted or checked their speed an instant. With diminished ranks, thinned by those thirty guns, which the Russians had laid with the most deadly accuracy, with a halo of flashing steel above their heads, and with a cheer which was many a noble fellow's death cry, they flew into the smoke of the batteries; but ere they were lost from view, the plain was strewed with their bodies and with the carcasses of horses. They were exposed to an oblique fire from the batteries on the hills on both sides, as well as to a direct fire of musketry.

Through the clouds of smoke we could see their sabres flashing as they rode up to the guns and dashed between them, cutting down the gunners as they stood. The blaze of their steel, as an officer standing near me said, was 'like the turn of a shoal of mackerel'. We saw them riding through the guns, as I have said; to our delight we saw them returning, after breaking through a column of Russian infantry, and scattering them like chaff, when the flank fire of the battery on the hill swept them down, scattered and broken as they were. Wounded men and dismounted troopers flying towards us told the sad tale – demigods could not have done what they had failed to do. At the very moment when they were about to retreat, an enormous mass of lancers was hurled upon their flank. Colonel Shewell, of the 8th Hussars, saw the danger, and rode his few men straight at them, cutting his way through with fearful loss. The other regiments turned and engaged in a desperate encounter. With courage too great almost for credence, they were breaking their way through the columns which enveloped them, when there took place an act of atrocity without parallel in the modern warfare of civilized nations. The Russian gunners, when the storm of cavalry passed, returned to their guns. They saw their own cavalry mingled with the troopers who had just ridden over them, and to the eternal disgrace of the Russian name the miscreants poured a murderous volley of grape and canister on the mass of struggling men and horses, mingling friend and foe in one common ruin. It was as much as our Heavy Cavalry Brigade could do to cover the retreat of the miserable remnants of that band of heroes as they returned to the place they had so lately quitted in all the pride of life.

At twenty-five to twelve not a British soldier, except the dead and dying, was left in front of these bloody Muscovite guns. Our loss, as far as it could be ascertained in killed, wounded, and missing at two o'clock today, was as follows:

	WENT INTO ACTION STRONG	RETURNED FROM ACTION	LOSS
4th Light Dragoons	118	39	79
8th Hussars	104	38	66
11th Hussars	110	25	85
13th Light Dragoons	130	61	69
17th Lancers	145	35	110
	607	198	409

DISCOVERING THE VICTORIA FALLS, AFRICA, 1856

Dr David Livingstone

Dr Livingstone was a Scottish explorer and missionary.

I resolved on the following day to visit the falls of Victoria, called by the natives Mosioatunya, or more anciently Shongwe. Of these we had often heard since we came into the country: indeed one of the questions asked by Sebituane was, 'Have you smoke that sounds in your country?' They did not go near enough to examine them, but, viewing them with awe at a distance, said, in reference to the vapour and noise, 'Mosi oa tunya' (smoke does sound there). It was previously called Shongwe, the meaning of which I could not ascertain. The word for a 'pot' resembles this, and it may mean a seething cauldron; but I am not certain of it. Being persuaded that Mr Oswell and myself were the very first Europeans who ever visited the Zambesi in the centre of the country, and that this is the connecting link between the known and unknown portions of that river, I decided to use the same liberty as the Makololo did, and gave the only English name I have affixed to any part of the country . . .

Sekeletu intended to accompany me, but, one canoe only having come instead of the two he had ordered, he resigned it to me. After twenty minutes' sail from Kalai, we came in sight, for the first time, of the columns of vapour, appropriately called 'smoke', rising at a distance of five or six miles, exactly as when large tracts of grass are burned in Africa. Five columns now arose, and bending in the direction of the wind, they seemed placed against a low ridge covered with trees; the tops of the columns at this distance appeared to mingle with the clouds. They were white below, and higher up became dark, so as to simulate smoke very closely. The whole scene was extremely beautiful; the banks and islands dotted over the river are adorned with sylvan vegetation of great variety of colour and form. At the period of our visit several trees were spangled over with blossoms. Trees have each their own physiognomy. There, towering over all, stands the great burly baobab, each of whose enormous arms would form the trunk of a large tree, beside groups of graceful palms, which, with their feathery-shaped leaves depicted on the sky, lend their beauty to the scene. As a hieroglyphic they always mean 'far from home', for one can never get over their foreign air in a picture or landscape. The silvery mohonono, which in the tropics is in form like the cedar of Lebanon, stands in pleasing contrast with the dark colour of the motsouri, whose cypress-form is dotted over at present with its pleasant scarlet fruit. Some trees resemble the great spreading oak, others assume the character of our own elms and chestnuts; but no one can imagine the beauty of the view from anything witnessed in England. It had never been seen before by European eyes; but scenes so lovely must have been gazed upon by angels in their flight. The only want felt is that of mountains in the background. The falls are bounded on three sides by ridges 300 or 400 feet in height, which are covered with forest, with the red soil appearing among the trees. When about half a mile from the falls, I left the canoe by which we had come thus far, and embarked in a lighter one, with men well acquainted with the rapids, who, by passing down the centre of the stream in the eddies and still places caused by many jutting rocks, brought me to an island situated in the middle of the river, and on the edge of the lip over which the water rolls. In coming hither, there was danger of being swept down by the streams which rushed along on each side of the island; but the river was now low, and we sailed where it is totally impossible to go when the water is high. But though we had reached the island, and were within a few yards of the spot, a view from which would solve the whole problem, I believe that no one could perceive where the vast body of water went; it seemed to lose itself in the earth, the opposite lip of the fissure into which it disappeared being only 80 feet distant. At least I did not comprehend it until, creeping with awe to the verge, I peered down into a large rent which had been made from bank to bank of the broad Zambesi, and saw that a stream of a thousand yards broad leaped down a hundred feet and then became suddenly compressed into a space of fifteen or twenty yards. The entire falls are simply a crack made in a hard basaltic rock from the right to the left bank of the Zambesi, and then prolonged from the left bank away through thirty or forty miles of hills. If one imagines the Thames filled with low, tree-covered hills immediately beyond the tunnel, extending as far as Gravesend; the bed of black basaltic rock instead of London mud; and a fissure made therein from one end of the tunnel to the other, down through the keystones of the arch, and prolonged from the left end of the tunnel through thirty miles of hills; the pathway being 100 feet down from the bed of the river instead of what it is, with the lips of the fissure from 80 to 100 feet apart; then fancy the Thames leaping bodily into the gulf; and forced there to change its direction, and flow from the right to the left bank; and then rush boiling and roaring through the hills – one may have some idea of what takes place at this, the most wonderful sight I had witnessed in Africa. In looking down into the fissure on the right of the island, one sees nothing but a dense white cloud, which, at the time we visited the spot, had two bright rainbows on it. (The sun was on the meridian, and the declination about equal to the latitude of the place.) From this cloud rushed up a great jet of vapour exactly like steam, and it mounted 200 or 300 feet high; there condensing, it changed its hue to that of dark smoke, and came back in a constant shower, which soon wetted us to the skin. This shower falls chiefly on the opposite side of the fissure, and a few yards back from the lip, there stands a straight hedge of evergreen trees, whose leaves are always wet. From their roots a number of little rills run back into the gulf; but as they flow down the steep wall there, the column of vapour, in its ascent, licks them up clean off the rock, and away they mount again. They are constantly running down, but never reach the bottom.

THE HANGING OF JOHN BROWN, HARPER'S FERRY, VIRGINIA, 1859

David Hunter Strother

The slave-abolitionist John Brown was captured by Virginian forces during a raid on the Harper's Ferry arsenal, and subsequently sentenced to death for treason.

At eleven o'clock, escorted by a strong column of soldiers, the prisoner entered the field. He wore the same seedy and dilapidated dress he had at Harper's Ferry and during his trial, but his rough boots had given place to a pair of parti-coloured slippers and he wore a low crown broad brimmed hat (the first time I had ever seen him with a hat) . . . He stepped from the waggon with surprising agility and walked hastily toward the scaffold pausing a moment as he passed our group to wave his pinioned arm and bid us good morning. I thought I could observe in this a trace of bravado – but perhaps I was mistaken, as his natural manner was short, ungainly and hurried. He mounted the steps of the scaffold with the same alacrity and there, as if by previous arrangement, he immediately took off his hat and offered his neck for the halter which was as promptly adjusted by Mr Avis the jailer. A white muslin cap or hood was then drawn over his face and the Sheriff not remembering that his eyes were covered requested him to advance to the platform. The prisoner replied in his usual tone, 'You will have to guide me there.'

The breeze disturbing the arrangement of the hood, the Sheriff asked his assistant for a pin. Brown raised his hand and directed him to the collar of his coat where several old pins were quilted in. The Sheriff took the pin and completed his work.

He was accordingly led forward to the drop, the halter hooked to the beam and the officers supposing that the execution was to follow immediately took leave of him. In doing so, the Sheriff enquired if he did not want a handkerchief to throw as a signal to cut the drop. Brown replied, 'No, I don't care; I don't want you to keep me waiting unnecessarily.'

These were his last words, spoken with that sharp nasal twang peculiar to him, but spoken quietly and civilly without impatience or the slightest apparent emotion. In this position he stood for five minutes or more, while the troops that composed the escort were wheeling into the positions assigned them. I stood within a few paces of him and watched narrowly during these trying moments to see if there was any indication of his giving way. I detected nothing of the sort . . .

Colonel Smith said to the Sheriff in a low voice, 'We are ready.'

The civil officers descended from the scaffold. One who stood near me whispered earnestly, 'He trembles, his knees are shaking.'

'You are mistaken,' I replied, 'it is the scaffold that shakes under the footsteps of the officers.'

GARIBALDI LIBERATES SICILY, 24–30 May 1860

Frank Vizetelly

Giuseppe Garibaldi's liberation of Sicily from the rule of the Bourbon King of Naples, Francis II, led to the eventual unification of Italy. Garibaldi's 'army' was a 1000-strong volunteer force, whose red-shirt uniform would become famous as a symbol of revolution.

On the morning of the 24th ult., as our vessel rounded Cape Mongerbino, we could distinctly perceive firing going on along the crest of hills above Palermo. Of course, everyone on board the

Vulture was on the *qui vive* in an instant, an interested group, of whom your humble servant formed one, congregated, with telescopes and double-barrelled glasses, on the taffrails; while the crew, leaving their work, struggled on the crosstrees for the best places. Immediately we dropped anchor in the bay we were boarded by numbers of people, who told us that an engagement between Garibaldi and the Royal troops had taken place near Monreale, and that they were anxious to purchase any arms we might have for sale. They also told us that, despite the precautions taken by the authorities, who had made it death for anyone to be found with a sword or musket, some thousand young fellows were prepared to fall upon the soldiers, and cut them to pieces, as soon as Garibaldi should drive them in. However, the fighting turned out to be a mere feint on the part of the Liberals, for the puffs of smoke retreated further and further into the hills till they were lost to view, and nothing decisive was gained on either side, except that the Neapolitans arrogated to themselves a victory, supposing the retiring column to be the whole of the patriot army. This was one of Garibaldi's famous 'sells', for he, in the meantime, with the bulk of his force, made a flank march from Pareo to Misilmeri, leaving the Neapolitan general under the impression that he had fled in an opposite direction. Of course the supposed triumph was made much of by the Government; and I am inclined to think, from what I saw on landing, the people were becoming discouraged at the reported discomfiture of their hero. This feeling, however, was soon dissipated by the 'committee', a secret revolutionary council, sitting in the heart of Palermo, who took active measures to revive the drooping spirits of their fellow-citizens. Apropos of this 'committee', I witnessed an incident connected with it on my first visit to the shore which provided me with material for a sketch.

You can easily imagine that the *sbirri* were very curious to find out the persons who composed this council of conspirators, and that they lost no opportunity of gaining information as to the whereabouts of the sitting and the names of the members. I had just passed through the Porta Felice when I saw an immense rush of people coming towards me from the direction of the 'Reale Finanze'. At their head was a man running at full speed with the blood streaming from numerous wounds about the head: one gash in particular was frightful; it extended from the temple to the chin, and gave an awful appearance to the wretched creature, who was shrieking as he ran for mercy.

But those who came behind had none for the spy who had been found lurking about the quarters of the 'committee', and, as the fleetest of his pursuers came up with him, stab after stab was made with their gleaming knives till the miserable spy sank exhausted in the doorway of a house near the American Consul's into which he was dragged by some passing soldiers.

On Saturday, the 26th ult., there was a great stir amongst the Neapolitan steamers in the bay; they all of them got their steam up and stood out to sea in various directions, as if their mission was to intercept a second landing on the coast. This was not the case, as I afterwards learned. General Letizia, the commander of the Royal troops, had been so taken in by Garibaldi's feigned retreat to the hills that he started all the steamers in pursuit of him, should be attempt to embark at any point of the coast, and he also dispatched a vessel to Naples with the news that all was over, and that he hoped soon to send the patriot in person to be tortured in some dark dungeon for His Majesty's gratification. As it happened, I received, about an hour after the departure of the steamers, a communication from Garibaldi's camp telling me where they were (only eight miles distant), and promising, if I would wait for a day or two, to find some means of getting me to them; but it was also hinted in the letter that they would come to me.

About half past three on Sunday morning (the 27th ult.) I was awoke by a rapid discharge of musketry, the ringing of church bells, and loud hurrahing, shouted by thousands of lungs. To jump up and dress was the work of but five minutes. Garibaldi with his men was fighting his way into the town by the Porta St Antonino, while Neapolitan officers, surprised at the sudden appearance of the man whom they thought far away and a fugitive, were galloping about, giving confused orders to the troops they had got together, and then countermanding them immediately afterwards. The first precaution taken by the military was to place sentinels at intervals along both sides of the streets and at the entrance of every thoroughfare, with instructions to fire on anyone offering to show himself either at the windows or the doors of the houses. Two guns have been brought up, and are sweeping the Strada Nuova from the Via Toledo to the Porta St Antonino. Every balcony in the former street has now become a fortress; citizens that were supposed to have been disarmed are now doing good service on the panic-stricken troops; while the small column of liberators are making sure progress, taking advantage as they advance of every projection which offers shelter. The men who drove the Austrians from Como and Varese know the value of every ounce of lead, and there is not one of their bullets that has not its billet on leaving the muzzles of their guns. Hurrah! The Toledo – the centre street of the town – is gained; and a strong breastwork of bedding, sacks of shumac, and paving-stones is raised midway between the Porta Nuova and the Porta Felice. The former, with the Piazza Reale and the Palace, is in possession of the troops, who are assembling there in strong bodies and collecting their guns. The fort has now begun to shell that portion of the town in possession of Garibaldi. No position one can take up is safe; loud explosions, followed by clouds of dust from falling houses, succeed each other without intermission. Women and children run shrieking about the streets, while here and there organized bands of labourers are dragging dead and wounded from beneath the heaps of smouldering ruins. Verily, Letizia, the Neapolitan general, should be complimented on his manly and valorous mode of fighting; it is a great achievement to kill unoffending old women and little children. Why, in one ruined house I saw the charred bodies of an entire family, averaging from the ages of sixty years to six months. But the firing is getting stronger in the Via Toledo; some field-pieces have been brought into position at the Porta Nuova, which sweep the street from end to end. However, at the Porta Felice a barricade has been raised, and on it one of Garibaldi's officers plants the Italian flag amidst a storm of grapeshot, that, wonderful to say, leaves him untouched. All the steeples in the vicinity have their bells ringing as a signal for all those who have arms to congregate at the spot, and soon the barricade has a host of defenders. In the meantime Garibaldi's own men and the *squadri*, or Sicilian mountaineers, have taken the troops in flank from some of the intersecting streets, and, in conjunction with those from the barricade of the Porta Felice, drive them well back on to the Piazza Reale. It is now night, and the scene in the Toledo baffles all attempt at description. A Neapolitan war-steamer has taken up her position off the quay at the foot of it, and is sending 13-inch shells up the pathway of houses. Flames are bursting forth in all directions, and walls are falling with a crash across the narrow thoroughfares, while the shrieks and yells of the wounded, as they are removed to more sheltered positions, combined with the hurrahing of the patriot soldiers, as they drive the troops step by step towards the Royal

Palace, realized to the beholder the idea of a dozen Pandemoniums in one. All through the night does the fighting continue uninterruptedly, and there is little or no sleep to be obtained by even a non-combatant, who at any moment may be awakened by a live shell in his bed.

On Tuesday the fighting was harder than ever. An attack was made on the Palace, and one wing was taken from the soldiers and held for a considerable period; this exploit was performed by young Garibaldi, at the head of fifteen men, and had he not been recalled I believe he would have established himself firmly.

When it is considered that Garibaldi entered the city with only a thousand of his own people whom he could depend upon, the result achieved is surprising.

Steam is up on board a vessel leaving with despatches for Naples, and I must get this off at once. I will only add now that we have had an armistice since Wednesday afternoon, which is to expire to-morrow (Sunday, 3 June), at twelve. It was the Neapolitan general who asked for it, and he has gone to Naples for instructions how to act.

THE AMERICAN CIVIL WAR: SHILOH, 6–7 April 1862

Anon

The author was a private soldier in the Union army.

It was quite dark, though still early in the night, when we moved on again. The men were in the best of spirits, rude witticisms, laughter and snatches of song ran along the whole line. Here and there some fellow boasted of the gallant deeds he would have performed had he been in the day's engagement. The officers, on the other hand, were more quiet than usual. They marched in silence or gathered in little knots and conversed in whispers. At length, the town of Savannah was entered. Every house in the place seemed to be illuminated; for each had been converted into an hospital and was packed from attic to basement with the dying and wounded who had been conveyed thither by the steamer.

Groans and cries of pain saluted our ears from all the buildings we passed. Through the windows, the sash of which were removed to give air to the injured, we could see the surgeons plying their horrid profession. The atmosphere was that of a vast dissecting room. The streets were crowded with ambulances, baggage trains, parties bearing the victims of the fight on stretchers, on rails, on rude litters of muskets and on their shoulders, and with batteries of artillery and long lines of infantry waiting to be taken to the scene of the struggle. The confusion everywhere visible, the shouting, cursing, quarrelling, beggars descriptions. Teams of mules, abandoned by their drivers, ran away trampling down every thing in their course. Quartermasters rode about at furious pace trying to extricate their transportation from the general mass. Doctors, one hand full of instruments, the other of bandages, and covered with blood, wildly rushed through the immense crowd in search of additional subjects of their art. Still, from all that could be gathered, the idea appeared to be that we had achieved a great victory. No one could exactly tell the events of the day; but the fact of our decisive triumph was unquestioned. The falsity of this common opinion every reader of the newspapers already knows.

Getting on board the *Hiawatha*, by midnight we were ploughing the turbid Tennessee river *en route* for Pittsburg Landing, by water a distance of fourteen miles. From the officers of the steamer we got other accounts of the battle, which we afterwards ascertained to be correct. Their statements were, that Johnston and Beauregard, hoping to destroy Grant before he was joined by Buell, then close at hand, made a furious attack upon him, in great strength, that Sunday morning immediately after daylight. There is some dispute whether or not we had outposts; those who maintain we had, admit that they were playing cards at the time of the assault. At all events our troops were completely and criminally surprised. Unable to form to resist the onslaught, hundreds of them were mercilessly shot down in their tents and company streets. Those who escaped fled in the greatest terror through the camps in their rear, spreading the panic and closely followed by the successful foe. At least two miles of the ground occupied by our forces was thus abandoned before the regiments near the river could be brought to present a front to the rebels. A temporary check was then given to the enemy's impetuous advance, but being strongly reinforced they pushed our army slowly and surely towards the landing. During the whole day the battle raged with violence. Several corps of our volunteers behaved with great gallantry; but others ran at the first fire, and with those surprised in the morning (at least 10,000 men) could not again be brought into action. But the Secessionists steadily gained upon us. Seven batteries of our light artillery and a large number of our soldiers fell into their hands, as well as thousands of tents, and immense quantities of Commissary and Quartermaster's stores. When night closed upon the struggle we were driven within three hundred yards of the river, and would have been pushed into it had not the spiteful little gunboats then been enabled to come to our relief. Our loss in the engagement was terrible; but it was not all we suffered. At times when the fortune of war was most decidedly against us, the skulkers under the bluff, would rush in crowds to reach the steamers moored in the Tennessee, and by jostling and pushing each other into and struggling together in the water, hundreds of them were drowned. Little pity is felt for their fate, of course; but still these help to swell the casualties of that disastrous day.

Regaled, as we were, during the entire passage from Savannah to Pittsburg Landing, with stories of defeat and forebodings of what would occur the next day, you may be certain that we were not as comfortable as if we were in the old barracks. It was plain to the dullest comprehension that McCook's, Nelson's and Crittenden's divisions of Buell's army, then arrived at the scene of action, would have work enough to do early in the morning, and that too against an enemy flushed with recent victory. It seemed like folly to hope for success; for our strength did not exceed thirty thousand. From Grant's badly beaten and demoralized force we expected nothing, unless it was a mere show of numbers. On the other hand, the rebels were estimated at from 60,000 to 80,000. These considerations did not do much to inspirit, whilst throughout the night our anxiety was kept alive and our consciousness of the immediate presence of the foe not permitted to slumber by the regular firing from the gunboats upon the camps of the enemy close beside those of our own.

At daybreak on Monday the 7th inst. our battalion was disembarked. Forcing its way with difficulty through the vast crowd of fugitives from the previous day's fight gathered on the river bank, we scrambled up the bluff in the best way we could and formed in the camp of the Missouri Artillery. Here there were more refugees, their officers riding among them and urging them to rally, but without the least success. I never witnessed such abject fear as these fellows exhibited. Without a single avenue of escape in the event of defeat, they were unable, even, to muster up the desperation of cornered cowards. It is said that several in high command set them the example of pusillanimity. As we moved among them they inquired 'what regiment is that?' '15th Regulars,' replied some of our men. 'Well, you'll catch regular hell today,' was their rejoinder. Others said 'Boys, it's of no use; we were beaten yesterday and you'll be beaten now.' But still our men got into line well, and were marched by the right flank a few hundred yards to the place where the action of the previous day had ended. Here Capt. Swaine and Major King joined us, knapsacks were unslung, and we made the final preparations for the conflict we knew to be imminent. Being informed that we were the reserve of Rousseau's Brigade, we were slowly moved forward in column at half distance, through camps our troops had abandoned in the fight of the 6th inst. Other corps, all the while, were passing us on either side, and disappearing from view in a dip of ground in front, but as yet the engagement had not begun.

Let me try, at this point, to give you as good an idea of the field of battle as I am able. The Tennessee river at Pittsburg Landing describes a considerable curve; in the neck formed by this bend and some distance outside of it were the camps of Gen. Grant's command. On the morning of the 7th, the rebels were posted some distance inside of the ground formerly occupied by us, so that the line of conflict was pretty nearly straight between the two points of the semi-circle. Nelson's division was on our extreme left, resting on the river; Crittenden was next to him on his right, then came McCook in the centre, and joined to him was McClernand, who had other of Grant's generals beyond him. This order continued unbroken until the struggle was over.

Nelson and Crittenden's commands having passed the left flank of our battalion speedily became engaged. A few scattering shots were heard from their direction, which were soon followed by such a heavy firing of small arms that it was plain our men had found the enemy. The field artillery also broke in with its thunder, increasing the din already so great that it was difficult to hear one's self speak. As further evidence that the battle had begun in earnest, a mounted officer dashed by, crying, 'bring on the ambulances,' and those vehicles were at once taken to the front, to return in a few minutes laden with mangled freight. Other wounded men, some on foot, others carried by their comrades, likewise now came to the rear. From these we learned that Nelson and Crittenden, although suffering severely, were steadily pushing the rebels back, a story attested by the frequent cheers that arose from their gallant fellows.

A sharp firing that now took place almost immediately in our front, showed that the left and centre of our (McCook's) division had got into action, and that the battle was rapidly becoming general. Our battalion was instantly deployed into line to receive the foe should the troops in advance give way. While in this position, Generals Buell and Rousseau rode up, ordered us to proceed to the right of the brigade, which was the right of the division, and be ready for any emergency, and to send out at the same time a company of skirmishers to provoke an attack. This converted us from a reserve into an assaulting party.

Forming in column by division on the first, we marched by the right flank to the position we were to occupy, Captain Haughey with his command, being thrown forward to feel the enemy. (I will state here that battalions of the 16th and 19th regiments US Infantry, the whole under Major John H. King, were with us and shared in all our operations.) At this place we again deployed, then moved by the right of companies to the front, until a little hill between us and the rebels was surmounted, when we were again brought into line. Rapid discharges of small arms forward of our left flank, now showed that our skirmishers were successful in their search. Again we were advanced, until having gained some distance, we were ordered to lie close to the ground. Immediately we were exposed to a cannonade and fire of musketry, whose severity defies description. From three batteries and their strong support of infantry just before us, masked by the underbrush, came a shower of grape, canister, spherical case, rifle balls, &c., that would have swept every one of us away had we been standing on our feet. An examination I have since made of the ground exhibits the fact that every tree and sapling bears the marks of shot. Protecting ourselves as we did, our loss was still severe. Among the injured were Capt. Acker of the 16th, killed, and Capt. Peterson of the 15th, wounded in the head. As yet, as I have said before, the foe was concealed in the thick woods so that we could not see them; but now emboldened, perhaps, by what they supposed their irresistible attack, they emerged from their cover. Never did they commit a more fatal mistake. Our men, restrained by their officers, had not discharged a piece up to this time. But now each coolly marked his man; and when Capt. Swaine, in a voice that could be heard along the whole line, gave the command to fire, our Springfield rifles dealt a destruction that was awful. After pelting the rebels a little while longer, we again moved forward to the sound of the bugle, taking to the earth once more when the enemy opened upon us. Here Lieut. Mitchell of the 16th was killed, and Lieut. Lyster of the 19th, and 1st Sergeants Williams and Kiggins of the 15th dangerously wounded. Halting a few moments to reply, we moved down upon the traitors a third time, subjected the while to a fearful storm of missiles, by which Capt. Curtiss and Lieut. Wykoff of the 15th were very severely hurt, and 1st Sergeant Killink of the same corps instantly killed. But at length the artillery of the enemy, that had been playing upon us so long, came in sight. Hastily fixing bayonets, we charged upon it at a double-quick. Capt. Keteltas of the 15th being then shot through the body. Unable to withstand our desperate assault, the rebel cannoneers abandoned their guns, and with the infantry supports fled across an open space into the woods beyond. An opportunity offered at this point to ascertain the havoc we had done. Every horse in each piece and caisson lay dead in his harness, and the ground was covered with the killed and dying. Among the latter was the Chief of the Artillery. As we came up he said, 'You have slain all my men and cattle, and you may take the battery and be damned.' But we had not leisure to stop and talk with him or any other person; for we were already being fired upon from the new covert of the foe. Pushing forward amid great danger across the field, we gained the edge of the timber and continued the fight in which we had then been engaged for more than five hours.

The foregoing was the state of affairs at high noon. Let us pause a moment to see what was the condition of the battle field at that hour. There was no fighting on the right of the centre; indeed it had not been severe in that quarter during the day. On the left, Nelson and Crittenden having repulsed the enemy, were resting on their arms; for the foe in their front had mysteriously disappeared. Our three battalions were our only troops then hotly engaged. You inquire, 'where were the rest of the rebels?' That is just what I propose telling you. Leaving only enough of men before the other divisions to mask their purpose, they were engaged massing their troops, those that had been engaged as well as their reserves, for an overwhelming onslaught upon the right of our centre, where we had contested all morning without support. I think it possible that Gen. Rousseau suspected their scheme; for whilst we strove in the edge of the timber, two regiments of volunteers took position on our right, and a section of a battery quietly unlimbered on our left. Scarcely were these dispositions completed, when down upon us came the enemy, pouring in a withering, staggering fire, that compelled the regiments just mentioned to break and fly, in such confusion that they could not be rallied again. This panic not only left us alone to sustain the dreaded onset, but in addition, put us in extraordinary peril by the total exposure of our left flank. The occasion was indeed critical. But before the enemy could take any advantage of the condition of things, Capt. Swaine averted the danger by causing our battalion to charge front, thus giving the 15th, 16th and 19th the form of two sides of a triangle. Here we fought for a time that seemed interminable, holding the rebel force in check, until Col. Gibson's brigade, hastily brought up to our relief, assisted by a flanking attack from Nelson and Crittenden's divisions started the foe in the retreat, that shortly became a rout. Falling back, then, only long enough to replenish our ammunition, we joined in the pursuit, keeping it up, notwithstanding our exhausted condition, until we got beyond the line of the camps captured from our troops the day before.

I do not undertake to say what body of troops engaged in the battle of Shiloh, is entitled to the most honor. But I unhesitatingly assert that the 1st Battalion of the 15th US Infantry did its whole duty. For seven hours it fought with out ceasing, that, too, after it had marched seventeen miles the day before, and been deprived of sleep the night previous. And when the dreadful attack upon our centre was made, which caused Willich's German veterans to scatter like cattle upon a thousand hills, it still stood up to its work as though there was no such word as defeat in its lexicon. Throughout the struggle, Major King, Capt. Swaine and the company officers conducted themselves with great gallantry. In our company, nine men are killed and wounded. The loss of the command is sixty-three. Curtenius escaped without a scratch.

Dr Parry informs me that our loss in killed and wounded, will not fall short of nine thousand men, and may exceed that number. From what I have seen myself, I give the fullest credence to his statement. On the evening of the engagement, the dead were everywhere. There never has been such carnage on this continent. I trust I may never again see anything of the kind.

The battle was fought in the woods, which were as serviceable to the enemy as fortifications. You may travel for a day around here and you will scarcely find a tree, sapling or twig, that has not been struck by a bullet. How any of us escaped is more than I can imagine.

THE ASSASSINATION OF PRESIDENT LINCOLN, WASHINGTON, AMERICA, 14 April 1865

Walt Whitman

Abraham Lincoln's murderer, John Wilkes Booth, was a pro-slavery fanatic.

The day, April 14, 1865, seems to have been a pleasant one throughout the whole land – the moral atmosphere pleasant too – the long storm, so dark, so fratricidal, full of blood and doubt and gloom, over and ended at last by the sunrise of such an absolute National victory, and utter breaking down of Secessionism – we almost doubted our own senses! Lee had capitulated beneath the apple-tree of Appomattox. The other armies, the flanges of the revolt, swiftly followed . . . And could it really be, then? Out of all the affairs of this world of woe and passion, of failure and disorder and dismay, was there really come the confirmed, unerring sign of plan, like a shaft of pure light – of rightful rule – of God? . . . So the day, as I say, was propitious. Early herbage, early flowers, were out. (I remember where I was stopping at the time, the season being advanced, there were many lilacs in full bloom. By one of those caprices that enter and give tinge to events without being at all a part of them, I find myself always reminded of the great tragedy of that day by the sight and odour of these blossoms. It never fails.)

But I must not dwell on accessories. The deed hastens. The popular afternoon paper of Washington, the little *Evening Star*, had spattered all over its third page, divided among the advertisements in a sensational manner in a hundred different places, *The President and his Lady will be at the Theatre this evening* . . . (Lincoln was fond of the theatre. I have myself seen him there several times. I remember thinking how funny it was that He, in some respects, the leading actor in the greatest and stormiest drama known to real history's stage, through centuries, should sit there and be so completely interested and absorbed in those human jack straws, moving about with their silly little gestures, foreign spirit, and flatulent text.)

On this occasion the theatre was crowded, many ladies in rich and gay costumes, officers in their uniforms, many well-known, citizens, young folks, the usual clusters of gas-lights, the usual magnetism of so many people, cheerful, with perfumes, music of violins and flutes – (and over all, and saturating all, that vast vague wonder, *Victory*, the Nation's Victory, the triumph of the Union, filling the air, the thought, the sense, with exhilaration more than all perfumes.)

The President came betimes, and, with his wife, witnessed the play, from the large stage-boxes of the second tier, two thrown into one, and profusely draped with the National flag. The acts and scenes of the piece – one of those singularly written compositions which have at least the merit of giving entire relief to an audience engaged in mental action or business excitements and cares during the day, as it makes not the slightest call on either the moral, emotional, aesthetic, or spiritual nature – a piece, (*Our American Cousin*) in which, among other characters, so called, a Yankee, certainly such a one as was never seen, or the least like it ever seen, in North America, is introduced in England, with a varied fol-de-rol of talk, plot, scenery, and such phantasmagoria as goes to make up a modern popular drama – had progressed through perhaps a couple of its acts, when in the midst of this comedy, or tragedy, or non-such, or whatever it is to be called, and to off-set it or finish it out, as if in Nature's and the Great Muse's mockery of those poor mimes, comes interpolated that Scene, not really or exactly to be described at all (for on the many hundreds who were there it seems to this hour to have left little but a passing blur, a dream, a blotch) – and yet partially to be described as I now proceed to give it . . . There is a scene in the play representing a modern parlour, in which two unprecedented English ladies are informed by the unprecedented and impossible Yankee that he is not a man of fortune, and therefore undesirable for marriage-catching purposes; after which, the comments being finished, the dramatic trio make exit, leaving the stage clear for a moment. There was a pause, a hush as it were. At this period came the murder of Abraham Lincoln. Great as that was, with all its manifold train, circling round it, and stretching into the future for many a century, in the politics, history, art, of the New World, in point of fact the main thing, the actual murder, transpired with the quiet and simplicity of any commonest occurrence – the bursting of a bud or pod in the growth of vegetation, for instance. Through the general hum following the stage pause, with the change of positions, came the muffled sound of a pistol shot, which not one hundredth part of the audience heard at the time – and yet a moment's hush – somehow, surely a vague startled thrill – and then, through the ornamented, draperied, starred and striped space-way of the

President's box, a sudden figure, a man raises himself with hands and feet, stands a moment on the railing, leaps below to the stage (a distance of perhaps fourteen or fifteen feet) falls out of position, catching his boot-heel in the copious drapery (the American flag), falls on one knee, quickly recovers himself, rises as if nothing had happened (he really sprains his ankle, but unfelt then) – and so the figure, Booth, the murderer, dressed in plain black broadcloth, bare-headed, with a full head of glossy, raven hair, and his eyes like some mad animal's flashing with light and resolution, yet with a certain strange calmness, holds aloft in one hand a large knife – walks along not much back from the footlights – turns fully toward the audience his face of statuesque beauty, lit by those basilisk eyes, flashing with desperation, perhaps insanity – launches out in a firm and steady voice the words, *Sic semper tyrannis* – and then walks with neither slow nor very rapid pace diagonally across to the back of the stage, and disappears . . . (Had not all this terrible scene – making the mimic ones preposterous – had it not all been rehearsed, in blank, by Booth, beforehand?)

A moment's hush, incredulous – a scream – the cry of *Murder* – Mrs Lincoln leaning out of the box, with ashy cheeks and lips, with involuntary cry, pointing to the retreating figure, *He has killed the President* . . . And still a moment's strange, incredulous suspense – and then the deluge! – then that mixture of horror, noises, uncertainty – (the sound, somewhere back, of a horse's hoofs clattering with speed) – the people burst through chairs and railings, and break them up – that noise adds to the queerness of the scene – there is inextricable confusion and terror – women faint – quite feeble persons fall, and are trampled on – many cries of agony are heard – the broad stage suddenly fills to suffocation with a dense and motley crowd, like some horrible carnival – the audience rush generally upon it – at least the strong men do – the actors and actresses are all there in their play costumes and painted faces, with mortal fright showing through the rouge, some trembling – some in tears – the screams and calls, confused talk – redoubled, trebled – two or three manage to pass up water from the stage to the President's box – others try to clamber up – etc., etc., etc.

In the midst of all this, the soldiers of the President's Guard, with others, suddenly drawn to the scene, burst in – (some two hundred altogether) – they storm the house, through all the tiers, especially the upper ones, inflamed with fury, literally charging the audience with fixed bayonets, muskets and pistols, shouting *Clear out! clear out! you sons of –* . . . Such the wild scene, or a suggestion of it rather, inside the playhouse that night.

Outside, too, in the atmosphere of shock and craze, crowds of people, filled with frenzy, ready to seize any outlet for it, come near committing murder several times on innocent individuals. One such case was especially exciting. The infuriated crowd, through some chance, got started against one man, either for words he uttered, or perhaps without any cause at all, and were proceeding at once to actually hang him on a neighbouring lamp-post, when he was rescued by a few heroic policemen, who placed him in their midst and fought their way slowly and amid great peril toward the Station House . . . It was a fitting episode of the whole affair. The crowd rushing and eddying to and fro – the night, the yells, the pale faces, many frightened people trying in vain to extricate themselves – the attacked man, not yet freed from the jaws of death, looking like a corpse – the silent resolute half-dozen policemen, with no weapons but their little clubs, yet stern and steady through all those eddying swarms – made indeed a fitting side-scene to the grand tragedy of the murder . . . They gained the Station House with the protected man, whom they placed in security for the night, and discharged him in the morning.

And in the midst of that night-pandemonium of senseless hate, infuriated soldiers, the audience and the crowd – the stage, and all its actors and actresses, its paint-pots, spangles, and gas-lights – the life-blood from those veins, the best and sweetest of the land, drips slowly down, and death's ooze already begins its little bubbles on the lips . . . Such, hurriedly sketched, were the accompaniments of the death of President Lincoln. So suddenly and in murder and horror unsurpassed he was taken from us. But his death was painless.

THE AMERICAN ASSAULT ON THE PYRAMIDS, EGYPT, June 1867

Mark Twain

Mark Twain covered the first organized Grand Tour by Americans for the *Alta California* newspaper.

A laborious walk in the flaming sun brought us to the foot of the great Pyramid of Cheops. It was a fairy vision no longer. It was a corrugated, unsightly mountain of stone. Each of its monstrous sides was a wide stairway which rose upward, step above step, narrowing as it went, till it tapered to a point far aloft in the air. Insect men and women – pilgrims from the *Quaker City* – were creeping about its dizzy perches, and one little black swarm were waving postage stamps from the airy summit – handkerchiefs will be understood.

Of course we were besieged by a rabble of muscular Egyptians and Arabs who wanted the contract of dragging us to the top – all tourists are. Of course you could not hear your own voice for the din that was around you. Of course the Sheiks said *they* were the only responsible parties; that all contracts must be made with them, all moneys paid over to them, and none exacted from us by any but themselves alone. Of course they contracted that the varlets who dragged us up should not mention bucksheesh once. For such is the usual routine. Of course we contracted with them, paid them, were delivered into the hands of the draggers, dragged up the Pyramids, and harried and be-deviled for bucksheesh from the foundation clear to the summit. We paid it, too, for we were purposely spread very far apart over the vast side of the Pyramid. There was no help near if we called, and the Herculeses who dragged us had a way of asking sweetly and flatteringly for bucksheesh, which was seductive, and of looking fierce and threatening to throw us down the precipice, which was persuasive and convincing. Each step being full as high as a dinner-table; there being very, very many of the steps; an Arab having hold of each of our arms and springing upward from step to step and snatching us with them, forcing us to lift our feet as high as our breasts every time, and do it rapidly and keep it up till we were ready to faint, who shall say it is not lively, exhilarating, lacerating, muscle-straining, bone-wrenching and perfectly excruciating and exhausting pastime, climbing the Pyramids? I beseeched the varlets not to twist *all* my joints asunder; I iterated, reiterated, even *swore* to them that I did not wish to beat any body to the top; did all I could to convince them that if I got there the last of all I would feel blessed above men and grateful to them forever; I begged them, prayed them, pleaded with them to let me stop and rest a moment – only one little moment: and they only answered with some more frightful springs . . . Twice, for one minute, they let me rest while they extorted bucksheesh, and then continued their maniac flight up the Pyramid. They wished to beat the other parties. It was nothing to them that I, a stranger, must be sacrificed upon the altar of their unholy ambition. But in the midst of sorrow, joy blooms. Even in this dark hour I had a sweet consolation. For I knew that except these Mohammedans repented they would go straight to perdition some day. And *they* never repent – they never forsake their paganism. This thought calmed me, cheered me, and I sank down, limp and exhausted, upon the summit, but happy, *so* happy and serene within.

GUNFIGHT IN DODGE CITY, KANSAS, AMERICA, *c.* 1868

Andy Adams

Quince Forrest was spending his winnings as well as drinking freely, and at the end of a quadrille gave vent to his hilarity in an old-fashioned Comanche yell. The bouncer of the dance hall of course had his eye on our crowd, and at the end of a change, took Quince to task. He was a surly brute, and instead of couching his request in appropriate language, threatened to throw him out of the house. Forrest stood like one absentminded and took the abuse, for physically he was no match for the bouncer, who was armed, moreover, and wore an officer's star. I was dancing in the same set with a redheaded, freckle-faced girl, who clutched my arm and wished to know if my friend was armed. I assured her that he was not, or we would have had notice of it before the bouncer's invective was ended. At the conclusion of the dance, Quince and The Rebel passed out, giving the rest of us the word to remain as though nothing was wrong. In the course of half an hour, Priest returned and asked us to take our leave one at a time without attracting any attention, and meet at the stable. I remained until the last, and noticed The Rebel and the bouncer taking a drink together at the bar – the former apparently in a most amiable mood. We passed out together shortly afterward, and found the other boys mounted and awaiting our return, it being now about midnight. It took but a moment to secure our guns, and once in the saddle, we rode through the town in the direction of the herd. On the outskirts of the town, we halted. 'I'm going back to that dance hall,' said Forrest, 'and have one round at least with that whore-herder. No man who walks this old earth can insult me, as he did, not if he has a hundred stars on him. If any of you don't want to go along, ride right on to camp, but I'd like to have you all go. And when I take his measure, it will be the signal to the rest of you to put out the lights. All that's going, come on.'

There were no dissenters to the programme. I saw at a glance that my bunkie was heart and soul in the play, and took my cue and kept my mouth shut. We circled round the town to a vacant lot within a block of the rear of the dance hall. Honeyman was left to hold the horses; then, taking off our belts and hanging them on the pommels of our saddles, we secreted our six-shooters inside the waistbands of our trousers. The hall was still crowded with the revelers when we entered, a few at a time, Forrest and Priest being the last to arrive. Forrest had changed hats with The Rebel, who always wore a black one, and as the bouncer circulated around, Quince stepped squarely in front of him. There was no waste of words, but a gun-barrel flashed in the lamplight, and the bouncer, struck with the six-shooter, fell like a beef. Before the bewildered spectators could raise a hand, five six-shooters were turned into the ceiling. The lights went out at the first fire, and amidst the rush of men and the screaming of women, we reached the outside, and within a minute were in our saddles. All would have gone well had we returned by the same route and avoided the town; but after crossing the railroad track, anger and pride having not been properly satisfied, we must ride through the town.

On entering the main street, leading north and opposite the bridge on the river, somebody of our party in the rear turned his gun loose into the air. The Rebel and I were riding in the lead, and at the clattering of hoofs and shooting behind us, our horses started on the run, the shooting by this time having become general. At the second street crossing, I noticed a rope of fire belching from a Winchester in the doorway of a store building. There was no doubt in my mind but we were the object of the manipulator of that carbine, and as we reached the next cross street, a man kneeling in the shadow of a building opened fire on us with a six-shooter. Priest reined in his horse, and not having wasted cartridges in the open air shooting, returned the compliment until he emptied his gun. By this time every officer in the town was throwing lead after us, some of which cried a little too close for comfort. When there was no longer any shooting on our flanks, we turned into a cross street and soon left the lead behind us. At the outskirts of the town we slowed up our horses and took it leisurely.

EASTER SUNDAY IN THE COUNTRY, CLYRO, WALES, 17 April 1870

Reverend Francis Kilvert

Diary: The happiest, brightest, most beautiful Easter I have ever spent. I woke early and looked out. As I had hoped the day was cloudless, a glorious morning. My first thought was 'Christ is Risen'. It is not well to lie in bed on Easter morning, indeed it is thought very unlucky. I got up between five and six and was out soon after six. There had been a frost and the air was rimy with a heavy thick white dew on hedge, bank and turf, but the morning was not cold. There was a heavy white dew with a touch of hoar frost on the meadows, and as I leaned over the wicket gate by the mill pond looking to see if there were any primroses in the banks but not liking to venture into the dripping grass suddenly I heard the cuckoo for the first time this year. He was near Peter's Pool and he called three times quickly one after another. It is very well to hear the cuckoo for the first time on Easter Sunday morning. I loitered up the lane again gathering primroses.

The village lay quiet and peaceful in the morning sunshine, but by the time I came back from primrosing there was some little stir and people were beginning to open their doors and look out into the fresh fragrant splendid morning.

There was a very large congregation at morning church, the largest I have seen for some time, attracted by Easter and the splendour of the day, for they have here an immense reverence for Easter Sunday. The anthem went very well and Mr Baskerville complimented Mr Evans after church about it, saying that it was sung in good tune and time and had been a great treat. There were more communicants than usual: 29. This is the fifth time I have received the Sacrament within four days. After morning service I took Mr V. round the churchyard and showed him the crosses on his mother's, wife's, and brother's graves. He was quite taken by surprise and very much gratified. I am glad to see that our primrose crosses seem to be having some effect for I think I notice this Easter some attempt to copy them and an advance towards the form of the cross in some of the decorations of the graves. I wish we could get the people to adopt some little design in the disposition of the flowers upon the graves instead of sticking sprigs into the turf aimlessly anywhere, anyhow and with no meaning at all. But one does not like to interfere too much with their artless, natural way of showing their respect and love for the dead. I am thankful to find this beautiful custom on the increase, and observed more and more every year. Some years ago it was on the decline and nearly discontinued. On Easter Day all the young people come out in something new and bright like butterflies. It is almost part of their religion to wear something new on this day. It was an old saying that if you don't wear something new on Easter Day, the crows will spoil everything you have on.

Between the services a great many people were in the churchyard looking at the graves. I went to Bettws Chapel in the afternoon. It was burning hot and as I climbed the hill the perspiration rolled off my forehead from under my hat and fell in drops on the dusty road. Lucretia Wall was in chapel looking pale and pretty after her illness. Coming down the hill it was delightful, cool and pleasant. The sweet suspicion of spring strengthens, deepens and grows more sweet every day. Mrs Pring gave us lamb and asparagus at dinner.

THE SIEGE OF PARIS, December 1870

Henry Labouchere

The French capital was besieged as a consequence of Napoleon III's declaration of war on Prussia in July 1870. The author was correspondent for the British *Daily News:* most of his reports were sent out of Paris by balloon.

When the Fenians in the United States meditate a raid upon Canada, they usually take very great care to allow their intentions to be known. Our sorties are much like these Hibernian surprises. If the Prussians do not know when we are about to attack, they cannot complain that it is our fault. The '*Aprés vous, Monsieurs les Anglais*', still forms the chivalrous but somewhat naif tactics of the Gauls. On Sunday, as a first step to military operations, the gates of the city were closed to all unprovided with passes. On Monday a Grand Council of generals and admirals took place at the Palais Royal. Yesterday and all last night drums were beating, trumpets were blowing, and troops were marching through the streets. The war battalions of the National Guard, in their new uniforms, spick and span, were greeted with shouts, to which they replied by singing a song, the chorus of which is 'Vive la guerre Piff-Paff', and which has replaced the 'Marseillaise'. As the ambulances had been ordered to be ready to start at six in the morning, I presumed that business would commence at an early hour, and I ordered myself to be called at 5.30. I was called, and got out of my bed, but, alas for noble resolutions! having done so, I got back again into it and remained between the sheets quietly enjoying that sleep which is derived from the possession of a good conscience, and a still better digestion, until the clock struck nine.

It was not until past eleven o'clock that I found myself on the outside of the gate of La Villette, advancing, as Grouchy should have done at Waterloo, in the direction of the sound of the cannon. From the gate a straight road runs to Le Bourget, having the Fort of Aubervilliers on the right, and St Denis on the left. Between the fort and the gate there were several hundred ambulance waggons, and above a thousand *brancardiers* stamping their feet and blowing on their fingers to keep themselves warm. In the fields on each side of the road there were numerous regiments of Mobiles drawn up ready to advance if required. The sailors, who are quartered here in great numbers, said that they had carried Le Bourget early in the morning, but that they had been obliged to fall back, with the loss of about a third of their number. Most of them had hatchets by their sides, and they attack a position much as if they were boarding a ship. About 100 prisoners had been brought into the town in the morning, as well as two *frères Chrétiens,* who had been wounded, and for whom the greatest sympathy was expressed. Little seemed to be known of what was passing. 'The Prussians will be here in an hour,' shouted one man; 'The Prussians are being exterminated,' shouted another. At a farm yard close by Drancy I saw Ducrot with his staff. The General had his hood drawn over his head, and both he and his aide-de-camp looked so glum, that I thought it just as well not to congratulate him upon the operations of the day. In and behind Drancy there were a large number of troops, who I heard were to camp there during the night. None seemed exactly to know what had happened. The officers and soldiers were not in good spirits. On my return into Paris, however, I found the following proclamation of the Government posted on the walls: – '2 p.m. – The attack was commenced this morning by a great deployment from Mount Valerein to Nogent, the combat has commenced, and continues everywhere, with favourable chances for us. – Schmitz.' The people on the Boulevards seem to imagine that a great victory has been gained.

When one asks them where? they answer 'everywhere'. I can only answer myself for what occurred at Le Bourget. I hear that Vinoy has occupied Nogent, on the north of the Marne; the resistance he encountered could not, however, have been very great, as only seven wounded have been brought into this hotel and only one to the American ambulance. General Trouchu announced this morning that 100 battalions of the National Guard are outside the walls, and I shall be curious to learn how they conduct themselves under fire. Far be it from me to say that they will not fight like lions. If they do, however, it will surprise most of the military men with whom I have spoken on the subject. As yet all they have done has been to make frequent 'pacts with death', to perform unauthorized strategical movements to the rear whenever they have been sent to the front, to consume much liquor, to pillage houses and – to put it poetically – toy with Amaryllis in the trench, or with the tangles of Nereas's hair. Their general, Clement Thomas, is doing his best to knock them into shape, but I am afraid that it is too late. There are cases in which, in defiance of the proverb, it is too late to mend.

In order to form an opinion with regard to the condition of the poorer classes, I went yesterday into some of the back slums in the neighbourhood of the Boulevard de Clichy. The distress is terrible. Women and children, half starved, were seated at their doorsteps, with hardly clothes to cover them decently. They said that, as they had neither firewood nor coke, they were warmer out-of-doors than in-doors. Many of the National Guards, instead of bringing their money home to their families, spend it in drink; and there are many families, composed entirely of women and children, who, in this land of bureaucracy, are apparently left to starve whilst it is decided to what category they belong. The Citizen Moltu, the ultra-Democratic Mayor, announced that in his *arrondissement* all left-handed marriages are to be regarded as valid, and the left-handed spouses of the National Guards are to receive the allowance which is granted to the legitimate wives of these warriors. But a new difficulty has arisen. Left-handed polygamy prevails to a great extent among the Citizen Moltu's admirers. Is a lady who has five husbands entitled to five rations, and is a lady who only owns the fifth of a National Guard to have only one-fifth of a ration? These are questions which the Citizen Moltu is now attempting to solve. A few days ago Madame Hamelin was discovered dead in bed in a garret of Belleville, of cold and starvation. Her husband has been, under Louis Philippe, ambassador at Constantinople. I went to see yesterday what was going on in the house of a friend of mine in the Avenue de l'Impératrice, who has left Paris. The servant who was in charge told me that up there they had been unable to obtain bread for three days, and that the last time that he had presented his ration ticket he had been given about half an inch of cheese. 'How do you live, then?' I asked. After looking mysteriously round to see that no one was watching us, he took me down into the cellar, and pointed to some meat in a barrel. 'It is half a horse,' he said, in the tone of a man who is showing someone the corpse of his murdered victim. 'A neighbouring coachman killed him, and we salted him down and divided it.' Then he opened a closet in which sat a huge cat. 'I am fattening her up for Christmas-day,' he observed.

THE PARIS COMMUNE: HUNTING DOWN THE COMMUNISTS, 24 May 1871

Archibald Forbes

The Commune was begun in February 1871 by Republican Parisians intent on resisting the Royalist-dominated government in Versailles. On 21 May, Versaillist troops entered the French capital. About 20,000 Communists died in the suppression that followed.

Wednesday, 24 May: The Versaillist troops collected about the foot of the Rue Saint-Honoré were enjoying the fine game of Communist hunting. The Parisians of civil life are caitiffs to the last drop of their thin, sour, white blood. But yesterday they had cried *Vive la Commune!* and submitted to be governed by this said Commune. Today they rubbed their hands with livid currish joy to have it in their power to denounce a Communist and reveal his hiding place. Very eager at this work are the dear creatures of women. They know the rat-holes into which the poor devils have got, and they guide to them with a fiendish glee which is a phase of the many-sided sex. *Voila!* the braves of France returned to a triumph after a shameful captivity! They have found him, the miserable! Yes, they drag him out from one of the purlieus which Haussmann had not time to sweep away, and a guard of six of them hem him round as they march him into the Rue Saint-Honoré. A tall, pale, hatless man, with something not ignoble in his carriage. His lower lip is trembling, but his brow is firm, and the eye of him has some pride and defiance in it. They yell – the crowd – 'Shoot him; shoot him!' – the demon women most clamorous, of course. An arm goes into the air; there are on it the stripes of a non-commissioned officer, and there is a stick in the fist. The stick falls on the head of the pale man in black. Ha! the infection has caught; men club their rifles, and bring them down on that head, or clash them into splinters in their lust for murder. He is down; he is up again; he is down again; the thuds of the gunstocks on him sounding just as the sound when a man beats a cushion with a stick. A certain British impulse, stronger than consideration for self, prompts me to run forward. But it is useless. They are firing into the flaccid carcass now thronging about it like blowflies on a piece of meat. His brains spurt on my boot and plash into the gutter, whither the carrion is bodily chucked, presently to be trodden on and rolled on by the feet of multitudes and wheels of gun carriages.

Womanhood, then, is not quite dead in that band of bedlamites who had clamoured 'Shoot him'. Here is one in hysterics; another with man, scared face, draws out of the press an embryo bedlamite, her offspring, and, let us hope, goes home. But surely all manhood is dead in the soldiery of France to do a deed like this. An officer one with a bull throat and the eyes of Algiers – stood by and looked on at the sport, sucking a cigar meanwhile.

The merry game goes on. Denouncing becomes fashionable, and denouncing is followed in the French natural sequence by braining Faugh! let us get away from the truculent cowards and the bloody gutters, and the yelling women, and the Algerian-eyed officers. Here is the Place Vendôme, held, as I learn on credible authority, by twenty-five Communists and a woman, against all that Versailles found it in its heart to do, for hours. In the shattered Central Place Versaillist sentries are stalking about the ruins of the column. They have accumulated, too, some forces in the rat-trap. There is one corpse in the gutter buffered and besmirched – the corpse, as I learn, of the Communist captain of a barricade who held it for half an hour single-handed against the braves of France, and then shot himself. The braves have, seemingly, made sure of him by shooting him and the clay, which was once a man, over and over again.

And how about the chained wildcats in the Hôtel de Ville? Their backs are to the wall, and they are fighting now, not for life, but that they may do as much evil as they can before their hour comes – as come it will before the minute hand of my watch makes many more revolutions. The Versaillists do not dare to rush at the barricades around the Hôtel de Ville; they are at once afraid of their skins and explosions. But they are mining, circumventing, burrowing, and they will be inside the cordon soon. Meanwhile the holders of the Hôtel de Ville are pouring out death and destruction over Paris in miscellaneous wildness. Now it is a shell in the Champs-Elysées; now one in the already shattered Boulevard Haussmann; now one somewhere about the Avenue Reine Hortense. It is between the devil and the deep sea with the people in the Hôtel de Ville. One enemy with weapons in his hand is outside; another, fire, the sunbeams struggle and surge ghastly swart waves and folds and pillars of dense smoke; not one or two, but I reckon them on my fingers till I lose the count. Ha! there is a sharp crack, and then a dull thud on the air. No artillery that, surely some great explosion which must have rocked Paris to its base. There rises a convolvulus shaped volume of whiter smoke, with a jetlike spurt, such as men describe when Vesuvius bursts into eruption, and then it break into fleecy waves and eddies away to the horizon all round as the ripple of a stone thrown into a pool spreads to the margin of the water. The crowds of Germans who sit by the Seine, stolidly watching, are startled into a burst of excitement – the excitement might well be worldwide. 'Paris the beautiful' is Paris the ghastly, Paris the battered, Paris the burning, Paris the blood-spattered now. And this is the nineteenth century, and Europe professes civilization, and France boasts of culture, and Frenchmen are braining one another with the butt ends of muskets, and Paris is burning. We want but a Nero to fiddle.

MEETING LIVINGSTONE, UJIJI, AFRICA, 10 November 1871

Sir Henry Morton Stanley

Dr Livingstone went missing during a search for the headwaters of the River Nile. The *New York Herald* sent Henry M. Stanley to find him.

We push on rapidly, lest the news of our coming might reach the people of Bunder Ujiji before we come in sight, and are ready for them. We halt at a little brook, then ascend the long slope of a naked ridge, the very last of the myriads we have crossed. This alone prevents us from seeing the lake in all its vastness. We arrive at the summit, travel across and arrive at its western rim, and –

pause, reader – the port of Ujiji is below us, embowered in the palms, only five hundred yards from us! At this grand moment we do not think of the hundreds of miles we have marched, of the hundreds of hills that we have ascended and descended, of the many forests we have traversed, of the jungles and thickets that annoyed us, of the fervid salt plains that blistered our feet, of the hot suns that scorched us, nor the dangers and difficulties, now happily surmounted. At last the sublime hour has arrived! – our dreams, our hopes, and anticipations are now about to be realized! Our hearts and our feelings are with our eyes as we peer into the palms and try to make out in which hut or house lives the white man with the grey beard we heard about on the Malagarazi.

We were now about three hundred yards from the village of Ujiji and the crowds are dense about me. Suddenly I hear a voice on my right side.

'Good morning, sir!'

Startled at hearing this greeting in the midst of such a crowd of black people, I turn sharply around in search of the man, and see him at my side, with the blackest of faces, but animated and joyous – a man dressed in a long white shirt, with a turban of American sheeting around his woolly head, and I ask:

'Who the mischief are you?'

'I am Susi, the servant of Dr Livingstone,' said he, smiling, and showing a gleaming row of teeth.

'What! Is Dr Livingstone here?'

'Yes, sir.'

'In this village?'

'Yes, sir.'

'Are you sure?'

'Sure, sure, sir. Why, I leave him just now.' . . .

'Now, you Susi, run, and tell the Doctor I am coming.'

'Yes, sir,' and off he darted like a madman . . .

Soon Susi came running back, and asked me my name; he had told the Doctor that I was coming, but the Doctor was too surprised to believe him, and, when the Doctor asked him my name, Susi was rather staggered.

But, during Susi's absence, the news had been conveyed to the Doctor that it was surely a white man that was coming, whose guns were firing and whose flag could be seen; and the great Arab magnates of Ujiji – Mohammed bin Sali, Sayd bin Majid, Abid bin Suleiman, Mohammed bin Gharib, and others

– had gathered together before the Doctor's house, and the Doctor had come out from his veranda to discuss the matter and await my arrival.

In the meantime, the head of the Expedition had halted, and the *kirangozi* was out of the ranks, holding his flag aloft, and Selim said to me, 'I see the Doctor, sir. Oh, what an old man! He has got a white beard.' And I – what would I not have given for a bit of friendly wilderness, where, unseen, I might vent my joy in some mad freak, such as idiotically biting my hand, turning a somersault, or slashing at trees, in order to allay those exciting feelings I that were well-nigh uncontrollable. My heart beats fast, but I must not let my face betray my emotions, lest it shall detract from the dignity of a white man appearing under such extraordinary circumstances.

So I did that which I thought was most dignified. I pushed back the crowds and, passing from the rear, walked down a living avenue of people, until I came in front of the semicircle of Arabs, in the front of which stood the white man with the grey beard. As I advanced slowly towards him I noticed he was pale, looked wearied, had a grey beard, wore a bluish cap with a faded gold band round it, had on a red-sleeved waistcoat, and a pair of grey tweed trousers. I would have run to him, only I was a coward in the presence of such a mob – would have embraced him, only, he being an Englishman, I did not know how he would receive me; so I did what cowardice and false pride suggested was the best thing – walked deliberately to him, took off my hat, and said:

'Dr Livingstone, I presume?'

'YES,' said he, with a kind smile, lifting his cap slightly.

I replace my hat on my head, and he puts on his cap, and we both grasp hands, and I then say aloud:

'I thank God, Doctor, I have been permitted to see you.'

He answered, 'I feel thankful that I am here to welcome you.'

I turn to the Arabs, take off my hat to them in response to the saluting chorus of 'Yambos' I receive, and the Doctor introduces them to me by name. Then, oblivious of the crowds, oblivious of the men who shared with me my dangers, we – Livingstone and I – turn our faces towards his *tembe*. He points to the veranda, or, rather, mud platform, under the broad overhanging eaves; he points to his own particular seat, which I see his age and experience in Africa has suggested, namely, a straw mat, with a goatskin over it, and another skin nailed against the wall to protect his back from contact with the cold mud. I protest against taking this seat, which so much more befits him than me, but the Doctor will not yield: I must take it.

We are seated – the Doctor and I – with our backs to the wall. The Arabs take seats on our left. More than a thousand natives are in our front, filling the whole square densely, indulging their curiosity, and discussing the fact of two white men meeting at Ujiji – one just come from Manyuema, in the west, the other from Unyanyembe, in the east.

BUFFALO BILL CODY ENTERTAINS GRAND DUKE ALEXIS OF RUSSIA, WYOMING, AMERICA, January 1872

Buffalo Bill Cody

William F. Cody was a Pony Express and buffalo hunter (hence the nickname). He eventually turned his natural talent for showmanship into a world famous Wild West circus.

At last, on the morning of the 12th of January, 1872, the Grand Duke and party arrived at North Platte by special train; in charge of a Mr Francis Thompson. Captain Hays and myself, with five or six ambulances, fifteen or twenty extra saddle-horses and a company of cavalry under Captain Egan, were at the dépôt in time to receive them. Presently General Sheridan and a large, fine-looking young man, whom we at once concluded to be the Grand Duke came out of the cars and approached us. General Sheridan at once introduced me to the Grand Duke as Buffalo Bill, for he it was, and said that I was to take charge of him and show him how to kill buffalo.

In less than half an hour the whole party were dashing away towards the south, across the South Platte and towards the Medicine; upon reaching which point we halted for a change of horses and a lunch. Resuming our ride we reached Camp Alexis in the afternoon. General Sheridan was well pleased with the arrangements that had been made and was delighted to find that Spotted Tail and his Indians had arrived on time. They were objects of great curiosity to the Grand Duke, who spent considerable time in looking at them, and watching their exhibitions of horsemanship, sham fights, etc. That evening the Indians gave the grand war dance, which I had arranged for.

General Custer, who was one of the hunting party, carried on a mild flirtation with one of Spotted Tail's daughters, who had accompanied her father thither, and it was noticed also that the Duke Alexis paid considerable attention to another handsome red-skin maiden. The night passed pleasantly, and all retired with great expectations of having a most enjoyable and successful buffalo hunt. The Duke Alexis asked me a great many questions as to how we shot buffaloes, and what kind of a gun or pistol we used, and if he was going to have a good horse. I told him that he was to have my celebrated buffalo horse Buckskin Joe, and when we went into a buffalo herd all he would have to do was to sit on the horse's back and fire away.

At nine o'clock next morning we were all in our saddles, and in a few minutes were galloping over the prairies in search of a buffalo herd. We had not gone far before we observed a herd some distance ahead of us crossing our way; after that we proceeded cautiously, so as to keep out of sight until we were ready to make a charge.

Of course the main thing was to give Alexis the first chance and the best shot at the buffaloes, and when all was in readiness we dashed over a little knoll that had hidden us from view, and in a few minutes we were among them. Alexis at first preferred to use his pistol instead of a gun. He fired six shots from this weapon at buffaloes only twenty feet away from him, but as he shot wildly, not one of his bullets took effect. Riding up to his side and seeing that his weapon was empty, I exchanged pistols with him. He again fired six shots, without dropping a buffalo.

Seeing that the animals were bound to make their escape without his killing one of them, unless he had a better weapon, I rode up to him, gave him my old reliable 'Lucretia,' and told him to urge his horse close to the buffaloes, and I would then give him the word when to shoot. At the same time I gave old Buckskin Joe a blow with my whip, and with a few jumps the horse carried the Grand Duke to within about ten feet of a big buffalo bull.

'Now is your time,' said I. He fired, and down went the buffalo. The Grand Duke stopped his horse, dropped his gun on the ground, and commenced waving his hat. When his *suite* came galloping up, he began talking to them in a tongue which I could not understand. Presently General Sheridan joined the group, and the ambulances were brought up. Very soon the corks began to fly from the champagne bottles, in honor of the Grand Duke Alexis, who had killed the first buffalo.

It was reported in a great many of the newspapers that I shot the first buffalo for Alexis, while in some it was stated that I held the buffalo while His Royal Highness killed it. But the way I have related the affair is the correct version.

It was thought that we had had about sport enough for one day, and accordingly I was directed by General Sheridan to guide the party back to camp, and we were soon on our way thither. Several of the party, however, concluded to have a little hunt on their own account, and presently we saw them galloping over the prairie in different directions in pursuit of buffaloes.

While we were crossing a deep ravine, on our way to camp, we ran into a small band of buffaloes that had been frightened by some of the hunters. As they rushed past us, not more than thirty yards distant, Alexis raised his pistol, fired and killed a buffalo cow. It was either an extraordinarly good shot or a 'scratch' – probably the latter for it surprised the Grand Duke as well as everybody else. We gave him three cheers, and when the ambulance came up we took a pull at the champagne in honor of the Grand Duke's success. I was in hopes that he would kill five or six more buffaloes before we reached camp, especially if a basket of champagne was to be opened every time he dropped one.

General Sheridan directed me to take care of the hides and heads of the buffaloes which Alexis had killed, as the Duke wished to keep them as souvenirs of the hunt. I also cut out the choice meat from the cow and brought it into camp, and that night at supper Alexis had the pleasure of dining on broiled buffalo steak obtained from the animal which he had shot himself.

We remained at this camp two or three days, during which we hunted most of the time, the Grand Duke himself killing eight buffaloes.

One day Alexis desired to see how the Indians hunted buffaloes and killed them with bow and arrow; so Spotted Tail, selecting some of his best hunters, had them surround a herd, and bring the animals down, not only with arrows, but with lances. The Grand Duke was told to follow upon the heels of one celebrated Indian hunter, whose name was 'Two Lance,' and watch him bring down the game; for this chief had the reputation of being able to send an arrow through and through the body of a buffalo. Upon this occasion he did not belie his reputation, for he sent an arrow *through* a buffalo, which fell dead at the shot, and the arrow was given to Alexis as a souvenir of his hunt on the American Plains.

When the Grand Duke was satisfied with the sport, orders were given for the return to the railroad. The conveyance provided for the Grand Duke and General Sheridan was a heavy double-seated open carriage, or rather an Irish dog-cart, and it was drawn by four spirited cavalry horses which were not much used to the harness. The driver was Bill Reed, an old overland stage driver and wagon master; on our way in, the Grand Duke frequently expressed his admiration of the skillful manner in which Reed handled the reins.

General Sheridan informed the Duke that I also had been a stage-driver in the Rocky Mountains, and thereupon His Royal Highness expressed a desire to see me drive. I was in advance at the time, and General Sheridan sang out to me:

'Cody, get in here and show the Duke how you can drive. Mr. Reed will exchange places with you and ride your horse.'

'All right, General,' said I, and in a few moments I had the reins and we were rattling away over the prairie. When we were approaching Medicine Creek, General Sheridan said: 'Shake 'em up a little, Bill, and give us some old-time stage-driving.'

I gave the horses a crack or two of the whip, and they started off at a very rapid gait. They had a light load to pull, and kept increasing their speed at every jump, and I found it difficult to hold them. They fairly flew over the ground, and at last we reached a steep hill, or divide, which led down into the valley of the Medicine. There was no brake on the wagon, and the horses were not much on the hold-back. I saw that it would be impossible to stop them. All I could do was to keep them straight in the track and let them go it down the hill, for three miles; which distance, I believe, was made in about six minutes. Every once in a while the hind wheels would strike a rut and take a bound, and not touch the ground again for fifteen or twenty feet. The Duke and the General were kept rather busy in holding their positions on the seats, and when they saw that I was keeping the horses straight in the road, they seemed to enjoy the dash which we were making. I was unable to stop the team until they ran into the camp where we were to obtain a fresh relay, and there I succeeded in checking them. The Grand Duke said he didn't want any more of that kind of driving, as he preferred to go a little slower.

CAPTAIN WEBB'S CHANNEL SWIM, 25 August 1875

Anon

At 3.22 a.m. he declined any refreshment, and half an hour later there was light enough to dowse lanterns . . . The breeze [then] produced a nasty bobble, but as the tide was at present setting to leeward it was not so bad as it might have been . . . Two bells found it very hazy over the land, but he still seemed in as good spirits as ever, and even had a little personal chaff with us. He did not seem strong enough, however, to make much way across the tide, and . . . it was a touch-and-go matter whether he would not be drifted too far to the eastward, and have to await another tide to fetch in . . . Some beef tea and a top-up of brandy were called for at 5.25 a.m., when his voice seemed faltering a bit. By four bells the lop had become really serious, but he declined to wear his spectacles. All hope of fetching in off Sangatte had to be abandoned. For the next hour he made literally no in-shore progress, although both the row boats were kept on his weather side, to ward off the sea as much as possible . . . at 7.25 the poor fellow complained bitterly of the sea, which of course increased greatly in crossing the broken water of the Ridens. It was cruel to think that this might be the cause of defeat when within actual hail of port, and nothing but unflinching bulldog pluck now kept the man going . . . At eight bells we sounded in ten fathoms, and had all but opened the entrance to Calais harbour. Luckily, however, the tide had by this time eased considerably, and he was enabled to get almost slack water and make a little headway for the shore instead of getting drifted to the eastward of Calais.

At 8.23 a.m. he took some brandy, and said he was 'as right as a bird, bar the sea.' He was swimming a quicker but shorter stroke of twenty-two to the minute . . . At 9.20 a.m. Capt. Dane was sighted coming out of Calais harbour in his gig, with all possible speed; and this was the best bit of luck we had met with since the same gallant skipper had left us at sea just before midnight. By 9.25 a.m. he had placed his gig in a capital position on Webb's weather side, where such a large craft made a far more effectual breakwater than our own two cockleshells of row boats. At 9.34 he seemed quite lively when Capt. Dane told him there was a grand reception waiting him ashore. Now, however, the S.W. stream had begun to make and the tide was going aweather, which further increased the brave swimmer's difficulties. At 9.40 a.m. we timed him at twenty-six strokes to the minute but they were short indeed compared to those of the first eighteen hours or so. However, the gig mended matters, somewhat, and her crew cheered him repeatedly in true British Jack Tar fashion . . . At 10.30 he laughingly hoped that 'the Frenchmen would give him some good grub ashore.' As a proof of how keen his intellect had remained throughout, he promptly requested us by name to immediately take in two or three feet of rope which had accidentally got overboard as he wished to take no unfair advantage. After a few more strokes the brave Matthew Webb stood upright in five feet of water on Calais sands abreast of the bathing establishment and half a mile to the westward of Calais pier at 10.40.15 a.m. English time on Wednesday, 25 August 1875, after having been in the water twenty-one hours forty-four minutes and fifty-five seconds without touching artificial support of any kind, and having swum as nearly as possible over thirty-nine miles and a half of ground.

Capt. Webb was assisted into a trap, driven to the Hotel de Paris, and at once put to bed, a medical man being in attendance. His pulse was at 72, and after three hours' sleep he woke up all right, bar weakness and hunger. At 10 p.m. he again turned in and slept soundly for twelve hours.

CUSTER'S LAST STAND, MONTANA, AMERICA, 25 June 1876

Two Moon

A little after 2 o'clock on the afternoon of 25 June, General Custer led his 7th US Cavalry battalion in an attack on a hostile Sioux–Cheyenne camp on the Little Bighorn River. His force numbered 255. The Indians sent around 3000 warriors into the field. The battle lasted an hour, perhaps less. Two moon was a Cheyenne chief.

Then the Sioux rode up the ridge on all sides, riding very fast. The Cheyenne went up the left way. Then the shooting was quick. Pop-pop-pop very fast. Some of the soldiers were down on their knees, some standing. Officers all in front. The smoke was like a great cloud, and everywhere the Sioux went the dust rose like smoke. We circled all round him – swirling like water round a stone. We shoot, we ride fast, we shoot again. Soldiers drop, and horses fall on them. Soldiers in line drop, but one man rides up and down the line – all the time shouting. He rode a sorrel horse with white face and white fore-legs. I don't know who he was. He was a brave man.

Indians keep swirling round and round, and the soldiers killed only a few. Many soldiers fell. At last all horses killed but five. Once in a while some man would break out and run towards the river, but he would fall. At last about a hundred men and five horsemen stood on the hill all bunched together. All along the bugler kept blowing his commands. He was very brave too. Then a chief was killed. I hear it was Long Hair [Custer], I don't know; and then the five horsemen and the bunch of men, may be forty, started toward the river. The man on the sorrel horse led them, shouting all the time. He wore a buckskin shirt, and had long black hair and mustache. He fought hard with a big knife. His men were all covered with white dust. I couldn't tell whether they were officers or not. One man all alone ran far down toward the river, then round up over the hill. I thought he was going to escape, but a Sioux fired and hit him in the head. He was the last man. He wore braid on his arms [sergeant].

All the soldiers were now killed, and the bodies were stripped. After that no one could tell which were officers. The bodies were left where they fell. We had no dance that night. We were sorrowful.

Next day four Sioux chiefs and two Cheyennes and I, Two Moon, went upon the battlefield to count the dead. One man carried a little bundle of sticks. When we came to dead men we took a little stick and gave it to another man, so we counted the dead. There were 388. There were thirty-nine Sioux and seven Cheyennes killed and about a hundred wounded.

Some white soldiers were cut with knives, to make sure they were dead; and the war women had mangled some. Most of them were left just where they fell. We came to the man with the big mustache; he lay down the hills towards the river. The Indians did not take his buckskin shirt. The Sioux said 'That is a big chief. That is Long Hair.' I don't know. I had never seen him. The man on the white-faced horse was the bravest man.

THE KELLY GANG IS DESTROYED BY POLICE, GLENROWAN, AUSTRALIA, 28 June 1880

Joe Melvin

The son of a transported Irish criminal, Ned Kelly (born 1855) was Australia's most notorious outlaw.

At last the Kelly gang and the police have come within shooting distance, and the adventure has been the most tragic of any in the bushranging annals of the colony. Most people will say that it is high time, too, for the murders of the police near Mansfield occurred as long ago as the 26th of October, 1878, the Euroa outrage on the 9th December of the same year, and the Jerilderie affair on the 8th and 9th of February, 1879. The lapse of time induced many to believe that the gang was no longer in the colony, but these sceptics must now be silent. The outlaws demonstrated their presence in a brutally effective manner by the murder of the unfortunate Aaron Sherritt at Sebastopol. Immediately on the news being spread the police were in activity. A special train was despatched from Melbourne at 10.15 on Sunday night. At Essendon Sub-inspector O'Connor and his five black trackers were picked up. They had come recently from Benalla, and were *en route* for Queensland again. Mr O'Connor, however, was fortunately staying with Mrs O'Connor's friends at Essendon for a few days before his departure. Mrs O'Connor and her sister came along thinking that they would be able to pay a visit to Beechworth. After leaving Essendon the train travelled at great speed, and before the passengers were aware of any accident having occurred, we had smashed through a gate about a mile beyond Craigieburn. All we noticed was a crack like a bullet striking the carriage. The brake of the engine had, however, been torn away, the footbridge of the carriage shattered, and the lamp on the guard's van destroyed. Guard Bell was looking out of the van at the time, and had a very narrow escape. The train had to be pulled up, but after a few minutes we started again, relying on the brake of the guard's van. Benalla was reached at half-past 1 o'clock, and there Superintendent Hare with eight troopers and their horses were taken on board. We were now about to enter the Kelly country, and caution was necessary. As the moon was shining brightly, a man was tied on upon the front of the engine to keep a lookout for any obstruction of the line. Just before starting, however, it occurred to the authorities that it would be advisable to send a pilot engine in advance, and the man on the front of our engine was relieved. A start was made from Benalla at 2 o'clock, and at 25 minutes to 3, when we were travelling at a rapid pace, we were stopped by the pilot engine. This stoppage occurred at Playford and Desoyre's paddocks, about a mile and a quarter from Glenrowan. A man had met the pilot and informed the driver that the rails were torn up about a mile and a half beyond Glenrowan, and that the Kellys were waiting for us near at hand. Superintendent Hare at once ordered the carriage doors on each side to be unlocked and his men to be in readiness. His orders were punctually obeyed, and the lights were extinguished. Mr Hare then mounted the pilot engine, along with a constable, and advanced. After some time he returned, and directions were given for the train to push on. Accordingly, we followed the pilot up to Glenrowan station, and disembarked.

No sooner were we out of the train, than Constable Bracken, the local policeman, rushed into our midst, and stated with an amount of excitement which was excusable under the circumstances, that he had just escaped from the Kellys, and that they were at that moment in possession of Jones's public house, about a hundred yards from the station. He called upon the police to surround the house, and his advice was followed without delay. Superintendent Hare with his men, and Sub-inspector O'Connor with his black trackers, at once advanced on the building. They were accompanied by Mr Rawlins, a volunteer from Benalla, who did good service. Mr Hare took the lead, and charged right up to the hotel. At the station were the reporters of the Melbourne press, Mr Carrington, of *The Sketcher*, and the two ladies who had accompanied us. The latter behaved with admirable courage, never betraying a symptom of fear, although bullets were whizzing about the station and striking the building and train. The first brush was exceedingly hot. The police and the gang blazed away at each other in the darkness furiously. It lasted for about a quarter of an hour, and during that time there was nothing but a succession of flashes and reports, the pinging of bullets in the air, and the shrieks of women who had been made prisoners in the hotel. Then there was a lull, but nothing could be seen for a minute or two in consequence of the smoke. In a few minutes Superintendent Hare returned to the railway-station with a shattered wrist. The first shot fired by the gang had passed through his left wrist. He bled profusely from the wound, but Mr Carrington, artist of *The Sketcher*, tied up the wound with his handkerchief, and checked the hemorrhage. Mr Hare then set out again for the fray, and cheered his men on as well as he could, but he gradually became so weak from loss of blood that he had reluctantly to retire and was soon afterwards conveyed to Benalla by a special engine. The bullet passed right through his wrist, and it is doubtful if he will ever recover the use of his left hand. On his departure Sub-inspector O'Connor and Senior-constable Kelly took charge, and kept pelting away at the outlaws all the morning. Mr O'Connor took up a position in a small creek in front of the hotel, and disposed his blackfellows one on each side, and stuck to this post gallantly throughout the whole encounter. The trackers also stood the baptism of fire with fortitude, never flinching for one instant.

At about 5 o'clock in the morning a heartrending wail of grief ascended from the hotel. The voice was easily distinguished as that of Mrs Jones, the landlady. Mrs Jones was lamenting the fate of her son, who had been shot in the back, as she supposed, fatally. She came out from the hotel crying bitterly and wandered into the bush on several occasions, and nature seemed to echo her grief. She always returned, however, to the hotel, until she succeeded, with the assistance of one of the prisoners, in removing her wounded boy from the building, and in sending him on to Wangaratta for medical treatment. The firing continued intermittently, as occasion served, and bullets were continually heard coursing through the air. Several lodged in the station building, and a few struck the train. By this time the hotel was completely surrounded by the police and the black trackers, and a vigilant watch of the hotel was kept up during the dark hours.

At daybreak police reinforcements arrived from Benalla, Beechworth, and Wangaratta. Superintendent Sadlier came from Benalla with nine more men, and Sergeant Steele, of Wangaratta, with six, thus augmenting the besieging force to about 30 men. Before daylight Senior-constable Kelly found a revolving rifle and a cap lying in the bush, about 100 yards from the hotel. The rifle was covered with blood, and a pool of blood lay near it. This was evidently the property of one of the bushrangers, and a suspicion therefore arose that they had escaped. That these articles not only belonged to one of the outlaws but to Ned Kelly himself was soon proved. When day was dawning the women and children who had been made prisoners in the hotel were allowed to depart. They were, however, challenged individually as they approached the police line, for it was thought that the outlaws might attempt to escape under some disguise.

At daylight the gang were expected to make a sally out so as to escape, if possible, to their native ranges, and the police were consequently on the alert. Close attention was paid to the hotel, as it was taken for granted that the whole gang were there. To the surprise of the police, however, they soon found themselves attacked from the rear by a man dressed in a long grey overcoat and wearing an iron mask. The appearance of the man presented an anomaly, but a little scrutiny of his appearance and behaviour soon showed that it was the veritable leader of the gang, Ned Kelly himself. On further observation it was seen that he was only armed with a revolver. He, however, walked coolly from tree to tree, and received the fire of the police with the utmost indifference, returning a shot from his revolver when a good opportunity presented itself. Three men went for him, viz., Sergeant Steele of Wangaratta, Senior-constable Kelly, and a railway guard named Dowsett. The latter, however, was only armed with a revolver. They fired at him persistently, but to their surprise with no effect. He seemed bullet-proof. It then occurred to Sergeant Steele that the fellow was encased in mail, and he then aimed at the outlaw's legs. His first shot of that kind made Ned Kelly stagger, and the second brought him to the ground with the cry, 'I am done – I am done.' Steele rushed up along with Senior-constable Kelly and others. The outlaw howled like a wild beast brought to bay, and swore at the police. He was first seized by Steele, and as that officer grappled with him he fired off another charge from his revolver. This shot was evidently intended for Steele, but from the smart way in which he secured the murderer the sergeant escaped. Kelly became gradually quiet, and it was soon found that he had been utterly disabled. He had been shot in the left foot, left leg, right hand, left arm, and twice in the region of the groin. But no bullet had penetrated his armour. Having been divested of his armour he was carried down to the railway station, and placed in a guard's van. Subsequently he was removed to the station-master's office, and his wounds were dressed there by Dr Nicholson, of Benalla. What statements he made are given below . . .

The siege was kept up all the forenoon and till nearly 3 o'clock in the afternoon. Some time before this the shooting from the hotel had ceased, and opinions were divided as to whether Dan Kelly and Hart were reserving their ammunition or were dead. The best part of the day having elapsed, the police, who were now acting under the direction of Superintendent Sadlier, determined that a decisive step should be taken. At 10 minutes to 3 o'clock another volley was fired into the hotel, and under cover of the fire Senior-constable Charles Johnson, of Violet Town, ran up to the house with a bundle of straw which (having set fire to) he placed on the ground at the west side of the building. This was a moment of intense excitement, and all hearts were relieved when Johnson was seen to regain uninjured the shelter he had left. All eyes were now fixed on the silent building, and the circle of besiegers began to close in rapidly on it, some dodging from tree to tree, and many, fully persuaded that everyone in the hotel must be *hors de combat*, coming out boldly into the open . . .

In the meantime the straw, which burned fiercely, had all been consumed, and at first doubts were entertained as to whether Senior-constable Johnson's exploit had been successful. Not very many minutes elapsed, however, before smoke was seen coming out of the roof, and flames were discerned through the front window on the western side. A light westerly wind was blowing at the time, and this carried the flames from the straw underneath the wall and into the house, and as the building was lined with calico, the fire spread rapidly. Still no sign of life appeared in the building.

When the house was seen to be fairly on fire, Father Gibney, who had previously started for it but had been stopped by the police, walked up to the front door and entered it. By this time the patience of the besiegers was exhausted, and they all, regardless of shelter, rushed to the building. Father Gibney, at much personal risk from the flames, hurried into a room to the left, and there saw two bodies lying side by side on their backs. He touched them, and found life was extinct in each. These were the bodies of Dan Kelly and Hart, and the rev. gentleman expressed the opinion, based on their position, that they must have killed one another. Whether they killed one another or whether both or one committed suicide, or whether both being mortally wounded by the besiegers, they determined to die side by side, will never be known. The priest had barely time to feel their bodies before the fire forced him to make a speedy exit from the room, and the flames had then made such rapid progress on the western side of the house that the few people who followed close on the rev. gentleman's heels dared not attempt to rescue the two bodies. It may be here stated that after the house had been burned down, the two bodies were removed from the embers. They presented a horrible spectacle, nothing but the trunk and skull being left, and these almost burnt to a cinder. Their armour was found near them. About the remains there was apparently nothing to lead to positive identification, but the discovery of the armour near them and other circumstances render it impossible to be doubted that they were those of Dan Kelly and Steve Hart. The latter was a much smaller man than the younger Kelly, and this difference in size was noticeable in their remains. Constable Dwyer, by-the-by, who followed Father Gibney into the hotel, states that he was near enough to the bodies to recognize Dan Kelly . . .

After the house had been burned Ned Kelly's three sisters and Tom Wright were allowed an interview with him. Tom Wright, as well as the sisters, kissed the wounded man, and a brief conversation ensued, Ned Kelly being to a certain extent recovered from the exhaustion consequent on his wounds. At times his eyes were quite bright, and, although he was of course excessively weak, his remarkably powerfull physique enabled him to talk rather freely. During the interview he stated:- 'I was at last surrounded by the police, and only had a revolver, with which I fired four shots. But it was no good. I had half a mind to shoot myself. I loaded my rifle, but could not hold it after I was wounded. I had plenty of ammunition, but it was no good to me. I got shot in the arm, and told Byrne and Dan so. I could have got off, but when I saw them all pounding away, I told Dan I would see it over, and wait until morning.'

'What on earth induced you to go to the hotel?' inquired a spectator.

'We could not do it anywhere else,' replied Kelly, eyeing the spectators who were strangers to him suspiciously. 'I would,' he continued, 'have fought them in the train, or else upset it if I had the chance. I didn't care a — who was in it, but I knew on Sunday morning there would be no usual passengers. I first tackled the line, and could not pull it up, and then came to Glenrowan station.'

'Since the Jerilderie affair,' remarked a spectator, 'we thought you had gone to Queensland.'

'It would not do for everyone to think the same way,' was Kelly's reply. 'If I were once right again,' he continued, 'I would go to the barracks, and shoot every one of the – traps, and not give one a chance.'

Mrs Skillion (to her brother) – 'It's a wonder you did not keep behind a tree.'

Ned Kelly – 'I had a chance at several policemen during the night, but declined to fire. My arm was broke the first fire. I got away into the bush, and found my mare, and could have rushed away, but wanted to see the thing out, and remained in the bush.'

He is very reserved as to anything connected with his comrades, but answered questions freely when his individual case was alone concerned. He appeared to be suffering from a severe shock and exhaustion, and trembled in every limb. Now and again he fainted, but restoratives brought him round, and in his stronger moments he made the following statements:-

'I was going down to meet the special train with some of my mates, and intended to rake it with shot; but it arrived before I expected, and I then returned to the hotel. I expected the train would go on, and I had the rails pulled up so that these – black-trackers might be settled. I do not say what brought me to Glenrowan, but it seems much. Anyhow I could have got away last night, for I got into the bush with my grey mare, and lay there all night. But I wanted to see the thing end. In the first volley the police fired I was wounded on the left foot; soon afterwards I was shot through the left arm. I got these wounds in front of the house. I do not care what people say about Sergeant Kennedy's death. I have made my statement of the affair, and if the public don't believe me I can't help it; but I am satisfied it is not true that Scanlan was shot kneeling. He never got off his horse. I fired three or four shots from the front of Jones's hotel, but who I was firing at I do not know. I simply fired where I saw police. I escaped to the bush, and remained there overnight. I could have shot several constables if I liked. Two passed close to me. I could have shot them before they could shoot. I was a good distance away at one time, but came back. Why don't the police use bullets instead of duck-shot? I have got one charge of duck-shot in my leg. One policeman who was firing at me was a splendid shot but I do not know his name. I daresay I would have done well to have ridden away on my grey mare. The bullets that struck my armour felt like blows from a man's first. I wanted to fire into the carriages, but the police started on us too quickly. I expected the police to come.'

Inspector Sadlier – 'You wanted, then, to kill the people in the train?'

Kelly – 'Yes, of course I did. God help them, but they would have got shot all the same. Would they not have tried to kill me?'

THE MASSACRE AT WOUNDED KNEE, SOUTH DAKOTA, AMERICA, 29 December 1890

Black Elk

The last major conflict in the 300-year war between the White Man and the Indians.

That evening before it happened, I went in to Pine Ridge and heard these things, and while I was there, soldiers started for where the Big Foots a band of Miniconjou Sioux were. These made about five hundred soldiers that were there next morning. When I saw them starting I felt that something terrible was going to happen. That night I could hardly sleep at all. I walked around most of the night.

In the morning I went out after my horses, and while I was out I heard shooting off toward the east, and I knew from the sound that it must be wagon-guns (cannon) going off. The sounds went right through my body, and I felt that something terrible would happen.

When I reached camp with the horses, a man rode up to me and said: 'Hey-hey-hey! The people that are coming are fired on! I know it!'

I saddled up my buckskin and put on my sacred shirt. It was one I had made to be worn by no one but myself. It had a spotted eagle outstretched on the back of it, and the daybreak star was on the left shoulder, because when facing south that shoulder is toward the east. Across the breast, from the left shoulder to the right hip, was the flaming rainbow, and there was another rainbow around the neck, like a necklace, with a star at the bottom. At each shoulder, elbow, and wrist was an eagle feather; and over the whole shirt were red streaks of lightning. You will see that this was from my great vision, and you will know how it protected me that day.

I painted my face all red, and in my hair I put one eagle feather for the One Above.

It did not take me long to get ready, for I could still hear the shooting over there.

I started out alone on the old road that ran across the hills to Wounded Knee. I had no gun. I carried only the sacred bow of the west that I had seen in my great vision. I had gone only a little way when a band of young men came galloping after me. The first two who came up were Loves War and Iron Wasichu. I asked what they were going to do, and they said they were just going to see where the shooting was. Then others were coming up, and some older men.

We rode fast, and there were about twenty of us now. The shooting was getting louder. A horseback from over there came galloping very fast toward us, and he said: 'Hey-hey-hey! They have murdered them!' Then he whipped his horse and rode away faster toward Pine Ridge.

In a little while we had come to the top of the ridge where, looking to the east, you can see for the first time the monument and the burying ground on the little hill where the church is. That is where the terrible thing started. Just south of the burying ground on the little hill a deep dry gulch runs about east and west, very crooked, and it rises westward to nearly the top of the ridge where we were. It had no name, but the Wasichus [white men], sometimes call it Battle Creek now. We stopped on the ridge not far from the head of the dry gulch. Wagon-guns were still going off over there on the little hill, and they were going off again where they hit along the gulch. There was much shooting down yonder, and there were many cries, and we could see cavalrymen scattered over the hills ahead of us. Cavalrymen were riding along the gulch and shooting into it, where the women and children were running away and trying to hide in the gullies and the stunted pines.

A little way ahead of us, just below the head of the dry gulch, there were some women and children who were huddled under a clay bank, and some cavalrymen were there pointing guns at them.

We stopped back behind the ridge, and I said to the others: 'Take courage. These are our relatives. We will try to get them back.' Then we all sang a song which went like this:

A thunder being nation I am, I have said.
A thunder being nation I am, I have said.
You shall live.
You shall live.
You shall live.
You shall live.

Then I rode over the ridge and the others after me, and we were crying: 'Take courage! It is time to fight!' The soldiers who were guarding our relatives shot at us and then ran away fast, and some more cavalrymen on the other side of the gulch did too. We got our relatives and sent them across the ridge to the northwest where they would be safe.

I had no gun, and when we were charging, I just held the sacred bow out in front of me with my right hand. The bullets did not hit us at all.

We found a little baby lying all alone near the head of the gulch. I could not pick her up just then, but I got her later and some of my people adopted her. I just wrapped her up tighter in a shawl that was around her and left her there. It was a safe place, and I had other work to do.

The soldiers had run eastward over the hills where there were some more soldiers, and they were off their horses and lying down. I told the others to stay back, and I charged upon them holding the sacred bow out toward them with my right hand. They all shot at me, and I could hear bullets all around me, but I ran my horse right close to them, and then swung around. Some soldiers across the gulch began shooting at me too, but I got back to the others and was not hurt at all.

By now many other Lakotas, who had heard the shooting, were coming up from Pine Ridge, and we all charged on the soldiers. They ran eastward toward where the trouble began. We followed down along the dry gulch, and what we saw was terrible. Dead and wounded women and children and little babies were scattered all along there where they had been trying to run away. The soldiers had followed along the gulch, as they ran, and murdered them in there. Sometimes they were in heaps because they had huddled together, and some were scattered all along. Sometimes bunches of them had been killed and torn to pieces where the wagon-guns hit them. I saw a little baby trying to suck its mother, but she was bloody and dead.

There were two little boys at one place in this gulch. They had guns and they had been killing soldiers all by themselves. We could see the soldiers they had killed. The boys were all alone there, and they were not hurt. These were very brave little boys.

When we drove the soldiers back, they dug themselves in, and we were not enough people to drive them out from there. In the evening they marched off up Wounded Knee Creek, and then we saw all that they had done there.

Men and women and children were heaped and scattered all over the flat at the bottom of the little hill where the soldiers had their wagon-guns, and westward up the drv gulch all the way to the high ridge, the dead women and children and babies were scattered.

When I saw this I wished that I had died too, but I was not sorry for the women and children. It was better for them to be happy in the other world, and I wanted to be there too. But before I went there I wanted to have revenge. I thought there might be a day, and we should have revenge.

After the soldiers marched away, I heard from my friend, Dog Chief, how the trouble started, and he was right there by Yellow Bird when it happened. This is the way it was:

In the morning the soldiers began to take all the guns away from the Big Foots, who were camped in the flat below the little hill where the monument and burying ground are now. The people had stacked most of their guns, and even their knives, by the tepee where Big Foot was lying sick. Soldiers were on the little hill and all around, and there were soldiers across the dry gulch to the south and over east along Wounded Knee Creek too. The people were nearly surrounded, and the wagon-guns were pointing at them.

Some had not yet given up their guns, and so the soldiers were searching all the tepees, throwing things around and poking into everything. There was a man called Yellow Bird, and he and another man were standing in front of the tepee where Big Foot was lying sick. They had white sheets around and over them, with eyeholes to look through, and they had guns under these. An officer came to search them. He took the other man's gun, and then started to take Yellow Bird's. But Yellow Bird would not let go. He wrestled with the officer, and while they were wrestling, the gun went off and killed the officer. Wasichus and some others have said he meant to do this, but Dog Chief was standing right there, and he told me it was not so. As soon as the gun went off, Dog Chief told me, an officer shot and killed Big Foot who was lying sick inside the tepee.

Then suddenly nobody knew what was happening, except that the soldiers were all shooting and the wagon-guns began going off right in among the people.

Many were shot down right there. The women and children ran into the gulch and up west, dropping all the time, for the soldiers shot them as they ran. There were only about a hundred warriors and there were nearly five hundred soldiers. The warriors rushed to where they had piled their guns and knives. They fought soldiers with only their hands until they got their guns.

Dog Chief saw Yellow Bird run into a tepee with his gun, and from there he killed soldiers until the tepee caught fire. Then he died full of bullets.

It was a good winter day when all this happened. The sun was shining. But after the soldiers marched away from their dirty work, a heavy snow began to fall. The wind came up in the night. There was a big blizzard, and it grew very cold. The snow drifted deep in the crooked gulch, and it was one long grave of butchered women and children and babies, who had never done any harm and were only trying to run away.

Around 200 Sioux were killed at Wounded Knee Creek. The Army suffered 25 casualties, most of them killed accidently by their own side in the frenzy of shooting.

Part Four

The Twentieth Century
1900–Present Day

INTRODUCTION

A man walks on the moon. To the crowds that gathered in London and New York to see in the new century on the winter's evening of 31 December 1899, such an event was the stuff of the wildest fantasy. The aeroplane itself was still on the drawing board of an obscure duo of North Carolina brothers, Orville and Wilbur Wright. Yet humankind's ability to escape from the confining gravity of Earth is neatly symbolic of how far the frontiers of technology and knowledge have been conquered in the twentieth century. The fact that many millions could watch the 1969 moon landing live at home through the medium of television only proves the point that this has been, without doubt, the most change-full century in history.

It has also been the most turbulent. On the eve of 1900 about a quarter of the world's population looked to Britain as their ruling nation. The Empire on which the 'sun never sets' stretched from Cardiff to Calcutta. Yet, even as the new century dawned, Britain's imperial grip was starting to slacken. The most prescient of the revellers in Trafalgar Square may have realized the future belonged to others; a portent of this was the surprising trouble the British were having in winning the then recent, remote war against uppity Dutch settlers in South Africa.

Paradoxically, the two great events which finished Britain as the world's premier power were the two she 'won': the World Wars of 1914–18 and 1939–45. The slaughter in the trenches in the First World War caused the rise of nationalism everywhere – including Britannia's own empire. It also, *inter alia*, ushered in the 1917

Communist revolution in Russia and led, almost inexorably, to the growth of Nazism in defeated Germany, the Holocaust and the Second World War – midnight in the century, its defining event. (It is one of the ironies of war, that its violence often stimulates potentially beneficial inventions: the Apollo rocket is a direct descendant of the V-1 'doodlebugs' which harassed London.) The nation which has emerged preeminent from these conflagrations is the USA; if the nineteenth century was British, the twentieth has been the American Century.

THE BOER WAR: SKIRMISH AT KARI SIDING, 29 March 1900

Rudyard Kipling

For the British the new century began as the old ended – fighting the Boer War (1899–1902) in South Africa. The war had initially been prompted by the discovery of vast quantities of diamonds and gold in a territory of South Africa that was outside Britain's jurisdiction. Although the British army outnumbered the Boers by more than five to one, the country in which they were fighting was difficult and hostile. The British campaign against the Afrikaner nationalists had been initially an exercise in humiliation, but the arrival of Generals Robert and Kitchener in January 1900 began to see the tide of war turn in imperial favour, with victories such as that at Kari Siding. At the time of the skirmish, the novelist Rudyard Kipling was working as a correspondent for the *Friend*, a newspaper for British soldiers.

So there had to be a battle, which was called the Battle of Kari Siding. All the staff of the Bloemfontein *Friend* attended. I was put in a Cape cart, with native driver, containing most of the drinks, and with me was a well-known war correspondent. The enormous pale landscape swallowed up 7,000 troops without a sign, along a front of seven miles. On our way we passed a collection of neat, deep and empty trenches well undercut for shelter on the shrapnel side. A young Guards officer, recently promoted to *Brevet-Major* – and rather sore with the paper that we had printed it *Branch* – studied them interestedly. They were the first dim lines of the dug-out, but his and our eyes were held. The Hun had designed them *secundum artem*, but the Boer had preferred the open within reach of his pony. At last we came to a lone farmhouse in a vale adorned with no less than five white flags. Beyond the ridge was a sputter of musketry and now and then the whoop of a field-piece. 'Here,' said my guide and guardian, 'we get out and walk. Our driver will wait for us at the farmhouse.' But the driver loudly objected. 'No, sar. They shoot. They shoot me.' 'But they are white-flagged all over,' we said. 'Yess, sar. That *why*,' was his answer, and he preferred to take his mules down into a decently remote donga and wait our return.

The farmhouse held two men and, I think, two women, who received us disinterestedly. We went on into a vacant world of sunshine and distances, where now and again a single bullet sang to himself. What I most objected to was the sensation of being under aimed fire – being, as it were, required as a head. 'What are they doing this for?' I asked my friend. 'Because they think we are the Something Light Horse. They ought to be just under this slope.' I prayed that the particularly Something Light Horse would go elsewhere, which they presently did, for the aimed fire slackened and a wandering Colonial, bored to extinction, turned up with news from a far flank. 'No; nothing doing and no one to see.' Then more cracklings and a most cautious move forward to the lip of a large hollow where sheep were grazing. Some of them began to drop and kick. 'That's both sides trying sighting-shots,' said my companion. 'What range do you make it?' I asked. 'Eight hundred, at the nearest. That's close quarters nowadays. You'll never see anything closer than this. Modern rifles make it impossible. We're hung up till something cracks somewhere.' There was a decent lull for meals on both sides, interrupted now and again by sputters. Then one indubitable shell – ridiculously like a pipsqueak in that vastness but throwing up much dirt. 'Krupp! Four or six pounder at extreme range,' said the expert. 'They still think we're the – Light Horse. They'll come to be fairly regular from now on.' Sure enough, every twenty minutes or so, one judgmatic shell pitched on our slope. We waited, seeing nothing in the emptiness,and hearing only a faint murmur as of wind along gas-jets, running in and out of the unconcerned hills.

Then pom-poms opened. These were nasty little one-pounders, ten in a belt (which usually jammed about the sixth round). On soft ground they merely thudded. On rock-face the shell breaks up and yowls like a cat. My friend for the first time seemed interested. 'If these are *their* pom-poms, it's Pretoria for us,' was his diagnosis. I looked behind me – the whole length of South Africa down to Cape Town – and it seemed very far. I felt that I could have covered it in five minutes under fair conditions – but *not* with those aimed shots up my back. The pom-poms opened again at a bare rock-reef that gave the shells full value. For about two minutes a file of racing ponies, their tails and their riders' heads well down, showed and vanished northward. 'Our pom-poms,' said the correspondent. 'Le Gallais, I expect. *Now* we shan't be long.' All this time the absurd Krupp was faithfully feeling for us, *vice* – Light Horse, and, given a few more hours, might perhaps hit one of us. Then to the left, almost under us, a small piece of hanging woodland filled and fumed with our shrapnel much as a man's moustache fills with cigarette-smoke. It was most impressive and lasted for quite twenty minutes. Then silence; then a movement of men and horses from our side up the slope, and the hangar our guns had been hammering spat steady fire at them. More Boer ponies on more skylines; a flurry of pom-poms on the right and a little frieze of far-off meek-tailed ponies, already out of rifle range.

'*Maffeesh*,' said the correspondent, and fell to writing on his knee. 'We've shifted 'em.'

Leaving our infantry to follow men on ponyback towards the Equator, we returned to the farmhouse. In the donga where he was waiting someone squibbed off a rifle just after we took our seats, and our driver flogged out over the rocks to the danger of our sacred bottles.

Then Bloemfontein, and Gwynne storming in late with his accounts complete – 125 casualties, and the general opinion that 'French was a bit of a butcher' and a tale of the General commanding the cavalry who absolutely refused to break up his horses by galloping them across raw rock – 'not for any dam' Boer'.

THE BOER WAR: THE SIEGE OF MAFEKING, CAPE PROVINCE, SOUTH AFRICA, April–May 1900

J. E. Neilly

Besieged by the Boers from October 1899, the British garrison and the civilian population at Mafeking was reduced to starvation levels by spring 1900.

Words could not portray the scene of misery. The best thing I can do is ask you to fancy 500–600 human frameworks of both sexes and all ages, from the tender infant upwards, dressed in the remains of tattered rags, standing in lines, each holding an old blackened can or beef tin, awaiting turn to crawl painfully up to the kitchen where the food was distributed. Having obtained the horse soup, fancy them tottering off a few yards and sitting down to wolf up the life-fastening mess, and lick the tins when they had finished. It was one of the most heart-rending sights I ever witnessed, and I have seen many . . .

When a flight of locusts came it was regarded as a godsend – this visitation that is looked upon by farmer as hardly less of a curse than the rinderpest or drought. The starving ones gathered the insects up in thousands, stripped them of their heads, legs, and wings, and ate the bodies. They picked up meat-tins and licked them; they fed like outcast curs. They went further than the mongrel. When a dog gets a bone he polishes it white and leaves it there. Day after day I heard outside my door continuous thumping sounds. They were caused by the living skeletons who, having eaten all that was outside the bones, smashed them up with stones and devoured what marrow they could find. They looked for bones on the dust-heaps, on the roads everywhere, and I pledge my word that I saw one poor fellow weakly follow a dog with a stone and with unerring aim strike him on the ribs, which caused the lean and hungry brute to drop a bone, which the Kaffir carried off in triumph to the kerb, where he smashed it and got what comfort he could from it.

THE BOER WAR: A BRITISH CONCENTRATION CAMP, SOUTH AFRICA, January 1901

Emily Hobhouse

After the tide of war began to turn, the British retaliated: they rounded up the Boers and their families and set fire to their farms. The Boers were herded into camps. The plight of the women and children in the filthy, insanitary, overcrowded camps became an international scandal – more than 20,000 were to die there.

Diary: January 31

Some people in town still assert that the camp is a haven of bliss. Well, there are eyes and no eyes. I was at the camp today, and just in one little corner this is the sort of thing I found. A girl of twenty-one lay dying on a stretcher – the father, a big, gentle Boer, kneeling beside her; while, next tent, his wife was watching a child of six, also dying, and one of about five drooping. Already this couple had lost three children in the hospital, and so would not let these go, though I begged hard to take them out of the hot tent. 'We must watch these ourselves,' he said. I sent – to fetch brandy, and got some down the girl's throat, but for the most part you must stand and look on, helpless to do anything because there is nothing to do anything with. Then a man came up and said, 'Sister, come and see my child, sick for three months.' It was a dear little chap of four, and nothing left of him but his great brown eyes and white teeth from which the lips were drawn back, too thin to close. His body was emaciated. The little fellow had craved for fresh milk, but of course there had been none until these last two days, and now the fifty cows only give four buckets. I can't describe what it is to see these children lying about in a state of collapse. It's just exactly like faded flowers thrown away. And one has to stand and look on at such misery and be able to do almost nothing.

QUEEN VICTORIA'S FUNERAL CORTÈGE, 1 February 1901

Countess of Denbigh

The death of Victoria, Queen of Great Britain and Ireland, Empress of India, on 22 January 1901 at Osborne on the Isle of Wight, truly marked the end of the old century. Her reign of almost sixty-four years had been the longest in British history, and she had spent the last forty years of it in mourning for her late husband, Prince Albert. She had imprinted her personality upon a whole era.

I think you will like to hear of my going down to Southampton to see the passing of our dear Queen from Osborne to Portsmouth.

I went on the *Scot*, where both Houses were embarked. We steamed out, and took up our position between the last British ship and the first foreign ships of war, on the south side of the double line down which the procession was to pass. The day was one of glorious sunshine, with the smoothest and bluest of seas. After a while a black torpedo destroyer came dashing down the line signalling that the *Alberta* was leaving Osborne and from every ship, both British and foreign, boomed out the minute guns for close on an hour before the procession reached us. The sun was now (three p.m.) beginning to sink, and a wonderful golden pink appeared in the sky and as the smoke slowly rose from the guns it settled in one long festoon behind them, over Haslar, a purple festoon like the purple hangings ordered by the King.

Then slowly down the long line of battleships came eight torpedo destroyers, dark gliding forms, and after them the white *Alberta* looking very small and frail next the towering battleships. We could see the motionless figures standing round the white pall which, with the crown and orb and sceptre, lay upon the coffin. Solemnly and slowly, it glided over the calm blue water, followed by the other three vessels, giving one a strange choke, and a catch in one's heart as memory flew back to her triumphal passage down her fleet in the last Jubilee review. As slowly and as silently as it came the cortège passed away into the haze: with the solemn booming of the guns continuing every minute till Portsmouth was reached. A wonderful scene and marvellously impressive, leaving behind it a memory of peace and beauty and sadness which it is impossible to forget.

THE FIRST RADIO SIGNAL ACROSS THE ATLANTIC, CANADA, 12 December 1901

Guglielmo Marconi

Marconi awaited the signal transmitted from Poldhu in Cornwall in a hut on the cliffs of Newfoundland. Until this time few scientists had believed that radio signals could follow the curvature of the earth for more than a hundred miles or so. Marconi's achievement created a sensation worldwide, and paved the way for the revolutionary development in radio communications and broadcasting.

Shortly before midday I placed the single earphone to my ear and I started listening. The receiver on the table before me was very crude – a few coils and condensers and a coherer – no valves, no amplifiers, not even a crystal. But I was at last on the point of putting the correctness of all my beliefs to test. The answer came at twelve-thirty when I heard, faintly but distinctly, *pip-pip-pip*. I handed the phone to Kemp: 'Can you hear anything?' I asked. 'Yes,' he said, 'the letter S' – he could hear it. I knew then that all my anticipations had been justified. The electric waves sent out into space from Poldhu had traversed the Atlantic – the distance, enormous as it seemed then, of 1,700 miles – unimpeded by the curvature of the earth. The result meant much more to me than the mere successful realization of an experiment. As Sir Oliver

Lodge has stated, it was an epoch in history. I now felt for the first time absolutely certain that the day would come when mankind would be able to send messages without wires not only across the Atlantic but between the farthermost ends of the earth.

THE FIRST POWERED FLIGHT, NORTH CAROLINA, AMERICA, 17 December 1903

Orville Wright

The feat of powered flight was finally achieved on a blustery winter's day at Kitty Hawk, North Carolina, by the brothers Orville and Wilbur Wright. In a telegram to their father Orville wrote: SUCCESS FOUR FLIGHTS THURSDAY MORNING ALL AGAINST TWENTY-ONE MILE WIND STARTED FROM LEVEL WITH ENGINE POWER ALONE AVERAGE SPEED THROUGH AIR THIRTY-ONE MILES LONGEST 59 SECONDS INFORM PRESS HOME CHRISTMAS. The longest flight was the last of the day, with Wilbur flying the 600-pound biplane. Orville later recorded in his diary:

At just twelve o'clock Will started on the fourth and last trip. The machine started with its up and downs as it had before, but by the time he had gone 300 or 400 feet he had it under much better control, and was travelling on a fairly even course. It proceeded in this manner till it reached a small hummock out about 800 feet from the starting ways, when it began pitching again and suddenly darted to the ground. The front rudder frame was badly broken up, but the main frame suffered none at all. The distance over the ground was 852 feet in 59 seconds. The engine turns was 1,071, but this included several seconds while on the starting ways and probably about half a second after landing. The jar of the landing had set the watch on the machine back, so we have no exact record for the 1,071 turns.

BLOODY SUNDAY, ST PETERSBURG, RUSSIA, 9 January 1905

The Times *correspondent*

Discontent at the autocratic Russian social and political system had long been mounting. On 9 January, a Russian Orthodox priest, Gregory Gapon, led a peaceful demonstration which hoped to present workers' requests for reforms directly to Tsar Nicholas II. He had forewarned the authorities of his plan. Workers carried icons, pictures of the Tsar and petitions citing their grievances. However, the Chief of Security, Grand Duke Vladimir, stopped the march and ordered the police to open fire as the workers approached the Winter Palace.

St Petersburg awoke this morning to find itself in a state of siege. A more perfect and lovely day never dawned. There were five degrees of frost. The air was crisp and invigorating and the sky almost cloudless. The gilded domes of the cathedrals and the churches and the frostencrusted roofs and façades of the houses, brilliantly illuminated by the sun, formed a superb panorama as I looked out of the hotel windows, wondering what the day would bring forth.

I noticed a significant change in the bearing of the passers-by. Instead of flocking up the steps of St Isaac's Cathedral, as usual on Sunday morning, they were all silently wending their way, singly or in small groups, in the direction of the Winter Palace. Joining in the steady stream of working men, I proceeded along the Admiralty Gardens in the direction of the Winter Palace. No observer could help being struck by the look of sullen determination on every face. As the people turning the corners came within view of the Winter Palace they craned their necks and with eager eyes directed on the square attempted to see what was happening.

Already a crowd of many thousands had collected, but was prevented from entering the square by mounted troops drawn up across each thoroughfare. Presently the masses began to press forward threateningly. The cavalry advanced at a walking pace, scattering the people right and left. Many curious observers at this point, thinking it prudent, disentangled themselves with some difficulty from the constantly swelling crowd and regained their homes. I myself returned to my headquarters to await reports from my staff of mounted correspondents stationed at all the important points throughout the city.

Event has succeeded event with such bewildering rapidity that the public is staggered and shocked beyond expression. Down to the last moment no one seemed to believe that anything serious was likely to happen. Clinging to their traditional trust in the efficiency of the knout, people shrugged their shoulders and said that there would probably be a few scuffles, but that the demonstrators would be easily dispersed.

Within a space of two hours the city has been plunged into a state of open revolution.

The first trouble began at eleven o'clock, when the military tried to turn back some thousands of Putiloff strikers at one of the bridges connecting the island, which is the great industrial quarter, with the central portions of the city. The same thing happened almost simultaneously at other bridges, where the constant flow of workmen pressing forward refused to be denied access to the common rendezvous in the Palace Square. The Cossacks at first used their knouts, then the flat of their sabres, and finally they fired.

The strikers in the front ranks fell on their knees and implored the Cossacks to let them pass, protesting that they had no hostile intentions. They refused, however, to be intimidated by blank cartridges, and orders were given to load with ball.

The passions of the mob broke loose like a bursting dam. The people, seeing the dead and dying carried away in all directions, the snow on the streets and pavements soaked with blood, cried aloud for vengeance.

Meanwhile, the situation at the Palace was becoming momentarily worse. The troops were reported to be unable to control the vast masses which were constantly surging forward. Reinforcements were sent, and at two o'clock here also the order was given to fire. Men, women, and children fell at each volley, and were carried away in ambulances, sledges, and carts. It was no longer a workman's question. The indignation and fury of every class were aroused. Students, merchants, all classes of the population alike were inflamed. At the moment of writing firing is going on in every quarter of the city.

Father Gapon, marching at the head of a large body of workmen, carrying a cross and other religious emblems, was wounded in the arm and shoulder.

The motor-car employed in carrying my telegrams to the cable office was seized and used to bear off the wounded.

The two forces of workmen are now separated. Those on the other side of the river are arming with swords, knives, and smiths' and carpenters' tools, and are busy erecting barricades.

Several officers have been severely injured on the Nevsky Prospect. Their swords were taken from them and their epaulettes torn off. Panic and consternation reign supreme. The troops are apparently reckless, firing right and left, with or without reason.

The rioters continue to appeal to them, saying 'You are Russians! Why play the part of bloodthirsty butchers?' As the killed and wounded are borne away, men reverently raise their caps and many shout 'Hurrah! Well done!' in honour of those stricken down.

I have passed through the Viborg district and the old part of St Petersburg. Troops are posted at various points, being specially concentrated at the Neva bridges.

The compact masses of workmen, among whom were many women and children, were calm, but they vigorously hissed the officers riding at the head of the troops.

On returning to the Nevsky Prospect, I ran into an enormous crowd composed of all classes of society. Strangers excitedly exchanged their news and impressions of the day's events, drawn into fellowship before a common danger. All were deeply moved and exasperated by the horrors committed by the soldiers at the Putiloff works, where the scene resembled a perfect shambles. There the workmen, anticipating firing, threw themselves flat on the ground, and the troops fired on them as they lay there.

At the Narva Gate, the troops fired on the demonstrators, who were led by Fathers Gapon and Sergius, bearing a cross and ikon and a portrait of the Tsar, which was shattered by the hail of bullets. Father Sergius was killed.

The police and soldiers guarding the Neva Bridge attempted to drive back the mob with the bayonet, but as it still pressed forward a bugle rang out and two volleys were fired haphazard into the struggling mass. Many were killed and wounded. Imprecations, curses, and vows of vengeance were hurled at the officers.

Dreadful anxiety prevails in every household where any members are absent. Distracted husbands, fathers, wives, and children are searching for those missing. The surgeons and Red Cross ambulances are busy. A night of terror is in prospect.

THE SAN FRANCISCO EARTHQUAKE, AMERICA, 17 April 1906

Jack London

Fires raged for four days after the earthquake. Some 28,000 buildings were destroyed; 700 people were killed; some quarter of a million made homeless.

San Francisco is gone! Nothing remains of it but memories and a fringe of dwelling houses on the outskirts. Its industrial section is wiped out. Its social and residential section is wiped out. The factories and warehouse, the great stores and newspaper buildings, the hotels and the palaces of the nabobs, are all gone. Remains only the fringe of dwelling houses on the outskirts of what was once San Francisco.

Within an hour after the earthquake shock the smoke of San Francisco's burning was a lurid tower visible a hundred miles away. And for three days and nights this lurid tower swayed in the sky, reddening the sun, darkening the sky, and filling the land with smoke.

On Wednesday morning at a quarter past five came the earthquake. A minute later the flames were leaping upward. In a dozen different quarters south of Market Street, in the working-class ghetto, and in the factories, fires started. There was no opposing the flames. There was no organization, no communication. All the cunning adjustments of a twentieth-century city had been smashed by the earthquake. The streets were humped into ridges and depression and piled with debris of fallen walls. The steel rails were twisted into perpendicular and horizontal angles. The telephone and telegraph systems were disrupted. And the great water mains had burst. All the shrewd contrivances and safeguards of man had been thrown out of gear by thirty seconds' twitching of the earth crust.

By Wednesday afternoon, inside of twelve hours, half the heart of the city was gone. At that time I watched the vast conflagration from out on the bay. It was dead calm. Not a flicker of wind stirred. Yet from every side wind was pouring in upon the city. East, west, north, and south, strong winds were blowing upon the doomed city. The heated air rising made an enormous suck. Thus did the fire of itself build its own colossal chimney through the atmosphere. Day and night this dead calm continued, and yet, near to the flames, the wind was often half a gale, so mighty was the suck.

The edict which prevented chaos was the following proclamation by Mayor E. E. Schmitz:

'The Federal Troops, the members of the Regular Police Force, and all Special Police Officers have been authorized to KILL any and all persons found engaged in looting or in the commission of any other crime.

'I have directed all the Gas and Electric Lighting Companies not to turn on gas or electricity until I order them to do so; you may therefore expect the city to remain in darkness for an indefinite time.

'I request all citizens to remain at home from darkness until daylight of every night until order is restored.

'I warn all citizens of the danger of fire from damaged or destroyed chimneys, broken or leaking gas pipes or fixtures, or any like cause.'

Wednesday night saw the destruction of the very heart of the city. Dynamite was lavishly used, and many of San Francisco's proudest structures were crumbled by man himself into ruins, but there was no withstanding the onrush of the flames. Time and again successful stands were made by the fire fighters, and every time the flames flanked around on either side, or came up from the rear, and turned to defeat the hard-won victory . . .

BLÉRIOT FLIES THE CHANNEL, 25 July 1909

Louis Blériot

In 1909, the London *Daily Mail* offered a prize of £1,000 to the first aviator to fly the English Channel. The prize was won by Frenchman Louis Blériot who achieved the crossing in a 28 hp monoplane. It took a little over forty minutes.

At four-thirty we could see all around: daylight had come. M. Le Blanc endeavoured to see the coast of England, but could not. A light breeze from the south-west was blowing. The air was clear.

Everything was prepared. I was dressed, as I am at this moment, in a khaki jacket lined with wool for warmth over my tweed clothes and beneath an engineer's suit of blue cotton overalls. My close-fitting cap was fastened over my head and ears. I had neither eaten nor drunk anything since I rose. My thoughts were only upon the flight, and my determination to accomplish it this morning.

Four-thirty five! *Tout est prêt!* Le Blanc gives the signal and in an instant I am in the air, my engine making 1,200 revolutions – almost its highest speed – in order that I may get quickly over the telegraph wires along the edge of the cliff. As soon as I am over the cliff I reduce my speed. There is now no need to force my engine.

I begin my flight, steady and sure, towards the coast of England. I have no apprehensions, no sensations, *pas du tout*.

The *Escopette* has seen me. She is driving ahead at full speed. She makes perhaps 42 kilometres [about 26 miles per hour]. What matters? I am making at least 68 kilometres [42 miles per hour].

Rapidly I overtake her, travelling at a height of 80 metres [about 260 feet].

The moment is supreme, yet I surprise myself by feeling no exultation. Below me is the sea, the surface disturbed by the wind, which is now freshening. The motion of the waves beneath me is not pleasant. I drive on.

Ten minutes have gone. I have passed the destroyer, and I turn my head to see whether I am proceeding in the right direction. I am amazed. There is nothing to be seen, neither the torpedo-destroyer, nor France, nor England. I am alone. I can see nothing at all – *rien du tout*!

For ten minutes I am lost. It is a strange position, to be alone, unguided, without compass, in the air over the middle of the Channel.

I touch nothing. My hands and feet rest lightly on the levers. I let the aeroplane take its own course. I care not whither it goes.

For ten minutes I continue, neither rising nor falling, nor turning. And then, twenty minutes after I have left the French coast, I see the green cliffs of Dover, the castle, and away to the west the spot where I intended to land.

What can I do? It is evident that the wind has taken me out of my course. I am almost at St Margaret's Bay and going in the direction of the Goodwin Sands.

Now it is time to attend to the steering. I press the lever with my foot and turn easily towards the west, reversing the direction in which I am travelling. Now, indeed, I am in difficulties, for the wind here by the cliffs is much stronger, and my speed is reduced as I fight against it. Yet my beautiful aeroplane responds. Still I fly westwards, hoping to cross the harbour and reach the Shakespear Cliff. Again the wind blows. I see an opening in the cliff.

Although I am confident that I can continue for an hour and a half, that I might indeed return to Calais, I cannot resist the opportunity to make a landing upon this green spot.

Once more I turn my aeroplane, and, describing a half-circle, I enter the opening and find myself again over dry land. Avoiding the red buildings on my right, I attempt a landing; but the wind catches me and whirls me round two or three times.

At once I stop my motor, and instantly my machine falls straight upon the land from a height of twenty metres [65 ft]. In two or three seconds I am safe.

Soldiers in khaki run up, and a policeman. Two of my compatriots are on the spot. They kiss my cheeks. The conclusion of my flight overwhelms me. I have nothing to say, but accept the congratulations of the representatives of the *Daily Mail* and accompany them to the Lord Warden Hotel.

Thus ended my flight across the Channel. The flight could be easily done again. Shall I do it? I think not. I have promised my wife that after a race for which I have entered I will fly no more.

A SUFFRAGETTE IN HOLLOWAY PRISON, LONDON, 1909

Lucy Burns

Ever since 1792, with the publication of Mary Wollstonecraft's plea, women had been demanding the right to vote. By the end of the nineteenth century their campaign had become a major political issue. Only New Zealand, Australia, the Western states of America, and Finland had granted women the right to vote by 1909, and in Britain they would not achieve it until 1918.

We remained quite still when ordered to undress, and when they told us to proceed to our cells we linked arms and stood with our backs to the wall. The Governor blew his whistle and a great crowd of wardresses reappeared, falling upon us, forcing us apart and dragging us towards the cells. I think I had twelve wardresses for my share, and among them they managed to trip me so that I fell helplessly to the floor. One of the wardresses grasped me by my hair, wound the long braid around her waist and literally dragged me along the ground. In the cell they fairly ripped the clothing from my back, forcing on me one coarse cotton garment and throwing others on the bed for me to put on myself. Left alone exhausted by the dreadful experience I lay for a time gasping and shivering on the floor. By and by a wardress came to the door and threw me a blanket. This I wrapped around me, for I was chilled to the bone by this time. The single cotton garment and the rough blanket were all the clothes I wore during my stay in prison. Most of the prisoners refused everything but the blanket. According to agreement we all broke our windows and were immediately dragged off to the punishment cells. There we hunger struck, and after enduring great misery for nearly a week, we were one by one released.

THE ARREST OF DR H. H. CRIPPEN, 31 July 1910

Captain H. G. Kendall

After murdering his wife – with the exotic poison, hyoscine – Crippen tried to flee to Canada with his paramour, Ethel LeNeve, but became the first criminal to be caught by use of the wireless. Captain Kendall was the master of the steamship *Montrose.*

The *Montrose* was in port at Antwerp when I read in the *Continental Daily Mail* that a warrant had been issued for Crippen and LeNeve. They were reported to have been traced to a hotel in Brussels but had then vanished again.

Soon after we sailed for Quebec I happened to glance through the porthole of my cabin and behind a lifeboat I saw two men. One was squeezing the other's hand. I walked along the boat deck and got into conversation with the elder man. I noticed that there was a mark on the bridge of his nose through wearing spectacles, that he had recently shaved off a moustache, and that he was growing a beard. The young fellow was very reserved, and I remarked about his cough.

'Yes,' said the elder man, 'my boy has a weak chest, and I'm taking him to California for his health.'

I returned to my cabin and had another look at the *Daily Mail.* I studied the description and photographs issued by Scotland Yard. Crippen was fifty years of age, 5 ft 4 ins high, wearing spectacles and a moustache; Miss LeNeve was twenty-seven, 5 ft 5 ins, slim, with pale complexion. I then examined the passenger list and ascertained that the two passengers were travelling as 'Mr Robinson and son'. I arranged for them to take meals at my table.

When the bell went for lunch I tarried until the coast was clear, then slipped into the Robinsons' cabin unobserved, where I noticed two things: that the boy's felt hat was packed round the rim to make it fit, and that he had been using a piece of a woman's bodice as a face flannel. That satisfied me. I went down to the dining saloon and kept my eyes open. The boy's manners at table were ladylike. Later, when they were promenading the saloon deck, I went out and walked behind them, and called out, 'Mr Robinson!' I had to shout the name several times before the man turned and said to me, 'I'm sorry, Captain, I didn't hear you – this cold wind is making me deaf.'

In the next two days we developed our acquaintance. Mr Robinson was the acme of politeness, quiet-mannered, a non-smoker; at night he went on deck and roamed about on his own. Once the wind blew up his coat tails and in his hip pocket I saw a revolver. After that I also carried a revolver, and we often had pleasant little tea parties together in my cabin, discussing the book he was reading, which was *The Four Just Men*, a murder mystery by Edgar Wallace – and when that little fact was wirelessed to London and published it made Edgar Wallace's name ring, so agog was everybody in England over the Crippen case.

That brings me to the wireless. On the third day out I gave my wireless operator a message for Liverpool: *One hundred and thirty miles west of Lizard . . . have strong suspicions that Crippen London cellar murderer and accomplice are among saloon passengers . . . Accomplice dressed as boy; voice, manner, and build undoubtedly a girl.*

I remember Mr Robinson sitting in a deckchair, looking at the wireless aerials and listening to the crackling of our crude spark-transmitter, and remarking to me what a wonderful invention it was.

I sent several more reports, but our weak transmitting apparatus was soon out of communication with land. We could hear other ships at a great distance, however, and you may imagine my excitement when my operator brought me a message he had intercepted from a London newspaper to its representative aboard the White Star liner *Laurentic* which was also heading westward across the Atlantic: *What is Inspector Dew doing? Is he sending and receiving wireless messages? Is he playing games with passengers? Are passengers excited over chase? Rush reply.*

This was the first I knew that my message to Liverpool had caused Inspector Dew to catch the first boat out – the *Laurentic*. With her superior speed. I knew she would reach the Newfoundland coast before me. I hoped that if she had any news for me the *Laurentic* would leave it at the Belle Island station to be transmitted to me as soon as I passed that point on my approach to Canada.

She had news indeed: *Will board you at Father Point . . . strictly confidential . . . from Inspector Dew, Scotland Yard, on board Laurentic.*

I replied: *Shall arrive Father Point about 6 a.m. tomorrow . . . should advise you to come off in small boat with pilot, disguised as pilot . . .*

This was confirmed. The last night was dreary and anxious, the sound of our fog-horn every few minutes adding to the monotony. The hours dragged on as I paced the bridge; now and then I could see Mr Robinson strolling about the deck. I had invited him to get up early to see the 'pilots' come aboard at Father Point in the River St Lawrence. When they did so they came straight to my cabin. I sent for Mr Robinson. When he entered I stood with the detective facing the door, holding my revolver inside my coat pocket. As he came in, I said, 'Let me introduce you.'

Mr Robinson put out his hand, the detective grabbed it, at the same time removing his pilot's cap, and said, 'Good morning, Dr Crippen. Do you know me? I'm Inspector Dew, from Scotland Yard.'

Crippen quivered. Surprise struck him dumb. Then he said, 'Thank God it's over. The suspense has been too great. I couldn't stand it any longer.'

Ethel LeNeve was acquitted of aiding Crippen in the murder of his wife. The doctor, however, was found guilty and sentenced to be hanged at Pentonville Prison.

ANTARCTIC EXPEDITION: THE FINAL DIARIES AND LETTERS OF CAPTAIN R. F. SCOTT, January 1912

Captain Scott

Scott had set out for the South Pole with eleven others on 24 October, only to find that Amundsen's Norwegians had arrived first. On their return journey, in 1912, Scott and his companions all perished. Their bodies were found by searchers later that year on 12 November. This diary entry leaves some confusion as to the date of his actual death, but it is now generally assumed that he mistakenly wrote 'March' for 'January'.

It is wonderful to think that two long marches would land us at the Pole. We left our depot today with nine days' provisions, so that it ought to be a certain thing now, and the only appalling possibility the sight of the Norwegian flag forestalling ours. Little Bowers continues his indefatigable efforts to get good sights, and it is wonderful how he works them up in his sleeping-bag in our congested tent. (Minimum for night – 27.5°.) Only 27 miles from the Pole. We *ought* to do it now.

Tuesday, 16 January . . . The worst has happened, or nearly, the worst . . . About the second hour of the march Bowers' sharp eyes detected what he thought was a cairn; he was uneasy about it, but argued that it must be a sastrugus. Half an hour later he detected a black speck ahead. Soon we knew that this could not be a natural snow feature. We marched on, found that it was a black flag tied to a sledge bearer; near by the remains of a camp; sledge tracks and ski tracks going and coming and the clear trace of dogs' paws – many dogs. This told us the whole story. The Norwegians have forestalled us and are first at the Pole. It is a terrible disappointment, and I am very sorry for my loyal companions. Many thoughts come and much discussion have we had. Tomorrow we must march on to the Pole and then hasten home with all the speed we can compass. All the daydreams must go; it will be a wearisome return. We are descending in altitude – certainly also the Norwegians found an easy way up.

Wednesday, 17 January . . . The Pole. Yes, but under very different circumstances from those expected. We have had a horrible day – add to our disappointment a head wind 4 to 5, with a temperature -22°, and companions labouring on with cold feet and hands.

We started at 7.30, none of us having slept much after the shock of our discovery. We followed the Norwegian sledge tracks for some way; as far as we make out there are only two men. In about three miles we passed two small cairns. Then the weather overcast, and the tracks being increasingly drifted up and obviously going too far to the west, we decided to make straight for the Pole according to our calculations . . . Great God! this is an awful place and terrible enough for us to have laboured to it without the reward of priority. Well, it is something to have got here, and the wind may be our friend tomorrow. We have had a fat Polar hoosh in spite of our chagrin, and feel comfortable inside – added a small stick of chocolate and the queer taste of a cigarette brought by Wilson. Now for the run home and a desperate struggle. I wonder if we can do it.

Thursday morning, 18 January . . . We have just arrived at this tent, 2 miles from our camp, therefore about 1½ miles from the Pole. In the tent we find a record of five Norwegians having been here, as follows: 'Roald Amundsen, Olav Olavson Bjaaland, Hilmer Hanssen, Sverre H. Hassel, Oscar Wisting; 16 Dec. 1911'. The tent is fine – a small, compact affair supported by a single bamboo. A note from Amundsen, which I keep, asks me to forward a letter to King Haakon!

The following articles have been left in the tent: three half-bags of reindeer containing a miscellaneous assortment of mitts and sleeping socks, very various in description, a sextant, a Norwegian artificial horizon and a hypsometer without boiling-point thermometers, a sextant and hypsometer of English make. Left a note to say I had visited the tent with companions . . .

This morning started with southerly breeze, set sail and passed another cairn at good speed; half-way, however, the wind shifted to W by S or WSW, blew through our wind clothes and into our mitts. Poor Wilson horribly cold, could not get off ski for some time. Bowers and I practically made camp, and when we got into the tent at last we were all deadly cold. Then temp. now midday down -43° and the wind strong. We *must* go on, but now the making of every camp must be more difficult and dangerous. It must be near the end, but a pretty merciful end. Poor Oates got it again in the foot. I shudder to think what it will be like tomorrow. It is only with greatest pains rest of us keep off frostbites. No idea there could be temperatures like this at this time of year with such winds. Truly awful outside the tent. Must fight it out to the last biscuit, but can't reduce rations.

Friday, 16 March or Saturday 17. Lost track of dates, but think the last correct. Tragedy all along the line. At lunch, the day before yesterday, poor Titus Oates said he couldn't go on; he proposed we should leave him in his sleeping-bag. That we could not do, and induced him to come on, on the afternoon march. In spite of its awful nature for him he struggled on and we made a few miles. At night he was worse and we knew the end had come.

Should this be found I want these facts recorded. Oates' last thoughts were of his mother, but immediately before he took pride in thinking that his regiment would be pleased with the bold way in which he met his death. We can testify to his bravery. He has borne intense suffering for weeks without complaint, and to the very last was able and willing to discuss outside subjects. He did not – would not – give up hope to the very end. He was a brave soul. This was the end. He slept through the night before last, hoping not to wake; but he woke in the morning – yesterday. It was blowing a blizzard. He said, 'I am just going outside and may be some time.' He went out into the blizzard and we have not seen him since.

I take this opportunity of saying that we have stuck to our sick companions to the last. In case of Edgar Evans, when absolutely out of food and he lay insensible, the safety of the remainder seemed to demand his abandonment, but Providence mercifully removed him at this critical moment. He died a natural death, and we did not leave him till two hours after his death. We knew that poor Oates was walking to his death, but though we tried to dissuade him, we knew it was the act of a brave man and an English gentleman. We all hope to meet the end with a similar spirit, and assuredly the end is not far.

I can only write at lunch and then only occasionally. The cold is intense, -40° at midday. My companions are unendingly cheerful, but we are all on the verge of serious frostbites, and though we constantly talk of fetching through I don't think any one of us believes it in his heart.

We are cold on the march now, and at all times except meals. Yesterday we had to lay up for a blizzard and today we move dreadfully slowly. We are at No. 14 pony camp, only two pony marches from One Ton Depot. We leave here our theodolite, a camera, and Oates' sleeping-bags. Diaries, etc., and geological specimens carried at Wilson's special request, will be found with us or on our sledge.

Sunday, 18 March. Today, lunch, we are 21 miles from the depot. Ill fortune presses, but better may come. We have had more wind and drift from ahead yesterday; had to stop marching; wind NW, force 4, temp. -35°. No human being could face it, and we are worn out *nearly*.

My right foot has gone, nearly all the toes – two days ago I was proud possessor of best feet. These are the steps of my downfall. Like an ass I mixed a small spoonful of curry powder with my melted pemmican – it gave me violent indigestion. I lay awake and in pain all night; woke and felt done on the march; foot went and I didn't know it. A very small measure of neglect and have a foot which is not pleasant to contemplate. Bowers takes first place in condition, but there is not much to choose after all. The others are still confident of getting through – or pretend to be – I don't know! We have the last *half* fill of oil in our primus and a very small quantity of spirit – this alone between us and thirst. The wind is fair for the moment, and that is perhaps a fact to help. The mileage would have seemed ridiculously small on our outward journey.

Monday, 19 March. Lunch. We camped with difficulty last night and were dreadfully cold till after our supper of cold pemmican and biscuit and a half a pannikin of cocoa cooked over the spirit. Then, contrary to expectation, we got warm and all slept well. Today we started in the usual dragging manner. Sledge dreadfully heavy. We are 15½ miles from the depot and ought to get there in three days. What progress! We have two days' food but barely a day's fuel. All our feet are getting bad – Wilson's best, my right foot worst, left all right. There is no chance to nurse one's feet till we can get hot food into us. Amputation is the least I can hope for now, but will the trouble spread? That is the serious question. The weather doesn't give us a chance – the wind from N to NW and -40° temp. today.

Wednesday, 21 March. Got within 11 miles of depot Monday night; had to lay up all yesterday in severe blizzard. Today forlorn hope, Wilson and Bowers going to depot for fuel.

Thursday, 22 and 23 March. Blizzard bad as ever – Wilson and Bowers unable to start – tomorrow last chance – no fuel and only one or two of food left – must be near the end. Have decided it shall be natural – we shall march for the depot with or without our effects and die in our tracks.

Thursday, 29 March. Since the 21st we have had a continuous gale from WSW and SW. We had fuel to make two cups of tea apiece and bare food for two days on the 20th. Every day we have been ready to start for our depot *11 miles* away, but outside the door of the tent it remains a scene of whirling drift. I do not think we can hope for any better things now. We shall stick it out to the end, but we are getting weaker, of course, and the end cannot be far.

It seems a pity, but I do not think I can write more.

R. SCOTT

For God's sake look after our people.

THE TITANIC SINKS, 15 April 1912

Harold Bride

Hailed by its builders and owners as 'unsinkable', the liner *Titanic* had a total complement of 2,224 passengers and crew but, it was to transpire; room for only 1,178 passengers in its lifeboats when it struck an iceberg in the Atlantic on its maiden voyage. A total of 1,513 lives were lost. Harold Bride was a *Titanic* wireless operator.

From aft came the tunes of the band. It was a ragtime tune. I don't know what. Then there was 'Autumn' . . . I went to the place I had seen the collapsible boat on the boat deck, and to my surprise I saw the boat, and the men still trying to push it off. I guess there wasn't a sailor in the crowd. They couldn't do it. I went up to them and was just lending a hand when a large wave came awash of the deck. The big wave carried the boat off. I had hold of an oarlock and I went with it. The next I knew I was in the boat. But that was not all. I was in the boat, and the boat was upside-down, and I was under it. And I remember realizing I was wet through and that whatever happened I must not breathe, for I was under water. I knew I had to fight for it, and I did. How I got out from under the boat I do not know but I felt a breath of air at last. There were men all around me – hundreds of them. The sea was dotted with them, all depending on their lifebelts. I felt I simply had to get away from the ship. She was a beautiful sight then. Smoke and sparks were rushing out of her funnel. There must have been an explosion, but we heard none. We only saw the big stream of sparks. The ship was turning gradually on her nose – just like a duck that goes for a dive. I had only one thing on my mind – to get away from the suction. The band was still playing. I guess all of them went down. They were playing 'Autumn' then. I swam with all my might. I suppose I was 150 feet away when the *Titanic*, on her nose, with her after-quarter sticking straight up in the air, began to settle – slowly.

When at last the waves washed over her rudder there wasn't the least bit of suction I could feel. She must have kept going just so slowly as she had been . . . I felt after a little while like sinking. I was very cold. I saw a boat of some kind near me, and put all my strength into an effort to swim to it. It was hard work. I was all done when a hand reached out from the boat and pulled me aboard. It was our same collapsible. The same crowd was on it. There was just room for me to roll on the edge. I lay there not caring what happened. Somebody sat on my legs. They were wedged in between slats and were being wrenched. I had not the heart left to ask the man to move. It was a terrible sight all around – men swimming and sinking.

I lay where I was, letting the man wrench my feet out of shape. Others came near. Nobody gave them a hand. The bottom-up boat already had more men than it would hold, and it was sinking. At first the larger waves splashed over my clothing. Then they began to splash over my head, and I had to breathe when I could. As we floated around on our capsized boat and I kept straining my eyes for a ship's lights, somebody said, 'Don't the rest of you think we ought to pray?' The man who made the suggestion asked what the religion of the others was. Each man called out his religion. One was a Catholic, one a Methodist, one a Presbyterian. It was decided the most appropriate prayer for all was the Lord's Prayer. We spoke it over in chorus with the man who first suggested that we pray as the leader. Some splendid people saved us. They had a right-side-up boat and it was full to capacity. Yet they came to us and loaded us all into it. I saw some lights off in the distance and knew a steamship was coming to our aid.

A SUFFRAGETTE COMMITS SUICIDE AT THE DERBY, ENGLAND, 1913

Anon.

They had just got round the Corner, and all had passed but the King's horse, when a woman squeezed through the railings and ran out into the course. She made straight for Anmer, and made a sort of leap for the reins. I think she got hold of them, but it was impossible to say. Anyway the horse knocked her over, and then they all came down in a bunch. They were all rolling together on the ground. The jockey fell with the horse, and struck the ground with one foot in the stirrup, but he rolled free. Those fellows know how to tumble. The horse fell on the woman and kicked out furiously, and it was sickening to see his hoofs strike her repeatedly. It all happened in a flash. Before we had time to realize it was over. The horse struggled to its feet – I don't think it was hurt – but the jockey and the woman lay on the ground.

The ambulance men came running up, put them on stretchers, and carried them away. Most of the other jockeys saw nothing of it. They were far ahead. It was a terrible thing.

The woman who died was Emily Wilding, a well-known activist in the cause of women's suffrage.

THE PREMIÈRE OF STRAVINSKY'S *RITE OF SPRING*, PARIS, FRANCE, 29 May 1913

Jean Cocteau

Stravinsky's ballet of pagan ritual has also been hailed as the beginning of Modernism in music. The opening night practically started a riot.

It was the first *scandale* ever witnessed. *The Rite of Spring* was performed . . . in a brash, brand-new theatre, too comfortable and too lacking in atmosphere for a Paris audience accustomed to experiencing its theatrical emotions while packed like sardines amidst the warmth of much red plush and gold. I have no thought that the *Rite* would have been more properly received in less pretentious surroundings; but this deluxe theatre symbolized very strikingly the mistake of pitting a strong, youthful work against a decadent public. An enervated public that spent its life lolling amid Louis XVI garlands and in Venetian gondolas, and on soft divans – and on pillows of an orientalism for which one can only say the Russian Ballet itself was responsible. Such an existence is like digesting one's lunch in a hammock; lying in a doze, you brush away anything really new as if it were a fly. It's troublesome.

I myself heard this historic work amid such a tumult that the dancers could no longer hear the orchestra and had to follow the rhythm as Nijinsky, stamping and shouting, beat it out for them from the wings.

Now come with me through the little metal door leading to the auditorium. Every seat is taken. The experienced eye perceives that every possible ingredient of a *scandale* is here: a society audience, décolleté, festooned with pearls, aigrettes, ostrich plumes; and, along with the tail-coats and the tulle, daytime jackets and women's hair that never saw a hairdresser – the ostentatiously drab trappings of that race of aesthetes who invariably acclaim the new out of mere hatred for the people in the boxes. (The ignorant applause of such aesthetes is more intolerable than the sincere boos of the society folk.) Then there were the feverish musicians, like so many Panurge's sheep, torn between the opinion expressed by the smart set and the respect due the Ballets Russes. No more of this: were I to continue, I would have to describe a thousand shades of snobbism, supersnobbism, counter-snobbism, which would fill a chapter by themselves.

The house played its appointed role: it rebelled, instantly. It laughed, booed, whistled, imitated the cries of animals: perhaps it would have tired more quickly if the crowd of aesthetes and some of the musicians, carried away by excessive enthusiasm, hadn't taken to insulting and even physically threatening the people in the boxes. What had begun as an uproar turned into a veritable battle.

Standing in her box, red in the face, her coronet askew, the old Comtesse de Pourtalès brandished her fan and shouted: 'This is the first time in sixty years that anyone has dared make fun of me.' The good lady was sincere: she thought the whole thing was a practical joke.

Practical requirements had obliged Diaghilev to present in the form of a gala a première that should have been for artists alone.

Quel bombe! Quel chef d'oeuvre!

THE ASSASSINATION OF THE ARCHDUKE FRANZ FERDINAND, SARAJEVO, YUGOSLAVIA, 28 June 1914

Borijove Jevtic

The murder of the heir to the Habsburg throne by Serb nationalist Gavrilo Princip was the incident which ignited the First World War. Austria made the assassination the pretext to declare war on Serbia, and within weeks the major powers had begun to mobilize. Jevtic was one of Princip's co-conspirators.

A tiny clipping from a newspaper mailed without comment from a secret band of terrorists in Zagreb, a capital of Croatia, to their comrades in Belgrade, was the torch which set the world afire with war in 1914. That bit of paper wrecked old proud empires. It gave birth to new, free nations.

I was one of the members of the terrorist band in Belgrade which received it and, in those days, I and my companions were regarded as desperate criminals. A price was on our heads. Today my little band is seen in a different light, as pioneer patriots. It is recognized that our secret plans hatched in an obscure café in the capital of old Serbia, have led to the independence of the new Yugoslavia, the united nation set free from Austrian domination.

The little clipping was from the *Srobobran*, a Croatian journal of limited circulation, and consisted of a short telegram from Vienna. This telegram declared that the Austrian Archduke Franz Ferdinand would visit Sarajevo, the capital of Bosnia, 28 June, to direct army manoeuvres in the neighbouring mountains.

It reached our meeting place, the café called Zeatna Moruana, one night the latter part of April, 1914 . . . At a small table in a very humble café, beneath a flickering gas jet we sat and read it. There was no advice nor admonition sent with it. Only four letters and two numerals were sufficient to make us unanimous, without discussion, as to what we should do about it. They were contained in the fateful date, 28 June.

How dared Franz Ferdinand, not only the representative of the oppressor but in his own person an arrogant tyrant, enter Sarajevo on that day? Such an entry was a studied insult.

28 June is a date engraved deeply in the heart of every Serb, so that the day has a name of its own. It is called the *vidovnan*. It is the day on which the old Serbian kingdom was conquered by the Turks at the battle of Amselfelde in 1389. It is also the day on which in the second Balkan War the Serbian arms took glorious revenge on the Turk for his old victory and for the years of enslavement.

That was no day for Franz Ferdinand, the new oppressor, to venture to the very doors of Serbia for a display of the force of arms which kept us beneath his heel.

Our decision was taken almost immediately. Death to the tyrant!

Then came the matter of arranging it. To make his death certain twenty-two members of the organization were selected to carry out the sentence. At first we thought we would choose the men by lot. But here Gavrilo Princip intervened. Princip is destined to go down in Serbian history as one of her greatest heroes. From the moment Ferdinand's death was decided upon he took an active leadership in its planning. Upon his advice we left the deed to members of our band who were in and around Sarajevo under his direction and that of Gabrinovic, a linotype operator on a Serbian newspaper. Both were regarded as capable of anything in the cause.

The fateful morning dawned. Two hours before Franz Ferdinand arrived in Sarajevo all the twenty-two conspirators were in their allotted positions, armed and ready. They were distributed 500 yards apart over the whole route along which the Archduke must travel from the railroad station to the town hall.

When Franz Ferdinand and his retinue drove from the station they were allowed to pass the first two conspirators. The motor cars were driving too fast to make an attempt feasible and in the crowd were Serbians: throwing a grenade would have killed many innocent people.

When the car passed Gabrinovic, the compositor, he threw his grenade. It hit the side of the car, but Franz Ferdinand with presence of mind threw himself back and was uninjured. Several officers riding in his attendance were injured.

The cars sped to the Town Hall and the rest of the conspirators did not interfere with them. After the reception in the Town Hall

General Potiorek, the Austrian Commander, pleaded with Franz Ferdinand to leave the city, as it was seething with rebellion. The Archduke was persuaded to drive the shortest way out of the city and to go quickly.

The road to the manoeuvres was shaped like the letter V, making a sharp turn at the bridge over the River Nilgacka. Franz Ferdinand's car could go fast enough until it reached this spot but here it was forced to slow down for the turn. Here Princip had taken his stand.

As the car came abreast he stepped forward from the kerb, drew his automatic pistol from his coat and fired two shots. The first struck the wife of the Archduke, the Archduchess Sofia, in the abdomen. She was an expectant mother. She died instantly.

The second bullet struck the Archduke close to the heart.

He uttered only one word; 'Sofia' – a call to his stricken wife. Then his head fell back and he collapsed. He died almost instantly.

The officers seized Princip. They beat him over the head with the flat of their swords. They knocked him down, they kicked him, scraped the skin from his neck with the edges of their swords, tortured him, all but killed him.

Then he was taken to the Sarajevo gaol. The next day he was transferred to the military prison and the round-up of his fellow conspirators proceeded, although he denied that he had worked with anyone.

He was confronted with Gabrinovic, who had thrown the bomb. Princip denied he knew him. Others were brought in, but Princip denied the most obvious things.

The next day they put chains on Princip's feet, which he wore till his death.

His only sign of regret was the statement that he was sorry he had killed the wife of the Archduke. He had aimed only at her husband and would have preferred that any other bullet should have struck General Potiorek.

The Austrians arrested every known revolutionary in Sarajevo and among them, naturally, I was one. But they had no proof of my connection with the crime. I was placed in the cell next to Princip's, and when Princip was taken out to walk in the prison yard I was taken along as his companion.

BRITAIN DECLARES WAR, 4 August 1914

King George V

Great Britain entered the First World War on 4 August 1914 after Germany refused to respect Belgian neutrality.

I held a council at 10.45 to declare war with Germany. It is a terrible catastrophe but it is not our fault. An enormous crowd collected outside the Palace; we went on the balcony both before and after dinner. When they heard that war had been declared, the excitement increased and May and I with David went on to the balcony; the cheering was terrific. Please to God it may soon be over and that He will protect dear Bertie's life.

King George V

JOINING UP, AUTUMN 1914

Oskar Kokoschka

Austrian by birth, Kokoschka went on to become one of Europe's most eminent painters.

In 1914 I was twenty-eight years old, and thus liable for military service. It seemed to me better to volunteer before I was conscripted. I had no wife or child to await my happy return. I had nothing to lose or to defend. I felt melancholy at the sight of the young bank clerks, the little office workers, whom I saw hurrying with their suitcases to enlist, and yet I did not share the doom-laden mood that prevailed on the streets. The air was thick with rumours that part of the army had gone into the field wearing peacetime clothing.

Arthur Conan Doyle

The British author of the *Sherlock Holmes* stories writes a letter to the War-Office.

I have been told that there may be some difficulty in finding officers for the New Army. I think I may say that my name is well-known to the younger men of this country and that if I were to take a commission at my age it might be of help. I can drill a company – I do so every evening. I have seen something of campaigning, having served as a surgeon in South Africa. I am fifty-five but I am very strong and hardy, and can make my voice audible at great distances which is useful at drill. Should you entertain my application, I should prefer a regiment which was drawn from the South of England – Sussex for choice.

Robert Graves

At the time of writing Robert Graves was a student. He later joined the Royal Welch Fusiliers, and wrote one of the classic memoirs of the conflict, *Goodbye to All That.*

I had just finished with Charterhouse and gone up to Harlech, when England declared war on Germany. A day or two later I decided to enlist. In the first place, though the papers predicted only a very short war – over by Christmas at the outside – I hoped that it might last long enough to delay my going to Oxford in October, which I dreaded. Nor did I work out the possibilities of getting actively engaged in the fighting, expecting garrison service at home, while the regular forces were away. In the second place, I was outraged to read of the Germans' cynical violation of Belgian neutrality. Though I discounted perhaps twenty per cent of the atrocity details as wartime exaggeration, that was not, of course, sufficient.

FLEEING THE GERMAN ADVANCE THROUGH FRANCE, October 1914

Frederick Delius

At the time of the German invasion of France, the composer Delius was living at Grez-sur-Loing, some sixty miles south of Paris.

We have been having very exciting times here – During the German advance there was an ever growing panic here caused, no doubt, by the refugees from Belgium & the North of France streaming thro' Grez – The high road to Nemours was a terrifying sight & we sat for hours watching this terrified stream of humanity pass by in every sort of vehicle possible – We had hundreds every night in Grez & they told terrible tales of German atrocities – On Sept 5th it got too much for us & we also could hear the booming of the canon [Battle of the Marne] so we decided to get out also, so we left for Orleans in a cattle truck with 50 or 60 others. We took 16½ hours to go 75 kilometres & arrived in Orleans at 3.30 in the morning & as there was not a room to be had in the whole town we spent the rest of the night on a bench on the boulevard near the railway station – We had the great luck to get a room at night so we decided to stay there & await further developments (*sic*) – We had a most interesting & exciting time in Orleans watching the soldiers going off to the front & the wounded coming back – trainload after trainload – this was awful – Some of the poor soldiers, carried on stretchers, with one or both legs shot off – As soon as we heard of the great Victory of the allies we quietly returned to Grez & found everything as quiet & peaceful as ever – Your uncle had gone off the same day as we did with his 2 servants en route for Guernsey – At Havre he got a steamer for Cherbourg & had a most fearful passage in a miserable little dirty boat. On arriving in some port or other they were fired on 3 times, it appears, as they had no flag up. I nearly died with laughter when Joe told me of his adventures – We are thinking of going to America until all this is over – I am entirely sick of it – We shall leave about Christmas probably from England – I may come to London a fortnight or 3 weeks before sailing & then I should just love to roam about London with you – I am glad you have not enlisted – I hate & loathe this German militarism & autocracy & hope it may be crushed for ever – but I can get up no enthusiasm whatever for the war. My sympathies are with the maimed & slaughtered on both sides. My North Country sketches are ready & also my 'Requiem'. I shall take them with me to America & perhaps conduct them myself – I shall have to make some money over there in some way or other. Music will be dead in Europe for a year or more & all countries will be ruined – It makes one despair of humanity – Lloyd Osbourne & his wife were here thro' the panic – They were seized with it 24 hours before we were & left for Nantes but they returned a fortnight ago here to Grez & are now on their way to London. We had great fun burying our best wine & silver – I would not have missed this experience for anything. The world has gone mad.

THE SOUND OF BULLETS, FRANCE, 2 October 1914

André Fribourg

It is understood that bullets whistle, just as horses neigh . . . But how poor the word is. How pale and niggardly in expressing the extraordinary richness of the music! . . . the differences of distance, of speed, of calibre, of direction, of the grouping of the guns . . . of dampness, heat, cold wind; the differences of the setting of the battle, whether in plain, valley, forest, glade or on a hill; the differences of intensity of fire are such that there is a veritable scale of sounds of an infinite variety of combinations . . . Very soon you learn to distinguish the sound of the Mannlicher from the sound of a Lebel. The S bullet leaves the rifle dryly, with a sharp note. The cry of the D is deeper, making many echoes . . .

A PILOT ENCOUNTERS THE ENEMY, WESTERN FRONT, 1914

Sholto Douglas, Royal Flying Corps

The first time I ever encountered a German plane in the air both the pilot, Harvey-Kelley, and myself were completely unarmed . . . We were taking photographs . . . of the trench system to the north of Neuve Chapelle when I suddenly espied a German two-seater about 100 yards away and just below us. The German observer did not appear to be shooting at us. There was nothing to be done. We waved a hand to the enemy and proceeded with our task. The enemy did likewise. At the time this did not appear to me in any way ridiculous – there is a bond of sympathy between all who fly, even between enemies. But afterwards just for safety's sake I always carried a carbine with me in the air. In the ensuing two or three months I had an occasional shot at a German engine. But these encounters can hardly be dignified by the name of 'fights'. We scarcely expected to shoot the enemy down . . .

CHRISTMAS IN THE TRENCHES, WESTERN FRONT, 1914

Private Frank Richards

On Christmas morning we stuck up a board with 'A Merry Christmas' on it. The enemy had stuck up a similar one. Platoons would sometimes go out for twenty-four hours' rest – it was a day at least out of the trench and relieved the monotony a bit – and my platoon had gone out in this way the night before, but a few of us stayed behind to see what would happen. Two of our men then threw their equipment off and jumped on the parapet with their hands above their heads. Two of the Germans done the same and commenced to walk up the river bank, our two men going to meet them. They met and shook hands and then we all got out of the trench. Buffalo Bill rushed into the trench and endeavoured to prevent it, but he was too late: the whole of the Company were now out, and so were the Germans. He had to accept the situation, so soon he and the other company officers climbed out too. We and the Germans met in the middle of no-man's-land. Their officers was also now out. Our officers exchanged greetings with them. One of the German officers said that he wished he had a camera to take a snapshot, but they were not allowed to carry cameras. Neither were our officers.

We mucked in all day with one another. They were Saxons and some of them could speak English. By the look of them their trenches were in as bad a state as our own. One of their men, speaking in English, mentioned that he had worked in Brighton for some years and that he was fed up to the neck with this damned war and would be glad when it was all over. We told him that he wasn't the only one that was fed up with it. We did not allow them in our trench and they did not allow us in theirs. The German Company-Commander asked Buffalo Bill if he would accept a couple of barrels of beer and assured him that they would not make his men drunk. They had plenty of it in the brewery. He accepted the offer with thanks and a couple of their men rolled the barrels over and we took them into our trench. The German officer sent one of his men back to the trench, who appeared shortly after carrying a tray with bottles and glasses on it. Officers of both sides clinked glasses and drunk one another's health. Buffalo Bill had presented them with a plum pudding just before. The officers came to an understanding that the unofficial truce would end at midnight. At dusk we went back to our respective trenches.

We had a decent Christmas dinner. Each man had a tin of Maconochie's and a decent portion of plum pudding. A tin of Maconochie's consisted of meat, potatoes, beans and other vegetables and could be eaten cold, but we generally used to fry them up in the tin on a fire. I don't remember any man ever suffering from tin or lead poisoning through doing them in this way. The best firms that supplied them were Maconochie's and Moir Wilson's, and we could always depend on having a tasty dinner when we opened one of their tins. But another firm that supplied them at this time must have made enormous profits out of the British Government. Before ever we opened the first tins that were supplied by them we smelt a rat. The name of the firm made us suspicious. When we opened them our suspicions were well founded. There was nothing inside but a rotten piece of meat and some boiled rice. The head of that firm should have been put against the wall and shot for the way they sharked us troops. The two barrels of beer were drunk, and the German officer was right: if it was possible for a man to have drunk the two barrels himself he would have bursted before he had got drunk. French beer was rotten stuff.

Just before midnight we all made it up not to commence firing before they did. At night there was always plenty of firing by both sides if there were no working parties or patrols out. Mr Richardson, a young officer who had just joined the Battalion and was now a platoon officer in my company wrote a poem during the night about the Briton and the Bosche meeting in no-man's-land on Christmas Day, which he read out to us. A few days later it was published in *The Times* or *Morning Post*, I believe. During the whole of Boxing Day we never fired a shot, and they the same, each side seemed to be waiting for the other to set the ball a-rolling. One of their men shouted across in English and inquired how we had enjoyed the beer. We shouted back and told him it was very weak but that we were very grateful for it. We were conversing off and on during the whole of the day. We were relieved that evening at dusk by a battalion of another brigade. We were mighty surprised as we had heard no whisper of any relief during the day. We told the men who relieved us how we had spent the last couple of days with the enemy, and they told us that by what they had been told the whole of the British troops in the line, with one or two exceptions, had mucked in with the enemy. They had only been out of action themselves forty-eight hours after being twenty-eight days in the front-line trenches. They also told us that the French people had heard how we had spent Christmas Day and were saying all manner of nasty things about the British Army.

GALLIPOLI, 25 April 1915

The landing of Allied troops – predominantly British and Anzac (Australian and New Zealand Army Corps) – at the entrance to the Dardanelles, the straits between the Mediterranean and Sea of Marmara, giving access to Istanbul (Constantinople), was intended to open a front against the Turks, and so lessen the pressure on the Russian Army. At the outset, it was regarded as a highly dangerous and almost unachievable move, and it proved one of the greatest military disasters of the First World

War, with the Allies slaughtered as they tried to struggle ashore. Even those that made it found themselves unable to break out of a narrow bridgehead on the rocky, sun-beaten Gallipoli peninsula.

Major Shaw

About 100 yards from the beach the enemy opened fire, and bullets came thick all around, splashing up the water. I didn't see anyone actually hit in the boats, though several were; e.g. my Quartermaster-Sergeant and Sergeant-Major sitting next to me; but we were so jammed together that you couldn't have moved; so that they must have been sitting there, dead. As soon as I felt the boat touch, I dashed over the side into three feet of water and rushed for the barbed wire entanglements on the beach; it must have been only three feet high or so, because I got over it amidst a perfect storm of lead and made for cover, sand dunes on the other side, and got good cover. I then found Maunsell and only two men had followed me. On the right of me on the cliff was a line of Turks in a trench taking pot shots at us, ditto on the left. I looked back. There was one soldier between me and the wire, and a whole line in a row on the edge of the sands. The sea behind was absolutely crimson, and you could hear the groans through the rattle of musketry. A few were firing. I signalled to them to advance. I shouted to the soldier behind me to signal, but he shouted back 'I am shot through the chest'. I then perceived they were all hit.

Chief Petty Officer Johnson, Royal Navy

For quite an hour the huge guns blazed away, whilst we in the trenches lay full length on the ground or stuffed ourselves into small holes cut in the trench side. It was good if two fellows could get together in one of these holes – it meant company. Your feet and legs stuck well out into the trench, but your back and head were safely protected by perhaps two feet of earth which any ordinary size of shell would cut a way through in the hundredth part of a second. You are both squeezed together, you don't dare think how easily a piece of shell would penetrate your shelter. You light a cigarette, look at each other, and wait . . . You press your back harder against the wall and your head harder into the roof. You know you are not safe, but you press harder and that seems to help a bit. You can only see in front of you the opposite side of the sandy trench, at which you gaze in a vacant stare. The shells scream louder and more often, the screeches, whistles and bangs are hopelessly intermingled, and the ground beneath and around you is rocking and trembling.

Thick fumes float into your hole and you cough and your pal coughs. Your knees and legs are covered with pieces of dirt and a layer of dust, and half of the ground that was above your head has gone by way of your neck to the seat of your trousers. You wonder if the bombardment will ever cease . . .

The crashes suddenly cease, the air becomes clearer at once, and you realize that for the time being at any rate the bombardment is over. You wait a few minutes to make quite sure, and then you struggle out of the hole into the trench . . . You look over the parapet, and see a stretch of country with no sign of life.

THE *LUSITANIA* IS TORPEDOED, 7 May 1915

McMillan Adams

The sinking of the British cruise liner *Lusitania* off the coast of Ireland by a German U-boat caused the drowning of over 1,000 people, including 100 Americans. It provoked outrage in the USA, and paved the way for America to enter the First World War. McMillan Adams was an American passenger aboard the liner.

I was in the lounge on A Deck . . . when suddenly the ship shook from stem to stern, and immediately started to list to starboard . . . I rushed out into the companionway . . . While standing there, a second, and much greater explosion occurred. At first I thought the mast had fallen down. This was followed by the falling on the deck of the water spout that had been made by the impact of the torpedo with the ship . . . My father came up and took me by the arm . . . We went to the port side . . . and started to help in the launching of the lifeboats. Owing to the list of the ship, the lifeboats . . . had a tendency to swing inwards across the deck and before they could be launched, it was necessary to push them over the side of the ship. While working there, the staff Captain told us that the boat was not going to sink, and ordered the lifeboats not to be lowered. He also asked the gentlemen to help in clearing the passengers from the boat deck (A Deck) . . . it was impossible to lower the lifeboats safely at the speed at which the *Lusitania* was still going . . . I saw only two boats launched from this side. The first boat to be launched, for the most part full of women, fell sixty or seventy feet into the water, all the occupants being drowned. This was owing to the fact that the crew could not work the davits and falls properly, so let them slip out of their hands, and sent the lifeboats to destruction . . . I said to my father 'We shall have to swim for it. We had better go below and get our lifebelts.'

When we got down to Deck D, our cabin deck, we found it was impossible to leave the stairs, as the water was pouring in at all the port holes . . . Finally, we reached the boat deck again, this time on the starboard side, and after filling a lifeboat with women and children, we jumped into it. The lifeboat [No. 19] was successfully lowered until we were about twelve feet from the water, when the man at the bow davit lost his nerve, and let the rope go. Most of the occupants were thrown into the water, but we, being in the stern, managed to stay in. The lifeboat was full of water, but the sailors said it would float if only we could get it away from the *Lusitania* which was now not far from sinking. My Father threw off his overcoat, and worked like a slave trying to help loose the falls from the boat. This, however, was impossible. B. Deck was then level with the water, and I suggested to my Father we should climb up and get into another lifeboat. He, however, looked up, saw the *Lusitania* was very near its end, and was likely to come over on us, and pin us beneath. He shouted to me to jump, which I did. We were both swimming together in the water, a few yards from the ship, when something separated us. That was the last I saw of him . . . After about an hour I was helped on to a collapsible boat which was upside down. It was at this time that we saw smoke coming towards us on the horizon out to sea, but as soon as the funnel was just in sight, it went away again from us. This must have been one of the boats that the German submarine stopped from coming to our rescue.

Later, another collapsible boat, full of water but right side up and with oars, came and picked us off our upturned boat. We rowed several miles in this sinking condition to [a] fishing boat.

ZEPPELIN RAID ON LONDON, Summer 1915

Freiharr Treusch von Buttlar Brandenfels

We were flying at a height of 15,000 feet. Suddenly the steersman called out to me: 'Searchlights on our starboard bow!' Then the whole car became alive, and with our binoculars to our eyes we leant out of the control car down to our waists.

What a magnificent sight! How wonderful to see the beams of the searchlights exploring the heavens inch by inch, intersecting one another, then collecting into groups of three, four and five from different directions, and cutting each other again, and at last, at the point where they intersected, possibly finding a Zeppelin hanging like a huge incandescent cigar in the sky!

In a moment red lights were scattered through the blackness. They were the shrapnel-bursts.

Soon corresponding red lights appeared below on the ground. They were our own bombs.

There could not be the slightest doubt that our ship, too, was now quite close to the English coast.

Suddenly I staggered and was enveloped in blackness. In the heat of the fight I had lost my liquid-air pipe. It had dropped off the mouthpiece. It grew darker and darker. I felt I was going to be sick. I groped madly about the floor and seized hold of legs, cables, machine-gun belts. At last, just as I felt I should faint from the leaden weight on my head, I found the pipe!

It was marvellous. The moment I was able to breathe in the liquid air again I felt I could have knocked down whole barricades of brick walls, or lifted our tender with my little finger, or juggled with the machine-gun as though it were a billiard-cue, so elemental and powerful is the sudden fresh breath of life that is breathed into one!

'Climb to 18,000 feet!'

Minus twenty-one degrees, thirty degrees, thirty-five degrees Centigrade! Splendid! We met with no inversion. On the contrary, the temperature decreased appreciably the higher we rose.

A quarter of an hour later we had made the coast. We could see the lights of towns and villages, and of railways with their red and green signals, quite plainly. Suddenly everything below went black again. The district was certainly very skilful at putting out or concealing lights. It knew all about airship raids!

Ahead of us, I should say about ten miles away, one of our ships was attacking, and it immediately occurred to me that I ought to keep a more southerly course. So I changed my direction, intending, as soon as I had the attacking ship on my starboard beam, to course about and, flying north-east, to attack the same objective.

Everything depended on our reaching our objective unobserved. We were lucky. It was not long before we located the brightly illumined ship four points abaft the starboard beam, and I gave the order to steer north-east with rudder hard aport. The attack could begin.

The trap-doors for the bombs, which were in the catwalk, could be opened by the *Wachoffizier* by simply pressing a button. We were on the western edge of our objective. I gave the order for action!

Schiller pressed the first button and the first ten-pounder bomb whistled down to the depths. In spite of the buzz of the engines we could hear it whizzing through the air. The whole thing happened in a flash; the next bomb followed, then the third and fourth.

The bombs were plainly visible. A tiny blob of light appeared 18,000 feet below us, a few seconds later we heard the dull thud above the hum of the engines.

There could be no doubt that we were well over our objective, so the heavier fellows, the one-hundred-weight and two-hundred-weight bombs, were also dropped. They were released at regular intervals and crashed down below with a loud whine, followed quite rhythmically by a heavy thud as they reached the ground. The last three bombs were released simultaneously, and a heavy roll of thunder resounded below.

The crew knew what to do. Out with the ammunition!

It was so light that my eyes began to smart. Immediately after the first burst the searchlights had found us. One, two, three, four! We were flying through a cloud of glaring light. I could read the smallest print on the map before me.

How magnificent the huge, dazzlingly bright form of the ship must have looked 18,000 feet up in the sky, as she steered her way across the heavens!

The shrapnel salvoes drew nearer and nearer. At first they burst 3,000 feet below us. Oh, so the man in front of us had been flying at 15,000 feet!

But they corrected their range damnably quickly. Now they were getting very close indeed. We could hear the shells bursting all round and the whine of the splinters as they hurtled through space – high-explosive shells.

Should we climb higher, exhaust our last reserve strength, and, for the sake of 300 feet, risk being brought down by a hit, in which case all would be lost?

Suddenly on our port bow we saw a brilliant light, but no searchlight beam. It was deep and broad, a regular bank of light. The searchlight was penetrating a cloud.

'All engines full throttle.' We were saved! Up we climbed into the cloud. The next salvo would certainly have hit the ship if we had not been able to hide.

SHOOTING DOWN A ZEPPELIN, POTTERS BAR, LONDON, October 1915

Lt W. J. Tempest, RFC

I decided to dive at her . . . firing a burst straight into her as I came. I let her have another burst as I passed under her and then banked my machine over, sat under her tail and flying along underneath her pumped lead into her for all I was worth . . . As I was firing, I noticed her begin to go red inside like an enormous Chinese lantern. She shot up about 200 feet, paused, and came roaring down straight on to me before I had time to get out of the way. I nose-dived for all I was worth, with the Zeppelin tearing after me . . . I put my machine into a spin and just managed to corkscrew out of the way as she shot past me, roaring like a furnace . . . then proceeded to fire off dozens of green Very lights in the exuberance of my feelings.

RETREAT FROM GALLIPOLI, 21 December 1915

H. W. Nevinson

The stores began to go first, slowly. Various ruses and accidents served to deceive the enemy, who even thought that the increased number of ships off the bay signified a strongly renewed attack about Christmas. To maintain this apprehension, parties of our men were taken off at night and returned by day, like a stage army. On the final day, an ironic order commanded that the immemorial custom of our men showing themselves on the skyline should be carefully maintained, and we all did our best to serve our country by walking everywhere round Suvla in the enemy's sight. Orders were further received that mule-carts were to be driven slowly up and down. The mules were singular fine animals; happily all were saved at Suvla, and nearly all at Anzac. Native Indians managed them as though mules were well-trained dogs, and served with great patience and fortitude, even under the severe trial of tempest and frost.

After the strain of carefully organized preparations, the excitement of the final hours was extreme, but no signs of anxiety were shown. Would the sea remain calm? Would the moon remain veiled in a thin cloud? Would the brigades keep time and place? Our own guns continued firing duly till the moment for withdrawal came. Our rifles kept up an intermittent fire, and sometimes came sudden outbursts from the Turks. An aeroplane whirred overhead, but was invisible. We could not be sure it was our own until we saw a green star blaze for a few seconds just below Saturn. On the earth a few fires still blazed where camps or dug-outs were once inhabited, but gradually they went out. Only far off the hospital tents along the curving shore showed lights, and there were only two of these. The sea glimmered white through a moonlit haze, and over its surface thin black lines kept moving. Could an enemy see, or could he possibly miss the significance of those thin black lines?

Mules neighed, chains rattled, steamers hooted low, and sailor men shouted into megaphones language strong enough to carry a hundred miles. Still the enemy showed no sign of life or hearing, though he lay almost visible in the moonlight across the familiar scene of bay and plain and hills to which British soldiers have given such unaccustomed names. So the critical hours went by slowly, and yet giving so little time for all to be done. At last the final bands of silent defenders began to come in from the nearest lines. Sappers began to come in, cutting all telephone wires and signals on their way. Some sappers came after arranging slow fuses to kindle our few abandoned stores of biscuits, bully beef, and bacon left in the bends of the shore. Silently the staffs began to go. The officers of the beach party, who had accomplished such excellent and sleepless work, collected. With a smile they heard the distant blast of Turks still labouring at the trenches – a peculiar instance of labour lost. Just before three a pinnace took me off to one of the battleships. At half-past three the last-ditchers put off. From our familiar northern point of Suvla Bay itself, I am told, the General commanding the Ninth Army Corps was himself the last to leave, motioning his chief of staff to go first. So the Suvla expedition came to an end after more than five months of existence. I do not discuss policy, but the leaving of the existence well became it.

THE SOMME, July 1916

Sergeant Major Ernest Shephard

The Battle of the Somme, which began on 1 July 1916, claimed 60,000 British casualties on the first day alone. By the battle's end in mid-November 1916, 420,000 British and 200,000 French lives had been lost. For all this, the Allies had gained only five miles of ground.

Diary: Saturday, 1 July

A lovely day, intensely hot. Lot of casualties in my trench. The enemy are enfilading us with heavy shell, dropping straight on us. A complete trench mortar battery of men killed by one shell, scores of dead and badly wounded in trench, now one p.m. Every move we make brings intense fire, as trenches so badly battered the enemy can see all our movements. Lot of wounded in front we got in, several were hit again and killed in trench. We put as many wounded as possible in best spots in trench and I sent a lot down, but I had so many of my own men killed and wounded that after a time I could not do this. Sent urgent messages to Brigade asking for RAMC bearers to be sent to evacuate wounded, but none came, although Brigade said they had been dispatched. Meanwhile the enemy deliberately shelled the wounded between the trenches with shrapnel, thus killing, or wounding, again most of them. Our own Regtl stretcher bearers worked like niggers to take cases away. Counted all Dorsets at one p.m. Total 53 all ranks. At three p.m. the Manchesters went through the Russian Sap and made an attack, captured a portion of the Leipzig Redoubt. Brigade sent message to say we would be relieved by 15th HLI as soon as possible. Meanwhile we were to hold tight.

We needed to; literally we were blown from place to place. Men very badly shaken. As far as possible we cleared trenches of debris and dead. These we piled in heaps, enemy shells pitching on them made matters worse.

Wounded suffering agonies. I got them water from bottles of dead, a few managed to crawl away to the Aid Post in wood. At dusk we got more wounded in from the front. Eight p.m. we got shelled intensely, and continued at intervals. I had miraculous escapes. The HLI arrived at midnight. I handed care of wounded to them, and took remnants of B and C Coys, only 10 NCOs and men, back via Mounteagle and Rock St, through Wood Post and over same track (Dumbarton) through Blighty

Wood, down the valley to Crucifix Corner. Arrived there at one a.m. on *Sunday 2 July*.

A WALK AMONG THE DEAD, THE SOMME, July 1916

Robert Graves

The next two days we spent in bivouacs outside Mametz Wood. We were in fighting kit and felt cold at night, so I went into the wood to find German overcoats to use as blankets. It was full of dead Prussian Guards Reserve, big men, and dead Royal Welch and South Wales Borderers of the New Army battalions, little men. Not a single tree in the wood remained unbroken. I collected my overcoats, and came away as quickly as I could, climbing through the wreckage of green branches. Going and coming, by the only possible route, I passed by the bloated and stinking corpse of a Gernan with his back propped against a tree. He had a green face, spectacles, close-shaven hair; black blood was dripping from the nose and beard. I came across two other unforgettable corpses: a man of the South Wales Borderers and one of the Lehr Regiment had succeeded in bayoneting each other simultaneously.

A TANK CHARGE, THE SOMME, 15 September 1916

Bert Chaney

The menacing rumble of a tank was heard for the first time in warfare when thirty-six British Mark is were used in an attack on the Somme on 15 September 1916. The Mark 1 weighed 30 tons and was developed from the agricultural tractor designed by American engineer Benjamin Holt. Its top speed was 5 mph.

We heard strange throbbing noises, and lumbering slowly towards us came three huge mechanical monsters such as we had never seen before. My first impression was that they looked ready to topple on their noses, but their tails and the two-little wheels at the back held them down and kept them level. Big metal things they were, with two sets of caterpillar wheels that went right round the body. There was a bulge on each side with a door in the bulging part, and machine-guns on swivels poked out from either side. The engine, a petrol engine of massive proportions, occupied practically all the inside space. Mounted behind each door was a motorcycle type of saddle seat and there was just about enough room left for the belts of ammunition and the drivers . . .

Instead of going on to the German lines the three tanks assigned to us straddled our front line, stopped and then opened up a murderous machine-gun fire, enfilading us left and right. There they sat, squat monstrous things, noses stuck up in the air, crushing the sides of our trench out of shape with their machine-guns swivelling around and firing like mad.

Everyone dived for cover, except the colonel. He jumped on top to the parapet, shouting at the top of his voice, 'Runner, runner, go tell those tanks to stop firing at once. At once, I say.' By now the enemy fire had risen to a crescendo but, giving no thought to his own personal safety as he saw the tanks firing on his own men, he ran forward and furiously rained blows with his cane on the side of one of the tanks in an endeavour to attract their attention.

Although, what with the sounds of the engines and the firing in such an enclosed space, no one in the tank could hear him, they finally realized they were on the wrong trench and moved on, frightening the Jerries out of their wits and making them scuttle like frightened rabbits.

THE RED BARON CLAIMS HIS THIRTY-SECOND VICTORY, FRANCE, 2 April 1917

Rittmeister Manfred Freiharr von Richthofen ('The Red Baron')

The legendary Baron von Richthofen was Germany's leading fighter pilot in the First World War, credited with the destruction of eighty Allied planes before his death in action in 1918. The nickname 'The Red Baron' derived from his affectation in having his Fokker aircraft painted brilliant red.

The second of April, 1917, was another hot day for my squadron. From our field we could hear the sounds of the bombardment, and it was certainly very heavy that day.

I was still in bed when the orderly rushed in crying: '*Herr Leutnant*, the English are here!' Still somewhat sleepy, I looked out of the window and there circling over the field were my dear 'friends'. I got out of bed, quickly put my things on and got ready.

My red bird was all set to begin the morning's work. My mechanics knew that I would not let this favourable moment go by without taking advantage of it. Everything was ready. I quickly donned my flying suit and was off.

Even so, I was the last to start. My comrades got much closer to the enemy. Then, suddenly, one of the impudent fellows fell on me, attempting to force me down. I calmly let him come on, and then we began a merry dance. At one point my opponent flew on his back, then he did this, then that. It was a two-seater. I was superior to him, and he soon realized that he could not escape me. During a pause in the fighting I looked around and saw that we were alone. Therefore, whoever shot better, whoever had the greatest calm and the best position in the moment of danger, would win.

It did not take long. I squeezed under him and fired, but without causing serious damage. We were at least two kilometres from the Front and I thought he would land, but I miscalculated my opponent. When only a few metres above the ground, he suddenly levelled off and flew straight ahead, seeking to escape me. That was too bad for him. I attacked him again and went so low that I feared I would touch the houses in the village beneath me. The Englishman kept fighting back. Almost at the end I felt a hit on my machine. I must not let up now, he must fall. He crashed at full speed into a block of houses, and there was not much left. It was again a case of splendid daring. He defended himself right up to the end.

Very pleased with the performance of my red 'bicycle' in the morning's work, I turned back. My comrades were still in the air and were very surprised when, as we later sat down to breakfast, I told them of my number thirty-two. A very young lieutenant had shot down his first, and we were all happy.

A FIRING SQUAD AT DAWN, WESTERN FRONT, 1917

Brig.-Gen. F. P. Crozier

During the 1914–18 war 307 British soldiers were executed for offences – mainly desertion – against the Army Act.

Now, in peace-time, I and the rest of us would have been very upset indeed at having to shoot a colleague, comrade, call him what you will, at dawn on the morrow. We would not, in ordinary circumstances, have slept. Now the men don't like it, but they have to put up with it. They face their ordeal magnificently. I supervise the preliminary arrangements myself. We put the prisoner in a comfortable warm place. A few yards away we drive in a post, in a back garden, such as exists with any villa residence. I send for a certain junior officer and show him all. 'You will be in charge of the firing-party,' I say; 'the men will be cold, nervous and excited, they may miss their mark. You are to have your revolver ready loaded and cocked; if the medical officer tells you life is not extinct you are to walk up to the victim, place the muzzle of the revolver to his heart and press the trigger. Do you understand?' 'Yes, sir,' comes the quick reply. 'Right,' I add, 'dine with me at my mess tonight.' I want to keep this young fellow engaged under my own supervision until late at night, so as to minimize the chance of his flying to the bottle for support. As for Crocker, he leaves this earth, in so far as knowing anything of his surroundings is concerned, by midnight, for I arrange that enough spirituous liquor is left beside him to sink a ship. In the morning, at dawn, the snow being on the ground, the battalion forms up on the public road. Inside the little garden on the other side of the wall, not ten yards from the centre of the line, the victim is carried to the stake. He is far too drunk to walk. He is out of view save from myself, as I stand on a mound near the wall. As he is produced I see he is practically lifeless and quite unconscious. He has already been bound with ropes. There are hooks on the post; we always do things thoroughly in the Rifles. He is hooked on like dead meat in a butcher's shop. His eyes are bandaged – not that it really matters, for he is already blind. The men of the firing-party pick up their rifles, one of which is unloaded, on a given sign. On another sign they come to the 'Present' and, on the lowering of a handkerchief by the officer, they fire – a volley rings out – a nervous ragged volley it is true, yet a volley. Before the fatal shots are fired I had called the battalion to attention. There is a pause, I wait. I see the medical officer examining the victim. He makes a sign, the subaltern strides forward, a single shot rings out. Life is now extinct. We march back to breakfast while the men of a certain company pay the last tribute at the graveside of an unfortunate comrade. This is war.

THE RUSSIAN REVOLUTION, PETROGRAD, 24 October 1917*

Leon Trotsky

In February 1917 strikes and demonstrations had brought down Tsar Nicholas II's regime, which was replaced by a republican provisional government led by the moderate reformer, Alexander Kerensky. The new body proved unwilling to extract Russia from the war and was quickly overtaken by the revolutionary left. On the evening of 24 October the Marxist Bolshevik party of V. I. Lenin seized power in Petrograd. Leon Trotsky was Lenin's chief comrade-in-arms and the main overseer of the insurrection, which was organized via the Bolshevik-dominated Military Revolutionary Committee. The Committee's headquarters was the Smolny building, where Trotsky spent the fateful night.

On the night of the 24th the members of the Revolutionary Committee went out into the various districts, and I was left alone. Later on Kamenev came in. He was opposed to the uprising, but he had come to spend that deciding night with me, and together we stayed in the tiny corner room on the third floor, so like the captain's bridge on that deciding night of the revolution.

There is a telephone booth in the large empty room adjoining us, and the bell rings incessantly about important things and trifles. Each ring heightens the alertness of the silence. One can readily picture the deserted streets of Petrograd, dimly lit, and whipped by the autumn winds from the sea; the bourgeois and officials cowering in their beds, trying to guess what is going on in those dangerous and mysterious streets; the workers' quarters quiet with the tense sleep of a war-camp. Commissions and conferences of the government parties are exhausting themselves in impotence in the Tsar's palaces, where the living ghosts of democracy rub shoulders with the still hovering ghosts of the monarchy. Now and again the silks and gildings of the halls are plunged into darkness – the supplies of coal have run short. In the various districts detachments of workers, soldiers, and sailors are keeping watch. The young proletarians have rifles and machine-gun belts across their shoulders. Street pickets are warming themselves at fires in the streets. The life of the capital, thrusting its head from one epoch into another on this autumn night, is concentrated about a group of telephones.

* 6 November in Western Calendar

Reports from all the districts, suburbs, and approaches to the capital are focused in the room on the third floor. It seems that everything has been foreseen; the leaders are in their places; the contacts are assured; nothing seems to have been forgotten.

Once more, let us go over it in our minds. This night decides. Only this evening in my report to the delegates of the second congress of the Soviets, I said with conviction: 'If you stand firm, there will be no civil war, our enemies will capitulate at once, and you will take the place that belongs to you by right. There can be no doubt about victory; it is as assured as the victory of any uprising can be. And yet these hours are still tense and full of alarm, for the coming night decides. The government while mobilizing cadets yesterday, gave orders to the cruiser *Aurora* to steam out of the Neva. They were the same Bolshevik sailors whom Skobelev, coming hat in hand, in August begged to protect the Winter Palace from Kornilov. The sailors referred to the Military-Revolutionary Committee for instructions, and consequently the *Aurora* is standing tonight where she was yesterday. A telephone call from Pavlovsk informs me that the government is bringing up from there a detachment of artillery, a battalion of shock troops from Tsarskoye Syelo, and student officers from the Peterhof military school. Into the Winter Palace Kerensky has drawn military students, officers, and the women shock troops. I order the commissaries to place dependable military defences along the approaches to Petrograd and to send agitators to meet the detachments called out by the government. All our instructions and reports are sent by telephone and the government agents are in a position to intercept them. Can they still control our communications?

'If you fail to stop them with words, use arms. You will answer for this with your life.'

I repeat this sentence time and time again. But I do not believe in the force of my order. The revolution is still too trusting, too generous, optimistic and light-hearted. It prefers to threaten with arms rather than really use them. It still hopes that all questions can be solved by words, and so far it has been successful in this – hostile elements evaporate before its breath. Earlier in the day (the 24th) an order was issued to use arms and to stop at nothing at the first sign of pogroms. Our enemies don't even dare think of the streets; they have gone into hiding. The streets are ours; our commissaries are watching all the approaches to Petrograd.

The officers' school and the gunners have not responded to the call of the government. Only a section of the Oraniembaum military students have succeeded in making their way through our defences, but I have been watching their movements by telephone. They end by sending envoys to the Smolny. The government has been seeking support in vain. The ground is slipping from under its feet.

The outer guard of the Smolny has been reinforced by a new machine-gun detachment. The contact with all sections of the garrison is uninterrupted. The companies on duty are on watch in all the regiments. The commissaries are in their places. Delegations from each garrison unit are in the Smolny, at the disposal of the Military-Revolutionary Committee, to be used in case the contact with that unit should be broken off. Armed detachments from the districts march along the streets, ring the bells at the gates or open the gates without ringing, and take possession of one institution after another. Nearly everywhere these detachments are met by friends who have been waiting impatiently for them. At the railway terminals, specially appointed commissaries are watching the incoming and outgoing trains, and in particular the movement of troops. No disturbing news comes from there. All the more important points in the city are given over into our hands almost without resistance, without fighting, without casualties. The telephone alone informs us: 'We are here!'

All is well. It could not have gone better. Now I may leave the telephone. I sit down on the couch. The nervous tension lessens. A dull sensation of fatigue comes over me.

'Give me a cigarette,' I say to Kamenev. (In those years I still smoked, but only spasmodically.) I take one or two puffs, but suddenly with the words, 'Only this was lacking!' I faint. (I inherited from my mother a certain susceptibility to fainting spells when suffering from physical pain or illness. That was why some American physician described me as an epileptic.) As I come to, I see Kamenev's frightened face bending over me. 'Shall I get some medicine?' he asks.

'It would be much better,' I answer after a moment's reflection, 'if you got something to eat.' I try to remember when I last had food, but I can't. At all events it was not yesterday.

THE RUSSIAN REVOLUTION: STORMING THE WINTER PALACE, PETROGRAD, 25 October 1917

John Reed

The Winter Palace was the seat of the moderate provisional government led by Alexander Kerensky. The so-called 'storming' of the Palace, like most of the early acts of the Russian Revolution, was a peculiarly bloodless affair. John Reed, an American socialist journalist, was later immortalized in the film *Reds*.

. . . It was absolutely dark, and nothing moved but pickets of soldiers and Red Guards, grimly intent. In front of the Kazan Cathedral a three-inch field-gun lay in the middle of the street, slewed sideways from the recoil of its last shot over the roofs. Soldiers were standing in every doorway talking in loud tones and peering down towards the Police Bridge. I heard one voice saying: 'It is possible that we have done wrong . . .' At the corners patrols stopped all passers-by – and the composition of these patrols was interesting, for in command of the regular troops was invariably a Red Guard . . . The shooting had ceased.

Just as we came to the Morskaya somebody was shouting: 'The *yunkers* have sent word that they want us to go and get them out!' Voices began to give commands, and in the thick gloom we made out a dark mass moving forward, silent but for the shuffle of feet and the clinking of arms. We fell in with the first ranks.

Like a black river, filling all the street, without song or cheer we poured through the Red Arch, where the man just ahead of me said in a low voice: 'Look out, comrades! Don't trust them. They will fire, surely!' In the open we began to run, stooping low and bunching together, and jammed up suddenly behind the pedestal of the Alexander Column.

'How many of you did they kill?' I asked.

'I don't know. About ten . . .'

After a few minutes huddling there, some hundreds of men, the Army seemed reassured and without any orders suddenly began again to flow forward. By this time, in the light that streamed out of all the Winter Palace windows, I could see that the first 200 or 300 men were Red Guards, with only a few scattered soldiers. Over the barricade of fire-wood we clambered, and leaping down inside gave a triumphant shout as we stumbled on a heap of rifles thrown down by the *yunkers* who had stood there. On both sides of the main gateway the doors stood wide open, light streamed out, and from the huge pile came not the slightest sound.

Carried along by the eager wave of men we were swept into the right-hand entrance, opening into a great bare vaulted room, the cellar of the East wing, from which issued a maze of corridors and staircases. A number of huge packing cases stood about, and upon these the Red Guards and soldiers fell furiously, battering them open with the butts of their rifles, and pulling out carpets, curtains, linen, porcelain, plates, glass-ware . . . One man went strutting around with a bronze clock perched on his shoulder; another found a plume of ostrich feathers, which he stuck in his hat. The looting was just beginning when somebody cried, 'Comrades! Don't take anything. This is the property of the People!' Immediately twenty voices were crying, 'Stop! Put everything back! Don't take anything! Property of the People!' Many hands dragged the spoilers down. Damask and tapestry were snatched from the arms of those who had them; two men took away the bronze clock. Roughly and hastily the things were crammed back in their cases, and self-appointed sentinels stood guard. It was all utterly spontaneous. Through corridors and up staircases the cry could be heard growing fainter and fainter in the distance, 'Revolutionary discipline! Property of the People . . .'

We crossed back over to the left entrance, in the West wing. There order was also being established. 'Clear the Palace!' bawled a Red Guard, sticking his head through an inner door. 'Come, comrades, let's show that we're not thieves and bandits. Everybody out of the Palace except the Commissars, until we get sentries posted.'

Two Red Guards, a soldier and an officer, stood with revolvers in their hands. Another soldier sat at a table behind them, with pen and paper. Shouts of 'All out! All out!' were heard far and near within, and the Army began to pour through the door, jostling, expostulating, arguing. As each man appeared he was seized by the self-appointed committee, who went through his pockets and looked under his coat. Everything that was plainly not his property was taken away, the man at the table noted it on his paper, and it was carried into a little room. The most amazing assortment of objects were thus confiscated; statuettes, bottles of ink, bed-spreads worked with the Imperial monogram, candles, a small oil-painting, desk blotters, gold-handled swords, cakes of soap, clothes of every description, blankets. One Red Guard carried three rifles, two of which he had taken away from *yunkers*; another had four portfolios bulging with written documents. The culprits either sullenly surrendered or pleaded like children. All talking at once the committee explained that stealing was not worthy of the people's champions; often those who had been caught turned around and began to help go through the rest of the comrades.

Yunkers came out in bunches of three or four. The committee seized upon them with an excess of zeal, accompanying the search with remarks like, 'Ah, Provocators! Kornilovists! Counter-revolutionists! Murderers of the People!' But there was no violence done, although the *yunkers* were terrified. They too had their pockets full of small plunder. It was carefully noted down by the scribe, and piled in the little room . . . The *yunkers* were disarmed. 'Now, will you take up arms against the People any more?' demanded clamouring voices.

'No,' answered the *yunkers*, one by one. Whereupon they were allowed to go free.

We came out into the cold, nervous night, murmurous with obscure armies on the move, electric with patrols. From across the river, where loomed the darker mass of Peter-Paul came a hoarse shout . . . Underfoot the sidewalk was littered with broken stucco, from the cornice of the Palace where two shells from the battleship *Aurora* had struck; that was the only damage done by the bombardment.

It was now after three in the morning. On the Nevsky all the street-lights were again shining, the cannon gone, and the only signs of war were Red Guards and soldiers squatting around fires. The city was quiet – probably never so quiet in its history; on that night not a single hold-up occurred, not a single robbery.

TORTURE, PALESTINE, November 1917

T. E. Lawrence

T. E. Lawrence (Lawrence of Arabia) was the British leader of an irregular Arab army fighting the Turks during the First World War.

Properly to round off this spying of the hollow land of Hauran, it was necessary to visit Deraa, its chief town. We could cut it off on north and west and south, by destroying the three railways; but it would be more tidy to rush the junction first and work outwards. Talal, however, could not venture in with me since he was too well known in the place. So we parted from him with many thanks on both sides, and rode southward along the line until near Deraa. There we dismounted. The boy, Halim, took the ponies, and set off for Nisib, south of Deraa. My plan was to walk round the railway station and town with Faris, and reach Nisib after sunset. Faris was my best companion for the trip, because he was an insignificant peasant, old enough to be my father, and respectable.

The respectability seemed comparative as we tramped off in the watery sunlight, which was taking the place of the rain last night. The ground was muddy, we were barefoot, and our draggled clothes showed the stains of the foul weather to which we had been exposed. I was in Halim's wet things, with a torn Hurani jacket, and was yet limping from the broken foot acquired when we blew up Jemal's train. The slippery track made walking difficult, unless we spread out our toes widely and took hold of the ground with them: and doing this for mile after mile was exquisitely painful to me. Because pain hurt me so, I would not lay weight always on my pains in our revolt: yet hardly one day in Arabia passed without a physical ache to increase the corroding sense of my accessory deceitfulness towards the Arabs, and the legitimate fatigue of responsible command.

We mounted the curving bank of the Palestine Railway, and from its vantage surveyed Deraa Station: but the ground was too open to admit of surprise attack. We decided to walk down the east front of the defences: so we plodded on, noting German stores, barbed wire here and there, rudiments of trenches. Turkish troops were passing incuriously between the tents and their latrines dug out on our side.

At the corner of the aerodrome by the south end of the station we struck over towards the town. There were old Albatros machines in the sheds, and men lounging about. One of these, a Syrian soldier, began to question us about our villages, and if there was much 'government' where we lived. He was probably an intending deserter, fishing for a refuge. We shook him off at last and turned away. Someone called out in Turkish. We walked on deafly; but a sergeant came after, and took me roughly by the arm, saying 'The Bey wants you'. There were too many witnesses for fight or flight, so I went readily. He took no notice of Faris.

I was marched through the tall fence into a compound set about with many huts and a few buildings. We passed to a mud room, outside which was an earth platform, whereon sat a fleshy Turkish officer, one leg tucked under him. He hardly glanced at me when the sergeant brought me up and made a long report in Turkish. He asked my name: I told him Ahmed ibn Bagr, a Circassian from Kuneitra. 'A deserter?' 'But we Circassians have no military service.' He turned, stared at me, and said very slowly 'You are a liar. Enrol him in your section, Hassan Chowish, and do what is necessary till the Bey sends for him.'

They led me into a guard-room, mostly taken up by large wooden cribs, on which lay or sat a dozen men in untidy uniforms. They took away my belt, and my knife, made me wash myself carefully, and fed me. I passed the long day there. They would not let me go on any terms, but tried to reassure me. A soldier's life was not all bad. Tomorrow, perhaps, leave would be permitted, if I fulfilled the Bey's pleasure this evening. The Bey seemed to be Nahi, the Governor. If he was angry, they said, I would be drafted for infantry training to the depot in Baalbek. I tried to look as though, to my mind, there was nothing worse in the world than that.

Soon after dark three men came for me. It had seemed a chance to get away, but one held me all the time. I cursed my littleness. Our march crossed the railway, where were six tracks, besides the sidings of the engine-shop. We went through a side gate, down a street, past a square, to a detached, two-storied house. There was a sentry outside, and a glimpse of others lolling in the dark entry. They took me upstairs to the Bey's room; or to his bedroom, rather. He was another bulky man, a Circassian himself, perhaps, and sat on the bed in a night-gown, trembling and sweating as though with fever. When I was pushed in he kept his head down, and waved the guard out. In a breathless voice he told me to sit on the floor in front of him, and after that was dumb; while I gazed at the top of his great head, on which the bristling hair stood up, no longer than the dark stubble on his cheeks and chin. At last he looked me over, and told me to stand up: then to turn round. I obeyed; he flung himself back on the bed, and dragged me down with him in his arms. When I saw what he wanted I twisted round and up again, glad to find myself equal to him, at any rate in wrestling.

He began to fawn on me, saying how white and fresh I was, how fine my hands and feet, and how he would let me off drills and duties, make me his orderly, even pay me wages, if I would love him.

I was obdurate, so he changed his tone, and sharply ordered me to take off my drawers. When I hesitated, he snatched at me; and I pushed him back. He clapped his hands for the sentry, who hurried in and pinioned me. The Bey cursed me with horrible threats: and made the man holding me tear my clothes away, bit by bit. His eyes rounded at the half-healed places where the bullets had flicked through my skin a little while ago. Finally he lumbered to his feet, with a glitter in his look, and began to paw me over. I bore it for a little, till he got too beastly; and then jerked my knee into him.

He staggered to his bed, squeezing himself together and groaning with pain, while the soldier shouted for the corporal and the other three men to grip me hand and foot. As soon as I was helpless the Governor regained courage, and spat at me, swearing he would make me ask pardon. He took off his slipper, and hit me repeatedly with it in the face, while the corporal braced my head back by the hair to receive the blows. He leaned forward, fixed his teeth in my neck and bit till the blood came. Then he kissed me. Afterwards he drew one of the men's bayonets. I thought he was going to kill me, and was sorry: but he only pulled up a fold of the flesh over my ribs, worked the point through, after considerable trouble, and gave the blade a half-turn. This hurt, and I winced, while the blood wavered down my side and dripped to the front of my thigh. He looked pleased and dabbled it over my stomach with his finger tips.

In my despair I spoke. His face changed and he stood still, then controlled his voice with an effort, to say significantly, 'You must understand that I know: and it will be easier if you do as I wish.' I was dumbfounded, and we stared silently at one another, while the men who felt an inner meaning beyond their experience, shifted uncomfortably. But it was evidently a chance shot, by which he himself did not, or would not, mean what I feared. I could not again trust my twitching mouth, which faltered always in emergencies, so at last threw up my chin, which was the sign for 'No' in the East; then he sat down, and half-whispered to the corporal to take me out and teach me everything.

They kicked me to the head of the stairs, and stretched me over a guard-bench, pommelling me. Two knelt on my ankles, bearing down on the back of my knees, while two more twisted my wrists till they cracked, and then crushed them and my neck against the wood. The corporal had run downstairs; and now came back with a whip of the Circassian sort, a thong of supple black hide, rounded, and tapering from the thickness of a thumb at the grip (which was wrapped in silver) down to a hard point finer than a pencil.

He saw me shivering, partly I think, with cold, and made it whistle over my ear, taunting me that before his tenth cut I would howl for mercy, and at the twentieth beg for the caresses of the Bey; and then he began to lash me madly across and across with all his might, while I locked my teeth to endure this thing which lapped itself like flaming wire about my body.

To keep my mind in control I numbered the blows, but after twenty lost count, and could feel only the shapeless weight of pain, not tearing claws, for which I had prepared, but a gradual cracking apart of my whole being by some too-great force whose waves rolled up my spine till they were pent within my brain, to clash terribly together. Somewhere in the place a cheap clock ticked loudly, and it distressed me that their beating was not in its time. I writhed and twisted, but was held so tightly that my struggles were useless. After the corporal ceased, the men took up, very deliberately, giving me so many, and then an interval during which they would squabble for the next turn, ease themselves, and play unspeakably with me. This was repeated often, for what may have been no more than ten minutes. Always for the first of every new series, my head would be pulled round, to see how a hard white ridge, like a railway, darkening slowly into crimson, leaped over my skin at the instant of each stroke, with a bead of blood where two ridges crossed. As the punishment proceeded the whip fell more and more upon existing weals, biting blacker or more wet, till my flesh quivered with accumulated pain, and with terror of the next blow coming. They soon conquered my determination not to cry, but while my will ruled my lips I used only Arabic, and before the end a merciful sickness choked my utterance.

At last when I was completely broken they seemed satisfied. Somehow I found myself off the bench, lying on my back on the dirty floor, where I snuggled down, dazed, panting for breath, but vaguely comfortable. I had strung myself to learn all pain until I died, and no longer actor, but spectator, thought not to care how my body jerked and squealed. Yet I knew or imagined what passed about me.

I remembered the corporal kicking with his nailed boot to get me up; and this was true, for the next day my right side was dark and lacerated, and a damaged rib made each breath stab me sharply. I remembered smiling idly at him, for a delicious warmth, probably sexual, was swelling through me: and then that he flung up his arm and hacked with the full length of his whip into my groin. This doubled me half-over, screaming, or, rather, trying impotently to scream, only shuddering through my open mouth. One giggled with amusement. A voice cried, 'Shame, you've killed him.' Another slash followed. A roaring, and my eyes went black: while within me the core of life seemed to heave slowly up through the rending nerves, expelled from its body by this last indescribable pang.

By the bruises perhaps they beat me further: but I next knew that I was being dragged about by two men, each disputing over a leg as though to split me apart: while a third man rode me astride. It was momently better than more flogging. Then Nahi called. They splashed water in my face, wiped off some of the filth, and lifted me between them retching and sobbing for mercy, to where he lay: but he now rejected me in haste, as a thing too torn and bloody for his bed, blaming their excess of zeal which had spoilt me: whereas no doubt they had laid into me much as usual, and the fault rested mainly upon my indoor skin, which gave way more than an Arab's.

So the crestfallen corporal, as the youngest and best-looking of the guard, had to stay behind, while the others carried me down the narrow stair into the street. The coolness of the night on my burning flesh, and the unmoved shining of the stars after the horror of the past hour, made me cry again. The soldiers, now free to speak, warned me that men must suffer their officer's wishes or pay for it, as I had just done, with greater suffering.

They took me over an open space, deserted and dark, and behind the Government house to a lean-to wooden room, in which were many dusty quilts. An Armenian dresser appeared to wash and bandage me in sleepy haste. Then all went away, the last soldier delaying by my side a moment to whisper in his Druse accent that the door into the next room was not locked.

I lay there in a sick stupor, with my head aching very much, and growing slowly numb with cold, till the dawn light came shining through the cracks of the shed, and a locomotive whistled in the station. These and a draining thirst brought me to life, and I found I was in no pain. Pain of the slightest had been my obsession and secret terror, from a boy. Had I now been drugged with it, to bewilderment? Yet the first movement was anguish: in which I struggled nakedly to my feet, and rocked moaning in wonder that it was not a dream, and myself back five years ago, a timid recruit at Khalfati, where something, less staining, of the sort had happened.

The next room was a dispensary. On its door hung a suit of shoddy clothes. I put them on slowly and unhandily, because of my swollen wrists: and from the drugs chose corrosive sublimate, as safeguard against recapture. The window looked on a long blank wall. Stiffly I climbed out, and went shaking down the road towards the village, past the few people already astir. They took no notice; indeed there was nothing peculiar in my dark broadcloth, red fez and slippers: but it was only by the full urge of my tongue silently to myself that I refrained from being foolish out of sheer fright. Deraa felt inhuman with vice and cruelty, and it shocked me like cold water when a soldier laughed behind me in the street.

THE RUSSIAN REVOLUTION: TSAR NICHOLAS II AND THE RUSSIAN ROYAL FAMILY ARE SHOT AT EKATERINBURG, 16 July 1918

Pavel Medvedev

In the evening of 16 July, between seven and eight p.m., when the time for my duty had just begun, Commandant Yurovsky [the head of the guard] ordered me to take all the Nagan revolvers from the guards and to bring them to him. I took twelve revolvers from the sentries as well as from some other of the guards, and brought them to the commandant's office. Yurovsky said to me, 'We must shoot *them all* tonight, so notify the guards not to be alarmed if they hear shots.' I understood, therefore, that Yurovsky had it in his mind to shoot the whole of the Tsar's family, as well as the doctor and the servants who lived with them, but I did not ask him where or by whom the decision had been made. I must tell you that in accordance with Yurovsky's order the boy who assisted the cook was transferred in the morning to the guardroom (in the Popov house). The lower floor of Ipatiev's house was occupied by the Letts from the Letts Commune, who had taken up their quarters there after Yurovsky was made commandant. They were ten in number. At about ten o'clock in the evening, in accordance with

Yurovsky's order, I informed the guards not to be alarmed if they should hear firing. About midnight Yurovsky woke up the Tsar's family. I do not know if he told them the reason they had been awakened and where they were to be taken, but I positively affirm that it was Yurovsky who entered the rooms occupied by the Tsar's family. Yurovsky had not ordered me or Dobrynin to awaken the family. In about an hour the whole of the family, the doctor, the maid and the waiters got up, washed and dressed themselves. Just before Yurovsky went to awaken the family, two members of the Extraordinary Commission [of the Ekaterinburg Soviet] arrived at Ipatiev's house. Shortly after one o'clock a.m., the Tsar, the Tsaritsa, their four daughters, the maid, the doctor, the cook and the waiters left their rooms. The Tsar carried the heir in his arms. The Emperor and the heir were dressed in *gimnasterkas* [soldiers' shirts] and wore caps. The Empress and her daughters were dressed but their heads were uncovered. The Emperor, carrying the heir, preceded them. The Empress, her daughters and the others followed him. Yurovsky, his assistant and the two above-mentioned members of the Extraordinary Commission accompanied them. I was also present. During my presence none of the Tsar's family asked any questions. They did not weep or cry. Having descended the stairs to the first floor, we went out into the court, and from there by the second door (counting from the gate) we entered the ground floor of the house. When the room (which adjoins the store room with a sealed door) was reached, Yurovsky ordered chairs to be brought, and his assistant brought three chairs. One chair was given to the Emperor, one to the Empress, and the third to the heir. The Empress sat by the wall by the window, near the black pillar of the arch. Behind her stood three of her daughters (I knew their faces very well, because I had seen them every day when they walked in the garden, but I didn't know their names). The heir and the Emperor sat side by side almost in the middle of the room. Doctor Botkin stood behind the heir. The maid, a very tall woman, stood at the left of the door leading to the store room; by her side stood one of the Tsar's daughters (the fourth). Two servants stood against the wall on the left from the entrance of the room.

The maid carried a pillow. The Tsar's daughters also brought small pillows with them. One pillow was put on the Empress's chair; another on the heir's chair. It seemed as if all of them guessed their fate, but not one of them uttered a single sound. At this moment eleven men entered the room: Yurovsky, his assistant, two members of the Extraordinary Commission, and seven Letts. Yurovsky ordered me to leave, saying, 'Go on to the street, see if there is anybody there, and wait to see whether the shots have been heard.' I went out to the court, which was enclosed by a fence, but before I got to the street I heard the firing. I returned to the house immediately (only two or three minutes having elapsed) and upon entering the room where the execution had taken place, I saw that all the members of the Tsar's family were lying on the floor with many wounds in their bodies. The blood was running in streams. The doctor, the maid and two waiters had also been shot. When I entered the heir was still alive and moaned a little. Yurovsky went up and fired two or three more times at him. Then the heir was still.

A BLACK DAY FOR THE GERMAN ARMY, 8 August 1918

General Ludendorff

August 8th was the black day of the German Army in the history of this War. This was the worst experience that I had to go through, except for the events that, from September 15th onwards, took place on the Bulgarian Front and sealed the fate of the Quadruple Alliance.

Early on 8 August, in a dense fog, rendered still thicker by artificial means, the English, mainly with Australian and Canadian divisions, and the French attacked between Albert and Moreuil with strong squadrons of tanks, but otherwise in no great superiority. Between the Somme and the Luce they penetrated deep into our positions. The divisions in line at that point allowed themselves to be completely overwhelmed. Divisional staffs were surprised in their headquarters by enemy tanks. The breach very soon extended across the Luce stream; the troops that were still gallantly resisting at Moreuil were rolled up. To the northward the Somme imposed a halt. Our troops in action north of the river had successfully parried a similar assault. The exhausted divisions that had been relieved a few days earlier and were now resting in the region south-west of Peronne, were immediately warned and set in motion by the commander of the Second Army. At the same time he brought forward into the breach all other available troops. The Rupprecht Army Group dispatched reserves thither by train. The Eighteenth Army threw its own reserves directly into the battle from the south-east, and pushed other forces forward in the region north-west of Roye. On an order from me, the Ninth Army too, although itself in danger, had to contribute. Days, of course, elapsed before the troops from more distant areas could reach the spot. For their conveyance the most extensive use was made of motor lorries.

By the early hours of the forenoon of 8 August I had already gained a complete impression of the situation. It was a very gloomy one. I immediately dispatched a General Staff officer to the battlefield, in order to obtain an idea of the condition of the troops.

The losses of the Second Army had been very heavy. Heavy demands had also been made on its reserves to fill up the gaps. The infantry of some divisions had had to go into action straight off the lorries, whilst their artillery had been sent to some other part of the line. Units were badly mixed up. It could be foreseen that a number of additional divisions would become necessary in order to strengthen the Second Army, even if the enemy continued the offensive, and that was not certain. Besides, our losses in prisoners had been so heavy that GHQ was again faced with the necessity of breaking up more divisions to form reserves. Our reserves dwindled. The losses of the enemy, on the other hand, had been extraordinarily small. The balance of numbers had moved heavily against us; it was bound to become increasingly unfavourable as more American troops came in. There was no hope of materially improving our position by a counter-attack. Our only course, therefore, was to hold on.

We had to resign ourselves now to the prospect of a continuation of the enemy's offensive. Their success had been too easily gained. Their wireless was jubilant, and announced – and with truth – that the morale of the German Army was no longer what it had been. The enemy had also captured many documents of inestimable value to them. The Entente must have gained a clear idea of our difficulty in finding reserves, a further reason why they should pursue the offensive without respite.

The report of the Staff Officer I had sent to the battlefield as to the condition of those divisions which had met the first shock of the attack on the 8th, perturbed me deeply. I summoned divisional commanders and officers from the line to Avesnes to discuss events with them in detail. I was told of deeds of glorious valour, but also of behaviour which, I openly confess, I should not have thought possible in the German Army; whole bodies of our men had surrendered to single troopers, or isolated squadrons. Retiring troops, meeting a fresh division going bravely into action, had shouted out things like 'Blackleg,' and 'You're prolonging the War,' expressions that were to be heard again later. The officers in many places had lost their influence and allowed themselves to be swept along with the rest. At a meeting of Prince Max's War Cabinet in October, Secretary Scheidemann called my attention to a Divisional Report on the occurrences of August 8th, which contained similar unhappy stories. I was not acquainted with this report, but was able to verify it from my own knowledge. A battalion commander from the front, who came out with a draft from home shortly before August 8th, attributed this to the spirit of insubordination and the atmosphere which the men brought back with them from home. Everything I had feared, and of which I had so often given warning, had here, in one place, become a reality. Our war machine was no longer efficient. Our fighting power had suffered, even though the great majority of divisions still fought heroically.

The 8th of August put the decline of that fighting power beyond all doubt, and in such a situation as regards reserves, I had no hope of finding a strategic expedient whereby to turn the situation to our advantage. On the contrary, I became convinced that we were now without that safe foundation for the plans of GHQ, on which I had hitherto been able to build, at least so far as this is possible in war. Leadership now assumed, as I then stated, the character of an irresponsible game of chance, a thing I have always considered fatal. The fate of the German people was, for me, too high a stake.

THE SIGNING OF THE TREATY OF VERSAILLES, 28 June 1919

Harold Nicolson

After the capitulation of Germany on 11 November 1918 she was required by the victorious Allies to sign a punitive peace treaty. The signing took place in the Hall of Mirrors at Versailles Palace – the Hall which had witnessed the humiliation of France and the proclamation of the German Empire in 1871.

La journée de Versailles. Lunch early and leave the Majestic in a car with Headlam Morley. He is a historian, yet he dislikes historical occasions. Apart from that he is a sensitive person and does not rejoice in seeing great nations humbled. I, having none of such acquirements or decencies, am just excited.

There is no crowd at all until we reach Ville d'Avray. But there are poilus at every crossroad waving red flags and stopping all other traffic. When we reach Versailles the crowd thickens. The avenue up to the Château is lined with cavalry in steel-blue helmets. The pennants of their lances flutter red and white in the sun. In the Cour d'Honneur, from which the captured German cannon have tactfully been removed, are further troops. There are Generals, Pétain, Gouraud, Mangin. There are St Cyriens. Very military and orderly. Headlam Morley and I creep out of our car hurriedly. Feeling civilian and grubby. And wholly unimportant. We hurry through the door.

Magnificent upon the staircase stand the Gardes Républicains – two caryatides on every step – their sabres at the salute. This is a great ordeal, but there are other people climbing the stairs with us. Headlam and I have an eye-meet. His thin cigaretted fingers make a gesture of dismissal. He is not a militarist.

We enter the two anterooms, our feet softening on to the thickest of savonnerie carpets. They have ransacked the Garde Meubles for their finest pieces. Never, since the Grand Siècle, has Versailles been more ostentatious or more embossed . . .

We enter the Galerie des Glaces. It is divided into three sections. At the far end are the Press already thickly installed. In the middle there is a horseshoe table for the plenipotentiaries. In front of that, like a guillotine, is the table for the signatures. It is supposed to be raised on a dais but, if so, the dais can be but a few inches high. In the nearer distance are rows and rows of tabourets for the distinguished guests, the deputies, the senators and the members of the delegations. There must be seats for over 1,000 persons. This robs the ceremony of all privilege and therefore of all dignity. It is like the Aeolian Hall.

Clemenceau is already seated under the heavy ceiling as we arrive. 'Le roi', runs the scroll above him, 'gouverne par lui-même.' He looks small and yellow. A crunched homunculus.

Conversation clatters out among the mixed groups around us. it is, as always on such occasions, like water running into a tin bath. I have never been able to get other people to recognize that similarity. There was a tin bath in my house at Wellington: one turned it on when one had finished and ran upstairs shouting

'Baath ready' to one's successor: 'Right ho!' he would answer: and then would come the sound of water pouring into the tin bath below, while he hurried into his dressing-gown. It is exactly the sound of people talking in undertones in a closed room. But it is not an analogy which I can get others to accept.

People step over the Aubusson benches and escabeaux to talk to friends. Meanwhile the delegates arrive in little bunches and push up the central aisle slowly. [Woodrow] Wilson and Lloyd George are among the last. They take their seats at the central table. The table is at last full. Clemenceau glances to right and left. People sit down upon their escabeaux but continue chattering. Clemenceau makes a sign to the ushers. They say 'Ssh! Ssh! Ssh!' People cease chattering and there is only the sound of occasional coughing and the dry rustle of programmes. The officials of the Protocol of the Foreign Office move up the aisle and say, 'Ssh! Ssh!' again. There is then an absolute hush, followed by a sharp military order. The Gardes Républicains at the doorway flash their swords into their scabbards with a loud click. 'Faîtes entrer les Allemands,' says Clemenceau in the ensuing silence. His voice is distant but harshly penetrating. A hush follows.

Through the door at the end appear two huissiers with silver chains. They march in single file. After them come four officers of France, Great Britain, America and Italy. And then, isolated and pitiable, come the two German delegates Dr Müller, Dr Bell. The silence is terrifying. Their feet upon a strip of parquet between the savonnerie carpets echo hollow and duplicate. They keep their eyes fixed away from those 2,000 staring eyes, fixed upon the ceiling. They are deathly pale. They do not appear as representatives of a brutal militarism. The one is thin and pink-eyelidded: the second fiddle in a Brunswick orchestra. The other is moon-faced and suffering: a privat-dozent. It is all most painful.

They are conducted to their chairs. Clemenceau at once breaks the silence. 'Messieurs,' he rasps, 'la sèance est ouverte.' He adds a few ill-chosen words. 'We are here to sign a Treaty of Peace.' The Germans leap up anxiously when he has finished, since they know that they are the first to sign. William Martin, as if a theatre manager, motions them petulantly to sit down again. Mantoux translates Clemenceau's words into English. Then St Quentin advances towards the Germans and with the utmost dignity leads them to the little table on which the Treaty is expanded. There is general tension. They sign. There is a general relaxation. Conversation hums again in an undertone. The delegates stand up one by one and pass onwards to the queue which waits by the signature table. Meanwhile people buzz round the main table getting autographs. The single file of plenipotentiaries waiting to approach the table gets thicker. It goes quickly. The officials of the Quai d'Orsay stand round, indicating places to sign, indicating procedure, blotting with neat little pads.

Suddenly from outside comes the crash of guns thundering a salute. It announces to Paris that the second Treaty of Versailles has been signed by Dr Müller and Dr Bell. Through the few open windows comes the sound of distant crowds cheering hoarsely. And still the signature goes on.

We had been warned it might last three hours. Yet almost at once it seemed that the queue was getting thin. Only three, then two, and then one delegate remained to sign. His name had hardly been blotted before the huissiers began again their 'Ssh! Ssh!' cutting suddenly short the wide murmur which had again begun. There was a final hush. 'La séance est levée,' rasped Clemenceau. Not a word more or less.

We kept our seats while the Germans were conducted like prisoners from the dock, their eyes still fixed upon some distant point of the horizon.

THE PUBLICATION OF *ULYSSES*, February 1922

James Joyce

James Joyce conceived the idea for his novel – now regarded by many as the greatest of the century – in 1906, but it was not until 1921 that he wrote the final word, battling desperately against poverty and failing eyesight. But this was not the end of the struggle. Episodes from *Ulysses* published in the United States had been confiscated on grounds of obscenity, and publication both there and in Britain was out of the question. Eventually, Sylvia Beach, who owned a bookshop in Paris, published a limited edition on 2 February 1922 (Joyce's fortieth birthday) – after the book had been reset six times, Joyce having almost entirely rewritten it in proof. It was not published in Britain until 1936.

Rue de l'Université 9, Paris VII

Dear Miss Weaver: Many thanks for your kind telegram. Two copies of *Ulysses* (nos. 901 and 902) reached Paris on 2 February and two further copies (nos. 251 and 252) on 5 February. One copy is on show, the other three were taken by subscribers who were leaving for different parts of the world. Since the announcement that the book was out the shop has been in a state of siege – buyers driving up two or three times a day and no copies to give them. After a great deal of telegraphing and telephoning it seems that 7 copies will come today and 30 tomorrow. A more nerveracking conclusion to the history of the book could scarcely have been imagined! The first 10 copies of the *edition de luxe* will not be ready before Saturday so that you will not receive your copy (no. 1) before Tuesday of next week at the earliest. I am glad for my own sake (though hardly for yours) that you are advertising an English edition. I hope it will be possible in that event to correct the numerous misprints. [Ezra] Pound says it is . . .

Thanks also for the prompt return of the *Penelope* episode (the name of which by another strange coincidence is your own). It did not arrive too late. Your description of it also coincides with my intention – if the epithet 'posthuman' were added. I have rejected the usual interpretation of her as a human apparition – that aspect being better represented by Calypso, Nausikaa and Circe, to say nothing of the pseudo Homeric figures. In conception and technique I tried to depict the earth which is prehuman and presumably posthuman.

With kindest regards

yours very sincerely and to the end importunately.

GERMAN INFLATION, September 1922

Ernest Hemingway

Once across the muddy Rhine you are in Germany, and the German end of the bridge is guarded by a couple of the meekest and most discouraged looking German soldiers you have ever seen. Two French soldiers with fixed bayonets walk up and down and the two German soldiers, unarmed, lean against a wall and look on. The French soldiers are in full equipment and steel helmets, but the Germans wear the old loose tunics and high peaked, peace-time caps.

I asked a Frenchman the functions and duties of the German guard.

'They stand there,' he answered.

There were no marks to be had in Strasbourg, the mounting exchange had cleaned the bankers out days ago, so we changed some French money in the railway station at Kehl. For ten francs I received 670 marks. Ten francs amounted to about ninety cents in Canadian money. That ninety cents lasted Mrs Hemingway and me for a day of heavy spending and at the end of the day we had one hundred and twenty marks left!

Our first purchase was from a fruit stand beside the main street of Kehl where an old woman was selling apples, peaches and plums. We picked out five very good looking apples and gave the old woman a fifty-mark note. She gave us back thirty-eight marks in change. A very nice looking, white bearded old gentleman saw us buy the apples and raised his hat.

'Pardon me, sir,' he said, rather timidly, in German, 'how much were the apples?'

I counted the change and told him twelve marks.

He smiled and shook his head. 'I can't pay it. It is too much.'

He went up the street walking very much as white bearded old gentlemen of the old regime walk in all countries, but he had looked very longingly at the apples. I wish I had offered him some. Twelve marks, on that day, amounted to a little under two cents. The old man, whose life's savings were probably, as most of the non-profiteer classes are, invested in German pre-war and war bonds, could not afford a twelve-mark expenditure. He is a type of the people whose incomes do not increase with the falling purchasing value of the mark and the krone.

With marks at 800 to the dollar, or eight to a cent, we priced articles in the windows of the different Kehl shops. Peas were 18 marks a pound, beans 16 marks; a pound of Kaiser coffee, there are still many 'Kaiser' brands in the German republic, could be had for 34 marks. Gersten coffee, which is not coffee at all but roasted grain, sold for 14 marks a pound. Flypaper was 150 marks a package. A scythe blade cost 150 marks, too, or eighteen and three-quarters cents! Beer was ten marks a stein or one cent and a quarter.

Kehl's best hotel, which is a very well turned out place, served a five-course table d'hôte meal for 120 marks, which amounts to fifteen cents in our money. The same meal could not be duplicated in Strasbourg, three miles away, for a dollar.

Because of the customs regulations, which are very strict on persons returning from Germany, the French cannot come over to Kehl and buy up all the cheap goods they would like to. But they can come over and eat. It is a sight every afternoon to see the mob that storms the German pastry shops and tea places. The Germans make very good pastries, wonderful pastries, in fact, that, at the present tumbling mark rate, the French of Strasbourg can buy for a less amount apiece than the smallest French coin, the one sou piece. This miracle of exchange makes a swinish spectacle where the youth of the town of Strasbourg crowd into the German pastry shop to eat themselves sick and gorge on fluffy, cream-filled slices of German cake at five marks the slice. The contents of a pastry shop are swept clear in half an hour.

In a pastry shop we visited, a man in an apron, wearing blue glasses, appeared to be the proprietor. He was assisted by a typical 'boche' looking German with close cropped head. The place was jammed with French people of all ages and descriptions, all gorging cakes, while a young girl in a pink dress, silk stockings, with a pretty, weak face and pearl earrings in her ears took as many of their orders for fruit and vanilla ices as she could fill.

She didn't seem to care very much whether she filled the orders or not. There were soldiers in town and she kept going over to look out of the window.

The proprietor and his helper were surly and didn't seem particularly happy when all the cakes were sold. The mark was falling faster than they could bake.

Meanwhile out in the street a funny little train jolted by, carrying the workmen with their dinner-pails home to the outskirts of the town, profiteers' motor cars tore by raising a cloud of dust that settled over the trees and the fronts of all the buildings, and inside the pastry shop young French hoodlums swallowed their last cakes and French mothers wiped the sticky mouths of their children. It gave you a new aspect on exchange.

As the last of the afternoon tea-ers and pastry eaters went Strasbourg-wards across the bridge the first of the exchange pirates coming over to raid Kehl for cheap dinners began to arrive. The two streams passed each other on the bridge and the two disconsolate looking German soldiers looked on. As the boy in the motor agency said, 'It's the way to make money.'

THE FASCISTS TAKE POWER, ITALY, October 1922

Benito Mussolini

The extreme right-wing Fascist party of Italy was formed by Benito Mussolini in 1919, taking a black shirt as its uniform and the slogan 'no discussion, only obedience' as its philosophy. The party thrived on the unrest and disillusion which swept Italy in the post-war period. In October Mussolini ordered his followers to march on Rome; the King gave-way before this show of force, and called on Mussolini to form a government.

I was in a terrible state of nervous tension. Night after night I had been kept awake, giving orders, following the compact columns of the Fascisti, restraining the battle to the knightly practices of Fascism.

A period of greater responsibilities was going to begin for me. I must not fail in my duty or in my aims. I gathered all my strength to my aid, I invoked the memory of the dead, I asked the assistance of God, I called upon the living faithful to assist me in the great task that confronted me.

That night of 31 October 1922, I left the direction of the *Popolo d' Italia*, and turned my fighting journal over to my brother Arnaldo. In the 1 November number I published the following declaration:

'From now on, the direction of the *Popolo d' Italia* is entrusted to Arnaldo Mussolini.

'I thank and salute with brotherly love all the editors, collaborators, correspondents, employees, workers, all those who have assiduously and faithfully laboured with me for the life of this paper and for love of our Country.

MUSSOLINI.

ROME 30 October 1922.'

I parted with regret from the paper that had been the most constant and potent element of our Victory. I must add that my brother Arnaldo has been able to maintain the editorship in a capable, dignified way.

When I had entrusted the paper to my brother, I was off for Rome. To the zealous people who wanted to get me a special train to go to Rome to speak with the King, I said that for me a compartment in the usual train was quite enough. Engines and coal should not be wasted. Economize! That is the first and acid test of a true man of Government. And after all, I could only enter Rome at the head of my Black Shirts now camping at Santa Marinella in the atmosphere and the shining rays of the Capital.

The news of my departure sped all over Italy. In every station where the train stopped there had gathered the Fascisti and the masses who wanted to bring me, even through the pouring rain, their cheers and their goodwill.

Going from Milan was painful. That city had given me a home for ten years; to me it has been prodigal in its satisfactions; it had followed me in every stress; it had baptized the most wonderful squads of action of Fascism; it had been the scene of historical political struggles. Now I was leaving it, called by destiny and by a greater task. All Milan knew of my going, and I felt that even in the feeling of joy for a going that was a symbol of victory, there was also a shade of sadness.

But this was not the hour for sentimentality. It was the time for quick, sure decisions. After the kisses and farewells of my family, I said good-bye to many prominent Milanese; and then I went away, running into the night, to take counsel with myself, to refresh my soul, to listen to the echoes of voices of friends and to envisage the wide horizons of tomorrow's possibilities.

The minor episodes of that trip and of those days are not important. The train brought me into the midst of the Fascisti, I was in view of Rome at Santa Marinella. I reviewed the columns. I established the formalities for the entrance into Rome. I established connections between the Quadriumvirate and the authorities.

My presence redoubled the great enthusiasm. I read in the eyes of those young men the divine smile of triumph of an ideal. With such elements I would have been inspired to challenge, if need be, not only the base Italian ruling class, but enemies of any sort and race.

In Rome there was waiting for me an indescribable welcome. I did not want any delay. Even before making contacts with my political friends I motored to the Quirinal. I wore a black shirt. I was introduced without formalities to the presence of His Majesty the King. The Stefani agency and the great newspapers of the world gave stilted or speculative details about this interview. I will limit myself, for obvious reasons of reserve, to declare that the conference was characterized by great cordiality. I concealed no plans, nor did I fail to make plain my ideas of how to rule Italy. I obtained the Sovereign's approbation. I took up lodgings at the Savoy Hotel and began to work. First I made agreements with the general command of the army to bring a militia into Rome and file them off in proper formation in a review by the King. I gave detailed and precise orders. One hundred thousand Black Shirts paraded in perfect order before the Sovereign. They brought to him the homage of Fascist Italy!

TUTANKHAMEN'S TOMB IS OPENED, LUXOR, EGYPT, 16 February 1923

The Times

Tutankhamen was born in about 1360 BC and succeeded to the Egyptian throne at the age of twelve. He died six years later.

This has been perhaps the most extraordinary day in the whole history of Egyptian excavation. Whatever anyone may have guessed or imagined of the secret of Tutankhamen's tomb, they surely cannot have dreamed the truth as now revealed. Entrance to-day was made into the sealed chamber, and yet another door opened beyond that. No eyes have yet seen the King, but to a practical certainty we now know that he lies there, close at hand, in all his original state, undisturbed.

Moreover, in addition to the great store of treasures which the tomb has already yielded, to-day has brought to light a new wealth of objects of artistic, historical, and even intrinsic value, which is bewildering. It is such a hoard as the most sanguine excavator can hardly have pictured even in visions in his sleep, and puts Lord Carnarvon's and Mr Carter's discovery in a class by itself above all previous finds.

Though the official opening of the sealed chamber had been fixed for Sunday it was obviously impossible to postpone until then the actual work of breaking in the entrance. This was a job involving some hours of work, because it had to be done with the greatest care, so as to keep intact as many of the seals as possible, and also to avoid injury to any of the objects on the other side which might be caused by the falling of the material dislodged. All this could not be done on Sunday while the official guests were kept waiting in the singularly unpleasant atmosphere of the tomb.

So an agreement was made with the Egyptian Government authorities by which the actual breaking through of the wall should be done in their presence to-day. Consequently, Mr Carter was very busy inside the tomb all the morning with Professor Breasted and Dr Alan Gardiner, whose assistance has been invaluable from the beginning in the work of examining the seals and deciphering and copying inscriptions of all kinds. They had finished by noon, and the tomb was closed till after lunch, at which Lord Carnarvon, Mr Carter and Lady Evelyn Herbert entertained all those invited to be present to-day.

It was after one o'clock when the official party entered the tomb and the operation was begun which was to result in such astounding discoveries. Of what followed I am able to give the following authoritative description.

To-day, between the hours of one and three in the afternoon, the culminating moment in the discovery of Tutankhamen's tomb took place, when Lord Carnarvon and Mr Howard Carter opened the inner sealed doorway in the presence of Lady Evelyn Herbert, Abdel Hamid Suliman Pasha, Under-Secretary of Public Works, M. Pierre Lacau, Director-General of thc Antiquities Department, Sir William Garstin, Sir Charles Cust, Mr Lythgoe, Curator of the Metropolitan Museum of Art, New York, Mr Winlock, Director of the Egyptian Expedition of the Metropolitan Museum, Professor Breasted, Dr Alan Gardiner, Messrs Alfred Lucas, Arthur C. Mace, Harry Burton, and R. Callander, the Hon. R. Bethell, and the inspectors of the Museum Department, together with other representative of the Government.

The process of opening this doorway bearing the royal insignia and guarded by protective statues of the King had taken several hours of careful manipulation under intense heat. It finally ended in a wonderful revelation, for before the spectators was the resplendent mausoleum of the King, a spacious, beautiful, decorated chamber, completely occupied by an immense shrine covered with gold inlaid with brilliant blue faïence.

This beautiful wooden construction towers nearly to the ceiling and fills the great sepulchral hall within a short span of its four walls. Its sides are adorned with magnificent religious texts and fearful symbols of the dead, and it is capped with a superb cornice and torus moulding like the propylaea of a temple; in fact, indeed a sacred monument. On the eastern end of this shrine are two immense folding doors closed and bolted.

Within it is yet another shrine, closed and sealed, and bearing the cipher of the royal necropolis. On this inner shrine hangs a funerary pall studded with gold, and by the evidence of the papyrus of Rameses IV there must be a series of these shrines within, covering the remains of the King lying in the sarcophagus. Around the outer canopy on the shrine stand great protective emblems of mystic type, finely carved and gilt, and upon the floor lie the seven oars for the King's use in the waters of the Elysian Fields.

In the farther end of the eastern wall of this sepulchral hall is yet another doorway, open and never closed. It leads to another chamber – the store chamber of the sepulchre. There at the end stands an elaborate and magnificently carved and gilded shrine of indescribable beauty. It is surmounted by tiers of 'uraei' (Royal serpents), and its sides are protected by open-armed goddesses of finest workmanship, their pitiful faces turned over their shoulders towards the invader. This is no less than the receptacle for the four canopic jars which should contain the viscera of the King.

Immediately at the entrance to this chamber stands the jackal Anubis, black and gold upon his shrine, which again rests upon a portable sled – strange and resplendent. Behind this, again, is the head of a bull, an emblem of the underworld. Stacked on the south side of the chamber in great numbers are black boxes and shrines of all shapes, all closed and sealed, save one with open doors, in which golden effigies of the King stand upon black leopards.

Similarly at the end of the chamber are more of these cases, including miniature coffins, sealed, but no doubt containing funerary statuettes of the monarch – the servants for the dead in the coming world. On the south side of the deity Anubis is a tier of wonderful ivory and wooden boxes, of every shape and design, studded with gold and inlaid with faïence, and beside them yet another chariot. This sight is stupendous, and its magnificence indescribable.

And as the time was fast creeping on and dusk falling in, the tomb was closed for further action and contemplation.

I WATCH TELEVISION, LONDON, 1 August 1928

Sydney Moseley

Diary

. . . I met a pale young man named Bartlett who is Secretary to the new Baird Television Company. *Television!* Anxious to see what it is all about . . . He invited me to go along to Long Acre where the new invention is installed. Now *that's* something! Television!

Met John Logie Baird; a charming man – a shy, quietly spoken Scot. He could serve as a model for the schoolboy's picture of a shock-haired, modest, dreamy, absent-minded inventor. Nevertheless shrewd. We sat and chatted. He told me he is having a bad time with the scoffers and sceptics – including the BBC and part of the technical press – who are trying to ridicule and kill his invention of television at its inception. I told him that if he would let me see what he has actually achieved – well, he would have to risk my damning it – or praising it! If I *were* convinced – I would battle for him. We got on well together and I have arranged to test his remarkable claim.

(Later) Saw television! Baird's partner, a tall, good-looking but highly temperamental Irishman, Captain Oliver George Hutchinson, was nice but very nervous of chancing it with me. He was terribly anxious that I should be impressed. Liked the pair of them, especially Baird, and decided to give my support . . . I think we really have what is called television. And so, once more into the fray!

THE WALL STREET CRASH, NEW YORK, 24 October 1929

Elliott V. Bell

Throughout the 1920s the USA had enjoyed a period of unparalleled prosperity; with the great stock-market crash of October 1929 the bubble burst, and the Great Depression was formally ushered in. The collapse of America's economy was soon followed by that of Europe's.

The day was overcast and cool. A light north-west wind blew down the canyons of Wall Street, and the temperature, in the low fifties, made bankers and brokers on their way to work button their topcoats around them. The crowds of market traders in the brokers' board rooms were nervous but hopeful as the ten o'clock hour for the start of trading approached. The general feeling was that the worst was over and a good many speculators who had prudently sold out earlier in the decline were congratulating themselves at having bought back their stocks a good deal cheaper. Seldom had the small trader had better or more uniform advice to go by.

The market opened steady with prices little changed from the previous day, though some rather large blocks, of 20,000 to 25,000 shares, came out at the start. It sagged easily for the first half-hour, and then around eleven o'clock the deluge broke.

It came with a speed and ferocity that left men dazed. The bottom simply fell out of the market. From all over the country a torrent of selling orders poured onto the floor of the Stock Exchange and there were no buying orders to meet it. Quotations of representative active issues, like Steel, Telephone, and Anaconda, began to fall two, three, five, and even ten points between sales. Less active stocks became unmarketable. Within a few moments the ticker service was hopelessly swamped and from then on no one knew what was really happening. By one-thirty the ticker tape was nearly two hours late; by two-thirty it was 147 minutes late. The last quotation was not printed on the tape until 7.08½ p.m., four hours, eight and one-half minutes after the close. In the meantime, Wall Street had lived through an incredible nightmare.

In the strange way that news of a disaster spreads, the word of the market collapse flashed through the city. By noon great crowds had gathered at the corner of Broad and Wall Streets where the Stock Exchange on one corner faces Morgan's across the way. On the steps of the Sub-Treasury Building, opposite Morgan's, a crowd of press photographers and newsreel men took up their stand. Traffic was pushed from the streets of the financial district by the crush.

It was in this wild setting that the leading bankers scurried into conference at Morgan's in a belated effort to save the day. Shortly after noon Mr Mitchell left the National City Bank and pushed his way west on Wall Street to Morgan's. No sooner had he entered than Albert H. Wiggin was seen to hurry down from the Chase National Bank, one block north. Hard on his heels came William C. Potter, head of the Guaranty Trust, followed by Seward Prosser of the Bankers Trust. Later George F. Baker, Jr, of the First National, joined the group.

The news of the bankers' meeting flashed through the streets and over the news tickers – stocks began to rally – but for many it was already too late. Thousands of traders, little and big, had gone 'overboard' in that incredible hour between eleven and twelve. Confidence in the financial and political leaders of the country, faith in the 'soundness' of economic conditions had received a shattering blow. The panic was on.

At Morgan's the heads of six banks formed a consortium – since known as the bankers' pool of October, 1929 – pledging a total of $240,000,000, or $40,000,000 each, to provide a 'cushion' of buying power beneath the falling market. In addition, other financial institutions, including James Speyer and Company and Guggenheim Brothers, sent over to Morgan's unsolicited offers of funds aggregating $100,000,000. It was not only the first authenticated instance of a bankers' pool in stocks but by far the largest concentration of pool buying power ever brought to bear on the stock market – but in the face of the panic it was pitifully inadequate.

After the bankers had met, Thomas W. Lamont, Morgan partner, came out to the crowd of newspaper reporters who had gathered in the lobby of his bank. In an understatement that has since become a Wall Street classic, he remarked:

'It seems there has been some disturbed selling in the market.'

It was at the same meeting that 'T.W.' gave to the financial community a new phrase – 'air pockets' – to describe the condition in stocks for which there were no bids, but only frantic offers. (Mr Lamont said he had it from his partner, George Whitney, and the latter said he had it from some broker.)

After the meeting, Mr Lamont walked across Broad Street to the Stock Exchange to meet with the governors of the Exchange. They had been called together quietly during trading hours and they held their meeting in the rooms of the Stock Clearing Corporation so as to avoid attracting attention. Mr Lamont sat on the corner of a desk and told them about the pool. Then he said:

'Gentlemen, there is no man nor group of men who can buy all the stocks that the American public can sell.'

It seems a pretty obvious statement now, but it had a horrid sound to the assembled governors of the Exchange. It meant that the shrewdest member of the most powerful banking house in the country was telling them plainly that the assembled resources of Wall Street, mobilized on a scale never before attempted, could not stop this panic.

The bankers' pool, in fact, turned out a sorry fiasco. Without it, no doubt, the Exchange would have been forced to close, for it did supply bids at some price for the so-called pivotal stocks when, because of the panic and confusion in the market, there were no other bids available. It made a small profit, but it did not have a ghost of a chance of stemming the avalanche of selling that poured in from all over the country. The stock market had become too big. The days that followed are blurred in retrospect. Wall Street became a nightmarish spectacle.

The animal roar that rises from the floor of the Stock Exchange and which on active days is plainly audible in the Street outside, became louder, anguished, terrifying. The streets were crammed with a mixed crowd – agonized little speculators, walking aimlessly outdoors because they feared to face the ticker and the margin clerk; sold out traders, morbidly impelled to visit the scene of their ruin; inquisitive individuals and tourists, seeking by gazing at the exteriors of the Exchange and the big banks to get a closer view of the national catastrophe; runners, frantically pushing their way through the throng of idle and curious in their effort to make deliveries of the unprecedented volume of securities which was being traded on the floor of the Exchange.

The ticker, hopelessly swamped, fell hours behind the actual trading and became completely meaningless. Far into the night, and often all night long, the lights blazed in the windows of the tall office buildings where margin clerks and bookkeepers struggled with the desperate task of trying to clear one day's business before the next began. They fainted at their desks; the weary runners fell exhausted on the marble floors of banks and slept. But within a few months they were to have ample time to rest up. By then thousands of them had been fired.

Agonizing scenes were enacted in the customers' rooms of the various brokers. There traders who a few short days before had luxuriated in delusions of wealth saw all their hopes smashed in a collapse so devastating, so far beyond their wildest fears, as to seem unreal. Seeking to save a little from the wreckage, they would order their stocks sold 'at the market', in many cases to discover that they had not merely lost everything but were, in addition, in debt to the broker. And then, ironic twist, as like as not the next few hours' wild churning of the market would lift prices to levels where they might have sold out and had a substantial cash balance left over. Every move was wrong, in those days. The market seemed like an insensate thing that was wreaking a wild and pitiless revenge upon those who had thought to master it.

The excitement and sense of danger which imbued Wall Street was like that which grips men on a sinking ship. A camaraderie, a kind of gaiety of despair, sprang up. The Wall Street reporter found all doors open and everyone snatched at him for the latest news, for shreds of rumour. Who was in trouble? Who had gone under last? Where was it going to end?

I remember dropping in to see a vice-president of one of the larger banks. He was walking back and forth in his office.

'Well, Elliott,' he said, 'I thought I was a millionaire a few days ago. Now I find I'm looking through the wrong end of the telescope.'

He laughed. Then he said: 'We'll get those bastards that did this yet.'

I never did find out whom he meant, but I learned later that he was not merely 'busted' but hopelessly in debt.

AN INTERVIEW WITH AL CAPONE, CHICAGO, 1930

Claud Cockburn

The Prohibition-era gangster Alphonse Capone was born in Brooklyn, but achieved his notoriety as a Mafia boss in Chicago.

The Lexington Hotel had once, I think, been a rather grand family hotel, but now its large and gloomy lobby was deserted except for a couple of bulging Sicilians and a reception clerk who looked at one across the counter with the expression of a speakeasy proprietor looking through the grille at a potential detective. He checked on my appointment with some superior upstairs, and as I stepped into the elevator I felt my hips and sides being gently frisked by the tapping hands of one of the lounging Sicilians. There were a couple of ante-rooms to be passed before you got to Capone's office and in the first of them I had to wait for a quarter of an hour or so, drinking whisky poured by a man who used his left hand for the bottle and kept the other in his pocket.

Except that there was a sub-machine-gun, operated by a man called MacGurn – whom I later got to know and somewhat esteem – poking through the transom of a door behind the big desk, Capone's own room was nearly indistinguishable from that of, say, a 'newly arrived' Texan oil millionaire. Apart from the jowly young murderer on the far side of the desk, what took the eye were a number of large, flattish, solid silver bowls upon the desk, each filled with roses. They were nice to look at, and they had another purpose too, for Capone when agitated stood up and dipped the tips of his fingers in the waters in which floated the roses.

I had been a little embarrassed as to how the interview was to be launched. Naturally the nub of all such interviews is somehow to get around to the question 'What makes you tick?' but in the case of this millionaire killer the approach to this central question seemed mined with dangerous impediments. However, on the way down to the Lexington Hotel I had had the good fortune to see, in I think the *Chicago Daily News*, some statistics offered by an insurance company which dealt with the average expectation of life of gangsters in Chicago. I forget exactly what the average expectation was, and also what the exact age of Capone at that time was – I think he was in his early thirties. The point was, however, that in any case he was four years older than the upper limit considered by the insurance company to be the proper average expectation of life for a Chicago gangster. This seemed to a offer a more or less neutral and academic line of approach, and after the ordinary greetings I asked Capone whether he had read this piece of statistics in the paper. He said that he had. I asked him whether he considered the estimate reasonably accurate. He said that he thought that the insurance companies and the newspaper boys probably knew their stuff. 'In that case,' I asked him, 'how does it feel to be, say, four years over the age?'

He took the question quite seriously and spoke of the matter with neither more nor less excitement or agitation than a man would who, let us say, had been asked whether he, as the rear machine-gunner of a bomber, was aware of the average incidence of casualties in that occupation. He apparently assumed that sooner or later he would be shot despite the elaborate precautions which he regularly took. The idea that – as afterwards turned out to be the case – he would be arrested by the Federal authorities for income-tax evasion had not, I think, at that time so much as crossed his mind. And, after all, he said with a little bit of corn-and-ham somewhere at the back of his throat, supposing he had not gone into this racket? What would he have been doing? He would, he said, 'have been selling newspapers barefoot on the street in Brooklyn'.

He stood up as he spoke, cooling his finger-tips in the rose bowl in front of him. He sat down again, brooding and sighing. Despite the ham-and-corn, what he said was quite probably true and I said so, sympathetically. A little bit too sympathetically, as immediately emerged, for as I spoke I saw him looking at me suspiciously, not to say censoriously. My remarks about the harsh way the world treats barefoot boys in Brooklyn were interrupted by an urgent angry waggle of his podgy hand.

'Listen,' he said, 'don't get the idea I'm one of these goddam radicals. Don't get the idea I'm knocking the American system. The American system . . .' As though an invisible chairman had called upon him for a few words, he broke into an oration upon the theme. He praised freedom, enterprise and the pioneers. He spoke of 'our heritage'. He referred with contemptuous disgust to Socialism and Anarchism. 'My rackets,' he repeated several times, 'are run on strictly American lines and they're going to stay that way.' This turned out to be a reference to the fact that he had recently been elected the President of the Unione Siciliano, a slightly mysterious, partially criminal society which certainly had its roots in the Mafia. Its power and importance varied sharply from year to year. Sometimes there did seem to be evidence that it was a secret society of real power, and at other times it seemed more in the nature of a mutual benefit association not essentially much more menacing than, say, the Elks. Capone's complaint just now was that the Unione was what he called 'lousy with blackhand stuff'. 'Can you imagine,' he said, 'people going in for what they call these blood feuds – some guy's grandfather was killed by some other guy's grandfather, and this guy thinks that's good enough reason to kill the other.' It was, he said, entirely unbusinesslike. His vision of the American system began to excite him profoundly and now he was on his feet again, leaning across the desk like the chairman of a board meeting, his fingers plunged in the rose bowls.

'This American system of ours,' he shouted, 'call it Americanism, call it Capitalism, call it what you like, gives to each and every one of us a great opportunity if we only seize it with both hands and make the most of it.' He held out his hand towards me, the fingers dripping a little, and stared at me sternly for a few seconds before reseating himself.

CIVIL DISOBEDIENCE, INDIA, 21 May 1930

Webb Miller

As part of their Civil Disobedience campaign to remove the British from India, the followers of Gandhi organized a protest against the Salt Tax in 1930.

After plodding about six miles across country lugging a pack of sandwiches and two quart bottles of water under a sun which was already blazing hot, inquiring from every native I met, I reached the assembling place of the Gandhi followers. Several long, open, thatched sheds were surrounded by high cactus thickets. The sheds were literally swarming and buzzed like a beehive with some 2,500 Congress or Gandhi men dressed in the regulation uniform of rough homespun cotton *dhotis* and triangular Gandhi caps, somewhat like American overseas soldiers' hats. They chattered excitedly and when I arrived hundreds surrounded me, with evidences of hostility at first. After they learned my identity, I was warmly welcomed by young college-educated, English-speaking men and escorted to Mme Naidu. The famous Indian poetess, stocky, swarthy, strong-featured, bare-legged, dressed in rough, dark homespun robe and sandals, welcomed me. She explained that she was busy martialling her forces for the demonstration against the salt pans and would talk with me more at length later. She was educated in England and spoke English fluently.

Mme Naidu called for prayer before the march started and the entire assemblage knelt. She exhorted them, 'Gandhi's body is in gaol but his soul is with you. India's prestige is in your hands. You must not use any violence under any circumstances. You will be beaten but you must not resist; you must not even raise a hand to ward off blows.' Wild, shrill cheers terminated her speech.

Slowly and in silence the throng commenced the half-mile march to the salt deposits. A few carried ropes for lassoing the barbed-wire stockade around the salt pans. About a score who were assigned to act as stretcher-bearers wore crude, hand-painted red crosses pinned to their breasts; their stretchers consisted of blankets. Manilal Gandhi, second son of Gandhi, walked among the foremost of the marchers. As the throng drew near the salt pans they commenced chanting the revolutionary slogan, *Inquilab zindabad*, intoning the two words over and over.

The salt deposits were surrounded by ditches filled with water and guarded by 400 native Surat police in khaki shorts and brown turbans. Half-a-dozen British officials commanded them. The police carried *lathis* – five-foot clubs tipped with steel. Inside the stockade twenty-five native riflemen were drawn up.

In complete silence the Gandhi men drew up and halted 100 yards from the stockade. A picked column advanced from the crowd, waded the ditches, and approached the barbed-wire stockade, which the Surat police surrounded, holding their clubs at the ready. Police officials ordered the marchers to disperse under a recently imposed regulation which prohibited gatherings of more than five persons in any one place. The column silently ignored the warning and slowly walked forward. I stayed with the main body about 100 yards from the stockade.

Suddenly, at a word of command, scores of native police rushed upon the advancing marchers and rained blows on their heads with their steel-shod *lathis*. Not one of the marchers even raised an arm to fend off the blows. They went down like ten-pins. From where I stood I heard the sickening whacks of the clubs on unprotected skulls. The waiting crowd of watchers groaned and sucked in their breaths in sympathetic pain at every blow.

Those struck down fell sprawling, unconscious or writhing in pain with fractured skulls or broken shoulders. In two or three minutes the ground was quilted with bodies. Great patches of blood widened on their white clothes. The survivors without breaking ranks silently and doggedly marched on until struck down. When every one of the first column had been knocked down stretcher-bearers rushed up unmolested by the police and carried off the injured to a thatched hut which had been arranged as a temporary hospital.

Then another column formed while the leaders pleaded with them to retain their self-control. They marched slowly toward the police. Although every one knew that within a few minutes he would be beaten down, perhaps killed, I could detect no signs of wavering or fear. They marched steadily with heads up, without the encouragement of music or cheering or any possibility that they might escape serious injury or death. The police rushed out and methodically and mechanically beat down the second column. There was no fight, no struggle; the marchers simply walked forward until struck down. There were no outcries, only groans after they fell. There were not enough stretcher-bearers to carry off the wounded; I saw eighteen injured being carried off simultaneously, while forty-two still lay bleeding on the ground awaiting stretcher-bearers. The blankets used as stretchers were sodden with blood . . .

In the middle of the morning V.J. Patel arrived. He had been leading the Swaraj movement since Gandhi's arrest, and had just resigned as President of the Indian Legislative Assembly in protest against the British. Scores surrounded him, knelt, and kissed his feet. He was a venerable gentleman of about sixty with white flowing beard and moustache, dressed in the usual undyed, coarse homespun smock. Sitting on the ground under a mango tree, Patel said, 'All hope of reconciling India with the British Empire is lost for ever. I can understand any government's taking people into custody and punishing them for breaches of the law, but I cannot understand how any government that calls itself civilized could deal as savagely and brutally with non-violent, unresisting men as the British have this morning.'

By eleven the heat reached 116 degrees in the shade and the activities of the Gandhi volunteers subsided. I went back to the temporary hospital to examine the wounded. They lay in rows on the bare ground in the shade of an open, palm-thatched shed. I counted 320 injured, many still insensible with fractured skulls, others writhing in agony from kicks in the testicles and stomach. The Gandhi men had been able to gather only a few native doctors, who were doing the best they could with the inadequate facilities. Scores of the injured had received no treatment for hours and two had died. The demonstration was finished for the day on account of the heat.

I was the only foreign correspondent who had witnessed the amazing scene – a classic example of *satyagraha* or non-violent civil disobedience.

HUNGER MARCHERS, WASHINGTON, December 1931

John Dos Passos

The Great Depression, which had begun with the Wall Street Crash in 1929, was the worst this century. By the early 1930s over twelve million people were unemployed in the United States – more than a quarter of the workforce.

Washington has a drowsy look in the early December sunlight. The Greco-Roman porticoes loom among the bare trees, as vaguely portentous as phrases about democracy in the mouth of a Southern Senator. The Monument, a finger of light cut against a lavender sky, punctuates the antiquated rhetoric of the Treasury and the White House. On the hill, above its tall foundation banked with magnolia trees, the dome of the Capitol bulges smugly. At nine o'clock groups of sleepy-looking cops in well-brushed uniforms and shiny-visored caps are straggling up the hill. At the corner of Pennsylvania Avenue and John Marshall Place a few hunger marchers stand around the trucks they came in. They looked tired and frowzy from the long ride. Some of them are strolling up and down the avenue. That end of the avenue, with its gimcrack stores, boarded-up burlesque shows, Chinese restaurants and flophouses, still has a little of the jerkwater, out-in-the-sticks look it must have had when Lincoln drove up it in a barouche through the deep mud or Jefferson rode to his inauguration on his own quiet nag.

Two elderly labouring men are looking out of a cigar-store door at a bunch of Reds, young Jewish boys from New York or Chicago, with the white armbands of the hunger marchers. 'Won't get nutten that a-way,' one of them says. 'Whose payin' for it anyway, hirin' them trucks and gasoline . . . Somebody's payin' for it,' barks the clerk indignantly from behind the cash register. 'Better'd spent it on grub or to buy 'emselves overcoats,' says the older man. The man who first spoke shakes his head sadly. 'Never won't get nutten that a-way.' Out along the avenue a few Washingtonians look at the trucks and old moving vans with *Daily Worker* cartoons pasted on their sides. They stand a good way off, as if they were afraid the trucks would explode; they are obviously swallowing their unfavourable comments for fear some of the marchers might hear them. Tough eggs, these Reds.

At ten o'clock the leaders start calling to their men to fall in. Some tall cops appear and bawl out drivers of cars that get into the streets reserved for the marchers to form up in. The marchers form in a column off ours. They don't look as if they'd had much of a night's rest. They look quiet and serious and anxious to do the right thing. Leaders, mostly bareheaded youngsters, run up and down, hoarse and nervous, keeping everybody in line. Most of them look like city dwellers, men and women from the needle trades, restaurant workers, bakery or laundry employees. There's a good sprinkling of Negroes among them. Here and there the thick shoulders and light hair of a truck driver or farm hand stand out. Motorcycle cops begin to cluster around the edges. The marchers are receiving as much attention as distinguished foreign officials.

Up on the hill, cordons of cops are everywhere, making a fine showing in the late-fall sunshine. There's a considerable crowd standing around; it's years since Washington has been interested in the opening of Congress. They are roping off the route for the hunger marchers. They stop a taxicab that is discovered to contain a small white-haired Senator. He curses the cops out roundly and is hurriedly escorted under the portals.

Inside the Capitol things are very different. The light is amber and greenish, as in an aquarium. Elderly clerks white as termites move sluggishly along the corridors, as if beginning to stir after a long hibernation. The elevator boy is very pale. 'Here comes the army of the unfed,' he says, pointing spitefully out of the window. 'And they're carrying banners, though Charlie Curtis said they couldn't.' A sound of music comes faintly in. Led by a band with silvery instruments like Christmas-tree ornaments that look cheerful in the bright sunlight, the hunger marchers have started up Capitol Hill. Just time to peep down into the Senate Chamber where elderly parties and pasty-faced pages are beginning to gather. Ever seen a section of a termite nest under glass?

There's a big crowd in the square between the Capitol and the Congressional Library. On the huge ramps of the steps that lead to the central portico the metropolitan police have placed some additional statuary; tastefully arranged groups of cops with rifles, riot guns and brand-new tear-gas pistols that look as if they'd just come from Sears, Roebuck. People whisper 'machine-gun nests', but nobody seems to know where they are. There's a crowd on the roof around the base of the dome, faces are packed in all the windows. Everybody looks cheerful, as if a circus had come to town, anxious to be shown. The marchers fill the broad semicircle in front of the Capitol, each group taking up its position in perfect order, as if the show had been rehearsed. The band, playing 'Solidarity Forever' (which a newspaper woman beside me recognizes as 'Onward Christian Soldiers'), steps out in front. It's a curious little band, made up of martini-horns, drums, cymbals and a lyre that goes tinkle, tinkle. It plays cheerfully and well, led by a drum major with a red tasselled banner on the end of his staff, and repeats again and again 'The Red Flag', 'Solidarity', and other tunes variously identified by people in the crowd. Above the heads of the marchers are banners with slogans printed out: IN THE LAST WAR WE FOUGHT FOR THE BOSSES: IN THE NEXT WAR WE'LL FIGHT FOR THE WORKERS . . . $150 CASH . . . FULL PAY FOR UNEMPLOYMENT RELIEF. The squad commanders stand out in front like cheerleaders at a football game and direct the chanting: 'We Demand – Unemployed Insurance, We Demand – Unemployed Insurance, WE DEMAND – UNEMPLOYED INSURANCE.'

A deep-throated echo comes back from the Capitol façade a few beats later than each shout. It's as if the statues and the classical-revival republican ornaments in the pediment were shouting too.

A small group leaves the ranks and advances across the open space towards the Senate side. All the tall cops drawn up in such fine order opposite the hunger marchers stick out their chests. Now it's coming. A tremor goes over the groups of statuary so tastefully arranged on the steps. The tear-gas pistols glint in the sun. The marchers stand in absolute silence.

Under the portal at the Senate entrance the swinging doors are protected by two solid walls of blue serge. Cameramen and reporters converge with a run. Three men are advancing with the demands of the hunger marchers written out. They are the centre of a big group of inspectors, sergeants, gold and silver braid of the Capitol and metropolitan police. A young fellow with a camera is hanging from the wall by the door. 'Move the officer out of the way,' he yells. 'Thank you . . . A little back, please lady, I can't see his face . . . Now hand him the petition.'

'We're not handing petitions, we're making demands,' says the leader of the hunger marchers. Considerable waiting around. The Sergeant at Arms sends word they can't be let in. Somebody starts to jostle, the cops get tough, cop voices snarl. The committee goes back to report while the band plays the 'Internationale' on marini-horns and lyre . . .

THE REICHSTAG FIRE, BERLIN, 23 February 1933

D. Sefton Delmer

The arson of the German parliament building was allegedly the work of a Communist-sympathizing Dutchman, van der Lubbe. More probably, the fire was started by the Nazis, who used the incident as a pretext to outlaw political opposition and impose dictatorship.

'This is a God-given signal! If this fire, as I believe, turns out to be the handiwork of Communists, then there is nothing that shall stop us now crushing out this murder pest with an iron fist.'

Adolf Hitler, Fascist Chancellor of Germany, made this dramatic declaration in my presence tonight in the hall of the burning Reichstag building.

The fire broke out at 9.45 tonight in the Assembly Hall of the Reichstag.

It had been laid in five different corners and there is no doubt whatever that it was the handiwork of incendiaries.

One of the incendiaries, a man aged thirty, was arrested by the police as he came rushing out of the building, clad only in shoes and trousers, without shirt or coat, despite the icy cold in Berlin tonight.

Five minutes after the fire had broken out I was outside the Reichstag watching the flames licking their way up the great dome into the tower.

A cordon had been flung round the building and no one was allowed to pass it.

After about twenty minutes of fascinated watching I suddenly saw the famous black motor car of Adolf Hitler slide past, followed by another car containing his personal bodyguard.

I rushed after them and was just in time to attach myself to the fringe of Hitler's party as they entered the Reichstag.

Never have I seen Hitler with such a grim and determined expression. His eyes, always a little protuberant, were almost bulging out of his head.

Captain Göring, his right-hand man, who is the Prussian Minister of the Interior, and responsible for all police affairs, joined us in the lobby. He had a very flushed and excited face.

'This is undoubtedly the work of Communists, Herr Chancellor,' he said.

'A number of Communist deputies were present here in the Reichstag twenty minutes before the fire broke out. We have succeeded in arresting one of the incendiaries.'

'Who is he?' Dr Goebbels, the propaganda chief of the Nazi Party, threw in.

'We do not know yet,' Captain Göring answered, with an ominously determined look around his thin, sensitive mouth. 'But we shall squeeze it out of him, have no doubt, doctor.'

We went into a room. 'Here you can see for yourself, Herr Chancellor, the way they started the fire,' said Captain Göring, pointing out the charred remains of some beautiful oak panelling.

'They hung cloths soaked in petrol over the furniture here and set it alight.'

We strode across another lobby filled with smoke. The police barred the way. 'The candelabra may crash any moment, Herr Chancellor,' said a captain of the police, with his arms outstretched.

By a detour we next reached a part of the building which was actually in flames. Firemen were pouring water into the red mass.

Hitler watched them for a few moments, a savage fury blazing from his pale blue eyes.

Then we came upon Herr von Papen, urbane and debonair as ever.

Hitler stretched out his hand and uttered the threat against the Communists which I have already quoted. He then turned to Captain Göring. 'Are all the other public buildings safe?' he questioned.

'I have taken every precaution,' answered Captain Göring. 'The police are in the highest state of alarm, and every public building has been specially garrisoned. We are waiting for anything.'

It was then that Hitler turned to me. 'God grant', he said, 'that this is the work of the Communists. You are witnessing the beginning of a great new epoch in German history. This fire is the beginning.'

And then something touched the rhetorical spring in his brain.

'You see this flaming building,' he said, sweeping his hand dramatically around him. 'If this Communist spirit got hold of Europe for but two months it would be all aflame like this building.'

By 12.30 the fire had been got under control. Two Press rooms were still alight, but there was no danger of the fire spreading.

Although the glass of the dome has burst and crashed to the ground the dome still stands.

So far it has not been possible to disentangle the charred debris and see whether the bodies of any incendiaries, who may have been trapped in the building, are among it.

At the Prussian Ministry of the Interior a special meeting was called late tonight by Captain Göring to discuss measures to be taken as a consequence of the fire.

The entire district from the Brandenburg Gate, on the west, to the River Spree, on the east, is isolated tonight by numerous cordons of police.

STALIN RIDES THE MOSCOW METRO, 23 April 1935

'Our Own Correspondent', London Daily Telegraph

M. Joseph Stalin, Dictator of Soviet Russia, has just taken his first journey by 'tube'.

Leaving the Kremlin after nightfall yesterday [23 April] he drove with his three principal lieutenants, M. Molotoff, M.

Orgonokidze and M. Kaganovich to the Crimea Square terminal station, and from there travelled over the full eight miles of Moscow's new underground.

Properly to appreciate the wide interest this has caused here one must go back to the opening of the first steam railways in England.

Stalin, we are officially informed, was 'wildly cheered' when he inspected the grandiose multi-coloured marbles which, in Moscow, replace London's plain but practical Underground stations.

This new Tube, although virtually ready these last three months, has not yet begun selling tickets or conveying ordinary passengers to and from their work. It is hoped, however, to begin a regular service on Thursday.

Stalin closely inspected the new escalators. These moving stairs are the chief source of astonishment to Moscow residents. Today a number of women and children who had been granted special 'joy-riding tickets' could only be persuaded to scale the escalator when a policeman undertook to accompany them.

Yesterday and today queues of these privileged ticket-holders waited hours for their turn to have a free ride with more eagerness than any crowds ever waited for rides on a scenic railway at Wembley. Again, disconsolate youngsters loitered in a vain hope of begging or stealing a pass.

As expected, the gorgeous marble pillars, and the floodlit tiling in the stations, which would be worthy of a setting for a grand opera, made a special appeal. As one of Moscow's oldest foreign inhabitants said to me, 'This Metro is ultra-modern in technique, but its gorgeous stations are the most characteristically Russian thing done here since the Revolution'.

JOE LOUIS FIGHTS MAX BAER, NEW YORK, October 1935

Jonathan Mitchell

These people are here, 95,000 of them, because they have money. Down there on the field, men have paid $150 and more for a pair of tickets. Twenty thousand seats were stamped 'ringside', and the customers out beyond third base were bilked. They should have known that Mike Jacobs, who is running this fight, is a smart man. No one can do anything to him, because he has the support of Hearst.

It feels good to have money again. Everyone in this crowd has money. The people who were swindled by Jacobs can afford it.

Happy days are here again. Of course, things aren't so good, with twenty million on relief. A man can be fired, and next morning there are ten men in line waiting for his job. But the unemployed have been around for a long time. No one can expect us to sit home and be sympathetic indefinitely.

It is a cold, clear night. The Stadium rises steeply around one half of the field. The floodlights on its upper edge are directed on the field and the bleachers, and the Stadium itself is black except for a steady row of red exit signs. Almost the whole of the immense field is covered with chairs. Jacobs has pushed the customers so closely together that all that can be seen of them, under the floodlights, is their microscopic, bright faces. They form neat rows, divided into plots by the aisles, like commercial Dutch tulip beds. There are acres of them, shining pinkly. Men in white, with high cardboard signs in their caps, move gravely about selling pop, like gardeners. The ring is at second base, and the movie operators' metal cage, high on a pole, that you used to see at fights is missing. The only movement comes from white tobacco smoke, rising in heavy waves. Through it you can see the American flags along the top of the Stadium, after the fashion of the opening verse of 'The Star-Spangled Banner'.

Near at hand the crowd is a respectable, bridge-playing one. About a fifth are Negroes, more carefully dressed and more mannerly than the whites. The little drunk with the long woollen muffler is certainly a Bronx dentist. He thinks correctly that the preliminary match now going on is poor, and keeps screaming, 'Lousy'. He brandishes a handful of crumpled bills and will give odds to anyone. There seems to be something painful in his past that he would like to explain, but the woollen muffler keeps blowing in his face, and communication between him and us is eternally frustrated.

There is a stirring in the aisles near the ring. The people who amount to something, and who are bowed through the police lines outside the Stadium, are entering. There are five state governors, the Republican National Committee, important business figures, and a large number of people whose press agents made them come so that their names would be in tomorrow's papers. Max Baer and his attendants are now at home plate. A dozen little pushing figures open up the crowd for him, and another dozen follow behind. Baer wears a white bathrobe, and has his hands on the shoulders of the state trooper in front of him. He nods to his many friends. Joe Louis, with another state trooper and other attendants, pushes in from third base. We learn afterwards that his bride, Marva Trotter, is in the first row in a bright-green dress and orchids. Louis seems to see no one.

The floodlights are extinguished. Nothing exists except the brightly glowing ring. That is old Joe Humphries being lifted through the ropes, the man who announced fights before the depression. Since then he has been sick, and had a bad time. We have all been having a bad time, for that matter. Jack Dempsey squats in Baer's corner, but no one notices him. Humphries's assistant is bawling into the microphones: 'Although Joe Louis is coloured, he is a great fighter, in the class of Jack Johnson and the giants of the past.' His voice fades away, and returns. 'American sportsmanship, without regard to race, creed or colour, is the talk of the world. Behave like gentlemen, whoever wins.' Nearly 2,000 police at the entrances of the Stadium are there to break up a possible race riot.

Baer has stripped. He has made a lot of money, Baer has. From all reports, he has spent a lot. He has played Broadway, Miami, and the other hot spots. Why shouldn't he have done so? Joe Louis takes off his flashing silk bathrobe, blue with a vermilion lining. It is the only extravagant gesture he makes. For all his youth, he is thick under the jaws, thick around the waist. His face is earnest, thoughtful, unsmiling.

Max Baer hasn't been, I suppose, what you would call a good boy. Joe Louis has, though. This is his greatest advantage. He once was taken to a night club, and it is reported that within ten minutes he wanted to go home. He said he was sleepy. He is supposed to have saved his money. Louis's father died when he was only two years old, down in Alabama. Until she married again, his mother had a hard struggle to support the children, and they were very dear to her. Louis is fond of his mother. She is a Lily of the Valley at her church in Detroit, where the family now lives. The Lilies are having a supper, or some such event, in a few days. She wants him there, and he is going with his new wife.

We are too far away to hear the gong. They are out in the middle of the ring, with a stubby little man in a white sweater moving softly around them. Baer holds both hands, open, clumsily in front of him. Look at Joe Louis. He is leading with a straight left arm, his right hand before his face ready to block, and his right elbow tucked in to his ribs. That is scientific. That is what they teach in correspondence courses, or the night gymnasium classes of the YMCA. In the first thirty seconds, you can tell that he reeks of study, practice, study. Any romantic white person who believes that the Negro possesses a distinctive quality ought to see Louis. He suggests a gorilla or a jungle lion about as much as would an assistant professor at the Massachusetts Institute of Technology.

Baer stands flat-footed, with his great death-dealing right fist doubled by his side. He swings, and you can almost count three while the fist sails through the air. Louis moves sidewise and back, because he has been taught that if you move with a blow it can never hurt you. Baer's glove slides up the side of Louis's head harmlessly. He swings again and again, and, carefully and unhurriedly, Louis slips away. Look! Louis at last is going in. A left, a right and another left in close. Louis has pulled in his head, and with both arms up before him, he looks like a brown crayfish. All you can see is the twitching of his shoulders. So incredibly fast he is that the blows themselves are almost invisible. His hands cannot possibly move more than a few inches. Look! Baer is backing into a neutral corner. Louis is raining down blows. Baer's nose spurts blood, his lower lip bleeds, his face is red pulp.

Baer must have meant something to many people. He made wisecracks and went to parties and was a harbinger of the return of the old days. He was Broadway, he was California and Florida, he represented the possession of money once more and spending it. This saddle-coloured, dour-faced, tongue-tied, studious youth, who is punishing Baer, punishing him more cruelly than human flesh and bones can endure, what does he represent? Baer stands with his hands hanging at his sides. He is helpless. He cannot hit the dissolving form before him, and he has never learned to protect himself. He holds his fine head, with its sweep of tightly curled hair and its great, brooding nose, high above his torturer. Pride alone keeps his head up, pride that has no tangible justification whatever. It was the same pride that kept Colonel Baratieri at Adowa, twenty years before Joe Louis was born.

It is the first round, and the fight is as good as over. Maybe it was foolish to spend money going to a fight. There must be many people, even down there in the ringside seats, who couldn't afford to spend what they did on tickets. No one can be sure of his job with twenty million on relief. This is a crazy country, with people handing out a million dollars to

Mike Jacobs and Hearst, while families right here in New York City are without enough to eat.

Round one is ended. Jack Dempsey vaults into the ring in a single, startling leap. Perhaps it is a trick. He must have vaulted from the ground to the edge of the ring platform, and from there into the ring itself. But from a distance, it seems one motion, and it is beautiful. Beside the man that Dempsey was, Baer and Louis and Schmeling are phonics. Nowadays everything, including men, is somehow different.

The next three rounds are slaughter. In the second, Baer makes a wild, swinging, purposeless attack. For probably fifteen seconds, he appears formidable, but his attack has no substance inside it. With the third round, he is beaten, but Louis does not rush in, as Dempsey would have, to kill. Deliberately he circles Baer, with his earnest, thoughtful face, seeking an opening through which to strike without possible risk of injury. He takes no chance of a last, desperate fling of Baer's prodigious right hand. He is a planner. He is a person who studies the basic aspects of a problem and formulates a programme. Apparently his studies are satisfactory, for he carefully steps up and knocks Baer down twice. Baer is on the canvas when time is called. Dempsey slides across the ring, picks Baer up like a mother, fusses over him until the fourth, and final, round. Baer once more is down. When the stubby referee, swinging his arm, reaches seven he tries to rouse himself. This turns out later to have been a fortunate gesture. The customers who suspected the honesty of the fight, and were unconvinced that a man could be half killed by fifty blows full on the jaw, were reassured as they watched Baer struggling to his feet. Had he been trying to throw the fight, they reasoned, he would have lain still. At the count of ten, Baer is on one knee his swollen face wearing a comical expression of surprise.

The floodlights return us to time and space. Near at hand, there is remarkably little cheering, even from Negroes. They act as if, despite the police, they think it more prudent to restrain their feelings. There in the ring, placing his hand on Baer's shoulder in a stiff gesture, is the best fighter living, and the first Negro whose backers and trainer are men of his race. No white man shares in Louis's winnings. If the whites of the Boxing Commission will permit the match, he will be champion of the world.

All across the Stadium, the neat tulip beds are being broken up as tiny figures push into the aisles and towards the exits. A man with a small blond moustache is sobbing: 'Maxie, why didn't you hit him?' Downtown in the Forties and Fifties, redecorated speakeasies will quickly be crammed to the doors and customers turned away. In Lenox Avenue in Harlem, Negroes will be tap-dancing from kerb to kerb, and singing: 'The Baer goes over the mountain', and 'Who won the fight?' Tomorrow the financial sections of the newspapers will report that business leaders regard the fight as final proof that the country's economic worries are past and a comfortable and prosperous future is assured.

JESSE OWENS TAKES GOLD IN THE 100-METRE DASH, BERLIN, 4 August 1936

New York Times *reporter*

The 1936 Berlin Olympics were intended by the Nazi regime to be a demonstration of the physical superiority of the Teuton. To Hitler's ill-concealed disgust, however, the games were dominated by black American athlete Jesse James Cleveland Owens, who won four track and field gold medals, including the gold for the garland event, the men's 100-metre dash.

Owens won today because he is the world's fastest human. No one ever ran a more perfect race. His start was perfect, his in-between running perfect and his finish perfect.

The Buckeye Bullet ripped out of his starting holes as though slung by a giant catapult. He was ahead in his first stride and let Osendarp and Wykoff battle behind him for what was left of the race.

Metcalfe, hardly the best starter in the world, was off in atrocious fashion. He was sixth in the six-man field at the getaway, but once in his stride he certainly moved. By sixty metres he had drawn even with the Hollander and begun to cut down the two-yard advantage Owens had on him.

It was then a speed duel between a streamlined express and an old-fashioned steam engine that exuded sheer, rugged power. Metcalfe cut those two yards to one at the wire, but it was as close as he could get.

Owens's time was a new world record of 10.3 seconds. Ralph Metcalfe was also a black American. Hitler left the stadium rather than have to congratulate Owens on his victory.

THE BATTLE OF CABLE STREET, LONDON, 7 October 1936

Phil Piratin

Following Mussolini's lead, Sir Oswald Mosley had founded the British Union of Fascists which advocated the abolition of free speech, greater interest in the Commonwealth, and anti-Semitism.

It was obvious that the Fascists and the police would now turn their attention to Cable Street. We were ready. The moment this became apparent the signal was given to put up the barricades. We had prepared three spots. The first was near a yard where there was all kinds of timber and other oddments, and also an old lorry. An arrangement had been made with the owner that this old lorry could be used as a barricade. Instructions had been given about this, but when someone shouted 'Get the lorry!' evidently not explaining that it was in the nearby yard, some of the lads, looking up the street, saw a stationary lorry about 200 yards away. They went along, brought it back, and pushed it over on its side before anyone even discovered that it was not the lorry meant to be used. Still it was a lorry, and supplemented by bits of old furniture, mattresses, and every kind of thing you expect to find in box-rooms, it was a barricade which the police did not find it easy to penetrate. As they charged they were met with milk bottles, stones, and marbles. Some of the housewives began to drop milk bottles from the roof tops. A number of police surrendered. This had never happened before, so the lads didn't know what to do, but they took away their batons, and one took a helmet for his son as a souvenir.

Cable Street was a great scene. I have referred to 'the lads'. Never was there such unity of all sections of the working class as was seen on the barricades at Cable Street. People whose lives were poles apart, though living within a few hundred yards of each other; bearded Orthodox Jews and rough-and-ready Irish Catholic dockers – these were the workers that the Fascists were trying to stir up against each other. The struggle, led by the Communist Party, against the Fascists had brought them together against their common enemies, and their lackeys.

Meanwhile, charges and counter-charges were taking place along 'the front' from Tower Hill to Gardner's Corner. Many arrests were made, many were injured. It was the police, however, who were carrying on the battle, while the Fascists lurked in the background, protected by a 'fence' of police. Mosley was late. As soon as he arrived, in a motor-car, a brick went clean through the window.

It was later rumoured that Sir Philip Game had been on the telephone to the Home Secretary, and had pleaded with Sir John Simon to forbid the march. Sir John was adamant. Sir Philip Game, however, made up his own mind. He forbade the march and told Mosley to argue it out with Sir John Simon. The Fascists lined up, saluted their leader, and marched through the deserted City to the Embankment, where they dispersed. The working class had won the day.

THE SPANISH CIVIL WAR: THE BOMBING OF GUERNICA, SPAIN, 26 April 1937

Noel Monks

The Civil War between Franco's Nationalists and Spain's elected Leftist government lasted from July 1936 to April 1939, and ended in Nationalist victory.

I passed through Guernica at about 3.30 p.m. The time is approximate, based on the fact that I left Bilbao at 2.30. Guernica was busy. It was market day. We passed through the town and took a road that Anton said would take us close to Marquina, where, as far as I knew, the front was. The front was there, all right, but Marquina was not. It had been smashed flat by bombers.

We were about eighteen miles east of Guernica when Anton pulled to the side of the road, jammed on the brakes and started shouting. He pointed wildly ahead, and my heart shot into my mouth when I looked. Over the tops of some hills appeared a flock of planes. A dozen or so bombers were flying high. But down much lower, seeming just to skim the treetops were six Heinkel 52 fighters. The bombers flew on towards Guernica, but the Heinkels, out for random plunder, spotted our car, and, wheeling like a flock of homing pigeons, they lined up the road – and our car.

Anton and I flung ourselves into a bomb hole, twenty yards to the side of the road. It was half filled with water, and we sprawled in mud. We half knelt, half stood, with our heads buried in the muddy side of the crater.

After one good look at the Heinkels, I didn't look up again until they had gone. That seemed hours later, but it was probably less than twenty minutes. The planes made several runs along the road. Machine-gun bullets plopped into the mud ahead, behind, all around us. I began to shiver from sheer fright. Only the day before Steer, an old hand now, had 'briefed' me about being strafed. 'Lie still and as flat as you can. But don't get up and start running, or you'll be bowled over for certain.'

When the Heinkels departed, out of ammunition I presumed, Anton and I ran back to our car. Nearby a military car was burning fiercely. All we could do was drag two riddled bodies to the side of the road. I was trembling all over now, in the grip of the first real fear I'd ever experienced. On occasions I'd been scared before – as when I'd crashed into the sea in the *Cutty Sark* – but here on the road to Guernica I was in a bad state of jitters indeed. Then suddenly the quaking passed and I felt exhilarated. These were the days in foreign reporting when personal experiences were copy, for there hadn't been a war for eighteen years, long enough for those who went through the last one to forget, and for a generation and a half who knew nothing of war to be interested. We used to call them 'I' stories, and when the Spanish war ended in 1939 we were as heartily sick of writing them as the public must have been of reading them.

At the foot of the hills leading to Guernica we turned off the main road and took another back to Bilbao. Over to our left, in the direction of Guernica, we could hear the crump of bombs. I thought the Germans had located reinforcements moving up from Santander to stem the retreat. We drove on to Bilbao.

At the Presidencia, Steer and Holme were writing dispatches. They asked me to join them at dinner at Steer's hotel. They said they, too, had seen flights of bombers, but didn't know where the bombs had dropped. The Torrontegui Hotel where I started to dine with Steer, Holme, Captain Roberts of the *Seven Seas Spray* and his game little daughter Fifi, that night was peopled mostly by Franco sympathizers. President Aguirre and his Government knew they were there, but they remained unmolested.

We'd eaten our first course of beans and were waiting for our bully beef when a Government official, tears streaming down his face, burst into the dismal dining-room crying: 'Guernica is destroyed. The Germans bombed and bombed and bombed.'

The time was about 9.30 p.m. Captain Roberts banged a huge fist on the table and said: 'Bloody swine.' Five minutes later I was in one of Mendiguren's limousines speeding towards Guernica. We were still a good ten miles away when I saw the reflection of Guernica's flames in the sky. As we drew nearer, on both sides of the road, men, women and children were sitting, dazed. I saw a priest in one group. I stopped the car and went up to him. 'What happened, Father?' I asked. His face was blackened, his clothes in tatters. He couldn't talk. He just pointed to the flames, still about four miles away, then whispered: 'Aviones . . . bombas . . . mucho, mucho.'

In the good 'I' tradition of the day, I was the first correspondent to reach Guernica, and was immediately pressed into service by some Basque soldiers collecting charred bodies that the flames had passed over. Some of the soldiers were sobbing like children. There were flames and smoke and grit, and the smell of burning human flesh was nauseating. Houses were collapsing into the inferno.

In the Plaza, surrounded almost by a wall of fire, were about a hundred refugees. They were wailing and weeping and rocking to and fro. One middle-aged man spoke English.

He told me: 'At four, before the market closed, many aeroplanes came. They dropped bombs. Some came low and shot bullets into the streets. Father Aronategui was wonderful. He prayed with the people in the Plaza while the bombs fell.' The man had no idea who I was, as far as I know. He was telling me what had happened to Guernica.

Most of Guernica's streets began or ended at the Plaza. It was impossible to go down many of them, because they were walls of flame. Debris was piled high. I could see shadowy forms, some large, some just ashes. I moved round to the back of the Plaza among survivors. They had the same story to tell, aeroplanes, bullets, bombs, fire.

Within twenty-four hours, when the grim story was told to the world, Franco was going to brand these shocked, homeless people as liars. So-called British experts were going to come to Guernica, weeks afterwards, when the smell of burnt human flesh had been replaced by petrol dumped here and there among the ruins by Mola's men, and deliver pompous judgements: 'Guernica was set on fire wilfully by the Reds.'

No Government official had accompanied me to Guernica. I wandered round the place at will. I drove back to Bilbao and had to waken the cable operator – it was nearly two in the morning – to send my message. Censorship had been lifted completely. The man who sent my dispatch couldn't read English. If the 'Reds' had destroyed Guernica and hundreds of their fellow Basques, I could have blown the whole story for all they knew – as I certainly would have done. I told the facts about the bombing of Guernica in my message and described the terrible scenes I'd witnessed.

The only things left standing were a church, a sacred Tree, symbol of the Basque people, and, just outside the town, a small munitions factory. There hadn't been a single anti-aircraft gun in the town. It had been mainly a fire raid. Steer and Holme picked up some dud incendiary bombs. They were branded with the German eagle. Some were handed to British agents and positively identified.

A sight that haunted me for weeks was the charred bodies of several women and children huddled together in what had been the cellar of a house. It had been a refugio. Franco's British apologists were going to proclaim that these people had been locked in the cellar by their own men while the house was dynamited and set alight.

Later that day I was to get a bomb addressed to me, personally. So was Steer. So was Holme. It was in the form of a cable from my office: 'Berlin denies Guernica bombing. Franco says he had no planes up yesterday owing fog. Quiepo de Llano [Franco's foul-mouthed broadcasting general in Seville] says Reds dynamited Guernica during retreat. Please check up soonest.'

Please check up!

Back we went to Guernica, all three of us. We compared notes. We checked each other's experiences the day before. Refugees from Guernica were pouring into Bilbao now. With an interpreter I took one family for a car ride to calm them down, soothe their shattered nerves. Then gently, quietly, I got from them their story. It was the same as the others. We asked Mendiguren to collect the weather reports for us from all fronts. No one had seen fog for a week on our front.

A MEETING WITH SIGMUND FREUD, VIENNA, AUSTRIA, 1938

Max Eastman

Berggasse 19 was a big roomy house full of books and pictures, the whole mezzanine floor padded with those thick rich rugs in which your feet sank like a camel's in the sand. I was not surprised to see hanging beside Rembrandt's *Anatomy Class*, without which no doctor's office would be recognizable, a picture of *The Nightmare* – a horrid monster with a semi-evil laugh or leer, squatting upon a sleeping maiden's naked breast. Freud's early specialty had been anatomy, and he had in him the hard scientific curiosity suggested by Rembrandt's picture. But he had too, in my belief, a streak of something closely akin to medieval superstition. He liked to talk about '*The* Unconscious', personifying the mere absence of a quality – and that the quality of awareness – and making it into a scheming demon for which anatomy certainly finds no place. Freud's discovery that impulses suppressed out of our thoughts can continue to control those thoughts, both waking and sleeping, and also our actions and bodily conditions, was certainly a major event in the history of science. But what a lot of purely literary mythology he built around it! Mental healing always did and always will run off into magic.

With such thoughts I sat there whetting my curiosity until the door opened and he came in.

Well – he was smaller than I thought, and slender-limbed, and more feminine. I have been surprised at the feminineness of all the great men I have met, including the Commander of the Red Army. Genius is a nervous phenomenon and, except for the steam-roller variety that struts the boards just now, it involves delicacy. Freud's nose was flatter than I expected, too, and more one-sided. It looked as if somebody with brass knuckles had given him a poke in the snout. It made him, when he threw his head clear back and laughed softly, as he frequently did, seem quaint and gnomelike. His voice was gentle too, gentle and a little thin, as though he were purposely holding back half his breath in order to be mischievous.

'What did you want?' he said in perfect English as we shook hands.

'Not a thing,' I said. 'I just wanted to look you over.'

THE PRIVATE LIFE OF ADOLF HITLER, BERCHTESGADEN, GERMANY, 1938

Anon.

The author of this account of the German dictator at home was one of the maids at his mountain retreat.

I had read in the German newspapers that Hitler lived a simple, unostentatious life. In a few minutes I realized how the trusting German people were being misled.

Keitner [an SS guard] was quite cynical about it. As he showed me the main dining room he smiled and said, 'You see, of course, how the Führer appreciates comfort. Only the best is good enough for him.' This particular room is sixty feet long by forty feet wide. A massive oak table runs down the centre. A soft glow comes from cunningly concealed lighting. Four etchings by Dürer hang on the walls. A vast Persian carpet covers the floor. Later on it was part of my duty, together with another girl, to lay the table. When the dinner was an informal one the service was of magnificent Dresden china, but when important guests were present they ate off solid silver – most of it plate from the Jewish merchants of Nuremberg, stolen from them by Himmler's agents.

The room in which Hitler receives his guests overlooks the Austrian Alps. This room houses his aviary of rare birds. One day I counted them. There were seventy-eight – all chattering and screaming at the same time. He always fed them himself. The death of one of them brought tears to his eyes. Its little corpse was buried in a small plot of ground with a tiny headstone of bronze placed on the grave.

Berchtesgaden has fourteen bedrooms for guests. Each bedroom has a private bathroom. The marble of Hitler's own bath comes from Italy. It was a present from Mussolini.

Every bedroom has a signed copy of *Mein Kampf*, together with pornographic French books imported from Paris. And every room has a portrait of Hitler over the bed.

The kitchens at Berchtesgaden are magnificent. All cooking is done by electricity. A former head chef of the Adlon Hotel in Berlin is in charge, with four younger men under him. He himself cooks only for Hitler. A Gestapo man is present night and day to ensure that no poison is introduced into the food.

Many walls are covered with rare Gobelin tapestries. 'Actually they are priceless,' declared Keitner, 'but if they were offered for sale in America they would fetch several million dollars.'

'But how can the Führer afford them?' I gasped.

'Well, there are ways and means,' smiled Keitner. 'The Führer can, for example, request a museum to "loan" him a tapestry, or he can suggest to a wealthy industrialist that it would be wise of him to send him a present. Then, some of them were just stolen from one of the ex-Kaiser's many castles.'

There are five rooms in Berchtesgaden which have never been photographed. I saw them once and once only. They are called the

Chambers of the Stars. They form a kind of penthouse on the roof. Only two people can enter them at any time – Hitler himself and his astrologer, one Karl Ossietz.

In the main room of this suite the ceiling is made of dark blue glass on which, by pressing a switch, the movements of the planets and constellations are shown. The best optical workers in Jena worked on this room for over a year before Hitler was satisfied with it. Designs of the zodiac form the patterns on the walls. In another of these rooms the only illumination comes from a brazier which burns night and day. Hitler often spends hours alone there, gazing into its angry glow or staring into a huge crystal globe.

In Germany no mention of Ossietz is allowed to be made, yet he is perhaps the most important man in the Third Reich outside Hitler himself. He just arrived at Berchtesgaden one day and has remained there ever since. He is the Rasputin of Nazi Germany.

Shortly after my arrival the Führer spent three days and nights in this suite alone with Ossietz. Göring arrived from Berlin with urgent news – but even the fat field marshal could not speak to Hitler until he emerged. He consults the stars before embarking upon any major activity. He would sooner listen to the advice of Ossietz than to counsel from his General Staff.

Every member of Hitler's staff hates Ossietz. They are all jealous of his influence. Göring, in particular, detests the man. He refused twice to stay in the same room with him. But Ossietz remains. Perhaps it is because he has told the Führer that he will still be ruling Germany when he himself dies, and he fixes the year of his death as 1962.

HITLER'S INSTRUCTIONS TO HIS GUESTS, BERCHTESGADEN, GERMANY, 1938

Instructions to Visitors

1. Smoking is forbidden, except in this bedroom.
2. The guest must not talk to servants or carry any parcel or message from the premises for any servant.
3. At all times the Führer must be addressed and spoken of as such and never as 'Herr Hitler' or other title.
4. Women guests are forbidden to use excessive cosmetics and must on no account use colouring material on their fingernails.

5. Guests must present themselves for meals within two minutes of the announcing bell. No one may sit at table or leave the table until the Führer has sat or left.
6. No one may remain seated in a room when the Führer enters.
7. Guests must retire to their rooms at 11 p.m. unless expressly asked to remain by the Führer.
8. Guests must remain in this wing of the house and must on no account enter the domestic quarters, the offices or the quarters of the SS officers, or the political police bureau.
9. On leaving Berchtesgaden, guests are absolutely forbidden to discuss their visit with strangers or to mention any remark made to them by the Führer. The conveying of information about the Führer's private life in this way will be visited by the severest penalties.

HITLER SPEAKS, NUREMBERG, GERMANY, 1938

Virginia Cowles

One night I went to the stadium with Jules Sauerwein to hear an address Hitler was making to Nazi political leaders gathered from all over Germany. The stadium was packed with nearly 200,000 spectators. As the time for the Führer's arrival drew near, the crowd grew restless. The minutes passed and the wait seemed interminable. Suddenly the beat of the drums increased and three motor-cycles with yellow standards fluttering from their windshields raced through the gates. A few minutes later a fleet of black cars rolled swiftly into the arena: in one of them, standing in the front seat, his hand outstretched in the Nazi salute, was Hitler.

The demonstration that followed was one of the most extraordinary I have ever witnessed. Hitler climbed to his box in the Grand Stand amid a deafening ovation, then gave a signal for the political leaders to enter. They came, a hundred thousand strong, through an opening in the far end of the arena. In the silver light they seemed to pour into the bowl like a flood of water. Each of them carried a Nazi flag and when they were assembled in mass formation, the bowl looked like a shimmering sea of swastikas.

Then Hitler began to speak. The crowd hushed into silence, but the drums continued their steady beat. Hitler's voice rasped into the night and every now and then the multitude broke into a roar of cheers. Some of the audience began swaying back and forth, chanting '*Seig Heil*' over and over again in a frenzy of delirium. I looked at the faces around me and saw tears streaming down people's cheeks. The drums had grown louder and I suddenly felt frightened. For a moment I wondered if it wasn't a dream; perhaps we were really in the heart of the African jungle. I had a sudden feeling of claustrophobia and whispered to Jules Sauerwein, asking if we couldn't leave. It was a silly question, for we were hemmed in on all sides, and there was nothing to do but sit there until the bitter end.

At last it was over. Hitler left the box and got back in the car. As soon as he stopped speaking the spell seemed to break and the magic vanish. That was the most extraordinary thing of all: for when he left the stand and climbed back into his car, his small figure suddenly became drab and unimpressive. You had to pinch yourself to realize that this was the man on whom the eyes of the world were riveted; that he alone held the lightning in his hands.

THE HOUSE OF COMMONS DISCUSSES WAR AND PEACE, LONDON, 2 September 1939

Mr Ralph Glyn, MP

Diary: September 3
Last night in London was one of the great times in modern history. The half-hour in the Commons – 7.30 to 8 – was perhaps the most decisive half-hour that we have known.

All through the day the House had been in a schoolboyish, almost hysterical mood; they were laughing and shuffling. There was a feeling that something fishy was happening in Downing Street. The Cabinet was still sitting. Ministers were telephoning Paris – and the Germans were bombing Poland. *Why* were we not at war?

At half-past seven we met again, this time subdued and tense. Chamberlain we knew would declare war. The Ambassadors were looking down; Count Edward Raczijnsky pale and worn. Chamberlain came in looking grey – a kind of whitish-grey – and glum, dour. Captain Margesson, the Secretary to the Treasury, came behind him, purple with anxiety. Chamberlain's statement! . . . In the house we thought he was only half way through when – he sat down. There was a gasp, first of horror, then anger. His own back-benchers leaned forward to cry, 'Munich, Munich!' The House seemed to rise to its feet with Mr Arthur Greenwood, the Labour leader.

Mr L. S. Amery, sitting very small near Anthony Eden, jumped up to shout at Greenwood – 'Speak for England.' Others took up the cry. Chamberlain white and hunched. Margesson with sweat pouring down his face, Sir John Simon, the Foreign Secretary, punctiliously looking holy.

Greenwood spoke slowly and very simply. He spoke for England and what is more he saved Chamberlain by most skilfully suggesting that it was the French who were delaying. Then one or two back-benchers, Chamberlain's own supporters, got up. It was not a joint Anglo-French pledge to Poland, they said, it was a *British* pledge – why were we not fulfilling it? The House swung against Chamberlain again. Winston Churchill, I saw, was getting whiter and grimmer. He turned round to look at Eden, who nodded as if to say, 'You speak, I'll follow.' I know that Churchill was about to move a vote of censure on the Government – which would have fallen. But Chamberlain looked across at Churchill: 'I'm playing straight,' his glance seemed to say, 'there really *are* reasons for delay.' Churchill sat back, relaxed, uneasy.

Then James Maxton, the pacifist, rose, gaunt, a Horseman from the Apocalypse, doom written across his face: 'Don't let's talk of national honour: what do such phrases mean? The plain fact is that war means the slaughter of millions. If the Prime Minister can still maintain the peace he will have saved those lives, he mustn't be rushed.' Again the House swung and was poised. We all thought in the curious hush: What if the gaunt figure of doom were right after all? Slaughter – misery – ruin – was he right? But the alternative: Hitler trading on our fears, Germany treading on freedom, Europe under terror. The whole House was swayed in unison with the drama which itself was living.

Another back-bencher spoke. 'We must keep our pledge – Hitler must be stopped.' Once again we were swinging against Chamberlain, when Margesson, damp and shapeless, rose to move the adjournment. In a kind of daze it was carried.

Britain declared war on Germany at 11 a.m. on the morning of 3 September.

THE *ROYAL OAK* IS TORPEDOED, SCAPA FLOW, SCOTLAND, 13 October 1939

Gunther Prien

The Second World War was barely six weeks old when German submarine U-47, commanded by Gunther Prien, penetrated the defences of the Royal Navy's base at Scapa Flow and sank the battleship *Royal Oak*.

. . . We are in Scapa Flow.

14.10.39. It is disgustingly light. The whole bay is lit up. To the south of Cava there is nothing. I go farther in. To port, I recognize the Hoxa Sound coastguard, to which in the next few minutes the boat must present itself as a target. In that event all would be lost; at present south of Cava no ships are to be seen, although visibility is extremely good. Hence decisions:

South of Cava there is no shipping; so before staking everything on success, all possible precautions must be taken. Therefore, turn to port is made. We proceed north by the coast. Two battleships are lying there at anchor, and further inshore, destroyers. Cruisers not visible, therefore attack on the big fellows.

Distance apart, 3,000 metres. Estimated depth, seven and a half metres. Impact firing. One torpedo fired on northern ship, two on southern. After a good three and a half minutes, a torpedo detonates on the northern ship; of the other two nothing is to be seen.

About! Torpedo fired from stern; in the bow two tubes are loaded; three torpedoes from the bow. After three tense minutes comes the detonation on the nearer ship. There is a loud explosion, roar, and rumbling. Then come columns of water, followed by columns of fire, and splinters fly through the air. The harbour springs to life. Destroyers are lit up, signalling starts on every side, and on land, 200 metres away from me, cars roar along the roads. A battleship had been sunk, a second damaged, and the other three torpedoes have gone to blazes. All the tubes are empty. I decide to withdraw, because: (1) With my periscopes. I cannot conduct night attacks while submerged . . . (2) On a bright night I cannot manoeuvre unobserved in a calm sea. (3) I must assume that I was observed by the driver of a car which stopped opposite us, turned around, and drove off towards Scapa at top speed. (4) Nor can I go farther north, for there, well hidden from my sight, lie the destroyers which were previously dimly distinguishable.

At full speed both engines we withdraw. Everything is simple until we reach Skildaenoy Point. Then we have more trouble. It is now low tide. The current is against us, Engines at slow and dead slow; I attempt to get away. I must leave by the south through the narrows, because of the depth of the water. Things are again difficult. Course, 058°, slow – ten knots. I make no progress. At full speed I pass the southern blockship with nothing to spare. The helmsman does magnificently. Full speed ahead both, finally three-quarter speed and full ahead all out. Free of the blockships – ahead a mole! Hard over and again about, and at 02.15 we are once more outside. A pity that only one was destroyed. The torpedo misses I explain as due to faults of course, speed and drift. In tube 4, a misfire. The crew behaved splendidly throughout the operation.

THE GERMAN BREAKTHROUGH IN THE WEST, 15 May 1940

Erwin Rommel

After the months of 'phony war,' Hitler sent his army sweeping into France and the Low Countries. The breakthrough by German armour at the River Meuse, in which Rommel's 7th Panzer Division played the key role, allowed the Wehrmacht to bypass France's heavily fortified Maginot Line.

The way to the west was now open. The moon was up and for the time being we could expect no real darkness. I had already given orders, in the plan for the breakthrough, for the leading tanks to scatter the road and verges with machine and anti-tank gunfire at intervals during the drive to Avesnes, which I hoped would prevent the enemy from laying mines. The rest of the Panzer Regiment was to follow close behind the leading tanks and be ready at any time to fire salvoes to either flank. The mass of the division had instructions to follow up the Panzer Regiment lorry-borne.

The tanks now rolled in a long column through the line of fortifications and on towards the first houses, which had been set alight by our fire. In the moonlight we could see the men of 7th Motor-Cycle Battalion moving forward on foot beside us. Occasionally an enemy machine-gun or anti-tank gun fired, but none of their shots came anywhere near us. Our artillery was dropping heavy harassing fire on villages and the road far ahead of the regiment. Gradually the speed increased. Before long we were 500–1000–2000–3000 yards into the fortified zone. Engines roared, tank tracks clanked and clattered. Whether or not the enemy was firing was impossible to tell in the ear-splitting noise. We crossed the railway line a mile or so south-west of Solre le Château, and then swung north to the main road which was soon reached. Then off along the road and past the first houses.

The people in the houses were rudely awoken by the din of our tanks, the clatter and roar of tracks and engines. Troops lay bivouacked beside the road, military vehicles stood parked in farmyards and in some places on the road itself. Civilians and French troops, their faces distorted with terror, lay huddled in the ditches, alongside hedges and in every hollow beside the road. We passed refugee columns, the carts abandoned by their owners, who had fled in panic into the fields. On we went, at a steady speed, towards our objective. Every so often a quick glance at the map by a shaded light and a short wireless message to Divisional HQ to report the position and thus the success of 25th Panzer Regiment. Every so often a look out of the hatch to assure myself that there was still no resistance and that contact was being maintained to the rear. The flat countryside lay spread out around us under the cold light of the moon. We were through the Maginot Line! It was hardly conceivable. Twenty-two years before we had stood for four and a half years before this selfsame enemy and had won victory after victory and yet finally lost the war. And now we had broken through the renowned Maginot Line and were driving deep into enemy territory.

DUNKIRK: THE VIEW FROM THE BEACHES, N. FRANCE, 30 May 1940

A British artillery officer

By 21 May the German army had reached the English Channel at Abbeville, encircling the Belgian army and the British Expeditionary Force sent to reinforce the Allied front. On 26 May Lord Gort, commander of the BEF, was authorized to re-embark his army back to Britain, and he began to concentrate the BEF and remnants of the French and Belgian armies – a total of some 400,000 men – at Dunkirk. The evacuation continued for nine days, from 26 May to June 3, all of them under ceaseless attack by the *Wehrmacht* and *Luftwaffe*.

We were now in the region of the dunes, which rose like humps of a deeper darkness. And these in their turn were dotted with the still blacker shapes of abandoned vehicles, half-sunk in the sand, fantastic twisted shapes of burned-out skeletons, and crazy-looking wreckage that had been heaped up in extraordinary piles by the explosions of bombs. All these black shapes were silhouetted against the angry red glare in the sky, which reflected down on us the agony of burning Dunkirk.

Slowly we picked our way between the wreckage, sinking ankle-deep in the loose sand, until we reached the gaunt skeletons of what had once been the houses on the promenade. The whole front was one long continuous line of blazing buildings, a high wall of fire, roaring and darting in tongues of flame, with the smoke pouring upwards and disappearing in the blackness of the sky above the roof-tops. Out seawards the darkness was as thick and smooth as black velvet, except for now and again when the shape of a sunken destroyer or paddle-steamer made a slight thickening on its impenetrable surface. Facing us, the great black wall of the Mole stretched from the beach far out into sea, the end of it almost invisible to us. The Mole had an astounding, terrifying background of giant flames leaping a hundred feet into the air from blazing oil tanks. At the shore end of the Mole stood an obelisk, and the high-explosive shells burst around it with monotonous regularity

Along the promenade, in parties of fifty, the remnants of practically all the last regiments were wearily trudging along. There was no singing, and very little talk. Everyone was far too exhausted to waste breath. Occasionally out of the darkness came a sudden shout:

'A Company, Green Howards . . .'

'C Company, East Yorks . . .'

These shouts came either from stragglers trying to find lost units, or guides on the look-out for the parties they were to lead on to the Mole for evacuation.

The tide was out. Over the wide stretch of sand could be dimly discerned little oblong masses of soldiers, moving in platoons and orderly groups down towards the edge of the sea. Now and again you would hear a shout:

'Alf, where are you? . . .'

'Let's hear from you, Bill . . .'

'Over this way, George . . .'

It was none too easy to keep contact with one's friends in the darkness, and amid so many little masses of moving men, all looking very much alike. If you stopped for a few seconds to look behind, the chances were you attached yourself to some entirely different unit.

From the margin of the sea, at fairly wide intervals, three long thin black lines protruded into the water, conveying the effect of low wooden breakwaters. These were lines of men, standing in pairs behind one another far out into the water, waiting in queues till boats arrived to transport them, a score or so at a time, to the steamers and warships that were filling up with the last survivors. The queues stood there, fixed and almost as regular as if ruled. No bunching, no pushing. Nothing like the mix-up to be seen at the turnstiles when a crowd is going into a football match. Much more orderly, even, than a waiting theatre queue.

About this time, afraid that some of our men might be tailing off, I began shouting, '2004th Field Regiment . . . 2004th Field Regiment . . .'

A group of dead and dying soldiers on the path in front of us quickened our desire to quit the promenade. Stepping over the bodies we marched down the slope on to the dark beach. Dunkirk front was now a lurid study in red and black; flames, smoke, and the night itself all mingling together to compose a frightful panorama of death and destruction. Red and black, all the time, except for an occasional flash of white low in the sky miles away to the left and right where big shells from coastal defence guns at Calais and Nieuport were being hurled into the town.

Down on the beach you immediately felt yourself surrounded by a deadly evil atmosphere. A horrible stench of blood and mutilated flesh pervaded the place. There was no escape from it. Not a breath of air was blowing to dissipate the appalling odour that arose from the dead bodies that had been lying on the sand, in some cases for several days. We might have been walking through a slaughter-house on a hot day. The darkness, which hid some of the sights of horror from our eyes, seemed to thicken this dreadful stench. It created the impression that death was hovering around, very near at hand.

We set our faces in the direction of the sea, quickening our pace to pass through the belt of this nauseating miasma as soon as possible.

'Water . . . Water . . .' groaned a voice from the ground just in front of us.

It was a wounded infantryman. He had been hit so badly that there was no hope for him. Our water-bottles had long been empty, but by carefully draining them all into one we managed to collect a mouthful or two. A sergeant knelt down beside the dying man and held the bottle to his lips. Then we proceeded on our way, leaving the bottle with the last few drains in it near the poor fellow's hand so that he could moisten his lips from time to time.

On either side, scattered over the sand in all sorts of positions, were the dark shapes of dead and dying men, sometimes alone, sometimes in twos and threes. Every now and then we had to pull ourselves up sharply in the darkness to avoid falling over a wooden cross erected by comrades on the spot where some soldier had been buried. No assistance that availed anything could be given to these dying men, The living themselves had nothing to offer them. They just pressed forward to the sea, hoping that the same fate would not be theirs. And still it remained a gamble all the time whether that sea, close though it was, would be reached in safety. Splinters from bursting shells were continually whizzing through the air, and occasionally a man in one of the plodding groups would fall with a groan.

DUNKIRK: THE VIEW FROM THE BOATS, 1 June 1940

Commander C. H. Lightoller, RNR (Retd)

The evacuation was carried by an armada of 222 naval units and 665 civilian craft. These vessels succeeded in bringing back to Britain 224,585 British and 112,546 French and Belgian troops. Among the civilian vessels was the yacht *Sundowner* owned by Commander Lightoller. Lightoller had been in history once: as the senior surviving officer of the *Titanic*.

Half-way across we avoided a floating mine by a narrow margin, but having no firearms of any description – not even a tin hat – we had to leave its destruction to someone better equipped. A few minutes later we had our first introduction to enemy aircraft, three fighters flying high. Before they could be offensive, a British destroyer – *Worcester*, I think – overhauled us and drove them off. At 2.25 p.m. we sighted and closed the twenty-five-foot motor-cruiser *Westerly*; broken down and badly on fire. As the crew of two (plus three naval ratings she had picked up in Dunkirk) wished to abandon ship – and quickly – I went alongside and took them aboard, giving them the additional pleasure of again facing the hell they had only just left.

We made the fairway buoy to the Roads shortly after the sinking of a French transport with severe loss of life. Steaming slowly through the wreckage we entered the Roads. For some time now we had been subject to sporadic bombing and machine-gun fire, but as the *Sundowner* is exceptionally and extremely quick on the helm, by waiting till the last moment and putting the helm hard over – my son at the wheel – we easily avoided every attack, though sometimes near lifted out of the water.

It had been my intention to go right on to the beaches, where my second son, Second-Lieutenant R. T. Lightoller, had been evacuated some forty-eight hours previously; but those of the *Westerly* informed me that the troops were all away, so I headed up for Dunkirk piers. By now divebombers seemed to be eternally dropping out of the cloud of enemy aircraft overhead. Within half a mile of the pierheads a two-funnelled grey-painted transport had over hauled and was just passing us to port when two salvoes were dropped in quick succession right along her port side. For a few moments she was hid in smoke and I certainly thought they had got her. Then she reappeared, still gaily heading for the piers and entered just ahead of us.

The difficulty of taking troops on board from the quay high above us was obvious, so I went alongside a destroyer (*Worcester* again, I think) where they were already embarking. I got hold of her captain and told him I could take about a hundred (though the most I had ever had on board was twenty-one). He, after consultation with the military C.O., told me to carry on and get the troops aboard. I may say here that before leaving Cubitt's Yacht Basin, we had worked all night stripping her down of everything movable, masts included, that would tend to lighten her and make for more room.

My son, as previously arranged, was to pack the men in and use every available inch of space – which I'll say he carried out to some purpose. On deck I detailed a naval rating to tally the troops aboard. At fifty I called below, 'How are you getting on?' getting the cheery reply, 'Oh, plenty of room yet.' At seventy-five my son admitted they were getting pretty tight – all equipment and arms being left on deck.

I now started to pack them on deck, having passed word below for every man to lie down and keep down; the same applied on deck. By the time we had fifty on deck I could feel her getting distinctly tender, so took no more. Actually we had exactly a hundred and thirty on board, including three *Sundowners* and five *Westerlys*.

During the whole embarkation we had quite a lot of attention from enemy planes, but derived an amazing degree of comfort from the fact that the *Worcester's* A.A. guns kept up an everlasting bark overhead.

Casting off and backing out we entered the Roads again; there it was continuous and unmitigated hell. The troops were just splendid and of their own initiative detailed lookouts ahead, astern, and abeam for inquisitive planes, as my attention was pretty wholly occupied watching the steering and giving orders to Roger at the wheel. Any time an aircraft seemed inclined to try its hand on us, one of the look-outs would just call quietly, 'Look out for this bloke, skipper', at the same time pointing. One bomber that had been particularly offensive, itself came under the notice of one of our fighters and suddenly plunged vertically into the sea just about fifty yards astern of us. It was the only time any man ever raised his voice above a conversational tone, but as that big black bomber hit the water they raised an echoing cheer.

My youngest son, Pilot Officer H. B. Lightoller (lost at the outbreak of war in the first raid on Wilhelmshaven), flew a Blenheim and had at different times given me a whole lot of useful information about attack, defence and evasive tactics (at which he was apparently particularly good) and I attribute in a great measure our success in getting across without a single casualty to his unwitting help.

On one occasion an enemy machine came up astern at about a hundred feet with the obvious intention of raking our decks. He was coming down in a gliding dive and I knew that he must elevate some ten to fifteen degrees before his guns would bear. Telling my son 'Stand by,' I waited till, as near as I could judge, he was just on the point of pulling up, and then 'Hard a-port.' (She turns 180 degrees in exactly her own length.) This threw his aim completely off. He banked and tried again. Then 'Hard a-starboard,' with the same result. After a third attempt he gave it up in disgust. Had I had a machine-gun of any sort, he was a sitter – in fact, there were at least three that I am confident we could have accounted for during the trip.

Not the least of our difficulties was contending with the wash of fast craft, such as destroyers and transports. In every instance I had to stop completely, take the way off the ship and head the heavy wash. The M.C. being where it was, to have taken one of these seas on either the quarter or beam would have at once put paid to our otherwise successful cruise. The effect of the consequent plunging on the troops below, in a stinking atmosphere with all ports and skylights closed, can well be imagined. They were literally packed like the proverbial sardines, even one in the bath and another on the WC, so that all the poor devils could do was sit and be sick. Added were the remnants of bully beef and biscuits. So that after discharging our cargo in Ramsgate at ten p.m., there lay before the three of us a nice clearing-up job.

FRANCE SURRENDERS, COMPIÈGNE, 21 June 1940

William L. Shirer

On 21 June France capitulated and signed a formal surrender to the Germans. The signing took place in the railway carriage at Compiègne, where Marshal Foch had dictated terms to the Germans in 1918.

On the exact spot in the little clearing in the Forest of Compiègne where, at five a.m. on 11 November 1918, the armistice which ended the World War was signed, Adolf Hitler today handed *his* armistice terms to France. To make German revenge complete, the meeting of the German and French plenipotentiaries took place in Marshal Foch's private [railway] car, in which Foch laid down the armistice terms to Germany twenty-two years ago. Even the same table in the rickety old *wagon-lit* car was used. And through the windows we saw Hitler occupying the very seat on which Foch had sat at that table when he dictated the other armistice.

The humiliation of France, of the French, was complete. And yet in the preamble to the armistice terms Hitler told the French that he had not chosen this spot at Compiègne out of revenge; merely to right an old wrong. From the demeanour of the French delegates I gathered that they did not appreciate the difference . . .

The armistice negotiations began at three-fifteen p.m. A warm June sun beat down on the great elm and pine trees, and cast pleasant shadows on the wooded avenues as Hitler, with the German plenipotentiaries at his side, appeared. He alighted from his car in front of the French monument to Alsace-Lorraine which stands at the end of an avenue about 200 yards from the clearing where the armistice car waited on exactly the same spot it occupied twenty-two years ago.

The Alsace-Lorraine statue, I noted, was covered with German war flags so that you could not see its sculptured work nor read its inscription. But I had seen it some years before – the large sword representing the sword of the Allies, and its point sticking into a large, limp eagle, representing the old Empire of the Kaiser. And the inscription underneath in French saying: 'TO THE HEROIC SOLDIERS OF FRANCE . . . DEFENDERS OF THE COUNTRY AND OF RIGHT . . . GLORIOUS LIBERATORS OF ALSACE-LORRAINE'.

Through my glasses I saw the Führer stop, glance at the monument, observe the Reich flags with their big swastikas in the centre. Then he strode slowly towards us, towards the little clearing in the woods. I observed his face. It was grave, solemn, yet brimming with revenge. There was also in it, as in his springy step, a note of the triumphant conqueror, the defier of the world. There was something else, difficult to describe, in his expression, a sort of scornful, inner joy at being present at this great reversal of fate – a reversal he himself had wrought.

Now he reaches the little opening in the woods. He pauses and looks slowly around. The clearing is in the form of a circle some 200 yards in diameter and laid out like a park. Cypress trees line it all round – and behind them, the great elms and oaks of the forest. This has been one of France's national shrines for twenty-two years. From a discreet position on the perimeter of the circle we watch.

Hitler pauses, and gazes slowly around. In a group just behind him are the other German plenipotentiaries: Göring, grasping his field-marshal's baton in one hand. He wears the sky-blue uniform of the air force. All the Germans are in uniform, Hitler in a double-breasted grey uniform, with the Iron Cross hanging from his left breast pocket. Next to Göring are the two German army chiefs – General Keitel, chief of the Supreme Command, and General von Brauchitsch, commander-in-chief of the German army. Both are just approaching sixty, but look younger, especially Keitel, who had a dapper appearance with his cap slightly cocked on one side.

Then there is Erich Raeder, Grand Admiral of the German Fleet, in his blue naval uniform and the invariable upturned collar which German naval officers usually wear. There are two non-military men in Hitler's suite – his Foreign Minister, Joachim von Ribbentrop, in the field-grey uniform of the Foreign Office; and Rudolf Hess, Hitler's deputy, in a grey party uniform.

The time is now three-eighteen p.m. Hitler's personal flag is run up on a small standard in the centre of the opening.

Also in the centre is a great granite block which stands some three feet above the ground. Hitler, followed by the others, walks slowly over to it, steps up, and reads the inscription engraved in great high letters on that block. It says: HERE ON THE ELEVENTH OF NOVEMBER 1918 SUCCUMBED THE CRIMINAL PRIDE OF THE GERMAN EMPIRE . . . VANQUISHED BY THE FREE PEOPLES WHICH IT TRIED TO ENSLAVE.'

Hitler reads it and Göring reads it. They all read it, standing there in the June sun and the silence. I look for the expression on Hitler's face. I am but fifty yards from him and see him through my glasses as though he were directly in front of me. I have seen that face many times at the great moments of his life. But today! It is afire with scorn, anger, hate, revenge, triumph. He steps off the monument and contrives to make even this gesture a masterpiece of contempt. He glances back at it, contemptuous, angry – angry, you almost feel, because he cannot wipe out the awful, provoking lettering with one sweep of his high Prussian boot. He glances slowly around the clearing, and now, as his eyes meet ours, you grasp the depth of his hatred. But there is triumph there too – revengeful, triumphant hate. Suddenly, as though his face were not giving quite complete expression to his feelings, he throws his whole body into harmony with his mood. He swiftly snaps his hands on his hips, arches his shoulders, plants his feet wide apart. It is a magnificent gesture of defiance, of burning contempt for this place now and all that it has stood for in the twenty-two years since it witnessed the humbling of the German Empire . . .

It is now three-twenty-three p.m. and the Germans stride over to the armistice car. For a moment or two they stand in the sunlight outside the car, chatting. Then Hitler steps up into the car, followed by the others. We can see nicely through the car windows. Hitler takes the place occupied by Marshal Foch when the 1918 armistice terms were signed. The others spread themselves around him. Four chairs on the opposite side of the table from Hitler remain empty. The French have not yet appeared. But we do not wait long. Exactly at three-thirty p.m. they alight from a car. They have flown up from Bordeaux to a nearby landing field. They too glance at the Alsace-Lorraine memorial, but it's a swift glance. Then they walk down the avenue flanked by three German officers. We see them now as they come into the sunlight of the clearing.

General Huntziger, wearing a bleached khaki uniform, Air General Bergeret and Vice-Admiral Le Luc, both in dark blue uniforms, and then, almost buried in the uniforms, M. Noël, French Ambassador to Poland. The German guard of honour, drawn up at the entrance to the clearing, snaps to attention for the French as they pass, but it does not present arms.

It is a grave hour in the life of France. The Frenchmen keep their eyes straight ahead. Their faces are solemn, drawn. They are the picture of tragic dignity.

They walk stiffly to the car, where they are met by two German officers, Lieutenant-General Tippelskirch, Quartermaster General, and Colonel Thomas, chief of the Führer's headquarters. The Germans salute. The French salute. The atmosphere is what Europeans call 'correct'. There are salutes, but no handshakes.

Now we get our picture through the dusty windows of that old *wagon-lit* car. Hitler and the other German leaders rise as the French enter the drawing-room. Hitler gives the Nazi salute, the arm raised. Ribbentrop and Hess do the same. I cannot see M. Noël to notice whether he salutes or not.

Hitler, as far as we can see through the windows, does not say a word to the French or to anybody else. He nods to General Keitel at his side. We see General Keitel adjusting his papers. Then he starts to read. He is reading the preamble to the German armistice terms. The French sit there with marble-like faces and listen intently. Hitler and Göring glance at the green table-top.

The reading of the preamble lasts but a few minutes. Hitler, we soon observe, has no intention of remaining very long, of listening to the reading of the armistice terms themselves. At three-forty-two p.m., twelve minutes after the French arrive, we see Hitler stand up, salute stiffly, and then stride out of the drawing-room, followed by Göring, Brauchitsch, Raeder, Hess, and Ribbentrop. The French, like figures of stone, remain at the green-topped table. General Keitel remains with them. He starts to read them the detailed conditions of the armistice.

Hitler and his aides stride down the avenue towards the Alsace-Lorraine monument, where their cars are waiting. As they pass the guard of honour, the German band strikes up the two national anthems, *Deutschland, Deutschland über Alles* and the *Horst Wessel* song. The whole ceremony in which Hitler has reached a new pinnacle in his meteoric career and Germany avenged the 1918 defeat is over in a quarter of an hour.

THE BATTLE OF BRITAIN, September 1940

Pilot Officer John Maurice Beard

After the fall of France, Britain stood alone against Germany. Hitler made a peace overture in June, which was dismissed by Winston Churchill, who had taken over from Chamberlain as Prime Minister. The blow came soon after with a full-scale air-attack by Göring's *Luftwaffe*: the Battle of Britain. Beginning in August, it lasted until November, although the peak of the fighting was in September. The RAF was outnumbered in planes and pilots four to one but nevertheless thwated the Germans' attempt to control the air over the channel. John Beard was one of 'The Few', a 21-year-old Hurricane pilot.

I was supposed to be away on a day's leave but dropped back to the aerodrome to see if there was a letter from my wife. When I found out that *all* the squadrons had gone off into action, I decided to stand by, because obviously something big was happening. While I was climbing into my flying kit, our Hurricanes came slipping back out of the sky to refuel, reload ammunition, and take off again. The returning pilots were full of talk about flocks of enemy bombers and fighters which were trying to break through along the Thames Estuary. You couldn't miss hitting them, they said. Off to the east I could hear the steady roll of anti-aircraft fire. It was a brilliant afternoon with a flawless blue sky. I was crazy to be off.

An instant later an aircraftsman rushed up with orders for me to make up a flight with some of the machines then reloading. My own Hurricane was a nice old kite, though it had a habit of flying left wing low at the slightest provocation. But since it had already accounted for fourteen German aircraft before I inherited it, I thought it had some luck, and I was glad when I squeezed myself into the same old seat again and grabbed the 'stick'.

We took off in two flights [six fighters], and as we started to gain height over the station we were told over the R. T. [radio-telephone] to keep circling for a while until we were made up to a stronger force. That didn't take long, and soon there was a complete squadron including a couple of Spitfires which had wandered in from somewhere.

Then came the big thrilling moment: ACTION ORDERS. Distantly I heard the hum of the generator in my R. T. earphones and then the voice of the ground controller crackling through with the call signs. Then the order 'Fifty plus bombers, one hundred plus fighters over Canterbury at 15,000 heading northeast. Your vector [steering course to intercept] nine zero degrees. Over!'

We were flying in four V formations of three. I was flying No. 3 in Red flight, which was the squadron leader's and thus the leading flight. On we went, wing tips to left and right slowly rising and falling, the roar of our twelve Marlins drowning all other sound. We crossed over London, which, at 20,000 feet, seemed just a haze of smoke from its countless chimneys, with nothing visible except the faint glint of the barrage balloons and the wriggly silver line of the Thames.

I had too much to do watching the instruments and keeping formation to do much thinking. But once I caught a reflected glimpse of myself in the windscreen – a goggled, bloated, fat thing with the tube of my oxygen supply protruding gruesomely sideways from the mask which hid my mouth. Suddenly I was back at school again, on a hot afternoon when the Headmaster was taking the Sixth and droning on and on about the later Roman Emperors. The boy on my right was showing me surreptitiously some illustrations which he had pinched out of his father's medical books during the last holidays. I looked like one of those pictures.

It was an amazingly vivid memory, as if school was only yesterday. And half my mind was thinking what wouldn't I then have given to be sitting in a Hurricane belting along at 350 miles an hour and out for a kill. *Me* defending London! I grinned at my old self at the thought.

Minutes went by. Green fields and roads were now beneath us. I scanned the sky and the horizon for the first glimpse of the Germans. A new vector came through on the R. T. and we swung round with the sun behind us. Swift on the heels of this I heard Yellow flight leader call through the earphones. I looked quickly toward Yellow's position, and there they were!

It was really a terrific sight and quite beautiful. First they seemed just a cloud of light as the sun caught the many glistening chromium parts of their engines, their windshields, and the spin of their airscrew discs. Then, as our squadron hurtled nearer, the details stood out. I could see the bright-yellow noses of Messerschmitt fighters sandwiching the bombers, and could even pick out some of the types. The sky seemed full of them, packed in layers thousands of feet deep. They came on steadily, wavering up and down along the horizon. 'Oh, golly,' I thought, 'golly, golly . . .'

And then any tension I had felt on the way suddenly left me. I was elated but very calm. I leaned over and switched on my reflector sight, flicked the catch on the gun button from 'Safe' to 'Fire', and lowered my seat till the circle and dot on the reflector sight shone darkly red in front of my eyes.

The squadron leader's voice came through the earphones, giving tactical orders. We swung round in a great circle to attack on their beam – into the thick of them. Then, on the order, down we went. I took my hand from the throttle lever so as to get both hands on the stick, and my thumb played neatly across the gun button. You have to steady a fighter just as you have to steady a rifle before you fire it.

My Merlin screamed as I went down in a steeply banked dive on to the tail of a forward line of Heinkels. I knew the air was full of aircraft flinging themselves about in all directions, but, hunched and snuggled down behind my sight I was conscious only of the Heinkel I had picked out. As the angle of my dive increased, the enemy machine loomed larger in the sight field, heaved toward the red dot, and then he was there!

I had an instant's flash of amazement at the Heinkel proceeding so regularly on its way with a fighter on its tail. 'Why doesn't the fool *move*?' I thought, and actually caught myself flexing my muscles into the action *I* would have taken had I been he.

When he was square across the sight I pressed the button. There was a smooth trembling of my Hurricane as the eight-gun squirt shot out. I gave him a two-second burst and then another. Cordite fumes blew back into the cockpit making an acrid mixture with the smell of hot oil and the aircompressors.

I saw my first burst go in and, just as I was on top of him and turning away, I noticed a red glow inside the bomber. I turned tightly into position again and now saw several short tongues of flame lick out along the fuselage. Then he went down in a spin, blanketed with smoke and with pieces flying off.

I left him plummeting down and, horsing back on my stick, climbed up again for more. The sky was clearing, but ahead toward London I saw a small, tight formation of bombers completely encircled by a ring of Messerschmitts. They were still heading north. As I raced forward, three flights of Spitfires came zooming up from beneath them in a sort of Prince-of-Wales's-feathers manoeuvre. They burst through upward and outward, their guns going all the time. They must have each got one, for an instant later I saw the most extraordinary sight of eight German bombers and fighters diving earthward together in flames.

I turned away again and streaked after some distant specks ahead. Diving down, I noticed that the running progress of the battle had brought me over London again. I could see the network of streets with the green space of Kensington Gardens, and I had an instant's glimpse of the Round Pond, where I sailed boats when I was a child. In that moment, and as I was rapidly overhauling the Germans ahead, a Dornier 17 sped right across my line of flight, closely pursued by a Hurricane. And behind the Hurricane came two Messerschmitts. He was too intent to have seen them and they had not seen me! They were coming slightly toward me. It was perfect. A kick at the rudder and I swung in toward them, thumbed the gun button, and let them have it. The first burst was placed just the right distance ahead of the leading Messerschmitt. He ran slap into it and he simply came to pieces in the air. His companion, with one of the speediest and most brilliant 'get-outs' I have ever seen, went right away in a half Immelmann turn. I missed him completely. He must almost have been hit by the pieces of the leader but he got away. I hand it to him.

At that moment some instinct made me glance up at my rear-view mirror and spot two Messerschmitts closing in on my tail. Instantly I hauled back on the stick and streaked upward. And just in time. For as I flicked into the climb, I saw the tracer streaks pass beneath me. As I turned I had a quick look round the 'office' [cockpit]. My fuel reserve was running out and I had only about a second's supply of ammunition left. I was certainly in no condition to take on two Messerschmitts. But they seemed no more eager than I was. Perhaps they were in the same position, for they turned away for home. I put my nose down and did likewise.

Only on the way back did I realize how hot I was. I had forgotten to adjust the ventilator apparatus in all the stress of the fighting, and hadn't noticed the thermometer. With the sun on the windows all the time, the inside of the 'office' was like an oven. Inside my flying suit I was in a bath of perspiration, and sweat was cascading down my face. I was dead tired and my neck ached from constantly turning my head on the lookout when going in and out of dogfights. Over east the sky was flecked with A. A. puffs, but I did not bother to investigate. Down I went, home.

At the station there was only time for a few minutes' stretch, a hurried report to the Intelligence Officer, and a brief comparing of notes with the other pilots. So far my squadron seemed to be intact, in spite of a terrific two hours in which we had accounted for at least thirty enemy aircraft.

But there was more to come. It was now about four p.m. and I gulped down some tea while the ground crew checked my Hurricane. Then, with about three flights collected, we took off again. We seemed to be rather longer this time circling and gaining height above the station before the orders came through on the R.T. It was to patrol an area along the Thames Estuary at 20,000 feet. But we never got there.

We had no sooner got above the docks than we ran into the first lot of enemy bombers. They were coming up in line about 5,000 feet below us. The line stretched on and on across the horizon. Above, on our level, were assorted groups of enemy fighters. Some were already in action, with our fellows spinning and twirling among them. Again I got that tightening feeling at the throat, for it really was a sight to make you gasp.

But we all knew what to do. We went for the bombers. Kicking her over, I went down after the first of them, a Heinkel 111. He turned away as I approached, chiefly because some of our fellows had already broken into the line and had scattered it. Before I got up he had been joined by two more. They were forming a V and heading south across the river.

I went after them. Closing in on the tail of the left one, I ran into a stream of crossfire from all three. How it missed me I don't know. For a second the whole air in front was thick with tracer trails. It seemed to be coming straight at me, only to curl away by the windows and go lazily past. I felt one slight bank, however, and glancing quickly, saw a small hole at the end of my starboard wing.

Then, as the Heinkel drifted across my sights, I pressed the button – once – twice . . . Nothing happened.

I panicked for a moment till I looked down and saw that I had forgotten to turn the safety-catch knob to the 'Fire' position. I flicked it over at once and in that instant saw that three bombers, to hasten their getaway, had jettisoned all their bombs. They seemed to peel off in a steady stream. We were over the southern outskirts of London now and I remember hoping that most of them would miss the little houses and plunge into fields.

But dropping the bombs did not help my Heinkel. I let him have a long burst at close range, which got him right in the 'office'. I saw him turn slowly over and go down, and followed to give him another squirt. Just then there was a terrific crash in front of me. Something flew past my window, and the whole aircraft shook as the engine raced itself to pieces. I had been hit by A.A. fire aimed at the bombers, my airscrew had been blown off, and I was going down in a spin.

The next few seconds were a bit wild and confused. I remember switching off and flinging back the sliding roof almost in one gesture. Then I tried to vault out through the roof. But I had forgotten to release my safety belt. As I fumbled at the pin the falling aircraft gave a twist which shot me through the open cover. Before I was free, the air stream hit me like a solid blow and knocked me sideways. I felt my arm hit something, and then I was falling over and over with fields and streets and sky gyrating madly past my eyes.

I grabbed at the rip cord on my chute. Missed it. Grabbed again. Missed it. That was no fun. Then I remember saying to myself, 'This won't do. Take it easy, take it slowly.' I tried again and found the rip cord grip and pulled. There was a terrific wrench at my thighs and then I was floating still and peacefully with my 'brolly' canopy billowing above my head.

The rest was lovely. I sat at my ease just floating gradually down, breathing deep, and looking around. I was drifting across London again at about 2,000 feet.

THE BLITZ, LONDON, September–November 1940

Thwarted in its attempt to destroy the RAF, the *Luftwaffe* switched its attention to mass-bombing raids on London. The first of the big raids came on 7 September, when 375 bombers unloaded their bombs on the capital.

Virginia Woolf

Tuesday, 10 September

Back from half a day in London – perhaps our strangest visit. When we got to Gower Street a barrier with diversion on it. No sign of damage. But coming to Doughty Street a crowd. Then Miss Perkins at the window. Mecklenburgh Square roped off. Wardens there. Not allowed in. The house about 30 yards from ours struck at one in the morning by a bomb. Completely ruined. Another bomb in the square still unexploded. We walked round the back. Stood by Jane Harrison's house. The house was still smouldering. That is a great pile of bricks. Underneath all the people who had gone down to their shelter. Scraps of cloth hanging to the bare walls at the side still standing. A looking glass I think swinging. Like a tooth knocked out – a clean cut. Our house undamaged. No windows yet broken – perhaps the bomb has now broken them. We saw Bernal with an arm band jumping on top of the bricks. Who lived there? I suppose the casual young men and women I used to see from my window; the flat dwellers who used to have flower pots and sit in the balcony. All now blown to bits. The garage man at the back – blear eyed and jerky – told us he had been blown out of his bed by the explosion: made to take shelter in a church. 'A hard cold seat,' he said, 'and a small boy lying in my arms. I cheered when the all clear sounded. I'm aching all over.' He said the Jerries had been over for three nights trying to bomb Kings Cross. They had destroyed half Argyll Street, also shops in Grays Inn Road. Then Mr Pritchard ambled up. Took the news as calm as a grig. 'They actually have the impertinence to say this will make us accept peace . . . !' he said: he watches raids from his flat roof and sleeps like a hog. So, after talking to Miss Perkins, Mrs Jackson – but both serene – Miss P. had slept on a camp bed in her shelter – we went on to Grays Inn. Left the car and saw Holborn. A vast gap at the top of Chancery Lane. Smoking still. Some great shop entirely destroyed: the hotel opposite like a shell. In a wine shop there were no windows left. People standing at the tables – I think drink being served. Heaps of blue-green glass in the road at Chancery Lane. Men breaking off fragments left in the frames. Glass falling. Then into Lincoln's Inn. To the *New Statesman* office: windows broken, but house untouched. We went over it. Deserted. Wet passages. Glass on stairs. Doors locked. So back to the car. A great block of traffic. The Cinema behind Madame Tussaud's torn open: the stage visible; some decoration swinging. All the Regent's

Park houses with broken windows, but undamaged. And then miles and miles of orderly ordinary streets – all Bayswater, and Sussex Square as usual – streets empty – faces set and eyes bleared. In Chancery Lane I saw a man with a barrow of music books. My typist's office destroyed. Then at Wimbledon a siren: people began running. We drove, through almost empty streets, as fast as possible. Horses taken out of the shafts. Cars pulled up. Then the all clear. The people I think of now are the very grimy lodging house keepers, say in Heathcote Street: with another night to face: old wretched women standing at their doors; dirty, miserable. Well – as Nessa said on the phone, it's coming very near. I had thought myself a coward for suggesting that we should not sleep two nights at 37. I was greatly relieved when Miss P. telephoned advising us not to stay, and L. agreed.

Edward Murrow, American journalist

All the fires were quickly brought under control. That's a common phrase in the morning communiqués. I've seen how it's done; spent a night with the London fire brigade. For three hours after the night attack got going, I shivered in a sandbag crow's-nest atop a tall building near the Thames. It was one of the many fire-observation posts. There was an old gun barrel mounted above a round table marked off like a compass. A stick of incendiaries bounced off rooftops about three miles away. The observer took a sight on a point where the first one fell, swung his gun-sight along the line of bombs, and took another reading at the end of the line of fire. Then he picked up his telephone and shouted above the half gale that was blowing up there, 'Stick of incendiaries – between 190 and 220 – about three miles away.' Five minutes later a German bomber came boring down the river. We could see his exhaust trail like a pale ribbon stretched straight across the sky. Half a mile downstream there were two eruptions and then a third, close together. The first two looked as though some giant had thrown a huge basket of flaming golden oranges high in the air. The third was just a balloon of fire enclosed in black smoke above the house-tops. The observer didn't bother with his gun sight and indicator for that one. Just reached for his night glasses, took one quick look, picked up his telephone, and said, 'Two high explosives and one oil bomb,' and named the street where they had fallen.

There was a small fire going off to our left. Suddenly sparks showered up from it as though someone had punched the middle of a huge camp-fire with a tree trunk. Again the gun sight swung around, the bearing was read, and the report went down the telephone lines: 'There is something in high explosives on that fire at 59.'

There was peace and quiet inside for twenty minutes. Then a shower of incendiaries came down far in the distance. They didn't fall in a line. It looked like flashes from an electric train on a wet night, only the engineer was drunk and driving his train in circles through the streets. One sight at the middle of the flashes and our observer reported laconically, 'Breadbasket at 90 – covers a couple of miles.' Half an hour later a string of fire bombs fell right beside the Thames. Their white glare was reflected in the black, lazy water near the banks and faded out in midstream where the moon cut a golden swathe broken only by the arches of famous bridges.

We could see little men shovelling those fire bombs into the river. One burned for a few minutes like a beacon right in the middle of a bridge. Finally those white flames all went out. No one bothers about the white light, it's only when it turns yellow that a real fire has started.

I must have seen well over a hundred fire bombs come down and only three small fires were started. The incendiaries aren't so bad if there is someone there to deal with them, but those oil bombs present more difficulties.

As I watched those white fires flame up and die down, watched the yellow blazes grow dull and disappear, I thought, what a puny effort is this to burn a great city.

THE HOME FRONT: A CHILD'S VIEW, SHEFFIELD, Autumn 1940

George Macbeth

In the morning, I would walk along Clarkehouse Road with my eyes glued to the pavement for shrapnel. It became the fashion to make a collection of this, and there were few days when I came home without a pocketful of jagged, rusting bits, like the unintelligible pieces from a scattered jigsaw of pain and violence.

Of course we didn't see them as this at the time. They were simply free toys from the sky, as available and interesting as the horse chestnuts in the Botanical Gardens, or the nippled acorns in Melbourne Avenue.

It must have been about this time that the British Restaurants were opening, with their austerity jam roll and meat balls; and our own meals were beginning to rely rather more on rissoles and home-made apple sponge. But my mother was always a good manager, and I have no sense of any sudden period of shortage or of going hungry.

Sweets were the great loss. There was no longer an everlasting, teeth-spoiling fountain of sherbet and liquorice, or of Boy Blue cream whirls, or of Cadbury's Caramello. Sweets were hard to come by, and then limited to a fixed ration.

One of the worst casualties was chocolate. The traditional division into milk and plain disappeared, and an awful intervening variety known as Ration Chocolate was born, issued in semi-transparent grease-proof wrappers, and about as appetizing as cardboard. In spite of a lifelong sweet tooth, I could never eat it.

MEDICAL EXPERIMENTS AT DACHAU, BAVARIA, GERMANY, 1941–5

Franz Blaha

Dachau was one of the principal Nazi concentration camps for the imprisonment – and frequently death – of 'undesirables', among them Jews, Slavs, political opponents and gypsies.

I, Franz Blaha, being duly sworn, depose and state as follows:

I was sent as a prisoner to the Dachau Concentration Camp in April 1941, and remained there until the liberation of the camp in April 1945. Until July 1941 I worked in a Punishment Company. After that I was sent to the hospital and subjected to the experiments in typhoid being conducted by Dr Mürmelstadt. After that I was to be made the subject of an experimental operation, and only succeeded in avoiding this by admitting that I was a physician. If this had been known before I would have suffered, because intellectuals were treated very harshly in the Punishment Company. In October 1941 I was sent to work in the herb plantation, and later in the laboratory for processing herbs. In June 1942, I was taken into the hospital as a surgeon. Shortly afterwards I was directed to conduct a stomach operation on twenty healthy prisoners. Because I would not do this I was put in the autopsy room, where I stayed until April 1945. While there I performed approximately 7,000 autopsies. In all, 12,000 autopsies were performed under my direction.

From mid-1941 to the end of 1942 some 500 operations on healthy prisoners were performed. These were for the instruction of the SS medical students and doctors and included operations on the stomach, gall bladder, spleen and throat. These were performed by students and doctors of only two years' training, although they were very dangerous and difficult. Ordinarily they would not have been done except by surgeons with at least four years' surgical practice. Many prisoners died on the operating table and many others from later complications. I performed autopsies on all these bodies. The doctors who supervised these operations were Lang, Mürmelstadt, Wolter, Ramsauer and Kahr. *Standartenführer* Dr Lolling frequently witnessed these operations.

During my time at Dachau I was familiar with many kinds of medical experiments carried on there with human victims. These persons were never volunteers but were forced to submit to such acts. Malaria experiments on about 1,200 people were conducted by Dr Klaus Schilling between 1941 and 1945. Schilling was personally asked by Himmler to conduct these experiments. The victims were either bitten by mosquitoes or given injections of malaria sporozoites taken from mosquitoes. Different kinds of treatment were applied, including quinine, pyrifer, neosalvarsan, antipyrin, pyramidon and a drug called 2516 Behring. I performed autopsies on bodies of people who died from these malaria experiments. Thirty to forty died from the malaria itself. Three to four hundred died later from diseases which proved fatal because of the physical condition resulting from the malaria attacks. In addition there were deaths resulting from poisoning due to overdoses of neosalvarsan and pyramidon. Dr Schilling was present at the time of my autopsies on the bodies of his patients.

In 1942 and 1943 experiments on human beings were conducted by Dr Sigismund Rascher to determine the effects of changing air pressure. As many as twenty-five persons were put at one time into a specially constructed van in which pressure could be increased or decreased as required. The purpose was to find out the effects of high altitude and of rapid parachute descents on human beings. Through a window in the van I have seen the people lying on the floor of the van. Most of the prisoners who were made use of died as a result of these experiments, from internal haemorrhages of the lungs or brain. The rest coughed blood when taken out. It was my job to take the bodies out and to send the internal organs to Munich for study as soon as they were found to be dead. About 400 to 500 prisoners were experimented on. Those not dead were sent to invalid blocks and liquidated shortly afterwards. Only a few escaped.

Rascher also conducted experiments on the effect of cold water on human beings. This was done to find a way for reviving aviators who had fallen into the ocean. The subject was placed in ice-cold water and kept there until he was unconscious. Blood was taken from his neck and tested each time his body temperature dropped one degree. This drop was determined by a rectal thermometer. Urine was also periodically tested. Some men lasted as long as twenty-four to thirty-six hours. The lowest body temperature reached was nineteen degrees C., but most men died at twenty-five degrees C., or twenty-six degrees C. When the men were removed from the ice water attempts were made to revive them by artificial warmth from the sun, from hot water, from electro-therapy or by animal warmth. For this last experiment prostitutes were used and the body of the unconscious man was placed between the bodies of two women. Himmler was present at one such experiment. I could see him from one of the windows in the street between the blocks. I have personally been present at some of the cold-water experiments when Rascher was absent, and I have seen notes and diagrams on them in Rascher's laboratory. About 300 persons were used in these experiments. The majority died. Of those who lived many became mentally deranged. Those not killed were sent to invalid blocks and were killed, just as were the victims of the air-pressure experiments. I only know two who survived – a Jugoslav and a Pole, both of whom have become mental cases.

Liver-puncture experiments were performed by Dr Brachtl on healthy people, and on people who had diseases of the stomach and gall bladder. For this purpose a needle was jabbed into the liver of a person and a small piece of liver was extracted. No anaesthetic was used. The experiment is very painful and often had serious results, as the stomach or large blood vessels were often punctured and haemorrhage resulted. Many persons died of these tests, for which Polish, Russian, Czech and German prisoners were employed. Altogether these experiments were conducted on about 175 people.

Phlegmone experiments were conducted by Dr Schütz, Dr Babor, Dr Kieselwetter and Professor Lauer. Forty healthy men were used at a time, of whom twenty were given intra-muscular, and twenty intravenous, injections of pus from diseased persons. All treatment was forbidden for three days, by which time serious inflammation and in many cases general blood poisoning had occurred. Then each group was divided again into groups of ten. Half were given chemical treatment with liquid and special pills every ten minutes for twenty-four hours. The rest were treated with sulphonamide and surgery. In some cases all of the limbs were amputated. My autopsy also showed that the chemical treatment had been harmful and had even caused perforations of the stomach wall. For these experiments Polish, Czech and Dutch priests were ordinarily used. Pain was intense in such experiments. Most of the 600 to 800 persons who were used finally died. Most of the others became permanent invalids and were later killed.

In the autumn of 1944 there were sixty to eighty persons who were subjected to salt-water experiments. They were locked in a room and for five days were given nothing to swallow but salt water. During this time their urine, blood and excrement were tested. None of these prisoners died, possibly because they received smuggled food from other prisoners. Hungarians and gypsies were used for these experiments.

It was common practice to remove the skin from dead prisoners. I was commanded to do this on many occasions. Dr Rascher and Dr Wolter in particular asked for this human skin from human backs and chests. It was chemically treated and placed in the sun to dry. After that it was cut into various sizes for use as saddles, riding breeches, gloves, house slippers and ladies' handbags. Tattooed skin was especially valued by SS men. Russians, Poles and other inmates were used in this way, but it was forbidden to cut out the skin of a German. This skin had to be from healthy prisoners and free from defects. Sometimes we did not have enough bodies with good skin and Rascher would say, 'All right, you will get the bodies.' The next day we would receive twenty or thirty bodies of young people. They would have been shot in the neck or struck on the head so that the skin would be uninjured. Also we frequently got requests for the skulls or skeletons of prisoners. In those cases we boiled the skull or the body. Then the soft parts were removed and the bones were bleached and dried and reassembled. In the case of skulls it was important to have a good set of teeth. When we got an order for skulls from Oranienburg the SS men would say, 'We will try to get you some with good teeth.' So it was dangerous to have a good skin or good teeth.

THE GERMAN AMBASSADOR HANDS OVER THE DECLARATION OF WAR ON THE USSR, MOSCOW, 22 June 1941

Ivan Krylov

At six o'clock in the morning of 22 June 1941, the German Ambassador, Count von Schulenburg, handed Molotov a Note of the German Government declaring war on the Soviet Union.

Both Count von Schulenburg and Molotov were pale with emotion. The Commissar for Foreign Affairs took the Note wordlessly, spat on it and then tore it up. He rang for his secretary Poskrebichev.

'Show this gentleman out through the back door.'

AN ENCOUNTER WITH RUSSIAN PRISONERS, EASTERN FRONT, July 1941

Benno Zieser, Wehrmacht

We suddenly saw a broad, earth-brown crocodile slowly shuffling down the road towards us. From it came a subdued hum, like that from a beehive. Prisoners of war. Russians, six deep. We couldn't see the end of the column. As they drew near the terrible stench which met us made us quite sick; it was like the biting stench of the lion house and the filthy odour of the monkey house at the same time.

But these were not animals, they were men. We made haste out of the way of the foul cloud which surrounded them, then what we saw transfixed us where we stood and we forgot our nausea. Were these really human beings, these grey-brown figures, these shadows lurching towards us, stumbling and staggering, moving shapes at their last gasp, creatures which only some last flicker of the will to live enabled to obey the order to march? All the misery in the world seemed to be concentrated here. There was also that gruesome barrage of shouts and wails, groans, lamentations and curses which combined with the cutting orders of the guards into a hideous accompaniment.

We saw one man shuffle aside from the ranks, then a rifle butt crash between his shoulder-blades and drive him gasping back into place. Another with a head wound lost in bloodstained bandages ran a few paces out with gestures almost ludicrous in their persuasiveness to beg one of the nearby local inhabitants for a scrap of bread. Then a leather thong fetched him a savage lash round his shoulders and yanked him, too, back into place. Another, a lanky fellow, a regular giant, stepped aside to pump ship, and when he too was forced back he could not stop nature and it all drenched the man in front, but he never even turned his head.

Stray dogs were legion, among them were the most unbelievable mongrels; the only thing they were all alike in was that they were thin. The Sheikh said one could have learned to play the harp on their ribs. That was no hindrance to the prisoners. They were hungry, so why not eat roast dog? They were always trying to catch the scary beasts. They would also beg us with gestures and *bow-wows* and *bang-bangs* to kill a dog for them. There it was, shoot it! And we almost always did; it was a bit of sport anyway, and at the same time it delighted those human skeletons. Besides, those wild dogs were a regular pest.

When we brought one down, there followed a performance that could make a man puke. Yelling like mad, the Russkies would fall on the animal and tear it in pieces with their bare hands, even before it was quite dead. The pluck they would stuff their pockets with, like tobacco, whenever they got hold of any of that – it made a sort of iron ration. Then they would light a fire, skewer shreds of the dog's meat on sticks and roast it. There were always fights over the bigger bits. The burnt flesh stank frightfully; there was almost no fat in it.

But they did not have roast dog every day. Behind the huts there was a big midden, a regular mountain of stinking waste, and if we did not look out they would poke about in it and eat such things as decaying onions, the mere sight of which was enough to turn you up. If one of us came near they would scatter like dung-flies. I once found one roasting dried pig's dung.

SIEGE OF LENINGRAD, August 1941–July 1942

Alexander Werth

For almost a year Leningrad was completely encircled by the *Wehrmacht* and a Finnish army under Mannerheim. It is estimated that a million Leningraders lost their lives, mostly from starvation.

One of the greatest examples of how Leningrad fought for its life was when in the spring [of 1942] 300,000 or 400,000 people came out into the street with shovels – people who were scarcely standing on their feet, so weak and hungry were they – and proceeded to clean up the town. All winter the drains and sewers had been out of action; there was a great danger of epidemics spreading with the coming of the warm weather. And in a few days these 300,000 or 400,000 weak, hungry people – many of them were very old people who had never handled a shovel in their lives – had shovelled away and dumped into the river and the canals all those mountains of snow and filth which, had they remained there, would have poisoned Leningrad. And it was a joy to see the city streets a few days later all clean and tidy. It had a great moral effect . . .

It was our people and not the soldiers who built the fortifications of Leningrad. If you added up all the antitank trenches outside Leningrad, made by the hands of our civilians, they would add up to as much as the entire Moscow–Volga canal. During the three black months of 1941, 400,000 people were working in three shifts, morning, noon and night, digging and digging. I remember going down to Luga during the worst days, when the Germans were rapidly advancing on Luga. I remember there a young girl who was carrying away earth inside her apron. It made no sense. I asked her what she was doing that for. She burst into tears, and said she was trying to do at least that – it wasn't much, but her hands simply couldn't hold a shovel any longer. And, as I looked at her hands, I saw that they were a mass of black and bloody bruises. Somebody else had shovelled the earth on to her apron while she knelt down, holding the corners of the apron with the fingers of her bruised, bloodstained hands. For three months our civilians worked on these fortifications. They were allowed one day off in six weeks. They never took their days off. There was an eight-hour working day, but nobody took any notice of it. They were determined to stop the Germans. And they went on working under shellfire, under machine-gun fire and the bombs of the Stukas.

THE RUSSIAN WINTER ARRIVES, 13 November 1941

Heinrich Haape, Wehrmacht

Like another previous invader of Russia, Napoleon Bonaparte, Hitler found that winter would undo his plans. Heinrich Haape was a medical officer with the *Wehrmacht*.

On 13 November we awoke and shivered. An icy blast from the north-east knifed across the snowy countryside. The sky was cloudless and dark blue, but the sun seemed to have lost its strength and instead of becoming warmer towards noon as on previous days, the thermometer kept falling and by sundown had reached minus twelve degrees Centigrade.

The soldiers, who up to now had not regarded the light frosts too seriously, began to take notice. One man who had been walking outside for only a short distance without his woollen *Kopfschutzer* or 'head-saver' came into the sick bay. Both ears were white and frozen stiff.

It was our first case of frost-bite.

We gently massaged the man's ears, taking care not to break the skin, and they thawed out. We powdered them and covered them with cotton-wool and made a suitable head-dressing. Perhaps we had managed to save the whole of the ears; we should have to wait and see.

This minor case of frost-bite was a serious warning. The icy winds from Siberia – the breath of death – were blowing across the steppes; winds from where all life froze, from the Arctic ice-cap itself. Things would be serious if we could not house ourselves in prepared positions and buildings, and I stopped to think of the armies marching on Moscow across open country at this very moment. All that those men had received so far were their woollen *Kopfschutzers*; the winter clothing had still not arrived. What was happening to the men's feet, for the ordinary army boot retained very little warmth?

Then, too, the thermometer showed only twelve degrees below zero. Temperatures would drop to minus twenty-four degrees – minus thirty-six degrees – minus forty-eight degrees – perhaps even lower. It was beyond comprehension – a temperature four times colder than a deep freezer. To attempt any movement without warm clothing in those conditions would be sheer suicide. Surely the older generals had been right when, after the battle of Vyasma and Bryansk, they had counselled: 'Dig in for the winter.' Some of them were men with experience of Russia during the 1914–1918 War. At the most they had said, continue the war through the winter only with a few thoroughly-equipped and well-provisioned divisions. Make the big push in the spring.

If only the battle for Moscow had started fourteen days earlier, the city would now have been in our hands. Or even if the rains had held off for fourteen days. If – if – if. If Hitler had started 'Barbarossa' six weeks earlier as originally planned; if he had left Mussolini on his own in the Balkans and had attacked Russia in May; if we had continued our sweeping advance instead of stopping at the Schutsche Lake; if Hitler had sent us winter clothing. Yes, if, if, if – but now it was too late.

Those Arctic blasts that had taken us by surprise in our protected positions had scythed through our attacking troops. In a couple of days there were 100,000 casualties from frost-bite alone; 100,000 first-class, experienced soldiers fell out because the cold had surprised them.

A couple of days later our winter clothing arrived. There was just enough for each company to be issued with four heavy fur-lined greatcoats and four pairs of felt-lined boots. Four sets of winter clothing for each company! Sixteen greatcoats and sixteen pairs of winter boots to be shared among a battalion of 800 men! And the meagre issue coincided with a sudden drop in the temperature to minus twenty-two degrees.

Reports reached us that the issue of winter clothing to the troops actually advancing on Moscow had been on no more generous scale. More and more reports were being sent to Corps and Army Headquarters recommending that the attack on Moscow by a summer-clad army be abandoned and that winter positions be prepared. Some of these reports were forwarded by Central Army Group to the Führer's Headquarters, but no reply or acknowledgement ever came. The order persisted: 'Attack!' And our soldiers attacked.

The attacks of the *Wehrmacht* brought them to within five miles of Moscow's city limits during the first week of December; a Red Army counter-attack on 6 December began to drive the Germans back, and they would never come so close to the prize again.

PEARL HARBOR, HAWAII, 7 December 1941

John Garcia

I was sixteen years old, employed as a pipe fitter apprentice at Pearl Harbor Navy Yard. On 7 December 1941, oh, around 8.00 a.m., my grandmother woke me. She informed me that the Japanese were bombing Pearl Harbor. I said, 'They're just practising.' She said, no, it was real and the announcer is requesting that all Pearl Harbor workers report to work. I went out on the porch and I could see the anti-aircraft fire up in the sky. I just said, 'Oh boy.'

I was four miles away. I got out on my motor-cycle and it took me five, ten minutes to get there. It was a mess.

I was working on the USS *Shaw*. It was on a floating dry dock. It was in flames. I started to go down into the pipe fitter's shop to get my toolbox when another wave of Japanese came in. I got under a set of concrete steps at the dry dock where the battleship *Pennsylvania* was. An officer came by and asked me to go into the *Pennsylvania* and try to get the fires out. A bomb had penetrated the marine deck, and that was three decks below. Under that was the magazines: ammunition, powder, shells. I said, 'There ain't no way I'm gonna go down there.' It could blow up any minute. I was young and sixteen, not stupid, not at sixty-two cents an hour. (Laughs.)

A week later, they brought me before a navy court. It was determined that I was not service personnel and could not be ordered. There was no martial law at the time. Because I was sixteen and had gone into the water, the whole thing was dropped.

I was asked by some other officer to go into the water and get sailors out that had been blown off the ships. Some were unconscious, some were dead. So I spent the rest of the day swimming inside the harbour, along with some other Hawaiians. I brought out I don't know how many bodies and how many were alive and how many dead. Another man would put them into ambulances and they'd be gone. We worked all day at that . . .

The following morning, I went with my tools to the *West Virginia*. It had turned turtle, totally upside down. We found a number of men inside. The *Arizona* was a total washout. Also the *Utah*. There were men in there, too. We spent about a month cutting the superstructure of the *West Virginia*, tilting it back on its hull. About 300 men we cut out of there were still alive by the eighteenth day. It took two weeks to get all the fires out. We worked around the clock for three days. There was so much excitement and confusion. Some of our sailors were shooting five-inch guns at the Japanese planes. You just cannot down a plane with a five-inch shell. They were landing in Honolulu, the unexploded naval shells. They have a ten-mile range. They hurt and killed a lot of people in the city.

When I came back after the third day, they told me that a shell had hit the house of my girl. We had been going together for, oh, about three years. Her house was a few blocks from my place. At the time, they said it was a Japanese bomb. Later we learned it was an American shell. She was killed. She was preparing for church at the time.

The surprise attack by Japan on the US Pacific Fleet sank ten ships and damaged many more. The action provoked America into joining the Second World War.

BATTLE OF MIDWAY, HAWAIIAN ISLANDS, THE PACIFIC, 7 June 1942

Captain Mitsuo Fuchida and Captain Masatake Okumiya, Imperial Japanese Navy

The naval struggle between Japan and the USA in the Pacific culminated in the battle of Midway. Virtually all the fighting was done by carrier-based aircraft and the engagement cost the Americans the carrier Yorktown and 147 planes; the Japanese lost four fast carriers and a similar number of aircraft. Midway completely changed the balance of power in the Pacific.

As our fighters ran out of ammunition during the fierce battle they returned to the carriers for replenishment, but few ran low on fuel. Service crews cheered the returning pilots, patted them on the shoulder, and shouted words of encouragement. As soon as a plane was ready again the pilot nodded, pushed forward the throttle, and roared back into the sky. This scene was repeated time and again as the desperate air struggle continued.

Preparations for a counter-strike against the enemy had continued on board our four carriers throughout the enemy torpedo attacks. One after another, planes were hoisted from the hangar and quickly arranged on the flight deck. There was no time to lose.

At 10.20 Admiral Nagumo gave the order to launch when ready. On *Akagi*'s flight deck all planes were in position with engines warming up. The big ship began turning into the wind. Within five minutes all her planes would be launched.

Five minutes! Who would have dreamed that the tide of battle would shift completely in that brief interval of time?

Visibility was good. Clouds were gathering at about 3,000 metres, however, and though there were occasional breaks, they afforded good concealment for approaching enemy planes. At 10.24 the order to start launching came from the bridge by voice-tube. The Air Officer flapped a white flag, and the first Zero fighter gathered speed and whizzed off the deck. At that instant a look-out screamed: 'Hell-Divers!' I looked up to see three black enemy planes plummeting towards our ship. Some of our machine-guns managed to fire a few frantic bursts at them, but it was too late. The plump silhouettes of the American Dauntless dive-bombers quickly grew larger, and then a number of black objects suddenly floated eerily from their wings. Bombs! Down they came straight towards me! I fell intuitively to the deck and crawled behind a command post mantelet.

The terrifying scream of the dive-bombers reached me first, followed by the crashing explosion of a direct hit. There was a blinding flash and then a second explosion, much louder than the first. I was shaken by a weird blast of warm air. There was still another shock, but less severe, apparently a near-miss. Then followed a startling quiet as the barking of guns suddenly ceased. I got up and looked at the sky. The enemy planes were already gone from sight.

The attackers had got in unimpeded because our fighters, which had engaged the preceding wave of torpedo planes only a few moments earlier, had not yet had time to regain altitude. Consequently, it may be said that the American dive-bombers' success was made possible by the earlier martyrdom of their torpedo planes. Also, our carriers had no time to evade because clouds hid the enemy's approach until he dived down to the attack. We had been caught flatfooted in the most vulnerable condition possible – decks loaded with planes armed and fuelled for an attack.

Looking about, I was horrified at the destruction that had been wrought in a matter of seconds. There was a huge hole in the flight deck just behind the amidship elevator. The elevator itself, twisted like molten glass, was dropping into the hangar. Deck plates reeled upwards in grotesque configurations, planes stood tail up, belching livid flame and jetblack smoke. Reluctant tears streamed down my cheeks as I watched the fires spread, and I was terrified at the prospect of induced explosions which would surely doom the ship. I heard Masuda yelling, 'Inside! Get inside! Everybody who isn't working! Get inside!'

Unable to help, I staggered down a ladder and into the ready room. It was already jammed with badly burned victims from the hangar deck. A new explosion was followed quickly by several more, each causing the bridge structure to tremble. Smoke from the burning hangar gushed through passageways and into the bridge and ready room, forcing us to seek other refuge. Climbing back to the bridge, I could see that *Kaga* and *Soryu* had also been hit and were giving off heavy columns of black smoke. The scene was horrible to behold.

Akagi had taken two direct hits, one on the after rim of the amidship elevator, the other on the rear guard on the port side of the flight deck. Normally, neither would have been fatal to the giant carrier, but induced explosions of fuel and munitions devastated whole sections of the ship, shaking the bridge and filling the air with deadly splinters. As fire spread among the planes lined up wing to wing on the after flight deck, their torpedoes began to explode, making it impossible to bring the fires under control. The entire hangar area was a blazing inferno, and the flames moved swiftly towards the bridge.

Because of the spreading fire, our general loss of combat efficiency, and especially the severance of external communication facilities, Nagumo's Chief of Staff, Rear-Admiral Kusaka, urged that the flag be transferred at once to light cruiser *Nagara*. Admiral Nagumo gave only a half-hearted nod, but Kusaka patiently continued his entreaty: 'Sir, most of our ships are still intact. You must command them.'

The situation demanded immediate action, but Admiral Nagumo was reluctant to leave his beloved flagship. Most of all he was loath to leave behind the officers and men of *Akagi*, with whom he had shared every joy and sorrow of war. With tears in his eyes, Captain Aoki spoke up: 'Admiral, I will take care of the ship. Please, we all implore you, shift your flag to *Nagara* and resume command of the Force.'

At this moment Lieutenant-Commander Nishibayashi, the Flag Secretary, came up and reported to Kusaka: 'All passages below are on fire, sir. The only means of escape is by rope from the forward window of the bridge down to the deck, then by the outboard passage to the anchor deck. *Nagara*'s boat will come alongside the anchor deck port, and you can reach it by rope ladder.'

Kusaka made a final plea to Admiral Nagumo to leave the doomed ship. At last convinced that there was no possibility of maintaining command from *Akagi*, Nagumo bade the Captain good-bye and climbed from the bridge window with the aid of Nishibayashi. The Chief of Staff and other staff and headquarters officers followed. The time was 10.46.

On the bridge there remained only Captain Aoki, his Navigator, the Air Officer, a few ratings, and myself. Aoki was trying desperately to get in touch with the engine room. The Chief Navigator was struggling to see if anything could be done to regain rudder control. The others were gathered on the anchor deck fighting the raging fire as best they could. But the unchecked flames were already licking at the bridge.

JEWS ARE ROUNDED UP, AMSTERDAM, 19 November 1942

Anne Frank

In pursuit of the 'final solution' – the mass extermination of the Jews – the Nazis deported some 500,000 West European Jews to the SS death camps at Auschwitz, Belsen, Treblinka, Sobibor and Majdanek, including 104,000 from the Netherlands.

Thursday, 19 November 1942
Apart from that, all goes well. Dussel has told us a lot about the outside world, which we have missed for so long now. He had very sad news. Countless friends and acquaintances have gone to a terrible fate. Evening after evening the green and grey army lorries trundle past. The Germans ring at every front door to enquire if there are any Jews living in the house. If there are, then the whole family has to go at once. If they don't find any, they go on to the next house. No one has a chance of evading them unless one goes into hiding. Often they go round with lists, and only ring when they know they can get a good haul. Sometimes they let them off

for cash – so much per head. It seems like the slave hunts of olden times. But it's certainly no joke; it's much too tragic for that. In the evenings, when it's dark, I often see rows of good, innocent people accompanied by crying children, walking on and on, in charge of a couple of these chaps, bullied and knocked about until they almost drop. No onc is spared – old people, babies, expectant mothers, the sick – each and all join in the march of death.

How fortunate we are here, so well cared for and undisturbed. We wouldn't have to worry about all this misery were it not that we are so anxious about all those dear to us whom we can no longer help.

I feel wicked sleeping in a warm bed, while my dearest friends have been knocked down or have fallen into a gutter somewhere out in the cold night. I get frightened when I think of close friends who have now been delivered into the hands of the cruellest brutes that walk the earth. And all because they are Jews!

Anne Frank was later taken to Belsen herself, where she died in 1945.

EL ALAMEIN, EGYPT, October–November 1942

Erwin Rommel

The battle of El Alamein was the turning point of the war in North Africa, a decisive victory for General Montgomery's British 8th Army over Erwin Rommel's Afrika Korps.

The supply situation was now approaching disaster. The tanker *Proserpina*, which we had hoped would bring some relief in the petrol situation, had been bombed and sunk outside Tobruk. There was only enough petrol left to keep supply traffic going between Tripoli and the front for another two or three days, and that without counting the needs of the motorized forces, which had to be met out of the same stocks. What we should really have done now was to assemble all our motorized units in the north in order to fling the British back to the main defence line in a concentrated and planned counter-attack. But we had not the petrol to do it. So we were compelled to allow the armoured formations in the northern part of our line to assault the British salient piecemeal.

Since the enemy was operating with astonishing hesitancy and caution, a concentrated attack by the whole of our armour could have been successful, although such an assembly of armour would of course have been met by the heaviest possible British artillery fire and air bombardment. However, we could have made the action more fluid by withdrawing a few miles to the west and could then have attacked the British in an all-out charge and defeated them in open country. The British artillery and air force could not easily have intervened with their usual weight in a tank battle of this kind, for their own forces would have been endangered.

But a decision to take forces from the southern front was unthinkable with the petrol situation so bad. Not only could we not have kept a mobile battle going for more than a day or two, but our armour could never have returned to the south if the British had attacked there. I did, however, decide to bring the whole of the 21st Panzer Division up north, although I fully realized that the petrol shortage would not allow it to return. In addition, since it was now obvious that the enemy would make his main effort in the north during the next few days and try for a decision there, half the Army artillery was drawn off from the southern front. At the same time I reported to the Führer's HQ that we would lose the battle unless there was an immediate improvement in the supply situation. Judging by previous experience, there was very little hope of this happening.

Relays of British bombers continued their attack throughout the night of the 26th. At about 02.00 hours a furious British barrage by guns of every calibre suddenly began in the northern sector. Soon it was impossible to distinguish between gun-fire and exploding shells and the sky grew bright with the glare of muzzle-flashes and shell-bursts. Continuous bombing attacks seriously delayed the approach march of the 21st Panzer Division and a third of the Ariete. By dawn the 90th Light Division and the Trieste had taken up position round the southern side of Sidi Abd el Rahman.

That morning [27 October] I gave orders to all formations to pin down the British assault forces during their approach by all-out fire from every gun they could bring to bear.

The tactics which the British were using followed from their apparently inexhaustible stocks of ammunition. Their new tank, the General Sherman, which came into action for the first time during this battle, showed itself to be far superior to any of ours.

Attacks against our line were preceded by extremely heavy artillery barrages lasting for several hours. The attacking infantry then pushed forward behind a curtain of fire and artificial fog, clearing mines and removing obstacles. Where a difficult patch was struck they frequently switched the direction of their attack under cover of smoke. Once the infantry had cleared lanes in the minefields, heavy tanks moved forward, closely followed by infantry. Particular skill was shown in carrying out this manoeuvre at night and a great deal of hard training must have been done before the offensive.

In contact engagements the heavily gunned British tanks approached to a range of between 2,000 and 2,700 yards and then opened concentrated fire on our anti-tank and anti-aircraft guns and tanks, which were unable to penetrate the British armour at that range. The enormous quantities of ammunition which the enemy tanks used – sometimes they fired over 30 rounds at one target – were constantly replenished by armoured ammunition carriers. The British artillery fire was directed by observers who accompanied the attack in tanks.

In the early hours of 27 October, the British attacked again towards the south-west at their old break-in point south of Hill 28. At about 10 a.m. I went off to Telegraph Track. Two enemy bomber formations, each of 18 aircraft, dropped their bombs inside ten minutes into our defence positions. The whole front continued to lie under a devastating British barrage.

Local counter-attacks were due to be launched that afternoon by the 90th Light Division on Hill 28 and by the 15th and 21st Panzer Divisions, the Littorio and a part of the Ariete, against the British positions between minefields L and I.

At 14.30 hours I drove to Telegraph Track again, accompanied by Major Ziegler. Three times within a quarter of an hour units of the 90th Light Division, which had deployed and were standing in the open in preparation for the attack, were bombed by formations of eighteen aircraft. At 15.00 hours our dive-bombers swooped down on the British lines. Every artillery and anti-aircraft gun which we had in the northern sector concentrated a violent fire on the point of the intended attack. Then the armour moved forward. A murderous British fire struck into our ranks and our attack was soon brought to a halt by an immensely powerful anti-tank defence, mainly from dug-in anti-tank guns and a large number of tanks. We suffered considerable losses and were obliged to withdraw. There is, in general, little chance of success in a tank attack over country where the enemy has been able to take up defensive positions; but there was nothing else we could do. The 90th Light Division's attack was also broken up by heavy British artillery fire and a hail of bombs from British aircraft. A report from the division that they had taken Hill 28 unfortunately turned out to be untrue.

That evening further strong detachments of the Panzer divisions had to be committed in the front to close the gaps. Several of the 90th Light Division's units also went into the line. Only 70 tons of petrol had been flown across by the *Luftwaffe* that day, with the result that the army could only refuel for a short distance, for there was no knowing when petrol would arrive in any quantity and how long the divisions would have to get along with the few tons we could issue to them. The watchword 'as little movement as possible' applied more than ever.

In the evening we again sent SOSs to Rome and the Führer's HQ. But there was now no longer any hope of an improvement in the situation. It was obvious that from now on the British would destroy us bit by bit, since we were virtually unable to move on the battlefield. As yet, Montgomery had only thrown half his striking force into the battle.

The end at El Alamein came on 2 November.

THE END AT STALINGRAD, RUSSIA, January 1943

Anon. German Soldiers

The battle for Stalingrad began on 15 September 1942 and was fought with the utmost ferocity, street by street, house by house, in what the Germans called the *Rattenkrieg* ('rat war'). The 270,000-strong German Sixth Army under von Paulus became completely surrounded by the Red Army, but Hitler refused to allow von Paulus to withdraw and ordered him to 'hedgehog' himself in. By the year's end the situation inside Stalingrad had deteriorated rapidly; rations had fallen below subsistence level, ammunition supplies had dwindled and cold and disease claimed thousands of *Wehrmacht* lives. On 10 January 1943 the Russians began a final assault on the doomed army.

Last letters home:

To return to the present position. Of the division there are only sixty-nine men still fit for action. Bleyer is still alive, and Hartlieb as well. Little Degen has lost both arms; I expect he will soon be in Germany. Life is finished for him, too. Get him to tell you the details which you people think worth knowing. D. has given up hope. I should like to know what he thinks of the situation and its consequences. All we have left are two machine-guns and 400 rounds. And then a mortar and ten bombs. Except for that all we have are hunger and fatigue

For a long time to come, perhaps for ever, this is to be my last letter. A comrade who has to go to the airfield is taking it along with him, as the last machine to leave the pocket is taking off tomorrow morning. The situation has become quite untenable. The Russians are only two miles from the last spot from which aircraft can operate, and when that's gone not even a mouse will get out, to say nothing of me. Admittedly several hundred thousand others won't escape either, but it's precious little consolation to share one's own destruction with other men.

On 24 January the Führer sent the following communiqué to the Sixth Army, Stalingrad:

Surrender is forbidden. 6th Army will hold their positions to the last man and the last round and by their heroic endurance will make an unforgettable contribution towards the establishment of a defensive front and the salvation of the Western world.

A week later, at five-forty-five, 31 January, the 6th Army HQ radio announced:

The Russians stand at the door of our bunker. We are destroying our equipment.

This station will no longer transmit.

Immediately after this transmission the Sixth Army laid down its arms and surrendered. Alongside von Paulus there surrendered 23 generals, 2,000 officers and 130,000 other ranks. Over 100,000 Germans were killed and wounded in the battle; many of the wounded were buried alive by the Red Army who dynamited their underground shelters.

THE DAMBUSTERS RAID, RUHR VALLEY, 16 May 1943

Guy Gibson, RAF

The famous 'bouncing bomb' attack on the Ruhr Valley dams by RAF 617 Squadron was intended to disrupt production in Germany's industrial heartland. Nineteen Lancaster bombers led by Wing Commander Guy Gibson took part in the raid, eight of which were lost. Two dams, the Möhne and Eder, were destroyed, bringing widespread flooding; a third dam, the Sorpe, survived the bomb that hit it. Here Guy Gibson describes the attack on the Möhne dam. He was killed in action a year later.

Down below, the Möhne Lake was silent and black and deep, and I spoke to my crew.

'Well boys, I suppose we had better start the ball rolling.' This with no enthusiasm whatsoever. 'Hello, all Cooler aircraft. I am going to attack. Stand by to come in to attack in your order when I tell you.'

Then to Hoppy: 'Hello, "M Mother". Stand by to take over if anything happens.'

Hoppy's clear and casual voice came back. 'OK, Leader. Good luck.'

Then the boys dispersed to the pre-arranged hiding-spots in the hills, so that they should not be seen either from the ground or from the air, and we began to get into position for our approach. We circled wide and came around down moon, over the high hills at the eastern end of the lake. On straightening up we began to dive towards the flat, ominous water two miles away. Over the front turret was the dam silhouetted against the haze of the Ruhr Valley. We could see the towers. We could see the sluices. We could see everything. Spam, the bomb-aimer, said, 'Good show. This is wizard.' He had been a bit worried, as all bomb-aimers are, in case they cannot see their aiming points, but as we came in over the tall fir trees his voice came up again rather quickly. 'You're going to hit them. You're going to hit those trees.'

'That's all right, Spam. I'm just getting my height.'

To Terry: 'Check height, Terry.'

To Pulford: 'Speed control, Flight-Engineer.'

To Trevor: 'All guns ready, gunners.'

To Spam: 'Coming up, Spam.'

Terry turned on the spotlights and began giving directions – 'Down – down – down. Steady – steady.' We were then exactly sixty feet.

Pulford began working the speed; first he put on a little flap to slow us down, then he opened the throttles to get the air-speed indicator exactly against the red mark. Spam began lining up his sights against the towers. He had turned the fusing switch to the 'ON' position. I began flying.

The gunners had seen us coming. They could see us coming with our spotlights on for over two miles away. Now they opened up and the tracers began swirling towards us; some were even bouncing off the smooth surface of the lake. This was a horrible moment: we were being dragged along at four miles a minute, almost against our will, towards the things we were going to destroy. I think at that moment the boys did not want to go. I know I did not want to go. I thought to myself, 'In another minute we shall all be dead – so what?' I thought again, 'This is terrible – this feeling of fear – if it is fear.' By now we were a few hundred yards away, and I said quickly to Pulford, under my breath, 'Better leave the throttles open now and stand by to pull me out of the seat if I get hit.' As I glanced at him I thought he looked a little glum on hearing this.

The Lancaster was really moving and I began looking through the special sight on my windscreen. Spam had his eyes glued to the bombsight in front, his hand on his button; a special mechanism on board had already begun to work so that the mine would drop (we hoped) in the right spot. Terry was still checking the height. Joe and Trev began to raise their guns. The flak could see us quite clearly now. It was not exactly inferno. I have been through far worse flak fire than that; but we were very low. There was something sinister and slightly unnerving about the whole operation. My aircraft was so small and the dam was so large; it was thick and solid, and now it was angry. My aircraft was very small. We skimmed along the surface of the lake, and as we went my gunner was firing into the defences, and the defences were firing back with vigour, their shells whistling past us. For some reason, we were not being hit.

Spam said, 'Left – little more left – steady – steady – steady – coming up.' Of the next few seconds I remember only a series of kaleidoscopic incidents.

The chatter from Joe's front guns pushing out tracers which bounced off the left-hand flak tower.

Pulford crouching beside me.

The smell of burnt cordite.

The cold sweat underneath my oxygen mask.

The tracers flashing past the windows – they all seemed the same colour now – and the inaccuracy of the gun positions near the power-station; they were firing in the wrong direction.

The closeness of the dam wall.

Spam's exultant, 'Mine gone.'

Hutch's red Very lights to blind the flak-gunners.

The speed of the whole thing.

Someone was saying over the RT, 'Good show, leader. Nice work.'

Then it was all over, and at last we were out of range, and there came over us all, I think, an immense feeling of relief and confidence.

Trevor said, 'I will get those bastards,' and he began to spray the dam with bullets until at last he, too, was out of range. As we circled round we could see a great 1000-feet column of whiteness still hanging in the air where our mine had exploded. We could see with satisfaction that Spam had been good, and it had gone off in the right position. Then, as we came closer, we could see that the explosion of the mine had caused a great disturbance upon the surface of the lake and the water had become broken and furious, as though it were being lashed by a gale.

THE RAILWAY OF DEATH, BURMA, May 1943

Jeffrey English

The author was captured by the Japanese at the fall of Singapore. In 1943 he was put to work on the Burma–Siam railway, where conditions caused the death of two out of every three POWs.

The work here was again on a rock cutting, about a mile from the camp and reached through the usual little track of churned-up mud. The shifts changed over down at the cutting, not back at camp, and so the men were paraded at 7 a.m. to be counted, and then had to march down to commence work at 8 a.m. The party coming off duty had to march back to the camp, and did not arrive until some time after 8.30 a.m. But that did not mean ten and a half hours for food and sleep. On five days a week rations had to be collected from the river, which involved going out at 1.30 p.m. and getting back between 5 p.m. and 6 p.m.

At our previous camp the ration parties had been drawn from the semi-sick, but here *all* men not bedded down had to go on the working parties to the cutting, and so the afternoon ration parties had to be found from the now off-duty night shift. A man would work or be going to and from work for the best part of fourteen hours, do a four-hour ration fatigue, and have only six hours out of twenty-four for feeding, cleaning himself up, and sleeping.

For the first week or so, when we still had over 300 'fit' in the combined Anglo-Australian camp, each individual only got two ration fatigues a week. It would have been even less, but of course one half of our 300 were on the day shift, and only the other half were on the unhappy night shift.

On three pints of rice a day, all this, of course, was impossible and flesh and blood could not stand the strain; and in addition to the overwork we had dysentery and other diseases spreading at a frightening pace. As the numbers of 'fit' men dwindled, the burden carried by the remainder consequently grew, until after only a few weeks the fitter men were doing all five ration fatigues a week as well as working the night shift in the cutting, and only having two days a week of real rest. As they gradually cracked up, more unfortunates, just past the crisis of their exhaustion or illnesses but in no way fully recovered, would be forced out in their place, lasting in their turn perhaps three or four days before they themselves had to be replaced by yet others not quite so ill.

Just as this gruelling programme put that at our previous camp in the shade, so did the new Nip Engineers make the last lot look like gentlemen. There, they had generally beaten only those whom they caught flagging or had somehow provoked their precariously balanced ill-humour; but here they beat up indiscriminately, beating every man in a gang if they wanted it to go faster, and two of them in particular were simply bloodthirsty sadists.

They were known to us as 'Musso' and 'The Bull', and they seemed to compete amongst themselves as to who could cause the most hurt. They were both on the night shift, and both would come on duty with a rope's end strapped to the wrist. These they plied liberally, and they also carried a split-ended bamboo apiece, whilst Musso in particular would lash out with anything which came handy, such as a shovel. Every morning two or three men would come back to camp with blood clotted on their faces and shoulders or matted in their hair, whilst others would return with puffy scarlet faces but no eye lashes or eye brows, these having been burnt off where they'd had a naked acetylene flare waved slowly across the eyes – a favourite trick of another Nip known to us as 'Snowdrop'.

They drove the men on, not just to make them work, but as a cruel master drives a beast of burden to force it on to further efforts greater than it can manage; and one would see half a dozen men staggering along with an 18-foot tree trunk, or rolling an outsize boulder to the edge of the cutting, with the Nip running alongside lashing out at them or kicking their knees and shins and ankles to keep them going.

Frequently men fainted, and to make sure that they weren't shamming, the Nip would kick them in the stomach, ribs or groin. If the man still didn't move, the favourite trick was to roll him over face downwards, and then jump up and down on the backs of his knees, so as to grind the kneecaps themselves into the loose gravel. If he fell on his side, a variation was to stand on the side of his face and then wriggle about, grinding and tearing his undercheek in the gravel: and as a way of telling a faked faint from a real one, both of these methods are, believe me, highly efficacious.

On one occasion a man was beaten up so badly by the Nips that they thought he wouldn't live, and so they got four prisoners and told them to bury him under a heap of rocks. The prisoners observed that he wasn't yet dead, but the Nips indicated that that didn't matter – they could bury him alive. It was only after a great deal of persuasion by a spunky Australian officer (who naturally took a personal bashing for his trouble, but didn't let that deter him) that the Nips eventually changed their minds and let the man be carried back to camp. He was carried on a stretcher, and came round later, but the beating had sent him almost off his head; he disappeared into the jungle and we couldn't find him for two days. On the third day he crept in for food; but he was now quite mental and became a gibbering idiot at the mere sight of a Nip. Had we bedded him down in a hospital tent, he could very well have simply popped off again; and so we found him a job in the cook-house where he would be working with others, and he worked there for a shaky fortnight before he packed it in and died.

MASS BOMBING, HAMBURG, GERMANY, Summer 1943

During the spring and summer of 1943, Hamburg, Berlin and the Ruhr Valley were bombed by the RAF and USAAF in a series of night raids the intensity of which was unparalleled in the history of warfare. Hamburg was almost obliterated by the bombing and the fire-storm it set off. A secret report prepared by the German government recorded that:

Trees three feet thick were broken off or uprooted, human beings were thrown to the ground or flung alive into the flames by winds which exceeded a hundred and fifty miles an hour. The panic-stricken citizens knew not where to turn. Flames drove them from the shelters, but high-explosive bombs sent them scurrying back again. Once inside, they were suffocated by carbon-monoxide poisoning and their bodies reduced to ashes as though they had been placed in a crematorium, which was indeed what each shelter proved to be. The fortunate were those who jumped into the canals and waterways and remained swimming or standing up to their necks in water for hours until the heat should die down.

D-DAY: EMBARKATION, 4 June 1944

Alan Moorehead

The Allied invasion of Normandy, 6 June 1944, was the greatest seaborne invasion in history. Some 160,000 troops – British, American, French, Polish and Canadian – embarked 5,000 craft in southern England to make the journey to 'the far shore'.

At three o'clock we were standing in a line on the path leading up to the gate. The young naval officer came by festooned with his explosives and rather surprisingly took up a position behind me. As each new group of troops turned up they exchanged wisecracks with the others already arrived. 'Blimey, 'ere's the Arsenal' . . . ''Ome for the 'olidays' . . . 'Wot's that, Arthur?' 'Them's me water-wings, dearie.' Even after waiting another hour there was still optimism in the ranks. Then we marched out through the gate and got on to the vehicles. An officer was running down the line making sure everyone was on board. He blew a whistle and we started off. Five miles an hour. Down Acacia Avenue. Round the park into High Street; a mile-long column of ducks and three-ton lorries, of Jeeps and tanks and bulldozers. On the sidewalk one or two people waved vaguely. An old man stopped and mumbled, 'Good luck.' But for the most part the people stared silently and made no sign. They knew we were going. There had been rehearsals before but they were not deceived. There was something in the way the soldiers carried themselves that said all too clearly 'This is it. This is the invasion.' And yet they were cheerful still. It was a relief to be out of the camp and moving freely in the streets again. Every now and again the column halted. Then we crept on slowly again towards the hards.

Two hours went by and the soldiers began to grow bored. They seized on anything for amusement. When a girl came by on a bicycle she was cheered with salacious enthusiasm from one end of the column to the other. An athlete dressed in a pink suit began to pace round the cricket field. The soldiers watched him with relish for a minute. Then, 'Hyah, Pinkie.' 'Careful, dearie.' Derisive shouting followed him round the ground. Towards the end of the column a soldier who was trained as a sniper took down his rifle with its telescopic sights and fixed them upon two lovers who were embracing at the farther end of the park. His friends gathered round him while he gave them a lewd commentary on what he saw. The soldiers were becoming very bored. It grew dark and the cricket match ended. Every hour or so a tea-waggon came round and the men ran towards it with their enamel mugs. One after another the lights in the houses were blacked out and the soldiers, left alone in the empty street, lapsed into complete listlessness and tiredness. Rumours kept passing back and forth from vehicle to vehicle. 'Our ship has fouled its anchor.' 'There has been a collision in the harbour.' Or more spectacularly, 'We have already made a landing on the Channel Islands.'

Towards ten o'clock the officers began running down the column shouting for the drivers to start. We began to edge forward slowly and presently came out on the dark promenade along the sea. There were many ships, both those moving in the sound and those which had brought their bows up on to the hard and had opened their gates to receive the vehicles. We were marked down for the Landing Ship Tank 816. A clamour of light and noise was coming out of its open bows. One after another the vehicles crept down the ramp and on to the great lift that took them to the upper deck. The sailors kept shouting to one another as they lashed down the trucks on the upper deck. All night the thump of army boots against the metal deck went on.

D-DAY: THE AIRBORNE LANDINGS, 6 June 1944

Guy Remington

At the airfield [on the evening of 5 June], we were directed to the planes that were to carry us over the Channel. I had seen some action before, so I had at least an idea of what to expect. Not many of the other men were so fortunate. The only thing that worried me, as we sat in the dark waiting for the takeoff, was the thought that I might break a leg in my jump. I tried not to think about that. We took off at ten-thirty, just as the moon was coming up. There appeared to be very little ground wind, and the weather seemed ideal for a night jump. Through the open door of my plane, I watched the other transports lifting heavily off the ground. They looked like huge, black bats as they skimmed slowly over the treetops and fell into formation. Before long, we took off too. Presently, near the coast of England, á squadron of fighters appeared below us. They flashed their lights on and off, and then wheeled away. That was *adiós*.

We had a two-hour run ahead of us, so I settled down in my seat. A major, sitting directly across from me, smiled, his teeth startlingly white in the dark. I smiled back. The noise of the plane made it impossible to talk. Suddenly the jump master shouted, 'Stand up and hook up!' I realized that I had been asleep, hard as it was to believe. The plane was rocking and bucking, trying to dodge the occasional bursts of flak from the dark, anonymous countryside below. A small red light gleamed in the panel by the door. We hooked up our parachutes, lined up close together, and waited. Then we stood there, waiting, for twelve and a half minutes. It seemed a long and terrible time.

The green light flashed on at seven minutes past midnight. The jump master shouted, 'Go!' I was the second man out. The black Normandy pastures tilted and turned far beneath me. The first German flare came arching up, and instantly machine-guns and forty-millimetre guns began firing from the corners of the fields, striping the night with yellow, green, blue, and red tracers. I pitched down through a wild Fourth of July. Fire licked through the sky and blazed around the transports heaving high overhead. I saw some of them go plunging down in flames. One of them came down with a trooper, whose parachute had become caught on the tailpiece, streaming out behind. I heard a loud gush of air: a man went hurtling past, only a few yards away, his parachute collapsed and burning. Other parachutes, with men whose legs had been shot off slumped in the harness, floated gently toward the earth.

I was caught in a machine-gun cross-fire as I approached the ground. It seemed impossible that they could miss me. One of the guns, hidden in a building, was firing at my parachute, which was already badly torn; the other aimed at my body. I reached up, caught the left risers of my parachute, and pulled on them. I went into a fast slip, but the tracers followed me down. I held the slip until I was about twenty-five feet from the ground and then let go the risers. I landed up against a hedge in a little garden at the rear of a German barracks. There were four tracer holes through one of my pants legs, two through the other, and another bullet had ripped off both my breast pockets, but I hadn't a scratch.

D-DAY: THE AIRBORNE LANDINGS, 6 June 1944

Major Friedrich Hayn, Wehrmacht staff officer

At 01.11 hours – an unforgettable moment – the field telephone rang. Something important was coming through: while listening to it the General stood up stiffly, his hand gripping the edge of the table. With a nod he beckoned his chief of staff to listen in. 'Enemy parachute troops dropped east of the Orne estuary. Main area Bréville-Ranville and the north edge of the Bavent forest. Counter-measures are in progress.' This message from 716 Intelligence Service struck like lightning.

Was this, at last, the invasion, the storming of '*Festung Europa*'? Someone said haltingly, 'Perhaps they are only supply troops for the French Resistance?' . . . The day before, in the St Malo area, many pieces of paper had been passing from hand to hand or had been dropped into the letterboxes; they all bore a mysterious announcement: *La carotte rouge est quittée*. Furthermore, our wireless operators had noticed an unusually large volume of coded traffic. Up till now, however, the Resistance groups had anxiously avoided all open action; they were put off by the danger of premature discovery and consequent extermination.

Whilst the pros and cons were still being discussed, 709 Infantry Division from Valognes announced: 'Enemy parachute troops south of St Germain-de-Varreville and near Ste Marie-du-Mont. A second drop west of the main Carentan–Valognes road on both sides of the Merderet river and along the Ste Mère-Eglise–

Pont-l'Abbé road. Fighting for the river crossings in progress.' It was now about 01.45 hours.

Three dropping zones near the front! Two were clearly at important traffic junctions. The third was designed to hold the marshy meadows at the mouth of the Dives and the bridge across the canalized Orne near Ranville. It coincided with the corps boundary, with the natural feature which formed our northern flank but would serve the same purpose for an enemy driving south. It is the task of parachute troops, as advance detachments from the air, to occupy tactically important areas and to hold them until ground troops, in this case landing forces, fight their way through to them and incorporate them into the general front. Furthermore in Normandy they could, by attacking the strong-points immediately west of the beach, paralyse the coastal defences. If it really was the task of the reported enemy forces to keep open the crossings, it meant that a landing would soon take place and they were really in earnest!

D-DAY: THE LANDINGS, 6 June 1944

Throughout the night of 5 June the Allied armada made its way across the Channel, arriving off the Normandy coast in the steely dawn of the 6th, when the troops were ordered into the assault craft in which they would make the final approach.

Lieutenant H. T. Bone, East Yorkshire Regiment

In the Mess decks we blacked our faces with black Palm Olive cream and listened to the naval orders over the loudhailer. Most of us had taken communion on the Sunday, but the padre had a few words to say to us. Then the actual loading into craft – swinging on davits – the boat lowering and finally 'Away boats'. While this was going on, all around could be seen the rest of the convoy, with battleships and cruisers firing their big guns every few minutes and destroyers rushing round. One had been hit by something and only the up-ended part of its bows remained in view. As our flotilla swung into line behind its leader we raised our flag, a black silk square with the white rose of Yorkshire in the centre . . . It was some distance to the beaches, and it was a wet trip. All of us had a spare gas-cape to keep us dry and we chewed our gum stolidly. Mine was in my mouth twelve or fourteen hours later and I usually hate the stuff and never touch it. Shielding ourselves from the spray and watching the fire going down from all the supporting arms and the Spits [Spitfires] overhead, the time soon passed . . . Suddenly there was a jarring bump on the left, and looking up from our boards we saw one of the beach obstacles about two feet above our left gunwale with a large mine on top of it, just as photographs had shown us. Again a bump, on the right, but still we had not grounded. The Colonel and the flotilla leader were piloting us in, and for a few brief minutes nothing happened except the music of the guns and the whang of occasional bullets overhead, with the sporadic explosions of mortar bombs and the background of our own heavy machine-gun fire. The doors opened as we grounded and the Colonel was out. The sea was choppy and the boat swung a good bit as one by one we followed him. Several fell in and got soaked through. I was lucky. I stopped for a few seconds to help my men with their wireless sets and to ensure they kept them dry. As we staggered ashore we dispersed and lay down above the water's edge.

The bloodiest fighting of the day came at Omaha beach, where the US 1st and 29th Infantry Divisions had the ill luck to encounter a crack *Wehrmacht* division, the 352nd, on a training manoeuvre. Omaha was also the most topographically difficult of the beaches, dominated as it is by a high cliff.

Captain Joseph T. Dawson, US 1st Infantry Division

We landed at H + 30 minutes [7.00 am] and found . . . both the assault units rendered ineffective because of the enormous casualties they suffered. Fortunately, when we landed there was some letup in the defensive fire from the Germans. Even so the boat containing assault unit Company G, which I commanded, took a direct hit from the artillery of the Germans, and I suffered major casualties. I lost about twenty men out of a total complement of 250 from that hit on my boat, and this included my naval officer who was communications link with the Navy, who were to support us with their fire from the battleships and cruisers some 8,000 yards out in the water.

As soon as we were able to assemble we proceeded off the beach through a minefield which had been identified by some of the soldiers who had landed earlier. We knew this because two of them were lying there in the path I selected. Both men had been destroyed by the mines. From their position, however, we were able to identify the path and get through the minefield without casualties and proceed up to the crest of the ridge which overlooked the beach. We got about halfway up when we met the remnants of a platoon of E Company, commanded by Lieutenant Spalding. This was the only group – somewhere less than twenty men – we encountered who had gotten off the beach. They had secured some German prisoners, and these were sent to the beach under escort. Above me, right on top of the ridge, the Germans had a line of defences with an excellent field of fire. I kept the men behind and, along with my communications sergeant and his assistant, worked our way slowly up to the crest of the ridge. Just before the crest was a sharp perpendicular drop, and we were able to get up to the crest without being seen by the enemy. I could now hear the Germans talking in the machine-gun nest immediately above me. I then threw two grenades, which were successful in eliminating the enemy and silencing the machine-gun which had been holding up our approach. Fortunately for me this action was done without them having any awareness of my being there, so I was no hero . . . it was an act of God, I guess.

D-DAY: MEETING THE LIBERATORS, VER-SUR-MER, FRANCE 6 June 1944

Anne de Vigneral, civilian

Diary: 6 June

12 noon. Relative calm, but we all run to find boards and branches to cover our trench. We fetch rugs, mattresses etc. On the last foray we meet a German officer who says to me, 'The sleep is ended.' He was naive! We try to have a disjointed lunch, but it is interrupted continually. The German officer stations himself in a farmer's hedge and forbids them to betray him . . . In any case bursts of fire are everywhere, the children run back into the house. I hadn't realized that in the field where we collected our wood the English were in one hedge, the Germans in the hedge opposite and they were shooting at each other!

1 p.m. I beg everyone to eat, but the noise gets worse and when I open the window I see all the Germans bent double going over the village bridge. We take our plates out, scuttle across the terrace and fall into the trench. The terrace is covered with bullets, the little maid feels one scrape her leg . . . we found it afterwards . . .

We see lots of Germans in the area between the property and the river. We don't know what to think.

1.15. We pop our heads out of the trench and see soldiers, but we can't recognize them. Is the uniform khaki or green? They are on their stomachs in the leaves . . .

1.30. To reassure myself I go to the kitchen to get some coffee (we had lunched in the trench) and come back quietly but very obviously carrying a coffee pot . . . and then the soldiers hidden in the laurels by the bridge come out. Hurrah, they are Canadians. We have lumps in our throats, we all speak at once, it is indescribable. Some laugh, some cry. They give the children chocolate; they are of course delighted. Themselves, they arrive calmly, chewing gum. (Isn't that typically English.)

2.00. Their officer arrives and tours the house with me looking for delayed action bombs. I, without a thought of danger, and all in a rush, open doors and cupboards. We find some bottles of champagne which we bring down. We sit on the steps and all drink. Even Jacques, seven years old, has a glass and drinks a toast with us. We all have already been given Capstan and Gold Flake cigarettes. Oh, don't they smell lovely!

PARIS CELEBRATES LIBERATION, FRANCE, September 1944

Simone de Beauvoir

The German forces in Paris surrendered on 25 August 1944, after attack by the Americans and Free French and an uprising by the citizens from within the city. The celebrations continued for a week or more.

We were liberated. In the streets, the children were singing:

Nous ne les reverrons plus,
C'est fini, ils sont foutus.

And I kept saying to myself: It's all over, it's all over. It's all over: everything's beginning. Patrick Walberg, the Leirises' American friend, took us for a jeep ride through the suburbs; it was the first time in years that I'd been out in a car. Once again I wandered after midnight in the mild September air. The bistros closed early, but when we left the terrace of the Rhumerie or the smoky little red inferno of the Montana, we had the sidewalks, the benches, the streets. There were still snipers on the roofs, and my heart would grow heavy when I sensed the vigilant hatred overhead. One night, we heard sirens. An airplane, whose nationality we never discovered, was flying over Paris; V-ls fell on the suburbs and blew houses to bits. Walberg, usually well-informed, said that the Germans were putting the finishing touches to new and even more terrifying secret weapons. Fear returned, and found its place still warm. But joy quickly swept it away. With our friends, talking, drinking, strolling, laughing, night and day we celebrated our deliverance. And all the others who were celebrating too, near or far, became our friends. An orgy of brotherhood! The shadows that had immured France exploded. The tall soldiers, dressed in khaki and chewing their gum, were living proof that you could cross the seas again. They ambled past, and often they stumbled. Singing and whistling, they stumbled along the sidewalks and the subway platforms; stumbling, they danced at night in the bistros and laughed their loud laughs, showing teeth white as children's. [Jean] Genet, who had no sympathy with the Germans but who detested idylls, declared loudly on the terrace of the Rhumerie that these costumed civilians had no style. Stiff in their black and green carapaces, the occupiers had been something else! For me, these carefree young Americans were freedom incarnate: our own and also the freedom that was about to spread – we had no doubts on this score – throughout the world.

SELECTION IN AUSCHWITZ, POLAND, October 1944

Primo Levi

Primo Levi was a member of the Italian anti-Fascist resistance, and was deported to the SS death camp at Auschwitz in 1944. He survived to write, amongst other books, memoirs of prison camp life, including *Survival in Auschwitz* from which the following extract is taken.

In the same way in which one sees a hope end, winter arrived this morning. We realized it when we left the hut to go and wash: there were no stars, the dark cold air had the smell of snow. In roll-call square, in the grey of dawn, when we assembled for work, no one spoke. When we saw the first flakes of snow, we thought that if at the same time last year they had told us that we would have seen another winter in Lager, we would have gone and touched the electric wire-fence; and that even now we would go if we were logical, were it not for this last senseless crazy residue of unavoidable hope.

Because 'winter' means yet another thing.

Last spring the Germans had constructed huge tents in an open space in the Lager. For the whole of the good season each of them had catered for over 1,000 men: now the tents had been taken down, and an excess 2,000 guests crowded our huts. We old prisoners knew that the Germans did not like these irregularities and that something would soon happen to reduce our number.

One feels the selections arriving. '*Selekcja*': the hybrid Latin and Polish word is heard once, twice, many times, interpolated in foreign conversations; at first we cannot distinguish it, then it forces itself on our attention, and in the end it persecutes us.

This morning the Poles had said '*Selekcja*'. The Poles are the first to find out the news, and they generally try not to let it spread around, because to know something which the others still do not know can always be useful. By the time that everyone realizes that a selection is imminent, the few possibilities of evading it (corrupting some doctor or some prominent with bread or tobacco; leaving the hut for Ka-Be or vice-versa at the right moment so as to cross with the commission) are already their monopoly.

In the days which follow, the atmosphere of the Lager and the yard is filled with '*Selekcja*': nobody knows anything definite, but all speak about it, even the Polish, Italian, French civilian workers whom we secretly see in the yard. Yet the result is hardly a wave of despondency: our collective morale is too inarticulate and flat to be unstable. The fight against hunger, cold and work leaves little margin for thought, even for this thought. Everybody reacts in his own way, but hardly anyone with those attitudes which would seem the most plausible as the most realistic, that is with resignation or despair.

All those able to find a way out, try to take it; but they are the minority because it is very difficult to escape from a selection. The Germans apply themselves to these things with great skill and diligence.

Whoever is unable to prepare for it materially, seeks defence elsewhere. In the latrines, in the washroom, we show each other our chests, our buttocks, our thighs, and our comrades reassure us: 'You are all right, it will certainly not be your turn this time . . . *du bist kein Muselmann* . . . more probably mine . . .' and they undo their braces in turn and pull up their shirts.

Nobody refuses this charity to another: nobody is so sure of his own lot to be able to condemn others. I brazenly lied to old Wertheimer; I told him that if they questioned him, he should reply that he was forty-five, and he should not forget to have a shave the evening before, even if it cost him a quarter-ration of bread; apart from that he need have no fears, and in any case it was by no means certain that it was a selection for the gas chamber; had he not heard the *Blockältester* say that those chosen would go to Jaworszno to a convalescent camp?

It is absurd of Wertheimer to hope: he looks sixty, he has enormous varicose veins, he hardly even notices the hunger any more. But he lies down on his bed, serene and quiet, and replies to someone who asks him with my own words; they are the command-words in the camp these days: I myself repeated them just as – apart from details – Chajim told them to me, Chajim, who has been in Lager for three years, and being strong and robust is wonderfully sure of himself; and I believed them.

On this slender basis I also lived through the great selection of October 1944 with inconceivable tranquillity. I was tranquil because I managed to lie to myself sufficiently. The fact that I was not selected depended above all on chance and does not prove that my faith was well-founded.

Monsieur Pinkert is also, *a priori*, condemned: it is enough to look at his eyes. He calls me over with a sign, and with a confidential air tells me that he has been informed – he cannot tell me the source of information – that this time there is really something new: the Holy See, by means of the International Red Cross . . . in short, he personally guarantees both for himself and for me, in the most absolute manner, that every danger is ruled out; as a civilian he was, as is well known, attaché to the Belgian embassy at Warsaw.

Thus in various ways, even those days of vigil, which in the telling seem as if they ought to have passed every limit of human torment, went by not very differently from other days.

The discipline in both the Lager and Buna is in no way relaxed: the work, cold and hunger are sufficient to fill up every thinking moment.

Today is working Sunday, *Arbeitssonntag*: we work until one p.m., then we return to camp for the shower, shave and general control for skin diseases and lice. And in the yards, everyone knew mysteriously that the selection would be today.

The news arrived, as always, surrounded by a halo of contradictory or suspect details: the selection in the infirmary took place this morning; the percentage was seven per cent of the whole camp, thirty, fifty per cent of the patients. At Birkenau, the crematorium chimney has been smoking for ten days. Room has to be made for an enormous convoy arriving from the Poznan ghetto. The young tell the young that all the old ones will be chosen. The healthy tell the healthy that only the ill will be chosen. Specialists will be excluded. German Jews will be excluded. Low Numbers will be excluded. You will be chosen. I will be excluded.

At one p.m. exactly the yard empties in orderly fashion and for two hours the grey unending army files past the two control stations where, as on every day, we are counted and recounted, and past the military band which for two hours without interruption plays, as on every day, those marches to which we must synchronize our steps at our entrance and our exit.

It seems like every day, the kitchen chimney smokes as usual, the distribution of the soup is already beginning. But then the bell is heard, and at that moment we realize that we have arrived.

Because this bell always sounds at dawn, when it means the reveille; but if it sounds during the day, it means '*Blocksperre*', enclosure in huts, and this happens when there is a selection to prevent anyone avoiding it, or when those selected leave for the gas, to prevent anyone seeing them leave.

Our *Blockältester* knows his business. He has made sure that we have all entered, he has the door locked, he has given everyone his card with his number, name, profession, age and nationality and he has ordered everyone to undress completely, except for shoes. We wait like this, naked, with the card in our hands, for the commission to reach our hut. We are hut 48, but one can never tell if they are going to begin at hut 1 or hut 60. At any rate, we can rest quietly at least for an hour, and there is no reason why we should not get under the blankets on the bunk and keep warm.

Many are already drowsing when a barrage of orders, oaths and blows proclaims the imminent arrival of the commission. The *Blockältester* and his helpers, starting at the end of the dormitory, drive the crowd of frightened, naked people in front of them and cram them in the *Tagesraum* which is the quartermaster's office. The *Tagesraum* is a room seven yards by four: when the drive is over, a warm and compact human mass is jammed into the *Tagesraum*, perfectly filling all the corners, exercising such a pressure on the wooden walls as to make them creak.

Now we are all in the *Tagesraum*, and besides there being no time, there is not even any room in which to be afraid. The feeling of the warm flesh pressing all around is unusual and not unpleasant. One has to take care to hold up one's nose so as to breathe, and not to crumple or lose the card in one's hand.

The *Blockältester* has closed the connecting door and has opened the other two which lead from the dormitory and the *Tagesraum* outside. Here, in front of the two doors, stands the arbiter of our fate, an SS subaltern. On his right is the *Blockältester*, on his left, the quartermaster of the hut. Each one of us, as he comes naked out of the *Tagesraum* into the cold October air, has to run the few steps between the two doors, give the card to the SS man and enter the dormitory door. The SS man, in the fraction of a second between two successive crossings, with a glance at one's back and front, judges everyone's fate, and in turn gives the card to the man on his right or his left, and this is the life or death of each of us. In three or four minutes a hut of 200 men is 'done', as is the whole camp of 12,000 men in the course of the afternoon.

Jammed in the charnel-house of the *Tagesraum*, I gradually felt the human pressure around me slacken, and in a short time it was my turn. Like everyone, I passed by with a brisk and elastic step, trying to hold my head high, my chest forward and my muscles contracted and conspicuous. With the corner of my eye I tried to look behind my shoulders, and my card seemed to end on the right.

As we gradually come back into the dormitory we are allowed to dress ourselves. Nobody yet knows with certainty his own fate, it has first of all to be established whether the condemned cards were those on the right or the left. By now there is no longer any point in sparing each other's feelings with superstitious scruples. Everybody crowds around the oldest, the most wasted-away, and most '*muselmann*'; if their cards went to the left, the left is certainly the side of the condemned.

Even before the selection is over, everybody knows that the left was effectively the '*schlechte Seite*', the bad side. There have naturally been some irregularities: René, for example, so young and robust, ended on the left; perhaps it was because he has glasses, perhaps because he walks a little stooped like a myope, but more probably because of a simple mistake: René passed the commission immediately in front of me and there could have been a mistake with our cards. I think about it, discuss it with Alberto, and we agree that the hypothesis is probable; I do not know what I will think tomorrow and later; today I feel no distinct emotion.

It must equally have been a mistake about Sattler, a huge Transylvanian peasant who was still at home only twenty days ago; Sattler does not understand German, he has understood nothing of what has taken place, and stands in a corner mending his shirt. Must I go and tell him that his shirt will be of no more use?

There is nothing surprising about these mistakes: the examination is too quick and summary, and in any case, the important thing for the Lager is not that the most useless prisoners be eliminated, but that free posts be quickly created, according to a certain percentage previously fixed.

The selection is now over in our hut, but it continues in the others, so that we are still locked in. But as the soup-pots have arrived in the meantime, the *Blockältester* decides to proceed with the distribution at once. A double ration will be given to those selected. I have never discovered if this was a ridiculously charitable initiative of the *Blockältester*, or an explicit disposition of the SS, but in fact, in the interval of two or three days (sometimes even much longer) between the selection and the departure, the victims at Monowitz-Auschwitz enjoyed this privilege.

Ziegler holds out his bowl, collects his normal ration and then waits there expectantly. 'What do you want?' asks the *Blockältester*: according to him, Ziegler is entitled to no supplement, and he drives him away, but Ziegler returns and humbly persists. He was on the left, everybody saw it, let the *Blockältester* check the cards; he has the right to a double ration. When he is given it, he goes quietly to his bunk to eat.

Now everyone is busy scraping the bottom of his bowl with his spoon so as not to waste the last drops of the soup; a confused, metallic clatter, signifying the end of the day. Silence slowly prevails and then, from my bunk on the top row, I see and hear old Kuhn praying aloud, with his beret on his head, swaying backward and forward violently. Kuhn is thanking God because he has not been chosen.

Kuhn is out of his senses. Does he not see Beppo the Greek in the bunk next to him, Beppo who is twenty years old and is going to the gas chamber the day after tomorrow and knows it and lies there looking fixedly at the light without saying anything and without even thinking any more? Can Kuhn fail to realize that next time it will be his turn? Does Kuhn not understand that what has happened today is an abomination, which no propitiatory prayer, no pardon, no expiation by the guilty, which nothing at all in the power of man can ever clean again?

If I were God, I would spit at Kuhn's prayer.

IWO JIMA, PACIFIC OCEAN, 19 February 1945

A US Marine Corps correspondent

Iwo Jima is a small volcanic island which lies at the southern end of a chain which stretches into Tokyo Bay. The Americans wanted to build an airbase on the island – which, in early 1945, was Japanese-held and heavily fortified – mainly to enable American fighters to support B29s in their raids over Japan. The invasion of Iwo Jima was launched on 19 February 1945. The fighting was expected to take eight days; it lasted five weeks.

When the 24th Marine Regiment's 2nd Battalion reached the scene, they called it 'the Wilderness', and there they spent four days on the line, with no respite from the song of death sung by mortars among those desolate crevices and gouged shell holes. The Wilderness covered about a square mile inland from Blue Beach 2, on the approaches to Airfield no. 2, and there was no cover. Here and there stood a blasted dwarf tree; here and there a stubby rock ledge in a maze of volcanic crevices.

The 2nd Battalion attacked with flame throwers, demolition charges, 37-millimetre guns, riflemen. A tank advancing in support was knocked out by a mortar shell. After every Japanese volley, Corsair fighter planes streamed down on the mortar positions, ripping their charges of bombs into the Wilderness. But after every dive was ended, the mortars started their ghastly song again.

Cracks in the earth run along the open field to the left of the Wilderness, and hot smoke seeped up through the cracks. Gains were counted in terms of 100 or 200 yards for a day, in terms of three or four bunkers knocked out. Losses were counted in terms of three or four men suddenly turned to bloody rags after the howl of a mortar shell, in terms of a flame-thrower man hit by a grenade as he poured his flame into a bunker. The assault platoon of flame throwers and demolitionists, spearheading the regiment's push through the Wilderness, lost two assistant squad leaders killed.

The Japs were hard to kill. Cube-shaped concrete blockhouses had to be blasted again and again before the men inside were silenced. Often the stunned and wounded Japs continued to struggle among the ruins, still trying to fire back. A sergeant fired twenty-one shots at a semi-concealed Jap before the latter was killed. Another Marine assaulting a pillbox found a seriously wounded Jap trying to get a heavy machine gun into action. He emptied his clip at him but the Jap kept reaching. Finally, out of ammunition, the Marine used his knife to kill him.

Forty-eight hours after the attack began, one element of the Third Division moved into the line under orders to advance at all costs.

Behind a rolling artillery barrage and with fixed bayonets, the unit leaped forward in an old-fashioned hell-bent-for-leather charge and advanced to the very mouths of the fixed Jap defences. Before scores of pillboxes the men flung themselves at the tiny flaming holes, throwing grenades and jabbing with bayonets. Comrades went past, hurdled the defences and rushed across Airfield no. 2. In three minutes one unit lost four officers. Men died at every step. That was how we broke their line.

Across the field we attacked a ridge. The enemy rose up out of holes to hurl our assault back. The squads re-formed and went up again. At the crest they plunged on the Japs with bayonets. One of our men, slashing his way from side to side, fell dead from a pistol shot. His comrade drove his bayonet into the Jap who had killed him. The Japs on the ridge were annihilated.

And now behind those proud and weary men, our whole previously stalled attack poured through. Tanks, bazookas and demolition men smashed and burned the by-passed fortifications. In an area 1,000 yards long and 200 deep, more than 800 enemy pillboxes were counted.

The survivors of this bold charge covered 800 yards in an hour and a half. Brave men had done what naval shelling, aerial bombardment, artillery and tanks had not been able to do in two days of constant pounding. What was perhaps the most intensively fortified small area ever encountered in battle had been broken.

Six thousand Americans died on Iwo Jima. Another 12,500 died in April in the seizure of Okinawa, an island in the Ryukyu chain in the Pacific, also designated as a USAAF fighter base. The Japanese dead numbered 21,000 on Iwo Jima, and around 100,000 on Okinawa.

CROSSING THE GERMAN BORDER, 9 February 1945

John Foley

After crushing Hitler's December offensive, the Allies made rapid progress in the West. By early February they had reached the border of Germany.

. . . 'What's this striped pole across the road, sir?' said Pickford.

'The frontier!' I said, pointing to the deserted hut which had housed the frontier police and customs men.

I stared curiously at my first German civilian. He was an old man, dressed in shabby serge and an engine-driver's sort of cap. His grizzled face regarded us from above a bushy white moustache as we clattered over the broken frontier barrier. And then I heard *Angler's* driver's hatch being thrown open, and when I looked over my shoulder I saw Smith 161 leaning out and staring questioningly at the old German.

'We on the right road for Berlin, mate?' asked Smith 161, with a perfectly straight face.

I swear the old blue eyes winked, as the man tugged at his grizzled moustache and said: '*Berlin? Ja, ja! Gerade aus!*'

'I thought the Germans had no sense of humour,' said Pickford, when we got moving again.

'I know,' I said. 'But he can remember Germany before Hitler, and probably before the Kaiser, too.'

A BOMB HITS THE PROPAGANDA MINISTRY, BERLIN, 13 March 1945

Joseph Goebbels

Joseph Goebbels was one of the principal ring-leaders of the Nazi party and head of the Nazi's Ministry of Public Enlightenment and Propaganda.

This evening's Mosquito raid was particularly disastrous for me because our Ministry was hit. The whole lovely building on the Wilhelmstrasse was totally destroyed by a bomb. The throne-room, the Blue Gallery and my newly rebuilt theatre hall are nothing but a heap of ruins. I drove straight to the Ministry to see the devastation for myself. One's heart aches to see so unique a product of the architect's art, such as this building was, totally flattened in a second. What trouble we have taken to reconstruct the theatre hall, the throne-room and the Blue Gallery in the old style! With what care have we chosen every fresco on the walls and every piece of furniture! And now it has all been given over to destruction. In addition fire has now broken out in the ruins, bringing with it an even greater risk since 500 bazooka missiles are stored underneath the burning wreckage. I do my utmost to get the fire brigade to the scene as quickly and in as great strength as possible, so as at least to prevent the bazooka missiles exploding.

As I do all this I am overcome with sadness. It is twelve years to the day – 13 March – since I entered this Ministry as Minister. It is the worst conceivable omen for the next twelve years.

A MEETING WITH HITLER, BERLIN, April 1945

Gerhard Boldt

The author was a junior *Wehrmacht* officer seconded to Hitler's Berlin HQ to prepare war maps.

It was now four p.m. and most of those who are to take part in the conference have assembled in the ante-room. They stand or sit together in groups, talk and eat sandwiches while drinking real coffee or brandy. The Chief beckons me forward to introduce me. He is surrounded by Field-Marshal Keitel, General Jodl, Grand-Admiral Dönitz, and Bormann. Next to them are grouped their ADCs. In one corner, near a small table holding a telephone, Himmler is talking to the General of the SS Fegelein, the permanent representative of Himmler with Hitler. Fegelein is married to a sister of Eva Braun, the future wife of Hitler. His whole attitude now already displays the brazen assurance of a brother-in-law of the head of the German Reich. Kalten-Brunner, the dreaded head of the Supreme Reich Security Office, stands apart, alone and reading a document. The permanent Deputy of the Reich Press Chief with Hitler, Lorenz, makes conversation with the Standard Leader Zander, Bormann's deputy. Reich Marshal Göring is sitting at a round table in the centre of the ante-room, together with the officers of his staff, the Generals Koller and Christians. Hitler's chief ADC, General Burgdorf, now crosses the ante-room and disappears into the studio. Shortly afterwards he reappears in the open doorway:

'The Führer requests your presence!' Göring leads and all the others follow behind him in their order of rank.

Hitler stands alone in the centre of the huge room, turned towards the ante-room. They approach in their order of entry, and he greets nearly everyone by a handshake, silently, without a word of welcome. Only once in a while he asks a question, which is answered by 'Yes, Führer' or 'No, Führer.' I remain standing near the door and wait for the things that are bound to come. It is certainly one of the most remarkable moments of my life. General Guderian speaks with Hitler apparently concerning myself, for he looks in my direction. Guderian beckons, and I approach Hitler. Slowly, heavily stooping, he takes a few shuffling steps in my direction. He extends his right hand and looks at me with a queerly penetrating look. His handshake is weak and soft without any strength. His head is slightly wobbling. (This struck me later on even more, when I had the leisure to observe him.) His left arm hangs slackly and his hand trembles a good deal. There is an indescribable flickering glow in his eyes, creating a fearsome and totally unnatural effect. His face and the parts round his eyes give the impression of total exhaustion. All his movements are those of a senile man.

A VISIT TO BELSEN DEATH CAMP, GERMANY, 19 April 1945

Richard Dimbleby

Alongside the 500,000 Jews from Western Europe who were killed by the SS, 5.5 million Jews from Eastern Europe were also executed. Some of these were shot on the spot by special SS squads; most, however, were transported to the extermination camps, Belsen among them, to be gassed.

I picked my way over corpse after corpse in the gloom, until I heard one voice raised above the gentle undulating moaning. I found a girl, she was a living skeleton, impossible to gauge her age for she had practically no hair left, and her face was only a yellow parchment sheet with two holes in it for eyes. She was stretching out her stick of an arm and gasping something, it was 'English, English, medicine, medicine', and she was trying to cry but she hadn't enough strength. And beyond her down the passage and in the hut there were the convulsive movements of dying people too weak to raise themselves from the floor.

In the shade of some trees lay a great collection of bodies. I walked about them trying to count, there were perhaps 150 of them flung down on each other, all naked, all so thin that their yellow skin glistened like stretched rubber on their bones. Some of the poor starved creatures whose bodies were there looked so utterly unreal and inhuman that I could have imagined that they had never lived at all. They were like polished skeletons, the skeletons that medical students like to play practical jokes with.

At one end of the pile a cluster of men and women were gathered round a fire; they were using rags and old shoes taken from the bodies to keep it alight, and they were heating soup over it. And close by was the enclosure where 500 children between the ages of five and twelve had been kept. They were not so hungry as the rest, for the women had sacrificed themselves to keep them alive. Babies were born at Belsen, some of them shrunken, wizened little things that could not live, because their mothers could not feed them.

One woman, distraught to the point of madness, flung herself at a British soldier who was on guard at the camp on the night that it was reached by the 11th Armoured Division; she begged him to give her some milk for the tiny baby she held in her arms. She laid the mite on the ground and threw herself at the sentry's feet and kissed his boots. And when, in his distress, he asked her to get up, she put the baby in his arms and ran off crying that she would find milk for it because there was no milk in her breast. And when the soldier opened the bundle of rags to look at the child, he found that it had been dead for days.

There was no privacy of any kind. Women stood naked at the side of the track, washing in cupfuls of water taken from British Army trucks. Others squatted while they searched themselves for lice, and examined each other's hair. Sufferers from dysentery leaned against the huts, straining helplessly, and all around and about them was this awful drifting tide of exhausted people, neither caring nor watching. Just a few held out their withered hands to us as we passed by, and blessed the doctor, whom they knew had become the camp commander in place of the brutal Kramer.

I have never seen British soldiers so moved to cold fury as the men who opened the Belsen camp this week.

SOVIET GUNS OPEN FIRE ON BERLIN, 22 April 1945

Soviet war correspondent

On the walls of the houses we saw Goebbels' appeals, hurriedly scrawled in white paint: 'Every German will defend his capital. We shall stop the Red hordes at the walls of our Berlin.' Just try and stop them!

Steel pillboxes, barricades, mines, traps, suicide squads with grenades clutched in their hands – all are swept aside before the tidal wave.

Drizzling rain began to fall. Near Bisdorf I saw batteries preparing to open fire.

'What are the targets?' I asked the battery commander.

'Centre of Berlin, Spree bridges, and the northern and Stettin railway stations,' he answered.

Then came the tremendous words of command: 'Open fire at the capital of Fascist Germany.'

I noted the time. It was exactly 8.30 a.m. on 22 April. Ninety-six shells fell in the centre of Berlin in the course of a few minutes.

The German capital fell to the Red Army on 2 May 1945. Hitler was already dead, having committed suicide in his underground bunker on 30 April.

VICTORY IN EUROPE CELEBRATIONS, LONDON, 8 May 1945

Mollie Panter-Downes

When the day finally came, it was like no other day that anyone can remember. It had a flavour of its own, an extemporaneousness which gave it something of the quality of a vast, happy village fête as people wandered about, sat, sang, and slept against a summer background of trees, grass, flowers, and water. It was not, people said, like the 1918 Armistice Day, for at no time was the reaction hysterical. It was not like the Coronation, for the crowds were larger and their gaiety, which held up all through the night, was obviously not picked up in a pub. The day also surprised the prophets who had said that only the young would be resilient enough to celebrate in a big way. Apparently the desire to assist in

London's celebration combusted spontaneously in the bosom of every member of every family, from the smallest babies, with their hair done up in red-white-and-blue ribbons, to beaming elderly couples who, utterly without self-consciousness, strolled up and down the streets arm in arm in red-white-and-blue paper hats. Even the dogs wore immense tricoloured bows: Rosettes sprouted from the slabs of pork in the butcher shops, which, like other food stores, were open for a couple of hours in the morning. With their customary practicality, housewives put bread before circuses. They waited in the long bakery queues, the string bags of the common round in one hand and the Union Jack of the glad occasion in the other. Even queues seemed tolerable that morning. The bells had begun to peal and, after the night's storm, London was having that perfect, hot, English summer's day which, one sometimes feels, is to be found only in the imaginations of the lyric poets.

The girls in their thin, bright dresses heightened the impression that the city had been taken over by an enormous family picnic. The number of extraordinarily pretty young girls, who presumably are hidden on working days inside the factories and government offices, was astonishing. They streamed out into the parks and streets like flocks of twittering, gaily plumaged cockney birds. In their freshly curled hair were cornflowers and poppies, and they wore red-white-and-blue ribbons around their narrow waists. Some of them even tied ribbons around their bare ankles. Strolling with their uniformed boys, arms candidly about each other, they provided a constant, gay, simple marginal decoration to the big, solemn moments of the day. The crowds milled back and forth between the Palace, Westminster, Trafalgar Square, and Piccadilly Circus, and when they got tired they simply sat down wherever they happened to be – on the grass, on doorsteps, or on the kerb – and watched the other people or spread handkerchiefs over their faces and took a nap. Everybody appeared determined to see the King and Queen and Mr Churchill at least once, and few could have been disappointed. One small boy, holding on to his father's hand, wanted to see the trench shelters in Green Park too. 'You don't want to see shelters today,' his father said. 'You'll never have to use them again, son.' 'Never?' the child asked doubtfully. 'Never!' the man cried, almost angrily. '*Never*! Understand?' In the open space before the Palace, one of the places where the Prime Minister's speech was to be relayed by loudspeaker at three o'clock, the crowds seemed a little intimidated by the nearness of that symbolic block of grey stone. The people who chose to open their lunch baskets and munch sandwiches there among the flower beds of tulips were rather subdued. Piccadilly Circus attracted the more demonstrative spirits.

By lunchtime, in the Circus, the buses had to slow to a crawl in order to get through the tightly packed, laughing people. A lad in the black beret of the Tank Corps was the first to climb the little pyramidal Angkor Wat of scaffolding and sandbags which was erected early in the war to protect the pedestal of the Eros statue after the figure had been removed to safekeeping. The boy shinnied up to the top and took a tiptoe Eros pose, aiming an imaginary bow, while the crowd roared. He was followed by a paratrooper in a maroon beret, who, after getting up to the top, reached down and hauled up a blonde young woman in a very tight pair of green slacks. When she got to the top, the Tank Corps soldier promptly grabbed her in his arms and, encouraged by ecstatic cheers from the whole Circus, seemed about to enact the classic role of Eros right on the top of the monument. Nothing came of it, because a moment later a couple of GIs joined them and before long the pyramid was covered with boys and girls. They sat jammed together in an affectionate mass, swinging their legs over the sides, wearing each other's uniform caps, and calling down wisecracks to the crowd. 'My God,' someone said, 'think of a flying bomb coming down on this!' When a firecracker went off, a hawker with a tray of tin brooches of Monty's head happily yelled that comforting, sometimes fallacious phrase of the blitz nights, 'All right, mates, it's one of ours!'

All day long, the deadly past was for most people only just under the surface of the beautiful, safe present, so much so that the Government decided against sounding the sirens in a triumphant 'all clear' for fear that the noise would revive too many painful memories. For the same reason, there were no salutes of guns – only the pealing of the bells, and the whistles of tugs on the Thames sounding the doot, doot, doot, dooooot of the 'V', and the roar of the planes, which swooped back and forth over the city, dropping red and green signals toward the blur of smiling, upturned faces.

It was without any doubt Churchill's day. Thousands of King George's subjects wedged themselves in front of the Palace throughout the day, chanting ceaselessly. 'We want the King' and cheering themselves hoarse when he and the Queen and their daughters appeared, but when the crowd saw Churchill there was a deep, full-throated, almost reverent roar. He was at the head of a procession of Members of Parliament, walking back to the House of Commons from the traditional St Margaret's Thanksgiving Service. Instantly, he was surrounded by people – people running, standing on tiptoe, holding up babies so that they could be told later they had seen him, and shouting affectionately the absurd little nurserymaid name, 'Winnie, Winnie!' One of two happily sozzled, very old, and incredibly dirty cockneys who had been engaged in a slow, shuffling dance, like a couple of Shakespearean clowns, bellowed, 'That's 'im, that's 'is little old lovely bald 'ead!' The crowds saw Churchill again later, when he emerged from the Commons and was driven off in the back of a small open car, rosy, smiling, and looking immensely happy. Ernest Bevin, following in another car, got a cheer too. One of the throng, an excited East Ender, in a dress with a bodice concocted of a Union Jack, shouted, 'Gawd, fancy me cheering Bevin, the chap who makes us work!' Herbert Morrison, sitting unobtrusively in a corner of a third car, was hardly recognized, and the other Cabinet Ministers did no better. The crowd had ears, eyes, and throats for no one but Churchill, and for him everyone in it seemed to have the hearing, sight, and lungs of fifty men. His slightly formal official broadcast, which was followed by buglers sounding the 'cease firing' call, did not strike the emotional note that had been expected, but he hit it perfectly in his subsequent informal speech ('My dear friends, this is your victory . . .') from a Whitehall balcony.

All day long, little extra celebrations started up. In the Mall, a model of a Gallic cock waltzed on a pole over the heads of the singing people. 'It's the Free French,' said someone. The Belgians in the crowd tagged along after a Belgian flag that marched by, its bearer invisible. A procession of students raced through Green Park, among exploding squibs, clashing dustbin lids like cymbals and waving an immense Jeyes Disinfectant poster as a banner. American sailors and laughing girls formed a conga line down the middle of Piccadilly and cockneys linked arms in the Lambeth Walk. It was a day and night of no fixed plan and no organized merriment. Each group danced its own dance, sang its own song, and went its own way as the spirit moved it. The most tolerant, self-effacing people in London on V E Day were the police, who simply stood by, smiling benignly, while soldiers swung by one arm from lamp standards and laughing groups tore down hoardings to build the evening's bonfires. Actually, the police were not unduly strained. The extraordinary thing about the crowds was that they were almost all sober. The number of drunks one saw in that whole day and night could have been counted on two hands – possibly because the pubs were sold out so early. The young service men and women who swung arm in arm down the middle of every street, singing and swarming over the few cars rash enough to come out, were simply happy with an immense holiday happiness. They were the liberated people who like their counterparts in every celebrating capital that night, were young enough to outlive the past and to look forward to an unspoilt future. Their gaiety was very moving.

Just before the King's speech, at nine Tuesday night, the big lamps outside the Palace came on and there were cheers and ohs from children who had never seen anything of that kind in their short, blacked-out lives. As the evening wore on most of the public buildings were floodlighted. The night was as warm as midsummer, and London, its shabbiness now hidden and its domes and remaining Wren spires warmed by lights and bonfires, was suddenly magnificent. The handsomest building of all was the National Gallery, standing out honey-coloured near a ghostly, blue-shadowed St Martin's and the Charles I bit of Whitehall. The illuminated and floodlighted face of Big Ben loomed like a kind moon. Red and blue lights strung in the bushes around the lake in St James's Park glimmered on the sleepy, bewildered pelicans that live there.

By midnight the crowds had thinned out some, but those who remained were as merry as ever. They went on calling for the King outside the Palace and watching the searchlights, which for once could be observed with pleasure . . .

'A Correspondent', The Hereford Times

Passing through the village of Stoke Lacy early on Tuesday afternoon one was startled to see an effigy of Hitler in the car park at the Plough. That evening a crowd began to gather, and word went round that Hitler was to be consumed in flames at 11 p.m. At that hour excitement was intense, when Mr W. R. Symonds called upon Mr S. J. Parker, the Commander of No. 12 Platoon of the Home Guard, to set the effigy alight. In a few minutes the body of Hitler disintegrated as this 1,000-year empire had done. First his arm, poised in the Hitler salute, dropped as smartly as it was ever raised in real life . . . then a leg fell off, and the flames burnt fiercely to the strains of 'Rule Britannia', 'There'll Always be an England', and 'Roll Out the Barrel'. The crowd spontaneously linked hands and in a circle 300-strong sang the National Anthem.

THE WORLD'S FIRST ATOM BOMB TEST, LOS ALAMOS, NEW MEXICO, 17 July 1945

Sir Geoffrey Taylor

If the war in Europe had ended, the war in the Far East was still being fought. The Allies, however, had developed a secret and deadly weapon. Code-named 'The Manhattan Project', the world's first atomic bomb was built by the Allies and detonated at a test in the New Mexico desert. The world had entered the nuclear age.

I was one of the group of British scientific men who worked at Los Alamos in New Mexico, where most of the recent experimental work on atomic bombs was carried out, and I saw the first bomb explode. Before I tell you about this; I ought to say that I have witnessed many ordinary bomb trials. In such trials the kind of result to be expected to always known beforehand, and the trial is designed to find out just how much damage the bomb will do. The first atomic bomb test had to be approached with a totally different outlook because it was not possible to make any previous experiment on a smaller scale. None of us knew whether we were going to witness an epoch-making experiment or a complete failure. The physicists had predicted that a self-propagating reaction involving neutrons was possible and that this would lead to an explosion. The mathematicians had calculated what mechanical results were to be expected. Engineers and physicists had set up an apparatus rather like that used in testing ordinary bombs, to measure the efficiency of the explosion. But no one knew whether this apparatus would be needed, simply because nobody knew whether the bomb would go off.

Our uncertainty was reflected in the bets which were made at Los Alamos on the amount of energy to be released. These ranged from zero to the equivalent of 80,000 tons of TNT. Those of us who were to witness the test assembled during a late afternoon in July at Los Alamos for the 230-mile drive to the uninhabited and desolate region where the test was to be made. We arrived about three o'clock in the morning at a spot twenty miles from the hundred-foot tower on which the bomb was mounted. Here we were met by a car containing a radio receiver. Round this we assembled, listening for the signal from the firing point which would tell us when to expect the explosion. We were provided with a strip of very dark glass to protect our eyes. This glass is so dark that at midday it makes the sun look like a little undeveloped dull green potato. Through this glass I was unable to see the light which was set on the tower to show us where to look. Remember, it was still dark. I therefore fixed my eyes on this light ten seconds before the explosion was due to occur. Then I raised the dark glass to my eyes two seconds before, keeping them fixed on the spot where I had last seen the light. At exactly the expected moment, I saw through the dark glass a brilliant ball of fire which was far brighter than the sun. In a second or two it died down to a brightness which seemed to be about that of the sun, so, realizing that it must be lighting up the countryside, I looked behind me and saw the scrub-covered hills, twenty-two miles from the bomb, lighted up as though by a midday sun. Then I turned round and looked directly at the ball of fire. I saw it expand slowly, and begin to rise, growing fainter as it rose. Later it developed into a huge mushroom-shaped cloud, and soon reached a height of 40,000 feet.

Though the sequence of events was exactly what we had calculated beforehand in our more optimistic moments, the whole effect was so staggering that I found it difficult to believe my eyes, and judging by the strong ejaculations from my fellow-watchers other people felt the same reaction. So far we had heard no noise. Sound takes over one and a half minutes to travel twenty miles, so we next had to prepare to receive the blast wave. We had been advised to lie on the ground to receive the shock of the wave, but few people did so, perhaps owing to the fact that it was still dark, and rattle-snakes and tarantulas were fairly common in the district. When it came it was not very loud, and sounded like the crack of a shell passing overhead rather than a distant high-explosive bomb. Rumbling followed and continued for some time. On returning to Los Alamos, I found that one of my friends there had been lying awake in bed and had seen the light of the explosion reflected on the ceiling of his bedroom, though the source of it was over 160 miles away in a straight line.

THE ALLIES DECIDE TO DROP THE ATOMIC BOMB ON JAPAN, POTSDAM, 25 July 1945

President Harry S. Truman

Diary: Potsdam 25 July 1945
We met at eleven today. That is Stalin, Churchill, and the US President. But I had a most important session with Lord Mountbatten and General Marshall before that. We have discovered the most terrible bomb in the history of the world. It may be the fire destruction prophesied in the Euphrates Valley Era, after Noah and his fabulous Ark.

Anyway we 'think' we have found the way to cause a disintegration of the atom. An experiment in the New Mexican desert was startling – to put it mildly. Thirteen pounds of the explosive caused the complete disintegration of a steel tower 60 feet high, created a crater 6 feet deep and 1,200 feet in diameter, knocked over a steel tower 1/2 mile away and knocked men down 10,000 yards away. The explosion was visible for more than 200 miles and audible for 40 miles and more.

This weapon is to be used against Japan between now and August 10th. I have told the Sec. of War, Mr Stimson, to use it so that military objectives and soldiers and sailors are the target and not women and children. Even if the Japs are savages, ruthless, merciless and fanatic, we as the leader of the world for the common welfare cannot drop this terrible bomb on the old capital or the new.

He and I are in accord. The target will be a purely military one and we will issue a warning statement asking the Japs to surrender and save lives. I'm sure they will not do that, but we will have given them the chance. It is certainly a good thing for the world that Hitler's crowd or Stalin's did not discover this atomic bomb. It seems to be the most terrible thing ever discovered, but it can be made the most useful.

The following day, 26 July, the Allies called upon Japan to surrender. The alternative they said was 'prompt and utter destruction'. Japan did not surrender.

HIROSHIMA, JAPAN, 6 August 1945

Colonel Tibbets, USAAF

The destruction promised by the Allies came on 6 August, when three B29s of the US air force took off from Tinian and flew to Hiroshima, the eighth largest city in Japan. One of the planes, the *Enola Gay*, carried an atomic bomb. The commander of the mission was Colonel Tibbets.

We started our take-off on time which was somewhere about two-forty-five I think, and the aeroplane went on down the runway. It was loaded quite heavily but it responded exactly like I had anticipated it would. I had flown this aeroplane the same way before and there was no problem and there was nothing different this night in the way we went. We arrived over the initial point and started in on the bomb run which had about eleven minutes to go, rather a long type of run for a bomb but on the other hand we felt we needed this extra time in straight and level flight to stabilize the air speed of the aeroplane, to get everything right down to the last-minute detail. As I indicated earlier the problem after the release of the bomb is not to proceed forward but to turn away. As soon as the weight had left the aeroplane I immediately went into this steep turn and we tried then to place distance between ourselves and the point of impact. In this particular case that bomb took fifty-three seconds from the time it left the aeroplane until it exploded and this gave us adequate time of course to make the turn. We had just made the turn and rolled out on level flight when it seemed like somebody had grabbed a hold of my aeroplane and gave it a real hard shaking because this was the shock wave that had come up. Now after we had been hit by a second shock wave not quite so strong as the first one I decided we'll turn around and go back and take a look. The day was clear when we dropped that bomb, it was a clear sunshiny day and the visibility was unrestricted. As we came back around again facing the direction of Hiroshima we saw this cloud coming up. The cloud by this time, now two minutes old, was up at our altitude. We were 33,000 feet at this time and the cloud was up there and continuing to go right on up in a boiling fashion, as if it was rolling and boiling. The surface was nothing but a black boiling, like a barrel of tar. Where before there had been a city with distinctive houses, buildings and everything that you could see from our altitude, now you couldn't see anything except a black boiling debris down below.

The first atomic bomb to be dropped in warfare killed 80,000 people – a quarter of Hiroshima's inhabitants.

NAGASAKI, JAPAN, 9 August 1945

Tatsuichiro Akizuki

Three days after Hiroshima a second atomic bomb was dropped, this time on Nagasaki. Tatsuichiro Akizuki was working in Nagasaki as a doctor when the bomb landed.

It was eleven o'clock. Father Ishikawa, who was Korean, aged about thirty-six and the hospital chaplain, was listening in the hospital chapel to the confession of those Catholics who had gone to him to confess, one after the other, before the great festival, on 15 August, of the Ascension of the Virgin Mary, which was only a week away. Brother Joseph Iwanaga was toiling outside the hospital with some farm workers, digging another air-raid shelter in the shrubbery in the centre of the hospital yard. Mr Noguchi had just begun to repair the apparatus used to lift water from the well. Other members of staff were busy providing a late breakfast. Some were filling big bowls with miso soup; others were carrying them through the corridors or up the stairs. The hospital was a hive of activity after the all-clear.

'Well, we'll soon be getting our breakfast,' I said to Miss Murai. 'The patients must be hungry.'

So was I, but before we had our breakfast we would have to finish treating all the out-patients.

I stuck the pneumo-thorax needle into the side of the chest of the patient lying on the bed. It was just after eleven a.m.

I heard a low droning sound, like that of distant aeroplane engines.

'What's that?' I said. 'The all-clear has gone, hasn't it?'

At the same time the sound of the plane's engines, growing louder and louder, seemed to swoop down over the hospital.

I shouted: 'It's an enemy plane! Look out – take cover!'

As I said so, I pulled the needle out of the patient and threw myself beside the bed.

There was a blinding white flash of light, and the next moment – *Bang! Crack!* A huge impact like a gigantic blow smote down upon our bodies, our heads and our hospital. I lay flat – I didn't know whether or not of my own volition. Then down came piles of debris, slamming into my back.

The hospital has been hit, I thought. I grew dizzy, and my ears sang.

Some minutes or so must have passed before I staggered to my feet and looked around. The air was heavy with yellow smoke; white flakes of powder drifted about; it was strangely dark.

Thank God, I thought – I'm not hurt! But what about the patients?

As it became brighter, little by little our situation grew clearer. Miss Murai, who had been assisting me with the pneumo-thorax, struggled to her feet beside me. She didn't seem to have been seriously injured, though she was completely covered with white dust. 'Hey, cheer up!' I said. 'We're not hurt, thank God!'

I helped her to her feet. Another nurse, who was also in the consulting room, and the patient, managed to stand up. The man, his face smeared white like a clown and streaked with blood, lurched towards the door, holding his bloody head with his hands and moaning.

I said to myself over and over again: Our hospital has suffered a direct hit – We've been bombed! Because the hospital stood on a hill and had walls of red brick, it must, I thought, have attracted the attention of enemy planes. I felt deeply and personally responsible for what had happened.

The pervading dingy yellow silence of the room now resounded with faint cries – 'Help!' The surface of the walls and ceiling had peeled away. What I had thought to be clouds of dust or smoke was whirling brick-dust and plaster. Neither the pneumo-thorax apparatus nor the microscope on my desk were anywhere to be seen. I felt as if I were dreaming.

I encouraged Miss Murai, saying: 'Come on, we haven't been hurt at all, by the grace of God. We must rescue the in-patients.' But privately I thought it must be all over with them – the second and third floors must have disintegrated, I thought.

We went to the door of the consulting room which faced the main stairway, and there were the in-patients coming down the steps, crying: 'Help me, doctor! Oh, help me, sir.' The stairs and the corridor were heaped with timbers, plaster, debris from the ceiling. It made walking difficult. The patients staggered down towards us, crying: 'I'm hurt! Help me!' Strangely, none seemed to have been seriously injured, only slightly wounded, with fresh blood dripping from their faces and hands.

If the bomb had actually hit the hospital, I thought, they would have been far more badly injured.

'What's happened to the second and third floors?' I cried. But all they answered was – 'Help me! Help!'

One of them said: 'Mr Yamaguchi has been buried under the debris. Help him.'

No one knew what had happened. A huge force had been released above our heads. What it was, nobody knew. Had it been several tons of bombs, or the suicidal destruction of a plane carrying a heavy bomb-load?

Dazed, I retreated into the consulting room, in which the only upright object on the rubbish-strewn floor was my desk. I went and sat on it and looked out of the window at the yard and the outside world. There was not a single pane of glass in the window, not even a frame – all had been completely blown away. Out in the yard dun-coloured smoke or dust cleared little by little. I saw figures running. Then, looking to the south-west, I was stunned. The sky was as dark as pitch, covered with dense clouds of smoke; under that blackness, over the earth, hung a yellow-brown fog. Gradually the veiled ground became visible, and the view beyond rooted me to the spot with horror.

All the buildings I could see were on fire: large ones and small ones and those with straw-thatched roofs. Further off along the valley, Urakami Church, the largest Catholic church in the east, was ablaze. The technical school, a large two-storeyed wooden building, was on fire, as were many houses and the distant ordnance factory. Electricity poles were wrapped in flame like so many pieces of kindling. Trees on the nearby hills were smoking, as were the leaves of sweet potatoes in the fields. To say that everything burned is not enough. It seemed as if the earth itself emitted fire and smoke, flames that writhed up and erupted from underground. The sky was dark, the ground was scarlet, and in between hung clouds of yellowish smoke. Three kinds of colour – black, yellow and scarlet – loomed ominously over the people, who ran about like so many ants seeking to escape. What had happened? Urakami Hospital had not been bombed – I understood that much. But that ocean of fire, that sky of smoke! It seemed like the end of the world.

I ran out into the garden. Patients who were only slightly hurt came up to me, pleading for aid.

I shouted at them: 'For heaven's sake! You're not seriously wounded!'

One patient said: 'Kawaguchi and Matsuo are trapped in their rooms! They can't move. You must help them!'

I said to myself: Yes, we must first of all rescue those seriously ill tubercular patients who've been buried under the ruins.

I looked southwards again, and the sight of Nagasaki city in a sea of flames as far as the eye could reach made me think that such destruction could only have been caused by thousands of bombers, carpet-bombing. But not a plane was to be seen or heard, although even the leaves of potatoes and carrots at my feet were scorched and smouldering. The electricity cables must have exploded underground, I thought.

And then at last I identified the destroyer – 'That's it!' I cried. 'It was the new bomb – the one used on Hiroshima!'

'Look – there's smoke coming from the third floor!' exclaimed one of the patients, who had fled for safety into the hospital yard.

I turned about and looked up at the roof.

The hospital was built of brick and reinforced concrete, but the main roof was tiled, sloping in the Japanese style, and in the middle of the roof was another small, ridged roof, from whose end a little smoke was issuing, as if something was cooking there. Almost all the tiles had fallen off, leaving the roof timbers exposed.

That's odd, I said to myself, not heeding what I saw.

The smoke from the hospital looked just like that of a cigarette in comparison with the masses billowing above the technical school, Urakami Church, nearby houses, and the Convent of the Holy Cross, which were now blazing with great ferocity. The sky was dark, as if it were threatening to rain.

'As soon as we have some rain,' I said, 'these fires will quickly be extinguished.' So saying, I began to dash about in the confusion.

The fire in the hospital roof spread little by little. It was rather strange how the roof was the first thing in the hospital to catch fire. But the temperature at the instant the bomb exploded would have been thousands of degrees Centigrade at the epicentre and hundreds of degrees Centigrade near the hospital. Wooden buildings within 1,500 metres of the epicentre instantly caught fire. Within 1,000 metres, iron itself melted. The hospital stood 1,800 metres away from the epicentre. Probably, coming on top of the scorching heat of the sun, which had shone for more than ten days running, the blasting breath of hundreds of degrees Centigrade had dried out the hospital timbers and ignited them. The attics under the roof were wooden and used as a store-house; the fire now spread through them. Upset as I was, at first I wasn't too concerned, thinking it was only a small fire. But before long the main roof of the building was enveloped in flames.

About ten minutes after the explosion, a big man, half-naked, holding his head between his hands, came into the yard towards me, making sounds that seemed to be dragged from the pit of his stomach.

'Got hurt, sir,' he groaned; he shivered as if he were cold. 'I'm hurt.'

I stared at him, at the strange-looking man. Then I saw it was Mr Zenjiro Tsujimoto, a market-gardener and a friendly neighbour to me and the hospital. I wondered what had happened to the robust Zenjiro.

'What's the matter with you, Tsujimoto?' I asked him, holding him in my arms.

'In the pumpkin field over there – getting pumpkins for the patients – got hurt . . .' he said, speaking brokenly and breathing feebly.

It was all he could do to keep standing. Yet it didn't occur to me that he had been seriously injured.

'Come along now,' I said. 'You are perfectly all right, I assure you. Where's your shirt? Lie down and rest somewhere where it's cool. I'll be with you in a moment.'

His head and his face were whitish; his hair was singed. It was because his eyelashes had been scorched away that he seemed so bleary-eyed. He was half-naked because his shirt had been burned from his back in a single flash. But I wasn't aware of such facts. I gazed at him as he reeled about with his head between his hands. What a change had come over this man who was stronger than a horse, whom I had last seen earlier that morning. It's as if he's been struck by lightning, I thought.

After Mr Tsujimoto came staggering up to me, another person who looked just like him wandered into the yard. Who he was and where he had come from I had no idea. 'Help me,' he said, groaning, half-naked, holding his head between his hands. He sat down, exhausted. 'Water . . . Water . . .' he whispered.

'What's the trouble? What's wrong with you? What's become of your shirt?' I demanded.

'Hot – *hot* . . . Water . . . I'm burning.' They were the only words that were articulate.

As time passed, more and more people in a similar plight came up to the hospital – ten minutes, twenty minutes, an hour after the explosion. All were of the same appearance, sounded the same. 'I'm hurt, *hurt!* I'm burning! Water!' They all moaned the same lament. I shuddered. Half-naked or stark naked, they walked with strange, slow steps, groaning from deep inside themselves as if they had travelled from the depths of hell. They looked whitish; their faces were like masks. I felt as if I were dreaming, watching pallid ghosts processing slowly in one direction – as in a dream I had once dreamt in my childhood.

These ghosts came on foot uphill towards the hospital, from the direction of the burning city and from the more easterly ordnance factory. Worker or student, girl or man, they all walked slowly and had the same mask-like face. Each one groaned and cried for help. Their cries grew in strength as the people increased in number, sounding like something from the Buddhist scriptures, re-echoing everywhere, as if the earth itself were in pain.

EXECUTION OF NAZI WAR CRIMINALS, NUREMBERG, 16 October 1946

Kingsbury Smith

The trials held by the International Military Tribunal at Nuremberg found twelve of the surviving leaders of Nazi Germany guilty of crimes against humanity. The twelve, who included Martin Bormann, tried *in absentia*, were sentenced to death by hanging. Kingsbury Smith represented the American press at the hangings.

Hermann Wilhelm Göring cheated the gallows of Allied justice by committing suicide in his prison cell shortly before the ten other condemned Nazi leaders were hanged in Nuremberg gaol. He swallowed cyanide he had concealed in a copper cartridge shell, while lying on a cot in his cell.

The one-time Number Two man in the Nazi hierarchy was dead two hours before he was scheduled to have been dropped through the trapdoor of a gallows erected in a small, brightly lighted gymnasium in the gaol yard, thirty-five yards from the cell block where he spent his last days of ignominy.

Joachim von Ribbentrop, foreign minister in the ill-starred regime of Adolf Hitler, took Göring's place as first to the scaffold.

Last to depart this life in a total span of just about two hours was Arthur Seyss-Inquart, former *Gauleiter* of Holland and Austria.

In between these two once-powerful leaders, the gallows claimed, in the order named, Field Marshal Wilhelm Keitel; Ernst Kaltenbrunner, once head of the Nazis' security police; Alfred Rosenberg, arch-priest of Nazi culture in foreign lands; Hans Frank, *Gauleiter* of Poland; Wilhelm Frick, Nazi minister of the interior; Fritz Sauckel, boss of slave labour; Colonel General Alfred Jodl; and Julius Streicher, who bossed the anti-Semitism drive of the Hitler Reich.

As they went to the gallows, most of the ten endeavoured to show bravery. Some were defiant and some were resigned and some begged the Almighty for mercy.

All except Rosenberg made brief, last-minute statements on the scaffold. But the only one to make any reference to Hitler or the Nazi ideology in his final moments was Julius Streicher.

Three black-painted wooden scaffolds stood inside the gymnasium, a room approximately 33 feet wide by 80 feet long with plaster walls in which cracks showed. The gymnasium had been used only three days before by the American security guards for a basketball game. Two gallows were used alternately. The third was a spare for use if needed. The men were hanged one at a time, but to get the executions over with quickly, the military police would bring in a man while the prisoner who preceded him still was dangling at the end of the rope.

The ten once great men in Hitler's Reich that was to have lasted for a thousand years walked up thirteen wooden steps to a platform eight feet high which also was eight feet square.

Ropes were suspended from a crossbeam supported on two posts. A new one was used for each man.

When the trap was sprung, the victim dropped from sight in the interior of the scaffolding. The bottom of it was boarded up with wood on three sides and shielded by a dark canvas curtain on the fourth, so that no one saw the death struggles of the men dangling with broken necks.

Von Ribbentrop entered the execution chamber at 1.11 a.m. Nuremberg time. He was stopped immediately inside the door by two Army sergeants who closed in on each side of him and held his arms, while another sergeant who had followed him in removed manacles from his hands and replaced them with a leather strap.

It was planned originally to permit the condemned men to walk from their cells to the execution chamber with their hands free, but all were manacled immediately following Göring's suicide.

Von Ribbentrop was able to maintain his apparent stoicism to the last. He walked steadily toward the scaffold between his two guards, but he did not answer at first when an officer standing at the foot of the gallows went through the formality of asking his name. When the query was repeated he almost shouted, 'Joachim von Ribbentrop!' and then mounted the steps without any sign of hesitation.

When he was turned around on the platform to face the witnesses, he seemed to clench his teeth and raise his head with the old arrogance. When asked whether he had any final message he said, 'God protect Germany,' in German, and then added, 'May I say something else?'

The interpreter nodded and the former diplomatic wizard of Nazidom spoke his last words in loud, firm tones: 'My last wish is that Germany realize its entity and that an understanding be reached between the East and the West. I wish peace to the world.'

As the black hood was placed in position on his head, von Ribbentrop looked straight ahead.

Then the hangman adjusted the rope, pulled the lever, and von Ribbentrop slipped away to his fate.

Field Marshal Keitel, who was immediately behind von Ribbentrop in the order of executions, was the first military leader to be executed under the new concept of international law – the principle that professional soldiers cannot escape punishment for waging aggressive wars and permitting crimes against humanity with the claim they were dutifully carrying out orders of superiors.

Keitel entered the chamber two minutes after the trap had dropped beneath von Ribbentrop, while the latter still was at the end of his rope. But von Ribbentrop's body was concealed inside the first scaffold; all that could be seen was the taut rope.

Keitel did not appear as tense as von Ribbentrop. He held his head high while his hands were being tied and walked erect toward the gallows with a military bearing. When asked his name he responded loudly and mounted the gallows as he might have mounted a reviewing stand to take a salute from German armies.

He certainly did not appear to need the help of guards who walked alongside, holding his arms. When he turned around atop the platform he looked over the crowd with the iron-jawed haughtiness of a proud Prussian officer. His last words, uttered in a full, clear voice, were translated as 'I call on God Almighty to have mercy on the German people. More than 2 million German soldiers went to their death for the fatherland before me. I follow now my sons – all for Germany.'

After his black-booted, uniformed body plunged through the trap, witnesses agreed Keitel had showed more courage on the scaffold than in the courtroom, where he had tried to shift his guilt upon the ghost of Hitler, claiming that all was the Führer's fault and that he merely carried out orders and had no responsibility.

With both von Ribbentrop and Keitel hanging at the end of their ropes there was a pause in the proceedings. The American colonel directing the executions asked the American general representing the United States on the Allied Control Commission if those present could smoke. An affirmative answer brought cigarettes into the hands of almost every one of the thirty-odd persons present. Officers and GIs walked around nervously or spoke a few words to one another in hushed voices while Allied correspondents scribbled furiously their notes on this historic though ghastly event.

In a few minutes an American army doctor accompanied by a Russian army doctor and both carrying stethoscopes walked to the first scaffold, lifted the curtain and disappeared within.

They emerged at 1.30 a.m. and spoke to an American colonel. The colonel swung around and facing official witnesses snapped to attention to say, 'The man is dead.'

Two GIs quickly appeared with a stretcher which was carried up and lifted into the interior of the scaffold. The hangman mounted the gallows steps, took a large commando-type knife out of a sheath strapped to his side and cut the rope.

Von Ribbentrop's limp body with the black hood still over his head was removed to the far end of the room and placed behind a black canvas curtain. This all had taken less than ten minutes.

The directing colonel turned to the witnesses and said, 'Cigarettes out, please, gentlemen.' Another colonel went out the door and over to the condemned block to fetch the next man. This was Ernst Kaltenbrunner. He entered the execution chamber at 1.36 a.m., wearing a sweater beneath his blue double-breasted coat.

With his lean haggard face furrowed by old duelling scars, this terrible successor to Reinhard Heydrich had a frightening look as he glanced around the room.

He wet his lips apparently in nervousness as he turned to mount the gallows, but he walked steadily. He answered his name in a calm, low voice. When he turned around on the gallows platform he first faced a United States Army Roman Catholic chaplain wearing a Franciscan habit. When Kaltenbrunner was invited to make a last statement, he said, 'I have loved my German people and my fatherland with a warm heart. I have done my duty by the laws of my people and I am sorry my people were led this time by men who were not soldiers and that crimes were committed of which I had no knowledge.'

This was the man, one of whose agents – a man named Rudolf Hoess – confessed at a trial that under Kaltenbrunner's orders he gassed 3 million human beings at the Auschwitz concentration camp!

As the black hood was raised over his head Kaltenbrunner, still speaking in a low voice, used a German phrase which translated means, 'Germany, good luck.'

His trap was sprung at 1.39 a.m.

Field Marshal Keitel was pronounced dead at 1.44 a.m. and three minutes later guards had removed his body. The scaffold was made ready for Alfred Rosenberg.

Rosenberg was dull and sunken-cheeked as he looked around the court. His complexion was pasty-brown, but he did not appear nervous and walked with a steady step to and up the gallows.

Apart from giving his name and replying 'no' to a question as to whether he had anything to say, he did not utter a word. Despite his avowed atheism he was accompanied by a Protestant chaplain who followed him to the gallows and stood beside him praying.

Rosenberg looked at the chaplain once, expressionless. Ninety seconds after he was swinging from the end of a hangman's rope. His was the swiftest execution of the ten.

There was a brief lull in the proceedings until Kaltenbrunner was pronounced dead at 1.52 a.m.

Hans Frank was next in the parade of death. He was the only one of the condemned to enter the chamber with a smile on his countenance.

Although nervous and swallowing frequently, this man, who was converted to Roman Catholicism after his arrest, gave the appearance of being relieved at the prospect of atoning for his evil deeds.

He answered to his name quietly and when asked for any last statement, he replied in a low voice that was almost a whisper, 'I am thankful for the kind treatment during my captivity and I ask God to accept me with mercy.'

Frank closed his eyes and swallowed as the black hood went over his head.

The sixth man to leave his prison cell and walk with handcuffed wrists to the death house was 69-year-old Wilhelm Frick. He entered the execution chamber at 2.05 a.m., six minutes after Rosenberg had been pronounced dead. He seemed the least steady of any so far and stumbled on the thirteenth step of the gallows. His only words were, 'Long live eternal Germany,' before he was hooded and dropped through the trap.

Julius Streicher made his melodramatic appearance at 2.12 a.m. While his manacles were being removed and his hands bound, this ugly, dwarfish little man, wearing a threadbare suit and a well-worn bluish shirt buttoned to the neck but without a tie (he was notorious during his days of power for his flashy dress), glanced at the three wooden scaffolds rising up menacingly in front of him. Then he glared around the room, his eyes resting momentarily upon the small group of witnesses. By this time, his hands were tied securely behind his back. Two guards, one on each arm, directed him to Number One gallows on the left of the entrance. He walked steadily the six feet to the first wooden step but his face was twitching.

As the guards stopped him at the bottom of the steps for identification formality he uttered his piercing scream: 'Heil Hitler!'

The shriek sent a shiver down my back.

As its echo died away an American colonel standing by the steps said sharply, 'Ask the man his name.' In response to the interpreter's query Streicher shouted, 'You know my name well.'

The interpreter repeated his request and the condemned man yelled, 'Julius Streicher.'

As he reached the platform, Streicher cried out, 'Now it goes to God.' He was pushed the last two steps to the mortal spot beneath the hangman's rope. The rope was being held back against a wooden rail by the hangman.

Streicher was swung around to face the witnesses and glared at them. Suddenly he screamed, '*Purim Fest 1946*.' [Purim is a Jewish holiday celebrated in the spring, commemorating the execution of Haman, ancient persecutor of the Jews described in the Old Testament.]

The American officer standing at the scaffold said, 'Ask the man if he has any last words.'

When the interpreter had translated, Streicher shouted, 'The Bolsheviks will hang you one day.'

When the black hood was raised over his head, Streicher said, 'I am with God.'

As it was being adjusted, Streicher's muffled voice could be heard to say, 'Adele, my dear wife.'

At that instant the trap opened with a loud bang. He went down kicking. When the rope snapped taut with the body swinging wildly, groans could be heard from within the concealed interior of the scaffold. Finally, the hangman, who had descended from the gallows platform, lifted the black canvas curtain and went inside. Something happened that put a stop to the groans and brought the rope to a standstill. After it was over I was not in a mood to ask what he did, but I assume that he grabbed the swinging body and pulled down on it. We were all of the opinion that Streicher had strangled.

Then, following removal of the corpse of Frick, who had been pronounced dead at 2.20 a.m., Fritz Sauckel was brought face to face with his doom.

Wearing a sweater with no coat and looking wild-eyed, Sauckel proved to be the most defiant of any except Streicher.

Here was the man who put millions into bondage on a scale unknown since the pre-Christian era. Gazing around the room from the gallows platform he suddenly screamed, 'I am dying innocent. The sentence is wrong. God protect Germany and make Germany great again. Long live Germany! God protect my family.'

The trap was sprung at 2.26 a.m. and, as in the case of Streicher, there was a loud groan from the gallows pit as the noose snapped tightly under the weight of his body.

Ninth in the procession of death was Alfred Jodl. With the black coat-collar of his *Wehrmacht* uniform half turned up at the back as though hurriedly put on, Jodl entered the dismal death house with obvious signs of nervousness. He wet his lips constantly and his features were drawn and haggard as he walked, not nearly so steady as Keitel, up the gallows steps. Yet his voice was calm when he uttered his last six words on earth: 'My greetings to you, my Germany.'

At 2.34 a.m. Jodl plunged into the black hole of the scaffold. He and Sauckel hung together until the latter was pronounced dead six minutes later and removed.

The Czechoslovak-born Seyss-Inquart, whom Hitler had made ruler of Holland and Austria, was the last actor to make his appearance in this unparalleled scene. He entered the chamber at 2.38 ½ a.m., wearing glasses which made his face an easily remembered caricature.

He looked around with noticeable signs of unsteadiness as he limped on his left clubfoot to the gallows. He mounted the steps slowly, with guards helping him.

When he spoke his last words his voice was low but intense. He said, 'I hope that this execution is the last act of the tragedy of the Second World War and that the lesson taken from this world war will be that peace and understanding should exist between peoples. I believe in Germany.'

He dropped to death at 2.45 a.m.

With the bodies of Jodl and Seyss-Inquart still hanging awaiting formal pronouncement of death, the gymnasium doors opened again and guards entered carrying Göring's body on a stretcher.

He had succeeded in wrecking plans of the Allied Control Council to have him lead the parade of condemned Nazi chieftains to their death. But the council's representatives were determined that Göring at least would take his place as a dead man beneath the shadow of the scaffold.

The guards carrying the stretcher set it down between the first and second gallows. Göring's big bare feet stuck out from under the bottom end of a khaki-coloured United States Army blanket. One blue-silk-clad arm was hanging over the side.

The colonel in charge of the proceedings ordered the blanket removed so that witnesses and Allied correspondents could see for themselves that Göring was definitely dead. The Army did not want any legend to develop that Göring had managed to escape.

As the blanket came off it revealed Göring clad in black silk pyjamas with a blue jacket shirt over them, and this was soaking wet, apparently the result of efforts by prison doctors to revive him.

The face of this twentieth-century freebooting political racketeer was still contorted with the pain of his last agonizing moments and his final gesture of defiance.

They covered him up quickly and this Nazi warlord, who like a character out of the days of the Borgias, had wallowed in blood and beauty, passed behind a canvas curtain into the black pages of history.

ISRAEL DECLARES INDEPENDENCE, TEL AVIV, ISRAEL, 14 May 1948

James Cameron

The Jews had been displaced from their homeland in Palestine in the second century AD by the Romans. Nearly two thousand years later, following Nazi persecution, many Jews began to emigrate to their ancient homeland, which caused friction with the Arab peoples who had since settled there. In 1947 the United Nations proposed that Palestine should be divided into Jewish and Arab states, with Jerusalem as a neutral zone. This plan was rejected by the Arabs but accepted by the Jews who, in May 1948, proclaimed the independent state of Israel.

In Rothschild Boulevard in the middle of Tel-Aviv stood the Museum Hall, a building as undistinguished as all others in the town; it had once been the home of Meir Dizengoff, first Mayor of Tel-Aviv. It was to be undistinguished no longer.

Outside the hall was drawn up a guard of honour of cadets from the Jewish Officers' School. A strong detachment of Haganah military police meticulously scrutinised the credentials of every soul entering up the steps from the Boulevard. In the steaming heat of that afternoon the atmosphere of crisis was almost tangibly neurotic. The Yishuv had waited six hundred generations for this day; Jewry had trod a long hard road from Babylon and Pharaoh's Egypt and the desert and the ghettos of the world; what had seemed endless was now at last to have an end. The moment could not and must not be wrecked now by a chance intruding enemy. Security was tense. Every arrival passed the cordons of guards who were men from Berlin and London and Cracow and South Africa and Iraq and Egypt, from the death-camps of Germany and Poland, from the farms of Galilee. No museum had ever been harder to enter.

The hall was crowded to suffocation, the heat magnified by the film-camera lights, the shadows broken by the flashbulbs. Above it all, against the blue and white hangings, looked down the portrait of the sombre-bearded Viennese journalist Theodor Herzl, who had dreamed it all how long ago? Just over fifty years.

Below the portrait of Herzl sat the eleven of the National Administration and the secretary. At the centre table sat the fourteen members of the National Council. Around them in a semi-circle were the Rabbis, Mayors, elders of the Yishuv, officers of the Haganah command, councillors, fund-raisers, the Zionist General Council. But from Jerusalem none could come, nor from Haifa and the north. Tel-Aviv was still an enclave in a hostile land.

At exactly four o'clock David Ben-Gurion, wearing a necktie for the only time in living memory, rapped his gavel on the table. The whole hall rose to its feet. The Philharmonic Orchestra concealed upstairs drew up its bows – but they were too late, already the crowd was singing the 'Hatikvah'.

It faded out, and Ben-Gurion said: 'The land of Israel was the birthplace of the Jewish people. Here their spiritual, religious and national identity was formed. In their exile from the land of Israel the Jews remained faithful to it in all the countries of their dispersal, never ceasing to hope and pray for the restoration of their national freedom.'

His white woolly halo danced, his face glistened in the heat, his eloquence mounted to a Hebraic fervour; he was speaking for Joshua and David, Nehemiah and Ezra the Writer, for the fugitives from the Crusaders and Saladin and Spain, for the survivors of Dachau and Ravensbruck, for the sabra Yishuv who had drained the Hulah swamps, the founders of Rehovot, the builders of Tel-Aviv itself, for the immigrant bus-drivers and the waiters in the cafés of Dizengoff Square, and those who were yet to come.

'Therefore by virtue of the natural and historic right of the Jewish people to be a nation as other nations, and of the Resolution of the General Assembly of the United Nations, we hereby proclaim the establishment of the Jewish nation in Palestine, to be called the Medinat Yisrael: the State of Israel.'

It was far from over; he had now to read the Articles arising from the declaration, the setting up of provisional authorities, the principles of 'social and political equality of all citizens distinguishing not between religions, races or sexes, providing freedom of religion, conscience, education, language and culture, the safeguarding of the Holy Places of all faiths.

'We appeal to the United Nations for help to the Jewish people in building their State, and to admit Israel into the family of nations. We offer only peace and friendship to all neighbouring states and people . . .'

And finally: 'With trust in God, we set our hand to this declaration, at this session of the Provisional State Council, on the soil of the Homeland, in the city of Tel-Aviv, on this Sabbath eve, the fifth of Iyar 5708, the fourteenth day of May 1948.'

It had taken exactly thirty-two minutes. Plus, of course, 2,000 years.

MARILYN MONROE IN HOLLYWOOD, AMERICA, 1950

Arthur Miller

The playwright – and future husband of Marilyn Monroe – describes his first meeting with the movie icon of the century.

A few days earlier I had gone to the Twentieth Century Fox studio with Kazan, who was under contract there and had many friends working on the sound stages. One of them, his former film editor, was now directing *As Young As You Feel*, a comedy with my father's *bête noire* Monty Woolley and, in a bit part, Marilyn. Moviemaking was still an exotic and fantastic affair for me, and full of mysteries. We had just arrived on a nightclub set when Marilyn, in a black open-work lace dress, was directed to walk across the floor, attracting the worn gaze of the bearded Woolley. She was being shot from the rear to set off the swivelling of her hips, a motion fluid enough to seem comic. It was, in fact, her natural walk: her footprints on a beach would be in a straight line, the heel descending exactly before the last toeprint, throwing her pelvis into motion.

When the shot was finished she came over to Kazan, who had met her with Hyde on another visit some time before. From where I stood, yards away, I saw her in profile against a white light, with her hair coiled atop her head; she was weeping under a veil of black lace that she lifted now and then to dab her eyes. When we shook hands the shock of her body's motion sped through me, a sensation at odds with her sadness amid all this glamour and technology and the busy confusion of a new shot being set up. She had been weeping, she would explain later, while telling Kazan that Hyde had died calling her name in a hospital room she had been forbidden by his family to enter. She had heard him from the corridor, and had left, as always, alone.

THE KOREAN WAR: LIEUTENANT PHILIP CURTIS WINS THE VICTORIA CROSS, IMJIN RIVER, N. KOREA 22 April 1951

Anthony Farrar-Hockley

The Communist regime of North Korea launched a major offensive in the Korean war on 22 April 1951, breaking through the line held by the United Nations west of Chungpyong Reservoir. The situation for the UN was saved only by the stand of the Gloucestershire Regiment at Imjin River.

The dawn breaks. A pale, April sun is rising in the sky. Take any group of trenches here upon these two main hill positions looking north across the river. See, here, the weapon pits in which the defenders stand: unshaven, wind-burned faces streaked with black powder, filthy with sweat and dust from their exertions, look towards their enemy with eyes red from fatigue and sleeplessness; grim faces, yet not too grim that they refuse to smile when someone cracks a joke about the sunrise. Here, round the weapons smeared with burnt cordite, lie the few pathetic remnants of the wounded, since removed: cap comforters; a boot; some cigarettes half-soaked with blood; a photograph of two small girls; two keys; a broken pencil stub. The men lounge quietly in their positions, waiting for the brief respite to end.

'They're coming back, Ted.'

A shot is fired, a scattered burst follows it. The sergeant calls an order to the mortar group. Already they can hear the shouting and see, here and there, the figures moving out from behind cover as their machine-guns pour fire from the newly occupied Castle Site. Bullets fly back and forth; overhead, almost lazily, grenades are being exchanged on either side; man meets man; hand meets hand. This tiny corner of the battle that is raging along the whole front, blazes up and up into extreme heat, reaches a climax and dies away to nothingness – another little lull, another breathing space.

Phil, is called to the telephone at this moment; Pat's voice sounds in his ear.

'Phil, at the present rate of casualties we can't hold on unless we get the Castle Site back. Their machine-guns up there completely dominate your platoon and most of Terry's. We shall never stop their advance until we hold that ground again.'

Phil looks over the edge of the trench at the Castle Site, two hundred yards away, as Pat continues talking, giving him the instructions for the counter attack. They talk for a minute or so; there is not much more to be said when an instruction is given to assault with a handful of tired men across open ground. Everyone knows it is vital: everyone knows it is appallingly dangerous. The only details to be fixed are the arrangements for supporting fire; and, though A Company's Gunners are dead, Ronnie will support them from D Company's hill. Behind, the machine-gunners will ensure that they are not engaged from the open eastern flank. Phil gathers his tiny assault party together.

It is time, they rise from the ground and move forward up to the barbed wire that once protected the rear of John's platoon. Already two men are hit and Papworth, the Medical Corporal, is attending to them. They are through the wire safely – safely! – when the machine-gun in the bunker begins to fire. Phil is badly wounded: he drops to the ground. They drag him back through the wire somehow and seek what little cover there is as it creeps across their front. The machine-gun stops, content now it has driven them back; waiting for a better target when they move into the open again.

'It's all right, sir,' says someone to Phil. 'The Medical Corporal's been sent for. He'll be here any minute.'

Phil raises himself from the ground, rests on a friendly shoulder, then climbs by a great effort on to one knee.

'We must take the Castle Site,' he says; and gets up to take it.

The others beg him to wait until his wounds are tended. One man places a hand on his side.

'Just wait until Papworth has seen you, sir –'

But Phil has gone: gone to the wire, gone through the wire, gone towards the bunker. The others come out behind him, their eyes all on him. And suddenly it seems as if, for a few breathless moments, the whole of the remainder of that field of battle is still and silent, watching amazed, the lone figure that runs so painfully forward to the bunker holding the approach to the Castle Site: one tiny figure, throwing grenades, firing a pistol, set to take Castle Hill.

Perhaps he will make it – in spite of his wounds, in spite of the odds – perhaps this act of supreme gallantry may, by its sheer audacity, succeed. But the machine-gun in the bunker fires directly into him: he staggers, falls, is dead instantly; the grenade he threw a second before his death explodes after it in the mouth of the bunker. The machine-gun does not fire on three of Phil's platoon who run forward to pick him up; it does not fire again through the battle: it is destroyed; the muzzle blown away, the crew dead.

APPEARING BEFORE THE HOUSE UN-AMERICAN ACTIVITIES COMMITTEE, WASHINGTON, AMERICA, 21 May 1952

Lillian Hellman

The internal politics of the USA in the early 1950s were conditioned by fears of the Cold War with the USSR. A witch-hunt led by Senator McCarthy attacked citizens suspected of left-wing views, many of whom were 'blacklisted' – prevented from working. A particular target for the attentions of McCarthyism was the entertainment industry; playwright Lillian Hellman was only one of many writers and artists to be asked to appear before Congress's House Un-American Activities Committee to admit their political belief and 'name names' of other suspected Communists.

The Committee room was almost empty except for a few elderly, small-faced ladies sitting in the rear. They looked as if they were permanent residents and, since they occasionally spoke to each other, it was not too long a guess that they came as an organized group or club. Clerks came in and out, put papers on the rostrum, and disappeared. I said maybe we had come too early, but Joe [Rauh, Hellman's lawyer] said no, it was better that I get used to the room.

Then, I think to make the wait better for me, he said, 'Well, I can tell you now that in the early days of seeing you, I was scared that what happened to my friend might happen to me.'

He stopped to tell Pollitt [Rauh's assistant] that he didn't understand about the press – not one newspaperman had appeared.

I said; 'What happened to your friend?'

'He represented a Hollywood writer who told him that he would under no circumstances be a friendly witness. That was why my friend took the case. So they get here, in the same seats we are, sure of his client, and within ten minutes the writer is one of the friendliest witnesses the Committee has had the pleasure of. He throws in every name he can think of, including his college roommate, childhood friend.'

I said, 'No, that won't happen and for more solid reasons than your honour or even mine. I told you I can't make quick changes.'

Joe told Pollitt that he thought he understood about no press and the half-empty room: the Committee had kept our appearance as quiet as they could. Joe said, 'That means they're frightened of us. I don't know whether that's good or bad, but we want the press here and I don't know how to get them.'

He didn't have to know. The room suddenly began to fill up behind me and the press people began to push toward their section and were still piling in when Representative Wood began to pound his gavel. I hadn't seen the Committee come in, don't think I had realized that they were to sit on a raised platform, the government having learned from the stage, or maybe the other way around. I was glad I hadn't seen them come in – they made a gloomy picture. Through the noise of the gavel I heard one of the ladies in the rear cough very loudly. She was to cough all through the hearing. Later I heard one of her friends say loudly, 'Irma, take your good cough drops.'

The opening questions were standard: what was my name, where was I born, what was my occupation, what were the titles of my plays. It didn't take long to get to what really interested them: my time in Hollywood, which studios had I worked for, what periods of what years, with some mysterious emphasis on 1937. (My time in Spain, I thought, but I was wrong.)

Had I met a writer called Martin Berkeley? (I had never, still have never, met Martin Berkeley, although Hammett* told me later that I had once sat at a lunch table of sixteen or seventeen people with him in the old Metro-Goldwyn-Mayer commissary.) I said I must refuse to answer that question. Mr Tavenner said he'd like to ask me again whether I had stated I was abroad in the summer of 1937. I said yes, explained that I had been in New York for several weeks before going to Europe, and got myself ready for what I knew was coming: Martin Berkeley, one of the Committee's most lavish witnesses on the subject of Hollywood, was now going to be put to work. Mr Tavenner read Berkeley's testimony. Perhaps he is worth quoting, the small details are nicely

*Dashiell Hammett. The detective-story writer, author of such private eye classics as *The Maltese Falcon*, was Hellman's long-time partner.

formed, even about his 'old friend Hammett', who had no more than a bowing acquaintance with him.

MR TAVENNER: . . . I would like you to tell the committee when and where the Hollywood section of the Communist Party was first organized.
MR BERKELEY: Well, sir, by a very strange coincidence the section was organized in my house . . . In June of 1937, the middle of June, the meeting was held in my house. My house was picked because I had a large living room and ample parking facilities . . . And it was a pretty good meeting. We were honoured by the presence of many functionaries from downtown, and the spirit was swell . . . Well, in addition to Jerome and the others I have mentioned before, and there is no sense in me going over the list again and again . . . Also present was Harry Carlisle, who is now in the process of being deported, for which I am very grateful. He was an English subject. After Stanley Lawrence had stolen what funds there were from the party out here, and to make amends had gone to Spain and gotten himself killed, they sent Harry Carlisle here to conduct Marxist classes . . . Also at the meeting was Donald Ogden Stewart. His name is spelled Donald Ogden S-t-e-w-a-r-t. Dorothy Parker, also a writer. Her husband Allen Campbell, C-a-m-p-b-e-l-l; my old friend Dashiell Hammett, who is now in jail in New York for his activities; that very excellent playwright, Lillian Hellman . . .

And so on.

When this nonsense was finished, Mr Tavenner asked me if it was true. I said that I wanted to refer to the letter I had sent, I would like the Committee to reconsider my offer in the letter.

MR TAVENNER: In other words, you are asking the committee not to ask you any questions regarding the participation of other persons in the Communist Party activities?

I said I hadn't said that.

Mr Wood said that in order to clarify the record Mr Tavenner should put into the record the correspondence between me and the Committee. Mr Tavenner did just that, and when he had finished Rauh sprang to his feet, picked up a stack of mimeographed copies of my letter, and handed them out to the press section. I was puzzled by this – I hadn't noticed he had the copies – but I did notice that Rauh was looking happy.

Mr Tavenner was upset, far more than the printed words of my hearing show. Rauh said that Tavenner himself had put the letters in the record, and thus he thought passing out copies was proper. The polite words of each as they read on the page were not polite as spoken. I am convinced that in this section of the testimony, as in several other sections – certainly in Hammett's later testimony before the Senate Internal Security Subcommittee – either the court stenographer missed some of what was said and filled it in later, or the documents were, in part, edited. Having read many examples of the work of court stenographers, I have never once seen a completely accurate report.

Mr Wood told Mr Tavenner that the Committee could not be 'placed in the attitude of trading with the witnesses as to what they will testify to' and that thus he thought both letters should be read aloud.

Mr Tavenner did just this, and there was talk I couldn't hear, a kind of rustle, from the press section. Then Mr Tavenner asked me if I had attended the meeting described by Berkeley, and one of the hardest things I ever did in my life was to swallow the words, 'I don't know him, and a little investigation into the time and place would have proved to you that I could not have been at the meeting he talks about.' Instead, I said that I must refuse to answer the question. The 'must' in that sentence annoyed Mr Wood – it was to annoy him again and again – and he corrected me: 'You might refuse to answer, the question is asked, do you refuse?'

But Wood's correction of me, the irritation in his voice, was making me nervous, and I began to move my right hand as if I had a tic, unexpected, and couldn't stop it. I told myself that if a word irritated him, the insults would begin to come very soon. So I sat up straight, made my left hand hold my right hand, and hoped it would work. But I felt the sweat on my face and arms and knew that something was going to happen to me, something out of control, and I turned to Joe, remembering the suggested toilet intermission. But the clock said we had only been there sixteen minutes, and if it was going to come, the bad time, I had better hang on for a while.

Was I a member of the Communist Party, had I been, what year had I stopped being? How could I harm such people as Martin Berkeley by admitting I had known them, and so on. At times I couldn't follow the reasoning, at times I understood full well that in refusing to answer questions about membership in the Party I had, of course, trapped myself into a seeming admission that I once had been.

But in the middle of one of the questions about my past, something so remarkable happened that I am to this day convinced that the unknown gentleman who spoke had a great deal to do with the rest of my life. A voice from the press gallery had been for at least three or four minutes louder than the other voices. (By this time, I think, the press had finished reading my letter to the Committee and were discussing it.) The loud voice had been answered by a less loud voice, but no words could be distinguished. Suddenly a clear voice said, 'Thank God somebody finally had the guts to do it.'

It is never wise to say that something is the best minute of your life, you must be forgetting, but I still think that unknown voice made the words that helped to save me. (I had been sure that not only did the elderly ladies in the room disapprove of me, but the press would be antagonistic.) Wood rapped his gavel and said angrily, 'If that occurs again, I will clear the press from these chambers.'

'You do that, sir,' said the same voice.

Mr Wood spoke to somebody over his shoulder and the somebody moved around to the press section, but that is all that happened. To this day I don't know the name of the man who spoke, but for months later, almost every day I would say to myself, I wish I could tell him that I had really wanted to say to Mr Wood: 'There is no Communist menace in this country and you know it. You have made cowards into liars, an ugly business, and you made me write a letter in which I acknowledged you power. I should have gone into your Committee room, given my name and address, and walked out.' Many people have said they liked what I did, but I don't much, and if I hadn't worried about rats in jail, and such . . . Ah, the bravery you tell yourself was possible when it's all over, the bravery of the staircase.

In the Committee room I heard Mr Wood say, 'Mr Walter does not desire to ask the witness any further questions. Is there any reason why this witness should not be excused from further attendance before the Committee?'

Mr Tavenner said, 'No, sir.'

My hearing was over an hour and seven minutes after it began. I don't think I understood that it was over, but Joe was whispering so loudly and so happily that I jumped from the noise in my ear.

He said, '*Get up. Get up.* Get out of here immediately. Pollitt will take you. Don't stop for any reason, to answer any questions from anybody. Don't run, but walk as fast as you can and just shake your head and keep moving if anybody comes near you.'

Some years later Hellman asked Rauh why she was not prosecuted by the Committee:

He said, 'There were three things they wanted. One, names which you wouldn't give. Two, a smear by accusing you of being a "Fifth Amendment Communist". They couldn't do that because in your letter you offered to testify about yourself. And three, a prosecution which they couldn't do because they forced us into taking the Fifth Amendment. They had sense enough to see that they were in a bad spot. We beat them, that's all.'

CONQUERING EVEREST, HIMALAYAS, 29 May 1953

Edmund Hillary

Mount Everest, at 29,028 feet the highest mountain in the world, was finally conquered in 1953, by New Zealander Edmund Hillary and Nepalese Sherpa, Tenzing Norgay. Here Hillary describes their assault on the final ridge.

Leaving Tenzing to belay me as best he could I jammed my way into this crack, then kicking backwards with my crampons I sank their spikes deep into the frozen snow behind me and levered myself off the ground. Taking advantage of every little rock-hold and the force of knee, shoulder and arms I could muster, I literally cramponed backwards up the crack with a fervent prayer that the cornice would remain attached to the rock. Despite the considerable effort involved, my progress although slow was steady, and as Tenzing paid out the rope I inched my way upwards until I could finally reach over the top of the rock and drag myself out of the crack on to a wide ledge. For a few moments I lay regaining my breath and for the first time really felt the fierce determination that nothing now could stop us reaching the top. I took a firm stance on the ledge and signalled to Tenzing to come on up. As I heaved hard on the rope Tenzing wriggled his way up the crack and finally collapsed exhausted at the top like a giant fish when it has just been hauled from the sea after a terrible struggle.

This great effort, at around 29,000ft, had come near to breaking both of them; but they went on, flanked by huge cornices.

I had been cutting steps continuously for two hours, and Tenzing too, was moving very slowly. As I chipped steps around still another corner, I wondered rather dully just how long we could keep it up. Our original zest had now quite gone and it was turning more into a grim struggle. I then realized that the ridge ahead, instead of still monotonously rising, now dropped sharply away, and far below I could see the North Col and the Rongbuk Glacier (on the Tibetan side). I looked upwards to see a narrow snow ridge running up to a snow summit. A few more whacks of the ice-axe in the firm snow and we stood on the top. My initial feelings were of relief – relief that there were no more steps to cut – no more ridges to traverse and no more humps to tantalize us with hopes of success. I looked at Tenzing and in spite of the balaclava, goggles and oxygen mask all encrusted with long icicles that concealed his face, there was no disguising his infectious grin of pure delight as he looked around him. We shook hands and then Tenzing threw his arm around my shoulders and we thumped each other on the back until we were almost breathless. It was 11.30 a.m. The ridge had taken us two and a half hours, but it seemed like a lifetime.

THE HUNGARIAN REVOLUTION, BUDAPEST, 23 October 1956

D. Sefton Delmer, London Daily Express

The Communists – with Russian backing – had taken power in Hungary in 1947, and made the country a one-party Stalinist state. Throughout the 1950s discontent with the regime grew, causing dissension within the Communists' ranks themselves, with a popular, liberal wing growing up around prime minister Imre Nagy. On 23 October 1956 an anti-Stalinist insurrection broke out in Budapest.

I have been the witness today of one of the great events of history. I have seen the people of Budapest catch the fire lit in Poznan and Warsaw and come out into the streets in open rebellion against their Soviet overlords. I have marched with them and almost wept for joy with them as the Soviet emblems in the Hungarian flags were torn out by the angry and exalted crowds. And the great point about the rebellion is that it looks like being successful.

As I telephone this dispatch I can hear the roar of delirious crowds made up of student girls and boys, of Hungarian soldiers still wearing their Russian-type uniforms, and overalled factory workers marching through Budapest and shouting defiance against Russia. 'Send the Red Army home,' they roar. 'We want free and secret elections.' And then comes the ominous cry which one always seems to hear on these occasions: 'Death to Rakosi.' Death to the former Soviet puppet dictator – now taking a 'cure' on the Russian Black Sea Riviera – whom the crowds blame for all the ills that have befallen their country in eleven years of Soviet puppet rule.

Leaflets demanding the instant withdrawal of the Red Army and the sacking of the present Government are being showered among the street crowds from trams. The leaflets have been printed secretly by students who 'managed to get access', as they put it, to a printing shop when newspapers refused to publish their political programme. On house walls all over the city primitively stencilled sheets have been pasted up listing the sixteen demands of the rebels.

But the fantastic and, to my mind, really super-ingenious feature of this national rising against the Hammer and Sickle, is that it is being carried on under the protective red mantle of pretended Communist orthodoxy. Gigantic portraits of Lenin are being carried at the head of the marchers. The purged ex Premier Imre Nagy, who only in the last couple of weeks has been readmitted to the Hungarian Communist Party, is the rebels' chosen champion and the leader whom they demand must be given charge of a new free and independent Hungary. Indeed, the Socialism of this ex-Premier and – this is my bet – Premier-soon-to-be-again, is no doubt genuine enough. But the youths in the crowd, to my mind, were in the vast majority as anti-Communist as they were anti-Soviet – that is, if you agree with me that calling for the removal of the Red Army is anti-Soviet.

In fact there was one tricky moment when they almost came to blows on this point. The main body of students and marchers had already assembled outside their university in front of the monument to the poet-patriot Petofi who led the 1848 rebellion against the Austrians. Suddenly a new group of students carrying red banners approached from a side street. The banners showed them to be the students of the Leninist–Marxist Institute, which trains young teachers of Communist ideology and supplies many of the puppet rulers' civil servants.

The immediate reaction of the main body, I noticed, was to shout defiance and disapproval of the oncoming ideologists.

But they were quickly hushed into silence and the ideologues joined in the march with the rest of them, happily singing the *Marseillaise* . . .

THE CRUSHING OF THE HUNGARIAN REVOLUTION, BUDAPEST, 4 November 1956

George Paloczi-Horvath, London Daily Herald

In response to the uprising, Soviet tanks and troops invaded Hungary, setting up a pro-Russian, orthodox Stalinist regime. These Soviet forces crushed the revolt, but only after bloody street-fighting in Budapest.

It was dawn . . . the day the Russians struck again.

We were awakened by the roar of heavy guns. The radio was a shambles. All we got was the national anthem, played over and over again, and continual repetition of Premier Nagy's announcement that after a token resistance we must cease fighting and appeal to the free world for help.

After our ten days' war of liberty; after the pathetically short period of our 'victory', this was a terrible blow. But there was not time to sit paralysed in despair. The Russians had arrested General Maleter, head of the Central Revolutionary Armed Forces Council. The Army had received ceasefire orders. But what of the fighting groups of workers and students?

These courageous civilian units now had to be told to put up only token resistance in order to save bloodshed. They had been instructed not to start firing.

I called up the biggest group, the 'Corvin regiment.' A deputy commander answered the phone. His voice was curiously calm:

'Yes, we realized we should not open fire. But the Russians did. They took up positions around our block and opened fire with everything they had. The cellars are filled with 200 wounded and dead. But we will fight to the last man. There is no choice. But inform Premier Nagy that we did not start the fight.'

This was just before seven in the morning. Premier Nagy, alas, could not be informed any more. He was not to be found.

The situation was the same everywhere. Soviet tanks rolled in and started to shoot at every centre of resistance which had defied them during our first battle for freedom.

This time, the Russians shot the buildings to smithereens. Freedom fighters were trapped in the various barracks, public buildings and blocks of flats. The Russians were going to kill them off to the last man. And they knew it. They fought on till death claimed them.

This senseless Russian massacre provoked the second phase of armed resistance. The installation of Kadar's puppet government was only oil on the fire. After our fighting days, after our brief span of liberty and democracy, Kadar's hideous slogans and stupid lies, couched in the hated Stalinite terminology, made everyone's blood boil. Although ten million witnesses knew the contrary, the puppet government brought forward the ludicrous lie that our war of liberty was a counter-revolutionary uprising inspired by a handful of Fascists.

The answer was bitter fighting and a general strike throughout the country. In the old revolutionary centres – the industrial suburbs of Csepel, Ujpest and the rest – the workers struck and fought desperately against the Russian tanks.

Posters on the walls challenged the lies of the puppet Government: '*The 40,000 aristocrats and fascists of the Csepel works strike on!*' said one of them.

'*The general strike is a weapon which can be used only when the entire working class is unanimous – so don't call us Fascists*,' said another.

Armed resistance stopped first. The Russians bombarded to rubble every house from which a single shot was fired. The fighting groups realized that further battles would mean the annihilation of the capital. So they stopped fighting.

But the strike went on.

The Workers' Councils, the Writers' Association and the Revolutionary Council of the Students decided at last that the general strike must be suspended if Hungary were not to commit national suicide . . .

THE SUEZ INVASION, EGYPT, 5–6 November 1956

Donald Edgar, London Daily Express

The nationalization of the Suez canal led to military intervention in Egypt by Britain and France, with airborne troops landing at Port Said on

5 November. Donald Edgar accompanied the seaborne troops, who landed at Port Said on the following day.

It was a sunny morning with a blue sky and our ship was in the centre of a great array of warships and transports which covered a great arc of sea from Port Fuad to the left of the Canal to Port Said in the centre and Gamil airfield on the right. Our ship was nearly stationary about three miles off shore, distant enough to reduce the scene to the size of a coloured picture postcard and the warships to toys on the Round Pond in Kensington Gardens.

It was only with an effort of will I could grasp that it was all for real, not a sequence from a film. It was really happening.

To the left of the Canal entrance a great cloud of black smoke from burning oil tanks was drifting over the city forming a sinister cloud. Along the sea-front puffs of white smoke were rising from shell-fire and red flames were taking hold on the right where the shanty town lay. Just off shore a line of elegant destroyers were moving along the beach firing into the city. As they had guns of only small calibre the reports at this distance were no more disturbing than the muffled woofs of a sleeping dog.

But to the extreme left, off Port Fuad, the French sector, lay a great battleship, the *Jean Bart*, and from time to time it fired a heavy shell from its great guns which made the air tremble a little where I stood.

Around us and further out to sea were cruisers and an aircraft carrier or two, waiting in ominous silence. Helicopters we were ferrying back and forth from the beach. I learned later they had carried the 45 Royal Marine Commando in to support 40 and 42 Commandos which had earlier landed in their Buffalos together with C Sqdn of the 6 Royal Tank Regiment. I watched one helicopter fall into the sea and a ship nearby suddenly leaped forward to the rescue with the speed of a greyhound. I learned it was HMS *Manxman*, the fastest ship in the Royal Navy at the time.

I took in everything I could and asked questions of the Captain, who tried to be helpful within his limits. He told us with a wry smile that there had been trouble with the American Sixth Fleet which was in the area, escorting a shipload of American refugees from Alexandria. In fact, I gathered the Anglo-French convoy was being closely shadowed by the Americans and the air had been filled with tough, rude radio exchanges. Hanson Baldwin smiled – but in somewhat wintry fashion. I did not really believe that Eisenhower would give orders to the Sixth Fleet to blow us out of the water, but I knew the political situation was so tense that even the impossible might happen.

I was busy making notes, drawing rough sketch-maps and then began to feel somewhat dispirited as the first excitement wore off.

I kept telling myself how lucky I was – standing on the bridge watching the most impressive military operation the British had put on for many a year, with parachutists, Marine Commandos, tanks, aircraft and a naval bombardment. What is more I was looking at it all in safety. In the cussed way of the English I think this last factor was beginning to have its effect on me. I was beginning to feel sorry for the people of Port Said who were on the receiving end.

I remembered only too well what it felt like. In 1940 in France it was the Germans who had the tanks, the aircraft and the overwhelming force and I was at the receiving end, taking shelter in ditches and cellars.

However, I fought these feelings back. A few miles away British troops were fighting their way through a city, perhaps against heavy opposition, suffering casualties. What is more in a few hours I could well be in danger myself.

The captain went to the radio room and came back to say that as it was taking longer than expected to clear the area round the jetties of the Canal we should not be landing until the afternoon. He suggested we had lunch.

It was a lunch to remember. A steward served us imperturbably with a drink while we studied the menu. Another took our order with the same solicitude as a head-waiter in the Savoy Grill. A wine-waiter suggested an excellent Burgundy. Outside, not far away, the marine Commandos with the Centurion tanks were fighting their way through the wrecked buildings of Port Said. No doubt men, women and children were dying in fear and anguish. Yet here was I sitting down to an excellent lunch as if I was a first-class passenger on a luxury Mediterranean cruise.

But I ate the lunch and drank the wine with enjoyment. All my instincts as an old soldier came to my aid – eat and drink whilst you can, you never know where the next meal is coming from. Whilst we were finishing our coffee and brandy the ship started to move gently towards the Canal.

We went up again to the bridge. The ship was easing its way towards the jetty on the right-hand of the entrance to the Canal and the scene of destruction along the water-front cleared through the smoke. Crumbled masonry, blackened walls still standing with nothing behind, burnt-out vehicles, debris scattered over the road. A few soldiers hurried to and fro, but the firing – rifle and machine-gun and mortar – seemed to be concentrated a few hundred yards down the Canal. The captain had a radio set on the bridge tuned to the BBC and we heard a bland voice announcing that all resistance had ceased in Port Said. It was just then when with a great scream that froze me in terror, a section of naval fighter-bombers dived down over us dropping their rockets and firing their cannon just ahead of us. Almost quicker than sight they wheeled away into the sky while clouds of grey smoke rose into the air. We were all silent on the bridge for a minute or two. This was the attack by Sea Furies on Navy House where 40 Commando had encountered tough resistance from a hundred-odd Egyptians who had barricaded themselves in. Even the tanks, firing at point-blank range had been unable to dislodge them so the Navy was called in to help with an air-strike. The Navy complied, but with some regret for the building had become over the years part of the Royal Navy's heritage. Even after this devastating attack, however, the Egyptians fought on and a Marine officer told me they had to clear them out room by room. 'They didn't know how to fight professionally,' he said to me. 'But by God they fought to the end.'

It was not until the next day that twenty survivors gave themselves up. Their bravery was another proof that the Egyptians, often abandoned by their officers, can fight magnificently.

By now it was late afternoon. In front of us a transport was unloading more tanks and paratroops who moved off down the Canal road. There were two barges from the *Jean Bart* filled with French paratroops lying down philosophically in the open holds. I noticed with a certain surprise, some female contours among the camouflage uniforms. I had not known till then that the French paratroops had women in their ranks among whose duties were cooking and first-aid. It was an imaginative re-creation of the traditional *vivandières!*

As I was looking at the quayside I saw a group of senior officers who seemed to be waiting for transport while snipers' bullets seemed to me to be getting uncomfortably close. Campbell recognized the leader – Lt General Sir Hugh Stockwell, the Allied Commander, who cheerily waved his swagger-stick at the passing troops. He had been spending a few hours looking at the situation and was trying to get back to the headquarters ship, HMS *Tyne.* I was not to know then that he had a hazardous journey back in a landing-craft which was nearly swamped and when he finally got aboard was greeted with the fateful order to cease-fire at midnight (two a.m. local time).

It grew dark and we were told that no one would be allowed to disembark until the morning to avoid confusion. Then Baldwin and I had a stroke of luck. The Brigadier in charge of Medical Services was a passenger and brusquely said he was going ashore whatever anyone said. He was determined to contact the airborne medical team which had landed the day before. He had seen stretchers going into the damaged Casino Palace Hotel about fifty yards away from us by the side of the Canal. Baldwin and I asked him if we could go along. He nodded and we picked up our bags and followed him ashore.

There were fires enough around to light our way across ropes, hose-pipes and debris to the hotel. The entrance-hall was filled with stretcher-cases. A big reception-room on the right had been cleared for the medical team. In another room along a passage an operating-room had been fixed up with emergency lighting and surgeons stripped to the waist wearing leather aprons were at their tasks. The British casualties had for the most part been flown back by helicopter to an aircraft-carrier. This team was dealing now with Egyptian casualties – some military, most civilian – men, women and children.

The dead were being carried out to the garden in the back to be buried in a shallow grave temporarily.

It was a sombre scene with few words spoken. The surgeons looked to me very young and very tired. They were working in relays, coming back to the main room to sit down and drink a glass of whisky in between operating.

Baldwin had dumped his bag and disappeared. He knew exactly where he was going – to the American consulate whose position further along the Canal he had pin-pointed on a street map before he had landed.

I went out to the road. Night had fallen and the fires had dimmed. Sentries had been posted. Out at sea there was not a light to give a hint of the great convoy and its accompanying warships.

A few shots sounded in the distance, but silence was enveloping the stricken city.

The Anglo-French Suez expedition was called off after joint pressure from Washington and Moscow. It marked a humiliating climb-down for the British, and many date 6 November 1956 as the point at which Britain ceased to be a world power.

LITTLE ROCK, ARKANSAS, 23 September 1957

Relman Morin, Associated Press

Passions erupted throughout the American south in the 1950s as black Americans sought equal educational opportunities. The most famous of the clashes between segregationists and anti-segregationists came at Little Rock, where Governor Orval E. Faubus used National Guard troops at Central High School to prevent integration. The troops were withdrawn after a federal court ruling, but replaced by a large crowd which declared its intention of keeping black children out. Relman Morin won a Pulitzer Prize for this dispatch from Little Rock.

It was exactly like an explosion, a human explosion.

At 8.35 a.m., the people standing in front of the high school looked like the ones you see every day in a shopping centre.

A pretty, sweet-faced woman with auburn hair and a jewel-green jacket. Another holding a white portable radio to her ear. 'I'm getting the news of what's going on at the high school,' she said. People laughed. A grey-haired man, tall and spare, leaned over the wooden barricade. 'If they're coming,' he said, quietly, 'they'll be here soon.' 'They better,' said another, 'I got to get to work.'

Ordinary people – mostly curious, you would have said – watching a high school on a bright blue-and-gold morning.

Five minutes later, at 8.40, they were a mob.

The terrifying spectacle of 200-odd individuals, suddenly welded together into a single body, took place in the barest fraction of a second. It was an explosion, savagery chain-reacting from person to person, fusing them into a white-hot mass.

There are three glass windowed telephone booths across the street from the south end of the high school.

At 8.35, I was inside one of them, dictating.

I saw four Negroes coming down the centre of the street, in twos. One was tall and big shouldered. One was tall and thin. The other two were short. The big man had a card in his hat and was carrying a Speed Graphic, a camera for taking news pictures.

A strange, animal growl rose from the crowd.

'Here come the Negroes.'

Instantly, people turned their backs on the high school and ran toward the four men. They hesitated. Then they turned to run.

I saw the white men catch them on the sidewalk and the lawn of a home, a quarter-block away. There was a furious, struggling knot. You could see a man kicking at the big Negro. Then another jumped on his back and rode him to the ground, forearms deep in the Negro's throat.

They kicked him and beat him on the ground and they smashed his camera to splinters. The other three ran down the street with one white man chasing them. When the white man saw he was alone, he turned and fled back toward the crowd.

Meanwhile, five policemen had rescued the big man.

I had just finished saying, 'Police escorted the big man away –'

At that instant, a man shouted, 'Look, the niggers are going in.'

Directly across from me, three Negro boys and five girls were walking toward the side door at the south end of the school.

It was an unforgettable tableau.

They were carrying books. White bobby-sox, part of the high school uniform, glinted on the girls' ankles. They were all neatly dressed. The boys wore open-throat shirts and the girls ordinary frocks.

They weren't hurrying. They simply strolled across perhaps fifteen yards from the sidewalk to the school steps. They glanced at the people and the police as though none of this concerned them.

You can never forget a scene like that.

Nor the one that followed.

Like a wave, the people who had run toward the four Negro men, now swept back toward the police and the barricades.

'Oh, God, the niggers are in the school,' a man yelled.

A woman – the one with the auburn hair and green jacket – rushed up to him. Her face was working with fury now.

Her lips drew back in a snarl and she was screaming, 'Did they go in?'

'The niggers are in the school,' the man said.

'Oh, God,' she said. She covered her face with her hands. Then she tore her hair, still screaming.

She looked exactly like the women who cluster around a mine head when there has been an explosion and men are trapped below.

The tall, lean man jumped up on one of the barricades. He was holding on to the shoulders of others nearby.

'Who's going through?' he roared.

'We all are,' the people shrieked.

They surged over and around the barricades, breaking for the police.

About a dozen policemen, in short-sleeved blue shirts, swinging billy clubs, were in front of them.

Men and women raced toward them and the policemen raised their clubs, moving this way and that as people tried to dodge around them.

A man went down, pole-axed when a policeman clubbed him.

Another, with crisp curly black hair, was quick as a rat. He dodged between two policemen and got as far as the schoolyard. There the others caught him.

With swift, professional skill, they pulled his coat half-way down his back, pinning his arms. In a flash they were hustling him back toward the barricades.

A burly, thick-bodied man wearing a construction worker's 'hard hat' charged a policeman. Suddenly, he stopped and held both hands high above his head.

I couldn't see it, but I assume the officer jammed a pistol in his ribs.

Meanwhile, the women – the auburn-haired one, the woman with the radio, and others – were swirling around the police commanding officers.

Tears were streaming down their faces. They acted completely distraught.

It was pure hysteria.

And they kept crying, 'The niggers are in our school. Oh, God, are you going to stand here and let the niggers stay in school?'

Then, swiftly, a line of cars filled with state troopers rolled toward the school from two directions. The flasher-signals or the tops of the cars were spurting red warnings.

REVOLUTION IN HAVANA, CUBA, 31 December 1958–1 January 1959

Edwin Tetlow

After fighting for two years in the mountains, Fidel Castro's revolutionaries reached the Cuban capital on the last day of 1958.

The approaches to the city from the airport seemed normal enough as viewed from a big old Buick taxi which I shared with the young American, who confided to me that he expected to find 'a lovely young thing' among those welcoming him to Cuba. The dark-complexioned driver hummed softly to the music from his radio as he piloted us skilfully through the turbulent traffic. The Hotel Nacional, a great oblong block of a place, had a few rooms available, at a hefty rate for those days. I settled in and had a leisurely dinner from an expansive menu in the hotel restaurant, which was filled with well-dressed, and obviously well-heeled, Cubans and a minority of foreigners. Feeling comfortable, I set out to stroll in the warm evening air, dropping in one some of the tourist haunts of suburban Vedado and upper midtown Havana, amassing material for the feature article I should be writing the following morning.

Eventually, around 11 p.m. [31 December 1958], I strolled into the Casino at the Hotel Nacional to await midnight. I noted that the bar was being heavily patronized. A four-piece band was playing in one corner of the ornate salon, accompanying a lusty and busty Cuban contralto who was singing at full strength to make herself heard above the band and the hubbub from the bar, and the softer, sleeker noises from the casino itself, so different from the rattle, slap and clap made by dice players as they thumped down their leathern cups on tables in the humbler haunts of the city. As the time passed towards midnight the noise became unbelievably piercing. How Cubans love noise! Eventually neither band nor contralto could be heard as separate entities.

Around the gaming tables, under glittering chandeliers bigger and more fanciful than any I had seen for years, guests both Cuban and foreign gambled with deep concentration. Only occasionally did head turn and envious smiles appear round tight-lipped mouths when somebody shrieked in ecstasy after hitting the jackpot at one of the fruit machines lining the walls of the casino. Also along the walls were several armed policemen stationed like sentries. I asked once or twice of seemingly knowledgeable guests why they were there. One man just shrugged and said languidly: 'Who knows?' One other man told me they had appeared for the first time only a few evenings earlier.

At midnight there came a token acknowledgement that 1959 had arrived. The intense proceedings at the gaming tables and the fruit machines were halted for but a few moments. A few men and women kissed and some people shook hands and smiled at each other before resuming the serious business of the night. At about 12.30 a.m. the members of the band quietly packed their instruments, the singer folded up her microphone stand, and she and the musicians walked off into the night. Only the bar and the gaming tables continued operations, the former being sustained mainly by a party of American and other foreigners who, growing more disarrayed almost by the minute, still managed to keep the tiring bartenders busy. At that hour I decided I had seen enough. I wanted to go to bed. Once there, I spent a few minutes jotting down facts and reminders for the writing I expected to be doing next morning. Satisfied that I had my assignment under control, I settled down and went to sleep.

I was awakened before 8 a.m. by an excited phone call from Robert Perez, my local correspondent, an energetic Puerto Rican who had lived for some years in Havana. 'He's gone,' he spluttered into the phone. 'Who's gone?' I asked, still half-asleep. 'Batista! Batista!' came the galvanizing answer from Perez. 'He went in the night.'

So he had. At about the time I was settling down to sleep he and a party of about forty, including many members of his family, had motored over to a military airfield at Camp Columbia, on the fringe of Havana, and – excessively heavily laden with baggage – had boarded an Army plane for a short hop eastwards across the water to the Dominican Republic, then still in the grip of Batista's fellow-dictator, Generalissimo Rafael Trujillo, later assassinated.

Pure luck had landed me in the very centre of a revolution while it was happening and being won. No hasty packing of a suitcase this time, no mad rush to catch the first plane to the scene of action, no hectic chase after news which was already growing old! This was a foreign correspondent's dream come true, and I was determined to make the most of it. First, on the sound recommendation of Robert Perez, I moved out of the lordly but isolated Hotel Nacional and into the Hotel Colina, a small and well-placed observation-post giving a view from my third-floor window of the approaches to the University of Havana, where Fidel Castro had been educated and where he was said to have substantial secret support.

The city was eerily quiet at about 8.45 a.m. as Perez and I made our cautious way to the Colina, not at all sure what might happen as we did so. Weren't revolutions affairs of wild shooting and melodramatic action? Not this one – yet. I felt as if I were in the eye of a hurricane, the centre where everything is still while furious winds whirl all around. Hardly anybody was moving. Perez told me as we inched our way towards the Colina that Cubans in the capital had done exactly what people in most countries of the Caribbean did when, as happens all too often in that steamy region, trouble threatened. They closed and locked their shutters, bolted all their doors, and holed up.

Once installed in my new strategic headquarters I implemented my plan of campaign. I dispatched Perez on a mission of news-gathering in the city, asking him to phone me as often as seemed necessary with any information he had. I calculated that because of his intimate knowledge of the city, contacts he had, plus his command of his native Spanish, he would have no trouble about keeping me in touch with what was happening. And he did so with great efficiency. As for myself, I stayed as a willing prisoner in my hotel room. I put in a telephone call to my newspaper after having been told by the local exchange that there was, predictably, 'long delay' in calls to the outside world, including distant London. While I waited I began assembling the story I would telephone as soon as the call came through. I listened to Radio Havana as it broadcast messages from Fidel Castro telling the populace to keep calm while it waited for him to take control of the nation. 'Don't worry, I shall come to you,' he said. I took messages from the assiduous Perez and as best I could I kept an eye on what was happening in the streets leading to the University.

In fact, very little happened all that morning. Only a very few people were to be seen hurrying along in order to carry out missions which presumably could not be put off. I noticed that almost all these scurrying pedestrians kept as close as possible to any nearby wall or other cover they were afforded. However, my heaven-sent story was shaping up well. It was helped greatly by word from Robert Perez that Fidel Castro had sent an amplified message to the people of Havana. Speaking from his field camp near Santa Clara, the last sizeable city between him and the capital, he said he did not accept as a bargaining agent a three-man junta of 'so called neutrals' whom Batista had left behind to represent him. 'I shall be coming into Havana soon,' Castro promised 'Keep the peace until then. I am sending a company of Barbudos [bearded ones] to administer Havana until I get there. They will preserve Havana – and you.'

This message galvanized the nervous population of the city. Reassured, thousands of them opened their shutters and doors and got into their cars, to celebrate their unexpected liberation. They staged a fantastic crawl-around of the city streets. They draped their vehicles, almost all of them American-made, with Cuban flags. If the car was a convertible, they wound down the top and then joined the follow-my-leader procession of their neighbourhood. As they did so, more and more people climbed up on and into the cars until, as I counted from my observation-point in the Hotel Colina, there were often as many as ten persons in one car. As each individual procession made its slow progress along the old, narrow streets, the ecstatic celebrants chanted the word *Li-ber-tad* and most of them added emphasis by pounding with their fists their car's side or roof in rhythm with the three syllables of the word for liberty. Very soon the din became hard to stand. I was staggered by the intensity, emotion and, I must add, childlike character of the manifestation of happy relief. Nobody could possibly foresee the tribulations in store for Cuba for the next forty years . . .

My telephone call to London came through at last in the early afternoon, in time for me to dictate over fifteen hundred words, many of them forming impromptu sentences, as thoughts occurred to me, across the bed of the Atlantic Ocean. Even my vigil the previous evening in the casino of the Hotel Nacional was not wasted; indeed the languid scene around the gaming tables and the jollity in the bar on the eve of one of the most startling and profound revolutionary upheavals of the century in Latin America added to the impact of the story I was able to tell. This was by far the most vivid first-hand report I had written in fifty years, during war as well as peace; and now that it was safely in the hands of my editors in Fleet Street, I was free to leave my bedroom at the Hotel Colina. I could spend the next couple of hours before my second phone call seeing for myself what was going on in the liberated city.

I permitted myself one substantial tot of Bacardi rum before I set out on the long walk from Vedado to midtown Havana. I had to thrust my way through the thick ranks of people watching, some with tears of joy coursing down their faces, the motorized crawl-around. But just as I was making the last turn into the Prado, which roughly marks the boundary between respectable bourgeois Havana and the livelier but sleazy down-town, I saw that something had happened to cut short the touching celebration. Panic was spreading among both Cubans in their cars and the onlookers who had been cheering them on. Vehicles were peeling off from the processions, screeching away into side-streets, and the crowds were scurrying for cover as quickly as their feet would race. In a matter of minutes I found myself uncomfortably alone in the mid-section of the broad Prado. What had happened?

The answer was forthcoming almost as soon as I asked myself the question. The underworld was taking over. One by one a party of dirty and ruffianly-looking young Cubans emerged from Calle Neptuno and other side-streets, Each was carrying a rifle or shotgun across his chest. They walked warily along the street, their gaze darting everywhere as they made sure that nobody was going to challenge them. Nobody did. Batista's hated armed policemen had fled into hiding once they heard that their protector had gone, (It transpired that by no means all of them escaped vengeance. Stories of beatings and murders of these men abounded during the next twenty-four hours.) The small-time gangsters now taking over central Havana were organized and ingenious. Some took up positions as watchdogs at strategic points, ordering away at gunpoint people such as myself, while their comrades went on a rampage of looting. Their first targets were parking-meters. These were smashed apart so that their contents could be rattled out and pocketed. Then came the turn of pinball machines and other gaming devices in arcades and deserted casinos which could easily be entered, including an especially lucrative one close to the Sevilla Biltmore Hotel. Here, from a discreet distance, I watched one gang of looters drag a slot-machine into the street and batter it open with jagged pieces of metal from a destroyed parking-meter. It struck me as a remarkable and possibly unique confirmation of the validity of the old saying that money makes money.

The physical hazards of remaining outdoors grew as the bandits got their hands on rum. They started shooting. Mostly it was the wildest kind of exhibitionism, but even so it claimed victims. Ambulances soon began making screaming runs through the streets on journeys to and from hospitals – and mortuaries. Late in the afternoon I went into one hospital and found it in chaos, overflowing with wounded persons and roughly bandaged out-patients. 'Some have been in street accidents, but mostly they seem to have been hit by flying bullets,' said one nurse to me.

There appeared to be no reason for most of the shooting. Indeed, one series of incidents which I ran into on my way back to the

Colina tended to show that Cubans just weren't to be trusted with weapons. A man's rifle would go off either because it was defective or because he had forgotten his finger was on the trigger, or even because of a need – common in Latin America – to show off. The trouble was that very often a haphazard shot would start a chain reaction. Men who heard the shot would start firing their own weapons, with the result that shotgun pellets and bullets began flying around an area, ricocheting off walls, smashing windows and occasionally hitting an unlucky pedestrian. Rarely did there seem to be a justifiable target. Alas, this kind of irresponsibility seemed to be occurring mostly near the University, and I was disturbed to deduced that the perpetrators were not underworld bandits of the kind I had met in the Prado but students who were supporters of Fidel Castro and were apparently obeying his broadcast admonitions to preserve the peace in Havana until he arrived. They were probably earnest enough in their devotion to his cause, but they wouldn't be much use if Batista's police and troops rallied. I reasoned that Fidel Castro would be well advised to get his trained Barbudos into Havana as quickly as he could. If they didn't come soon, there would probably be a confrontation between his amateur followers and the downtown bandits, and if the latter won, which seemed likely, unimaginable bloody chaos would follow.

The most senseless shooting spree of all happened on the afternoon of 2 January, the second day of the revolution. I was standing in the shelter of a shopping arcade near the Parque Centrale, in the centre of Havana, and was looking at the debris of splintered windows and doors and ransacked shelves left by yesterday's looters when I became aware of a noisy commotion on a street corner close to the Sevilla Biltmore. The cracks made by ragged rounds of gunshots were coming from somewhere close at hand. I crept cautiously forward to investigate. A squad of about half a dozen young men wearing armbands to show that they were members of a pro-Castro group which had come out of hiding during the past forty-eight hours were firing rifles and automatic pistols from the west side of the Prado at an upper window of a building on the opposite side of the wide thoroughfare. Their collective aim was atrocious. I could see bullets squelching into stonework far above, below and around the window, and only one or two were flying through it into the room beyond. The attack lasted at least half an hour, without, as I noted most carefully, a single shot coming back in reply. This one-sided 'battle' was happening so close to the Sevilla Biltmore that a party of American tourists, wisely obeying a recommendation from the US Embassy not to venture outdoors, could hear all the shooting but had no more idea of what it all meant than, it emerged, did the men involved.

The facts came to me eventually. Word had reached a volunteer unit of Castro supporters that some fugitives of the Batista regime were hiding in a room on the top floor of the building now being attacked. There were said to be at least dozen armed followers of Rolando Masferrer, a notorious henchman of Batista, locked inside the room. When the shooting ended, one militiaman said gloatingly to me; We got the lot.' In truth, as I was able to confirm for myself little later, there had been nobody at all in the whole building.

As taxis had vanished from the streets, we were walking on foot when we ran into trouble. A voice called out suddenly in grating Spanish from somewhere in the darkness a few feet ahead of us: 'Halt. Hands up!' Peering ahead, I could see three men with rifles pointed straight at us. Two of them were kneeling side by side on the pavement while the third, their leader, stood barring the way directly ahead. He had a revolver in his right hand – and an armed Cuban was no man to be trifled with. His gun might very well go off by chance.

But I have never had much time for amateur warriors anywhere. Tonight, also, I was tired, hungry and consequently bad-tempered and of fallible judgement. I was tempted to bluff my way through and I was slow to comply with the orders of our interceptors. My American companions were perhaps wiser. They all raised their hands and one of them muttered impatiently to me as he did so: 'Come, man. You'll get us all shot!' Unwillingly, I complied.

Our captors motioned us into the passageway of an apartment house. There, blocking the way, sat an unshaven young fellow at a desk. We were in the unit's rough and ready headquarters. The man at the desk started questioning the two Americans nearest to him. I was very hot indeed in that passageway. I sidled back into the street, leaving it to others who spoke far better Spanish than I to argue and protest against this unwarranted interference with the free movement of foreign civilians pursuing their daily task in extremely difficult circumstances, and so on. As I breathed the welcome fresh air I mentally assessed the odds about being able to make a dash for it and go up the hill to my hotel. I decided against trying to do so. Several of these amateur gunmen were still around, for I could hear them talking close to me. Even though there was a good chance that if they fired after me as I ran away they might very well miss me, I considered the risk not worth taking. If I were wounded or killed, my newspaper would be the innocent loser.

Meanwhile our negotiators were making no impression whatever on the man at the desk. He told them he was chief of one of the paramilitary units which had been ordered by Fidel Castro to keep the city peaceful, and he couldn't in good conscience let us go on our way. 'My authority doesn't extend very far,' he confessed. 'There are a lot of bandits still roaming around out there. You might get robbed – or worse – if I let you go off into the night.' It availed nothing that our spokesman told him we were well able to take care of ourselves and anyway intended to hole up in our hotels as soon as we got there. 'Sorry, you'll have to spend tonight under our protection,' the man insisted.

We were bundled into two cars and driven to a dingy-looking house in one of the streets running diagonally off the Malecon boulevard on the sea front. It turned out to have been a 'safe' house used by revolutionary agents and couriers as well as by fugitives from Batista's police. I was shown to a small and none-too-savoury bedroom immediately underneath a rooftop water cistern. Dumping my typewriter, my only luggage, resignedly in a corner of the room, I obeyed my captors' order to go down to the desk, sign my name in a register and claim a key.

As I did so, the good fortune which had sent me to Havana in the first place and had attended me for forty-eight hours thereafter worked again. I was walking away from the hotel desk when I noticed a big utility truck standing in the street outside the hotel entrance. Half a dozen laughing soldiers – real soldiers this time – were unloading their kit and other baggage from it. I was astonished to observe that two of them standing with their backs facing me had black hair hanging down so long below their shoulders that I should have said they were girls if they obviously had not been blessed with thick black beards. I walked forward and began talking with them. They were, they said, the very first detachment of Barbudos which Castro had promised to send into Havana.

So the seeming ill-luck that had landed me into being arrested had also brought me another lively segment for the morrow's story.

This is yet another example of how compensations have so frequently offset what seemed initially to be setbacks in my profession as a journalist. A missed train or plane, failure to establish contact by phone or cable with London, somebody's refusal to tell me something, were irritating when encountered, but so often were followed by a piece of unexpected good fortune. Perhaps this helps to explain my perennial optimism.

The Barbudos were among the fittest and happiest young warriors I have ever seen. They had good reason for being so. They had had very little serious fighting and, as the never-robust morale had seeped away from Batista's conscripts during the past few months in the Sierra Maestra, an astonishingly easy victory had fallen to them. They told me that they had enjoyed a leisurely, unchallenged advance upon the capital from the eastern province of Oriente, through Camagüey and Las Villas. The peasants in these mostly rural areas had welcomed them with increasing ardour as the reality of Castro's total victory had become manifest. People had been eager to give them anything they wanted. One Barbudo told me he couldn't remember when he had been last paid. 'The one thing we didn't need was money,' he said. 'People couldn't do enough for us. They lavished everything, especially food, on us.'

Proof of this was forthcoming as some of the contents of the truck were arrayed on the counter of the hotel reception desk. There were hams, strings of sausages, cottage-made bread, butter, beer and many other such good provender. We were all invited to tuck into a midnight feast – rebel soldiers, our captors, American reporters, including one lone Englishman, and anybody else who happened to be about. Good fellowship bloomed with every mouthful. There was much hearty back-slapping, joking, talk and toasting of international understanding, and some glowing forecasts from the Barbudos of the future Cuba once Fidel Castro took charge.

MASSACRE AT SHARPEVILLE, SOUTH AFRICA, 21 March 1960

Humphrey Taylor, Drum *magazine*

A demonstration by black South Africans against the Apartheid law which required them to carry a pass, or ID card, was fired upon by police, killing 56, wounding 152, at the township of Sharpeville. Humphrey Taylor was the only journalist to witness the shootings.

We went into Sharpeville the back way, around lunch time last Monday, driving along behind a big grey police car and three Saracen armoured cars.

As we went through the fringes of the township many people were shouting the Pan Africanist slogan '*Izwe Lethu*' (Our Land). They were grinning and cheerful. Some kids waved to the policemen sitting on the Saracens and two of the policemen waved back.

It was like a Sunday outing – except that Major A. T. T. Spengler, head of the Witwatersrand Security Branch, was in the front car and there were bullets in the Saracens' guns.

At the main gates of the fenced-off location, policemen were stopping all cars coming in from the outside. Spengler and the Saracens headed for the police station which is deep inside the settlement, and we followed. The policemen were by now all inside the Saracens, with the hatches battened down, looking at Sharpeville through chinks of armour plating. Yet the Africans did not appear to be alarmed by the cars. Some looked interested and some just grinned.

There were crowds in the streets as we approached the police station. There were plenty of police, too, well armed.

A constable shoved the butt of his rifle against my windshield. Another pointed his rifle at my chest. Another leaned into the car, shouting: 'Have you got a permit to be in this location?'

I said no, whereupon he bellowed: 'Then get out, get out, get out! or I will arrest you on the spot. Understand?'

He had a police gun in his holster and a black pistol tucked into his belt. We decided to go around the other side of the police station, where we parked in a big field.

We could see a couple of the Saracens, their tops poking starkly above the heads of the crowd, just over 100 yards away from us. This was about seven minutes before the police opened fire.

The crowd seemed to be loosely gathered around them and on the fringes people were walking in and out. The kids were playing. In all there were about 3,000 people. They seemed amiable.

I said to Ian Berry, *Drum's* chief photographer: 'This is going to go on all day.' He replied: 'Let's hang on for a bit.'

Suddenly there was a sharp report from the direction of the police station.

'That's a shot,' Berry said.

There were shrill cries of *Izwe Lethu* – women's voices, I thought. The cries came from the police station and I could see a small section of the crowd swirl around the Saracens. Hands went up in the Africanist salute.

Then the shooting started. We heard the chatter of a machine-gun, then another, then another.

'Here it comes,' said Berry. He leaped out of the car with two cameras and crouched in the grass, taking pictures.

The first rush was on us, then past.

There were hundreds of women, some of them laughing. They must have thought that the police were firing blanks.

One woman was hit about ten yards from our car. Her companion, a young man, went back when she fell. He thought she had stumbled.

Then he turned her over and saw that her chest had been shot away. He looked at the blood on his hand and said: 'My God, she's gone!'

Hundreds of kids were running, too. One little boy had on an old black coat which he held up behind his head, thinking perhaps that it might save him from the bullets. Some of the children, hardly as tall the grass, were leaping like rabbits. Some of them were shot, too.

Still the shooting went on. One of the policemen was standing on top of a Saracen, and it looked as though he was firing his sten gun into the crowd. He was swinging it around in a wide arc from his hip as though he were panning a movie camera. Two other police officers were on the truck with him, and it looked as though they were firing pistols.

Most of the bodies were strewn in the road running through the field in which we were. One man who had been lying still, dazedly got to his feet, staggered a few yards then fell in a heap. A woman sat with her head cupped in her hands.

One by one the guns stopped. Nobody was moving in our field except Berry. The rest were wounded – or dead. There was no longer a crowd and it was very quiet.

Berry ran back to the car, saying: 'Let's go before they get my film.' We drove out through the main gate, looking straight ahead.

Before the shooting, I heard no warning to the crowd to disperse. There was no warning volley. When the shooting started, it did not stop until there was no living thing on the huge compound in front of the police station.

The police have claimed they were in desperate danger because the crowd was stoning them. Yet only three policemen were reported to have been hit by stones – and more than 200 Africans were shot down.

The police also have said that the crowd was armed with 'ferocious weapons' which littered the compound after they fled.

I saw no weapons, although I looked very carefully, and afterwards studied the photographs of the death scene. While I was there I saw only shoes, hats and a few bicycles left among the bodies.

It seemed to me that tough stuff was behind the killings at Sharpeville. The crowd gave me no reason to feel scared, though I moved among them without any distinguishing mark to protect me, quite obvious with my white skin.

I think the police were scared, though, and I think the crowd knew it.

That final shrill cry from the women before the shooting started certainly sounded much more like a jeer than a battle-cry. And the first Africans who fled past me after the shooting started were still laughing.

A VISIT TO THE WHITE HOUSE, WASHINGTON, AMERICA, 25 January 1961

J. K. Galbraith

Just appointed US ambassador to India by President Kennedy, Galbraith writes in his diary:

After the meeting, Mac Bundy told me 'The Boss' (a new term) had been asking for me. I went into Ken O'Donnell's office and presently the President came through, grabbed me by the arm, and we had an hour-and-a-half chat which included a tour of the upstairs of the White House. We saw where Ike's golf shoes had poked innumerable holes in his office floor. When we left the office in the West Wing for the house proper, we went headlong into a closet. The President turned over furniture to see where it was made, dismissed some as Sears, Roebuck and expressed shock that so little – the Lincoln bed apart – consisted of good pieces. Only expensive reproductions. The effect is indeed undistinguished although today the house was flooded with sunlight and quite filled with flowers.

THE BERLIN WALL, GERMANY, November 1961

Mark Arnold-Foster, London Observer

In August 1961 the Soviet authorities began the building of a massive concrete wall to divide off their sector of conquered Berlin from those occupied by the Western powers. Ostensibly, the wall was to prevent spying by the West; more truthfully, it was to prevent the mass escape to the West of East Germans disaffected with Stalinism.

The wall starts in a bird sanctuary on the banks of a stream called the Tegeler Fliess. It flows through a marshy valley 200 yards from the village of Lubars, which has four big farms, a policeman, a duck pond – now frozen – and an inn called The Merry Finch. The village is reputed to be the coldest place in Berlin. It might have been moved here from Wiltshire.

It belongs, all the same, to the French sector of the city and the high road leading out of it leads only to the Russian sector. The barrier is seven minutes from The Merry Finch, but the East German People's Police can see you sooner. Here, as everywhere along the wall, they operate in pairs, one man with field glasses, the other with a gun.

At this point the barrier consists of three barbed-wire fences supported on concrete posts seven feet high and six inches thick. The first fence is on the border itself; the second is ten feet behind the first; the third is 150 yards behind the second. Each fence has up to ten strands of barbed wire and the ground between the first and second is obstructed with more barbed wire coiled over wooden supports consisting of two crosses linked together and resembling, but for the wire, gigantic devices for keeping carving knives off table-cloths.

The ground between the second and third fences has been cleared and can be lit at night. A line of poles thirty feet high, spaced thirty yards apart, carries a power line; each pole has a cluster of electric lights. There is a line of watchtowers twenty feet high spaced 600 yards apart which has been manned throughout this week.

Farther south, where the suburbs become denser, the border is marked by a railway embankment. In Berlin, as in Surrey, railway lines in leafy suburbs tend to be flanked by gardens. By this week the People's Police had managed to get rid of most of the gardens that were in their way on the east side of the tracks. On Wednesday they were burning the rubbish, the tool sheds along with cherry trees, at the Bornholmerstrasse Station, four and three-quarter miles south of the point at which the railway becomes the frontier.

Five hundred yards further south, at the back of the Hertha football stadium, the wall itself begins.

For most of its length it is eight feet high. It is made of pink prefabricated concrete slabs measuring three feet four inches by three feet eight inches. They are one foot thick. Smaller prefabricated concrete blocks, the size of four English bricks, have been used to fill in awkward corners.

In most places the wall has now been capped with one or two rows of grey cement posts, eleven feet eight inches long and a foot square and laid on their sides. Cemented into them are Y-shaped welded rods carrying seven strands of barbed wire, two of which overhang the wall on the Western ride and two on the other. In the city the People's Police have cleared as much ground as they can on their side of the wall and have, in places, reinforced it with fences.

At one point in the south-eastern borough of Neukolln they have planted two seven-foot fences on the Western side of the wall – the first four feet from it and the second four feet from the first – and a third fence, only five feet high, 100 feet behind the wall. The power line and the lights run down the middle of the open ground.

This kind of clearance is neither necessary nor possible in most places. A mile south of the Hertha football stadium is the Bernauerstrasse, in the borough of Wedding, where the sector boundary runs east and west and coincides with the building line on the south side of the street. Here, as in other places, the People's Police have made their wall out of houses. At first they bricked up the front door and the ground-floor windows: people who lived on the south side of the street were talking to people who lived on the north side.

Some of them were doing more than that. At a bus stop opposite No. 44 neighbours have put a cross in memory of a student called Bernd Lunser who, pursued by the People's Police, jumped off the roof on 4 October. The West Berlin Fire department tried, but failed, to catch him in a jumping sheet. No. 44 is five storeys high. This week, all the roofs on the southern side of the Bernauerstrasse have been fenced with barbed wire.

Two hundred yards down the road from No. 44 the wall has been heightened to ten feet. Behind it, at this point, is the graveyard of the Church of Reconciliation. Farther west again the graveyard of the Church of St Sophia has also been walled in to a height of ten feet. Neither section carries the usual barbed wire superstructure. Churchyards get broken glass instead.

The new wall round the French cemetery in the Lisenstrasse has barbed wire, but is even higher. It was the highest section of wall I saw.

Round the corner in the Invalidesstrasse is a crossing point for the 500-odd West Berliners still allowed to visit East Berlin. A poster across the road says: THE STRONGER THE GERMAN DEMOCRATIC REPUBLIC GETS THE GREATER IS THE CERTAINTY OF PEACE IN GERMANY. It was here that an East German railway policeman shot and killed an unknown man who had dived into the neighbouring Humboldt Dock from the grounds of the Charite Hospital.

From the Humboldt Dock the wall follows the bank of the Spree to skirt the Reichstag building (at present occupied, in part, by the Durham Light Infantry) and to join this week's new works at the Brandenburg Gate. Here the wall is now thicker than anywhere else and its construction is more solid.

When they built it the East Germans began by sinking a row of steel posts into the roadway and cementing them in. They then laid slotted prefabricated concrete slabs over the posts, which projected through the slabs and held them steady. They then poured wet cement over the slabs and laid another layer on top, repeating the process until they had made a multi-decker sandwich in which slabs of concrete had been substituted for bread, the wet cement for butter.

The wall follows to the inch the western boundary of East Berlin which, in front of the Gate, bulges out into the roadway in a segment of a circle 100 yards wide and fifty deep. The East German construction workers – few, so it is said, come from Berlin – began the job at half-past five last Sunday evening and finished at half past ten on Tuesday night. They were heavily guarded by People's Police, dressed for the most part in camouflaged combat uniforms. They ate at a field kitchen parked beneath the Gate.

From the gate down the Ebertstrasse to the Potsdamerplatz they added, in the same period, two rows of heavy welded steel tripods, fixed in the roadway with cement. These have been camouflaged, ineffectively, with the sort of netting used round tennis courts. Their military purpose seems to be to deter the Western Powers from attacking with tanks the site of the Wertheim department store, an undertaking once regarded here as Germany's answer to Harrods.

From the Potsdamerplatz the wall runs south to include the ruins of the Potsdam Station, then north again, then east towards the Spree. It bisects the Wilhelmstrasse immediately south of what used to be Göring's Air Ministry. This week, early on Tuesday morning, about 200 young West Berliners gathered here to protest against the reinforcement of the wall. Some of them threw burning torches into the Russian sector. The People's Police replied with a jet of water and ninety-seven tear-gas bombs. The West Berliners replied, in turn, with 107.

The next street east is Friedrichstrasse where foreigners may cross the border. It is a narrow place of tension where only one tank can operate at a time. Here, for a day and two nights last month, the United States and Russia faced each other with their guns loaded. The whole might and purpose of Nato was represented by the gunner of a single Patton tank, Private Baker, aged twenty, of Michigan.

The next gap in the wall is at the Heinrich Heine Strasse. Coffins are exchanged here on Wednesdays. The Wall runs thence along the northern boundary of the borough of Kreuzberg round the back of the Bethany Hospital to the banks of the River Spree.

From the Spree for rather more than half a mile the border follows the Landwehrkanal, forty yards wide and a once-useful waterway.

In Neukolln, the wall twists between blocks of flats, shops, houses, gardens. In two streets the boundary follows the building line, but here the situation that obtains in the Bernauerstrasse is reversed. The houses belong to the West, the pavement to the East.

Where this happens the People's Police have built their wall in the gutter. A notice at the end of one such street reads: CITIZENS OF SEBASTIANSTRASSE! WE DRAW YOUR ATTENTION TO THE FACT THAT THE PAVEMENT YOU USE BELONGS TO THE TERRITORY OF THE GERMAN DEMOCRATIC REPUBLIC AND THAT THE BUILDING LINE IS THE STATE FRONTIER. WE EXPECT YOU TO REFRAIN FROM ANY PROVOCATION ON THE TERRITORY BECAUSE OTHERWISE WE WILL TAKE THE SECURITY MEASURES THAT ARE NECESSARY.

There is an artificial mound in a children's playground in the courtyard between the two blocks of flats in the Wildenbruchstrasse in Neukolln which provides a better view across the wall than any other eminence in the borough. The People's Police across the way have once or twice reacted angrily to sightseers watching from its grassy summit. The people in the flats complain that the gas still lingers in their children's sandpit.

The wire ends four miles on in Rudow, a distant, pleasant southern suburb on State Highway 179, the road that leads to East Berlin Airport and to the site of Hitler's most powerful broadcasting station. Under its local name, Waltersdorfer Chausee, the road now ends in two rows of barbed wire and a slit-trench.

The last house in West Berlin is No. 197: small, neat and loved. What must have been No. 199 has been bulldozed away. It was, by all accounts, as neat and modest as 197. In the place where it used to stand the earth has been cleared away and flattened. The cherry trees have been flung aside to make way for the wire.

THE CIVIL RIGHTS MARCH ON WASHINGTON, AMERICA, 29 August 1963

Vincent Ryder and David Shears, London Daily Telegraph

The Great Negro March on Washington yesterday turned out to be an orderly, good-humoured stroll around the Lincoln Memorial by the 200,000 Civil Rights demonstrators.

Only two arrests were made. One was of a follower of George Rockwell, the United States Nazi leader. Police hustled him away when he tried to make a speech.

Before the 200,000-strong Civil Rights march in Washington today was half over, Mr Bayard Rustin, deputy organizer and the real moving spirit, spoke of the next move.

He said: 'Already one of our objectives has been met. We said we would awaken the conscience of the nation and we have done it.'

The next move would be a 'counter-filibuster' if opponents in the Senate tried to talk the proposed Civil Rights Bill to death. On every day of this 'filibuster' 1,000 Negroes would be brought into Washington to stage a demonstration.

A great roar of approval met the warning by the Rev. Martin Luther King, the integrationist leader, that America was in for 'a rude awakening' if she thought she could go back to business as usual.

'Let us not seek to satisfy our thirst for freedom by drinking from the cup of hatred and bitterness,' said Mr King. Negroes would go on with the struggle until 'justice flows like water and righteousness like a stream'.

The cheers rolled over the crowd, jammed in front of the Lincoln Memorial and along the shallow reflecting pool.

It was a day of quiet triumph, a mingling of fervent demands with a show of orderly, relaxed calm. Earlier fears of disorder seemed almost laughably out of place.

Personalities in the march included Marlon Brando, Burt Lancaster, Lena Horne, Judy Garland, Sammy Davis, Sidney Poitier and Josephine Baker, who flew from Paris.

For two hours the marchers' numbers swelled around the monument within sight of the White House and the Capitol, which houses Congress.

They were entertained by singers and by brief speeches from their heroes, Jackie Robinson, the baseball player, and a man who roller-skated all the way from Chicago, and admitted his legs were tired.

The organizers expected that this sort of distraction would be necessary to keep tempers under control. They need not have worried. The crowd seemed almost as determined to be respectable as to demand civil rights.

Black suits and dresses predominated. A group of poor Negroes from Parksville, Mississippi, were in well-pressed overalls.

There were clerical collars by the dozen. Clergymen of every denomination joined the demonstration.

THE ASSASSINATION OF PRESIDENT JOHN F. KENNEDY, DALLAS, AMERICA, 23 November 1963

Merriman Smith

It was a balmy, sunny noon as we motored through downtown Dallas behind President Kennedy. The procession cleared the centre of the business district and turned into a handsome highway that wound through what appeared to be a park.

I was riding in the so-called White House press 'pool' car, a telephone company vehicle equipped with a mobile radio-telephone. I was in the front seat between a driver from the telephone company and Malcom Kilduff, acting White House press secretary for the President's Texas tour. Three other pool reporters were wedged in the back seat.

Suddenly we heard three loud, almost painfully loud cracks. The first sounded as if it might have been a large firecracker. But the second and the third blasts were unmistakable. Gunfire.

The President's car, possibly as much as 150 or 200 yards ahead, seemed to falter briefly. We saw a flurry of activity in the secret service follow-up car behind the chief executive's bubble-top limousine.

Next in line was the car bearing Vice-President Lyndon B. Johnson. Behind that, another follow-up car bearing agents assigned to the vice-president's protection. We were behind that car.

Our car stood still for probably only a few seconds, but it seemed like a lifetime. One sees history explode before one's eyes and for even the most trained observer, there is a limit to what one can comprehend.

I looked ahead at the President's car but could not see him or his companion, Gov. John Connally. Both had been riding on the right side of the limousine. I thought I saw a flash of pink that would have been Mrs Jacqueline Kennedy.

Everybody in our car began shouting at the driver to pull up closer to the President's car. But at this moment, we saw the big bubbletop and a motorcycle escort roar away at high speed.

We screamed at our driver, 'get going, get going'. We careened around the Johnson car and its escort and set out down the highway, barely able to keep in sight of the President's car and the accompanying secret service car.

They vanished around a curve. When we cleared the same curve we could see where we were heading – Parkland Hospital. We spilled out of the pool car as it entered the hospital driveway.

I ran to the side of the bubbletop.

The President was face down on the back seat. Mrs Kennedy made a cradle of her arms around the President's head and bent over him as if she were whispering to him.

Gov. Connally was on his back on the floor of the car, his head and shoulders resting in the arms of his wife, Nellie, who shook with dry sobs. Blood oozed from the front of the governor's suit. I could not see the President's wound. But I could see blood spattered around the interior of the rear seat and a dark stain spreading down the right side of the President's dark grey suit.

From the telephone car, I had radioed the Dallas UPI Bureau that three shots had been fired at the Kennedy motorcade.

Clint Hill, the secret service agent in charge of the detail assigned to Mrs Kennedy, was leaning over into the rear of the car.

'How badly was he hit, Clint?' I asked.

'He's dead,' Hill replied curtly.

BEATLEMANIA HITS AMERICA, NEW YORK, 7 February 1964

Tom Wolfe, New York Herald Tribune

John, Paul, Ringo and George arrive in New York on their first US tour.

By six-thirty a.m. yesterday [7 February], half the kids from South Orange, NJ to Seaford LI, were already up with their transistors plugged in their skulls. It was like a civil defence network or something. You could turn anywhere on the dial, WMCA, WCBS, WINS, almost any place, and get the bulletins: 'It's B-Day! Six-thirty a.m.! The Beatles left London thirty minutes ago! They're thirty minutes out over the Atlantic Ocean! Heading for New York!'

By one p.m. about 4,000 kids had finished school and come skipping and screaming into the international terminal at Kennedy Airport. It took 110 police to herd them. At one-twenty p.m., the Beatles' jet arrived from London.

The Beatles left the plane and headed for customs inspection and everybody got their first live look at the Beatles' hair style, which is a mop effect that covers the forehead, some of the ears and most of the back of the neck. To get a better look, the kids came plunging down the observation deck, and some of them already had their combs out, raking their hair down over their foreheads as they ran.

Then they were crowding around the plate-glass windows overlooking the customs section, stomping on the floor in unison, some of them beating time by bouncing off the windows.

The Beatles – George Harrison, 20; John Lennon, 23; Ringo Starr, 23; and Paul McCartney, 21 – are all short, slight kids from Liverpool who wear four-button coats, stovepipe pants, ankle-high black boots with Cuban heels. And droll looks on their faces. Their name is a play on the word 'beat'.

They went into a small room for a press conference, while some of the girls tried to throw themselves over a retaining wall.

Somebody motioned to the screaming crowds outside. 'Aren't you embarrassed by all this lunacy?'

'No,' said John Lennon. 'It's crazy.'

'What do you think of Beethoven?'

'He's crazy,' said Lennon. 'Especially the poems. Lovely writer.'

In the two years in which they have risen from a Liverpool rock-and-roll dive group to the hottest performers in the record business, they had seen much of this wildness before. What really got them were the American teenage car sorties.

The Beatles left the airport in four Cadillac limousines, one Beatle to a limousine, heading for the Plaza Hotel in Manhattan. The first sortie came almost immediately. Five kids in a powder blue Ford overtook the caravan on the expressway, and as they passed each Beatle, one guy hung out the back window and waved a red blanket.

A white convertible came up second, with the word BEETLES scratched on both sides in the dust. A police car was close behind that one with the siren going and the alarm light rolling, but the kids, a girl at the wheel and two guys in the back seat, waved at each Beatle before pulling over to the exit with the cops gesturing at them.

In the second limousine, Brian Sommerville, the Beatle's press agent, said to one of the Beatles, George Harrison: 'Did you see that, George?'

Harrison looked at the convertible with its emblem in the dust and said, 'They misspelled Beatles.'

But the third sortie succeeded all the way. A good-looking brunette, who said her name was Caroline Reynolds, of New Canaan, Conn., and Wellesley College, had paid a cab driver $10 to follow the caravan all the way into town. She cruised by each Beatle, smiling faintly, and finally caught up with George Harrison's limousine at a light at Third Avenue and 63rd St.

'How does one go about meeting a Beatle?' she said out of the window.

'One says hello,' said Harrison out of the window.

'Hello!' she said. 'Eight more will be down from Wellesley.' Then the light changed and the caravan was off again.

At the Plaza Hotel, there were police everywhere. The Plaza, on Central Park South just off Fifth Avenue, is one of the most sedate hotels in New York. The Plaza was petrified. The Plaza accepted the Beatles' reservations months ago, before knowing it was a rock-and-roll group that attracts teenage riots.

About 500 teenagers, most of them girls, had shown up at the Plaza. The police herded most of them behind barricades in the square between the hotel and the avenue. Every entrance to the hotel was guarded. The screams started as soon as the first limousine came into view.

The Beatles jumped out fast at the Fifth Avenue entrance. The teenagers had all been kept at bay. Old ladies ran up and touched the Beatles on their arms and backs as they ran up the stairs.

After they got to the Plaza the Beatles rested up for a round of television appearances (the Ed Sullivan Show Sunday), recordings (Capitol Records), concerts (Carnegie Hall, Wednesday) and a tour (Washington, Miami). The kids were still hanging around the Plaza hours after they went inside.

One group of girls asked everybody who came out, 'Did you see the Beatles? Did you touch them?'

A policeman came up, and one of them yelled, 'He touched a Beatle! I saw him!'

The girls jumped on the cop's arms and back, but it wasn't a mob assault. There were goony smiles all over their faces.

THE KILLING OF GEORGE CORNELL AT THE BLIND BEGGAR PUBLIC HOUSE, LONDON, ENGLAND, 9 March 1966

Ronald Kray

The Kray twins, Ronnie and Reggie, ran a Mafia-type gang or 'firm' in the East End of London in the 1960s. George Cornell was a member of the rival Richardson firm, and had been implicated in the shooting of a Kray associate, Richard Hart.

Richard Hart had to be avenged. No one could kill a member of the Kray gang and expect to get away with it. The problem was, both of the Richardsons and Mad Frankie Fraser were in custody and likely to remain so. That left Cornell. He would have to be the one to pay the price. And, let's face it, who better? All I had to do was find him. The next night, 9 March, I got the answer. He was drinking in the Blind Beggar.

Typical of the yobbo mentality of the man. Less than twenty-four hours after the Catford killing and here he was, drinking in a pub that was officially on our patch. It was as though he wanted to be killed.

I unpacked my 9mm Mauser automatic. I also got out a shoulder holster. I called Scotch Jack Dickson and told him to bring the car round to my flat and to contact Ian Barrie, the big Scot, and to collect him on the way. As we drove towards the Blind Beggar, I checked that Barrie was carrying a weapon, just in case.

At eight-thirty p.m. precisely we arrived at the pub and quickly looked around to make sure that this was not an ambush. I told Dickson to wait in the car with the engine running, then Ian Barrie and I walked into the Blind Beggar. I could not have felt calmer, and having Ian Barrie alongside me was great. No general ever had a better right-hand man.

It was very quiet and gloomy inside the pub. There was an old bloke sitting by himself in the public bar and three people in the saloon bar: two blokes at a table and George Cornell sitting alone on a stool at the far end of the bar. As we walked in the barmaid was putting on a record. It was the Walker Brothers and it was called 'The Sun Ain't Gonna Shine Any More'. For George Cornell that was certainly true.

As we walked towards him he turned round and a sort of sneer came over his face. 'Well, look who's here,' he said.

I never said anything. I just felt hatred for this sneering man. I took out my gun and held it towards his face. Nothing was said, but his eyes told me that he thought the whole thing was a bluff. I shot him in the forehead. He fell forward on to the bar. There was some blood on the counter. That's all that happened. Nothing more. Despite any other account you may have read of this incident, that was what happened.

It was over very quickly. There was silence. Everyone had disappeared – the barmaid, the old man in the public and the blokes in the saloon bar. It was like a ghost pub. Ian Barrie stood next to me. He had said nothing.

I felt fucking marvellous. I have never felt so good, so bloody alive, before or since. Twenty years on and I can recall every second of the killing of George Cornell. I have replayed it in my mind millions of times.

After a couple of minutes we walked out, got into the car and set off for a pub in the East End run by a friend called Madge. On the way there we could hear the screaming of the police car sirens. When we got to the pub I told a few of my friends what had happened. I also told Reg, who seemed a bit alarmed.

Then we went to a pub at Stoke Newington called the Coach and Horses. There I gave my gun to a trusted friend we used to call the Cat and told him to get rid of it. I suddenly noticed my hands were covered in gunpowder burns, so I scrubbed them in the washroom. I showered and put on fresh clothing – underwear, a suit, a shirt and tie. (We had spare sets of 'emergency' clothes at several places.) All my old clothing was taken away to be burned. Upstairs in a private room I had a few drinks with some of the top members of the firm – Reg, Dickson, Barrie, Ronnie Hart and others. We listened to the radio and heard that a man had been shot dead in the East End. As the news was announced I could feel everyone in the room, including Reg, looking at me with new respect. I had killed a man. I had got my button, as the Yanks say. I was a man to be feared. I was now the Colonel.

ENGLAND WIN THE WORLD CUP, LONDON, 30 July 1966

David Miller

They had fetched him, three and a half years ago, from quiet Ipswich, a taciturn, shy, deeply reserved man, and calmly leading with his chin, as they say, he had promised to win them the World Cup. There were those who laughed, and some were still laughing when the tournament began. Yet by the finish, with a relentless inflexibility of will, with sterling courage, with efficiency that brought unbounded admiration, his team, England's team, helped to keep that promise.

They did it, Alf Ramsey and England, after just about the worst psychological reverse possible on an unforgettable afternoon. With victory dashed from their grasp, cruelly only seconds from the final whistle, they came again in extra time, driving weary limbs across the patterned turf beyond the point of exhaustion, and crowned the ultimate achievement with a memorable goal with the last kick of all by Hurst, making him the first player to score a hat-trick in the World Cup Final.

We had all often talked of the thoroughness of preparation of the deposed champions, Brazil, but England's glory this day, to be engraved on that glinting, golden trophy, was the result of the most patient, logical, painstaking, almost scientific assault on the trophy there had perhaps ever been – and primarily the work and imagination of one man.

For those close to him through the past three exciting seasons, Ramsey's management had been something for unending admiration, and the unison cry of the 93,000 crowd, 'Ram-sey, Ram-sey' as his side mounted the steps to collect Jules Rimet's statuette from the Queen was the final rewarding vindication for one who had unwaveringly pursued his own, often lonely, convictions.

As the crowd stood in ovation, Greaves looked on wistfully. Injury had cost him his place, and though he recovered, Ramsey had resisted the almost overpowering temptation to change a winning side. This, too, was vindication, his whole aim since 1963 having been to prepare not a team but a squad, so that at any moment he might replace an out of form or injured man without noticeable deterioration in the side. When the time came, the luckless Greaves's omission caused hardly a stir of pessimism.

At the start of the tournament, I had written that if England were to win, it would be with the resolution, physical fitness and cohesion of West Germany in 1954, rather than with the flair of Brazil in the two succeeding competitions. And so it proved, with the added coincidence that it was the Germans themselves, as usual bristling with all these same characteristics in profusion, who were the unlucky and brave victims of England's methodical rather than brilliant football. Before the semi-finals I said that the deciding factor of this World Cup, when all others had cancelled out in the modern proficiency of defensive systems, would be character, and now the character of every England player burned with a flame that warmed all those who saw it. The slightest weakening, mentally or physically, in any position, could have lost this match a hundred times over, but the way in which Ball, undoubtedly the man of the afternoon, Wilson, Stiles, Peters, Bobby Charlton and above all Moore, impelled themselves on, was something one would remember long after the tumult of excitement and the profusion of incidents had faded. Justifiably, Moore was voted the outstanding player of the competition; his sudden, surging return to form on tour beforehand had helped cement the castle at the critical hour.

All assessments of great events should be measured by absolute standards along with the quality of contemporaries, and therefore one had to say that England were not a great team, probably not even at that moment the best team in the world, depending on what you mean by best.

What matters is that they were the best there at Wembley in July, on that sunny, showery afternoon, best when the chips were down in open combat, and that, after all, is what counts – the result, rather than its manner, goes into the record books. Besides, Ramsey had not set about producing the most entertaining but the most successful team. Could he afford to be the one romantic in a world of hard-headed, win-at-all-costs efficiency? Could he favour conventional wingers who promised much and produced little? A manager is ultimately only as good as the players at his disposal; handicapped by a shortage of world class, instinctive players of the calibre of the South Americans, Italians, Hungarians, or his own Bobby Charlton, and by an over-abundance of average competence, Ramsey had slowly eliminated all those who lacked what he needed for cohesion. What greater demonstration of unity of purpose could there have been than the insistence of the winners, for all the emotion of the moment, that the eleven reserves join them on the lap of honour, and after share equally the £22,000 bonus.

Some complained England were helped by playing all their matches at Wembley, yet certainly in that mood and form they could and would have won anywhere in the country. Besides, under Ramsey, England had had more success abroad than ever before. If nothing else, this World Cup, penetrating almost every home in the land, should have persuaded the doubters, the detractors and the cynics that this is the greatest spectator sport there is, and the Final was a fitting climax.

At the start England asserted themselves – Bobby Charlton exerting a telling influence in midfield, even though closely watched by Beckenbauer sent Peters streaming through with fine anticipation, into spaces behind the German midfield trio. Suddenly, however, in the thirteenth minute, England found themselves a goal down for the first time in the competition. It was not an error under pressure, it was unforced. As a centre from the left came over, Wilson stood alone, eyes riveted on the dropping ball. He made to head it down to Moore, but his judgement betrayed him, sending it instead straight to Haller, who whipped in a low skidding shot past an unsighted, helpless Banks.

The strapping Germans and their flag-waving supporters bounced with joy, but within six minutes England were level. Midway inside the German half, on the left, Overath tripped Moore, and even before the referee had finished wagging his finger at Overath, Moore had spotted a gaping hole in the German rearguard. He placed the ball and took the kick almost in one move, a dipping floater that carried thirty-five yards and was met by Hurst, streaking in from the right, with another graceful, expertly-timed header like that which beat Argentina.

The pattern swung once more in the ten minutes before half-time. The three German strikers, nosing in and out like carnivorous fish, began to create havoc that was only averted after extreme anxiety. In between, Hunt, from a glorious pass by Bobby Charlton, hammered a thundering shot, a difficult one running away to his left, straight at Tilkowski. On the stroke of half-time, it was England who were desperately lucky, when a fast dipper by Seeler was tipped over by Banks, arched in mid-air like a stalling buzzard.

Little happened for nearly twenty-five minutes after halftime, the lull punctuated only by 'Oh, oh, what a referee,' as Mr Dienst went fussily about his business. Then, with twenty minutes to go, England's rhythm began to build up again, Bobby Charlton, Ball and Peters stretching the Germans to the extreme of their physical endurance with passes that again and again almost saw Hurst and Hunt clear. With eleven minutes to go, Ball won a corner, put it across, the ball was headed out, and hit back first-time by Hurst. It struck a defender, fell free, and Peters swooped to lash it home.

England, sensing victory, played it slow, slow, but Hunt wasted a priceless chance when it was three red England shirts to one white German on the edge of the penalty area, by misjudging his pass. With a minute left, all was disaster as Jack Charlton was most harshly penalized for 'climbing' over the top of Held. Emmerich blasted the free kick. A German in the penalty area unquestionably pulled the ball down with his hand, and after a tremendous scramble, Weber squeezed the ball home to level the match.

You could see England's spirits sink as the teams changed over for extra time but, quickly calmed and reassured by the emotionless Ramsey, they rallied themselves instantly. Ball, still unbelievably dynamic, going like the wind right to the finish, had a shot tipped over, Bobby Charlton hit a post and with twelve minutes gone, England were once more in front as Stiles slipped the ball up the wing to Ball, whose cross was thumped hard by Hurst. The ball hit the bar, bounced down and came out, and after consultation with the Russian linesman, Bakhramov, a goal was given. I had my doubts, doubled after later seeing television, but that surely had to be the winner, for now, socks rolled down, both teams were physically in distress. Again England sought economy with gentle passes, keeping precious possession, wearing the Germans down yet further, Poor Wilson hardly knew where he was after a blow on the head. Slowly the minutes ticked away, agonisingly, until with the referee looking at his watch, Hurst staggered on alone from yet one more of Moore's perceptive passes, to hit the ball into the roof of the net with what, little strength he had left, and make England's victory, like their football, solid and respectable. Whether Ramsey, as silent in victory as defeat, could achieve the impossible and adapt these same characteristics to win in Mexico in 1970 was a chapter that would unfold over the next four years.

ENGLAND: – Banks (*Leicester*); Cohen (*Fulham*), Charlton J. (*Leeds*), Moore (*W. Ham*), Wilson (*Everton*); Stiles (*Manchester United*), Charlton R. (*Manchester United*), Peters (*W. Ham*); Ball (*Blackpool*), Hunt (*Liverpool*), Hurst (*W. Ham*).

WEST GERMANY: – Tilkowski; Hoettges, Schulz, Weber, Schnellinger; Beckenbauer, Haller, Overath; Seeler, Held, Emmerich.

Referee: – G. Dienst (Switzerland).

Linesmen: – K. Galba (Czechoslovakia), T. Bakhramov (USSR).

THE LAST JOURNEY OF CHE GUEVARA, VALLEGRANDE, BOLIVIA, 10 October 1967

Richard Gott, Guardian

After playing a leading role in the Cuban Revolution, the Argentinian-born Guevara left Cuba in 1965 to lead a guerilla movement in Bolivia. He was captured and executed by government troops and the American CIA while trying to foment a revolt there.

The body of Che Guevara was flown into this small hill town in south-eastern Bolivia at five o'clock last night.

From the moment the helicopter landed bearing the small figure strapped in a stretcher to the landing rails, the succeeding operation was to a large extent left in the hands of a man in battledress, who, all the correspondents here agree, was unquestionably a representative of one of the United States intelligence agencies.

He was probably a Cuban exile and so Che Guevara, who in life had declared war almost singlehanded on the United States, found himself in death face to face with his major enemy.

The helicopter purposely landed far from where a crowd had gathered and the body of the dead guerilla leader was hastily transferred to a van. We commandeered a jeep to follow it and the driver managed to get through the gates of the hospital grounds where the body was taken to a small colour-washed hut that served as a mortuary.

The doors of the van burst open and the American agent leapt out, emitting a war cry of 'Let's get the hell out of here.' One of the correspondents asked him where he came from. 'Nowhere,' was the surly response.

The body, dressed in olive green fatigues with a zippered jacket, was carried into the hut. It was undoubtedly that of Che Guevara. Ever since I first reported in January that Che was probably in Bolivia I have not shared the general scepticism about his whereabouts.

I am probably one of the few people here who have seen him alive. I saw him in Cuba at an Embassy reception in 1963 and there is no doubt in my mind that this body was that of Che. It had a black wispy beard, long matted hair, and the shadow of a scar on the right temple, probably the result of an accident in July when he was grazed by a rifle shot.

On his feet he wore moccasins as though he had been shot down while running fleet-footed through the jungle. He had two wounds in the lower part of the neck and possibly one in the stomach. It is believed that he was captured when seriously wounded, but died before a helicopter could arrive to take him out of the battle zone.

My only doubts about the identity arose because Che was much thinner and smaller than I had recalled, but it is hardly surprising that after months in the jungle he had lost his former heavy appearance.

As soon as the body reached the mortuary the doctors began to pump preservative into it, and the American agent made desperate efforts to keep off the crowds. He was a very nervous man and looked furious whenever cameras were pointed in his direction. He knew that I knew who he was and he also knew that I knew that he should not be there, for this is a war in which the Americans are not supposed to be taking part. Yet here was this man, who has been with the troops in Vallegrande, talking to the senior officers on familiar terms.

One can hardly say that this was the factor with which Che failed to reckon, for it was his very purpose to provoke United States intervention in Latin America as a way of bringing help and succour to the embattled Vietnamese. But he certainly did fail to estimate correctly the strength and pervasiveness of the US intelligence agencies in this continent, and this more than anything else has been the cause of his downfall and that of the Bolivian guerillas.

And so he is dead. As they pumped preservative into his half-naked, dirty body and as the crowd shouted to be allowed to see, it was difficult to recall that this man had once been one of the great figures of Latin America.

It was not just that he was a great guerrilla leader, he had been a friend of Presidents as well as revolutionaries. His voice had been heard and appreciated in inter-American councils as well as in the jungle. He was a doctor, an amateur economist, once Minister of Industries in revolutionary Cuba, and Fidel Castro's right-hand man. He may well go down in history as the greatest continental figure since Bolivar. Legends will be created around his name.

He was a Marxist but impatient of the doctrinal struggles between the Russians and the Chinese. He was perhaps the last person who tried to find a middle way between the two and attempted to unite radical forces everywhere in a concerted campaign against the US. He is now dead, but it is difficult to feel that his ideas will die with him.

VIETNAM WAR: THE CITADEL OF HUÉ, VIETNAM, February 1968

Michael Herr

On 30 January 1968, the North Vietnamese marked the beginning of the Tet (lunar new year) by launching an offensive against 125 locations held by the South Vietnamese and US troops, including Khe Sahn Saigon and Hué. This account of Hué during the fighting of February 1968 is from Michael Herr's classic of war journalism, *Dispatches*.

Going in, there were sixty of us packed into a deuce-and-a-half, one of eight trucks moving in convoy from Phu Bai, bringing in over 300 replacements for the casualties taken in the earliest fighting south of the Perfume River. There had been a harsh, dark storm going on for days, and it turned the convoy route into a mudbed. It was terribly cold in the trucks, and the road was covered with leaves that had either been blown off the trees by the storm or torn away by our artillery, which had been heavy all along the road. Many of the houses had been completely collapsed, and not one had been left without pitting from shell fragments. Hundreds of refugees held to the side of the road as we passed, many of them wounded. The kids would laugh and shout, the old would look on with that silent tolerance for misery that made so many Americans uneasy, which was usually misread as indifference. But the younger men and women would often look at us with unmistakable contempt, pulling their cheering children back from the trucks.

We sat there trying to keep it up for each other, grinning at the bad weather and the discomfort, sharing the first fear, glad that we weren't riding point or closing the rear. They had been hitting our trucks regularly, and a lot of the convoys had been turned back. The houses that we passed so slowly made good cover for snipers, and one B-40 rocket could have made casualties out of a whole truckload of us. All the grunts were whistling, and no two were whistling the same tune, it sounded like a locker room before a game that nobody wanted to play. Or almost nobody. There was a black Marine called Philly Dog who'd been a gang lord in Philadelphia and who was looking forward to some street fighting after six months in the jungle, he could show the kickers what he could do with some city ground. (In Hue he turned out to be incredibly valuable. I saw him pouring out about a hundred rounds of .30-calibre fire into a breach in the wall, laughing, 'You got to bring some to get some'; he seemed to be about the only man in Delta Company who hadn't been hurt yet.) And there was a Marine correspondent, Sergeant Dale Dye, who sat with a tall yellow flower sticking out of his helmet cover, a really outstanding target. He was rolling his eyes around and saying, 'Oh, yes, oh yes, Charlie's got his shit together here, this will be *bad*,' and smiling happily. It was the same smile I saw a week later when a sniper's bullet tore up a wall two inches above his head, odd cause for amusement in anyone but a grunt.

Everyone else in the truck had that wild haunted going-West look that said it was perfectly correct to be here where the fighting would be the worst, where you wouldn't have half of what you needed, where it was colder than Nam ever got. On their helmets and flak jackets they'd written the names of old operations, of girlfriends, their war names (FAR FROM FEARLESS, MICKEY'S MONKEY, AVENGER V, SHORT TIME SAFETY MOE), their fantasies (BORN TO LOSE, BORN TO RAISE HELL, BORN TO KILL, BORN TO DIE), their ongoing information (HELL SUCKS, TIME IS ON MY SIDE, JUST YOU AND ME GOD

RIGHT?). One kid called to me, 'Hey man! You want a story, man? Here man, write this: I'm up there on 881, this was May, I'm just up there walkin' the ridgeline like a movie star and this Zip jumps up smack into me, lays his AK-47 fucking right *into* me, only he's so *amazed* at my *cool* I got my whole clip off' fore he knew how to thank me for it. Grease one.' After twenty kilometers of this, in spite of the black roiling sky ahead, we could see smoke coming up from the far side of the river, from the Citadel of Hué.

The bridge was down that spanned the canal dividing the village of An Cuu and the southern sector of Hué, blown the night before by the Viet Cong, and the forward area beyond the far bank wasn't thought to be secure, so we bivouacked in the village for the night. It had been completely deserted, and we set ourselves up in empty hootches, laying our poncho liners out over broken glass and shattered brick. At dusk, while we all stretched out along the canal bank eating dinner, two Marine gunships came down on us and began strafing us, sending burning tracers up along the canal, and we ran for cover, more surprised than scared. 'Way to go, motherfucker, way to pinpoint the fuckin' enemy,' one of the grunts said, and he set up his M-60 machine-gun in case they came back. 'I don't guess we got to take *that* shit,' he said. Patrols were sent out, guards posted, and we went into the hootches to sleep. For some reason, we weren't even mortared that night.

In the morning we crossed the canal on a two-by-four and started walking in until we came across the first of the hundreds of civilian dead that we were to see in the next weeks: an old man arched over his straw hat and a little girl who'd been hit while riding her bicycle, lying there with her arm up like a reproach. They'd been lying out like that for a week; for the first time we were grateful for the cold.

Along the Perfume River's south bank there is a long, graceful park that separates Hué's most pleasant avenue, Le Loi, from the river-front. People will talk about how they'd sit out there in the sun and watch the sampans moving down the river, or watch the girls bicycling up Le Loi, past the villas of officials and the French-architected University buildings. Many of those villas had been destroyed and much of the University permanently damaged. In the middle of the street a couple of ambulances from the German Mission had been blown up, and the Cercle Sportif was covered with bullet holes and shrapnel. The rain had brought up the green, it stretched out cased in thick white fog. In the park itself, four fat green dead lay sprawled around a tall, ornate cage, inside of which sat a small, shivering monkey. One of the correspondents along stepped over the corpses to feed it some fruit. (Days later, I came back to the spot. The corpses were gone, but so was the monkey. There had been so many refugees and so little food then, and someone must have eaten him.) The Marines of 2/5 had secured almost all of the central south bank and were now fanning out to the west, fighting and clearing one of the major canals. We were waiting for some decision on whether or not US Marines would be going into the Citadel itself, but no one had any doubts about what that decision would be. We sat there taking in the dread by watching the columns of smoke across the river, receiving occasional sniper rounds, infrequent bursts of .50-calibre, watching the Navy LCUs on the river getting shelled from the wall. One Marine next to me was saying that it was just a damned shame, all them poor people, all them nice-looking houses, they even had a Shell station there. He was looking at the black napalm blasts and the wreckage along the wall. 'Looks like the Imperial City's had the schnitz,' he said.

THE VIETNAM WAR: THE PACIFICATION OF MY LAI, 16 March 1968

Time *magazine correspondent*

Throughout the 1960s the USA became steadily more embroiled in the civil war in Vietnam between the Communist North and non-Communist South, and in 1965 took the fateful decision of committing troops to help the embattled South Vietnamese regime. The My Lai massacre, committed by C Company of the US 11th Infantry Brigade, resulted in the court martial of Lieutenant William Calley for the murder of 109 Vietnamese citizens.

West, a squad leader in a platoon commanded by Lieutenant Jeffrey La Cross, followed Calley's platoon into My Lai. 'Everyone was shooting,' he said. 'Some of the huts were torched. Some of the *yanigans* [young soldiers] were shooting kids.' In the confusion, he claims, it was hard to tell 'mama-sans from papa-sans', since both wore black pyjamas and conical hats. He and his squad helped round up the women and children. When one of his men protested that 'I can't shoot these people', West told him to turn a group over to Captain Medina. On the way out of the village, West recalls seeing a ditch filled with dead and dying civilians. His platoon also passed a crying Vietnamese boy, wounded in both a leg and an arm. West heard a GI ask, 'What about him?' Then he heard a shot and the boy fell. 'The kid didn't do anything,' said West, 'He didn't have a weapon' . . .

Another soldier in the group following Calley's was SP4 Varnado Simpson, twenty-two. 'Everyone who went into the village had in mind to kill,' he says. 'We had lost a lot of buddies and it was a VC stronghold. We considered them either VC or helping the VC.' His platoon approached from the left flank. 'As I came up on the village there was a woman, a man and a child running away from it towards some huts. So I told them in their language to stop, and they didn't, and I had orders to shoot them down and I did this. This is what I did. I shot them, the lady and the little boy. He was about two years old.'

A detailed account came from Paul David Meadlo, twenty-two, a member of Calley's platoon . . . Meadlo says his group ran through My Lai, herding men, women, children and babies into the centre of the village – 'like a little island'.

'Lieutenant Calley came over and said, "You know what to do with them, don't you?" And I said, "Yes." And he left and came back about ten minutes later, and said, "How come you ain't killed them yet?" And I told him that I didn't think he wanted us to kill them, that he just wanted us to guard them. He said, "No, I want them dead." So he started shooting them. And he told me to start shooting. I poured about four clips [68 shots] into them. I might have killed ten or fifteen of them.

'So we started to gather more people, and we had about seven or eight, and we put them in the hootch [hut] and then we dropped a hand grenade in there with them. And then they had about seventy to seventy-five people all gathered up by a ravine, so we threw ours in with them and Lieutenant Calley told me, "Meadlo, we got another job to do." And so he walked over to the people, and he started pushing them off and started shooting. We just pushed them all off and just started using automatics on them.'

According to SP5 Jay Roberts, the rampaging GIs were not interested solely in killing, although that seemed foremost in their minds. Roberts told *Life*, 'Just outside the village there was this big pile of bodies. This really tiny kid – he had only a shirt on, nothing else – he came over to the pile and held the hand of one of the dead.

One of the GIs behind me dropped into a kneeling position thirty metres from this kid and killed him with a single shot.' Roberts also watched while troops accosted a group of women, including a teenage girl. The girl was about thirteen, wearing black pyjamas: 'A GI grabbed the girl and with the help of others started stripping her,' Roberts related. 'Let's see what she's made of,' a soldier said. 'VC boom-boom,' another said, telling the thirteen-year-old girl that she was a whore for the Vietcong. 'I'm horny,' said a third. As they were stripping the girl, with bodies and burning huts all around them, the girl's mother tried to help her, scratching and clawing at the soldiers.

Continued Roberts: 'Another Vietnamese woman, afraid for her own safety, tried to stop the woman from objecting. One soldier kicked the mother, and another slapped her up a bit. Haeberle [the photographer] jumped in to take a picture of the group of women. The picture shows the thirteen-year-old girl hiding behind her mother, trying to button the top of her pyjamas. When they noticed Ron, they left off and turned away as if everything was normal. Then a soldier asked, "Well, what'll we do with 'em?" "Kill 'em," another answered. I heard an M60 go off, a light machine-gun, and when we turned all of them and the kids with them were dead.'

THE NIGHT OF THE BARRICADES, PARIS, 10 May 1968

Hans Koning

A minor dispute involving students at Nanterre and Sorbonne universities escalated into a mass student revolt in favour of reform of the authoritarian French educational system.

The Quartier Latin on the left bank of the Seine is a marvellously thick soup of college buildings, France's more famous middle schools, parks, cafés, boulevards and little streets: perfect headquarters for a new French revolution. There is nothing like that in American cities. I remember sitting in a Paris Left Bank café on the evening of 10 May which was going to be the Night of the Barricades: the night of 10 May to 11 May was to turn the tide against the police and put the students well-nigh in control of that part of the city. Before it had got really dark, there was already a wild excitement in the air. You could almost taste it; it affected everyone. Waiters distractedly put coffees and drinks down and didn't bother to check the money. As the evening wore on, tourist types and older people from other areas looked around, got their things together, and left in a hurry. But don't think that there was fear in the air, that people felt threatened. There was elation, not worry.

Some future rightist French government may bulldoze the Latin Quarter into wide-open spaces with scattered glass-and-concrete high rises – just as in the nineteenth century Baron Haussmann got rid of all the narrow workmen's streets and alleyways for Louis Napoleon and replaced them by the star pattern of the great boulevards, each one as straight as the path of a cannonball. When I got back to Paris in 1970, I found that the city had already asphalted over the paving stones of many streets and squares. The cobblestoned touristy charm had gone, but no future students would have paving stones to hand to heave at the cops.

The fighting of the 10–11 May night was astounding. It was astounding to watch the students being unafraid of police with tear gas and CS gas, concussion grenades, nightsticks, pistols, helmets, visors, shields, grenade rifles, and the famous leaded capes. It was equally astounding to find their courage 'rewarded', so to speak, by sympathy and even admiration not only from the radio reporters of the independent radio stations (Europe One and Radio Luxembourg) but also from the public at large. The fight was so unequal, the police so brutal that you had to be a very determined Law & Order person to feel sympathy for the authorities.

The students had made three demands: that the police get out of the Sorbonne, that the university be reopened, and that the arrested students and other demonstrators be released. They decided to try to enforce their case not 'by writing letters to the papers' but by protest marches. That night, with the police barring their way wherever they went, they built their barricades where they found themselves stuck, in the Rue St-Jacques, the Rue Gay-Lussac, and some other narrower streets south of the Panthéon. They dug in. It was the police, the CRS, and the Gardes Mobiles from the army who attacked.

Through the night various professors, famous scientists, and men of letters appealed (often on the radio) for the police to let up. When a statement of the Sorbonne rector blamed the students for not negotiating, Radio Luxembourg put an almost immediate student reaction on the air, repeating the three basic demands and inviting Rector Roche to answer them. The only answer was a repeat of Roche's original statement. When dawn came, the last barricades fell to the police, and the remaining young men, and some young women, were dragged, often clubbed, into the police vans. An unknown number was taken to the hospital by volunteers who had to fight the police to get through.

It was a cold morning. The streets were littered with stones, with debris of all sorts, burned-out cars, shoes, and lost pieces of clothing. A restless crowd of young people, probably mostly students too, filled the streets. It looked as if the police had won, but actually they had lost. The mood of the city and the country had turned against them.

By the end of May, workers too had launched a vast movement of strikes, paralysing the country. Eventually General De Gaulle, after securing the backing of the army, succeeded in re-establishing his authority and the revolution petered out.

MAN LANDS ON THE MOON, 20 July 1969

Neil Armstrong, Buzz Aldrin

At 10.56 p.m., EDT, on 20 July 1969, Neil A. Armstrong stepped down from the bottom rung of *Apollo II*'s landing craft and became the first person to walk on the moon. Seconds later he was followed by his crewmate, Edwin (Buzz) Aldrin. Through the miracle of modern communications, hundreds of millions of people witnessed the event via TV. Below is Armstrong and Aldrin's commentary on the landing, as spoken to mission control at Houston.

ARMSTRONG: I'm at the foot of the ladder. The LM [lunar module] foot beds are only depressed in the surface about one or two inches, although the surface appears to be very, very fine grained as you get close to it. It's almost like a powder. It's very fine. I'm going to step off the LM now.

That's one small step for man, one giant leap for mankind.

The surface is fine and powdery. I can pick it up loosely with my toe. It does adhere in fine layers like powdered charcoal to the sole and the sides of my boots. I only go in a small fraction of an inch, maybe an eighth of an inch but I can see the footprints of my boots and the treads in the fine sandy particles.

There seems to be no difficulty in moving around this and we suspect that it's even perhaps easier than the simulations of 1/6 G that we performed in various simulations on the ground. Actually no trouble to walk around. The descent engine did not leave a crater of any size. It has about one-foot clearance on the ground. We're essentially on a very level place here. I can see some evidence of rays emanating from the descent engine, but a very insignificant amount.

HOUSTON: Neil, this is Houston did you copy about the contingency sample? Over.

ARMSTRONG: Roger. Going to get to that just as soon as I finish these picture series.

ALDRIN: Are you going to get the contingency sample? Okay. That's good.

ARMSTRONG: The contingency sample is down and it's up. Like it's a little difficult to dig through the crust. It's very interesting. It's a very soft surface but here and there where I plug with the contingency sample collector I run into very hard surface but it appears to be very cohesive material of the same sort. I'll try to get a rock in here.

HUSTON: Oh, that looks beautiful from here, Neil.

ARMSTRONG: It has a stark beauty all its own. It's like much of the high desert of the United States. It's different but it's very pretty out here. Be advised that a lot of the rock samples out here, the hard rock samples have what appear to be vesicles in the surface. Also, as I look at one now that appears to have some sort of feenacres [spelled phonetically].

HOUSTON: Roger. Out.

ARMSTRONG: This has been about six or eight inches into the surface. It's easy to push on in. I'm sure I could push it in further, but it's hard for me to bend down further than that.

ALDRIN: I didn't know you could throw so far, Neil.

ARMSTRONG: See me throw things? Is my pocket open?

ALDRIN: Yes it is. It's not up against your suit, though. Hit it back once more. More toward the inside. Okay that's good.

ARMSTRONG: Put it in the pocket.

ALDRIN: Yes. Push down. Got it? No it's not all the way in. Push. There you go.

ARMSTRONG: The sample is in the pocket. My oxygen is 81 per cent. I have no flags and I'm in minimum flow.

HOUSTON: Roger, Neil.

ALDRIN: How far are my feet from the . . .

ARMSTRONG: Okay, you're right at the edge of the porch.
ALDRIN: Now I want to back up and partially close the hatch – making sure not to lock it on my way out.
ARMSTRONG: . . . Good thought.
ALDRIN: That's our home for the next couple hours; we want to take good care of it. Okay, I'm on the top step and I can look down over the ICU and landing-gear pad. It's a very simple matter to hop down from one step to the next.
ARMSTRONG: Yes, I found that to be very comfortable, and walking is also very comfortable, Houston.
ARMSTRONG: You've got three more steps and then a long one.
ALDRIN: Okay. I'm going to leave that one foot up there and both hands down to about the fourth rung up.
ARMSTRONG: Now I think I'll do the same.

A little more. About another inch. There you got it. That's a good step.

About a three footer.

Beautiful view.

Ain't that somethin'?

THE WOODSTOCK FESTIVAL, AMERICA, September 1969

Greil Marcus, Rolling Stone

Friday was the first day of the Woodstock Music and Arts Fair, now moved to White Lake near Bethel, New York, a hundred miles from New York City and fifty miles from Woodstock proper. The intrepid *Rolling Stone* crew thought it would be bright to beat the traffic, so we left the city early in the morning and headed up. When we got to Monticello, a little town eight miles from the festival, the traffic was light. Then we hit it. Eight miles of two-lane road jammed with thousands of cars that barely moved. Engines boiling over, people collapsed on the side of the road, everyone smiling in common bewilderment.

Automotive casualties looked like the skeletons of horses that died on the Oregon Trail. People began to improvise, driving on soft shoulders until they hit the few thousand who'd thought of the same thing, then stopping again. Finally the two lanes were transformed into four and still nothing moved. Bulbous vacationers (for this was the Catskills, laden with chopped liver and bad comedians) stared at the cars and the freaks and the nice kids, their stomachs sticking out into the road. Here we were, trying to get to the land of Hendrix and the Grateful Dead, all the while under the beady eyes of Mantovani fans.

There wasn't any traffic control. We sat still in our car and figured out all sorts of brilliant solutions to the transportation problem, everything from one-way roads to hired buses (a plan that failed at the last minute), but we still weren't getting anywhere, and it had been four hours now. This was the road on the map, right? No other way to get there? A lot of kids were pulling over and starting to walk through the fields. We had six miles to go. It was a cosmic traffic jam, where all the cars fall into place like pieces in a jigsaw puzzle and stay there for ever.

The police estimated that there were a million people on the road that day trying to get to the festival. A million people; 186,000 tickets had been sold; the promoters figured that maybe 200,000, tops, would show. That seemed outlandish, if believable. But no one was prepared for what happened, and no one could have been.

Perhaps a quarter of a million never made it. They gave up and turned back, or parked on the highway and set up tents on the divider strip and stuck it out. Shit, they'd come to camp out for three days, and they were gonna do it. Many had walked fifteen miles in the rain and the mud, only to give up a mile or so before the festival and turn back, but they were having fun. Camped on the highway with no idea where White Lake was or what was going on, they were making friends, dancing to car radios and making their own music on their own guitars.

'Isn't it pretty here, all the trees and the meadows? And whenever it gets too hot, it rains and cools everyone off. Wow.' 'Yeah, but you paid eighteen dollars and drove all the way from Ohio and you can't even get to the festival. Aren't you disappointed? Or pissed off?' 'No, man. Everyone is so friendly, it's like being stuck in an elevator with people when the power goes off. But it's much nicer here than in an elevator.'

It was an amazing sight, the highway to White Lake: it looked, as someone said, like Napoleon's army retreating from Moscow. It looked like that for three days. Everywhere one looked one saw tents and campfires, cars rolled into ditches, people walking, lying down, drinking, eating, reading, singing. Kids were sleeping, making love, wading in the marshes, trying to milk the local cows and trying to cook the local corn. The army of New York State Quickway 17B was on manoeuvres.

Thinking back to Saturday, one image sticks in my mind, an image that I doubt is shared by many but one that I will never forget. Friday night, folk music had been played – Joan Baez, Arlo Guthrie, Sweetwater and Ravi Shankar. But by the next morning the future was unclear, and rumours that the area had been declared an official disaster seemed quite credible. Many left Saturday morning, oppressed by water shortages, ninety-degree heat, ninety-nine per cent humidity and the crush of bodies.

'I love all these people,' said a young girl, 'they're all beautiful, and I never thought I'd be hassled by so many beautiful people, but I am, and I'm going home.' Faces were drawn and tired, eyes blank, legs moving slowly on blistered and sore feet. The lack of water, food and toilets was becoming difficult, though everyone shared, and many simply roamed the area with provisions with the sole purpose of giving them away. But it got hotter and hotter, and a boy was running toward the lake in a panic, cradling his little puppy in his arms. The dog was unconscious, its tongue out of its mouth but not moving. The boy thought the dog was going to die, and he was scared. He kept running, and I stared after him, and then I left the festival and decided to go home. I couldn't get a plane, and I was lucky to stay, but that scene was real, and it too was part of the festival at White Lake.

Everyone in the country has seen pictures of the crowd. Was it bigger than it looked? Whoever saw so many people in the same spot, all with the same idea? Well, Hitler did, and General MacArthur, and Mao, but this was a somewhat better occasion. They came to hear the music, and they stayed to dig the scene and the people and the countryside. Any time, no matter who was playing, one could see thousands moving in every direction and more camped on every hill and all through the woods. The magnificent sound system was clear and audible long past the point at which one could no longer see the bands.

The outstanding thing was the unthinkable weight of the groups that played. Take Saturday night and Sunday morning (the music was scheduled to begin at one in the afternoon and run for twelve hours, but it began at three or four and went until the middle of the next morning). Here's the line-up: Joe Cocker, Country Joe and the Fish, Ten Years After, the Band, Johnny Winter, Blood, Sweat and Tears, Crosby, Stills, Nash and Young, the Paul Butterfield Blues Band, Sha Na Na and Jimi Hendrix. It's like watching God perform the Creation. 'And for My next number . . .'

Sometime around four in the morning the stage crew began to assemble the apparatus for the festival's most unknown quantity, Crosby, Stills, Nash and Young. This was not exactly their début – they'd played once or twice before – but this was a national audience, both in terms of the composition of the crowd and the press and because of the amazing musical competition with which they were faced.

It took a very long time to get everything ready, and the people on stage crowded around the amplifiers and the nine or ten guitars and the chairs and mikes and organ, more excited in anticipation than they'd been for any other group that night. A large semicircle of equipment protected the musicians from the rest of the people. The band was very nervous. Neil Young was stalking around, kissing his wife, trying to tune his guitar off in a corner, kissing his wife again, staring off away from the crowd. Stills and Nash paced back and forth and tested the organ and the mikes, and drummer Dallas Taylor fiddled with his kit and kept trying to make it more than perfect. Finally, they went on.

They opened with 'Suite Judy Blue Eyes', stretching it out for a long time, exploring the figures of the song for the crowd, making their quiet music and flashing grimaces at each other when something went wrong. They strummed and picked their way through other numbers, and then began to shift around, Crosby singing with Stills, then Nash and Crosby, back and forth. They had the crowd all the way. They seemed like several bands rather than one.

Then they hit it. Right into 'Long Time Gone', a song for a season if there ever was one: Stills on organ, shouting out the choruses; Neil snapping out lead; Crosby aiming his electric twelve-string out over the edge of the stage, biting off his words and stretching them out – lyrics as strong as any we are likely to hear.

There's something, something, something
Goin' on around here
That surely, surely, surely
Won't stand

The light of day
Oooooohhh!
And it appears to be a long time . . .

I have never seen a musician more involved in his music. At one point Crosby nearly fell off the stage in his excitement.

Deep into the New York night they were, early Sunday morning in the dark after three days of chaos and order, and it seemed like the last of a thousand and one American nights. Two hundred thousand people covered the hills of a great natural amphitheatre, campfires burning in the distance, the lights shining down from the enormous towers on to the faces of the band. Crosby, Stills, Nash and Young were just one of the many acts at this festival, and perhaps they wouldn't top the bill if paired with Hendrix or the Airplane or Creedence Clearwater or the Who or the Band, but this was their night. Their performance was scary, brilliant proof of the magnificence of music, and I don't believe it could have happened with such power anywhere else. This was a festival that had triumphed over itself, as Crosby and his band led the way toward the end of it.

'BLOODY SUNDAY' IN LONDONDERRY, NORTHERN IRELAND, 30 January 1972

Sean Collins

Soldiers from the British Paratroop Regiment opened fire on a civil rights protest by Irish Catholics, killing thirteen.

Oh at the time of Bloody Sunday I was only a wain, a child of nine. There were seven in our family: my mother, my father, and five of us kids. We all lived in a two-bedroomed flat on the eighth floor of one of the blocks in Rossville Street. We didn't know then of course, but that was going to be right overlooking where the shootings were. The flats had been built to be occupied by Catholic families: there was a strict policy of segregation of areas on a religious basis in Derry, and the one we were in was called Bogside. Everybody more or less knew everyone else there, and everyone was poor.

The police used to patrol the Bogside a lot. I remember the police from the beginning, they were part of the everyday scenery. I don't recall much animosity towards them though. As a kid you knew there were occasions when there was trouble, protests and riots and all that, but you'd no idea what it was really about.

Sometimes the police'd appear in armoured cars which were called 'pigs': you'd see them firing gas or rubber bullets at people if there was a crowd. But it was something which had nothing to do with you: that was the adults' world, and what happened in it was what happened, that's all. I remember one of our favourite games we played was to imitate it: we didn't play 'cowboys and indians', we played 'cops and rioters'. Today it was your turn to be one, then the next day you were the other.

We'd never any understanding at all what it was about. My family wasn't Republican: all they cared for was we should keep out of trouble and not get hurt. They always told us if we saw something going on anywhere, we were to come straight home and stop inside. 'Course we never did though: we used to try and find good places to watch from, then afterwards we'd run round all the streets to see if we could find rubber bullets as souvenirs. An empty gas canister, well that'd be a great prize.

I remember it clearly when the soldiers came: our parents told us they were there to protect us and they were our friends. The first ones I ever saw were standing around in the street, and women were going up to them and talking to them and giving them cups of tea. To us wains they soon became sort of like hero figures: they gave us sweets, and asked our names, talked to us about different places in the world they'd been. The biggest thrill of all would be if one specially liked you and would let you touch his rifle, and hold it while you had a look along its sights. To me the soldiers were fascinating. I thought they were wonderful. None of us feared them at all in any way: grown-ups as well, we were all pleased and glad they were there.

The day of Bloody Sunday itself, all kids were told that after morning Mass we had to be home by 12 o'clock latest, and afterwards there'd be no going out playing for the rest of the day. Our parents said there was going to be a big march, it was going to come down from the Creggan and go to the Guildhall. If we were good we could go out on the balcony of the flat to watch it in the distance, but that was all. No one knew beforehand it was going to be diverted down Rossville Street and come right towards us. So there was great excitement then when it was, when it started to come right in our direction.

At first it looked peaceful enough. There was some shouting but only a little: but then after a while we began to hear some shooting from somewhere towards the back. I thought it was going to be an ordinary riot, and the police'd try to contain it as they usually did, by shooting off some rubber bullets and perhaps sending in some gas. But then suddenly I realized there was something different about the sound. It wasn't like one I'd ever heard before. When rubber bullets are fired, you hear 'Bang, bang, bang' like that. This wasn't that noise: it was much sharper, going 'Crack, Crack, Crack'. Then somebody on the balcony said, it was one of the adults I think, 'Jesus, that's rifle fire, they're using real bullets they are!' And we saw the marching column start to break up, people beginning to run away from it as hard as they could.

What I saw next after that I couldn't believe, not really at first at all. An army troop carrier appeared, and it started coming slowly towards us down the street. A man was running away from it and they were chasing him and trying to pin him against the wall. He escaped somehow, I think he dodged off somehow to the side. So then the troop carrier stopped, and out of it, or from out of another one that'd come along by its side, half a dozen soldiers jumped out. They stood by the vehicle a minute: and then slowly and deliberately each one of them went down on one knee and started to fire steadily into the crowd. It was like as if they were doing a sort of training demonstration, that's the only way I can describe it.

People were falling hit, and there was complete pandemonium. Some were stopping to try and help those who'd been hurt to get up, and others had for their only thought to get away. I saw a priest crouching down at the end of a wall: and when I looked at him I knew him, he was our own priest, Father Daly. He crawled from behind the wall to go to a man who was lying in the open a few yards away from him. I looked back where the soldiers were, and I saw one of them look up and he saw us watching from the balcony. He brought his gun up and took aim, but I didn't wait to see if he was really going to shoot or not; like everyone else there I ducked down. So whether that soldier fired or not, I don't know. Afterwards though nine bullet holes were found in the brickwork of the front of the flats, some of them as high up as the floor above ours.

Most of all what comes clearly back to me was my feeling of

surprise. It was surprise that these men, the soldiers who I'd liked so much and admired – suddenly they weren't good people or heroes like I'd thought. They were cruel and heartless causing death and panic, putting terror into the hearts of the ordinary people of the community I lived in. It's difficult to judge the effect of it afterwards, but I'd say for me it was like the smashing up of a dream: sort of the end to my innocence somehow, the innocence of a child who till then had thought there was something noble and romantic about soldiers. I didn't think that afterwards, not ever again.

NIXON RESIGNS AS US PRESIDENT, WASHINGTON, 8 August 1974

Richard Nixon

Richard Milhous Nixon, 37th President of the USA, resigned office under the threat of impeachment, when several leading members of his government were found guilty of organizing a break into the Democratic National Committee's headquarters in the Watergate Hotel, Washington.

Two minutes before nine o'clock I went into the Oval Office. I sat in my chair behind the desk while the technicians adjusted the lighting and made their voice check.

At forty-five seconds after nine, the red light on the camera facing my desk went on – it was time to speak to America and the world.

I began by saying how difficult it was for me to leave the battle unfinished, but my lack of congressional support would paralyse the nation's business if I decided to fight on.

> In the past few days . . . it has become evident to me that I no longer have a strong enough political base in the Congress to justify continuing that effort. As long as there was such a base, I felt strongly that it was necessary to see the constitutional process through to its conclusion, that to do otherwise would be unfaithful to the spirit of that deliberately difficult process, and a dangerously destabilizing precedent for the future.
>
> But with the disappearance of that base, I now believe that the constitutional purpose has been served, and there is no longer a need for the process to be prolonged.

Then I came to the most difficult sentence I shall ever have to speak. Looking directly into the camera, I said,

> Therefore, I shall resign the presidency effective at noon tomorrow.

I continued:

> By taking this action, I hope that I will have hastened the start of that process of healing which is so desperately needed in America.
>
> I regret deeply any injuries that may have been done in the course of the events that led to this decision. I would say only that if some of my judgements were wrong – and some were wrong – they were made in what I believed at the time to be in the best interest of the nation.

I talked briefly about America and about the world. I talked about my own attempts in twenty-five years of public life to fight for what I believed in. I recalled that in my first inaugural address I had pledged to consecrate myself and my energies to the cause of peace among nations. I went on:

> I have done my very best in all the days since to be true to that pledge. As a result of these efforts, I am confident that the world is a safer place today, not only for the people of America, but for the people of all nations, and that all of our children have a better chance than before of living in peace rather than dying in war.
>
> This, more than anything, is what I hoped to achieve when I sought the presidency. This, more than anything, is what I hope will be my legacy to you, to our country, as I leave the presidency.

Throughout the speech I looked down at the pages of the text, but I did not really read it. That speech was truly in my heart. At the end, I said: 'To have served in this office is to have felt a very personal sense of kinship with each and every American. In leaving it, I do so with this prayer: May God's grace be with you in all the days ahead.'

The red light blinked off. One by one the blinding television lights were switched off. I looked up and saw the technicians respectfully standing along the wall, pretending that they were not waiting for me to leave so that they could dismantle their equipment. I thanked them and left the Oval Office.

Kissinger was waiting for me in the corridor. He said, 'Mr President, after most of your major speeches in this office we have walked together back to your house. I would be honoured to walk with you again tonight.'

As we walked past the dark Rose Garden, Kissinger's voice was low and sad. He said that he thought that historically this would rank as one of the great speeches and that history would judge me one of the great Presidents. I turned to him and said, 'That depends, Henry, on who writes the history.' At the door of the Residence I thanked him and we parted.

I quickly headed for the elevator that would take me to the Family Quarters. The long hall was dark and the police and Secret Service had mercifully been removed or were keeping out of sight. When the doors opened on the second floor, the family was all waiting there to meet me. I walked over to them. Pat put her arms around me. Tricia. Julie. Ed. David. Slowly, instinctively, we embraced in a tender huddle, drawn together by love and faith.

We sat talking for a few minutes about the day and the speech. Suddenly I began to shake violently, and Tricia reached over to hold me. 'Daddy!' she exclaimed, 'the perspiration is coming clear through your coat!' I told them not to worry. I had perspired heavily during the speech, and I must have caught a chill walking over from the office. In a minute it had passed.

THE RUMBLE IN THE JUNGLE: MUHAMMAD ALI KNOCKS OUT GEORGE FOREMAN IN EIGHT, KINSHASA, ZAÏRE, 30 October 1974

Norman Mailer

Well, George came off the ropes and pursued Ali like a man chasing a cat. The wild punch seemed to have refreshed him by its promise that some of his power was back. If his biggest punches were missing, at least they were big. Once again he might be his own prodigy of strength. Now there were flurries on the ropes which had an echo of the great bombardment in the fifth round. And still Ali taunted him, still the dialogue went on. 'Fight hard,' said Ali, 'I thought you had some punches. You're a weak man.

You're all used up.' After a while, Foreman's punches were whistling less than his breath. For the eighteenth time Ali's corner was screaming, 'Get off the ropes. Knock him out. Take him home!' Foreman had used up the store of force he transported from the seventh to the eighth. He pawed at Ali like an infant six feet tall waving its uncoordinated battle arm.

With twenty seconds left to the round, Ali attacked. By his own measure, by that measure of twenty years of boxing, with the knowledge of all he had learned of what could and could not be done at any instant in the ring, he chose this as the occasion and lying on the ropes, he hit Foreman with a right and left, then came off the ropes to hit him with a left and a right. Into this last right hand he put his glove and his forearm again, a head-stupefying punch that sent Foreman reeling forward. As he went by, Ali hit him on the side of the jaw with a right, and darted away from the ropes in such a way as to put Foreman next to them. For the first time in the entire fight he had cut off the ring on Foreman. Now Ali struck him a combination of punches fast as the punches of the first round, but harder and more consecutive, three capital rights in a row struck Foreman, then a left, and for an instant on Foreman's face appeared the knowledge that he was in danger and must start to look to his last protection. His opponent was attacking, and there were no ropes behind the opponent. What a dislocation: the axes of his existence were reversed! He was the man on the ropes! Then a big projectile exactly the size of a fist in a glove drove into the middle of Foreman's mind, the best punch of the startled night, the blow Ali saved for a career. Foreman's arms flew out to the side like a man with a parachute jumping out of a plane, and in this doubled-over position he tried to wander out to the center of the ring. All the while his eyes were on Ali and he looked up with no anger as if Ali, indeed, was the man he knew best in the world and would see him on his dying day. Vertigo took George Foreman and revolved him. Still bowing from the waist in this uncomprehending position, eyes on Muhammad Ali all the way, he started to tumble and topple and fall even as he did not wish to go down. His mind was held with magnets high as his championship and his body was seeking the ground. He went over like a six-foot sixty-year-old butler who has just heard tragic news, yes, fell over all of a long collapsing two seconds, down came the Champion in sections and Ali revolved with him in a close circle, hand primed to hit him one more time, and never the need, a wholly intimate escort to the floor.

The referee took Ali to a corner. He stood there, he seemed lost in thought. Now he raced his feet in a quick but restrained shuffle as if to apologize for never asking his legs to dance, and looked on while Foreman tried to rouse himself.

Like a drunk hoping to get out of bed to go to work, Foreman rolled over, Foreman started the slow head-agonizing lift of all that foundered bulk God somehow gave him and whether he heard the count or no, was on his feet a fraction after the count of ten and whipped, for when Zack Clayton guided him with a hand at his back, he walked in docile steps to his corner and did not resist. Moore received him. Sadler received him. Later, one learned the conversation.

'Feel all right?'

'Yeah,' said Foreman.

'Well, don't worry. It's history now.'

'Yeah.'

'You're all right,' said Sadler, 'the rest will take care of itself.'

SAIGON: THE FINAL DAY, VIETNAM, 29 April 1975

John Pilger

As the victorious Communist forces closed in on Saigon, the last Americans were being evacuated from the compound of the US embassy. Also awaiting a helicopter out was Australian journalist John Pilger.

People were now beginning to come over the wall. The Marines, who had orders not to use their guns, had been up all night and were doped with 'speed' – methedrine – which provides a 'high' for twenty-four hours before the body craves sleep. But methedrine also whittles the nerve ends, and some of the young Marines were beginning to show the effects. As the first Chinook helicopter made its precarious landing, its rotors slashed into a tree, and the snapping branches sounded like gunfire. '*Down! Down!*' screamed a corporal to the line of people crouched against the wall, waiting their turn to be evacuated, until an officer came and calmed him.

The helicopter's capacity was fifty, but it lifted off with seventy. The pilot's skill was breathtaking as he climbed vertically to two hundred feet, with bullets pinging against the rotors and shredded embassy documents playing in the downdraft. However, not all the embassy's documents were shredded and some were left in the compound in open plastic bags. One of these I have. It is dated 25 May, 1969 and reads, 'Top Secret . . . memo from John Paul Vann, counter insurgency':

> . . . 900 houses in Chau Doc province were destroyed by American air strikes without evidence of a single enemy being killed . . . the destruction of this hamlet by friendly American firepower is an event that will always be remembered and never forgiven by the surviving population . . .

From the billowing incinerator on the embassy roof rained twenty, fifty and one hundred dollar bills. Most were charred; some were not. The Vietnamese waiting around the pool could not believe their eyes; former ministers and generals and torturers scrambled for their bonus from the sky or sent their children to retrieve the notes. An embassy official said that more than five million dollars were being burned. 'Every safe in the embassy has been emptied and locked again,' said the official, 'so as to fool the gooks when we've gone.'

The swishing of rotors now drowned the sounds of the dusk: the crump of artillery, the cries of women attempting to push young children over the wall. Two Marines watched a teenage girl struggle through the barbed wire. At first they did nothing, then as her hands clawed the last few inches one of them brought his rifle butt down on one hand, while the other brought his boot down on the other. The girl fell, crying, back into the mob. Somehow, most of one family had managed to get over the wall: a man, his wife, and her father. Their sons and his grandmother were next, but the barrel of an M-16 spun them back to the other side. The wife pleaded with a Marine to let the rest of her family over, but he did not hear her.

At least a thousand people were still inside the embassy, waiting to be evacuated, although most of the celebrities, like 'Giggles' Quang, had seen themselves on to the first helicopters; the rest waited passively, as if stunned. Inside the embassy itself there was champagne foaming on to polished desks, as several of the embassy staff tried systematically to wreck their own offices: smashing water coolers, pouring bottles of Scotch into the carpets, sweeping pictures from the wall. In a third-floor office a picture of the late President Johnson was delivered into a wastepaper basket, while a framed quotation from Lawrence of Arabia was left on the wall. The quotation read:

> Better to let them do it imperfectly, than to do it perfectly yourself, for it is their country, their war, and your time is short.

From the third floor I could see the British embassy across the road. It was being quietly ransacked now. The Union Jack, which had been spread across the main entrance, perhaps to ward off evil spirits, had been torn away and looters were at work with little interference from the police. I derived some small satisfaction from the sight of this. It was there, a few days earlier, that the British Ambassador, a spiffy chap called John Bushell, had shredded his own papers and mounted his own little evacuation without taking with him a dozen very frightened British passport holders. Before he drove away, Mr Bushell gave an impromptu press conference.

'We are pulling out for reasons of safety,' he said. 'Our main responsibility is the safety of the British community in Saigon.'

I asked him about people who were waving their British passports outside the gates of the British embassy. Why were they not even allowed into the compound?

'Look here,' he replied, 'we gave ample warning. We put advertisements in the local papers. The trouble with these people, as I understand it, was that they didn't have tax clearance, which takes ten days, as well as exit visas from the Vietnamese government.'

Exit visas? Tax clearances? But wasn't this an emergency evacuation for reasons, as he had just said, of protecting life?

'Well, yes,' he replied, 'but we really can't break the rules laid down by government, can we?'

But surely this government had ceased to exist and there might be anarchy and a great deal of danger, which was why he was getting out?

'That may be true,' said the Ambassador, 'but we gave these people a reasonable time to get the paperwork done, and you really can't expect us to help them at such short notice . . . look here, the Americans surely will pick up any stray palefaces.'

But 'these people' were Indians and Chinese. The Ambassador looked confused.

'Oh, you mean Hong Kongers,' he said. 'They should have heeded our warnings . . . they'll have just to work hard at it, won't they?' At this, he turned to another British official and said, 'How many coolies . . . Vietnamese . . . are we leaving, do you know?'

The official replied, 'Coolies? Oh, about thirty-six in all.'

At six-fifteen p.m. it was my turn for the Jolly Green Giant as it descended through the dark into the compound. The loadmaster stopped counting at sixty; people were in each other's arms. The helicopter tilted, rose, dropped, sharply, then climbed as if laden with rocks; off to the starboard there were shots. We flew low over the centre of the city, over the presidential palace where 'Big' Minh awaited his fate, and the Caravelle Hotel, where I owed for two days, then out along the Saigon River, over the Rung Sat, the 'swamp of death' which lay between the city and the sea. The two gunners scanned the ground, as they always used to, looking for 'Charlie'. Some of us had on our minds the heat-seeking missile which had brought a helicopter down as we watched in the early hours. There was small arms fire around us, but they were letting us go; and when the South China Sea lay beneath us, the pilot, who was red-eyed with fatigue and so young he had acne, lit up a cigarette and handed the packet around. In the back of the helicopter there was a reminder of what we had left: a woman, who had left her daughter on the other side of the wall, cried softly.

THE SEX PISTOLS PLAY THEIR FIRST CONCERT, LONDON, 6 November 1975

Adam Ant

The harbingers of punk rock played for the first time in public at St Martins School of Art, London. The band was formed by entrepreneur Malcom McLaren initially as a means of publicizing a clothes shop he ran with designer Vivienne Westwood.

For their first ever gig . . . the Sex Pistols were support group to the band I was in, Bazooka Joe. I'll never forget it. They came in as a gang: they looked like they couldn't give a fuck about anybody. John had baggy pinstripe trousers with braces and a ripped-up T-shirt saying 'Pink Floyd' with 'I Hate' over it. Jonesy was tiny, he looked like a young Pete Townshend. Matlock had paint-spattered trousers and a woman's pink leather top. Paul Cook looked like Rod Stewart, like a little Mod really.

I watched them play: Malcolm was at the front, orchestrating them, telling them where to stand. Viv was there. There weren't many there: maybe a dozen of their people – Jordan, Michael Collins, Andy Czezowski. They did 'Substitute', and 'Whatcha Gonna Do About It' with the lyrics changed: 'I want you to know that I *hate* you baby.' Then John lost interest. He'd eat sweets, pull them out and suck them and just spit them out: he just looked at the audience, glazed.

There were no guitar solos, it was just simple songs. They did five and that was it: goodnight. The rest of my band hated them because they thought they couldn't play: in fact somebody said as much to Glen and he said: 'So what?' But I thought they were very tight. It was only John who hadn't learned how to make the voice last, but over a fifteen-minute burst, he was very clear. At the end Rotten slagged off Bazooka Joe as being a bunch of fucking cunts and our guitarist Danny Kleinman leapt from the front row and pinned John against the back wall: he made him apologize.

The impression they left on me was total . . . They had a certain attitude I'd never seen: they had bollocks and they had very expensive equipment and it didn't look like it belonged to them. They had the look in their eyes that said: 'We're going to be massive.' I stood there transfixed. When Danny jumped John, I didn't jump in to help him. I left Bazooka Joe the next day: I came out of that gig thinking, 'I'm tired of Teddy Boys' and it seemed to me that the Sex Pistols were playing simple songs that I could play. I just wanted to go away and form my own band.

THE FALKLANDS WAR: THE FIRST MAN INTO PORT STANLEY, 14 June 1982

Max Hastings

The war between Britain and Argentina for the South Atlantic Falkland Islands (Malvinas) came to an end on 14 June 1982, with the surrender of the Argentine forces led by General Menendez. The first Briton into Port Stanley, the Falkland's capital, was the war correspondent, Max Hastings.

British forces are in Port Stanley. At 2.45 p.m. British time today, men of the 2nd Parachute Regiment halted on the outskirts at the end of their magnificent drive on the capital pending negotiations.

There, we sat on the racecourse until, after about twenty minutes I was looking at the road ahead and there seemed to be no movement. I thought, well I'm a civilian so why shouldn't I go and see what's going on because there didn't seem to be much resistance.

So I stripped off all my combat clothes and walked into Stanley in a blue civilian anorak with my hands in the air and my handkerchief in my hand.

The Argentinians made no hostile movement as I went by the apparently undamaged but heavily bunkered Government House.

I sort of grinned at them in the hope that if there were any Argentinian soldiers manning the position they wouldn't shoot at me.

Nobody took any notice so I walked on and after a few minutes I saw a group of people all looking like civilians a hundred yards ahead and I shouted at them.

I shouted: 'Are you British?' and they shouted back: 'Yes, are you?' I said 'Yes.'

They were a group of civilians who had just come out of the civil administration building where they had been told that it looked as if there was going to be a ceasefire.

We chatted for a few moments and then I walked up to the building and I talked to the senior Argentinian colonel who was standing on the steps. He didn't show any evident hostility.

They were obviously pretty depressed. They looked like men who had just lost a war but I talked to them for a few moments and I said: 'Are you prepared to surrender West Falkland as well as East?'

The colonel said: 'Well, maybe, but you must wait until four o'clock when General Menendez meets your general.'

I said: 'May I go into the town and talk to civilians?' He said: 'Yes,' so I started to walk down the main street past Falklanders who were all standing outside their houses.

They all shouted and cheered and the first person I ran into was the Catholic priest, Monsignor Daniel Spraggon, who said: 'My God, it's marvellous to see you.'

That wasn't directed at me personally but it was the first communication he had had with the British forces.

I walked on and there were hundreds, maybe thousands, of Argentinian troops milling around, marching in columns through the streets, some of them clutching very badly wounded men and looking completely like an army in defeat with blankets wrapped around themselves.

There were bits of weapons and equipment all over the place and they were all moving to central collection points before the surrender or ceasefire.

Eventually I reached the famous Falklands hotel, the Upland Goose. We had been dreaming for about three months about walking into the Upland Goose and having a drink, and I walked in and again it was marvellous that they all clapped and cheered.

They offered me gin on the assumption that this is the traditional drink of British journalists, but I asked if they could make it whisky instead and I gratefully raised my glass to them all.

Owner of the Upland Goose, Desmond King said: 'We never doubted for a moment that the British would turn up. We have just been waiting for the moment for everybody to come.'

The last few days had been the worst, he said, because Argentinian guns had been operating from among the houses of Stanley and they had heard this terrific, continuous battle going on in the hills.

They were afraid that it was going to end up with a house-to-house fight in Stanley itself. The previous night when I had been with the Paras we were getting a lot of shell fire coming in on us and eventually we sorted out the co-ordinates from which it was firing. Our observation officer tried to call down to fire on the enemy batteries and the word came back that you could not fire on them because they are in the middle of Stanley.

So the battalion simply had to take it and suffer some casualties.

Anyway, there we were in the middle of the Upland Goose with about twenty or thirty delighted civilians who said that the Argentinians hadn't done anything appalling. It depends what one means by appalling, but they hadn't shot anybody or hung anybody up by their thumbs or whatever.

They had looted a lot of houses that they had taken over. At times they got very nervous and started pushing people around with submachine guns in their backs and the atmosphere had been pretty unpleasant.

Robin Pitaleyn described how he had been under house arrest in the hotel for six weeks, since he made contact by radio with the *Hermes*. He dismissed criticism of the Falkland Island Company representatives who had sold goods to the occupiers.

'We were all selling stuff,' he said. 'You had a simple choice – either you sold it or they took it. I rented my house to their air force people. They said – either you take rent or we take the house. What would you have done?'

Adrian Monk described how he had been compulsorily evicted from his own house to make way for Argentinian soldiers who had then totally looted it. There appears to have been widespread looting in all the houses of Stanley to which the Argentinians had access.

The houses on the outskirts of the town in which the Argentinians had been living were an appalling mess full of everything from human excrement all over the place to just property lying all over the place where soldiers had ransacked through it. But they were all alive and they all had plenty of food and plenty to drink and they were all in tremendous spirits.

It wasn't in the least like being abroad. One talks about the Falklanders and yet it was as if one had liberated a hotel in the middle of Surrey or Kent or somewhere.

It was an extraordinary feeling just sitting there with all these girls and cheerful middle-age men and everybody chatting in the way they might chat at a suburban golf club after something like this had happened.

I think everybody did feel a tremendous sense of exhilaration and achievement. I think the Paras through all their tiredness knew they had won a tremendous battle.

It was the Paras' hour and, after their heavy losses and Goose Green and some of the fierce battles they had fought, they had made it all the way to Stanley and they were enjoying every moment of their triumph.

A question that has to be answered is how the Argentinian troops managed to maintain their supplies of food and ammunition.

I think it's one of the most remarkable things. I think intelligence hasn't been one of our strong points throughout the campaign.

Even our commanders and people in London agree that we have misjudged the Argentinians at several critical points in the campaign.

Our soldiers have been saying in the last couple of days how astonished they were when they overran enemy positions. We have been hearing a great deal about how short of food and ammunition they were supposed to be but whatever else they lacked it certainly was not either of those.

They had hundreds of rounds of ammunition, masses of weapons and plenty of food.

The civilians told me they had been running Hercules on to the runway at Port Stanley despite all our efforts with Naval gunnery, with Vulcans, with Harriers up to and including last night and, above all, at the beginning of May they ran a very big container ship called the *Formosa* through the blockade and got her back to Buenos Aires again afterwards. She delivered an enormous consignment of ammunition which really relieved the Argentinians' serious problems on that front for the rest of the campaign.

I think in that sense we have been incredibly lucky. The British forces have been incredibly lucky.

Considering the amount of stuff the Argentinians got in, we have done incredibly well in being able to smash them when they certainly had the ammunition and equipment left to keep fighting for a long time.

So why did they surrender? I think their soldiers had simply decided that they had had enough. Nobody likes being shelled and even well-trained troops find it an ordeal.

Even the Paras freely admit that it's very, very unpleasant being heavily shelled.

The last two nights, the Argentinian positions had been enormously heavily shelled by our guns. They gave them a tremendous pounding and when an Army starts to crumble and collapse it's very, very difficult to stop it.

I think that the Argentinian generals simply had to recognize that their men no longer had the will to carry on the fight.

This story of the fall of Port Stanley begins last night, when men of the Guards and the Gurkhas and the Parachute Regiment launched a major attack supported by an overwhelming British bombardment on the last line of enemy positions on the high ground above the capital.

Three civilians died in British counter-battery fire the night before last, as far as we know the only civilian casualties of the war. Mrs Doreen Burns, Mrs Sue Whitney and 82-year-old Mrs Mary Godwin were all sheltering together in a house hit by a single shell. Altogether only four or five houses in Stanley have been seriously damaged in the battle.

At first light the Paras were preparing to renew their attack in a few hours after seizing all their objectives on Wireless Ridge under fierce shell and mortar fire. Suddenly, word came that enemy troops could be seen fleeing for their lives in all directions around Port Stanley. They had evidently had enough. The decision was taken to press on immediately to complete their collapse.

Spearheaded by a company of the Parachute Regiment commanded by Major Dare Farrar-Hockley, son of the regiment's colonel, British forces began a headlong dash down the rocky hills for the honour of being first into Stanley.

I marched at breakneck speed with Major Farrar-Hockley through the ruins of the former Royal Marine base at Moody Brook, then past the smoking remains of buildings and strongpoints destroyed by our shelling and bombing.

Our route was littered with the debris of the enemy's utter defeat.

We were already past the first houses of the town, indeed up to the War Memorial beside the sea, when the order came through to halt pending negotiations and to fire only in self-defence.

The men, desperately tired after three nights without sleep, exulted like schoolboys in this great moment of victory.

The Parachute Regiment officer with whom I was walking had been delighted with the prospect that his men who had fought so hard all through this campaign were going to be the first British troops into Stanley. But they were heartbroken when, just as we reached the racecourse the order came to halt.

Major Farrar-Hockley ordered off helmets, on red berets. Some men showed their sadness for those who hadn't made it all the way, who had died even during the last night of bitter fighting.

The Regiment moved on to the racecourse and they tore down the Argentinian flag flying from the flagpole. Afterwards they posed for a group photograph . . . exhausted, unshaven but exhilarated at being alive and having survived a very, very bitter struggle.

After half an hour with the civilians I began to walk back to the British lines. Scores of enemy were still moving through the town, many assisting badly wounded comrades, all looking at the end of their tether.

Damaged enemy helicopters were parked everywhere among the houses and on the racecourse. Argentine officers still looked clean and soldierly, but they made no pretence of having any interest in continuing the struggle.

Each one spoke only of 'four o'clock', the magic moment at which General Moore was scheduled to meet General Menendez and the war presumably come to a halt.

Back in the British lines, Union Jacks had been hoisted and Brigadier Julian Thompson and many of his senior officers had hastened to the scene to be on hand for the entry into the capital.

Men asked eagerly about the centre of Stanley as if it was on the other side of the moon.

By tomorrow, I imagine, when everyone has seen what little there is of this little provincial town to be seen, we shall all be asking ourselves why so many brave men had to die because a whimsical dictator, in a land of which we knew so little, determined that his nation had at all costs to possess it.

MASSACRE AT CHATILA CAMP, BEIRUT, LEBANON, 16–17 September 1982

Robert Fisk

After the Israeli army invaded South Lebanon in June 1982, PLO (Palestine Liberation Organization) forces were evacuated to Syria. Many Palestinian refugees and non-combatants, however, remained behind in their camps. At the end of August, control of the camps was passed by the Israelis over to the Lebanese Christian militia.

What we found inside the Palestinian Chatila camp at ten o'clock on the morning of 18 September 1982 did not quite beggar description, although it would have been easier to retell in the cold prose of a medical examination. There had been massacres before in Lebanon, but rarely on this scale and never overlooked by a regular, supposedly disciplined army. In the panic and hatred of battle, tens of thousands had been killed in this country. But these people, hundreds of them, had been shot down unarmed. This was a mass killing, an incident – how easily we used the word 'incident' in Lebanon – that was also an atrocity. It went beyond even what the Israelis would have in other circumstances called a *terrorist* atrocity. It was a war crime.

Jenkins and Tveit and I were so overwhelmed by what we found in Chatila that at first we were unable to register our own shock. Bill Foley of AP had come with us. All he could say as he walked round was 'Jesus Christ!' over and over again. We might have accepted evidence of a few murders; even dozens of bodies, killed in the heat of combat. But there were women lying in houses with their skirts torn up to their waists and their legs wide apart, children with their throats cut, rows of young men shot in the back after being lined up at an execution wall. There were babies – blackened babies because they had been slaughtered more than twenty-four hours earlier and their small bodies were already in a state of decomposition – tossed into rubbish heaps alongside discarded US army ration tins, Israeli army medical equipment and empty bottles of whisky.

Where were the murderers? Or, to use the Israelis' vocabulary, where were the 'terrorists'? When we drove down to Chatila, we had seen the Israelis on the top of the apartments in the Avenue Camille Chamoun but they made no attempt to stop us. In fact, we had first driven to the Bourj al-Barajneh camp because someone told us that there was a massacre there. All we saw was a Lebanese soldier chasing a car thief down a street. It was only when we were driving back past the entrance to Chatila that Jenkins decided to stop the car. 'I don't like this,' he said. 'Where is everyone? What the fuck is that smell?'

Just inside the southern entrance to the camp, there used to be a number of single-storey concrete-walled houses. I had conducted many interviews inside these hovels in the late 1970s. When we walked across the muddy entrance of Chatila, we found that these buildings had all been dynamited to the ground. There were cartridge cases across the main road. I saw several Israeli flare canisters, still attached to their tiny parachutes. Clouds of flies moved across the rubble, raiding parties with a nose for victory.

Down a laneway to our right, no more than fifty yards from the entrance, there lay a pile of corpses. There were more than a dozen of them, young men whose arms and legs had been wrapped around each other in the agony of death. All had been shot at point-blank range through the cheek, the bullet tearing away a line of flesh up to the ear and entering the brain. Some had vivid crimson or black scars down the left side of their throats. One had been castrated, his trousers torn open and a settlement of flies throbbing over his torn intestines.

The eyes of these young men were all open. The youngest was only twelve or thirteen years old. They were dressed in jeans and coloured shirts, the material absurdly tight over their flesh now that their bodies had begun to bloat in the heat. They had not been robbed. On one blackened wrist, a Swiss watch recorded the correct time, the second hand still ticking round uselessly, expending the last energies of its dead owner.

On the other side of the main road, up a track through the debris, we found the bodies of five women and several children. The women were middle-aged and their corpses lay draped over a pile of rubble. One lay on her back, her dress torn open and the head of a little girl emerging from behind her. The girl had short, dark curly hair, her eyes were staring at us and there was a frown on her face. She was dead.

Another child lay on the roadway like a discarded doll, her white dress stained with mud and dust. She could have been no more than three years old. The back of her head had been blown away by a bullet fired into her brain. One of the women also held a tiny baby to her body. The bullet that had passed through her breast had killed the baby too. Someone had slit open the woman's stomach, cutting sideways and then upwards, perhaps trying to kill her unborn child. Her eyes were wide open, her dark face frozen in horror.

Tveit tried to record all this on tape, speaking slowly and unemotionally in Norwegian. 'I have come to another body, that of a woman and her baby. They are dead. There are three other women. They are dead . . .' From time to time, he would snap the 'pause' button and lean over to be sick, retching over the muck on the road. Foley and Jenkins and I explored one narrow avenue and heard the sound of a tracked vehicle. 'They're still here,' Jenkins said and looked hard at me. They were still there. The murderers were still there, in the camp. Foley's first concern was that the Christian militiamen might take his film, the only evidence – so far as he knew – of what had happened. He ran off down the laneway.

Jenkins and I had darker fears. If the murderers were still in the camp, it was the witnesses rather than the photographic evidence that they would wish to destroy. We saw a brown metal gate ajar; we pushed it open and ran into the yard, closing it quickly behind us. We heard the vehicle approaching down a neighbouring road, its tracks clanking against pieces of concrete. Jenkins and I looked at each other in fear and then knew that we were not alone. We *felt* the presence of another human. She lay just beside us, a young, pretty woman lying on her back.

She lay there as if she was sunbathing in the heat, and the blood running from her back was still wet. The murderers had just left. She just lay there, feet together, arms outspread, as if she had seen her saviour. Her face was peaceful, eyes closed, a beautiful woman whose head was now granted a strange halo. For a clothes line hung above her and there were children's trousers and some socks pegged to the line. Other clothes lay scattered on the ground. She must have been hanging out her family's clothes when the murderers came. As she fell, the clothes pegs in her hand sprayed over the yard and formed a small wooden circle round her head.

Only the insignificant hole in her breast and the growing stain across the yard told of her death. Even the flies had not yet found her. I thought Jenkins was praying but he was just cursing again and muttering 'Dear God' in between the curses. I felt so sorry for this woman. Perhaps it was easier to feel pity for someone so young, so innocent, someone whose body had not yet begun to rot. I kept looking at her face, the neat way she lay beneath the clothes line, almost expecting her to open her eyes.

She must have hidden in her home when she heard the shooting in the camp. She must have escaped the attention of the Israeli-backed gunmen until that very morning. She had walked into her yard, heard no shooting, assumed the trouble was over and gone about her daily chores. She could not have known what had happened. Then the yard door must have opened, as quickly as we had just opened it, and the murderers would have walked in and killed her. Just like that. They had left and we had arrived, perhaps only a minute or two later.

We stayed in the yard for several more minutes. Jenkins and I were very frightened. Like Tveit, who had temporarily disappeared, he was a survivor. I felt safe with Jenkins. The militiamen – the murderers of this girl – had raped and knifed the women in Chatila and shot the men but I rather suspected they would hesitate to kill Jenkins, an American who would try to talk them down. 'Let's get out of here,' he said, and we left. He peered into the street first, I followed, closing the door very slowly because I did not want to disturb the sleeping, dead woman with her halo of clothes pegs.

Foley was back in the street near the entrance to the camp. The tracked vehicle had gone, although I could still hear it moving on the main road outside, moving up towards the Israelis who were still watching us. Jenkins heard Tveit calling from behind a pile of bodies and I lost sight of him. We kept losing sight of each other behind piles of corpses. At one moment I would be talking to Jenkins, at the next I would turn to find that I was addressing a young man, bent backwards over the pillar of a house, his arms hanging behind his head.

I could hear Jenkins and Tveit perhaps a hundred yards away, on the other side of a high barricade covered with earth and sand that had been newly erected by a bulldozer. It was perhaps twelve feet high and I climbed with difficulty up one side of it, my feet slipping in the muck. Near the top, I lost my balance and for support grabbed a hunk of dark red stone that protruded from the earth. But it was no stone. It was clammy and hot and it stuck to my hand and when I looked down I saw that I was holding a human elbow that protruded, a triangle of flesh and bone, from the earth.

I let go of it in horror, wiping the dead flesh on my trousers, and staggered the last few feet to the top of the barricade. But the smell was appalling and at my feet a face was looking at me with half its mouth missing. A bullet or a knife had torn it away and what was left of the mouth was a nest of flies. I tried not to look at it. I could see, in the distance, Jenkins and Tveit standing by some more corpses in front of a wall but I could not shout to them for help because I knew I would be sick if I opened my mouth.

I walked on the top of the barricade, looking desperately for a place from which to jump all the way to the ground on the other side. But each time I took a step, the earth moved up towards me. The whole embankment of muck shifted and vibrated with my weight in a dreadful, springy way and, when I looked down again, I saw that the sand was only a light covering over more limbs and faces. A large stone turned out to be a stomach. I could see a man's head, a woman's naked breast, the feet of a child. I was walking on dozens of corpses which were moving beneath my feet.

The bodies had been buried by someone in panic. They had been bulldozed to the side of the laneway. Indeed, when I looked up, I could see a bulldozer – its driver's seat empty – standing guiltily just down the road.

I tried hard but vainly not to tread on the faces beneath me. We all of us felt a traditional respect for the dead, even here, now. I kept telling myself that these monstrous cadavers were not enemies, that these dead people would approve of my being here, would want Tveit and Jenkins and me to see all this and that therefore I should not be frightened. But I had never seen so many corpses before.

I jumped to the ground and ran towards Jenkins and Tveit. I think I was whimpering in a silly way because Jenkins looked around, surprised. But the moment I opened my mouth to speak, flies entered it. I spat them out. Tveit was being sick. He had been staring at what might have been sacks in front of a low stone wall. They formed a line, young men and boys, lying prostrate. They had been executed, shot in the back against the wall and they lay, at once pathetic and terrible, where they had fallen.

This wall and its huddle of corpses were reminiscent of something we had all seen before. Only afterwards did we realize how similar it was to those old photographs of executions in occupied Europe during the Second World War. There may have been twelve or twenty bodies there. Some lay beneath others. When I leaned down to look at them closely, I noticed the same dark scar on the left side of their throats. The murderers must have marked their prisoners for execution in this way. Cut a throat with a knife and it meant the man was doomed, a 'terrorist' to be executed at once.

As we stood there, we heard a shout in Arabic from across the ruins. 'They are coming back,' a man was screaming. So we ran in fear towards the road. I think, in retrospect, that it was probably anger that stopped us leaving, for we now waited near the entrance to the camp to glimpse the faces of the men who were responsible for all this. They must have been sent in here with Israeli permission. They must have been armed by the Israelis. Their handiwork had clearly been watched – closely observed – by the Israelis, by those same Israelis who were still watching us through their field-glasses.

Another armoured vehicle could be heard moving behind a wall to the west – perhaps it was Phalangist, perhaps Israeli – but no one appeared. So we walked on. It was always the same. Inside the ruins of the Chatila hovels, families had retreated to their bedrooms when the militiamen came through the front door and there they lay, slumped over the beds, pushed beneath chairs, hurled over cooking pots. Many of the women here had been raped, their clothes lying across the floor, their naked bodies thrown on top of their husbands or brothers, all now dark with death.

'SLIM': AIDS IN UGANDA, AFRICA, February 1987

Peter Murtagh

Around 10 million people are expected to die from Acquired Immune Deficiency Syndrome by the end of the century, most of them in Africa where the disease is thought to have originated.

Josephine Nnagingo lives in a mud and wattle farmhouse in the middle of her family's field of banana trees not far from Kyotera, a few miles from the shores of Lake Victoria in southern Uganda.

Nearby is a small building, used by the local Elim Pentecostal Church where, two Sundays ago, the congregation of women sang praise the Lord to the beat of homemade skin-covered drums. We made our way to Josephine's home as the chorus of happy voices in beautiful harmony wafted gently through the banana trees.

The church women believe that faith in God and adherence to his Gospel will protect them from Aids. Perhaps it will; but not Josephine.

She is dying from what her people call Slim, the Ugandan word for Aids. It was coined in late 1984 by the district medical officer of Masaka, Dr Anthony Lergaba, who noticed the appearance of a new disease which appeared to waste people away.

Josephine, who is 27, first felt ill about three years ago shortly after the birth of her fifth child. She got cramps in her stomach, began to vomit and developed chronic diarrhoea. She also has pains in her throat and chest and a skin rash covers much of her body. 'I have rashes which I scratch they are so painful. The disease came slowly and then started to weaken me,' she explained through an interpreter.

Because of the vomiting and diarrhoea, Josephine's body is not able to get the nourishment to keep it alive. She is slowly starving to death and does not expect to survive much longer.

The wasting of her shrunken body has made her head appear outsized, and her dress is now too big for her. Her arms and legs are desperately thin, and she moves only with pain.

Josephine is not unique in her family. Her sister died of Aids three years ago, as did Josephine's first husband the year before that. He fathered her first two children but her second husband, who fathered the other three, vanished after the birth of their last child. The baby was vomiting and had diarrhoea when it was born but appears now to be all right.

Behind the house and beneath a mound of stones is the grave of Josephine's grandfather whom the family believe also died of Aids. Josephine's mother, Folomela, says that he had the symptoms of Slim and lost a lot of weight before fading away seven years ago. A similarly appalling catalogue of death can be heard in almost every home in the Masaka and Rakai districts of southern Uganda. The disease has so devastated some of the tiny ports on the western shores of Lake Victoria that houses have been abandoned.

In some cases the occupants have returned to their family homes to die, while in others, deaths in the houses have prompted the survivors to flee in the belief that the buildings themselves are in some way responsible for the illness.

According to a doctor in Kyotera, five people a day died of Aids last December. The day before I visited the village there were three funerals, and two more on the day we were there. 'The situation is bad, very bad,' said the doctor. 'At the beginning, it used to be a young man's disease, but now it is no longer age specific. My landlord has lost four people in the last year, three brothers and a nephew. People have stopped working. Their job now is burying every day. Every day.'

About one million people live in the Masaka and Rakai districts, and the Aids virus is conservatively estimated to have infected 50,000 of them, or five per cent of the population. People are aware of the fatal consequences of the disease and many no longer bother to go to hospital when they fall ill.

One result is that a fatalistic approach has developed to all illnesses. Some people who contract curable tropical diseases are dying because they no longer seek medical help in the belief that they have Aids.

In a desperate search for help, people in the area have turned to witchdoctors and herbalists. Some of the men around Kyotera who believe that Aids is witchcraft have sex with the widows of victims. The widows almost certainly have the virus as well but, tragically, the men hope that the mysterious power which has apparently kept the widow alive will be transferred to them.

'They look at this good-looking woman and say why is she so good-looking and still alive? She must have some special power,' said the doctor.

When people go to witchdoctors, they are asked first if there is any person with whom they have ever had a row. Invariably there is and this person is then identified as the source of evil making the patient sick.

Herbs are prescribed and the patient is given talismans to wear. Animal bones may be hung on the front door of the patient's home, and the witchdoctor may prescribe dog soup. One witchdoctor made his patient throw out all the goods he had bought from the man identified as the source of his troubles. It did not work, however, and the patient died.

However, village faith in the witchdoctors was shaken recently. One of them had proudly put up a notice outside his home proclaiming that he had the cure for Slim. People believed it until he too contracted the disease.

THE SHOOTING OF THE STUDENTS AT TIANANMEN SQUARE, BEIJING, CHINA, 7 June 1989

Anon. Beijing student

I am a student at Qinghua University. I am twenty years old. I spent last night sitting on the steps of the Monument to the Heroes of the People. I witnessed from start to finish the shooting and suppression by the army of students and citizens.

Many of my fellow students have already been shot dead. My clothes are still stained with their blood. As a lucky survivor and an eyewitness, I want to tell peace-loving and good people across the world about the massacre.

Frankly speaking, we knew early on in the evening that the troops intended to suppress us. Someone whose status I can't reveal phoned us at four o'clock on Saturday afternoon. (The call was to a neighbourhood phone station in an alley near the Square.) The caller told us that the Square was about to be invaded and cleared. We went on to the alert. After a discussion we took some measures. We did our best to alleviate contradictions and avoid a bloodbath.

We had twenty-three submachine-guns and some incendiary bombs that we'd snatched from soldiers during the previous two days. The Autonomous Students' Union called a meeting and decided to return these weapons forthwith to the martial law troops to show that we intended to promote democracy by non-violent means. On the rostrum at Tiananmen Square beneath the portrait of Chairman Mao we liaised with troops about this, but an officer said that he was under higher orders not to accept the weapons.

So the negotiations failed. At around one in the morning, when things had become really critical, we destroyed the guns and dismantled the bombs. We poured away the petrol so that bad people couldn't use it and the authorities couldn't point to it as 'proof' that we were out to kill soldiers. After that, the Union told everyone in the Square that the situation was extremely grave, that bloodshed seemed inevitable, and that they wanted students and citizens to leave the Square. But there were still 40,000-50,000 students and about 100,000 citizens determined not to go. I, too, decided not to go.

The mood was extraordinarily tense. This was the first time we'd ever experienced such danger. I'd be lying if I said we weren't afraid, but everyone was psychologically braced and tempered. (Some students, of course, didn't believe that the troops would shoot to kill.) In a word, we were imbued with a lofty sense of mission. We were prepared to sacrifice ourselves for China's democracy and progress.

After midnight, after two armoured cars had sped down each side of the Square from the Front Gate, the situation became increasingly serious. Official loudspeakers repeatedly blared out 'notices'. Dense lines of steel-helmeted troops ringed the Square. Despite the darkness, you could clearly see the machine-guns mounted on top of the History Museum. There was not the slightest attempt to hide them.

We students crowded round the Monument to the Heroes of the people. I carefully estimated the crowd. Two-thirds were men, one-third were women; about 30 per cent from universities and colleges in Beijing. Most were students from other cities.

At four o'clock sharp, just before daybreak, the lights in the Square suddenly went out. The loudspeakers broadcast another order to 'clear the Square'. I suddenly had a tight feeling in my stomach. There was only one thought in my head: the time has come, the time has come.

The hunger-strike Hou Dejian (a Taiwan pop-singer now working on the mainland) and some other people negotiated with the troops and agreed to get the students to leave peacefully. But just as they were about to go, at 4.40 a.m., a cluster of red signal flares rose into the sky above the Square and the lights came on again.

I saw that the front of the Square was packed with troops. A detachment of soldiers came running from the east entrance of the Great Hall of the People. They were dressed in camouflage. They were carrying light machine-guns and wearing steel helmets and gas-masks.

As soon as these troops had stormed out, they lined up a dozen or so machine-guns in front of the Monument to the Heroes of the People. The machine-gunners lay down on their stomachs. Their guns pointed toward the Monument. The rostrum was behind them. When all the guns were properly lined up, a great mass of soldiers and armed police, wielding electric prods, rubber truncheons, and some special weapons of a sort I'd never seen before suddenly rushed us. We were sitting quietly. There were two differences between the troops and the armed police: their uniforms were different, and so were their helmets. The police helmets were bigger than the troops' and had steel flaps going down over the ears. The soldiers and the policemen started violently laying about us. They split our ranks down the middle and opened up a path to the Monument. They stormed up to its third tier. I saw forty or fifty students suddenly spurt blood. Armoured troop carriers and an even greater number of troops that had been waiting in the Square joined the siege. The troop carriers formed a solid blockade, except for a gap on the museum side.

The troops and policemen who had stormed the monument smashed our loudspeaker installations, our printing equipment, and our supply of soda water. Then they beat and threw down the steps the students still occupying the third tier. We'd stayed put all along, holding hands and singing the Internationale. We'd been shouting. 'The people's army won't attack the people'. The students packing the third tier had no choice but to retreat under the blows and kicks of such a large body of men. While this was going on, the sound of machine-guns started up. Some troops were kneeling down and firing. Their bullets whizzed above our heads. The troops lying on their stomachs shot up into the students' chests and faces. We had no choice but to retreat back up onto the Monument. When we reached it the machine-guns stopped. But the troops on the Monument beat us back down again. As soon as we'd been beaten down, the machine-guns started up again.*

The dare-to-die brigade of workers and citizens picked up anything that served as a weapon – bottles, pieces of wood – and rushed towards the troops to resist them. The Students' Union gave the order to retreat to places outside the Square. It was not yet five o'clock.

A great crowd of students rushed toward the gap in the line of troop carriers. The heartless drivers closed the gap. Thirty-odd carriers drove into the crowd. Some people were crushed to death.

*This manoeuvre was plainly designed to avoid troops firing directly onto the Monument, and chipping or pocking the stone fresco of heroes (though, as television news has shown, they did hit a few).

Even the flagpole in front of the Monument was snapped off. The whole Square was in massive chaos. I'd never thought my fellow-students could be so brave. Some started to push at the troop carriers. They were mown down. Others clambered over their corpses and pushed too. Finally they managed to push one or two carriers aside and open up a gap. I and 3,000 other students rushed through under a hail of fire. We ran across to the entrance to the History Museum.

There were large numbers of citizens in front of the Museum. We joined up with them. Seeing how bad things were, we immediately ran off to the north in the direction of the Gate of Heavenly Peace. But we'd only gone a few steps when rifle fire broke out from a clump of bushes alongside the road. We saw no people – just the bursts of fire from the gun-barrels. So we turned and ran off south towards the Front Gate.

I was running and weeping. I saw a second batch of students running off under machine-gun fire. I saw lots of people lying on their stomachs on the road that we were trying to escape along. We were all crying – running and crying. When we reached the Front Gate, we were suddenly confronted by a batch of troops. They didn't open fire. They were armed with big wooden staves. They beat us furiously,

Then a large crowd of citizens came pouring out of the Front Gate. They clashed violently with these troops. They protected us while we escaped in the direction of Beijing railway station. The troops pursued us. It was five o'clock. Dawn was breaking. The gunfire on the Square seemed to have died down a little.

THE FALL OF THE BERLIN WALL, GERMANY, 11 November 1989

Peter Millar and Richard Ellis, Sunday Times

After days of protest, the East German Communist regime was forced to open the country's borders, including the infamous Wall in Berlin.

More than one million Germans from East and West held the world's biggest non-stop party in Berlin yesterday, as their sober leaders tried in vain to dampen the euphoria by warning that a united Germany was not yet on the political agenda.

East Berliners poured into West Berlin to celebrate their liberty on free beer and wine, and late last night one 24-year-old visitor from the East gave birth to a baby girl on one of the city's bustling streets, to the delight of the partying crowds.

The new life seemed symbolic. Berlin was itself a city reborn. The party clogged the streets as the barriers that divided Germany melted like the ice of the cold war. Officials said well over a million people had passed the frontiers from East Germany into West Berlin and West Germany in a matter of hours.

After nightfall, as the party proved unstoppable, police shut off traffic from several main streets, and sealed off the Wall at the Brandenburg Gate to prevent demonstrators from dancing on it. West Berlin police said they were in constant touch with their East German colleagues on the other side of the wall.

Tension gave way to heated but good-natured banter between West Berliners and the normally sullen East German guards standing on the wall.

'I'm not here talking to you because I have to or because I've been told to,' one policeman said. 'I'm here because I want to (be).'

'What's your name, what's your name?' shouted the crowd.

'Call me Karl-Heinz,' he answered.

'Tell me, what will happen when there's no more use for the wall?' he was asked.

'Well, if it goes that far, I suppose we'll get to know each other.'

Along the Kurfürstendamm, tens of thousands of East and West Berliners linked their arms to sing songs celebrating their newly gained solidarity.

To the tune of Glory Glory Hallelujah, they chorused *Berlin ist ein Stadt, Deutschland is ein Land* (Berlin is one city, Germany is one country). As they sang, people held up cigarette lighters, matches and candles and sparklers to demonstrate their feelings.

For the benefit of American television crews, there were songs even in English: 'We shall overcome' and 'This land is my land'.

Street poets regaled the crowds with jokes and verses that concentrated on the collapse of the Berlin Wall. 'Die Maur', as the wall is known in German, is in two, said one, but no longer is Berlin.

Sales of beer and champagne soared as East Berliners continued to come over to the West to join the festivities, and traffic in West Berlin was at a standstill . . .

The first new border crossing point came into use just after dawn after a night of activity by workmen with bulldozers. East Berliners filed on foot from Bernauer Strasse into the West.

This had been the scene of some of the most dramatic and emotional events of August 1961 when the wall was built – East Berliners dropping from upper storey windows while troops bricked up their front doors. Several died.

On Potsdamer Platz, once the Piccadilly Circus of the German empire and a hundred yards from the unmarked site of Hitler's bunker, the bulldozers were creating a crossing to be opened this morning.

Elsewhere, official teams were knocking down the wall to create eighteen new crossing points. At one new site, East Berlin engineers shook hands with their western counterparts through the gap they had created in the six-inch thick, steel-reinforced concrete.

Tourists watched in amazement, their cameras recording the historic moments. One American borrowed a hammer from a Berliner and told his wife: 'Get one of me hitting the wall, honey.'

Every small piece chipped off was seized as a souvenir. At one partly destroyed section near the Tiergarten, young West Berliners sold off chunks of the wall for DM10.

In the gift shops, newly printed T-shirts were selling well the most popular bearing the slogan *Der Letze Macht Das Licht Aus!* (the last one turns out the light).

'THE MUSEUM OF MADNESS': A TOUR OF CEAUSESCU'S PALACE, BUCHAREST, ROMANIA, December 1989

Simon Haydon

Nicolae Ceausescu was among the many East European Stalinist dictators to fall in 1989. As Simon Haydon found on visiting Ceausescu's palace after his execution, the Romanian leader lived in a style far at odds with his simple working man image.

Nicolae Ceausescu lived in a dream house dripping with gold and silver and packed with art treasures, while his nation starved. Even his nuclear bunker was lined with marble.

The new Romanian leadership yesterday gave western journalists their first view of the Ceausescu home since he was deposed. The sprawling two-storey villa with forty rooms stands at the centre of a compound of a dozen houses for Ceausescu's ministers, generals and friends in northern Bucharest.

'I cannot even imagine a billionaire in the West living in such style,' said Octavio Badea, a musician who has joined about 500 soldiers and civilians guarding the house, which was briefly plundered last weekend during battles between Ceausescu loyalists and government troops.

The Ceausescus slept in separate apartments – and Elena's bore startling similarities to that of Imelda Marcos, unveiled after she and her husband fled their Manila palace in 1986. Rows of shoes were on display, some with diamond-encrusted heels made by Charles Jourdan. Elena's fur coats, part of a wardrobe that also included hundreds of dresses, were strewn over her large unmade bed.

Her husband's pyjamas still lay on the bed he last slept in a week ago. Three telephones stood on his bedside tables. 'It is almost too hard to understand. I hope one day this place will be turned into a museum of madness,' said Major Stancu Valentin, who escorted the journalists.

The visitors to the villa were met in an entry hall decorated with precious vases, topped by a golden dome. Further inside the ground floor was the piano room, with a Vienna-made Buchner grand piano, badly out of tune. All the rooms were crammed with paintings, valuable ornaments and gilded furniture. 'They had amazingly good taste considering he was not much more than a tyrannical peasant,' said Mr Badea.

One Christmas card was from the Ceausescus' daughter, Zoia, who was caught as she tried to flee with large sums of money – since stored upstairs for safe keeping. 'Happy Christmas to my dearly beloved parents from your daughter Zoia,' the card read.

Mrs Ceausescu had been learning English. BBC English-language videotapes were scattered round her room. And her husband was apparently a fan of Western films. Every room boasted a West German television set, on which he could show French or American films from a stack piled high in one of his flats.

Warm water flowed from gold-plated taps in the Italian-tiled bathrooms. On the balcony downstairs, where exquisite fountains once splashed, a soldier had left his dirty boots, exchanged for a pair of Ceausescu's.

Soldiers, fearing the Securitate may try to recapture the house, have taken up residence in the marble-lined nuclear bunker, which can sleep sixteen and has enough provisions for a long wait.

Major Valentin said the Ceausescus kept a relatively small staff because the dictator was mean. Documents in the kitchen showed he sent unused fruit and meat back to the markets to reclaim his money. The couple kept to a strict diet, with the ruler's daily food intake and calorie intake specially printed out for him.

Outside the house, the couple and their children – Nicu, Zoia and Valentin – enjoyed a swanky fitness centre for the compound's residents, with a swimming pool, boxing ring, volleyball court and several tennis courts.

Ceausescu's 102-year-old mother, who lived in a bungalow near the main house, was taken to hospital when her home was overrun last Friday. Her house is now a barracks for the troops protecting the plush residence.

THE GULF WAR: THE BOMBING OF BAGHDAD, IRAQ, 17 January 1991

John Simpson, BBC

John Simpson, Foreign Affairs Editor of the BBC, was in the Iraqi capital when Operation Desert Storm, the Allied operation against Saddam Hussein and his occupation of Kuwait, began.

It had taken us much too long to get our gear together. I was angry with myself as we ran across the marble floor of the hotel lobby, scattering the security men and Ministry of Information minders.

A voice wailed after us in the darkness: 'But where are you going?' 'There's a driver here somewhere,' said Anthony Wood, the freelance cameraman we had just hired. When I saw which driver it was, I swore. He was the most cowardly of them all. The calmer, more rational voice of Eamonn Matthews, our producer, cut in: 'We'll have to use him. There's no one else.' It was true. The other drivers knew there was going to be an attack, and had vanished.

We had no idea where we wanted to go. There was no high ground, to give us a good shot of the city. We argued as the car screeched out of the hotel gate and down into the underpass. 'No bridges,' I said. 'He's heading for 14 July Bridge. If they bomb that we'll never get back.'

The driver swerved alarmingly, tyres squealing. At that moment, all round us, the anti-aircraft guns started up. Brilliant red and white tracers arched into the sky, then died and fell away. There was the ugly rumble of bombs. I looked at my watch: 2.37

a.m. The bombing of Baghdad had begun twenty-three minutes earlier than we had been told to expect. For us, those minutes would have made all the difference.

The sweat shone on the driver's face in the light of the flashes. 'Where's he going now?' He did a wild U-turn, just as the sirens started their belated wailing. Anthony wrestled with the unaccustomed camera. 'I'm getting this,' he grunted. The lens was pointing at a ludicrous angle into the sky as another immense burst of fireworks went off beside us. It was hard not to flinch at the noise.

'The bloody idiot – he's heading straight back to the hotel.' The driver had had enough. He shot in through the gates and stopped. We had failed ignominiously in our effort to escape the control of the authorities and now we were back.

I had become obsessed with getting out of the Al Rasheed Hotel. It smelled of decay, and it lay between five major targets: the presidential palace, the television station, an airfield, several Ministries. I had no desire to be trapped with 300 people in the underground shelters there, and I wanted to get away from the government watchers. Television requires freedom of action, and yet we were trapped again.

In the darkness of the lobby angry hands grabbed us and pushed us downstairs into the shelter. The smell of frightened people in a confined space was already starting to take over. Anthony held the camera over his head to get past the sobbing women who ran against us in the corridor. Children cried. Then the lights went out, and there was more screaming until the emergency power took over. Most of the Western journalists were hanging round the big shelter. I was surprised to see one of the cameramen there: he had a reputation for courage and independence, but now he was just looking at the waves of frightened people with empty red eyes. Anthony, by contrast was neither worried nor elated. He was mostly worried about getting his equipment together.

Not that it *was* his equipment. Anthony had stepped in to help us because our own cameramen had to leave. It had been a difficult evening. As more and more warnings came in from New York, Paris and London, about the likelihood of an attack, almost every news organization with people in Baghdad was instructing them to leave. The personal warnings President Bush had given to American editors suggested that the coming onslaught would be the worst since the Second World War.

I remembered my grandfather's stories of men going mad under the bombardment at the Somme and Passchendaele. This would be the first high-tech war in history and most newspapers and television companies were reluctant to expose their employees to it. The BBC, too, had ordered us out. Some wanted to; others didn't. In the end it came to a four–three split: Bob Simpson, the radio correspondent and a good friend of mine for years, decided to stay; so did Eamonn Matthews. I was the third. In our cases the BBC, that most civilized of British institutions, came up with a sensible formula: it was instructing us to leave, but promised to take no action against us if we refused.

We still needed a cameraman. But by now there were several people whose colleagues had decided to move out, but who were determined to stay themselves. We found two who were prepared to work with us: Nick Della Casa and Anthony Wood.

There seemed to be no getting out of the shelter. Guards, some of them armed with Kalashnikovs, stood at each of the exits from the basement. They had orders to stop anyone leaving. The main shelter was now almost too full to sit or lie down. Some people seemed cheerful enough, and clapped and sang or watched Iraqi television. Children were crying, and guests and hotel staff were still arriving all the time from the upper floors.

In the general panic, the normal patterns of behaviour were forgotten. A woman in her thirties arrived in a coat and bath towel, and slowly undressed and put on more clothes in front of everyone. Nobody paid her the slightest attention. The heavy metal doors with their rubber linings and the wheel for opening and closing them, as in a submarine, stayed open.

Even so, I felt pretty bad. From time to time it seemed to me that the structure of the hotel swayed a little as if bombs were landing around us. Perhaps it was my imagination. To be stuck here, unable to film anything except a group of anxious people, was the worst thing I could imagine. Anthony and I got through the submarine door and tried to work our way up the staircase that led to the outside world. A guard tried to stop us, but I waited till the next latecomer arrived and forced my way through. Anthony followed.

The upper floors were in darkness. We laboured along the corridor, trying to work out by feel which was our office. Listening at one door, I heard the murmur of voices and we were let in. The sky was lit up by red, yellow and white flashes, and there was no need for us to light torches or candles. Every explosion had us cowering and ducking. I wandered round a little and asked a friendly cameraman to film what's called in the trade 'a piece to camera' for me.

Despite the crash and the whine of bombs and artillery outside we whispered to each other. By now, though, I was acclimatizing to the conditions, and sorted out the words in my head before I started. You are not popular with cameramen if you need too many takes under such circumstances.

Back in the corridor there was a flash from a torch, and an Iraqi called out my name. A security man had followed me up from the shelter. In order to protect the others I walked down towards him in the yellow torchlight. I had no idea what I was going to do, but I saw a partly open door to my left and slipped inside. I was lucky. The vivid flashes through the window showed I was in a suite of rooms which someone was using as an office.

I worked my way past the furniture and locked myself in the bedroom at the end. Lying on the floor, I could see the handle turning slowly in the light from the battle outside. When the security man found the door was locked he started banging on it and calling out my name, but these doors were built to withstand rocket attacks; a mere security man had no chance.

Close by, a 2,000-pound penetration bomb landed, but contrary to the gossip in the hotel neither my eyeballs nor the fillings in my teeth came out. I switched on the radio I found by the bed and listened to President Bush explaining what was going on. It was 5.45, and I was soon asleep.

At nine o'clock there was more banging on the door, and more calling of my name. It was Eamonn, who had tracked me down to tell me he had got our satellite telephone to work. Smuggling the equipment through the airport two weeks before had been a smart piece of work, and in a city without power and without communications we now had both a generator and the means to broadcast to the outside world.

Eamonn moved the delicate white parasol of the dish around until it locked on to the satellite. It was hard to think that something so complex could be achieved so easily. We dialled up the BBC and spoke to the pleasant, cool voice of the traffic manager. It was just as if we were somewhere sensible, and not sheltering against a brick wall from the air raids. I gave a brief account to the interviewer at the other end about the damage that the raids had caused in the night: the telecommunications tower damaged, power stations destroyed. I had less idea what was happening on the streets. Directly the broadcast was over, I headed out with Anthony for a drive around. 'Not good take picture now, Mr John,' said the driver. He was an elderly crook but I had an affection for him all the same. 'Got to work, I'm afraid, Ali.' He groaned.

It was extraordinary: the city was in the process of being deprived of power and communications, and yet the only sign of damage I could see was a broken window at the Ministry of Trade. The streets were almost empty, except for soldiers trying to hitch a lift. 'Going Kuwait, Basra,' said Ali. Some were slightly wounded, and their faces seemed completely empty.

Iraqis are normally animated and sociable, but there was no talking now, even in the bigger groups. A woman dragged her child along by its arm. A few old men squatted with a pile of oranges or a few boxes of cigarettes in front of them. An occasional food shop or a tea-house was open; that was all.

'Allah.' A white car was following us. 'He see you take picture.' I told Ali to take a sudden right turn, but he lacked the courage. The security policeman waved us down. 'Just looking round,' I said, as disarmingly as I could. 'He say you come with him.' 'Maybe,' said Anthony.

We got back into the car, and followed the white car for a little. The Al Rasheed Hotel was in the distance. 'Go there,' I said loudly, and Ali for once obeyed. The policeman waved and shouted, but by now the sirens were wailing again and the Ministry of Defence, on the left bank of the river, went up in a column of brown and grey smoke.

Ali put his foot down, and made it to the hotel. The policeman in his white car arrived thirty seconds after us, but obediently searched for a place in the public car park while the three of us ran into the hotel and lost ourselves in the crowd which filled the lobby.

In a windowless side office, where our minders sat for safety, I spotted a face I knew: Jana Schneider, an American war photographer, completely fearless. Throughout the night she had wandered through Baghdad filming the falling missiles. Near the Sheraton she had watched a 'smart' bomb take out a Security Ministry building while leaving the houses on either side of it undamaged.

I found it hard to believe, and yet it tied in with my own observation. This extraordinary precision was something new in warfare. As the day wore on, Baghdad seemed to me to be suffering from an arteriosclerosis – it appeared unchanged, and yet its vital functions were atrophying with each new air raid. It was without water, power and communication.

I was putting together an edited report for our departing colleagues to smuggle out when someone shouted that a cruise missile had just passed the window. Following the line of the main road beside the hotel and travelling from south-west to north-east, it flashed across at 500 miles an hour, making little noise and leaving no exhaust. It was twenty feet long, and was a good hundred yards from our window. It undulated a little as it went, following the contours of the road. It was like the sighting of a UFO.

LOS ANGELES RIOT, AMERICA, 30 April–1 May 1992

'West Coast Correspondent', Economist

The acquittal of four policemen who beat black motorist Rodney King torched off the most lethal urban riot in American history, leaving 50 dead and over $1 billion worth of damage in the South Central area of Los Angeles.

In front of the smoking electronics store, the small black boy had a problem. He had looted six items, but he could carry only five. For around fifteen minutes he hesitated, shielding them from other, older pillagers, while he tried to arrange them. Then flames spouted from the shop, driving out the remaining looters. A scuffle broke out across the street and the boy loped off down an alley, leaving a radio-alarm clock behind. It was probably his most valuable booty and it would have made a good present for a friend. A bearded (white) hippie, muttering an apology, picked it up instead.

Barely twenty-four hours before, Los Angeles had seemed its usual smoggy, complacent self. The first news of the acquittals in the Rodney King beatings arrived in the late afternoon. When asked for their reaction, two policemen parked opposite *The Economist* office at the *Los Angeles Times* gave a non-committal grunt. At first, the most distraught people seemed to be guilty liberals (some journalists burst into tears). Then a young mob appeared downtown. They smashed the windows and doors of the *Times* building and burnt the local coffee shop. But the television pictures from South Central were much more frightening.

After that first angry night, what followed in most parts of Los Angeles was more pillage than riot. The fires were started by thugs (supposedly gang members who had pledged to add ten new fires every hour), but the looting was done by petty thieves. The atmosphere was usually like a disorganized rock concert: at its worst, it resembled an angry English soccer crowd – with guns. One Hispanic man scurried away carrying several cartons of tampons. Television coverage, with its maps and pictures of defenceless stores, provide a looter's guide to the best local bargains.

Gradually the fires spread northwards and westwards towards the prosperous 'Westside' that tourists visit. There a different type of riot was taking place. A supermarket on the border of West Hollywood and Beverly Hills was packed with queues 30-deep. Each shopper seemed to be carrying enough provisions to last a month. There was a screaming match at the kosher food counter. Gossip spread that a British billionaire's daughter had said the riots were boring, 'but if they ever heave a brick through Tiffany's window, I might join them.'

She never got her chance: West Los Angeles survived largely untouched. Even in heavily looted areas like Korea-town and Mid-Wilshire, many of the rioters like the small black boy, seemed almost innocently childlike. However, in South Central, the atmosphere changed. The shops – particularly those owned by Asians – were stripped bare. The crowds hanging on street corners seemed to be looking for victims rather than bargains. Women screamed about their neighbourhood being destroyed; onlookers were no more welcome than at a funeral.

The most enduring memory from the riots was the signs in shop windows. In South Central, they pleaded pathetically. 'Black owned business'. Some stooped lower, putting 'blak owned business' in an attempt to mollify one gang, the Bloods, who dislike the letter 'c' because it reminds them of their arch-enemies, the Crips. On Rodeo Drive, where there are fewer black-owned businesses, shops at first bravely sported signs saying 'No Justice' to show that their sympathies lay with Mr King. When the riots died down the signs disappeared.

'ETHNIC CLEANSING' IN BOSNIA, YUGOSLAVIA, July 1992

Roy Gutman, Newsday

Hasnija Pjeva witnessed the execution of her husband Nenad, from the terrace of her house outside Visegrad.

It was 7.30 a.m., June 24, and Nenad was returning from his overnight factory shift when the armed men in Serbian paramilitary uniforms spotted him. Nenad started running to the nearby riverbank, but the irregulars shot him dead on the spot. They dragged the corpse onto the bridge, then threw it into the green water of the Drina.

'I didn't bury him,' Hasnija said of her husband two days later, tears welling in her eyes. 'The river took him away.'

Abdulahu Osmanagulis was at his home in Visegrad, a virtual prisoner since Serb forces seized the predominantly Muslim town three months before. They burned down the two ancient mosques and roamed the streets, firing small arms day and night. Early last week three of his neighbours were shot in their home.

'The bodies were just left lying there in the courtyard,' Osmanagulis said. He knew it was time to get out of his house.

Emina Hodzic's husband was abducted one noon, her son that same evening. Mediha Tira's husband was taken away by men with blackened faces.

The killings all happened last week in the Bosnian town whose Turkish-built 'bridge on the Drina' was immortalized by Yugoslavian novelist Ivo Andric. There are now two bridges, and after last week's events, both will find their place in the literature of war atrocities.

Except for an unknown but apparently small number who escaped, all the able-bodied Muslim men and youths of Visegrad who had not fled the occupiers were shot, according to a dozen survivors.

'Most of the executions were committed on the bridge. Their bodies were thrown into the river,' said Osmanagulis, the unofficial leader of the survivors. It appears that dozens were executed, perhaps hundreds. No one knows exactly.

'If the Drina River could only speak, it would say how many dead were taken away,' said Hasnija Pjeva.

Visegrad (pronounced VEE-shih-grad), with a population of about 30,000, is one of a number of towns where Serb forces carried out 'ethnic cleansing' of Muslims in the past two weeks, according to the Bosnian government.

'There was chaos in Visegrad. Everything was burned, looted and destroyed,' said a Visegrad expellee, 43, who spoke of the terrible events over coffee in the Miratovac café but would give neither his name nor his profession. He escaped only because he was an invalid with a gangrenous leg.

The survivors of the massacre are the old, the infirm, the women and the children. They are traumatized by what they witnessed, barely able to speak or to control their emotions. Two of the women had been raped, Osmanagulis said. But the heartbreak was compounded by the humiliation they endured at the hands of the local Serbian Red Cross.

Against their wishes, 280 people were shipped in a convoy of five buses across Serbia, the principal state in the new Yugoslavia, to Macedonia, a breakaway state, a journey of about 275 miles. The Serbian Red Cross gave them food and clothes but insisted they sign papers saying they had been well treated and wanted to go to Macedonia.

'We all wanted to go to Kosovo or Sandzak,' two mainly Muslim areas of southern Serbia, said Osmanagulis, 'but they directed us exclusively to Macedonia. There was no other choice.'

He carried a paper requesting that the Macedonian border authorities provide passports and admit the entire group. But Macedonia, which has more than 30,000 Bosnian refugees but has yet to be recognized by Western countries or to receive any real assistance, has stopped accepting any refugees, particularly Muslims, due to substantial problems with its own Muslim minority, according to Mira Jankovska, a government spokeswoman in Skopje.

And so the Macedonians refused to allow the survivors of the Visegrad massacre to cross the border. It was 4 a.m.

Osmanagulis conferred with the drivers, and they agreed that everyone should disembark and try to enter on foot, but the Macedonian police turned them away. 'I ran back to the buses and everyone followed, but when the drivers saw us, they turned the buses around and left,' he said.

For sixteen hours on June 25 the survivors found themselves stranded in a no-man's-land on an international highway without food, water, shelter or assistance, abandoned by the Red Cross and welcomed nowhere. Fifteen of them were over eighty, and there were at least as many children under the age of two. They stood and sat from 4 a.m. until 8 p.m. through the hot midday sun and a fierce summer rainstorm.

Albanian Muslims in this impoverished farm village in southern

Serbia, about a twenty-minute drive from the border crossing, brought bread, water and tomatoes. Then in the evening they arrived with tractors and taxis and took them to a small mosquc here. On the advice of a local doctor who feared the spread of disease, the survivors were moved to private homes two days later.

'If the people of the village hadn't helped us, half of us would be dead of starvation or illness,' said Osmanagulis. One woman, ninety-two, died after the ordeal. She was buried on Sunday.

Now the survivors of Visegrad sit in this village at the end of a potholed dirt road, sleeping on the floors and couches of its simple houses, caught between the hostility of Serbia and Macedonia, unattended by any refugee organization, unable even to contact anyone outside, for there is no telephone.

'We have a saying,' said Osmanagulis, summing up their plight: 'The sky is too high, and the ground is too hard.'

THE END OF APARTHEID: NELSON MANDELA VOTES IN THE SOUTH AFRICAN ELECTION, INANDA, 27 April 1994

Karl Maier

'Out of the darkness into the glorious light' reads the inscription on the tombstone of the African National Congress's founding president, John Dube, who was buried at the Ohlange High School where Nelson Mandela fulfilled a life-long ambition yesterday by casting a vote in South Africa's first all-race elections.

Sunlight had just broken over the hills of Natal province when a motorcade escorted by South African Defence Force troops and police brought Mr Mandela to the sight of the tomb.

Mr Mandela, 76, laid a wreath then walked down towards the high school where 300 journalists were cajoling officials of the ANC and the Independent Electoral Commission to set up the ballot box to capture the most famous vote in South Africa's history in the best possible position.

As he moved towards a verandah where the ballot box was poised, Mr Mandela was asked which party he planned to vote for. 'I have been agonizing over that question,' he replied, and went inside to mark his ballot.

Mr Mandela returned beaming. His was probably the most choreographed vote in history. Lifting the ballot paper above the box, Mr Mandela turned to face photographers then deposited the answer to his agonizing question.

'An unforgettable occasion,' he called it. 'We are moving from an era of resistance, division, oppression, turmoil and conflict and starting a new era of hope, reconciliation and nation-building.

'I sincerely hope that the mere casting of a vote . . . will give hope to all South Africans,' he said. Hope perhaps, but that vote yesterday gave officials at Ohlange a big headache. Hundreds of voters boycotted their local voting station and headed to the school, demanding to cast their ballots where Nelson Mandela did.

THE BODY OF DIANA, PRINCESS OF WALES, IS FLOWN HOME, RAF NORTHOLT, ENGLAND, 31 August 1997

Jonathan Freedland, Guardian

The icon of the latter half of the twentieth century, Diana Spencer, ex-wife of the Princes of Wales, was killed in a car crash in Paris, 30 August 1997.

In the end, they let her go quietly. No drum, no funeral note – only a dumb silence as the body of Diana, Princess of Wales, returned to the land she might have ruled as queen.

There was no crowd to meet her, none of the hordes of flagwavers she so delighted in life. Instead the flat, grey tarmac of RAF Northolt, windy as a prairie, a line-up of dignitaries – and a hearse.

She had made the journey from Paris by plane, on an RAF BAe 126. They kept the coffin in the passenger cabin, within sight of her two sisters, Lady Jane Fellowes and Lady Sarah McCorquodale, and her former husband, the Prince of Wales.

The skies themselves seemed to make way for her arrival, the clouds parting like an honour guard. Once the plane had landed, it nudged toward the welcoming party hesitantly, as if weighed down by its tragic cargo. Waiting there was the kind of receiving line Diana met every day. In the middle, arms by his sides, fists clenched tight, the Prime Minister. A cleric stood close by, bright in scarlet cassock. None of them said a word.

Eventually the plane door opened, and the Prince appeared head down, hands clasped behind his back. He was guided by the Lord Chamberlain, the Earl of Airlie. In another context it might have been a standard royal visit: Charles shown round a new factory or hospital wing. But he had come on a more baleful duty. He took his place in line – as he has done so often.

By now, the team of coffin bearers, each one in the crisp uniform of the Queen's Colour Squadron, had completed its precise march toward the other side of the aircraft. At the stroke of seven o'clock, the hatch opened revealing a glimpse of colour, the Royal Standard clinging to the hard, square outline of the coffin. It seemed an unforgiving shape: just a box, with none of the curve or sparkle of the woman whose body lay within.

The silence of the air was cut, and not just by the sound of distant traffic – which rumbled on, as if to prove that the clocks never stop, even for the death of a princess.

The air was filled with the *chickageev, chickageev* of the thousand camera lenses pointed at the scene ahead. Even now the world's telephoto eye was still staring at her, more focused than ever. Despite everything, everyone still wanted a piece of Diana. The cameras kept up their din, but there was an eerie silence from the men who held them. Once they would cry out, 'Diana! Diana!' – urging her to look their way or to flash just one more of those million-dollar smiles. But there was no shouting yesterday. And no smiles either.

The bearers of the body inched their way to the hearse. They stood, swivelled on their heels, and clasping tight with their white gloved hands, lowered the coffin as smoothly as a hydraulic pump. They were about to turn away, but a bit of the flag was still spilling out; it had to be tucked in, just like the train of one of Diana's more lavish ball gowns.

The sisters stepped forward, each one turning to curtsy for the man whom Diana had once loved. Charles kissed each one before they stepped into the royal Daimler. The next car was filled with bouquets.

The Prince himself did his duty, talking to each one of the VIPs who had stood beside him. Tony Blair clasped both royal hands in a double handshake, nodding intently. Charles made a gesture with upturned palms, as if to say What Can I Do? He thanked the RAF guard and disappeared back inside the plane, heading for Balmoral and his newly bereaved young sons. 'He's going back to the boys,' said his spokesman.

And then, on the final day of August, the sky darkened, and the wind whipped harder. It felt like the last day of summer, and the beginning of a long winter.

SOURCES AND ACKNOWLEDGEMENTS

The editor has made every effort to locate all persons having any rights in the selections appearing in this anthology and to secure permission from the holders of such rights. Any queries regarding the use of material should be addressed to the editor c/o the publishers.

The editor acknowledges the following sources: 'Nagasaki' comes from *Nagasaki 1945* by Tatsuichiro Akizuki, Quartet, copyright © 1981 Tatsuichiro Akizuki and Keiichi Nagata; 'The Anarchy of the Barons', from *Anglo Saxon Chronicles*, trans G. N. Garmonsway, Everyman, J. M. Dent, 1953, copyright © 1994 J. M. Dent; 'The Vikings Raid Britain', from *Anglo-Saxon Chronicles*, trans. G. N. Garmonsway, Everyman, J. M. Dent, 1953, copyright © 1994 J. M. Dent; 'Winning the Race for the South Pole', from *The South Pole* by Roald Amundsen, trans. A. G. Chater, John Murray 1912; 'The Shooting of the Students in Tiananmen Square' by Anon. Beijing student is from *New Statesmen & Society*, 16 June 1989, copyright © Guardian Syndication 1989; 'The Private Life of Adolf Hitler by Anon, from *Eyewitness Adolf Hitler*, edited by Allen Churchill, 1979; 'The martyrdom of Polycarp' by Anon, from *Letter from the Church of Smyrna to the Church of Philomelium*, trans. J. B. Lightfoot; 'The Sex Pistols Play their First Concert' by Adam Ant from *England's Dreaming* by Jon Savage, Faber & Faber, copyright © 1991 Jon Savage; 'My Cock is like a Drawbridge', from *Centuries of Childhood* by Philip Aries, Random House 1961, copyright © 1961 Random House; 'The Berlin Wall' by Mark Arnold-Foster from *The Observer*, 26 November 1961, copyright © Guardian Syndication 1961; 'The Death of Alexander', from the *Anabasis of Alexander* by Arrian, trans. E. J. Robson, Loeb Classical Library; 'Peterloo', from *Passages in the Life of a Radical* by Samuel Bamford, 1840–5; 'The Battle of Britain' by John Beard, from *Their Finest Hour* by Allan Machie and Walter Graebner, Harcourt Brace, copyright © 1941 Harcourt Brace & Co.; 'The Battle of Trafalgar: The Death of Lord Nelson' by William Beatty, from *Despatches and Letters of Nelson*, ed. Nicholas, 1845; 'Paris Celebrates the Liberation', from *Force of Circumstance* by Simone de Beauvoir, English translation copyright © 1964, 1965 by G. P. Putnam's Sons, copyright © 1963 by Librairie Gallimard, rights outside the US administered by André Deutsch, George Weidenfeld & Nicholson Ltd; 'The Wall Street

Crash' by Elliott V. Bell, from *We Saw It Happen*, 1938, copyright © 1938 Simon & Shuster Inc.; 'The Massacre at Wounded Knee' by Black Elk, from *Black Elk Speaks*, ed. John G. Neihardt, 1932; 'Medical Experiments at Dachau' by Franz Blaha, from *The Trial of Major German War Criminals: The Proceedings of the International Military Tribunal at Nuremberg*, 1946, copyright © 1946 HMSO; 'A Meeting with Hitler', from *In the Shelter with Hitler*, by Gerhrd Boldt, Citadel Books; 'D-Day: The landings' by H. T. Bone, from an unpublished memoir, Imperial War Museum, reprinted in *Eye-witness D-Day* by Jon E. Lewis, Robinson 1994; 'The Titanic Sinks' by Harold Bride, from *The New York Times*, 19 April 1912; 'The Great Exhibition' by Charlotte Brontë, from *The Brontes' Life and Letters*, ed. Clement Shorter, 1907; 'Julius Caesar Invades Britain', from *Gallic War* by Julius Caesar, Loeb Classical Library; 'The Death of Queen Elizabeth', from *Memoirs* by Sir Robert Carey, 1759; 'A Feast with a Mandan Chief', from *Letters and Notes on the Manners, Customs and Conditions of the North American Indian* by George Catlin, 1841; 'How to Keep a Slave', from *De Agri Cultura* by Cato, trans W. D. Hooper and H. R. Ash, Loeb Classical Library; 'The Sack of Rome' from *The Autobiography of Benvenuto Cellini*, trans. George Bull, Penguin, copyright © 1956 George Bull; 'A Dictatror Comes to Dinner', from *Letters to Atticus XIII* by Cicero, trans. G. E. Jeans, reprinted in *Voices from the Past* by James and Janet Maclean Todd, Readers Union, 1956; 'A Tank Charge' by Bert Chaney, from *People at War*, ed. Michael Moynihan, David and Charles, 1973; 'The Peasants' Revolt reaches London', from the *City Letter-Book* in *Memorals of London*, ed. H. T. Riley, 1868; 'An Interview with Al Capone' from *I, Claud* by Claud Cockburn, copyright © 1956, 1967 Claud Cockburn; 'Buffalo Bill Cody Entertains', from *The Life of Buffalo Bill* by William F. Cody, Senate, 1977; 'Bloody Sunday' by Sean Collins (interview by Tony Parker), from *New Statesman & Society*, January 1992, copyright © 1992 Guardian Syndication; 'Michelangelo Paints the Ceiling of the Sistine Chapel', from *Life of Michelangelo* by A. Condivi, 1553; 'Hitler Speaks', from *Looking for Trouble* by Virginia Cowles, Hanish Hamilton, 1941; 'The English Civil War: The Battle of Marston Moor' by Thomas Cromwell, from *Cromwell's Letters and Speeches*, ed. T. Carlyle, 1845; 'The English Civil War: The Storming of Drogheda' by Thomas Cromwell from *Cromwell's Letters and Speeches*, ed. T. Carlyle, 1845; 'A Firing Squad at Dawn', from *A Brass Hat in No-Man's Land* by Brig.-Gen. Crozier, Jonathan Cape; 'D-Day: The Landings', from *Eye-Witness D-Day* by Jon E. Lewis, 1994; 'The Reichstag Fire' by D. Sefton Delmer is from the *Daily Express*, 22 February 1933; 'The Conquistadores enter Mexico City', from *The Conquest of New Spain* by Bernal Diaz, trans. J. M. Cohen, Penguin, copyright © 1963 J. M. Cohen; 'A Visit to Belsen' by Richard Dimbleby, from *Richard Dimbleby: Broadcaster*, ed. Leonard Miall, copyright © 1956 BBC; 'Hunger Marchers' by John Dos Passos, from *New Republic*, 1931, copyright © Harrison-Blaine Inc.; 'A Pilot Encounters the Enemy' by Sholto Douglas, from *They Fought for the Sky* by Quentin Reynolds, 1957; 'A Meeting with Freud' by Max Eastman, from *New Republic*, May 1938, copyright © 1938 Harrison-Blaine Inc.; 'The Suez Invasion', from *Express '56* by Donald Edgar, John Clare Books, 1957; 'The Industrial Revolution: Working-Class Manchester', from *The Condition of the Working Class in England* by Friedrich Engels, Foreign Language Publishing House, Moscow, 1962; 'The Railway of Death', from *One for Every Sleeper* by Jeffrey English, Robert Hale, 1989, copyright © 1989 Jeffrey English; 'Captured by a Slave Trader', from *The Interesting Narrative of the Life of Olaudah Equiano or Gustavus Vassa the African* by Olaudah Equiano, 1789; 'Cremation of a Viking Chieftain' by Ibn Fadlan, from *The Religions of Northern Europe* by Regis Boyer, 1973; 'Highway Robbery', from *Diary* by John Evelyn, ed. E. S. de Beer, OUP 1959; 'The Stand of the Gloucesters at Imjin River,' from *The Edge of the Sword* by Anthony Farrar-Hockley, copyright © 1956 A. Farrar-Hockley; 'The Gunpowder Plot' by Guy Fawkes, from *King's Book*, 1605, reprinted in *They Saw It Happen 1485–1688*, ed. C. R. N. Routh, Blackwell, 1956; 'Children Playing' by Minucius Felix, from *War, Women and Children in Ancient Rome* by John K. Evans, Routledge, 1991; 'Cannibalism at the Donner Camps' by

Captain Fellun, from *Overland in 1846*, ed. Dale Morgan, University of Nebraska Press, Nebraska and London, 1963; 'Massacre at Chatilla Camp', from *Pity the Nation* by Robert Fisk, André Deutsch, 1990, copyright © 1990 Robert Fisk; 'Crossing the German Border' from *Mailed Fist* by John Foley, Panther Books, 1951; 'The Paris Commune: Hunting down the Communists' by Archibald Forbes, from *Memorials of War and Peace*, 1894; 'A Traveller's London' from *Itinerarium* by Andreas Franciscus, trans. C. V. Malfatti, copyright © 1953 C. V. Malfatti, reprinted in *They Saw It Happen 1485–1688*, ed. C. R. N. Routh, Blackwell, 1956; 'The Jews are Rounded Up', from *Anne Frank's Diary*, copyright © 1956 Valentine Mitchell & Co. Ltd; 'The Body of Diana, Princess of Wales is Flown Home' by Jonathan Freedland, from the *Guardian*, 1 September 1997, copyright © 1997 Guardian Syndication; 'The Battle of Crécy', and 'Pageants for the Wedding of Isabella and Charles V', from *Chronicles of England, France and Spain* by Sir John Froissart, trans. John Bourchier, Lord Berners, ed. G. C. Macaulay, London 1899; 'Battle of Midway', from *Midway* by Mitsuo Fuchida and Masatake Okumiya, copyright © 1955 US Naval Institute, Maryland; 'Pearl Harbor' by John Garcia, from *The Good War: An Oral History of World War II* by Studs Terkel, copyright © 1984 Studs Terkel; 'The Torture of a Jesuit Priest', from *John Gerard: The Autobiography of an Elizabethan*, trans. Philip Caraman, Longmans, 1951; 'The Dambusters Raid', from *Enemy Coast Ahead* by Guy Gibson, copyright © 1956 Guy Gibson; 'A Walk Among the Dead' by Robert Graves, from *Goodbye to All That* by Robert Graves, Cassell, 1929, reprinted by permission of A. P. Watt on behalf of the Robert Graves Copyright Trust; 'The Murder of Thomas à Becket' by Edward Grim, from *English Historical Documents, 1042–1189*, ed. David C. Douglas and George W. Greenaway, Eyre & Spottiswoode, 1953; 'Ethnic Cleansing' originally published as 'The River Took Him' by Roy Gutman from *Newsday*, 3 July 1993, copyright © 1993 Newsday Inc; 'The Russian Winter Arrives', from *Moscow Tram Stop* by Heinrich Haape, Collins, 1957; 'The Falklands War' by Max Hastings, from the *Evening Standard*, 15 June 1982, copyright © 1982 *Evening Standard* and Max Hastings; 'The Armada' by Sir John Hawkins, from *Defeat of the Spanish Armada*, ed Laughton; 'The Museum of Madness' by Simon Haydon from *The Sunday Correspondent*, December 1989; 'Appearing before the House Un-American Activities Committee', from *Scoundrel Time*, Macmillan, 1976, copyright © Lillian Hellman; 'German Inflation' by Ernest Hemingway, from *By-Line: Ernest Hemingway*, ed. William White, 1967, reprinted by permission of HarperCollins; 'Vietnam War: The Citadel of Hué', from *Dispatches* by Michael Herr, copyright © 1977 Michael Herr; 'The Virtues of Tobacco' by Thomas Herriot, from *Principal Voyages* by R. Hakluyt, 1600; 'Emperor Septimius Severus is Made a God', from *Histories* by Herodian, trans. B. K. Workman in *They Saw it Happen in Classical Times*, Basil Blackwell Ltd, 1964. 'Hunting Crocodiles' by Herodotus from *Herodotus II*, Loeb Classical Library; 'Conquering Everest', from *High Adventure* by Edmund Hillary, Hodder & Stoughton, 1955; 'The Black Hole of Calcutta' by J. Z. Holwell, from *Annual Register*, 1758; 'An Audience with Queen Elizabeth, by André Hurault, from the *Journal of Sieur de Maisse*, trans. Harrison and Jones, The Nonesuch Press, 1931; 'Visiting a Slave Market', from *The South-West by a Yankee* by Joseph Ingraham, 1835; 'The Assassination of the Archduke Franz Ferdinand' by Borijov Jevtic, from *New York World*, June 1924; 'The Crusades: A French Knight in Combat', from *Chronicles of the Crusades* by Joinville & Villhardouin, Penguin, copyright © 1963 M. R. B. Shaw; 'The Destruction of the Temple at Jerusalem', from *The Jewish Wars* by Josephus, trans. H. St J. Thackeray, Loeb Classical Library; 'The English Love of Hunting' by Philip Julius, from *The Diary of the Duke of Stettin*, comp. Frederic Gerschow, Royal Historical Society, 1892; 'First Excursion on the London-Manchester Railway', from *Record of a Girlhood* by Fanny Kemble, 1878; 'The Arrest of Dr H. H. Crippen' by Captain H. G. Kendall from *Scrapbook 1900–1914*, ed. Leslie Bailey, Muller, 1957; 'Easter Sunday in the Country' by Francis Kilvert, from *Kilvert's Diary 1870–78*, ed. William Plomer, Cape, 1939; 'Skirmish at Kari Siding', from *Something of Myself* by Rudyard Kipling, Macmillan & Co, 1937;

'Neither Beast nor Bird Would Touch Them', from *Chronicles* by Henry Knighton, reprinted in *Chaucer's World*, ed. Clair C. Olson and Martin M. Crow, Oxford, 1948; 'The Night of the Barricades', from *Ninety Sixty Eight: A Personal Report* by Hans Koning, Unwin Hyman, 1988; 'The Killing of George Cornell', from *Our Story* by Reginald and Ronald Kray (with Fred Dineage), Sidgwick & Jackson Ltd, copyright © 1988 Bejubob Ltd; 'The German Ambassador Hands Over the Declaration of War', from *Soviet Staff Officer* by Ivan Krylov, Falcon Press, 1941; 'Strange Cruelties' by Bartolome de Las Casas, from *Brief Report on the Destruction of the Indians*, 1542, trans. in *Purchas His Pilgrimes*, reprinted in *The Faber Book of Reportage*, ed. John Carey, Faber & Faber, 1987; 'Torture', from *Seven Pillars of Wisdom* by T. E. Lawrence, 1926, copyright © 1926, 1935 Doubleday & Co.; 'Selection in Auschwitz', from *Survival in Auschwitz* by Primo Levi, copyright © 1986 Primp Levi; 'Dunkirk: The View from the Boats' by Commander C. H. Lightoller, from *Dunkirk* by A. D. Devine, Faber & Faber, 1945; 'The San Francisco Earthquake' by Jack London, from *Collier's Weekly*, 5 May 1906; 'The Reformation in England' by John London *et al*, from *Original Letters Illustrative of English History*, ed. H. Ellis, Dawsons, 1969; 'A Black Day for the German Army', from *My War Memories* by General Ludendorff, Hutchinson & Co.; 'Friends Divided', from *The Memoirs of Edmund Ludlow*, ed. C. H. Firth; 'The First Aerial Voyage in England', from *The First Aerial Voyage in England* by Vincent Lunardi, 1784; 'Martin Luther Protests Against the Sale of Indulgences', from *The Life of Martin Luther, Told by Himself*, ed. Jules Michelet; 'The Home Front: A Child's View', from *A Child's War* by George Macbeth; 'The End of Apartheid' by Karl Maier, from the *Independent*, 28 April 1994, copyright © 1992 Newspaper Publishing plc; 'The Rumble in the Jungle', from *The Fight* by Norman Mailer, 1974, copyright © 1974 Norman Mailer; 'The Huns' by Ammianus Marcellinus, from *Vol. XXVI*, trans, J. C. Rolfe, Loeb Classical Library, 'The First Radio Signal Across the Atlantic' by G. Marconi, from *Scrapbook 1900–14*, ed. Leslie Bailey, Muller, 1957; 'The Woodstock Festival' by Greil Marcus, from *Rolling Stone*, September 1969, copyright © 1969 Greil Marcus; 'The Russian Revolution: Tsar Nicholas II and . . . Family are Shot' by Pavel Medvedev, from *The Last Days of the Romanovs* by Robert Wilton, 1920; 'Marilyn Monroe in Hollywood', from *Timebends* by Arthur Miller, Methuen 1987, copyright © 1987 Arthur Miller; 'Civil Disobedience', is from *I Found No Peace* by Webb Miller, Gollancz, 1937; 'The French Revolution: The Condemned are Sent to the Guillotine' by J. G. Millingen, from *English Witnesses of the French Revolution*, J. M. Thompson, Blackwell, 1938; 'Joe Louis Fights Max Baer' by Jonathan Mitchell, from the *New York Republic*, October 1935; 'The Spanish Civil War: The Bombing of Guernica', from *Eyewitness* by Noel Monks, Muller, 1955; 'Smallpox-Ingrafting', from *The Complete Letters of Lady Mary Wortley Montagu*, ed. Robert Halsband, Clarendon Press, 1965; 'D-Day: Embarkation', from *Eclipse* by Alan Moorhead, Hamish Hamilton, copyright © 1945 Alan Moorehead; 'I Watch Television', from *The Private Letters and Diaries of Sydney Moseley* by Sydney Moseley, Max Parish Publishers, 1960; 'The Blitz', from *This is London*' by Edward R. Murrow, Cassell, 1941; 'Slim' by Peter Murtagh, from the *Guardian*, February 1987, copyright © Guardian Syndication 1987; 'The Fascists Take Power', from *My Autobiography* by Benito Mussolini, 1931; 'The Industrial Revolution: The Black Country' by James Nasmyth, from *James Nasmyth, Engineer: An Autobiography*, ed. Samuel Smiles, 1833; 'The Assassination of Julius Caesar' by Nicholas of Damascus, from *Historici Graeci Minores*, ed. Dindorf, trans. B. K. Workman in *They Saw It Happen in Classical Times*, Blackwell, 1964; 'The Signing of the Treaty of Versailles, from *Peacemaking 1919* by Harold Nicholson, Constable, 1933; 'Nixon Resigns as US President', from *The Memoirs of Richard Nixon*, Sidgwick & Jackson, copyright © 1978 Richard Nixon; 'Victory in Europe Celebrations' by Mollie Panter-Downes, from *New Yorker*, May 1945; 'The Great Fire of London', from *Diary* by Samuel Pepys, ed. Robert Latham and William Matthews, G. Bell & Sons, 1970–83; 'A Prisoner of the Inquisition' by Miles Phillips, from *Principal Voyages* by R. Hakluyt, 1589; 'The Battle of Cable Street', from *Our Flag*

Stays Red by Phil Piratin, 1948, copyright © 1948 Lawrence & Wishart; 'The Execution of the Philosopher Socrates', from *Phaedo* by Plato, trans. B. Jowett, reprinted in *Voices from the Past*, ed. James and Janet Maclean Todd, Readers Union, 1956; 'Saigon: The Final Day', from *The Last Day* by John Pilger, Syndication International, copyright © 1975 John Pilger; 'The Eruption of Vesuvius', from *Letters of the Younger Pliny*, trans. Betty Radice, Penguin, copyright © 1959, 1963 Betty Radice; 'Kublai-Khan's Summer Palace', from *The Travels* by Marco Polo, trans. William Marsden, Wordsworth, 1997; 'The American War of Independence: In Action Against the British' by Israel Potter, from 'Life and Adventures of Israel R Potter', *The Magazine of History*; 1911; 'The Royal Oak is Torpedoed' by Gunther Prien, from *Hitler and His Admirals* by Anthony Martienssen, Secker & Warburg, 1948; 'Dinner with Atilla the Hun' by Priscus, from *Historici Graeci Minores* ed. Dindorf, trans. B. K. Workman in *They Saw It Happen in Classical Times*, Blackwell, 1964; 'The Russian Revolution: Storming the Winter Palace', from *Ten Days That Shook the World* by John Reed, 1919; 'D-Day: The Airborne Landings' by Guy Remington, from *New Yorker*, July 1944; 'Christmas in the Trenches', from *Old Soldiers Never Die* by Frank Richards, A. Mott, 1933; 'A Public Execution' by Samuel Richardson, from *Familiar Letters on Important Occasions*, ed. B. W. Downs, Routledge & Sons, 1928, reprinted in *The Oxford Book of Letters*, ed. Frank Kermode and Anita Kermode, OUP, 1996; 'The Red Baron Claims his 32nd Victory', from *The Red Baron* by Manfred von Richthofen, copyright © 1963 Doubleday & Co.; 'The Black Death' by Robert of Avebury, from *Translations and Reprints from Original Sources of European History*, University of Pennsylvania, 1902; 'Flagellants' by Robert of Avebury, from *British Latin Selections AD 500–1400*, ed. R. A. Browne, Blackwell, 1954; 'A Perfect Steam Engine', from 'Narrative of Mr Watt's Invention of the Improved Engine' by John Robinson in *The Origins and Progress of the Mechanical Inventions of James Watt*, ed. J. P. Muirhead, 1855; 'The Breakthrough in the West' and 'El Alamein' by Erwin Rommel, from *The Rommel Papers*, ed. B. H. Liddell-Hart, copyright © 1953 B. H. Liddell-Hart, renewed 1981 Lady Kathleen Liddell-Hart, Fritz Beyerlain-Dittmar and Manfred Rommel; 'The Battle of Balaclava' by William Howard Russell, from *The Times*, November 1854; 'The Murder of Rizzio', from 'The Narrative of Lord Ruthven' in *History of the Affairs of Church and State in Scotland*; 'Antarctic Expedition' by R. F. Scott from *Scott's Last Expedition*, 1913; 'Gladiatorial Games', from *Letters* by Seneca, trans R. H. Gummer; 'The Somme', from *A Sergeant-Major's War* by Ernest Shepherd, copyright © The Crowood Press; 'France Surrenders', from *Berlin Diary: The Journal of a Foreign Correspondent, 1934–41* by William L. Shirer, copyright © 1940, 1941, renewed 1968 by William L. Shirer, reprinted by permission of Don Congdon Associates Inc; 'The Gulf War: The Bombing of Baghdad' by John Simpson, from the *Observer*, January 1991; 'The Irish Potato Famine' by Elizabeth Smith, from *The Irish Journals of Elizabeth Smith, 1840–50*, ed. David Thomson and Moyra McGusty, Clarendon Press, 1980; 'Execution of Nazi War Criminals' by Kingsbury Smith, from *It Happened in 1946*, ed. Clark Kinnaird; 'The Assassination of President John F. Kennedy' by Merriman Smith, copyright © UPI 1963; 'How I Found Livingstone' by H. M. Stanley, from the *New York Herald*, 10 August 1872; 'The Boyhood Genius of Sir Isaac Newton' by Dr Stukely, from *Collections for the History of the Town . . . of Grantham*, ed. Edmund Turnor, 1806; 'The Fire of Rome', from *The Annals of Imperial Rome* by Tacitus, trans. Michael Grant, Penguin, copyright © 1951, 1959, 1971 Michael Grant Publications Ltd; 'The World's First Atom-Bomb Test' by Geoffrey Taylor, from *Voices from Britain*, ed. Henning Krabbe, Allen & Unwin, 1947; 'Massacre at Sharpeville' by Humphrey Taylor from the *Observer*, 27 March 1960; 'Revolution in Havana', from *As It Happened* by Edwin Tetlow; 'Shipwrecked by a Hurricane' by Anthony Thacher, from *Original Letters of Eminent Literary Men of the Sixteenth, Seventeenth and Eighteenth Centuries*, ed. Henry Ellis, Camden Society, 1843; 'The Plague in Athens', from *Thucydides II*, trans. C. F. Smith, Loeb Classical Library; 'Hiroshima' by Colonel Tibbetts, from *The World at War* by Mark Arnold-Foster, William Collins & Sons. copyright © 1973, 1981 Thames

TV Ltd; 'The Vietnam War: The Pacification of My Lai', from *Time* magazine, 5 December 1969; 'Bloody Sunday' by '*Times* correspondent', from *The Times*, January 1905; 'The Russian Revolution', from *My Life* by Leon Trotsky; 'The Allies Decide to Drop the Atomic Bomb' by Harry S. Truman from *Off The Record: The Private Papers of Harry S. Truman*, Harper & Row, 1986; 'The American Assault on the Pyramids', from *Innocents Abroad* by Mark Twain, 1875; 'Paedophilia' by Arnaud de Verniolles, from *Montaillou* by E. Le Roy Ladurie, Penguin, 1973; 'D-Day: Meeting the Liberators', from a unpublished diary by Anne de Vigneral, Imperial War Museum, reprinted in *Eye-Witness D-Day* by Jon E. Lewis, 1994; 'The Marriage of Victoria and Albert' by Queen Victoria, from 'Victoria's Diary' in *In Their Own Words*, ed. Randall Gibbons, Random House, 1995; 'Garibaldi Liberates Sicily' by Frank Vizetelly, from *The Illustrated London News*, June 1860; 'A Portrait of Oliver Cromwell', from *Memoirs of the Reign of Charles I* by Sir Phillip Warwick; The English Longbow Wins the Battle of Agincourt', from *Collection of Chronicles* by Jehan de Waveran, trans. William Hardy and E. L. C. P. Hardy, Rother Series, 1864–91; 'The Mob Destroy the Machines' by Thomas Bentley, from *A Group of Englishmen* by Eliza Meteyard, 1871; 'Siege of Leningrad', from *Moscow War Diary* by Alexander Werth, Alfred K Knopf, 1942; 'Waterloo' by Edmund Wheatley, from *The Wheatley Diary: A Journal and Sketchbook kept during the Peninsular War and Waterloo Campaign*, ed. C. Hibbert, Longman, 1961; 'The Assassination of President Lincoln', from *Memoranda During the War* by Walt Whitman, 1875; 'The Devils Take the Soul of the Witch of Berkeley', from *Chronicles of the Kings of England* by William of Malmesbury, trans. J. A. Giles, Bohn's Antiquarian Library, 1847; 'The Blitz' by Virginia Woolf, from *A Writer's Diary* by Virginia Woolf, copyright © 1954 Leonard Woolf, renewed 1982 by Quentin Bell and Angelica Garnett; 'The First Powered Flight' by Orville Wright, from *Miracle at Kitty Hawk* by Fred C. Kelly, Farrar Strauss & Co.; 'The Execution of Mary Queen of Scots by Robert Wynfielde, from *Original Letters Illustrative of English History*, ed. H. T. Ellis, Hardy, Triphook & Lepard, 1825; and 'An Encounter with Russian Prisoners', from *In Their Shallow Graves* by Benno Zieser, Elek Books, 1956.